Advanced Cases
in
Multinational
Business
Operations

S. PRAKASH SETHI

School of Business Administration
University of California, Berkeley

GOODYEAR PUBLISHING COMPANY, INC.
Pacific Palisades, California

To My Wife,
Donna

Contents

Preface

The phenomenon of large European and American corporations and their multinational operations is not of recent origin. However, their growth—of which American multinational corporations account for a large part—has been so explosive that our understanding of the complexities has not kept pace with our need for such understanding. A multinational corporation operates under different sets of political, economic, and sociocultural environments in diverse countries and regions whose aims and objectives may not only differ from those of the corporation, but among themselves as well. Thus in striving to maximize its gains and to also contribute to general economic welfare—by efficient allocation of scarce economic resources on a global basis—the multinational corporation may be subjected to a multiplicity of pressures. These pressures call for development of skills to reconcile disparate interests, to make the corporations profitable, and to contribute to the long-run economic growth of the host countries.

There is a basic difference between the operating environment of a firm whose business is primarily confined to one country and that of the firm which operates internationally. The one-country firm treats the sociocultural, political, and economic environment of the country as constant and therefore given. These variables are considered exogenous to the firm's decision-making matrix. The primary concern of the firm is then to develop those strategies which would provide maximum scope for adaptation to these exogenous circumstances, and to exploit their strengths and weaknesses to the firm's advantage. The situation is quite different, however, for the multicountry firm. The external environment is different in each country and must be considered in developing operating strategies. The problem of adaptation is no longer simple since the exogenous variables of the one-country firm must now be treated as inputs and incorporated into the decision-making matrix.

To operate in this complex and changing environment, the multinational corporation must develop and retain those managerial skills which can operate under cross-cultural conditions. For the student of international business, there is need to develop those conceptual frameworks which can explain these complex phenomena and can provide a basis for understanding their working and a tool for explaining and predicting changes in the outcome given a change in the variable input. To do this we must draw heavily from such basic disciplines as cultural anthropology, social psychology, comparative sociology, and political science, in addition to economics. Although the need for constructing such a theoretical framework exists, its development would be a long-term project.

Another alternative is to take an inductive approach to our study of the subject. This can be done by carefully collecting existing data—in the form of successes and failures of various business practices currently followed by multinational corporations in their overseas operations—and through careful analysis and evaluation, building a body of knowledge which can be applied to the development of general principles. This book is a modest attempt in this direction.

The objective of this book is through a series of case studies, to expose the student and the business manager to a variety of operating and policy issues involving large multinational corporations. It is aimed at developing in the reader a sensitivity to the issues involved, an awareness of the complexity of the external environment and of the differences in the perceptual biases of the various parties, and familiarity with successes and failures of assorted strategies and tactics used by different companies under supposedly similar circumstances. It is primarily designed for use in executive development programs and by graduate students in courses dealing with various facets of international business such as international management, international marketing, international financial management, international industrial relations, international business-government relations, and international operations.

Many corporations and their executives cooperated generously to make these case studies possible. Some corporations, because they furnished current data and because their business is briskly competitive, chose not to be identified. Their names and data have been disguised appropriately. To them I can offer sincere thanks only anonymously. To the corporations who accepted identification, thanks are due especially to: AB Svenska Telegramnyrån, Stockholm, Sweden; Agro-Industrial Development Corporation, New York; The Calabrian Company, New York; Caterpillar Tractor Company, Peoria, Illinois; Celanese Fibers International Corporation, New York; Chase Manhattan Bank, New York; Chevron Chemical Company, San Francisco, California; Hewlett-Packard Company, Palo Alto, California; Johns-Manville Company, New York; National Cash Register Company, Dayton, Ohio; and Raytheon Corporation, Lexington, Massachusetts.

I also acknowledge with gratitude the help of many persons and administrative bodies within the University of California at Berkeley. The Professional Schools' Program financed the major portion of the work on these cases. The Institute of Business and Economic Research, the Committee on Research, and the School of Business Administration supplied partial research funds and the needed typing and clerical assistance for preparation of the manuscript. The continuing encouragement and support of Dean Richard H. Holton of the Schools of Business Administration is deeply appreciated. In addition to the help of my research assistants, Elliot Stevenson and John Hogle, other students also contributed in varying degrees. Notable among them are David Curry, Charles Golson, Sonny Tsuboi, and

Woodrow Wilson Hoffman. I am also grateful to my editor, Mrs. Jan Seibert, who contributed greatly to the readability of the manuscript, and to Patricia Murphy and Mrs. Betty Kendall, who typed its many drafts.

And finally, I am grateful to my wife, Donna, who in the months immediately preceding and following our marriage was immensely patient and affectionately encouraging while I worked on the book.

The international corporation operates in a kind of governmental vacuum . . . it is constantly exposed to the danger of expropriations, discriminatory legislation and the hatred and opprobrium of the people and countries whom on the whole it serves. It seems to be one of the unfortunate facts of society that being merely useful is a poor source either of prestige or of legitimacy.

Kenneth E. Boulding

1

Environmental Operating Conditions–Business Government Interface

---

THE CALABRIAN (CALTHAI) CO., LTD., THAILAND
U. S. Private Enterprise-Dealing with Two Political Entities: The Governments of the United States and Thailand

"As long as I sit in this chair, Calabrian will not get another penny from the government,"[1] said Herbert Salzman, director of AID (U. S. Agency for International Development). It was a death sentence for the privately owned company that had set up shop in Thailand with support from the U. S. AID program. Without financial support, Calabrian could not continue to operate and in May 1970, the company became inoperative.

THE CALABRIAN COMPANY

Calabrian, a New York commodity import-export firm, had acquired vast experience in twenty-one years of worldwide trading. Though modest by international standards, the company had built up a steady business in marketing grains, sugar, coconut, and other commodities. It operated a pharmaceutical plant in the Virgin Islands and had branches or affiliates in Johannesburg, Tokyo, and Saigon. Charles Cogliandro, president of Calabrian, estimated the company's current assets at $600,000. Because of its expertise in the trading aspects of business, however, much of its resources lay in know-how and ability. Calabrian, therefore, had been able to generate an annual turnover of $20 million. Furthermore, Calabrian had a good reputation with banks, and financing had never hindered any of its projects.

---

1. *Baltimore News American.* 19 November 1969.

1

CALABRIAN AND AID IN THAILAND

Calabrian, in Thailand since 1963, initiated its business activities with sugar exporting. In 1965 to 1966 a sugar surplus brought a crisis. Calabrian helped Thailand dispose of the surplus by expediting sugar shipments to the U. S. As a result of this effort, Thailand obtained a U. S. sugar import quota of 16,000 tons. Calabrian shipped the remaining surplus to Vietnam under AID's purchase program. In all, 50,000 tons were affected and Thailand's sugar crisis was eliminated.

AID, interested in developing the sugar industry in Thailand, contracted with Calabrian to conduct a feasibility study. In this study, the commodity trading company concluded that the development of a sugar refinery was premature. Calabrian therefore turned its attention to corn trading in which it had been interested since 1963. In 1964 to 1965 efforts were confined to setting up corn-drying installations. But in 1966, as a consequence of the sugar study, the trading company's endeavors became completely directed to corn.

Mr. Cogliandro said that Thailand's future was in corn. Sugar was traditionally a surplus-type commodity in the world, but corn was in great demand and was increasingly consumed in the countries bordering Thailand.[2] Calabrian realized that if the company was to expand its corn operations, it must stabilize its sources of supply. This meant providing some sort of financial assistance to the Thai farmer during the production and harvest phases to keep him free from the bondage of the local merchant-money lenders. Calabrian, therefore, decided to go into a pilot project farm assistance program.

In 1966 Calabrian initiated a loan program for Thai farmers in agreement with the Krung Thai Bank, an institution wholly owned by the Royal Thai Government. The basis of this agreement was that Krung Thai and Calabrian would assume equal risks in a $400,000 program to loan money directly to farmers. Since Calabrian did not have the organization to do so, Krung Thai was to supervise the actual loans.

CALABRIAN RUNS INTO PROBLEMS

"Once the project began," Mr. Cogliandro said, "the Krung Thai Bank's interpretation of joint risk became different from what was originally intended." The agreement implied a fifty-fifty sharing of risk which Calabrian interpreted to mean equal risk sharing from the first dollar loaned. However, the bank interpreted this proviso to mean that Calabrian would assume total risk on the first 50 percent of the loans and the bank on the remainder! And Krung Thai did not screen farmers for the loans.

As a result the program ran into heavy initial losses on uncollectible loans, some of which were to be expected. The lack of adequate infrastructure hindered

---

2. Unless otherwise specified, all quotations and references to company spokesmen are from written or oral communication with the author.

operations from progressing smoothly. Transportation, communication, and financing were nonexistent. Everything had to be built from the ground up.

At the end of 1966 Calabrian decided not to pursue the project, feeling that an all-inclusive farm-assistance program was not in their line and that they should stick to commodity trading or get out entirely. The farmers' rudimentary stage required a great deal more development. Considering the overall magnitude of the situation, it was decided that it was too much for a small company like Calabrian. Although the project concept was bold and promised long-term benefits to the economy, its execution needed considerable amounts of money.

At this time Calabrian's losses amounted to approximately $200,000, of which Mr. Cogliandro believed that with a vigorous collection program, he could have recovered about half. But as the sorely needed program progressed, Calabrian became hailed as the "champion" of the farmers. To default would be contrary to expectation. Mr. Cogliandro explains, "After gaining the acceptance and confidence of farmers, we couldn't turn around and call the loans in. Taking legal action was out of the question." However, Calabrian's corn trading was quite successful and there was every reason to expect that future profits would more than cover this loss.

By this time the project had generated considerable favorable publicity. The program was widely, although mistakenly, associated with the American government, as the large level of social and political impact of such a program could not be ignored.

The problems incurred with the pilot project persuaded Mr. Cogliandro to see the U. S. Ambassador to Thailand, Graham Martin. Because of the bad experience with loaning money to farmers, in addition to the activities of corn trading, Mr. Cogliandro thought the lending program should be discontinued.

In looking back, Mr. Cogliandro described his visit with Ambassador Martin:

The Ambassador was not happy that after starting the program Calabrian should just walk away from it. He encouraged us to ask AID for a loan. The potential remuneration of such a program would not only accrue to the company but benefit the country in a manner attributable to the U. S. Government.

The Ambassador was very adamant in his request. His full support to continue persuaded us to comply with his wishes. No one put a gun to our heads. It was our own decision—but he certainly asked us very hard.

THE CORN PROGRAM PROPOSAL
FOR AN AID LOAN

Mr. Cogliandro then developed a proposal for an ambitious investment scheme that would combine trading in corn with farm assistance.

We had a concept and wrote it on a piece of paper and gave it to the Thai and U. S. governments. It involved a series of country stations and elevators and a port elevator. But it also went further than that. It went into the agribusiness aspects. From this basic concept, the whole plan evolved.

The central idea was to deal directly with the farmers, advising them on planting, weeding, and fertilizing. Also, Calabrian would develop more suitable strains for the prevailing soil and weather conditions. At the same time, the farmers would be assured of a market for the increased production. Further, loans would be made to the farmers so they could (1) buy seed corn and fertilizers, (2) rent farm equipment, and (3) acquire title to their land. The basic objective was to increase corn production by giving farmers the means and determination to do so.

On November 28, 1966, Calabrian submitted a formal request to AID for a complete, extended, all-purpose risk guarantee for the following exposures:

1.	Farm loans	$ 7,500,000
2.	Construction of six silos	3,000,000
3.	Four flat storage facilities	200,000
4.	Agricultural equipment	5,000,000
		$15,700,000

An extended-risk guarantee makes the government liable for 75 percent of a company's investment in a private foreign enterprise. The company pays an annual 1.75 percent premium to the government for the privilege of the guarantee,[3] in addition to the going bank interest rate.

PROJECT SCALED DOWN

The substantial risks involved in a venture of this sort made the project even more impressive, once the benefits to the Thai farmer were fully appreciated. By mutual agreement the project was reevaluated and the projected cost of Mr. Cogliandro's proposal was scaled down from $15 million to $4.5 million (Table 1). He agreed to the reduction because of the bureaucratic nature of the situation and the time element.

We went in on the basis that this concept would cost about $15 million. We ended up with $4.5 million.[4] The bureaucracy that we confronted was formidable and we did not have time for any alterations. Any revisions had to be approved not only by AID but by the governmental agencies concerned with such an international project—the Treasury for money, the State Department for political reasons, and the Agricultural Department because agricultural commodities were involved.

The time element was very important to us at this stage. The harvest season for corn is September. If this project were to be instigated at all, it had to be done and the construction completed by then to be of any use.

3. "Foreign Aid Through Private Initiative," Report of the Advisory Committee on Private Enterprise in Foreign Aid, AID, Washington, D. C., July, 1965.
4. The guarantee covered only $3.4 million. It did not apply to each investor's money, but to the total project investment. AID could guarantee 100 percent of the institutional loans as long as they did not exceed 75 percent of the total investment.

TABLE 1

Nature and Sources of Funds

	Planned	Actual
Chemical Bank New York Trust Co. (guaranteed loan)	$3,000,000	$3,000,000
Krung Thai Bank loan to finance farmers	1,000,000	–
Bangkok Bank loan (secured by mortgages on facilities financed with Chemical Bank)	–	1,045,000
Calabrian equity investment	255,000	248,000[a]
Equity from other investors	245,000	100,000
Total	$4,500,000	$4,393,500

[a]$7,000 was returned to the company because it was not needed to pay for the agreed number of stock shares at the prevailing foreign exchange rate.

SOURCE: "Questionable Support of a Private Venture in Thailand Under the Investment Guaranty Program," Report to Committee on Foreign Relations, U. S. Senate, General Accounting Office of the Comptroller General of the United States, April 1, 1970, p. 23.

The insurgency problem was also blossoming at that time. The U. S. was sending troops into Thailand, and the Chinese were sending forces through Laos into Thailand.

The whole U. S. Embassy, the AID people, and the Thai Embassy were very anxious for the project to be launched because of the insurgency. Everyone wanted us to begin the project immediately. We concurred because we felt the remaining loans would be available as the project progressed. Our conception of the project's cost was still about $15 million.

AID *ACCEPTS THE PROJECT*

In Washington, Mr. Cogliandro's scheme was accepted and welcomed by AID in April 1967. If it were successful, an important agricultural development, consistent with U. S. government objectives in Thailand, would be accomplished at no cost to the U. S. government. AID expected the project to:

Increase Thailand's export earnings through high-quality corn production.

Provide supervised credit to Thai farmers for supplies and materials.

Furnish privately managed extension services to increase farmers' crop yields.

Assist farm owners in perfecting land titles and acquiring basic farm machinery.

Establish grading of Thai corn to make it salable at higher average prices in world markets.[5]

To Mr. Cogliandro's surprise, the project was accepted rather quickly, considering that "we initiated the project in November 1966, only five months ago. But even

5. "Private Loan Guaranty Helps Thai Farm Project," Press Release, Agency for International Development, Information Staff, Washington, April 21, 1967.

so, it wasn't fast enough to have all the construction completed and have it operating." Washington lost no time in garnering favorable publicity and the project was announced to the press with much fanfare and in glowing terms:

PRIVATE LOAN GUARANTY HELPS THAI FARM PROJECT

A major private enterprise project to spur the growth of Thailand's rural economy will be helped by the U. S. Agency for International Development and the Chemical Bank New York Trust Co.

AID is issuing an extended risk guaranty for a $3 million loan by the bank to provide principal start-up financing for the Calabrian (Thailand) Co., Ltd. This is a joint venture between Thai shareholders and the Calabrian Co., Inc., a New York firm with long experience in world-wide commodity trading.

The project, which supports War on Hunger objectives, will benefit some 7,000 farmers, using the familiar "county agent" concept of U. S. agriculture in providing advice on use of fertilizers, seed selection, cultivation, and other aspects of successful farming. . . .

The five-year loan by the U. S. bank protected by AID's "all-risk" insurance, may be used only to purchase U. S. goods and services. Additional financing for the project will be provided to the Calabrian (Thailand) Co. by the Krung Thai Bank and the shareholders.

The private financing will cover costs of construction and initial operation of the corn merchandising project, including grain storage and processing facilities. Operations will include crop loans and technical services to farmers, together with shelling, drying, grading, transporting, and storing corn, and finally sale in foreign trade.

The Krung Thai Bank portion of the financing will cover loans "in kind"—commodities and services—to the farmers to assist them in planting, cultivating, and harvesting. The farmers, in groups, will mutually guaranty [*sic*] repayment of the loans.

The company will establish up-country farm centers to provide technical services to the farmers, including farm equipment maintenance. A number of demonstration farms to be established this year will promote use of fertilizers and new hybrid seed. Among objectives of the training program throughout the system will be institution of row-crop planting, crucial to improving yield (a doubling is foreseen) from present "hill" planting methods.[6]

AID—*CALABRIAN, OPTIMISTIC VIEWS*

AID believed that, given an adequate flow of capital, Calabrian would be successful in establishing a viable business.[7] Furthermore, the scheme coincided with the Thai government policy that encouraged the establishment of industries processing raw materials. Calabrian thought it could also make its profits, by simplifying handling operations, introducing economies of scale, and relying upon its international network for a superior knowledge of market conditions. It was believed that the farmer could hope for higher profits by raising productivity and eliminating the middlemen.

6. Ibid.
7. "The Calabrian Maze," *Investor*, March 1969, p. 240.

CALABRIAN'S POLITICAL AND IDEOLOGICAL INVOLVEMENT

In December 1966, Kenneth Van de Laar stated that

the central and Northern areas may not be as explosive as the "Northeast," but are highly sensitive to communist influence and are important areas which should be concentrated upon to build stability and progress for the security of Thailand, and the government of Thailand recognizes this. Any program which would improve the conditions for these farmers would therefore meet the objectives of the U. S. foreign policy for South East Asia, and should therefore be supported and given equal priority status with any agricultural program for the "Northeast."[8]

Van de Laar set the mood of the company and its state of involvement when he issued this statement:

The first and most important conclusion is that a program of assistance to the Thai farmer is essential to the stability of Thailand. Support of such a program by the U. S. agencies involved is therefore almost mandatory and our program would be an ideal vehicle for the attainment of U. S. foreign policy objectives through private enterprise.[9]

In his conclusion, Van de Laar became emotionally involved in this project which he deemed so American and so spiritually right:

In supporting us [Private Enterprise] to successfully carry through this project the U. S. government will achieve a highly satisfactory objective, namely to help these people to progress without feeling that they are receiving "give aways" or charity. The farmers of Thailand are now suffering under a heavy burden of "indebtedness." We should aim to relieve their burden, *not change the debt from a financial to a moral one!*[10]

THE THAI CORN INDUSTRY IN 1967

Thailand was expected to produce about 1,250,000 tons of corn and approximately 100,000 tons of sorghum during 1967, with more than 70 percent coming from the central and northern plains. Thailand is the fourth largest exporter of corn, almost the entire crop being exported because few or no facilities exist for local consumption of feed grains.

In units of kilograms per rai, the national average corn yield is only about 250 (about twenty-five bushels per acre), with some areas averaging around 300 to 350, and a few progressive farms producing up to 700. Almost no

---

8. Kenneth Van de Laar, Managing Director, CalThai, Ltd., in a letter to Charles Cogliandro, dated December 24, 1968, p. 1.
9. Ibid., p. 8.
10. Ibid.

fertilizers, herbicides, or insecticides are used, and in most areas field preparation leaves much to be desired.

Due to local price-fixing and high duty, chemical fertilizers cost three times what they do in the U. S. Farmers are perpetually in debt to local merchants, who advance them money for seeds, tools, and food—at annual interest rates of up to 120 percent—against the year's corn crop. Due to low yields, lack of technical assistance, and the cost of financing (when available), farmers are unable to invest in the implements and fertilizers necessary to improve their crops.

More than 80 percent of the corn farmers in these central and northern areas have no title to the land they farm or, at best, they hold only a "right-to-occupy" document which can be revoked at any time. Many of these farmers could qualify to obtain a clear title but are (1) unable to afford the required fees to secure a registered title, (2) ignorant of the process that should be followed, or (3) unaware of the fact that there are methods by which they can obtain title.

THE MERCHANT SYSTEM

The market mechanism used to deliver corn from the farmer to export markets is the merchant system. It is both archaic and inefficient. It consists of five classes of merchants, from the general-store merchant in the country to the final link in Bangkok. Each level is dependent upon the next one.

Loans to farmers come down this chain. At each level the loan becomes more expensive, ending with the farmer paying from 60 to 120 percent interest. This was the whole crux of the problem. As a result, the farmers were always in debt to the money-lenders. The rate of nonpayment was great, and the whole system was really a bartering transaction where debts were paid in harvested corn.

CALTHAI

The Calabrian (Thailand) Company, Ltd.—CalThai, as it came to be known—registered on November 16, 1966, took over operations from Calabrian. Since July 1966, Calabrian had incurred losses of $300,000 on the project. The original directors were Charles Cogliandro; Irving Sverdlik, an attorney who became managing director; David Safer; and Albert Lyman, a leading lawyer.

Project facilities. Construction of ten small collection and storage facilities began in the middle of 1967 and was completed in November of that year. Each had a silo with a capacity of 1,600 tons of maize. These storage points acted as centers from which CalThai advisers loaned money, hired out tractors, and dispensed seeds, fertilizers, pesticides, and other agricultural material. Two additional storage facilities (country elevators) were completed in 1968. A major terminal elevator was built at Tha Rua and completed on November 10, 1967. Its capacity of 65,000 tons was the largest ever constructed in Thailand. The addition of a third building to the Tha Rua complex later increased its storage capacity to 73,900 tons (*see* Table 2). Tha Rua, situated by an inlet, is accessible to barges for eventual export of accumulated maize.

TABLE 2

Grain Elevator Capacities (in Metric Tons)

	1967	*1968*	*Total*
Terminal Elevators:			
Tha Rua	61,700	12,200	73,900
Payuhakiri	–	60,700	60,700
Khao Ya Kata	–	60,700	60,700
	61,700	133,600	195,300
12 Country Elevators	16,700	4,390	21,090
Total	78,400	137,990	216,390

SOURCE: "Questionable Support of a Private Venture in Thailand Under the Investment Guaranty Program," Report to Committee on Foreign Relations, U. S. Senate, General Accounting Office of the Comptroller General of the United States, April 1, 1970, p. 40.

Mr. Cogliandro cited three reasons for starting the project with eleven storage facilities:

1. In 1967, $1.8 million was allotted to facilities construction. It was understood by CalThai that further loans would be forthcoming as the project progressed. The initial loan of $4.5 million was the first installment to finance a $15 million program. It in no way was meant as a reduction in the magnitude of the project.
2. CalThai meant the project to be a significant force in modernizing the backward agricultural sector. To show its intent and determination, CalThai proposed to make a large visual impact upon the country.
3. The prefabricated storage facilities were shipped from Houston, Texas. To minimize transportation costs, the equipment and prefabricated parts were shipped in a single load and saved an estimated $500,000.

Grading.   CalThai made plans to introduce grading for Thai corn which would raise its reputation and price in world markets. The ratings, based primarily on shelling and drying processes, would correspond roughly to U. S. grades 1, 2, and 3. Far East Superintendence Co. and OMIC of Japan were to certify grading standards to ensure uniformity.

CalThai's managing director, Irving Sverdlik, said:

With just a little effort, the grade of Thai corn could be excellent, and with a certified standard, it would command higher prices in foreign markets outside Japan. Calabrian expects to help the farmer cash in on the higher prices in order to change the subsistence cycle and to give the farmers a little economic impetus.

At that time Thailand sold 80 percent of its corn at grade 2. The difference due to up-grading could amount to a considerable sum, since the 1968 crop of 1.3 million tons was expected to double within the next three years.

Farm loans. In May 1967 Calabrian signed an agreement to provide corn crop loans through the Bank of Agricultural Cooperatives at 1 percent a month. The $1.0 million program, to expand as other bank branches were set up, might be opened to other crops in the future. "These low-interest loans will enable farmers to break away from traditional reliance on middleman merchants," said Mr. Sverdlik.

AID's ALL-RISK INSURANCE PROGRAM

The financing necessary for such bold steps in a highly uncertain venture would be too risky for a profit-making company. However, AID felt that its "all-risk" insurance, with 75 percent of all investments eligible for a 100 percent extended-risk guarantee, would induce private enterprise to venture into uncertain situations. In this way the company's resources might be directed toward goals that would coincide with the aims of AID.

AID's risk-insurance program started in 1963. However, until 1964, insurable risks were limited by law to situations in the less developed areas, including those commonly called specific risks:

1. Inconvertibility of earnings or of repayment of principal.
2. Losses due to expropriation or confiscation.
3. Losses due to war or revolution, and those known as extended risk.
4. Losses and loans made for housing mortgages.
5. Up to 75 percent of the loss on an investment arising out of any such other kind of risk as the President might determine.[11]

The AID guarantee did not, in fact, require output of any American funds unless the privately run project went under because of legitimate business failure and the above-mentioned causes.

AID PERSONNEL

Herbert Salzman and Graham Williams were two key figures for AID at the inception of this project. They were the link between AID and Calabrian and the ones with whom Mr. Cogliandro negotiated. Mr. Salzman was assistant administrator of AID, and Mr. Williams worked specifically with Calabrian and the Thailand project. Concerning Calabrian, Mr. Salzman pointed out: "This project is a good example of what private initiative and resource—United States and local—can do to increase world food production and reduce the world food crisis. It is also a practical demonstration of government-business cooperation in the war on hunger."[12] He described AID as "a catalyst in

11. "Foreign Aid Through Private Initiative," op. cit.
12. Felix Belair, Jr., "Private Aid to Thais Guaranteed by U. S.," *New York Times*, 21 April 1967, p. 1.

helping to get this project started by making our extended-risk guarantee available."

GOVERNMENT VS. PRIVATE BUSINESS INTERESTS

The U. S. Embassy in Thailand and AID were anxious for the project to begin. The U. S. government was primarily interested in the program from the political point of view. Cogliandro said, "The U. S. government didn't care whether or not you made a profit; it was only interested in the political aspects. It encouraged us to go into it at all costs because much could be accomplished more quickly." He also said that everybody wanted to do something to help the farmers, but Calabrian was the first to do something tangible by giving them money.

CALTHAI's PLANS—PROGRESS AND PROBLEMS

Between the project's acceptance in April and the corn season beginning in September, there was little time to construct the necessary facilities. This delayed the corn-buying and put Calabrian at a disadvantage. Company buyers found that 90 percent of the farmers had already committed their crops to local merchants. If CalThai wanted corn to sell, it would have to buy it from the middlemen and pay their high prices. The company felt impelled to plunge ahead with corn purchases anyway. The facilities already constructed would stand idle for many months if no corn were purchased until the next buying season. However, CalThai's construction costs, farm programs, and overhead had taken a large share of the loans and as early as August 1967 CalThai executives told the New York office, "Our financial resources are already stretched at the seams." It became apparent that with such heavy construction and organizational costs, CalThai would sustain a loss for the year. By the close of 1967 Calabrian and AID were estimating that CalThai's loss during its first accounting year, which ended in March 1968, would be about $465,000. A loss of this size would have exceeded the total equity capital invested in cash by CalThai's stockholders.

Besides these large expenses, other exogenous factors created unfavorable results for the organization's plans:

1. A bumper American crop had depressed the world price of maize.
2. A threatened drought in Thailand caused the government to place an embargo on maize exports to everywhere except Japan (under JFTA agreement).
3. CalThai had great plans for developing the European and Taiwan market. However, with the closure of the Suez Canal, the expectations of shipping corn to Europe did not materialize.
4. Another disadvantage was the requirement that all guaranteed loans were to be spent in the U. S., even when materials were 25 to 30 percent more expensive.

ADDITIONAL FINANCIAL SUPPORT

CalThai, feeling that these setbacks should not impede the project, continued to think optimistically. It planned to construct more country stations and increase the volume of maize that could be handled to give the company the advantage of buying more corn during the next season. (Mr. Cogliandro said later that "this action was taken on the premise that the Farm Assistance program was to continue. If AID had indicated at that time its lack of interest, as it did late in 1968, a new approach would have been taken.")

The company's thinking was confirmed by a specialist assigned by AID when CalThai turned to it for additional financial support.

In a March 1968 telegram to AID/Bangkok, AID/Washington explained that the

November 1967 proposal from Cogliandro, which was basis for consideration of loan and equity guaranties to support 1968 expansion, called for additional U. S. equity in the amount of $2 million. During negotiations in December 1967, AID/W agreed to equity coverage of 75 cents of every dollar against loss due to bankruptcy or sale to third party at a loss. The entire U. S. equity would be covered by specific risks.

In the same telegram, it was stated that Van de Laar indicated "Calabrian/NY unable to raise new Calabrian/NY equity for investment in CalThai. It appears that little effort has been made to raise new equity." But Van de Laar proposed that new equity be raised from the following sources:

1.	Chemical Bank (loan)	$4,000,000
2.	Chemical Bank (for equity)	1,500,000
3.	Calabrian (stock)	2,000,000
		$7,500,000

Calabrian/NY, on AID/W insistence that it find real equity, made contact with a prominent New York investment banker who reported interest in trying to place control of Cal/NY with new corporate shareholders but uncertainty about its possibility. The inevitable result was, as AID/W put it, "If equity can be found, Cogliandro will lose control of Cal/NY and CalThai, and if project flounders, CalThai must liquidate." The telegram was not on a strictly "hard-nose" basis. AID/W sympathized with the situation and said, ". . . we fully appreciate [the] need to find a fast solution to keep project afloat. Do you [AID/Bangkok] have ideas on possible local sources, government or private, of new equity, for necessary working capital, to substitute for Cal/NY shortfall?"

Calabrian was unable to raise the $2 million from American sources. AID/Washington then concluded that, based on all the above, it was inclined to postpone extended guaranties to assist additional financing for expansion. However, other developments were taking place that were unknown to AID/W. In November 1967 the Bangkok Bank sent in its own auditors to evaluate Calabrian's situation. Mr. Cogliandro said:

They knew we were losing money, but reviewed the project and came to the conclusion that it was worth continuing. As a condition of getting any support from the Bangkok Bank, we decided to overhaul the whole situation—putting it on a strictly commercial basis. At this time I couldn't see ourselves worrying about the Thai farmers if nobody else did.

On May 27, 1968 CalThai signed a letter of intent with the Bangkok Bank to underwrite $1 million worth of shares. The overhaul included the reduction of American personnel. Mr. Cogliandro said, "This was a big burden on us. We were still carrying out certain farm-assistance aspects of the program." The equity arrangement with the Bangkok Bank was finally approved after certain modifications to conform to Thai laws.

After learning that CalThai's operating losses through January 31, 1968 exceeded $1 million, and that CalThai was unable to obtain the $2 million for its planned equity investment, AID modified the financing plan for 1968:

1. Calabrian, from:
   (a) Bangkok Bank (equity) $1,000,000
   (b) Chemical Bank (guaranteed)   1,500,000
   (c) A & S Steel (facilities contractor)   500,000   3,000,000
2. Bank of America (guaranteed)   3,000,000
                                               $6,000,000

The modified financing plan was dictated by what AID thought was essential to get CalThai into a profitable position by providing additional storage capacity and deferring farmer assistance until it could be paid for out of earnings. AID believed that the losses sustained could be recouped through tighter management of the business and increased volumes of corn.

In conjunction with the guaranteed arrangement Calabrian agreed to two possible dispositions of its $2.5 million in CalThai stock.

1. If Calabrian did not repay $1 million of the $1.5 million Chemical Bank loan by October 1, 1968, AID would acquire the right to sell the stock for such consideration as AID deemed appropriate.
2. To pledge the stock to the Chemical Bank as security for the $1.5 million loan.

The loan from the Bank of America was issued a 100 percent guarantee. AID's justification was that the total amount guaranteed for the project equaled less than 75 percent of the total contemplated investment in the project. This justification relied on the proposed equity investment by the Bangkok Bank as well as the unguaranteed loans which had been made possible by the expenditure of guaranteed funds. AID therefore needed to ensure that the Bangkok Bank was prepared to honor its underwriting agreement. AID conducted extensive negotiations with the bank which delayed implementing the 1968 financing plan. This delay, together with the approaching October 1 deadline, created maximum uncertainty in the trade. It made AID's continuing support doubtful to present to other potential investors.

The October 1 date became immediately known throughout the trade, and rumors were persistent that AID was trying to interest outside investors to take over CalThai management. This had a disastrous effect upon the confidence of the trade and convinced other investors to do nothing until that date had passed, whereupon they could obtain most lenient terms from AID.

Loans became available to CalThai on the following dates:

April 5, 1968: Loan from Chemical Bank to Calabrian for CalThai equity
June 7, 1968: Loan from facilities contractor to Calabrian for CalThai equity
June 19, 1968: Loan from Bank of America
July 1968: Bangkok Bank for CalThai equity

With financing temporarily settled, CalThai embarked on a vigorous building program to increase to twelve the number of grain storage units. Construction was also begun on two huge 20-rai terminal complexes to complement the Tha Rua facility (*see* Table 2).

STRIFE BETWEEN CALABRIAN AND AID

As the project progressed, differing views and conflicting attitudes clashed periodically, resulting in uneasy relations between Calabrian and AID. Mr. Cogliandro describes the situation as "a revolving door." He explains:

When we went in, we dealt with one group of people in Washington. Graham Williams was taken off the project, and each month thereafter, somebody else would come in and be put in charge of this project. Each had his own concept of what should be done and what should not be done. Finally, they brought in a man from Turkey who knew all the answers—everyone was out of step but him. I would say there was definitely a clash of personalities.

However, continuity between AID/Bangkok and CalThai was maintained, even during these monthly changeovers. Mr. Cogliandro said:

AID/Washington and AID/Bangkok had always been diametrically opposed. AID/Bangkok knew our problems and what we were trying to accomplish. AID/Washington had their eyes on Congress [Foreign Relations Committee] and what their reaction might be rather than what was being accomplished in Bangkok. My frank opinion is that AID's main concern was to appease Senator Fulbright. In early 1968 a new director was assigned to AID/Bangkok and after that, everything CalThai did was wrong. It seemed AID had made up its mind to discourage the project from continuing.

CALTHAI's PROBLEMS WITH AID

Just when one crisis seemed to be solved, another appeared and became, in turn, an irritating nuisance to the continuation of the project. One such problem arose concerning the treaty between the U. S. government and the Thai government under the extended-risk program. Under this treaty, the Thai government is not to place any obstacles in the way of any project that is guaranteed by the U. S. government. "Therefore," Mr. Cogliandro explains, "the Thai government had no right to impose the corn embargo."

CalThai wanted to break the embargo and was sure the U. S. government would offer support. Refusing to do business with Japan was CalThai's method of objecting to and demonstrating to the Thai government its resentment of the embargo. Holding corn at that time was not wise due to its shrinkage and weight loss. It turned out to be CalThai's largest single financial loss. Mr. Cogliandro explained this strategy as "what was thought to be the politically right thing to do."

As it turned out, when CalThai asked AID for support, there was no response. In Mr. Cogliandro's opinion,

It was a politically created situation and Japan was too important to the U. S. to get involved in such a minor matter. When the U. S. government deserted us, we sold 35,000 tons to the Japanese in one month. But by then, it was too late because the prices had dropped. The damage had already been done.

THE JFTA AGREEMENT

The Japanese Feed Trade Association had an agreement with Thailand to buy 720,000 tons of corn annually at a set (1968) price of $42 per ton. The prices set between the two countries were consistently below world prices by $10 to $15. Also as a result of this agreement, an embargo was placed on corn shipments to anywhere but Japan if it was felt that Thailand's corn crop was large enough to fill only Japan's quota. Under this agreement, Japan also acquired preferential treatment in paying set packing charges. In Bangkok corn was shipped in bags rather than bulk. All buyers paid a minimum of $5 per ton packing charge. But the JFTA agreement allowed only $2 per ton.

CalThai had been fighting this agreement to no avail. Despite Japan's purchase of 8 million tons annually, the Thai government was afraid buying would stop.

We tried to demonstrate to the Thai government that Japan was buying Thai corn at prices lower than from other sources and the only party that suffers is the farmers. We could have sold corn to Japan at JFTA prices and still shown a profit. But we wanted to help the farmers establish the principle of independence. Selling corn to Japan would perpetuate that agreement.

CalThai was interested in the welfare of the farmer and fought in his behalf. Mr. Cogliandro said:

> We thought we could do something with the U. S. government behind us. As crusaders, we thought we were doing what the U. S. government wanted us to do. In fact, we were known as an arm of the U. S. government. We were, at that time, guided by political reasoning and not by commercial rationalization.

AID's VIEW OF THE JFTA AGREEMENT

The feelings of AID/W on the JFTA agreement are reflected in a telegram to AID/Bangkok, reproduced below in part:

> We are asking suitable advice from you concerning Thai-Japanese agreement.... Although CalThai in 1967 was burdened with excessive salary costs and preincorporation expenses and charges and suffered from ineffective management, main cause for losses was failure to get a better price for corn. This was caused by the 1967 Thai-Japanese trade agreement. In light of substantial U. S. and U. S. government financial involvement in CalThai project as it now exists and as proposed for expansion . . . AID/W thinks it essential that Thai government understand we are supporting project solely for Thailand's benefit. We, therefore, need assurances from the Thai government that final trade agreement and arrangements thereunder permit CalThai to sell corn at competitive world prices. Please discuss this with appropriate Thai government officials and advise us [on] their position.
>
> The Thai position is essential to our decision whether to go ahead with new U. S. government financial commitments to CalThai. If we cannot be satisfied on this, only possibility would be holding action with little, if any, additional U. S. capital.

In a reply by AID/Bangkok, Ambassador Unger stated that "It appears the Japanese trade agreement [is a] long-term problem about which little can be done now except plant suggestions for improvement of pricing and location formula with Thai Board."

CORN EMBARGO SQUEEZE

The corn embargo hindered the free functioning of the project. CalThai depended upon access to free markets to sell its corn, but again the U. S. government did not intervene. "Because we could not diversify our market," Mr. Cogliandro said, "we were at the mercy of the Japanese."

UNWISE BUSINESS DECISIONS?

Calabrian's buying procedure was to deal directly with the farmer, thus bypassing the middleman and eliminating the extra step in getting the corn to market. The merchants were not happy about this, nor were they pleased when CalThai purchased corn at prices higher than those prevailing in the Bangkok market. As a consequence of buying at inflated prices, the trade viewed the company's motives suspiciously. Bangkok dealers proceeded to buy up maize in large quantities, hoarding stocks so that prices rose. CalThai therefore had to pay increasingly higher prices. The strategy employed by CalThai is explained by Mr. Cogliandro:

> The grain business in Thailand is like anywhere else in the world. The person who pays the highest prices gets the goods. The rumor that we paid too much to the farmer is nonsense. Basically in Thailand, the grain price follows a traditional pattern where the price that exists during harvest season is the lowest of the whole year, and whether you pay 1/2 baht or 1 baht more per picul [60 kilos] is not going to make or break the project. This is not a significant factor.

The marketing strategy worked in this manner. Calabrian, with expertise in grain trading, developed estimates of the trends in world corn prices. They realized that the price fluctuates during the year and is lowest during harvest seasons.

CALTHAI's PLACEMENT OF SILOS

AID/W criticized CalThai for constructing a major grain elevator behind a sand bar in the port of Tha Rua. An American agronomist said:

> It hampers ships from coming up the river to load corn. Other ships load off the bank below the sand bar, but CalThai has to send small boats out to transfer the corn. The Japanese must have paid off the fellow who picked the site.

Mr. Cogliandro retorted,

> All grain elevators in Thailand, including the three port elevators in Bangkok (not Calabrian-owned) have been built "behind sand bars." It is the nature of the country, one well known and carefully considered before construction began. As it happens in this particular instance:
>
> 1. The site was recommended to management by an AID-approved grain consultant who had been involved with grains all his life. The recommendation was accepted as it confirmed the finding of the company after thousands of hours of study and operation.
> 2. AID has distributed widely, and published in its own publications, a photograph showing barges of about 250 tons floating past Tha Rua. The normal size barge in use today ranges from 50 to 100 tons.
> 3. Anyone familiar with the corn trade in Thailand knows that about 500,000 tons of corn have been moved from that exact area for shipment to Bangkok annually for many years, and that the locality is perhaps the most important interior corn market of Thailand, next only to Bangkok in importance.

CALTHAI's TRADING WITH
CHINESE MERCHANTS

CalThai has constantly been criticized for its handling of the shrewd Chinese merchants. AID felt that CalThai was naive and unaware of the way these people did business. When purchasers went out to acquire ten truckloads of maize, ten would be loaded, but only eight or nine might reach the warehouse. Mr. Cogliandro explained:

> You hear so many things—the merchants stole from us, they pulled something on us, or they gave us bad corn. The grain comes into the installation and is paid for after being weighed by our own staff. We always knew what the merchant was doing, his techniques, and way of doing things. You can't be in the country for five years and not know this.

CalThai's strategy was not to compete and eventually to eliminate the merchants. In its long-range plans CalThai proposed to utilize the merchants' network to collect and deliver corn to established storage sites. They could do it much cheaper and there would be mutual benefits. They would be paid immediately rather than having to wait two to four weeks as in the old system.

CALTHAI's OVERHEAD

Starting costs had been high and the operation continued to carry too high an overhead—$1 million a year. Too many Americans were paid by U. S. standards (agronomists, for example, had salaries of $18,000 per year, plus expenses). CalThai eventually reduced its American personnel from twenty-two agronomists to ten, and later to six. The company felt that by paying its local staff monthly salaries in excess of customary levels, corruption would be avoided, but it did not work out that way. Mr. Cogliandro said, "Sometimes corn just disappeared. Without proper communication among eleven silos and installations, it was very hard to control the activities of the 200 employees."

BANGKOK BANK FREEZES
CALTHAI's ACCOUNT

On August 6, 1968 it was learned that the Bangkok Bank had blocked the CalThai account into which the bank's equity contribution had been paid. They refused to release the funds to CalThai until U. S. funds were transferred to Thailand. CalThai then sought to transfer to Thailand, as working capital, the $1.4 million balance left in the Bank of America loan commitment. Although AID had previously permitted guaranteed funds to be transferred to Thailand, its position now was that these funds could only be used for procurement in the U. S. AID prohibited further drawdowns of the Bank of America loan and the transfer of guaranteed funds to Thailand.

AID/Bangkok requested that Bank of America guaranteed loan funds be transferred to Thailand in lieu of the equity capital funds, but AID/Washington maintained that the forecasted cash flows indicated that adequate local currency working capital would be available when the Bangkok Bank's contemplated equity investment was made.

AID refused to permit the transfer because in the sixteen months preceding July 1968 CalThai had recorded losses of $2.6 million. AID had the authority to deny the grant because Calabrian had defaulted on two interest payments to the banks making the initial $6.1 million loans—Chemical Bank New York Trust Company and Bank of America. Faced with the potential loss of even more money, AID decided to abandon the project rather than allow additional capital to be used in an effort to see Calabrian through another year.

CalThai's accounts were frozen at a very bad time. Grain prices were rising above normal levels and foreign buyers were able to consume more than Thailand could supply. Despite higher prices, bankruptcy threatened, because CalThai had not sold enough corn in its first eighteen months of operation to meet its interest payments.

AID's REPUTATION AT STAKE

The people at AID were worried not only about the failure of the program itself, but also about what it represented. CalThai's collapse would represent the first major failure in the agency's seven-year program of high-risk loan guarantees.[13] What had promised to be a significant contribution to Thailand's stability had become a bitter memory of unfulfilled American promises to Thai farmers.

COGLIANDRO's POSITION
AND ATTITUDE

Charles Cogliandro, President of CalThai, found it difficult to work with AID/ Washington. He said, "AID had a preconceived impression of what I would do and not do." This he felt was totally wrong. "I would have welcomed direction and advice from AID and would earnestly attempt to solve basic differences between us." But as AID handled the situation, CalThai was left entirely on its own in an environment with many political overtones. Mr. Cogliandro, along with Senator Fulbright, charged that AID's investment in the Thai scheme was undertaken "in order to accomplish certain political objectives." He felt CalThai became involved in a political situation where a private company could not cope without U. S. government assistance.

AID's delay in the second financing created uncertainty in the trade and discouraged new equity going into the project. Strenuous effort was made to locate interested participants to invest in CalThai, but AID cast doubt on the project's outlook, and potential investors were frightened away.

13. Peter A. Hornbostel, "Investment Guaranties: Bureaucracy Clogs the Flow," *Columbia Journal of World Business* (March-April 1969).

There were many people talking and criticizing but very few knew the actual situation in Thailand. AID/Washington based many of their decisions on prevailing impressions. They knew so little of the situation that they listened to these rumors. The controversy over the location of the Tha Rua installation is illustrative of this. You don't have to be in Thailand long to know that the biggest shipping point from the interior is from Tha Rua.

Although it is true that AID assumed the major portion of the risk of loss, from the start all parties were informed that the total capital of Calabrian was somewhat over $500,000. But later AID acted as though Calabrian was to assume the financial burden. "AID says one thing and does another—it's difficult to rely on them."

AID's FINANCIAL ARRANGEMENTS

The financing arrangements AID agreed upon for the project were unique compared with the financing arrangements for other comparable projects supported with extended-risk investment guarantees. The basic deviations were:

1. AID guaranteed 100 percent of U. S. bank loans which constituted almost all the U. S. investment in the project. Calabrian was not required to guarantee the normal portion of the loans or to make a significant unguaranteed investment. In the General Accounting Office opinion, AID should, in all cases, require the owner who controls a project supported with guarantees of the Calabrian type to assume a meaningful portion of the total risk involved in the project, since to do otherwise would not be conducive to good financial management.[14] Calabrian contended that it invested $750,000 of actual cash directly from its own funds; therefore Calabrian invested more than its own net worth into the project. This $750,000 did not include any indirect investments, although they were considerable. AID issued its first guarantee for the project to Chemical Bank for $3 million. As justification, the required 75 percent relation with the total project had to be maintained. CalThai then borrowed $1 million from the Krung Thai Bank.
2. AID allowed CalThai to borrow $1 million from the Bangkok Bank by mortgaging the principal grain facilities constructed with the guaranteed funds. But the loan agreement covering the Chemical Bank guarantee prohibited any mortages, pledges, or liens on other property or assets of CalThai. Calabrian emphasized that CalThai had not entered into any mortgage without AID's prior approval.
3. AID allowed CalThai to draw down guaranteed loan with only $255,000 of the pledged $500,000 subscribed to CalThai's stock.
4. Calabrian agreed to repay by 1 October 1968 $1 million of the $1.5 million Chemical Bank guaranteed loan or AID would acquire control of CalThai's stock.

14. "Questionable Support of a Private Venture in Thailand Under the Investment Guaranty Program," General Accounting Office of the Comptroller General of the U. S., April 1, 1970, p. 2.

THE IMPORTANCE OF BANGKOK
BANK's EQUITY INVESTMENT

The accumulation of these requirements for future adjustments to the financial structure made AID sensitive to a need to ensure that the Bangkok Bank was prepared to honor its underwriting agreement to purchase $1 million in preferred stock of CalThai. Up to that time, $7.5 of the $9.5 million were guaranteed loans. For AID to justify the amount of the guaranteed portion, that portion must equal less than 75 percent of total investment. Without Bangkok Bank's unguaranteed investment, the proportion of guaranteed to unguaranteed investment was $7.5 million/$9.5 million = 78.94 percent; 3.94 percent above the limit. With Bangkok Bank's equity investment, the percentage would drop to: $7.5 million/$10.5 million = 71.5 percent (*see* Table 3).

TABLE 3

Equity and Loan Financing

	Amount (millions)	Percentage
Guaranteed Loan Funds:		
1967 Chemical Bank loan	$3.0	
1968 Bank of America loan	3.0	
1968 Chemical Bank loan used for equity[a]	1.5	
	$ 7.5	71.4
Unguaranteed Loan Funds:		
1967 Bangkok Bank loan secured by a grain facility mortgage	1.0	1.5	14.3
1968 Facilities contractor (A&S steel) loan used for equity[a]	0.5	
	1.5	14.3
Unguaranteed Equity Capital:		
Existing equity (excluding $2.0 million shown as loan above)[a]	0.5	
Proposed equity of Bangkok Bank	1.0	
	1.5	14.3
Total Contemplated Investment	$10.5	100.0

[a]The 1968 Chemical Bank loan and the 1968 loan from the facilities contractor were invested in CalThai by Calabrian.

AID believed that it was justified in giving greater than usual assistance to the Calabrian project because it was intended to achieve important development objectives in Thailand. AID made its decision to underwrite almost all the initially planned investment with the knowledge that Calabrian's total net worth, which AID understood to be about $500,000, prevented Calabrian's making a meaningful investment in the project.

CALTHAI's ACCOMPLISHMENTS
IN THAILAND

A report from Ambassador Unger to AID/Washington described what Calabrian had achieved during its first half year, ending December 15, 1967:

1. Calabrian-Thailand Farm Service Center managers and extension agronomists have assisted, advised, and demonstrated to thousands of farmers the most effective plowing and cultivating methods with modern farm machinery.
2. CalThai has experimented with many grades and application rates of fertilizers. From these test-demonstration experiments, they have been able to develop a great deal of data that they are making available to the corn farmers.
3. CalThai has tested about twenty-five varieties of hybrid corn and grain sorghums with outstanding results. This information is also being presented to individual farmers and associations.
4. CalThai has disrupted the institutionalized merchant system by using moisture meters and accurate weighing. This has built a great deal of good will and confidence for CalThai and the program. Previous methods used by merchants consisted of squeezing a handful of corn or biting a kernel to test its moisture. Farmers were also dubious of the accuracy of the scales used.
5. CalThai began a daily posting of its buying price that reflected the day's world market price for Thai corn. CalThai had assumed all costs of gathering, evaluating, transmitting and publicly posting the information—the first such service ever given the farmers. Providing these services has accounted for a relatively high percentage of CalThai's overhead expense.
6. The world market price of corn is off up to $10 per ton. Thai farmers' price is up about $6 per ton, compared to 1966. Assuming a total corn crop of 1 million tons, the increased income to Thailand will be $6 million. With an average farm size of ten acres and a yield of thirty bushels per acre, the $6 million would net the average farmer about $45.75 (915 baht) additional income from his crop.
7. The construction of large grain facilities in the interior of Thailand (*see* Table 2).
8. Overall impact upon the Thai farm economy:
   (a) Introduction of modern farming methods
   (b) Less dependence upon merchants
   (c) Better financing and extension of credit through various banks
   (d) Exposing innate inequities of JFTA agreement
   (e) Increasing corn production:

1960 to 1964	Average:	720,000
1966		1,100,000
1967		1,200,000
1968		1,375,000*

   *Second crop; first crop damaged by drought.

Even though considerable progress had been achieved, and its presence in Thailand was acknowledged to be important, CalThai was unable to get access to the funds already guaranteed them, nor could it secure loans elsewhere. As Herbert Salzman had promised, "As long as I sit in this chair, Calabrian will not get another penny from the government. We're going to shut them down."

LOOKING BACKWARD

Even with the exogenous factors that inhibited CalThai in the marketing of corn (e.g., bumper American crops, corn embargo, etc.), Mr. Cogliandro stated that CalThai could always sell any quantity processed. He said, "The three biggest buyers in the area—Japan, Taiwan, and Singapore—were our steadiest customers."

CalThai made about $100,000 profit on the project by December 1967, about $10,000 in January 1968, and expected to show good profits in February and March. But from then onward, the whole project went rapidly downhill as a result of AID's handling of the situation.[15]

In retrospect, Mr. Cogliandro said:

If we had to start over again, we would run a business and not a welfare program. We could have operated strictly on a business basis, being cold-blooded and having no regard for the farmer. What the hell do we care if the Thai farmer gets $10 or $20 for his corn! If the price of corn was $50, we would buy for $40. But we did not do this—we were champions of the farmer! We were fighting for him. And we were completely and hopelessly deserted by the U. S. government.

He went on to explain what he felt ruined the efforts of CalThai:

Basically, what destroyed the project was the attitude and actions of the U. S. government and the Bangkok Bank. You cannot rely on the U. S. government. If you try to, it's just like playing Russian roulette.

15. Comments on *Investor* article, written by United States Operations Mission (AID) Bangkok, and published in the *Investor*.

ARGO-INDUSTRIAL DEVELOPMENT CORP., S. A. (AGRIDCO), U. S. A.

A Unique Private American Enterprise to Assist in the Economic Development of the Dominican Republic Through the Development of Agribusiness

The Agro-Industrial Development Company (AGRIDCO) was officially incorporated on January 1, 1968. This agribusiness corporation is a consortium of five large, internationally oriented firms including International Minerals and Chemical Corporation (IMC), ADELA Investment Company, Worthington Corporation, International Harvester Company, and Dow Chemical Co.

AGRIDCO was allotted over 400,000 acres of Dominican Republic land in April 1967 to conduct feasibility studies for developing agriculture and the economic infrastructure of that nation. The preliminary study was completed in the first quarter of 1968, and contract negotiations with the Dominican government for the complete development project seemed to be nearing completion by January 1969. AGRIDCO's chairman and primary moving force, Mr. Kenneth Mueller, was quite optimistic that AGRIDCO would be in full operation by April 1969. In a recent interview in his home office in New York City Mr. Mueller said:[1]

> I have hopes that we will have it [AGRIDCO] off the ground in probably ninety days. This may be somewhat optimistic, but we are moving very, very rapidly.

However, by February 1969, AGRIDCO's progress had been slowed appreciably. Despite Mr. Mueller's extensive experience with both Dominican Republic and Latin American business and politics, the corporate chairman could not foresee the volatile nature of public opinion in the Dominican nation and the numerous internal power struggles which repeatedly upset and restructured contract negotiations for the project.

The first signs that AGRIDCO's attempts to aid the underdeveloped nation would be compromised were evident in February and March 1967. A legislative subcommittee—an offshoot of the government's National Development Commission (CND)—rejected the consortium's original development proposal and submitted a counterproposal which placed the entire financial burden for the preliminary land studies upon AGRIDCO, thus lowering AGRIDCO's effective profit expectations from the project. The counterproposal consisted of five points.[2]

1. That AGRIDCO pay for the feasibility studies of the project: an expected cost of $300,000.
2. That AGRIDCO contribute a reasonable share of the total capital investment; it was explained that the amount of this share had not been determined and was subject to negotiation.
3. That AGRIDCO reduce its percentage of the profits: discussion had been based on 40 percent, of which 37 percent was to be reinvested in the country.
4. That the purchases and acquisitions of equipment or inputs be made under competitive conditions, by any company, and not only the members of the AGRIDCO consortium.
5. That all classes of losses that may apply to the state be guaranteed. This implies that the state will never be able to lose on an investment.

A spokesman for CND said that the counterproposal was drawn up in a radical form in a "manner that any concessions made to AGRIDCO by the government would not harm the national interest." The spokesman assured that the project

---

1. All further references to Mr. Mueller's comments pertain to interviews with the author conducted during 1969.
2. "Replace AGRIDCO Exploitation Project," *El Listin,* 13 March 1967. *El Listin* is a privately owned newspaper published in the Dominican Republic.

would be approved by the government if AGRIDCO accepted the modifications and if public opinion considered it favorable.

AGRIDCO representatives accepted these modifications, and interaction between the development agents and the Dominican government subsided while the preliminary land research progressed. The completed research marked the need for further negotiations and contract settlement during 1968. However, on February 6, 1969, the government decided that the project should be reappraised, and later that month contract negotiations had reached a standstill.

Listin Diario[3] commented on the latest project criticism: "Luis Julian Perez, president of the National Development Commission, lamented that the project must be abandoned by the government's plans because 'public scandal provoked the publication of misleading news on the project.'" Perez pointed out that, "the subcommittee that studied the project demanded AGRIDCO make various modifications before the project would be accepted for discussion."[4]

The newest modifications suggested by the CND subcommittee, considered substantial, consisted of two major elements.[5] The first element represented the latest stage in the evolution of the project, profit negotiations, initiated in the 1967 CND counterproposal. In the two-year interim between active negotiations, the profit distribution for the project had fluctuated wildly.

1. AGRIDCO would receive 40 percent of the profits generated by the project rather than the original 50 percent stipulated. Of this 40 percent, 37 percent must be reinvested in the country.
2. The formation of a totally autonomous Corporation of Agricultural Development (CODESA) directed by a council formed by:
   (a) a representative of the President of the Republic who would preside;
   (b) the director and subdirector of the Dominican Agrarian Institute (IAD);
   (c) the Secretary of Agriculture, the president-administrator of the Institute of Development and Cooperative Credit, the director of the Institute of Hydraulic Resources, and the director of the Office of Community Development.

AGRIDCO accepted these modifications. However, four days later in the February 10, 1969 issue of *Listin Diario!*

The government has decided to study once again the project discussed for agricultural development presented by the AGRIDCO Consortium. . . . This information was presented yesterday by the President of the Republic, Doctor Joaquin Balaguer.

The project had been abandoned indefinitely from government plans according to previous statements by Balaguer and Luis Perez, president of the National Development Commission. The President stated that the project would have to be studied again to see if there was anything acceptable.[6]

3. Another newspaper published in the Dominican Republic.
4. "Luis Julian Perez Defends the AGRIDCO Project," *Listin Diario*, 6 February 1969.
5. Antolin Montas, "Firm Would Obtain Forty Million Dollars," *El Caribe*, 7 February 1969.
6. "CND Maintains They Will Study the AGRIDCO Plan," *Listin Diario*, 10 February 1969.

HISTORY OF THE CONSORTIUM

International Minerals and Chemical Corporation, the prime force behind AGRIDCO, had been in operation for over sixty years and had grown nationally and internationally to become the world's leading producer of fertilizer products, marketing in sixty foreign countries. At this time IMC's Director of Overseas Development, Kenneth Mueller, was interested in discovering new ideas or new ways that would expand the scope of the company's future activities and creative use of executive abilities. Mr. Mueller expressed this interest by saying: ". . . we were considering here in IMC different forms, different kinds of arrangements by which IMC could, in conjunction with other agribusiness companies, more efficiently use the kind of internal talents we had." (At the time of AGRIDCO's incorporation, Kenneth Mueller became the Chairman of the Board of Directors of the new company, while simultaneously holding his other position with IMC.)

Mr. Mueller also recognized the mounting need in many foreign nations for outside help in combating the food-shortage problem. The application of modern techniques and machinery in underutilized land areas contributes to the country's national development by feeding more people as well as by aiding the balance of payments problem that arises from importing foodstuffs. IMC was in a position to help fight global food shortage and in a manner which would employ the company's talents and products extensively and creatively.

FOREIGN MARKET ENTRY—
SOME PROVEN METHODS

IMC's experience in international operations had demonstrated that there are at least four reliable methods for entering a foreign market.

1. The company can build a plant in the host nation, establishing a foreign branch which produces and distributes its products semi-autonomously. The branch plant may use the established foreign distribution channels or attempt to develop its own distribution net.
2. Rather than make a large initial investment in plant and equipment, the company can offer a patent licensing agreement to a local producer. The agreement provides the foreign firm with the right and knowledge (through consultation) for carrying on production. In this situation the licensee would distribute the finished goods.
3. International markets can also be penetrated by importing finished or semi-finished goods and simply establishing warehousing and distribution facilities in the host nation. Such a plan is most economical and efficient when shipping costs are low or import tariffs are reasonable. However, it is rare that both of these conditions are met.
4. Rather than developing a mutually exclusive relationship, the corporation might work closely with the host nation's government, acting as a consultant and providing plant(s), equipment and management for a development corporation suited to the government's estimates of national needs.

Not only had IMC used each of these four methods for establishing business internationally, it would combine the most favorable elements from the plans to meet the special needs of a new project.

FOREIGN MARKET ENTRY—
THE NEED FOR A NEW APPROACH

Although IMC could attack the food shortage and land development problem alone, Mr. Mueller envisioned a joint effort involving other members of the world business community. The nature of such a partnership, however, was quite vague. One type of organization that had been tried with reasonable success was found in India. Mr. Mueller stated: "There is a British combined agribusiness plant in India, and this is essentially complementary countries providing raw materials, management, marketing, production, distribution, and planning facilities."

By mid-1965 the idea of a multination partnership had been tentatively overruled. The involvement of several nations in a development project usually compounds the organization's problems by introducing divergent concepts of management philosophy and of legal and contractual obligations. Meaningful communications between the national representatives is difficult to maintain. Mr. Mueller elaborated on the alternative approach subsequently pursued.

> I took the initiative to talk to a series of companies who have international involvements to find out if some of them would be willing in some way to cooperate with one another towards the development of an aggregate of their techniques and talents, aggregating them in such a way as to help a foreign country develop its agriculture.

Mr. Mueller proposed that each member of the partnership contribute expertise toward the development of a specific land parcel or parcels in a given country. The basic idea was to innovate a corporate form which required not only the financial merging of the interested parties, but also the effective merger of their objectives and desires to aid a developing nation. An innovative approach that could meet these requirements would likely avoid 100 percent ownership of the production and distributing facilities and rather than paternalize the nation's people, attempt to involve them in the project through education, training, and profit sharing. Clearly, the organizational structure needed to garner both technical and social rapport with a nation's people would have to be unique.

THE SEARCH FOR PARTNERS—
NEGOTIATION AND RESPONSE

More than twenty-five large firms were approached by IMC. Mr. Mueller himself, conducted most of the exploratory search for interest in a development project. Responses from the management of contacted companies ranged from interest to bewilderment. One executive with whom Mr. Mueller spoke remarked:

Ken seemed sure that there was a potential for several U. S. firms to get together and help an underdeveloped country. Of course, I tried to get him to clarify what he meant by "get together" but I'm not sure if Ken had really thought his plan out for any great length. We were semi-cooperative of course. Most of the men that Ken talked with appreciated the need for advice and help outside the U. S. The clearest impression I ever got of the IMC plan was that they were proposing some kind of amalgam of company talents in some form which would help and potentiate a less-developed country's agriculture. But to be truthful, having the conversation with Ken was an exercise in futility. The agenda was just too loosely drawn.

Early in 1966 it became apparent that IMC and Mr. Mueller would have to clarify the development proposal if they hoped to gain the interest and cooperation of other internationally diverse firms. The proposal was outlined that IMC would find "a country with a land mass which needed developing and form a kind of land mass developing corporation in which every one could take an equity position and use this as the developing instrument."

Several questions arose immediately. What kind of a developing instrument should be used? Would it act autonomously? How then would it utilize the talents inhering in each of the companies?

An agreement was proposed which replaced the usual corporate description of specific policies with an *Agreement of Consortium* among members. The proposal attempted to clarify how each member would contribute its expertise toward the development of a specific land parcel or parcels in a given country under a given set of circumstances. Response to Mueller's persistence in meeting with the management and boards of many companies had created increased interest in the approach; the executive comment following is not atypical:

We don't even believe in the Consortium. It's a ridiculous kind of thing. All you do is compound problems that any one company has throughout its own management structure. You always have difficulties in management even within a company. You have the Vice-President of Purchasing who doesn't necessarily agree with the Vice-President of Sales, etc. Why should we compound these problems by forming a consortium of diverse companies with divergent interests and hope that the thing can hold together? What purpose does it serve? We believe that we can do the job as well as any group of companies.

Other companies viewed the consortium as an unwieldy way of trying to develop an agricultural endeavor. A single company could do the job more efficiently and quickly by simply contracting for the inputs needed.

IMC's arguments for a multifirm consortium were stated by Mr. Mueller. He believed that "we had the benefits of both the single company approach (because the consortium could be incorporated as a single company), while having the additional benefit of being able to call upon the expertise of the member companies, which no other single company would have. We have the best of both possible worlds." The fact that Mr. Mueller had by now specified a corporate form for his developing agent, with members dividing stock ownership equally among themselves, facilitated IMC's negotiations for partners.

THE CHOICE OF PARTNERS

The specific choice of partners in the IMC joint venture presented decisions concerning both the functional and legal aspects of amalgamation. United States companies collaborating in overseas markets had been cited by the Justice Department for violation of antitrust legislation and for restraining trade.

Table 1 indicates the nature and attributes of IMC's partners in the consortium. IMC had selected the four firms from a much larger list which included companies with functional expertise in many diverse areas including food processing, construction, research, promotion, and finance. Although a multinational consortium had been tentatively ruled out in the earlier stages of planning the development project, the negotiations leading to the formation of AGRIDCO resulted in essentially a bi-national corporation. ADELA Investment Co., S. A., of Luxembourg proved to be an essential element of the new structure and was a charter member of AGRIDCO along with the four U. S. based firms: International Harvester, IMC, Dow Chemical, and the Worthington Corporation.

WHAT COUNTRY TO DEVELOP?

IMC and each of the consortium members had a wide range of experience in international business, hence there was no lack of suggestions of countries suitable for development. Some of the most important alternatives are discussed below.

India

IMC had worked closely with the Indian government since 1963 in a program to promote private investment in fertilizer plants.[7] In conjunction with Standard Oil of California, IMC formed the Coromandel Fertilizers Co., investing $80 million to ease the crushing food problem in India. The primary objectives of the Indian project were to supply the country with two significant inputs: high quality fertilizer and the education necessary for its effective use. Coromandel Fertilizers proved highly successful, in part because the Indian government was highly cooperative and supported foreign investments by extending generous tax and export concessions. By 1966, the Indian government had approved five large investment projects, and groundwork for a sixth was laid coincidentally with the consortium's search for projects. The new proposal was to establish a $100 million complex at Mithapur in Western India which would turn out 2.3 million tons of fertilizer annually after ten years. The Mithapur project had been approved in principle by the Indian Cabinet, and agreement on certain modifications requested by New Delhi was reportedly near. Ultimately, the Mithapur project was to be tied in with a $160 million government-owned nuclear power plant and was to be expanded into an agro-industrial complex.

7. "Business Abroad," *Business Week*, 27 July 1968, p. 82.

TABLE 1

Member Companies and Descriptions

Company Name	Products	Plant Locations and Size	Contributions to AGRIDCO
Adela Investments Co., S. A.	Provides investment consultation to promote profitable economic development in Latin America.	61 investments in 17 Latin American countries. 150 shareholders.	Investment know-how; managerial and professional services through ADELATEC, the firm's research branch.
International Harvester Co.	Farm, industrial, and construction equipment and trucks.	47 plants and 350 offices worldwide, $2,542 million sales 1967. Does business in 153 countries and employs 111,400.	Seven years experience in applying the most advanced technology in research and engineering. Will provide service and equipment.
International Minerals and Chemical Corp.	Chemical and fertilizer products as well as many other related products for agriculture, industry and the consumer.	200 plants and offices worldwide, $330 million sales in 1967. Does business in 60 countries and employs 9,000.	Sixty years experience and continuing worldwide growth in production, effective marketing and research and computer services for agribusiness.
The Dow Chemical Co.	Chemical, pharmaceutical, biological, packaging materials; systems and consulting services.	125 plants and offices worldwide, $1,383 million sales 1967. 35,000 employees.	A broad research base as well as a great variety of products.
Worthington Corp., a subsidiary of Studebaker-Worthington	Water, health and sanitation, energy, transportation and food.	62 plants and 316 offices worldwide, $750 million sales in 1967, 33,000 employees, does business in 150 countries.	Broad technical and geographic experience in developing water supplies for irrigation, human and industrial consumption; electric power generation and refrigeration, including allied services for food processing and storage.

Pakistan

International Harvester's experience in the Middle East suggested that Eastern and Western Pakistan offered large areas of underutilized land. Considering the obstacles that Pakistan had had to overcome, its economic progress had been notable. The basic problems of a geographically divided country, a high population growth rate, and a heavy dependence on traditional agriculture were compounded in recent years by a costly war, followed by two years of drought.[8]

The Pakistani government was willing to rely heavily on private industry to bolster the economy. The Government stimulated private investment by means of tax holidays, which eased the burden of a complicated income tax structure, and by favorable depreciation allowances and facilities for medium- and long-term credits. Foreign investment was also encouraged by the government's policy which provided guarantees on profit remittances and capital repatriation. The inflow of private foreign capital was expected to contribute to Pakistan's agri-industrial development.

Puerto Rico

In 1964, 1965, and 1966, American investment and enthusiasm in Puerto Rico were running high. A successful promotional campaign of the Ogilvy Advertising agency had stirred tourist interest in the semi-tropical island, and land and investment values were skyrocketing. Although IMC and the consortium would not be investing early in Puerto Rican agriculture, the Island's potential was far from exhausted. USAID (United States Agency for International Development) was guaranteeing investments, and capital was available locally or from Chase-Manhattan Bank loans.

Other Possibilities

Many other eastern and Latin American countries were using primitive agricultural methods and would benefit from the technical and managerial skills the group had to offer.

In 1966 one of the least likely alternatives for harboring development was the Dominican Republic. President Trujillo had been assassinated in 1961; the government was traditionally unstable and unfriendly toward foreign investors; and the economy faced a *severe* balance-of-payments problem. USAID was trying to encourage investment in the Dominican Republic, and Mr. Mueller spoke of a chance meeting.

At this point, USAID became very deeply involved in the Dominican Republic in trying to help it get on its feet again, through our own government's involvement and interest there. It was coincidental that at the same time they were thinking of how to stimulate U. S. corporate interest again in the Dominican Republic, we were thinking about the consortium. And it just so happened that I ran into the USAID Agricultural Officer in Washington, who said to me, "Say, I understand you people are talking about some sort of consortium, a group of

---

8. *World Business,* October 1968, p. 21.

companies ... to get together and develop the agricultural potential of a country or of part of a country." I said, "Yes, we're trying to do something of that sort. I'm not sure we've found the formula yet, but we're working on it!" He said, "Well, as soon as you find the formulas, let me know, because I would be very interested if you people would show any interest at all in the Dominican Republic."

Investigations and contacts with the Agricultural Officer to the Dominican Republic convinced Mr. Mueller and the consortium that the country did offer a real potential for improvement in agriculture.

THE ENVIRONMENT FOR ENTRY

The Agricultural Environment

The Dominican Republic is approximately 18,700 square miles in area; about 200 miles long and 160 miles wide at the widest point. The country is located 900 miles southeast of Miami, due east of Jamaica, and has a semi-tropical climate suitable for agricultural production.

In 1965 and 1966 the Dominican agricultural products included tobacco, coffee, bananas, sugar, and cocoa. The food industry was the primary source of national income, but both the production and export value of crops and livestock had been decreasing since 1960 as shown in Figures 1 through 3 and Table 2. Figure 1 illustrates these trends in the country's major farm crops. Figure 2 indicates that the sharp declines were also evident in the production of livestock. During the 1960s the number of hogs declined nearly 50 percent and all other livestock including goats, sheep, and horses experienced declines of this magnitude. The production of cattle was down slightly during the six-year period. Improved breeding and management requiring highly trained specialists would be essential to promote the recovery of these economic sectors.

Figure 3 emphasizes the impact of declining agricultural production on the value of Dominican Republic exports. Since 1964 the value of both sugar and tobacco exports was down more than 50 percent and of bananas and coffee more than 40 percent. Only coffee had shown the potential of regaining pre-1964 levels of export value by rebounding during 1965. Table 2 is a prospectus of the export demand for Dominican agricultural commodities for 1967.

In addition to the primary agricultural products, the Dominican Republic produced "back-up" crops. The farm production of these crops reached a plateau in 1961 and has remained relatively stable since that time. Back-up crops included potatoes, dry beans, peanuts, cotton, coconuts, and vegetables. A summary of five-year production for four of these crops is shown in Table 2. The acreage, production and yields for each back-up crop were about constant from 1961 to 1965. Improved technological methods were available for increasing the yield of these crops but Dominican farmers had not been educated to use the new techniques.

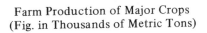

FIGURE 1

Farm Production of Major Crops
(Fig. in Thousands of Metric Tons)

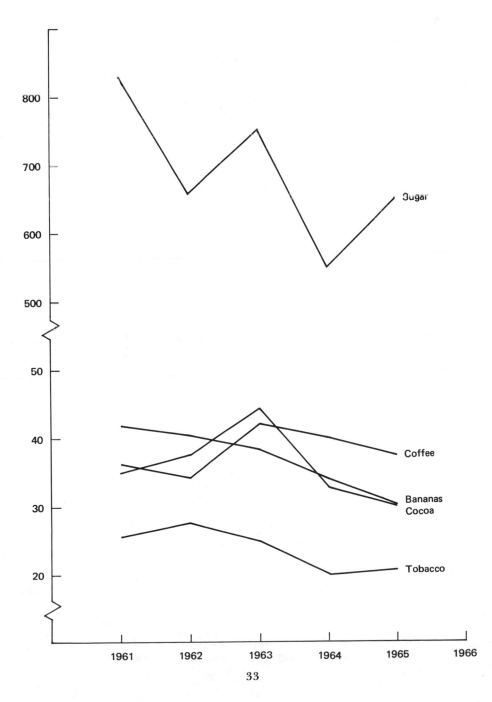

33

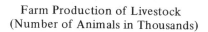

FIGURE 2

Farm Production of Livestock
(Number of Animals in Thousands)

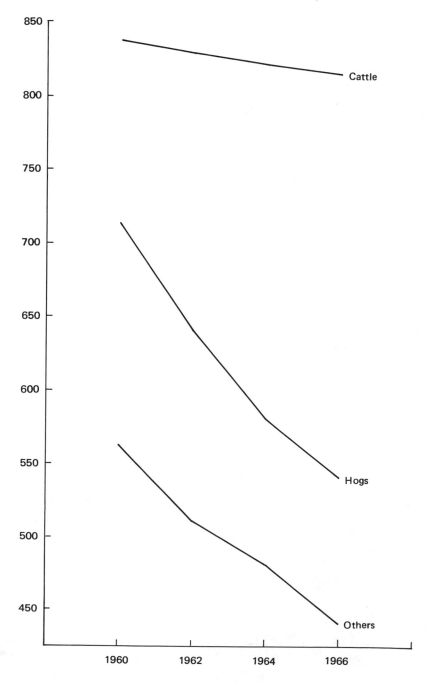

34

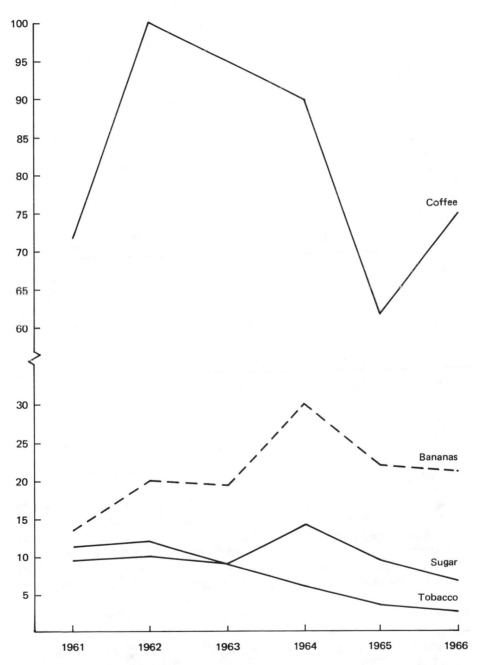

FIGURE 3

Declining Value of Dominican Republic Exports
(Value in Millions of D.R. Dollars)

TABLE 2

Prospective Dominican Republic Export Demand

	Cattle and Meat	Cereals	Fruits and Vegetables	Animal Feeds	Oil Seeds	Edible Oils	Fibers (Cotton)
Imports of some neighboring islands—1965 (in $100,000 U. S. Dollars)							
Antigua	6	11	5	1	—	2	—
Bahamas	70	26	22	10	—	—	—
Barbados	52	34	23	17	7	5	1
Bermuda	42	8	19	10	—	—	—
Granada	3	8	—	1	—	—	—
Guadalupe	36	58	30	5	—	16	—
Jamaica	92	215	40	25	—	4	16
Martinica	42	54	25	6	1	15	1
Netherland Antilles	68	35	40	9	—	6	—
Trinidad	77	178	51	37	7	12	—
Total	488	627	255	121	15	60	18

TABLE 3

Farm Output—Back-up Crops
(in Thousands of Metric Tons, Except Cotton in Metric Tons)

Crop	1961	1962	1963	1964	1965
Rice	126	145	146	146	147
Peanuts	44	52	48	53	53
Vegetables	241	255	262	262	261
Cotton	1,000	2,100	2,100	2,100	2,100

The Political Environment

The basic structure underlying politics in the Dominican Republic[9] is akin to the political framework found in the United States. The government, a constitutional democracy, consists of executive, legislative, and judicial branches. The legislature is bicameral. The nation's chief executive is chosen in the national elections which are now held once every four years. Candidates for the election represent a specific political party and platform. Although the Dominican Revolutionary Party and the Dominican Reform Party were in the limelight during the 1966 elections, a multitude of political parties are

9. Area Handbook for the Dominican Republic (Washington, D. C.: American University, U.S. Government Printing Office, 1967), pp. 40-85.

evident in the country. These parties tend to be small clusters of individuals backing a specific candidate rather than a basic and long-standing political philosophy.

The similarity between the government of the Dominican Republic and the government of the United States ends in structure. Between 1844 (when the country was freed from Haitian dominance) and 1964, twenty-four distinct constitutions were enacted. The country has been both an independent republic as well as a protectorate of foreign states including Spain and the United States.

A Brief Political History

Over the years the Dominican Republic has been a deeply torn and troubled land. Its history is one of turmoil, civil war, and foreign intervention, interrupted only when dictators managed to impose uneasy and sullen peace. Rafael Leonidas Trujillo, such a dictator, controlled the Republic for more than thirty years.

Trujillo rose to power during the six years of the Horacio Vasquez administration between 1924 to 1930. After organizing a political revolution, Trujillo was elected president in an unopposed election in 1930. Trujillo achieved an impressive record of material development in the Dominican Republic while gaining monopolistic control both economically and politically. Although "free" elections were held regularly throughout the Trujillo reign, when Trujillo was not in office the chiefs-of-state were his political puppets.

Early in 1960 Venezuela requested that the Organization of American States investigate the charge of the denial of human rights in the Dominican Republic. The Inter-American Peace Commission assigned to the investigation indicted that Trujillo regime and the dictator's control of the domestic situation steadily declined.

The political, economic, and social forces built by Trujillo crumbled soon after his 1961 assassination. Early in 1966 the country had a provisional government established by an agreement between the two opposing factions that were seeking to govern the Republic. The Act of Dominican Reconciliation, a peacemaking measure signed in December 1965, was essentially a summary of the country's constitutions of 1962 and 1963.

As provided in the Act of Reconciliation, national elections were held on June 1, 1966, and were reportedly free from coercion and manipulation. Joaquin Balaguer, representing the Dominican Reform Party, won by a wide majority over Juan Bosch of the Dominican Revolutionary Party. Balaguer has a reputation for integrity and popularity due to the reforms he instituted as President during the last days of the Trujillo era.[10] However, Dr. Balaguer faced strong criticism before the election for his alleged favoring of the United States.

10. Dr. Balaguer was also president of the Republic for six months in 1961.

The Economic Environment in 1967 and 1968

Joaquin Balaguer attempted foremost to achieve economic stability for his country. His economic strategy for 1967, "the Year of Development" had two major elements.

First, the Dominican Republic would limit the imports of noncapital goods. Affected were imported "sumptuary" goods and those which competed with locally manufactured products. The import controls applied to an estimated 30 percent of annual imports and were expected to trim an expected $8 million from adverse capital flow.

Second, Balaguer's "Austerity Law" imposed wage and price controls on the internal economy. The Dominican budget was to experience cutbacks in many areas including military expenditures, public works, industry and commerce, finance, and the Congress. Tax collections were up 20 percent.

Beginning estimates for fiscal 1967 showed an expected deficit of from $30 to $40 million. However, Balaguer's "austere budget" showed signs of decreasing the budget deficit. By late 1967 estimates of the deficit had dwindled, and some government officials were even hopeful that a slight surplus would be achieved.

The Dominican strategy for 1968 eased the import restriction but tightened budgetary constraints. Import controls were relaxed to the extent that those goods whose imports were to be cut in half would be allowed to expand to 75 percent of the 1967 base for the first six months of fiscal 1968.

The austere budget for 1968 passed through congress after only two hours of debate, with the opposition deputies declining to vote. Total expenditures, at P176.8 million, were P1.4 million less than those budgeted for 1967. The biggest cutback was in public works, down almost 20 percent to P12.4 million. Other departments receiving cutbacks were industry and commerce, agriculture and finance. The office of the president received P23 million, up 1 million from 1967, and increased allocations were assigned to public debt service, education, labor, and the courts.

Balaguer also achieved a difficult and important cut in military spending. A P2.8 million reduction in the Armed Forces budget offset a P1.5 million increase for Interior and Police, giving the total military expenditures P55.3 million, down slightly from 1967.

APPROACHING THE DOMINICAN REPUBLIC—THE NEGOTIATING STRATEGY

Mr. Mueller approached the Dominican Republic by personal contact with government officials, including five visits with the country's newly elected President, and through AID and the Dominican Embassy.[11] Mueller states:

> We called AID and the State Department who made the introductions and arrangements for me to meet with certain Dominican officials. The Dominican officials I met with expressed immediate interest; they were very interested in having us help in some way in their agricultural development plans. They were unsure of what way we could help; we hadn't described the consortium or how it would operate, but nonetheless, on a general basis, they were interested.

Although a majority of government officials were willing to cooperate with the consortium, strong opposition emanated from several other factions. The Dominican Sugar Council was charged with the responsibility of organizing more and more land for the production of sugar, an important export crop. The Council administered all the sugar estates that had been taken over by the government after Trujillo's assassination.

The Sugar Council was unprepared to hear a proposal about taking over a large portion of their land to reevaluate it and change the crop make-up, diversifying the land away from sugar. The consortium's approach seemed quite unreasonable, especially in light of the Council's increasing success in late 1966 and 1967. In 1967 the Dominican sugar crop was expected to exceed the record levels set in 1964 and the sugar complex showed a profit for fiscal 1967 after the prevalent losses throughout the early 1960s.[12]

The Dominican people were also less than enthusiastic over the consortium's development plans and, following the nation's experience with the United Fruit Company, were wary of foreign investors. United Fruit had at one time taken over much of the agricultural sector of the economy in a plantation-type agricultural development. The company gradually gained 100 percent ownership in nearly every agricultural venture, but due to crop difficulties, large increases in labor costs, and political turmoil, United Fruit was forced to withdraw its interest in the Republic by 1962. The company's withdrawal fostered mistrust and resentment toward American firms among many Dominicans because it represented severe economic hardship for families accustomed to the patron method of management.

11. Mr. Mueller indicates the nature of his relationship with the remainder of the AGRIDCO board of directors in the following passage.

All of the decisions regarding policy of AGRIDCO have always been made with the concurrence of the full board of directors. Proposals have originated with any one of the members of the companies and have been considered at directors meetings or, if not, by conference phone calls between the companies.

From the beginning, each of the companies understood and agreed that within the general structure of AGRIDCO philosophy I would have the privilege and the right to make whatever decisions were necessary in negotiations with the Dominicans to bring the project into being.

Mr. Mueller met with government officials frequently. AGRIDCO's full board of directors convened for such a meeting only on rare and important occasions.

12. *Business Abroad*, 25 December 1967, p. 18.

The consortium directors were aware that public opinion would be unfavorable toward any large American company attempting to do business in the country. The AGRIDCO project, they knew, would not be paternalistic and was designed to involve the people and government of the country in the earliest stages. Mr. Mueller felt that the good intentions of AGRIDCO and the project's potential benefit to the nation were apparent, minimizing the need for a public relations program. Therefore, in the early stages of negotiating, the consortium's strategy was to present the project plans and growth projections in a relatively unembellished, technical manner.

The Dominican people demonstrated a fear of repeating the United Fruit situation after the press reports concerning the preliminary land studies were released. In an interview with the author, Mr. Mueller was asked:

> Did the government have any problems, since it is a democratic one, in selling this project to the people because of the opposition political parties and the inevitable charge of collaborating with the Yankee Imperialists?
>
> **Mueller:** Oh yes. There was a great deal of opposition. In the first instance, the press reports were generally negative because they seized upon the preliminary study done by the consortium on the lands [*see* Figure 4 and Table 4], and the preliminary study laid out some preliminary plans as to what lands would be taken under control, what probable changes would be forthcoming. They seized upon these as being overt imperialistic grabs at land. We allowed the flurry to die down and later on put out a different kind of publicity with a different set of figures, a different set of facts. Our public relations program was less than successful because it was introduced at an inopportune time and there were political problems that were manifested in the difficulties in the agricultural industry down there. These problems didn't help the project to grow in stature.

Consortium representatives tended to minimize the importance of the internal power struggles between the government departments. The internal political problems were considered atypical of the country and "probably not as prominent as those problems in other countries."[13]

President Balaguer was then just completing his first term of office in 1968, the first Dominican president to complete an elected term.

AGRIDCO'S *OFFER OF DEVELOPMENT TO THE DOMINICAN REPUBLIC*

After more than a year of questioning, advising, and negotiating, IMC and its four associates announced formally in January 1968 the formation and incorporation of the Agro-Industrial Development Co., S. A. (AGRIDCO) and the consortium's intent to help the Dominican Republic develop potential farm-lands and infrastructure.

Traditionally, development is brought about by educating the local farmers in improved farming and business methods. Secondly, the developing interests supply

13. Interview with the author.

FIGURE 4

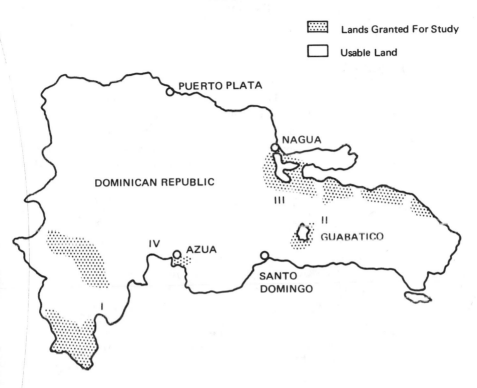

initial credit to the farmers to establish purchasing power for farm supplies and equipment. Land reform programs are instituted if necessary, and prices are controlled to give the farmers the incentive to increase production. This system accomplishes desirable long-range development goals while leaving final business decisions to the farmer. The time required to increase output significantly is usually at least one generation.

AGRIDCO officials felt that they could reduce the time period necessary to realize increased production by using what they called the "accelerated technological system."[14] This system is comprised of:

1. The immediate introduction of improved technology in agriculture.
2. Development of a comprehensive input supply and marketing system.
3. Evaluation of native labor, infrastructure, and land resources.
4. Provision of management and coordination.
5. Matching supply and demand.
6. Passing on technology and skills to the local labor.
7. Provision of capital.

14. *A Dominican Republic Agribusiness Consortium*, a monograph published by AGRIDCO to explain the consortium project, January 1969.

The accelerated plan would be administered by an agribusiness operating entity (AGRIDCO) and could reduce the time taken to significantly increase output to 3 to 5 years.

The Offer of Jobs—Labor and Labor Relations

The total labor force in the Dominican Republic (pop. 4 million) is about 1.3 million, consisting primarily of unskilled agricultural workers. Unemployment had been averaging between 33 and 35 percent of the labor force since 1961.

AGRIDCO was expected to adopt many of IMC's labor relations policies because Kenneth Mueller would continue to be the consortium's guiding force. IMC's relations with its foreign distributors indicated this attitude.

Normally, IMC would allow an independent distributor (i.e., international trader) to establish the company's initial contract in a new market. Following the market's development period, IMC would transfer the distributorship from the independent trader to its own staff. A new market area might require anywhere from four months to several years before its development and size warranted IMC's takeover and full channel staffing. Normally, IMC's distributor agreements contained the basic components listed:

1. Fixed the parties to the agreement.
2. Stated that the contract supersedes all previous agreements.
3. Fixed the duration (perhaps after a 3 to 6 months trial agreement).
4. Assigned territorial rights
   (a) exclusive
   (b) nonexclusive
   (c) sole
   (d) stipulated that the manufacturer would make no special price concessions to the government unless warranted by the size or nature of the purchase and where cost-savings could be demonstrated.
5. Identified the products covered.
6. Expressed the intent to comply with government regulations.
7. Limited sales forbidden by the U. S. Export Act.

Mr. Mueller described the establishment of a distributorship by saying:

> Our first attempt is always to end up getting people in the local area representing the company and the products. And as things develop and we see the development pattern mature, we make a change.
>
> I look upon this whole thing as a series of stair steps with successive plateaus. A company in this country doing no business whatsoever outside the U. S. is up on a zero plateau, zero level. They get some international orders—what do they do? They can throw them in the basket or they can answer them. If they answer them, then they're going to sell some products. So they get in touch with an export agent somewhere, an international trader. Now they're on plateau 1, and there's a limit to what you can do there, because the export agent has diverse interests. The people he has in foreign areas are not necessarily those who would handle your product line best.

A second plateau comes when you change off and set up your own sales organization, having people in your company who are looking after this. Next you break from the international trader; set up your own organization, a sales organization completely independent from the home offices. That's a third plateau. Of course if you manufacture for a foreign area, that's another plateau.

AGRIDCO estimated that their ventures would produce, directly and indirectly, a total of approximately 42,500 jobs in three to five years in the Dominican Republic.

Directly	*Indirectly*
2,500 jobs in three years	10,000 jobs in three years
5,000 jobs in five years	25,000 jobs in five years

THE AGREEMENT BETWEEN THE DOMINICAN GOVERNMENT AND AGRIDCO

AGRIDCO's program captivated the interest of President Balaguer. The project was lauded as a means not only to accelerate the Dominican economy and social development, but also the chance to take a leadership position in the world community by giving impetus and direction to comparable undertakings in other developing countries. The government and IMC, on behalf of the consortium, signed a Statement of Principles testifying that AGRIDCO is designed to achieve:

1. The rapid development of up to 200,000 acres of crop and pasture land through the application of modern agricultural and commercial techniques.
2. The efficient transfer of land ownership from the Dominican government to Dominican *campesinos*, in a way which will fulfill man's territorial instinct to own his home and land, and yet assure the intensive application of large-scale efficient agribusiness techniques necessary for profitable farming.
3. The development and financing of the infrastructure needed (including education, communications, transportation, and community economic health and social facilities) and providing for a system to transfer land ownership to Dominican farmers through the application of the Dominican government profit share in the projects.
4. The development of agro-industrial investments related to the project, such as fertilizer, processing and packaging plants, as well as domestic and export marketing facilities and by-product plants, through the application of AGRIDCO's profit share, on a joint venture basis with Dominican investors, including farmers acquiring project land interests.
5. The rapid amortization from project profits of the long-term financing needed for the projects, which will be sought by the Dominican government in the form of a long-term loan from USAID.

Table 4 indicates the profit and reinvestment plan AGRIDCO and the Dominican government had adapted after initial negotiations in October, November, and December 1968.

TABLE 4
Projected Income from AGRIDCO Projects
(Prior to 1969 Contract Negotiations)

Net annual income from AGRIDCO projects (50% to D.R. government, 50% to AGRIDCO)	$ 9,480,000[a]
Export sales value	40,000,000
Estimated number of jobs created directly and indirectly	30,000

The $9,480,000 net income will be divided and used as follows:

$4,740,000 to D. R. government	$4,740,000 to AGRIDCO
to improve:	25 percent committed to reinvest to improve:
Infrastructure	Processing
Medical services	Storage
Land ownership	Distribution
Municipal water	Credit
Transportation	Industrial Development
Communication	Manufacturing
Housing	Packing
Power	Canning
Schools	25 percent optional for reinvestment:
Recreation	AGRIDCO could supply new capital

[a]For a detailed breakdown of fifth year income *see* Table 6.

The government was also to reserve the right to inspect the books of the consortium to assure fair pricing of materials and equipment.[15]

AGRIDCO's *INITIAL SURVEY*

Practical phases of the project began in October 1967, when the Dominican Institute of Agriculture made available to AGRIDCO for preliminary study more than 400,000 acres of land located in several parts of the country. The research branch of **ADEIA**, **ADEIATEC**, performed the detailed feasibility study in order to determine optimal land usage, cost, employment and sales, and profits.

The results of this preliminary study are shown in Table 5. Of the total land granted for research, only 87,500 acres were thought to be usable.

AGRIDCO: *1969*

An interview in March 1969 with AGRIDCO chairman Ken Mueller indicated that the consortium was in the process of finalizing its contractual agreement with the Dominican government. AGRIDCO members had signed a joint statement agreeing to total involvement in the program.

Each of the five members was expected to contribute equipment, services, supplies, capital, and executive talent on an equal basis. Executive talent was to be provided free of charge by any of the member firms, and IMC altruistically offered the excess

15. *Business in Latin America*, 18 January 1968, p. 20.

TABLE 5

Summary of Land Potential

Land Areas Evaluated	Land Area			Best Crop Potential
	Total Evaluated	Usable	Description	
1. Enriquillo	107	10.0	Nearly level; low rainfall. Some irrigation probable. Cotton chief crop. Non-usable land is hilly, rocky.	Cotton Sorghum Vegetables Peanuts Sesame
2. Guabatico	50	25.0	Savanna-grass. Good rainfall. Ideal pasture. Some privately owned.	Pasture for cattle
3. Nagua-Yuna	101	27.5	High rainfall. Non-usable land is swamp and mountains. Drainage required.	Rice Plantain Cacao Oil palm
4. Azua (requested)	50	25.0	Arid, near-level plain. Water needed. Partly developed. Nonusable land is rocky or land reform.	Cotton Sorghum Vegetables Fruit Beans
5. Other tracts (seven)	106	–	Usable parts too small, widely scattered, or inaccessible for large-scale development.	
Total Acreage	414	87.5		

Of the land areas in the D. R. evaluated by the Consortium to determine potential for farm production, four tracts were of adequate size and quality to be economically used for the proposed system of development.

total land in the four tracts was about 300,000 acres

87,500 acres were found suitable for crop and pasture development

25,000 suited for pasture only

62,500 for crops

other land was too steep, rocky, salty, swampy, or already occupied

The usable parts of the seven other tracts evaluated were too small, widely scattered, or inaccessible to be economically feasible for large-scale development.

time and cost of project organization. The latest profit-sharing plan provided AGRIDCO with 40 percent of the total project profits with the stipulation that 37 percent of this share (or 15 percent of the total) be reinvested in the Dominican Republic. Equal profit shares would go to each consortium member. Table 6 is a detailed statement of projected sales and income by crop for the third and fifth years of development.

Mr. Mueller explained the consortium's approach to development as "catalytic."

We devote a percentage of our crops to investments in agribusiness enterprises, such as packing houses, canning plants, warehouses, meat storage and slaughter houses—this kind of thing. So that what we are really building is an agri-industrial complex.

TABLE 6

Estimated Income and Sales by Crops

Crop	Thousands of Acres Farmed	Net Farm Income per Acre (Dollars)	Total Net Farm Income (Thousands of Dollars)	Gross Receipt per Acre (Dollars)	Gross Farm Value of Production (Millions of Dollars)
3rd Year Projections (129,000 Acres)					
Pasture	35	18	630	100	3.5
Rice	8	100	800	225	1.8
Cotton	20	50	1000	200	4.0
Fruits and vegetables	6	200	1200	600	3.6
Sorghum and other grain	25	35	875	100	2.5
Peanuts and other oilseed crops	35	40	1400	90	3.15
Total	129		5905		18.55
5th Year Projections (200,000 Acres)					
Pasture	60	18	1080	100	6.0
Rice	20	100	2000	225	4.5
Cotton	20	50	1000	200	4.0
Fruits and vegetables	10	200	2000	600	6.0
Sorghum and other grain	40	35	1400	100	4.0
Peanuts and other oilseed crops	50	40	2000	90	4.5
Total	200		9480		29.0

aAfter direct and variable production expenses, but with no expense for land or taxes; charging direct business management, but no overhead for off-island consortium company services.

AGRIDCO's development policies stated that the consortium would:

1. Not hold title to the land it developed.
2. Use local personnel to the maximum extent possible.
3. Train and educate the local people for project skills.
4. Introduce appropriate types of farm product marketing and company skills when needed.
5. Foster related social and community development.
6. Encourage the investment and growth of related business and industry and related projects.
7. Have a management contract covering farm production and related projects.
8. Help plan a smooth transition from commercial food production to local private food production.

AGRIDCO's profit share was modified in February 1969 and negotiations approached a standstill. Two forces in the country caused the contract impasse. Campaigning for the national elections in May 1970 had tentatively begun, and the attention of each possible candidate focused sharply on the AGRIDCO project. Second, the Dominican government wished to assign to CODESA an ever-enlarging scope of power. Four CODESA policies were especially important in this respect.[16]

1. CODESA will direct, orient, and dictate policy on all the economic and commercial operations necessary to fulfill the objectives of the AGRIDCO project. To this end CODESA will be responsible for the establishment of better norms and administrative techniques and internal controls for the more efficient operation of the program, leading to the better utilization of resources that it holds at its disposal.
2. CODESA will contract with AGRIDCO to provide the technical administration of the whole program for a period of ten years, under the unified responsibility of the members of the consortium.
3. CODESA will coordinate the programs and make agreements of action with public organizations concerned directly with the project, in accord with the inherent functions of these organizations.
4. The cost of the programs resulting from the agreements made will be paid with the resources provided by AID credit for the project with the periodic approval of the council of directors of CODESA and AID.

Besides slowed contract negotiations, AGRIDCO was meeting heavy competition for the favors of the Dominican government because of an increasingly competitive investment climate in the Republic. American Can Company hopes to have a new metal-can factory operating in the Republic in 1969. A Stokely-Van Camp venture is seen as one can buyer. Other U. S. food packers may be drawn to the area for both local and export sales. Gulf and Western Industries South Puerto Rican Sugar Company is the largest private Dominican sugar firm. Central Aguirre Sugar Co., from a Puerto Rican base, now also has a Dominican project to harvest grain and other crops. U. S. bank support has recently helped finance cattle-herd upgrading and improvement of grazing lands. Beyond the food field: Pittsburg Plate Glass is doing a study of salt deposits which could lead to a Dominican deal to mine salt.

16. *El Caribe,* op. cit., 7 February 1969.

APPENDIX A

Agro-Industrial Development Co., S. A. (AGRIDCO) Organization Chart

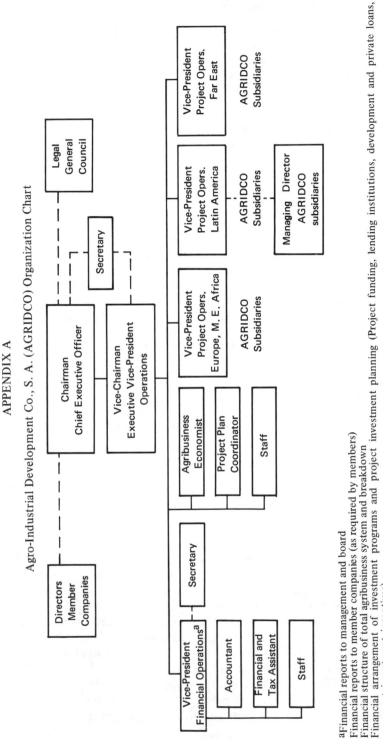

aFinancial reports to management and board
Financial reports to member companies (as required by members)
Financial structure of total agribusiness system and breakdown
Financial arrangement of investment programs and project investment planning (Project funding, lending institutions, development and private loans, government investment incentives)
Barter and arbitrage
Corporate member company and other private investment promotion
Taxes and financial—incentives, programs, policies, and evaluation
Moniter financial position (Member companies—participation, performance, return, and benefits)
Accounting and bookkeeping systems and standards: All projects and subsidiary companies; All profit centers; Member company activities; Purchasing standards.

48

APPENDIX B

Economic Benefits—Exports

Estimated 1967 D. R. Exports	*Million $*
Total	156
90% - Agriculture	140
50% - Sugar	77
14% - Coffee	22
8% - Cocoa	13
8% - Tobacco	13
80% - 4 major crops	

Estimated Consumer Sales Value of AGRIDCO Production in 5th Year —
$80,000,000—about 50% (40,000,000) is estimated for exports
(diversified products)

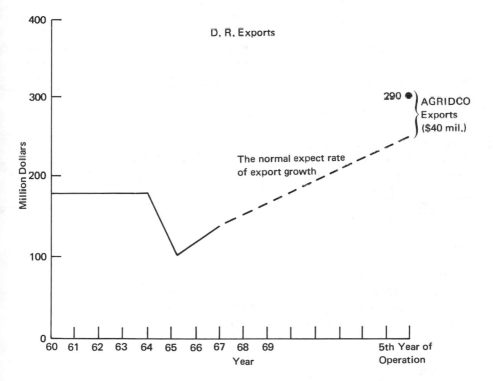

RAYTHEON-ELSI S. p. A., ITALY

Dealing with Local and Federal Governments in a Foreign Country Concerning Labor Problems and Government Contracts

On March 29, 1968, after twelve years in operation, Raytheon-Elsi, S.p.A., an electronics component manufacturing subsidiary of the Raytheon Company of Lexington, Mass. closed its doors in Palermo, Sicily. On the advice of its stockholders and legal staff, the parent company acted for the subsidiary in filing a petition of voluntary bankruptcy on April 26, 1968. On May 16 the bankruptcy was adjudicated by the Tribunal of Palermo. In the wake of this affair came numerous reports from Europe, especially Italy, that all financial institutions were reviewing their loan portfolios, subjecting them to a rigorous examination of the debtor's creditworthiness.

The events preceding these actions and their repercussions are still being discussed in international management and financial circles. The "Elsi Affair" raised serious questions concerning the roles to be played by government and private industry in the progress of underdeveloped countries.

RAYTHEON COMPANY

Raytheon Company, an electronics manufacturing firm, ranks 113th on *Fortune's* list of the 500 largest U. S. manufacturing companies.[1]

Through the years, the company's sales have been concentrated primarily in military hardware and software. The 1964 through 1968 sales to the U. S. government as a percent of total sales are shown in Table 1.[2]

Raytheon had extensive international operations and was operating in Europe, Asia, and Canada. The company's international position as of December 1968 appears in Table 2.

In addition, as of December 1966, the company maintained sales representatives in Taiwan, Panama, Kenya, Nigeria, Lebanon, Switzerland, France, Italy, England, and Japan; and sold its products through more than 100 distributors located in key markets throughout the world.[3] Appendix I gives a summary of the contribution to company profit made by both consolidated and unconsolidated foreign companies as well as data on Raytheon's investments in unconsolidated foreign companies.

1. *See* Appendix I.
2. Annual Reports, 1965 to 1968, Raytheon Company, Lexington, Massachusetts.
3. Annual Report, 1966, Raytheon Company.

TABLE 1

Ratio of Sales to U.S. Government to Total Sales

Year	Total Sales	Percentage of Total Sales to U.S. Government
1964	$ 454,121,862	83
1965	534,384,586	75
1966	875,615,880	66
1967	1,114,277,417	55
1968	1,157,963,165	58

TABLE 2

Raytheon's International Position, December 1968

International Markets	Company	Production	Location
Radar, Communications, and Power Cables	A.C. Cossor	Air traffic control radar, transponders, marine equipment, VHF radios, instruments, displays.	Harlow, Essex, England
	Sterling Cable Company	Electric power cables for military and industrial use.	Aidermaston, Berkshire, England
	Selenia S.p.A.	Radar systems, microwave communications, digital display systems.	Rome and Naples, Italy
Electronic Components	Sorensen AG	Power supplies.	Zurich, Switzerland
	Semiconductors Limited	Semiconductor devices.	Bombay, India
	New Japan Radio Limited		Tokyo, Japan
	Transistor AG		Zurich, Switzerland
Natural Resources	Seismograph Service Limited Compagnie Francaise de Prospection Sismique	Seismic exploration services to the petroleum industry.	Holwood, Kent, England Paris, France
	Badger Limited Badger N.V.	Design, engineering, and construction of petroleum and chemical processing plants.	London, England The Hague, Netherlands
	Canadian Badger Co., Ltd.		Toronto, Ontario, Canada
	Badger (France) S.a.r.l.		Paris, France
	Badger Italiana S.p.A.		Milan, Italy
	Badger-Tomoe Co. Ltd.		Tokyo, Japan

RAYTHEON-ELSI S.p.A., ITALY

In 1956 the Raytheon Company accepted 14 percent of the equity of Eletronica Sicula (Elsi) of Palermo, Sicily, in lieu of cash payment for management and technical services. Before this Elsi had been a small, nondescript electronics firm producing military equipment for the NATO alliance. Elsi's principal products included television and x-ray tubes, and semiconductors. Because of the kinds of products produced and the market conditions in Sicily, "most of the venture's output was exported."[4] Elsi's products were sold out of Geneva and Milan sales offices,[5] with an estimated 60 percent of the sales going to European governments.[6] At the time Raytheon first participated in Elsi, the company was owned by "La Centrale," an Italian holding company. Raytheon continued to increase its equity in Elsi until by 1967 it owned 98 percent of the outstanding stock, the remaining 2 percent being held by Raytheon's wholly owned domestic subsidiary, the Machlett Laboratories.[7] Table 3 gives a schedule of Raytheon's acquisition of Elsi.

TABLE 3

Raytheon's Holdings in Elsi

Year	Percentage of Raytheon's Equity in Elsi
1956	14
1959	30
1961	49
1962	60
1964	80
1967	98

"In 1962, at the time it became the majority owner, Raytheon assumed the management responsibility for Elsi, which employed some 1200 people at the peak." Prior to 1967, Raytheon-Elsi had a Sicilian management.

The reasons for Raytheon's take-over of Elsi were stated in an interview with a company spokesman.[8]

One, because we felt at that time that we could make an economic contribution in southern Italy and Sicily which was the most backward,

3. Annual Report, 1966, Raytheon Company.
4. "Raytheon's Italian Lesson," *Business Week,* 7 September 1968, p. 35.
5. Interview with author.
6. Ibid.
7. "Memorandum for Financial Institutions Concerning Elsi, S.p.A., Palermo, Sicily, a Subsidiary of Raytheon Company," Raytheon Co., Lexington, Massachusetts, July 17, 1968, p. 1.
8. Unless otherwise stated all comments attributed to Raytheon's spokesmen were made in interviews with the author.

economically, of all Italy. Also the fact that the company wasn't getting anywhere with the ownership it had at the time; there was very little technology available to the company. They had a relatively narrow product base, and there was not a very active participation on the part of the Italian partners in the enterprise, particularly by Centrale. So I think the answer to why the build-up over the period of years and why the eventual total ownership is that Raytheon felt that the only way to make it a viable business was to increase the ownership until it had full management control and could inject the technology, the advanced production methods, cost control, and so on.

During Raytheon's twelve years of participation in the Elsi venture, its aggregate dollar value of capital investment grew to approximately $12 million. When operations ceased in 1968, Elsi was valued at between $23 and $25 million. It has been estimated that Elsi contributed, "in the course of a year, approximately 8 billion lire to the important industrial development of the autonomous region of Sicily."[9] In 1968 Raytheon was allowed a $13 million tax benefit against a $14.3 million write-off of its investment and accounts receivables in Elsi S.p.A., leaving an actual net loss of $1.3 million.[10]

THE ELSI AFFAIR

From its inception Raytheon-Elsi was not profitable, according to a Raytheon spokesman, "Elsi was operated from 1954 to 1960 with comparatively small losses . . . ."[11] In 1967 Elsi sustained losses of $4.4 million and during the first quarter of 1968, losses in excess of $650,000 were accumulated.[12]

When questioned why Raytheon allowed a subsidiary to incur losses for twelve consecutive years, a company spokesman noted:

When Mr. Phillips [Thomas L. Phillips] became president of Raytheon, he dealt with three problem areas, one of which was Elsi. He dealt with them in order of their relative seriousness to the company. One was the problem of closing down a plant. . . . The other was to get us out of the production of receiving tools. . . . So, management attention was devoted to solving those two problems while at the same time trying to improve and deal with the Elsi situation. Once those two problems were solved and behind us, the management attention got focused on the third problem which was Elsi.

MARKETING PROBLEMS

Raytheon's attention was focused on Elsi in 1967, after it had assumed complete ownership of the company. A team of Italian-speaking American executives went from the home office to Palermo. Raytheon-Elsi had been accused of not making a concerted effort to sell the company's products. Silvio Laurin, a former Raytheon

9. "The Closing of the Raytheon Works in Sicily," *New Zurich Times,* 28 March 1968.
10. Annual Report, 1968, Note J., Raytheon Co.
11. "The Closing of the Raytheon Works in Sicily," op. cit.
12. "Raytheon Venture in Italy in a Triangle," *New York Times,* 26 August 1968.

employee, remarked that he felt ". . . that Raytheon didn't effectively put together a Europe-wide sales force to sell the plant's products. And, indeed, company brochures list only two sales offices in Italy, plus two 'marketing representatives' to cover the rest of Europe."[13] A company spokesman denied Mr. Laurin's comments contending,

> . . . that the so-called Raytheon executive who made that observation to the Italian press wasn't even close enough to the situation to be able to make such an observation. He was not involved in it himself, he had no background of fact or knowledge from which to make such an observation. On the other hand, I wouldn't say unequivocally that our marketing effort was all it should have been or might have been, but it was by no means as sparse as this quote indicates. . . . What we had done, and this is what this fellow had overlooked, was to move marketing operations up to where they could be effective, partly in Geneva and partly in Milan.

Acting on the advice of the management team, Raytheon embarked on a sales expansion program. "More concerted effort was made in the marketing, in calling on customers and potential customers, and working with the various agencies of the Italian government in the interest of trying to get more directed purchases coming to Elsi." In addition, Raytheon salesmen in Europe who were handling only Raytheon products were set to work selling Elsi's products as well.

PRODUCTION PROBLEMS

In addition to Mr. Laurin's comments on Elsi's marketing, he also saw problems in the production process. "Equipment installed to produce semiconductors became obsolete in about eighteen months, as technology advanced. At the same time, the semiconductor market began to be plagued by excess capacity."[14] Further difficulties were encountered in the television tube department. "Raytheon doesn't make television tubes in the U. S. It had little advanced technology to supply to its subsidiary. So Elsi was just another company in a highly competitive field."[15]

Raytheon also encountered difficulties in attracting executive talent to Elsi. "American executives appeared to be unwilling to settle in Palermo largely because the Sicilian town offered no adequate English-language schooling facilities for their children."[16]

The management team, feeling that excess personnel was the biggest bottleneck to increased efficiency, suggested dismissing approximately 250 to 300 workers. To prevent the dismissal—a practice frowned upon in Italy—the Italian government suggested that Elsi set up a retraining program for those affected. In mid-1967 the

---

13. "U. S. Companies Find That Foreign Ventures Don't Always Succeed," *Wall Street Journal,* 20 August 1968, p. 1.
14. Ibid., p. 1.
15. Ibid.
16. Ibid., p. 21.

retraining program was instituted for approximately 300 workers with the understanding that sufficient business would be directed to Elsi to justify the additional labor force. Commenting on this understanding, a spokesman from Raytheon noted that,

> There was not a contract as such to direct the business. However, the background of the agreement was that we were going to lay those people off and they [the Italian government] didn't want us to—it was socially unacceptable to lay people off. They said we [Raytheon] will provide training funds for these people with the understanding that there will be jobs available at the end. Now they never said how they were going to make the jobs available, but the verbal understanding was that there would be directed purchases made to us.

GOVERNMENT RELATIONS

The "directed purchases" were to be made under the Mezzogiorno laws in effect in Italy.[17] Among these laws is a provision which states that the Italian government must make at least 30 percent of its purchases in the Mezzogiorno (South Italy) when the product is available. Unfortunately, Elsi did not receive orders for these directed purchases. According to a company spokesman "Elsi was the only Italian manufacturer of x-ray tools. So one of the things the Italian government should have done was to purchase their x-ray tools for their hospitals in Sicily. Well, they never did that." In addition, Elsi was entitled to subsidies, i.e., transportation subsidies, capital write-offs, and the like, but the company received only a long-term loan from IRFIS—the Sicilian Development Corporation—in the amount of $4 million at 4 percent.

In early 1967 Raytheon started to search intensively for an Italian partner to assist Elsi. Raytheon felt that such a partner would facilitate Elsi's receiving directed purchases and subsidies. "Its all very well for an Italian company to go into Sicily and get subsidies from the Italian government; but it's a lot harder for a foreign investor to do the same thing. . . . We were simply not getting access to the marketplaces that our competitors had access to . . . . Basically we felt that without a government partner in this thing, Elsi would not survive.[18] Elsi's search for partners "involved contacts with private industry, many meetings with government officials at both the national and regional levels, as well as detailed reports concerning Elsi."[19] One possible partner approached was the Instituto per la Ricostruzione Industriale—IRI (Appendix III) with whom Raytheon was already associated in another company, Selenia of Rome.[20] According to Italian law, IRI is obliged to put 40 percent of its new investments into the Mezzogiorno.

17. *See* Appendix II.
18. Much of Elsi's competition was from companies which were wholly or partly owned by the Italian government. "Memorandum for Financial Institutions Concerning Elsi, S.p.A., Palermo, Sicily, a Subsidiary of Raytheon Company," op. cit., p. 3.
19. "Memorandum for Financial Institutions Concerning Elsi, S.p.A., Palermo, Sicily, a Subsidiary of Raytheon Company," op. cit., p. 2.
20. "Banks Study Solvency of U. S. Companies in Italy," *The Financial Times* (Rome), 19 June 1968.

When IRI did not respond to Elsi's advances, the Italian press condemned IRI's actions. An article in *L'Ora*,[21] a communist newspaper, deplored the attitude of some members of the regional government who were seeking posts for themselves rather than support from the central government. The bad "undergovernment" states the article, caused IRI to refuse to assist the region in general and Elsi in particular. From other sources came claims that the Elsi case gave evidence of IRI's policy of disengagement vis-à-vis Sicily.

> In the last few days, on the occasion of his annual press conference, the IRI President, Professor Petrilli, was asked by a journalist to clarify IRI's attitude in the Raytheon-Elsi case. The answer given by Professor Petrilli was that the Elsi case is not demonstrative of disengagement, but is a proof of the caution with which the Institute studies its investments and the economic conditions involved. As a matter of fact there is no possibility of "rescuing" Elsi as this is the case of a company which is failing and which is asking for public assistance. IRI, instead, has decided to participate in the setting up of a new sound and vital company, to be located in Palermo, which will operate in the electro-telephonic field, which is evidence of IRI's sincere will to support the Sicilian economy.[22]

In addition to the search for Elsi's partner, Raytheon's management team advised investing an additional $4 million in Elsi. This additional investment was in vain, however, for in 1967 Raytheon-Elsi sustained losses of $4.4 million.

THE SITUATION WORSENS

In January of 1968 Raytheon-Elsi announced its intent to close the television tube division of the plant. This move would have resulted in the dismissal of approximately one-fourth of Elsi's 1,200 personnel, all of whom were members of a communist affiliated union. The immediate result of Raytheon's announcement was a wildcat strike by the workers in the affected division. In the ensuing two months, Elsi was the target of an estimated twenty-four strikes.[23]

A company spokesman discussed the reasons for the wildcat strike:

> There were minor labor standard arguments and things like that. Any wildcat strike has some justification. . . . It's apt to be a work distribution thing or a labor stand . . . . This was and is a communist-run union. Now they handle themselves in a pretty principled fashion. I think there was some political motivation, but I don't know that that's the key to the whole thing. It doesn't hurt them to make things embarrassing for a U. S. company . . . .

In February of 1968 Mr. C. F. Adams, Chairman of Raytheon, advised officials of the Sicilian government that the situation was most urgent, and stated Elsi's minimum requirements to enable it to stay in operation,

---

21. *L'Ora* (Palermo), 19 June 1968.
22. "Bulletin of the News Agency of the Chamber of Deputies (Rome), 20 June 1968, p. 2.
23. "U. S. Companies Find that Foreign Ventures Don't Always Succeed," op. cit., p. 1.

These requirements included: A majority participation by one or more Italian entities; an investment by them of approximately $10 million, thereby eliminating the need for Raytheon's guarantees [Raytheon had guaranteed loans made to Elsi in the amount of $8 million]; and an understanding that no further financial investment would be required of Raytheon. In return for this Raytheon was willing, among other things, to continue to provide management and technical assistance to Elsi and to defer amounts owing by Elsi to Raytheon.[24]

As a result of the frequent wildcat strikes, Raytheon announced in early March 1968 that the entire television tube division would be shut down. According to a company spokesman:

There was a scream of lockout, but there was no lockout. The strike was started before we shut the line down. We told them that we simply could not continue to run that line if they were going to walk-out. . . . Finally, the decision had to be made that we couldn't live with that situation as it cost more to keep the division running with work stoppages than it cost to shut it down.

This resulted in a complete strike at the plant on March 4.

At that point, Elsi was faced with two alternatives: The injection of new capital, as required under Italian law, to replenish the prior year's losses, or a liquidation of the business. The Raytheon shareholders had advised the management of Elsi that both for business reasons and because of U. S. investment limitations, no more capital would be invested. . . . On March 16, the Board voted to cease trading on March 29 and to dismiss all but about 120 key employees, unless, of course, Elsi's long time goal of finding a suitable partner could be achieved prior to that date.[25]

No proposals were received before March 29, so on that day dismissal notices were sent out.

"On April 1, at a meeting with its banks, Elsi proposed an orderly liquidation of its assets in accordance with an agreement to be worked out with the major creditors."[26] Unfortunately, the company's announcement of its intention to liquidate was ill timed.

The dismissal of over 1,000 men working in a plant in Palermo would have been likely to have serious repercussions on the General Election which was due on May 19. Under an 1865 law which has been invoked only on one other occasion since the end of the war, the mayor of Palermo, on April 2, requisitioned the Raytheon-Elsi plant for six months. . . .[27]

The confiscation of Elsi's assets effectively put a halt to the planned liquidation of the firm. "On April 15, a $1,280,000 unguaranteed obligation matured

---

24. "Memorandum for Financial Institutions Concerning Elsi, S.p.A., Palermo, Sicily, a Subsidiary of Raytheon Company," op. cit., p. 3.

25. Ibid., p. 4.

26. Ibid.

27. "Banks Study Solvency of U. S. Companies in Italy," op. cit.

at one of the banks. Elsi was unable to meet this obligation, and the bank refused to extend it."[28]

During the month of April, Elsi management continued to negotiate with the president of the Sicilian Region. These negotiations were not successful and culminated in a memorandum from the President of Sicily to Elsi.

MEMO OF THE PRESIDENT OF THE REGION
[President of Sicily]
TO THE COMPANY RAYTHEON-ELSI

I deem it my duty, in the situation as it has developed, to provide Raytheon Company with some fundamental elements of judgment so that the irreparable can be avoided.

On the premise that the intent of the Company is that of liquidating Elsi, I shall herein explain the reasons why it is absolutely impossible that this can take place for the time being.

1. Nobody in Italy shall purchase, that is to say IRI shall not purchase either for a low or for a high price, the Region shall not purchase, private enterprise shall not purchase. Let me add that the Region and IRI and anybody else who has any possibility to influence the market will refuse in the most absolute manner to favor any sale *while the plant is closed*.

2. The banks, which have outstanding credits for approximately 16 billion Lire, can not and will not accept any settlement even at the cost of dragging the Company into litigation on an international level. I mean to refer to Raytheon and not to Elsi because the distinction between Elsi and Raytheon is not found to be admissible since any and all financing was granted to Elsi based on the moral guarantee of Raytheon, whose executives have always negotiated said financing.

3. Anyway, it is known in Italy that one can enforce the claims directly against Raytheon because it has interests and revenues in our country also outside Elsi.

   It is obvious that every attempt will be made (even at the cost of long litigation) to obtain from Raytheon what is owned by Elsi.

4. In the event that the plant shall be kept closed, waiting for Italian buyers who will never materialize, the requisition shall be maintained at least until the courts will have resolved the case. Months shall go by.

On the other hand the Italian Government has responsibly solicited the U. S. Government to make a cordial intervention with Raytheon Company at the time the latter was readying itself to send the letters of dismissal [of employees and workers].

The U. S. Government had a negative reply and· forwarded it curtly to the Italian Government which was seriously disappointed.

Taking into account all the above reasons which would put Raytheon into an obvious situation of moral isolation, I shall now illustrate the reasons which in my opinion would improve the situation in every respect both moral and financial.

---

28. "Memorandum for Financial Institutions Concerning Elsi, S.p.A., Palermo, Sicily, a Subsidiary of Raytheon Company," op. cit., p. 5.

1. A plant in full operation is worth much more than a closed one or one which is in the midst of a great conflict morally isolating Raytheon both in Italy and in Europe.
2. The plant can be kept open through the formation of a provisional management company organized by IRI, the Region, and Raytheon. In such case there shall not be necessary any further capital investment since the nature and the purposes of the management company would not require it necessarily. At the end of each fiscal year the operational losses shall be computed and allocated amongst the shareholders. Taking into account the fact that IRI would have a participation of 10-20 percent, the Region a participation of 40 percent and Raytheon a participation of 40 percent, Raytheon would make an initial gain represented by a diminution of 60 percent of the losses incurred until today.
3. In the meantime the Region has approved a law taking on itself the burden of paying for a period of five months the salaries of the workers that were dismissed at an earlier date, that is to say in December.
4. In the climate of new cordiality the situation also can improve because of a greater willingness to help by the Region, by IRI itself, by the Banks, by private enterprise that have shown certain interest in Elsi. It is known that the Italian Ministry of Defense must place orders for microwave tubes and it can also place orders with Elsi, thereby increasing its sales and diminishing its losses.
5. Everybody, including the Region and IRI, shall be ready to help Raytheon in the meantime to liquidate Elsi through a useful sale in the shortest possible time.

In substance, any losses, even if allocated in rather reduced terms to Raytheon, shall certainly be diminished with regard to the losses of the prior years because of the concurrence of so many favorable circumstances represented by the commitments of the Region, IRI, the Banks and private enterprise.

The gain shall be certain for Raytheon as far as the figures go and the prospective gain shall be greater taking into account the fundamental objective of Raytheon which remains after all the liquidation.

For these reasons I take the liberty of suggesting and recommending the formation of the management company through the natural and necessary participation of Raytheon in a proportion of at least 40 percent.

The proposal in the memorandum did nothing to resolve Elsi's financial situation, and moreover threatened to prevent for an indefinitely long period any sales of Elsi's assets.[29] Faced with this situation, the Board of Directors of Raytheon elected to file the petition of voluntary bankruptcy.

AFTERMATH

During the period that Raytheon-Elsi was in operation the company received approximately $20 million in loans from Italian financial institutions. The terms of these loans varied but can be classed under three general headings:

1. More than $8 million in loans to Elsi by Italian banks and guaranteed by Raytheon.
2. Approximately $6.5 million in loans secured by Elsi plant, equipment, and inventories.

29. Ibid., p. 5.

3. Approximately $6 million in unsecured loans.

When Raytheon-Elsi filed for a petition of voluntary bankruptcy, Raytheon announced its intention to honor the $8 million in guaranteed loans but said that its obligations did not extend to the $6 million in unsecured loans. Payment of the remaining $6 million depended on the liquidation of Elsi's assets which was blocked by the requisition of the plant. The $6 million in unsecured loans became a major source of trouble.

Up until this time it had been common practice in Italian banking circles to grant loans to the subsidiaries of foreign corporations as a matter of convenience. "Italian banks . . . are used to the idea that parent American companies, in particular find it difficult or awkward to guarantee loans made to foreign-based subsidiaries, because they do not want such loans to appear in the parent's balance sheet, or because they might prevent new borrowings by the parent, or because permission might be needed from owners of other fixed interest debt. So instead of a guarantee some sort of letter of agreement is generally obtained."[30] According to Raytheon spokesmen, the loans in question were negotiated by Elsi personnel and much of the indebtedness was incurred by Elsi well before Raytheon acquired 98 percent ownership. The company further denied one bank's contention that its loans were made on the basis of a letter of agreement.[31]

It will be up to the courts to decide whether any of the loans in question were predicated on a letter of agreement. Regardless of the outcome of judicial proceedings, the Raytheon-Elsi affair has caused a serious reappraisal of the loaning practices of Italian financial institutions. The *Rome Financial Times* noted that "Until now American investments have been welcomed in every possible way. Henceforth, they will be scrutinized much more closely. There is little doubt that the repercussions of the Raytheon affair will spread to other European nations."[32] An Article in *Il Sole* noted that "The American corporations are increasingly drawing on the European capital market and should be the first to see to it that the Raytheon case does not recur but will, rather, be settled to the full satisfaction of all creditors. Otherwise, what is the significance of the well-known 'letter of intent' which should correspond at least to a moral engagement."[33] The *London Financial Times* noted that "The parent Raytheon's behavior in relation to its Italian offshoot will be held to demonstrate that it is no longer entirely safe to make large sums of money available to the subsidiaries of American companies on the assumption that the 'letter of agreement' signed by the parent will stand the creditor in good stead should things go wrong."[34] Finally, in an article in *Business Week* it was noted that the reappraisal of loaning practices had taken place: "Other U. S. companies in Italy are already feeling the consequences of the Raytheon bankruptcy, for Italian banks will no longer grant them unsecured loans. They can still borrow all they want but they must get ironclad guarantees from the parent company in the U. S."[35]

30. "Raytheon and the Mayor of Palermo," *Economist* (London), 22 June 1968.

31. "Memorandum for Financial Institutions Concerning Elsi, S.p.A., Palermo, Sicily, a subsidiary of Raytheon Company," op. cit., p. 6.

32. "Banks Study Solvency of U. S. Companies in Italy," op. cit.

33. "New Anxieties on Credit," *Il Sole-24 Ore* (Italy), 12 May 1968.

34. "The Important Affair of Raytheon-Elsi's Debts," *Financial Times* (London), 17 June 1968.

35. "Raytheon's Italian Lesson," op. cit., p. 36.

APPENDIX I

Raytheon Company, Lexington, Massachusetts
Statistical Summary (Dollars in Thousands Except per Share Statistics)

Raytheon Company and Consolidated Subsidiaries	1968	1967	1966	1965	1964
Sales					
Net sales	$ 1,157,963	$ 1,106,049	$ 708,993	$ 487,834	$ 454,122
Income					
Income before taxes	$ 59,960	$ 54,405	$ 36,478	$ 19,956	$ 15,589
Income before extraordinary items	$ 30,845	$ 28,602	$ 18,443	$ 11,021	$ 8,243
Net income	$ 29,569	$ 28,602	$ 18,443	$ 11,021	$ 8,243
Earnings per common share (2):					
Income before extraordinary items	$2.10	$1.98	$1.45	$1.13	$ .98
Extraordinary items	$ (.09)	–	–	–	–
Net income	$2.01	$1.96	$1.45	$1.13	$ .98
Income before extraordinary items as % of sales	2.7%	2.6%	2.5%	2.3%	1.8%
Income before extraordinary items as % of average total stockholders' equity	14.4%	15.1%	11.9%	8.9%	7.6%
Dividends Paid					
On preferred stock (cash)	$ 867	$ 885	$ –	$ 234	$ 248
On common stock (stock)	–	–	–	–	–
On common stock (cash)	$ 6,271	$ 5,023	$ 4,055	$ 2,662	$ 1,850
Assets					
Current	$ 361,151	$ 364,492	$ 301,429	$ 210,870	$ 180,272
Property, plant and equipment (net)	$ 91,087	$ 78,255	$ 63,949	$ 44,790	$ 39,317
Investments and other	$ 13,428	$ 17,298	$ 16,592	$ 18,088	$ 16,099
Total	$ 465,666	$ 460,045	$ 381,970	$ 273,748	$ 235,688
Working Capital					
Working capital	$ 160,391	$ 148,042	$ 122,880	$ 104,556	$ 93,375
Ratio of current assets to current liabilities	1.80	1.68	1.69	1.98	2.07

61

APPENDIX I—*continued*

Raytheon Company and Consolidated Subsidiaries

Financial Structure	1968	1967	1966	1965	1964
Short-term debt	$ 77,314	$ 112,496	$ 98,061	$ 39,231	$ 39,385
Long-term debt	39,254	42,647	42,379	41,670	39,707
Total debt	116,568	155,143	140,440	80,901	79,092
Preferred stock	—	—	—	4,202	4,325
Common stockholders' equity	—	—	—	121,561	104,759
Total equity	225,652	200,948	161,042	125,763	109,084
Common stockholders' equity per share	$14.93(3)	$13.48(3)	$12.48(3)	$12.68	$12.84
Debt/equity ratio	.52	.77	.87	.64	.73

General	1968	1967	1966	1965	1964
Funded backlog of U. S. Government orders	$ 429,151	$ 380,287	$ 354,379	$ 262,287	$ 238,195
Number of employees	51,588	50,146	41,821	32,559	30,173
Building space (square feet)	12,000,000	10,500,000	9,100,000	8,100,000	7,600,000
Research and development (company sponsored)	26,163	22,560	19,536	14,616	14,221
Depreciation and amortization on property, plant and equipment	19,585	16,694	12,422	8,504	7,655
Additions and replacements in property, plant and equipment	33,130	26,545	23,567	11,616	8,430
Shares outstanding (after deducting shares in treasury):					
Preferred	770,403	788,948	792,023	84,048	86,505
Common	14,347,131	14,123,872	12,115,450	9,585,248	8,158,792
Common stockholders of record	24,582	23,512	25,011	24,103	26,443

	1963	1962	1961	1960	1959
Sales					
Net sales	$ 510,516	$ 599,019	$ 562,901	$ 539,975	$ 494,278
Income					
Income before taxes	$ 13,339	$ 18,715	$ 13,067	$ 15,845	$ 21,801
Income before extraordinary items	6,332	9,553	6,877	8,105	10,481
Net income	92	9,553	6,877	11,536	13,481

Raytheon Company and Consolidated Subsidiaries

	1963	1962	1961	1960	1959
Earnings per common share (2):					
Income before extraordinary items	$ .73	$1.16	$ .85	$1.05	$1.51
Extraordinary items	$ (.76)	–	–	$ .46	$ .44
Net income	$ (.03)	$1.16	$ .85	$1.51	$1.95
Income before extraordinary items as % of sales	1.2%	1.6%	1.2%	1.5%	2.1%
Income before extraordinary items as % of average total stockholders' equity	5.8%	9.2%	7.2%	9.4%	14.4%
Dividends Paid					
On preferred stock (cash)	$ 281	$ 284	$ 315	$ 315	$ 148
On common stock (stock)	3%	3%	3%	5%	5%
On common stock (cash)	$ –	$ –	$ –	$ –	$ –
Assets					
Current	$ 187,217	$ 201,862	$ 193,687	$ 184,966	$ 174,552
Property, plant and equipment (net)	$ 39,978	$ 48,257	$ 44,781	$ 35,139	$ 26,127
Investments and other	$ 12,983	$ 14,375	$ 14,171	$ 5,689	$ 5,559
Total	$ 240,178	$ 264,494	$ 252,639	$ 225,794	$ 206,238
Working Capital					
Working capital	$ 96,854	$ 89,219	$ 84,865	$ 61,661	$ 59,854
Ratio of current assets to current liabilities	2.07	1.79	1.78	1.50	1.52
Financial Structure					
Short-term debt	$ 37,118	$ 49,451	$ 49,358	$ 75,698	$ 68,935
Long-term debt	$ 40,979	$ 42,502	$ 44,188	$ 10,350	$ 11,327
Total debt	$ 78,097	$ 91,953	$ 93,546	$ 86,048	$ 80,262
Preferred stock	$ 4,956	$ 5,127	$ 5,738	$ 5,738	$ 5,738
Common stockholders' equity	$ 103,402	$ 103,935	$ 93,890	$ 86,400	$ 74,474
Total equity	$ 108,358	$ 109,062	$ 99,628	$ 92,138	$ 80,212
Common stockholders' equity per share	$12.53	$12.94	$12.07	$11.59	$10.88
Debt/equity ratio	.72	.84	.94	.93	1.00

APPENDIX I—continued

Raytheon Company and Consolidated Subsidiaries

General	1963	1962	1961	1960	1959
Funded backlog of U. S. Government orders	$ 245,672	$ 340,657	$ 362,723	$ 288,350	$ 294,937
Number of employees	35,777	42,574	43,713	40,078	41,371
Building space (square feet)	8,100,000	8,100,000	8,200,000	7,900,000	7,200,000
Research and development (company sponsored)	$ 13,128	$ 15,294	$ 13,596	$ 10,997	$ 7,354
Depreciation and amortization on property, plant and equipment	$ 8,938	$ 8,379	$ 7,091	$ 5,349	$ 4,392
Additions and replacements in property, plant and equipment	$ 8,083	$ 9,382	$ 17,594	$ 14,468	$ 9,528
Shares outstanding (after deducting shares in treasury):					
Preferred	99,120	102,549	114,769	114,769	114,769
Common	8,253,710	8,034,976	7,783,344	7,456,494	6,847,134
Common stockholders of record	27,341	28,678	27,783	28,096	23,903

APPENDIX I—*continued*

1. The above tabulations summarize the company's financial statements as contained in its annual reports for each of the years 1959 through 1968, which include the operations of businesses acquired under the pooling of interests concept from the beginning of the year in which the acquisition is reported. On the basis of including operations of pooled businesses prior to their years of acquisition, operating results would have been as follows:

Year	Net Sales	Net Income	Net Income per Common Share
1967	$1,114,277,000	$28,938,000	$1.99
1966	$ 882,295,000	$21,482,000	$1.48
1965	$ 707,785,000	$18,059,000	$1.22
1964	$ 632,888,000	$12,546,000	$ .81

2. Earnings per share statistics computed: for 1968 through 1965, on average number of shares; for 1964 and prior on the number of shares outstanding at end of each period; on earnings reduced by preferred stock dividends where applicable.

3. Assuming full conversion of Series A preferred stock.

4. Statistics for all years prior to 1968, relating to the number of common shares outstanding, have been adjusted to give effect to the two-for-one common stock split on June 4, 1968.

5.   Results of Operations in Unconsolidated and Consolidated Foreign Companies (Other than Canadian)

	1964	*1965*	*1966*	*1967*	*1968*
Operating Income (Loss)	(33,353)	1,945,513	711,171	(1,678,769)	1,046,873
Other Income (Loss)				(539,597)[a]	
Less: Amortization of Investments	1,043,515	923,610	(927,059)	(994,668)	(584,855)
Contribution (Loss) to Profits Net of Foreign and Domestic Taxes	(1,076,868)	1,021,903	(215,888)	(3,213,034)	462,018

[a]Devaluation of British pound

6.   Investments in Unconsolidated Foreign Companies

	1964	*1965*	*1966*	*1967*	*1968*
Majority Owned or Controlled	8,982,849	9,402,771	7,407,389	6,817,504	4,194,434
Other	349,676	2,128,943	2,350,047	2,255,324	2,966,757

7. The investments in unconsolidated foreign companies which are majority owned or otherwise controlled are stated at cost, increased or decreased by the company's share in their net earnings or losses since acquisition of a majority interest or effective control and decreased by the amortization

over a ten-year period of the excess of cost over equity in underlying net tangible assets at the time of acquisition. Investments in other unconsolidated foreign companies are stated at cost.

Raytheon Company Annual Reports, 1965-1968.

8. Under Raytheon Company's Principles of Consolidation, consolidated financial data includes:

1964—financial accounts for the parent company, wholly owned domestic, Canadian and British subsidiaries

1965—same as 1964

1966—same as 1965 plus all foreign subsidiaries of Seismograph Service Corporation

1967—same as 1966 plus all foreign subsidiaries of the Badger Company, Inc.

1968—parent company, and all wholly owned domestic and foreign subsidiaries

APPENDIX II

Cassa Per Il Mezzogiorno

Southern Italy Development Fund

Piazzale Kennedy 20, Eur, Rome

President: Prof. Gabriele Pescatore.

The Fund was set up in 1950 to develop the Southern areas of the country. By the end of 1965 contracts for public works worth 1,522,000 million lire had been awarded. The Fund was extended in June 1965 until 1980, with the task of implementing five-year plans coordinated with the national economic plan. During the 1965-1969 period, the Fund has been endowed with 1,640,000 million lire. The following are completed projects supervised by the Fund:

Land Reclamation and Irrigation: More than 6,800 kilometres of river channel control, embankments and drains have been completed. Over 928,000 hectares of land have been drained or protected from floods, and 10,867 kilometres of irrigation canals and networks laid, 6,901 kilometres of new agricultural roads constructed and 2,007 kilometres improved.

Aqueducts: The Fund has tackled the drinking water supply problem by laying 12,532 kilometres of mains and constructing 2,535 water towers with a capacity of about 1,435,676 cubic metres.

Transport and Communications: 3,371 kilometres of new trunk roads have been built and 15,978 kilometres improved; also the construction of 572 kilometres of motor highways is nearing completion. The tracks of numerous railway lines have been doubled. Fifty-one port improvements have been approved with an expenditure of 29,000 million lire. Construction is nearing completion.

Hospitals: 54 hospitals are under construction, with an approved expenditure of 32,500 million lire, in centres of the Southern Regions.

Industry: 186 projects have been approved for setting up industrial estates in selected areas, the Fund's contributions towards this total, 37,848 million lire. In the private sector the Fund has operated a two-fold industrialization project: (a) credit is extended through three specialized institutes in the South

(ISVEIMER for Southern Italy, IRFIS for Sicily, and CIS for Sardinia); 5,902 loans of 1,229,275 million lire were approved. (b) Straight grants to 7,145 small and medium-sized enterprises of about 177,847 million lire. 84,016 loans valued at 22,725 million lire have been granted to the handicraft industries.

Private Land Improvements: By the end of 1967 the Fund had approved the construction of: 7,238 kilometres of farm roads; 62,863 wells, tanks and reservoirs; 2,006 kilometres of transmission lines; 71 cheese factories; 422 olive oil mills; 519 wine factories. In addition, about 244,200 hectares have been prepared for farming and 220,600 hectares have been irrigated. A large portion of coastal population has been supported with 14,108 contributions totaling 33,179 million lire for the fishing industry.

Education: The Fund has completed 147 schools for industrial training and 21 agricultural schools with 120 branches have been opened. 604 kindergartens have been completed to a value of over 14,000 million lire. 5,345 loans for school buildings to a value of 7,300 million lire have been granted.

Tourism: Projects to the value of 53,763 million lire have been completed. They include: local and sightseeing roads, archeological excavations, modern museums, monument restorations, and improvements to grottoes and spas. The Fund has also financed 1,072 loans for the construction of 41,462 rooms with 76,011 beds in a hotel project.

Cassa Per Il Mezzogiorno
Southern Italy Development Fund
(1950 to 1967, Extended to 1980)

	Number of Projects	*Cost (Thousand Million Lire)*
Land Reclamation and Mountain Reservoirs	11,185	882
Drains and Water Supply	2,453	398
Communications	2,642	299
Tourism	957	68
Railways and Ports	212	106
Hospitals	54	34

APPENDIX III
State Holdings and Nationalized Bodies

Istituto Per La Ricostruzione Industriale—IRI
(Institute for Industrial Reconstruction)
89 Via Veneto, Rome
President: Prof. Giuseppe Petrilli

Established 1933 as an autonomous government agency controlling banking and credit institutions as well as many of the largest industrial undertakings. IRI is a state holding responsible for the management of a great number of companies in which the state participates. There are five sectorial holding companies:

STET: Thirteen companies providing urban and trunk line telephone services, telecommunications, manufactured products and implementing research and development activities catering for 5,500,000 subscribers. Length of urban circuits: 13,900,000 km. Length of trunkline circuits: 4,100,000 km.

FINMARE: Four large shipping lines. The companies account for about 61 percent of Italy's passenger and mixed passenger-cargo carrying capacity.

FINSIDER: Nine major iron and steel firms producing pig iron, steel, tubes, plates, sections, structural steel, cement and other products.

FINMECCANICA: Twelve major engineering firms, including aircraft, motor vehicles, industrial machinery, *electronics* and optical instruments.

FINCANTIERI: f. 1966; one shipbuilding firm accounting for almost 80 percent of total Italian capacity. Six ship repairing firms.

A number of other companies are also under direct IRI control. These include the national airline Alitalia; the Autostrade company, which is responsible for the construction and operation of about half of the Italian motorway network; the RAI television service; the three main Italian commercial banks: Banca Commerciale Italiana, Credito Italiano and Banco di Roma; the Banco di Santo Spirito; and the financial holding company SME.

Ente Nazionale Idrocarburi—ENI

(Italian State Petroleum Company)

72 Viale dell'Arte, Rome

President: Dott. Eugenio Cefis

A state holding company with subsidiaries including AGIP, SNAM and ANIC, operating in petroleum exploration and production, refining, petroleum products marketing, petrochemicals and scientific research.

Ente Nazionale Per L'Energia

Elettrica—ENEL

(National Electricity Board)

Via del Triton 181, Rome

Chairman: Vitantonio di Cagno

Set up in 1962 to generate and distribute electrical power throughout various areas of the country and to work in conjunction with the Ministry of Industry and Trade.

COCA-COLA COMPANY

Coca-Cola and the Middle East Crisis: International Politics and Multinational Corporations

In late 1964 the management of Coca-Cola Company was faced with a crucial policy decision concerning its overseas business—whether to grant a bottling franchise in Israel to its then distributor, the Tempo Bottling Company of Israel—thereby antagonizing its Arab customers who were, in effect, at war with Israel.[1]

In 1951—three years after the modern State of Israel was founded (May 14, 1948)—the Arab nations set up an economic boycott against certain companies doing business with the Israelis.[2] In most instances the Arabs have not objected to ordinary trade with Israel but have enforced the ban when capital goods or military equipment was involved.[3]

Had Coca-Cola accepted Tempo's application for the bottling franchise, the Israeli company would have built its own bottling plant and purchased syrup but not the finished product from Coca-Cola.

In January 1965, the company decided that the potential demand for Coca-Cola in Israel did not justify a bottling plant at that time and therefore refused the franchise. Several important considerations were responsible for the company's decision.

The principal reason was profits: the potential Israeli market for Coke—some 2.5 million Israelis—was dwarfed by the 104.7 million Arab population in the Arab League countries.[4] The Arabs had been among Coke's heaviest consumers since the soft drink arrived in the Middle East during World War II. Even tiny Kuwait had a per capita consumption of 175 bottles a year—nearly double the average United States rate. The hot desert climate and the Arab taboo against alcoholic spirits combined to make Coke a widely consumed beverage in the Middle East.[5]

In contrast, early governments of Israel, to minimize their exchange problems, had yielded to local citrus fruit lobbyists and abrogated Abraham Feinberg's

---

1. Irving Spiegal, "Coca-Cola Refuses Israelis a Franchise," *New York Times*, 8 April 1966, 1:7.

2. *MSU Business Topics*, Spring 1968, p. 74.

3. "Business in Mideast Walks on Shifting Sands," *Business Week*, 2 July 1966, pp. 26, 28.

4. Luman H. Long, ed., *The World Almanac and Book of Facts, 1967*, New York: Newspaper Enterprise Association, 1966, p. 630.

5. "Bottled Up," *Newsweek*, 18 April 1966, p. 78. *See also* Thomas Buckley, "Coca-Cola Grants Israeli Franchise," *New York Times*, 16 April 1966, 1:2.

contract to bottle Coke in 1949. Coca-Cola knew that American companies such as Zenith Radio Corp. and Ford Motor Co. had been barred from doing business in the Arab countries because they sold their products in Israel. Therefore, it seemed that Coca-Cola might be able to operate either in the Arab countries or in Israel, but not in both.[6] If business firms have an obligation to their customers as well as their stockholders, then Coca-Cola certainly owed such an obligation to the Arabs because of their long devotion to its products.

Moreover, in view of the competitive conditions, the danger of losing the lucrative Arab market appeared very real. The Arab countries could shut down the twenty-nine franchised Coca-Cola bottling plants because they could easily substitute Pepsi-Cola for Coca-Cola. Psychologists have tested panels of regular cola drinkers and concluded that people could not differentiate between colas by taste alone.[7] Pepsi competed with Coke in the Arab market, and most probably would capitalize on Coke's fall from Arab-leader favor.

A second consideration in refusing the franchise to Tempo was the company's dissatisfaction with its Israeli distributor. In 1963, Coke filed suit in a Tel Aviv court against Tempo for infringing upon the Coca-Cola trademark. Coca-Cola also was unhappy with Tempo because it bottled other soft drinks. By custom, Coca-Cola franchises are granted in perpetuity as long as the bottlers uphold rigid quantity standards specified by the company. Although many Coca-Cola bottlers also manufacture and sell other soft drinks, the company's tradition of granting franchises of indefinite duration made it necessary for them to choose only those firms with whom they could get along.[8] Obviously, Tempo's past record did not meet this criterion.

FRANCHISE REPERCUSSIONS IN ISRAEL

Tempo was not satisfied with Coca-Cola's contention of insufficient market in Israel. They averred that Coca-Cola's management had set arbitrary and unusually high quotas for Tempo, which were impossible to meet. They charged that the main reason for the refusal of the franchise was to support the Arab boycott, and asked the Anti-Defamation League of the B'nai B'rith to undertake an investigation.[9] If Coca-Cola was indeed supporting the boycott, it would be violating U. S. government foreign policy.[10]

In April 1966, after a fifteen-month investigation, the Anti-Defamation League released a report noting that Israel was one of the few countries in the free world without a Coca-Cola bottling plant. The reason for this, the report alleged, was that the Coca-Cola Export Corporation was cooperating with the Arab League boycott.

6. *Business Week*, op. cit.
7. James A. Myers and William H. Reynolds, *Consumer Behavior and Marketing Management*, Boston: Houghton Mifflin Co., 1967, Ch. 2.
8. E. J. Kahn, Jr., "Profiles," *The New Yorker*, 14 February 1959, pp. 37-40.
9. "Capping the Crisis; Israeli Franchise," *Time*, 22 April 1966, p. 75.
10. Irving Spiegal, op. cit.

The report cited the three major prerequisites Coca-Cola had for granting a bottling plant franchise: a $1 million minimum investment; a "viable market," and "practically exclusive manufacture of Coke." Tempo, which had $2.2 million in sales in 1965, had supposedly met the first two requirements and had agreed to the third.[11] The League stated that the Israeli market was potentially more profitable than that of the Arab franchise. Therefore, "The deducible facts seem strongly to indicate that, while submitting to the Arab boycott, Coca-Cola has assiduously attempted to camouflage its submission as a pure nonpolitical, economic decision."[12]

The aftermath of the report was sheer confusion. James A. Farley (former U. S. Postmaster General), Chairman of the Coca-Cola Export Corporation, vigorously denied the charge of honoring "any boycott." He said that detailed surveys of economic and market conditions evidenced a low success potential to the Israeli market, but indicated that "All decisions of this kind are constantly under assessment and reassessment." Farley also said that the Tempo Company "had been found guilty in a Tel Aviv court of infringing the Coca-Cola trademark and bottle design in the marketing of its own product, Tempo Cola."[13] Denying yielding to the threat of an Arab boycott, Robert L. Gunnels, Coca-Cola Export vice president, said that an Israeli bottling plant would not be "mutually profitable" to Tempo and Coca-Cola, and added that a similar decision had been made regarding bottling franchises in Jordan and Syria.

Some of the information advanced by Coca-Cola was unknown to the Anti-Defamation League. Arnold Foster, who prepared the report, said the League was unaware of Coca-Cola's granting Abraham Feinberg's earlier application for a franchise and also of Tempo's infringement on the Coke trademark. He said that these facts had not been mentioned when the League contacted Coca-Cola in regard to the franchise denial to Tempo.[14]

The managing director of Tempo, in turn, objected to Coca-Cola's statements, saying that Tempo had not been found guilty by the court as the case had been settled out of court; and that the shape of the Tempo Cola bottle was not at issue. According to the *New York Times*, court records bore out the Tempo statement.[15]

Coca-Cola's basic position was, if it is to operate profitably at home and abroad, it must cater to everybody. A year before the Anti-Defamation League report, Coca-Cola president, J. Paul Austin, had received a human relations award from the American Jewish Association. The company had a record of being a goodwill ambassador for the United States. In 1949, as a result of left-wing agitation, an anti-Coke bill had become law in France. This aroused anti-France feelings in the United States, leading to several proposals of boycotts of French products. However, the company refused to exploit the anti-France feelings; and James

11. *Newsweek,* 18 April 1966.
12. Irving Spiegal, op. cit.
13. Thomas Buckley, op. cit.
14. "Coca-Cola Unit Denies Charge It Is Supporting Arab Boycott of Israel," *Wall Street Journal,* 13 April 1966, 11:3.
15. Thomas Buckley, op. cit.

Farley succeeded, through persuasion and diplomatic negotiations, in getting France to repeal the law.[16] The company had also begun operations in Bulgaria in response to the U. S. government's policy of "building bridges to the East."[17]

Coca-Cola, of course, was aware that Congress went on record opposing foreign initiated boycotts in the Williams-Javits law of 1965,[18] and pointed out that its decision was based solely on economic grounds, and that it was not violating the statute nor the intent of Congress.

THE ANTI-DEFAMATION LEAGUE

The Anti-Defamation League has, since its founding, become a powerful force in the use of reason and moral suasion to eradicate prejudice against Jews. Despite Coca-Cola's arguments, and the League's admission of ignorance of some of the facts, the firm stood to lose the patronage of some 5.6 million Jewish people in America—since word got around that Coca-Cola was possibly anti-Jewish. (It should be noted, however, that the 104.7 million Arab population dwarfs the 13.3 million worldwide Jewish population; so, from the standpoint of income, the Arabs appear to be more desirable friends than the Israelis.)[19]

Mount Sinai Hospital in New York stopped taking delivery of Coca-Cola for its cafeteria. A New York theater chain and Coney Island's Nathan's Famous Hot Dog Emporium threatened to follow suit, and the New York City Human Rights Commission called for an investigation of Coca-Cola. Within a week of the League's charges, and despite Coca-Cola's denial of them, the company again issued a bottling franchise for Israel to Abraham Feinberg, now a New York banker, president of the Israel Development Corporation, and a promoter of Bonds for Israel. The Anti-Defamation League said that Coca-Cola's decision "will show other American corporations the sham the Arab boycott really is."[20]

Actually, Feinberg had contacted Coca-Cola about his "renewed interest" a week before the League's charges were made public. Feinberg commented that he would not have accepted any franchise "if I believed Coca-Cola bows to Arab boycott threats."[21]

Now it remained to be seen what the Arabs would do. Israeli officials predictably reported that the boycott's influence had declined in recent years since the Arab governments had not invariably backed up their threats. The Israeli Consulate General stated there were more than 200 American companies doing business with both Israel and the Arab League nations. *Business Week* reported that although the rich nations—Saudi Arabia, Kuwait, Libya—were the strictest enforcers of the boycott, Egypt often "winks at boycotts," and Tunisia, Algeria, and Morocco "ignore the boycott more than they observe

16. E. J. Kahn, Jr., op. cit.
17. "Thaw That Refreshes," *Time*, 3 December 1965, p. 98.
18. Irving Spiegal, op. cit.
19. Luman H. Long, op. cit., pp. 332, 594-670.
20. *Time*, op. cit.
21. Thomas Buckley, op. cit.

it."[22] Despite these reassurances, however, the possibility of large sale losses was real.

THE ARAB REACTION

The reprisals from the Arab countries were not long in coming. In July 1966, the Central Office for the Boycott of Israel of the Arab League asked the company about its plans for setting up bottling plants in Israel and warned Coca-Cola that it faced a ban on its product; saying that the bottling plants would be closed within three months if the Israeli plant was approved. In November the thirteen-country Arab League Boycott Conference met in Kuwait.[23] The Boycott Bureau told the conference it had received unsatisfactory replies from Coca-Cola.

The conference then passed a resolution to stop the production and sale of Coca-Cola within Arab League countries. Enforcement of the ban, however, was left to the discretion of the individual countries.[24] The Boycott Bureau established a nine-month time limit to allow Arab bottling plants to use up Coke concentrates in stock.

The company made some belated efforts to placate Arab opinion. One month before the Arab League meeting, the company ran an advertisement in a Cairo newspaper showing the important economic and social role played by Coca-Cola in the Arab countries. However, a month was apparently not enough time for the advertisement to have any effect. In December 1966, Bagdad Radio announced that Iraq had begun its ban on Coca-Cola. The company said it had received no official notification from Iraq, but that in the three months since the ban was announced by the League the boycott "has not manifested itself in production sales."[25]

In September 1967, nine months after Arab League representatives met to approve the boycott, the Boycott Bureau announced that the ban was effective. Despite the ban and the Arab's increased hatred of Israel after the six-day war, Coke was not deterred and a Coca-Cola bottling plant opened for business in Tel Aviv in February 1968.

---

22. *Business Week*, op. cit.
23. Composed of the United Arab Republic, Iraq, Jordan, Lebanon, Saudi Arabia, Syria, Morocco, Yemen, Algeria, Kuwait, Libya, Sudan, and Tunisia.
24. Thomas F. Brady, op. cit. *See also*, *Business Week*, 26 November 1966.
25. "Iraq Plans to Boycott Three U. S. Companies," *Wall Street Journal*, 20 December 1966, p. 11.

2

Organization and Management

HEWLETT-PACKARD COMPANY U. S. A. (A)

Early History, Growth, and Organization

Hewlett-Packard Company (H-P) of Palo Alto, California is the world's largest manufacturer of precision electronic measuring instruments.[1] The 1968 *Fortune* list of 500 United States manufacturing enterprises ranked H-P 313th in terms of sales ($270 million) and 230th in terms of after-tax profits ($22 million). Its 1968 earned return on invested capital was 14.6 percent (compared to the industry's average of 11.7 percent). H-P's most impressive statistic, however, is sales growth. From 1958 through 1968 its average annual increase was 21.34 percent, placing it 37th among U. S. manufacturing companies (Table 1).

PRODUCT LINE

H-P's catalog, the largest in the industry, lists over 2,000 products which can be broadly classified under the following categories.[2]

1. *Microwave equipment.* Consists of signal generators, power meters, and items for use in waveguide and coaxial systems. These products are used in research and development, production and maintenance of microwave communications, military and commercial radar, air navigation and guided missile control.
2. *Electronic counters and frequency time standards.* Principal instruments here are digital frequency counters, digital time interval meters and time standards. Applications are in electronics, nuclear science and industrial automation.

1. *Standard & Poor's Listed Stock Reports*, 25 June 1969, p. 1137.
2. Ibid., p. 1139.

TABLE 1

Income Statistics (Million Dollars) and per Share (Dollars) Data[a]

Year Ended Oct. 31	*Net Sales*	*Percent Operating Income of Sales*	*Operating Income*	*Depreciation and Amortization*	*Net Before Taxes*	*Net Income*	*Earnings*	*Common Share (Dollars) Data*: *Dividends Paid*[b]	*Common Share (Dollars) Data*: *Price Range*[c]	*Price–Earnings Ratios High-Low*
1969	–	–	–	–	–	–	–	0.10	95 –75¼	–
1968	268.85	18.4	49.59	9.49	42.94	20.83	1.66	0.20	91⅜–59⅛	56–36
1967	243.36	18.5	45.02	7.77	38.19	20.12	1.62	0.20	89¾–48¾	55–30
1966	203.34	18.3	37.30	5.50	32.68	17.45	1.42	0.20	55¾–35⅛	37–35
1965	163.62	18.5	30.26	4.22	27.36	13.91	11.12	0.20	38⅞–22½	35–20
1964	134.07	16.0	21.48	3.43	18.97	10.04	0.80	Nil	23⅜–17	29–21
1963	115.93	14.8	17.17	3.17	15.10	7.25	0.60	Nil	27¼–18½	45–31
1962	110.96	14.0	15.59	2.45	15.69	7.59	0.65	Nil	37 –15¼	57–23
1961	87.27	15.5	13.53	9.92	11.98	6.04	0.53	Nil	53 –26	100–49
1960	76.81	14.5	11.14	1.45	10.00	4.99	0.44	Nil	30¼–13⅞	69–32
1959	47.75	18.5	8.82	0.84	8.15	3.90	0.40	Nil	16⅞–12½	42–31

[a]Consolidated; including Sanborn Co. after 1959, Harrison Laboratories after 1960, field sales organizations from 1962, and Datamec Corp. and F & M Scientific after 1963.

[b]Adjustment for 200 percent stock dividend in 1960.

[c]Calendar year.

TABLE 1—continued

Pertinent Balance Sheet Statistics (Million Dollars)[a]

Oct. 31	Gross Prop.	Capital Expenditures	Cash Items	Inventories	Receiv-ables	Current Assets	Current Liabilities	Net Working Capital	Current Ratio Assets to Liabilities	Long-Term Debt	Book Value Common Share[a] (Dollars)
1968	93.22	15.85	4.69	58.33	50.83	117.50	41.22	76.28	2.9–1	1.23	11.23
1967	80.87	19.95	3.38	52.19	43.86	102.08	43.37	58.71	2.4–1	1.96	9.37
1966	63.61	18.66	2.27	53.59	40.62	98.61	50.99	47.62	1.9–1	0.79	7.62
1965	46.76	10.03	3.53	35.53	31.95	72.56	29.47	43.09	2.5–1	0.47	6.15
1964	38.89	7.32	9.84	30.15	21.35	62.59	20.03	42.56	3.1–1	0.23	5.09
1963	32.69	4.60	4.92	25.15	17.82	48.78	15.08	33.70	3.2–1	0.29	4.19
1962	28.37	8.65	3.52	24.22	16.98	45.50	16.97	28.54	2.9–1	0.34	4.16
1961	20.21	4.24	3.32	18.52	12.51	34.78	12.87	21.91	2.7–1	0.24	2.54
1960	17.30	8.46	2.63	16.51	10.60	30.05	13.65	16.40	2.2–1	0.50	1.92
1959	10.46	2.54	1.66	10.15	6.71	18.68	8.09	10.59	2.3–1	0.63	1.78

[a]Consolidated; including Sanborn Co. after 1959, Harrison Laboratories after 1960, field sales organizations from 1962, and Datamec Corp. and F & M Scientific after 1963.

SOURCE: *Standard & Poor's Listed Stock Reports*, 25 June 1969, p. 1137.

3. *Oscillators and vacuum tube voltmeters.* Instruments in this field find general use throughout industry and government. Uses range from maintenance of telephone systems to industrial and defense needs.
4. *Oscilloscopes.* These instruments provide means of visual presentation of electrical phenomena and as such are basic equipment in research and development laboratories.
5. *Graphic recording devices and accessories.* These instruments consist of various strip chart and X-Y recorders for measuring and recording physical events.
6. *Power supplies.* This equipment provides voltage and current sources for electronic laboratories.
7. *Measurement systems.* Digital data systems and radio frequency systems are designed for a wide range of military and industrial uses.
8. *Medical electronic apparatus.* This equipment measures and records various biophysical events.
9. *Gas chromatographs and C-H-N analyzers.* These instruments are used to analyze chemical compounds.
10. *Electronic calculators and computers.* An electronic calculator is manufactured for scientific and engineering uses, while small digital computers and computer-based systems have been developed for the industrial control industry, education, and for general scientific purposes.

Other products include special purpose transformers and potentiometers, miscellaneous measuring equipment, and solid-state components.

Direct sales to the U. S. Government represented about 12 percent of the 1967 to 1968 total, while another 25 percent of orders came from foreign customers. Research and development expenditures approximated 11 percent of sales.

HISTORY

1937 Two former Stanford classmates—William R. Hewlett and David Packard—meet in Palo Alto, California on August 23 to discuss "tentative organization plans and a tentative work program for a proposed business venture." They consider "high frequency systems including receivers," medical equipment, and television. Hewlett was in graduate school at Stanford, Packard working for General Electric in New York.

1938 Packard takes a job as research assistant at Stanford and rents a house with a one-car garage. Together they rig a laboratory in the garage and begin to experiment. Here they successfully design and build such diverse devices as "a weight reducing machine, an electronic harmonica tuner, a bowling alley foul line indicator, and a diathermy machine."[3] The diathermy, a high-frequency, deep-heat therapeutic apparatus, is their first sale.

   The next commercial development is a resistance capacity oscillator. Walt Disney buys eight of these to use in the movie

3. *Hewlett-Packard in Perspective*, Hewlett-Packard Company, Palo Alto, California, p. 2.

classic "Fantasia." This oscillator makes use of Hewlett's research for his master's thesis, an important historical document in the field of electronic instrumentation.

1939   Proceeds from oscillator sales added to original $535 investment; partnership formed. New instruments developed and built.

1940 to 1945   By mid-year 1940 new quarters rented, seven employees hired, production bonus and paid vacations given. "Every nickel" plowed back into company. Defense contracts obtained to produce and develop military related products. Growth and expansion continues. H-P manufacturing 25 different measuring instruments, has over 100 employees.

1945 to 1946   Employment drops, picks up again. This period is used for conversion from defense to commercial products.

1947   Concentration begins on commercial products.

1950   Development increases significantly.

1951   Palo Alto Engineering Company (PAECO) established to manufacture special transformers. Company later acquired by H-P.

1954   Manufacturing and marketing 225 instruments with sales of over a million dollars a month.

1956   Dymec set up in Palo Alto to design and manufacture data-processing and radar simulator systems. Corporation later acquired by H-P.

1957   H-P stock sold to the public and traded over-the-counter.

1958   F. L. Moseley Company of Pasadena, California acquired—manufacturer of high quality graphic recorders.

1959   Boonton Radio Corporation of New Jersey acquired—manufacturer of precision instruments for measuring electrical circuits and checking aircraft guidance systems.

1960   H-P manufacturing facilities constructed on 80-acre site in Loveland, Colorado (fifty miles north of Denver).

1961   March 17, H-P common stock listed on New York and Pacific Coast stock exchanges.

1961   October, Sanborn Company of Waltham, Massachusetts acquired—manufacturers of medical diagnostic instruments and systems. This, H-P's largest single expansion up to this time, firmly established the company in the medical field.

1961   Late in year, Harrison Laboratories of Berkeley Heights, New Jersey acquired—manufacturer of top quality power supplies.

1964   H-P manufacturing facilities constructed in Colorado Springs, Colorado (fifty miles south of Denver).

1964 to 1965 More companies acquired: Mechrolab, Inc.—manufacturer of vapor pressure and automatic membrane-type osmometers; Delcon— producers of ultrasonic detection and test devices; Datamec Corporation of Mountain View, California—manufacturer of digital magnetic tape units and other data acquisition electromechanical equipment; F&M Scientific Corporation of Avondale, Pennsylvania—manufacturer of gas chromatographs (precision instruments for chemical analyses).

1967 H-P purchases plant site in Santa Clara, California and begins construction.

1968 71-acre manufacturing site purchased in San Diego, California. Also purchased an existing plant in Cupertino, California.

1969 February, David Packard leaves his H-P interest in trust and becomes U. S. Deputy Secretary of Defense.

INTERNATIONAL EXPANSION

H-P's international expansion followed the traditional pattern of exports, overseas sales offices, and finally overseas manufacturing facilities. In the early years H-P exports represented such a small part of total sales that relatively little attention was paid to them. At this time Canadian sales were handled directly by the company, while other sales went through an international trader. By 1954, exports had expanded sufficiently so that H-P cancelled its arrangements with the international trader and began handling all its international sales directly.

By 1959 exports represented 11 percent of total sales and Hewlett-Packard, S. A. was established with headquarters in Geneva, a branch office in Frankfurt, and a warehouse in Basel. Hewlett-Packard, GmbH was set up as a wholly owned manufacturing subsidiary of Hewlett-Packard, S. A. with a factory in leased facilities at Boblingen, West Germany (near Stuttgart).

In 1961 a new and larger plant was constructed at Boblingen, and Hewlett-Packard Ltd., was formed as a wholly owned U. K. manufacturing subsidiary located in leased facilities in Bedford, England, outside London. Later a marketing arm of H-P Ltd., took over the sales of H-P products in the United Kingdom. Also, in 1961, Electronic Marketing Company, SA/NV, with offices in Brussels and Amsterdam, was formed to promote sales in the Benelux Countries. Hewlett-Packard, S. A. was responsible for coordinating the marketing effort in Europe. Hewlett-Packard (Canada) Ltd., was formed as a sales subsidiary in Canada in 1961.

By 1962 sales were being made in over 70 foreign countries. H-P received national recognition for its overseas sales in September 1962 with the presentation of the President's E-for-Export Award, an honor initiated by the U. S. Department of Commerce.

In 1963 H-P entered into a joint venture with Yokogawa Electric Works, Ltd., Tokyo, Japan, to form Yokogawa-Hewlett-Packard, Ltd., a manufacturing and marketing endeavor. Construction was begun on a 60,000 square foot production facility in Tokyo. H-P held 49 percent of the equity, Yokogawa the remaining 51 percent. Also in 1963, new marketing organizations were formed in France and Sweden.

In 1964, manufacturing facilities were again expanded at Boblingen, West Germany. United Kingdom manufacturing operations were also moved to South Queensberry, Scotland, because expansion was restricted at Bedford. A new sales organization was established in France with headquarters in Paris, and in 1964 French sales jumped 70 percent over 1963. Also in 1964, a sales subsidiary, Hewlett-Packard Italiana, S. p. A., was formed in Italy with headquarters at Milan. Despite increased manufacturing in Europe, export sales from the U. S. to Europe were 25 percent greater in 1964 than in 1963.

In 1966, the company established a Mexican sales subsidiary. In 1967, international orders received for U. S. products rose 13 percent higher than 1966—to $39.4 million—despite significant increases in overseas manufacturing output. At the end of 1967, seventeen instruments developed in H-P's overseas research facilities were being marketed in several different countries, including the United States. Also by 1967, marketing organizations were established in Finland, Norway, Denmark, Australia, New Zealand, Argentina, Brazil, and Venezuela. Overseas operations employed more than 2,100 persons.

In 1968, a sales subsidiary was established in South Africa.

The distribution of H-P sales between domestic and international territories is given in Figure 1.

DOMESTIC ORGANIZATION

H-P's domestic organization is depicted in Figures 2 through 5. Figure 2 reflects the outline of overall organization while Figures 3 through 5 represent the organizations which are typical for a staff division (Finance), manufacturing division (Microwave), and a geographical region (Eastern United States).

Each manufacturing division (domestic and international) enjoys a large degree of autonomy in its operations. Each division has its own research and development group, its own production facilities, its own marketing support effort, and all other activities associated with the company with *the exception of its own field sales force*. The products of each manufacturing division are sold through the company's various domestic and international sales offices so that as far as a customer is concerned one sales engineer represents the entire corporation to him; regardless of whether the products are manufactured in the U. S. or abroad, his contact with H-P is that sales engineer. There exists, therefore, tremendous direct communication between various people in the manufacturing divisions and sales offices all over the world. These communications are largely channelled horizontally. Informal communication and interaction among all factions are heavily emphasized. These numerous dotted line relationships developed as growth required and are not shown on the organization charts. In general, only questions involving major policy decisions or requiring solutions of conflicts are referred to the administrators at the corporate level.

FIGURE 1

Percentage Distribution of Hewlett-Packard Company's Business

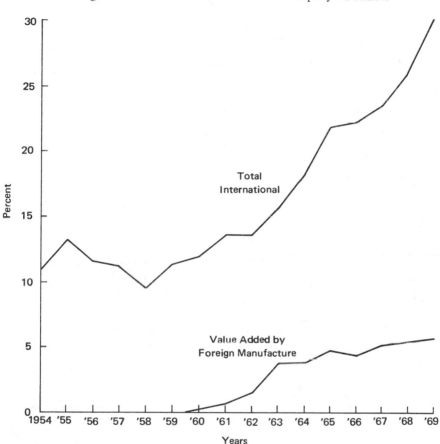

In its operations, H-P places heavy emphasis on R & D and manufacturing efforts. However, the marketing function is becoming increasingly significant. H-P explained this trend in the company's 1967 annual report:

> Because of the growing diversity of our products and markets, we are moving toward more specialization in our marketing structure and program. This is an important transition which will receive considerable management attention in 1968. Our objective is to maintain the marketing effectiveness we have demonstrated in our traditional areas and build equivalent strength which we can apply to areas that are new to us.

Since H-P was founded, its products were sold domestically through a nationwide network of independent representatives. The increasing complexity and breadth of its product line made it necessary for H-P to establish its own field sales organizations. By 1962, H-P reached acquisition agreement with ten of its fourteen

FIGURE 2

General Organization

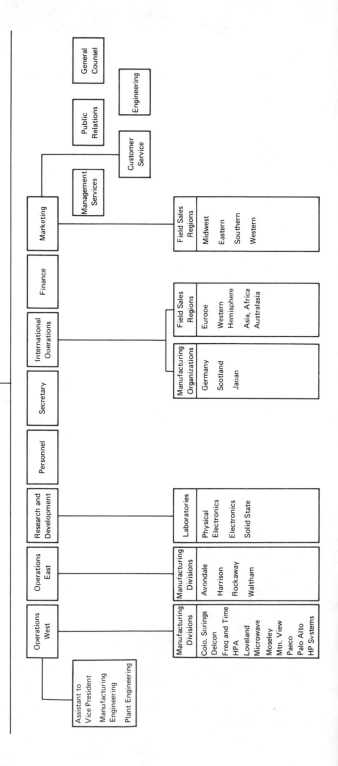

Executive Council Major executive acting as a group to advise and assist the Chief Executive Office in establishing objectives and policies for all corporate affairs and in evaluating performance of the Corporation at all levels. Membership consists of all corporate officers and others who are appointed by the Chief Executive Office.

Corporate Executive Group The corporate executive group consists of those offices within this shaded area on the chart which have responsibility for corporate wide affairs. Each office has responsibility in its functional area to:

1. Establish corporate wide objectives and policies.
2. Coordinate objectives and policies of all operating units.
3. Evaluate the performance of each operating unit.
4. Coordinate evaluation and reporting procedures for all operating units.
5. Provide advice and counsel and encourage exchange of information throughout the corporation on all affairs relating to area of functional responsibility.

Each office has the responsibility to administer approved corporate policies in areas where corporate wide uniformity and conformance is required. Where conflicts occur the question may be referred through the appropriate Vice President for resolution.

Channels of Contact The chart provides a picture of the general lines of responsibility, authority and accountability. Flow of information is expected to be upward as well as downward. All must recognize that this chart does not indicate or limit chances of contact or flow of information between or among the officers, managers, supervisors, and other personnel of HP.

In line with HP philosophy and practice, organization policy continues to permit, encourage and even expects the exercise of common sense and sound judgment, at all levels, in determining the best and most appropriate channels of contact for successful and expeditious follow through on HP work.

Contacts, and flow of information, between personnel within a group or between groups are to be carried out in the simplest, most obvious and direct way practicable. Of course, in making such contacts it is the responsibility of each person to keep his manager informed promptly regarding such matters as:

1. Those for which his manager may be held properly accountable by others.
2. Those in which there are or could likely be cause for disagreement or controversy, especially between different groups within HP.
3. Those in which the advice of his manager or coordination by his manager is required with other HP groups.
4. Those in which recommendations are involved for change, or in variance from established policies.
5. Those for which his good sense tells him his manager should know in order to be more effective in his day-to-day actions aas well as his planning for his group.

Each manager, as he believes there is a need, is expected to guide his staff as to matters that fall in the above category.

83

FIGURE 3

Financial Division

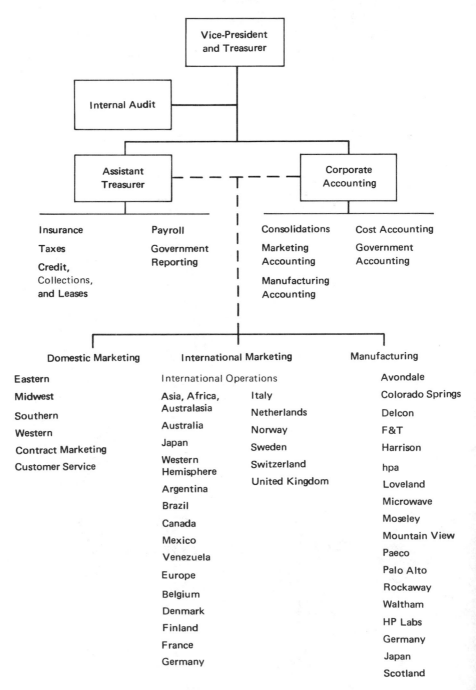

Vice-President and Treasurer

Internal Audit

Assistant Treasurer

Corporate Accounting

Insurance
Taxes
Credit, Collections, and Leases

Payroll
Government Reporting

Consolidations
Marketing Accounting
Manufacturing Accounting

Cost Accounting
Government Accounting

Domestic Marketing
Eastern
Midwest
Southern
Western
Contract Marketing
Customer Service

International Marketing
International Operations
Asia, Africa, Australasia
Australia
Japan
Western Hemisphere
Argentina
Brazil
Canada
Mexico
Venezuela
Europe
Belgium
Denmark
Finland
France
Germany

Italy
Netherlands
Norway
Sweden
Switzerland
United Kingdom

Manufacturing
Avondale
Colorado Springs
Delcon
F&T
Harrison
hpa
Loveland
Microwave
Moseley
Mountain View
Paeco
Palo Alto
Rockaway
Waltham
HP Labs
Germany
Japan
Scotland

FIGURE 4

Microwave Division

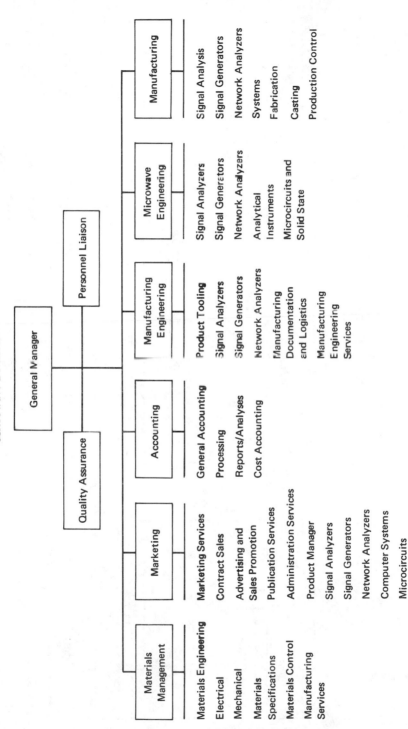

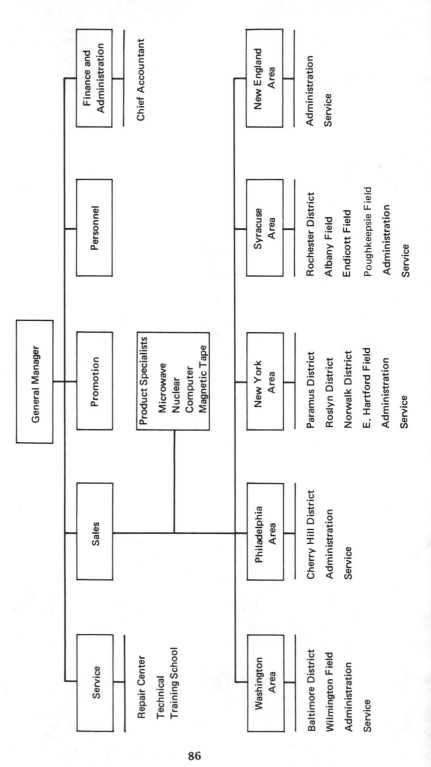

FIGURE 5
Eastern Region

General Manager

Service | Sales | Promotion | Personnel | Finance and Administration

Repair Center
Technical
Training School

Product Specialists
Microwave
Nuclear
Computer
Magnetic Tape

Chief Accountant

Washington Area | Philadelphia Area | New York Area | Syracuse Area | New England Area

Baltimore District
Wilmington Field
Administration
Service

Cherry Hill District
Administration
Service

Paramus District
Roslyn District
Norwalk District
E. Hartford Field
Administration
Service

Rochester District
Albany Field
Endicott Field
Poughkeepsie Field
Administration
Service

Administration
Service

86

sales representatives, and they were assimilated into H-P. These sales organizations were acquired by direct purchase or by an exchange of stock.

By 1966, H-P's domestic marketing effort was grouped into four regions. Domestic regions and their headquarters were established at: east, Englewood, New Jersey; midwest, Skokie, Illinois; south, Atlanta, Georgia; west, North Hollywood, California. Recently the control and administration of product development and marketing efforts have become increasingly complex, and so a new organizational pattern is emerging. The domestic organization has moved to a "group concept," or "group control system" of segmentation. The group concept is designed to decentralize the company's policy making activities and bring them closer to their point of impact. As one official explains it:

Notice the number of changes that have been made recently in our organization chart. What kinds of problems does this raise? One is coordination. It is tough to keep track of all these organizations to make sure they are not developing the same things or things which are not mutually supportive. Many instruments are used jointly and it is important to have the right oscilloscope to work with the proper microwave unit. So we have set up a group arrangement recently whereby the microwave division and the frequency and time division and HPA (another division) are grouped together under one man, who has been appointed a vice-president. He was the former head of the microwave division. This "super-group" will have engineering and manufacturing responsibilities. It will also have a much stronger marketing voice than the manufacturing division had in the past and will work with the marketing organizations both inside and outside the U. S.

INTERNATIONAL ORGANIZATION

H-P's overseas marketing operations for administrative purposes have been divided into three regional groups which have direct control over their particular regions. The first, and by far the largest in terms of sales volume, is the European complex, which encompasses all of Europe, including the United Kingdom. This region is administered from Geneva. The second region, the Western Hemisphere outside of United States—Canada and Latin America—is administered from Palo Alto. The third region, called the Triple A region, includes Australia, New Zealand, Asia, and Africa. This region is also administered from Palo Alto. The organization of H-P's international activities are depicted in Figures 6 through 12.

Grouping activities by region was done to deal with the increasing complexity of a growing organization: by the end of 1968, H-P had twenty-two sales companies and three factories outside of the United States. Also, company policy has been to decentralize throughout the world whenever possible to facilitate the personal interest and involvement that local autonomy brings.

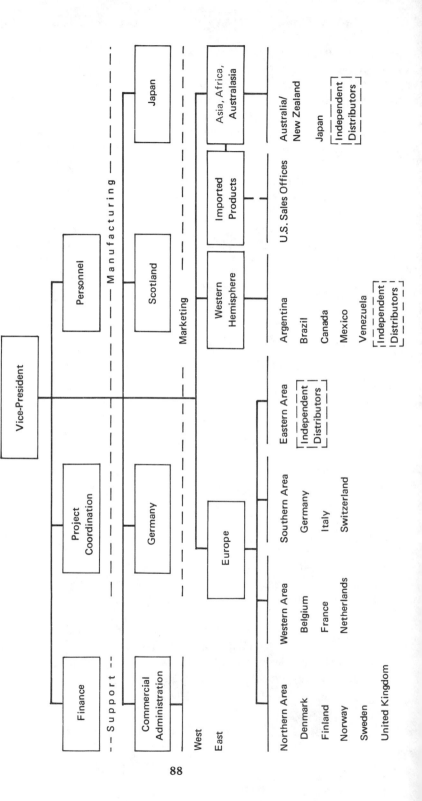

FIGURE 6

International Operations

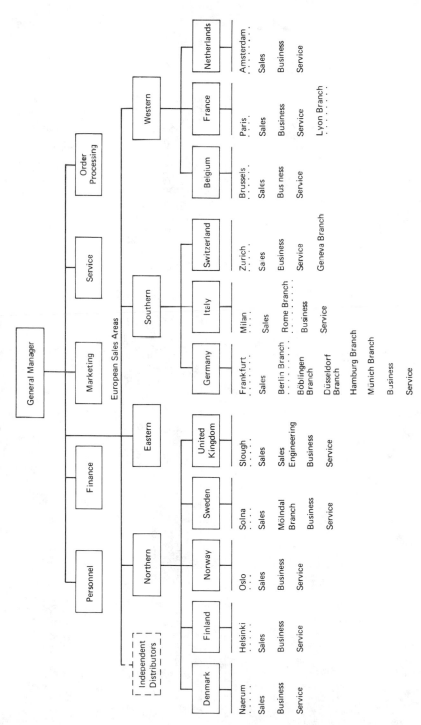

FIGURE 7

Europe Hewlett-Packard, S. A.

FIGURE 8

Scotland Hewlett-Packard Ltd.

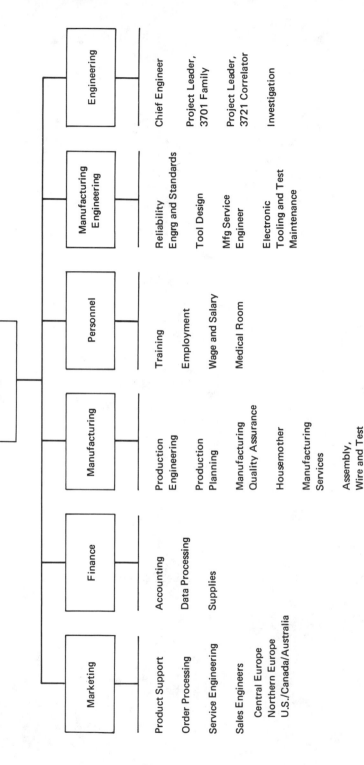

FIGURE 9

Germany Hewlett-Packard GmbH

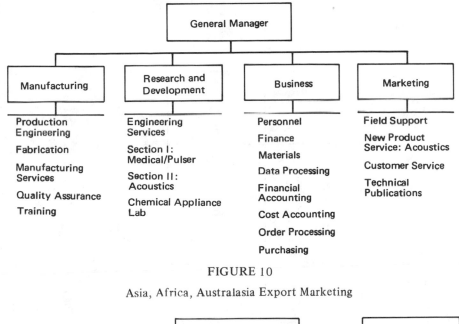

FIGURE 10

Asia, Africa, Australasia Export Marketing

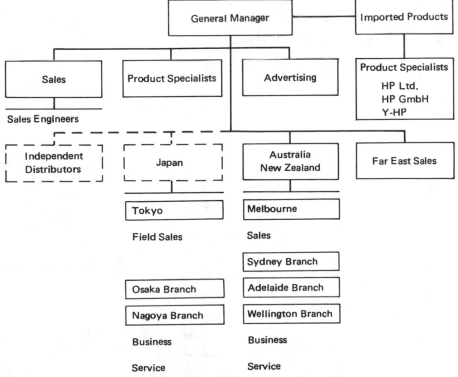

91

FIGURE 11

Yokogawa-Hewlett-Packard Ltd.

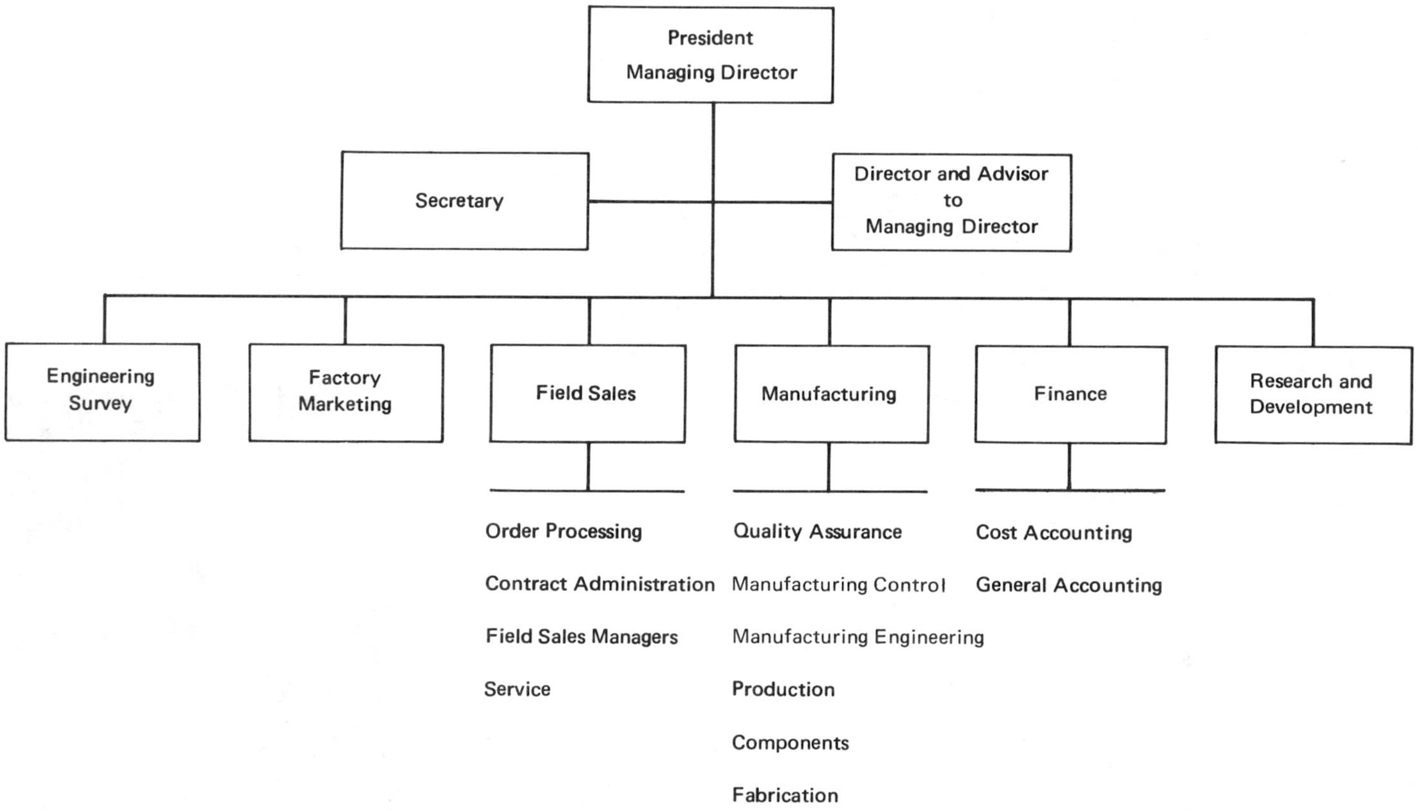

FIGURE 12

Western Hemisphere

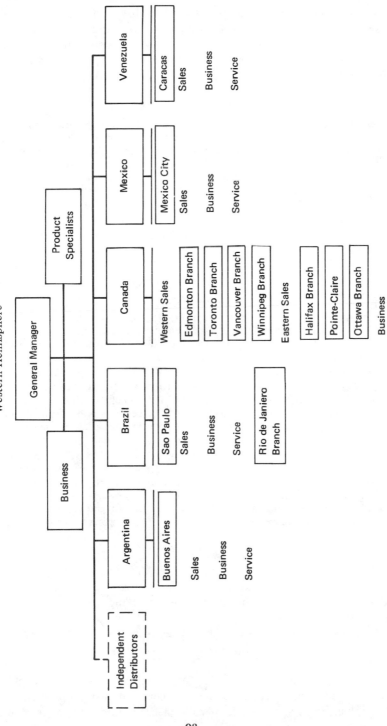

In its international activities the company has had to pay considerable attention to country and regional differences. For example, as early as 1957 H-P felt that the European Common Market would come into existence and, what is more, would be successful. Consequently, H-P moved aggressively and set up manufacturing facilities in Germany. According to one company official:

> It then became apparent that in order to sell the products of this factory we had to do a considerably better job of marketing in Europe, we had to ride much closer herd on our independent distributors than we could do from Palo Alto, six thousand miles away. So then the thought was to set up a regional marketing organization in Geneva to shephard the factory in its initial stages, and more importantly, to develop the market in Europe.

The company officials stated that although exhaustive studies were not conducted before manufacturing operations were established in Germany, several factors entered into the consideration:

1. There was a desire to jump the tariff wall and locate within the boundaries of the Common Market. It was foreseen that a united common market would offer a sales potential nearly equal to that of the U. S. and if the company did not manufacture in the common market someone else would.
2. The transportation costs of shipping all products from the U. S. were quite high and were considered likely to make H-P products overpriced. A company official, however, admitted recently that in view of developments in bulk air cargo, H-P, if faced with the same problem now, might think differently about locating manufacturing facilities abroad.
3. It was later recognized that the future growth of business in Europe could not be handled adequately through independent representatives even though they were supervised through a European headquarters. These representatives were private entrepreneurs who wished to make quicker profits and were reluctant to plow money back into the business, invest in services, or to maintain low prices to build volume business.

Recently there has been some criticism within the company that natural geographic regions were used excessively as decision bases without considering the potential of different regions, the complexities of selling within the region's areas, or the difference in demand for various individual products. For example, the "Asia, Australia, and Africa" sales region covers a large number of disparate areas, some highly industrialized and some not at all. This has created some problems of coordination.

The company, eventually hopes to introduce the "group concept" in its international operations. Nevertheless, it is recognized that the "group concept" will have to be *adapted* to meet the peculiar needs of international division. It will be a combination of group-region concepts.

FUNCTIONAL SPLITS

H-P's international marketing operations have three basic aspects: the marketing effort—the working with the field sales people and the customers, the administrative activities—financial analysis and control, policy guidance, etc., and the support function—accepting orders, placing orders on the manufacturing organizations, gathering equipment, preparing documentation, export licensing, packaging, and anything else entailing in getting the product out. This function is performed at the headquarters of the International Division in Palo Alto and also in Geneva. Centralizing this function with each regional marketing organization is designed to coordinate world-wide ordering and supply of H-P products to its customers.

APPENDIX I

Hewlett-Packard Company—Corporate Offices and Locations of
Domestic and International Operations

CORPORATE OFFICES
  1501 Page Mill Road, Palo Alto, California 94304
DOMESTIC OPERATIONS
Manufacturing
  Avondale Division (formerly F & M Scientific), Avondale, Pennsylvania.
    Gas chromatographs, other analytical instruments
  Colorado Springs Division, Colorado Springs, Colorado.
    Oscilloscopes, pulse generators
  Delcon Division, Mountain View, California.
    Ultrasonic industrial detectors, cable fault locators
  Frequency & Time Division, Palo Alto, California, and Beverly, Massachusetts.
    Electronic counters, time and frequency standards, synthesizers, nuclear instrumentation
  Harrison Division, Berkeley Heights, New Jersey.
    Regulated power supplies, television picture monitors
  HP Associates, Palo Alto, California.
    Diodes, microwave components, optoelectronic devices, photoconductors
  Loveland Division, Loveland, Colorado.
    Analog and digital meters, signal sources, standards, wave and distortion analyzers, telephone test equipment
  Microwave Division, Palo Alto, California.
    Microwave instruments, sweep and signal generators, spectrum and network analyzers
  Moseley Division, Pasadena, California.
    Laboratory and industrial recorders and plotters
  Mountain View Division, Mountain View, California.
    Analog and digital magnetic instrumentation recorders
  Paeco Division, Palo Alto, California.
    Magnetic components, tape heads

Palo Alto Division (formerly Dymec), Palo Alto, California.
    Computers, data acquisition systems
Rockaway Division, Rockaway, New Jersey.
    Impedance meters, signal sources
Waltham Division (formerly Sanborn), Waltham, Massachusetts.
    Medical and biophysical instrumentation, oscillographs and other recorders
Marketing
Eastern Sales Region, Paramus, New Jersey.
Midwest Sales Region, Skokie, Illinois.
Neely (Western) Sales Region, North Hollywood, California.
Southern Sales Region, Atlanta, Georgia.
    48 sales offices throughout the United States
INTERNATIONAL OPERATIONS

Manufacturing
Hewlett-Packard G.m.b.H., Böblingen, West Germany.
    Wholly owned subsidiary
Hewlett-Packard Ltd., South Queensberry, Scotland.
    Wholly owned subsidiary
Yokogawa-Hewlett-Packard, Ltd., Tokyo, Japan.
    A joint venture
Marketing
Export Marketing, Palo Alto, California.
    Africa, Asia, Australasia
Hewlett-Packard Inter-Americas, Palo Alto, California.
    Canada, Latin America
Hewlett-Packard S.A., Geneva, Switzerland.
    Western Europe
    115 sales offices throughout the Free World

INTERNATIONAL FOODS, INC., U. S. A. (A)

Organizational and Subsidiary Operating Budget Development

International Foods Incorporated, U. S. A. (IFI),[1] headquartered in New York, is a wholly owned division of Herbert Kingsbury Foods, Inc. (HKF), specializing in the production and distribution of dairy products and other processed foods. As of

---

1. All the names and figures in this study are fictitious in order to disguise the identity of the company and to protect its competitive position. Unless otherwise noted, quoted material is from verbal or written communication between the author and IFI management.

January 1970, IFI's activities, which exclude HKF operations in Canada and the U. S., included forty wholly owned manufacturing plants in seventeen countries, joint ventures in ten countries, sales in approximately 135 countries, and 6,000 overseas employees. In 1969, sales outside the U. S. and Canada were close to $200 million of which 65 percent came from the sale of one product, namely, evaporated milk. The percentages of sales derived from different regions were: Far East, 25; Latin America, 15; Europe, 50; and Middle East and Africa, 10.

ORGANIZATION OF INTERNATIONAL FOODS, INC.

Although IFI is autonomous, it and HKF maintain headquarters at the same location. Their only direct relationships are in top management and product lines, the IFI line being similar to but less comprehensive than the HKF line.

The IFI board of directors consists of the chairman of the board, president, and senior financial vice-president of the parent company (HKF), plus the president, executive vice-president, and the vice presidents of the finance and legal departments of IFI. It is with this body, but particularly the chairman and president of the parent company, that final decision-making authority relating to IFI operations rests. Each year the board must approve capital spending plans, marketing plans, and profit and loss projections for the ensuing fiscal year. The processes of affiliate budgeting and approval are described later.

Headquarters Staff

On IFI headquarters staff are approximately sixty-five persons who, broadly speaking, are responsible for "overall planning, approval of annual budgets, review of current operations, approval of major capital expenditures, approval of key executive salaries, provision of specialized services such as engineering and consolidation of accounts, and export sales." The headquarters operation is organized into four departments on a functional basis. Within each department tasks have been assigned on the basis of geographical regions and an even distribution of the workload to be performed by each department (Figures 1 through 3).

Departmental Staff Functions

Finance. As shown in Figure 1, the responsibilities of the four controllers are apportioned on a functional and geographical basis. Controllers are assigned a specific geographical area and within this area are responsible for aiding affiliate operations in solving any financial problems, for monitoring the financial status of the various operations, and for assisting affiliates in the preparation of annual financial plans.

In some cases the controllers' functional responsibilities cut across geographical responsibilities as is the case with worldwide consolidation of accounts which utilizes information gathered from all foreign operations. By far the most important functional responsibility in terms of value of information relayed from affiliates to the IFI board of directors is the President's Report. This report is presented

FIGURE 1

IFI Headquarters—Finance Department

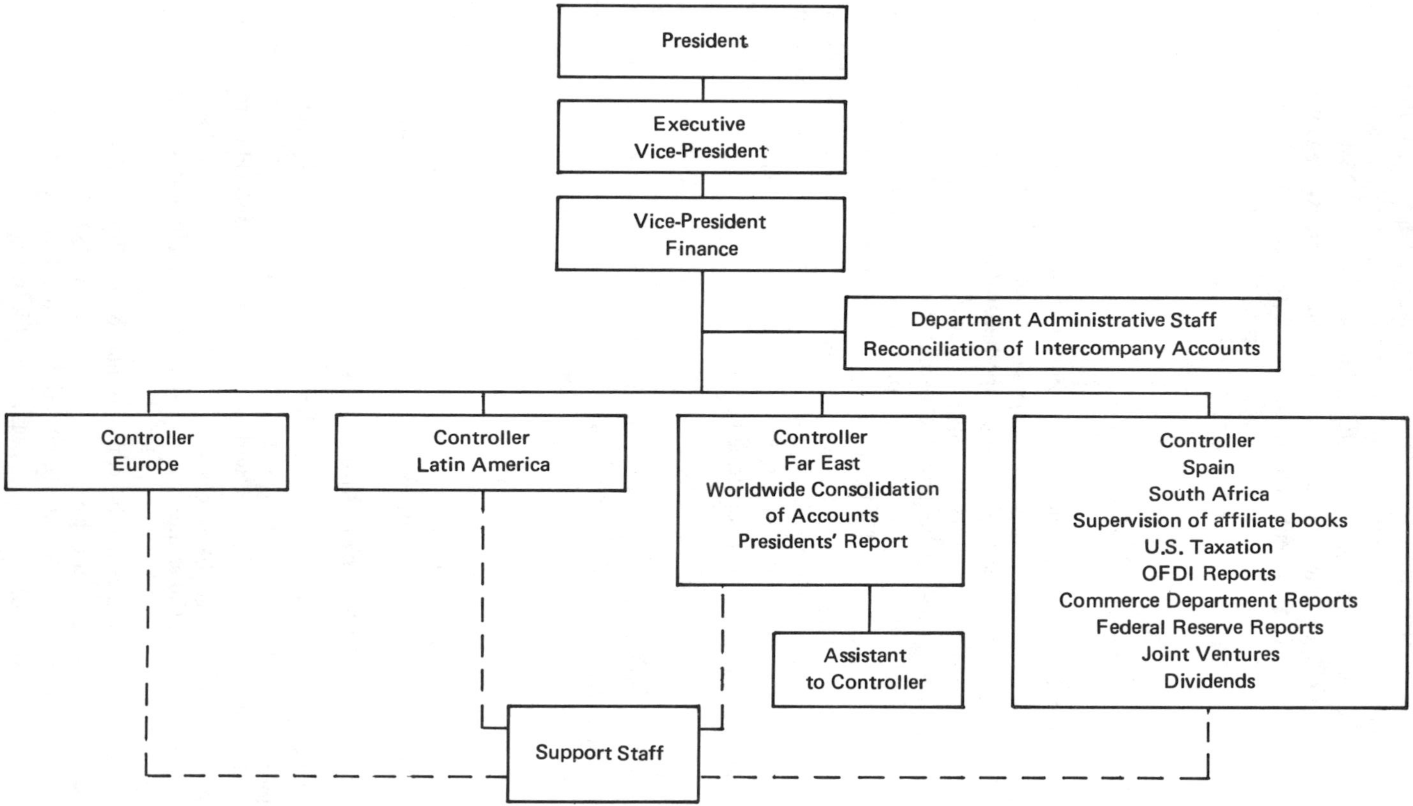

President

Executive Vice-President

Vice-President Finance

Department Administrative Staff
Reconciliation of Intercompany Accounts

Controller Europe

Controller Latin America

Controller Far East
Worldwide Consolidation of Accounts
Presidents' Report

Assistant to Controller

Support Staff

Controller
Spain
South Africa
Supervision of affiliate books
U.S. Taxation
OFDI Reports
Commerce Department Reports
Federal Reserve Reports
Joint Ventures
Dividends

98

FIGURE 2

IFI Headquarters—Production Department

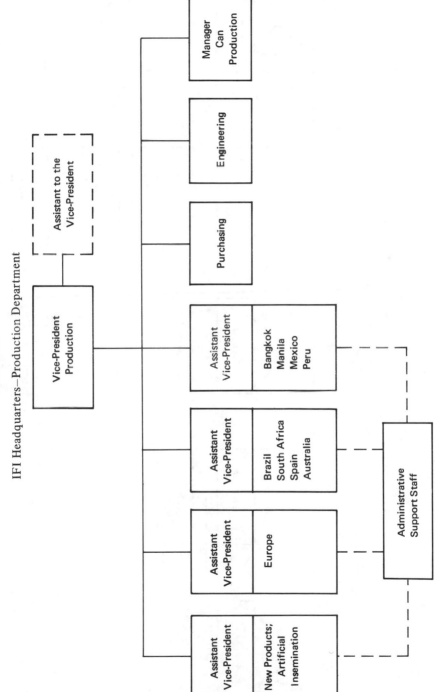

FIGURE 3

IFI Headquarters—Marketing Department

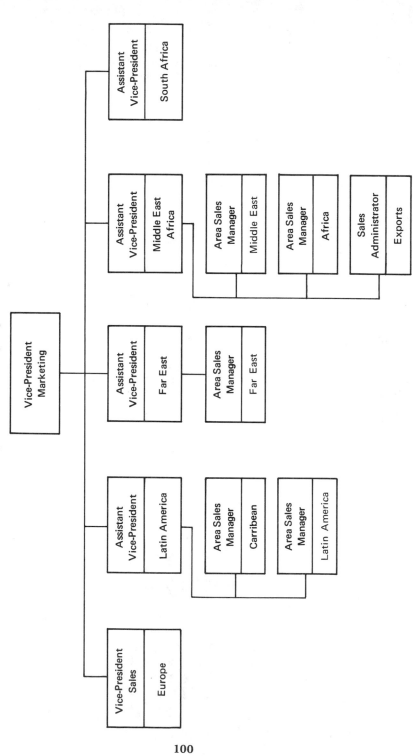

quarterly by the president of IFI and contains a summary by quarter of profit and loss statistics for each foreign operation.

The departmental support staff assists the four controllers and the vice-president on an "as needed" basis. The administration staff is primarily concerned with the reconciliation of intercompany accounts and has little to do with foreign operations.

Production. Broadly speaking, the headquarters' production staff (Figure 2) develops and coordinates overseas production policies and assists in production problem solving. The staff also conducts studies on acquisitions, investigates new products, aids affiliates in the preparation of production budgets and profit and loss statements, assists affiliates in programs of production cost reduction and employee training, conducts plant expansion studies, and monitors overseas production operations.

The production department has four assistant vice-presidents, one with worldwide responsibility for new products and artificial insemination. The remaining three assistant vice-presidents with duties apportioned on a geographical basis, maintain a close working relationship with affiliate production departments, aiding them in problem solving and preparing production budgets and reports in addition to monitoring current operations.

The purchasing agent has worldwide responsibility for the purchase of certain production equipment and some raw materials by some foreign affiliates. (This includes intercompany purchases of tin cans which are normally sold at cost to affiliates by the can-making division.) The purchasing agent is responsible for making affiliate purchases at the lowest possible cost. A program is being developed for a centralized purchasing department for European operations.

The engineering department works very closely with the assistant vice-presidents and has both engineering and production responsibilities.

IFI operates eleven foreign can-manufacturing plants which supply the can needs of all foreign operations. The manager of the can-making division coordinates the foreign production of cans to ensure that they are available when and where they are needed. Can needs are determined on the basis of sales estimates for finished goods which are contained in the marketing plans. The headquarter's manager of can-making acts only in an advisory capacity to the foreign can-making operations. All purchases of raw materials for can production are handled by the individual foreign can-producing operations.

The executive staff member is in charge of the internal operation of the department and assists the assistant vice-presidents on an "as needed" basis. The assistant to the vice-president is assigned on a permanent basis to aid the vice-president in the performance of his duties.

Marketing. The responsibilities of the four assistant vice-presidents of marketing and the vice-president of sales are apportioned on a geographical basis (Figure 3). These men are responsible for improving the marketing mix, transmitting marketing information to the affiliates, aiding the affiliates in preparing the annual marketing plan, and approving these plans at the affiliate level before they are reviewed by the vice-president of marketing. In addition, they monitor affiliate marketing operations.

During fiscal year 1968 to 1969, approximately 15 percent of IFI gross sales were accounted for by exports originating from the United States, Canada, Holland, France, and Australia. The marketing of these exports is the responsibility of the five area sales managers. More specifically, the area sales managers have profit and loss responsibilities for their assigned export markets, marketing budget planning and implementation, new product planning and introduction, pricing, and sales-agent selection. There is no formal, direct link between the area sales managers and the foreign affiliate marketing departments; the area sales managers report directly to the headquarter's assistant vice-presidents of marketing in charge of the area which receives the exports.

The sales administrator-exports is in charge of accounting, invoicing (generally C.I.F. or C. and F.), credit control, preparation of advertising budgets, and shipping for all IFI export operations. The sales administrator-exports has no direct, formal relationship to affiliate exporting operations either in the country of origin or destination of exports; he reports directly to the assistant vice-president of marketing for the Middle East and Africa.

The vice-president of sales—Europe (located in Brussels, Belgium) acts as a liaison between European affiliate marketing departments and the IFI headquarters marketing department. This individual has no decision-making authority, he acts only in an advisory capacity, helping European affiliate marketing departments in such areas as budget preparation and operational problem solving. The vice-president of sales—Europe reports directly to the headquarter's assistant vice-president of marketing for Europe.

IFI does not have its own market research department. Instead, the company employs a U. S.-based market research firm which determines the methodology of a market study and, with the vice-president, affiliate managing director, and assistant vice-president for the area of interest, determines its overall objectives. With methodology and objectives set, the firm chooses a market research firm near the market under scrutiny to conduct the actual study. Field-work data are transmitted to the U. S. market research firm where they are tabulated and evaluated, and the results reported to the IFI vice-president of marketing and the affiliate. IFI spends approximately $250,000 per year on market research. In 1969 some forty studies were conducted.

DEPARTMENTAL PLANNING, BUDGETING, AND REVIEW

This section is addressed to the role played by the headquarters staff in affiliate budgeting procedures. It is important to keep in mind that all departments of the IFI headquarters operation act in a staff and consultant capacity with regard to affiliate budgeting. In practice, this means that final decision-makind authority rests solely with the IFI board of directors which must approve any plans or budgets submitted by the affiliates before they may become operative.

Finance

Each year, beginning in June, the affiliates must prepare the Comprehensive Profit and Loss Forecast for the ensuing fiscal year. This forecast is prepared locally in consultation with the headquarters finance staff and is based on the projections contained in the marketing plans for the same time period. Headquarters involvement in drawing up this forecast is kept at a minimum and is usually called on only where there is some question at the affiliate level about how headquarters would like certain components of the forecast handled, such as procedural or reporting questions. The headquarters staff takes an active role in the financial operations of affiliates located in countries with unstable currencies, sometimes to the point of actually dictating to the affiliate which exchange rate to use. In general, the headquarters financial staff acts as a financial consulting service for the affiliates.

After completing the Comprehensive Profit and Loss Forecast and receiving the affiliate managing director's approval, the affiliate submits it to the headquarters finance department for review. If questions arise at the headquarters level, the controller responsible for the affiliate's area works out the difficulties with the head of the affiliate finance department. The forecast must receive the approval of the appropriate controller and the vice president of finance before the latter presents it for approval to the board of directors.

Once the forecast has been approved by the board and becomes operative, the affiliate finance department must see that the forecast is met. The headquarters finance department monitors the performance of the affiliates through a series of reports submitted by the affiliates. By far the most important report is the Quarterly Profit and Loss Statement which is a summary of the affiliates financial status for the current fiscal year and a month-by-month projection for the next quarter. This report, presented to the board of directors by the vice-president of finance, is used as a basis for evaluating the affiliate's financial status. The projections contained in this report are prepared by the affiliate finance department in consultation with the affiliate marketing and production departments.

The evaluation process is carried out by the headquarters finance department by comparing the quarterly projections to actual results which are reported in the Monthly Profit and Loss Statement. The quarterly statement is adjusted to reflect actual results and in this way is continuously revised and kept up to date. In the analysis of variances between projected and actual results "there is no statistical, mechanical type of evaluation. There is no formula that we apply which, for example, would say that anytime you have over 3 percent variance, a review of operations is necessary. We don't get that rigid."

In addition to the Monthly Profit and Loss Statement the affiliates submit a monthly Treasury Summary which is in effect a cash-flow summary of the previous month's operations. This report is used internally by the headquarters finance department to keep tabs on the liquidity position of the various affiliates. Its importance is underscored by the fact that all affiliate operations are actively encouraged to finance themselves locally. The Monthly Profit and Loss Statement and Treasury Summary are routed to all IFI officers and directors.

Production

As previously mentioned, the headquarters production department maintains a staff and consultant relationship with the IFI affiliate production operations. To insure that IFI will be able to produce the amount of products forecast by the affiliate marketing departments, the affiliate production departments prepare a five-year production schedule and budget. This document uses as a base the approved five-year sales projections of the marketing department. On the basis of the five-year sales projections, the production department calculates needed raw material supplies. In addition, plant and equipment needs for production and packaging are forecast. This process is done at the affiliate levels with close coopera-tion between the production and marketing departments and, once completed, it is reviewed by the headquarters staff. The five-year budget and production plans are for internal information and use. The board of directors only approves plans for twelve months ahead.

Monitoring of affiliate production operations by headquarters appears to be minimal. According to interviews, "the department is just starting to get into this type of thing. Previously, this was handled by the finance people in conjunction with the production people. There is a program currently being instituted whereby affiliate production departments will review their operations on a month-by-month basis. This program does not yet exist in all countries but attempts are being made to implement it." Production managers at the affiliate level are evaluated on the basis of cost minimization. In addition to the five-year production forecast, the affiliates submit to the head office a monthly PSI (Production, Sales, Inventory) Report which carries a projection of these three variables for the remainder of the current fiscal year and the year immediately following. Also, the affiliates submit a monthly Standard Cost Projection of production costs on a month-by-month basis for one year.

IFI has direct access to HKF's research and development department, where a man is assigned to handle IFI R and D work.

Marketing

Each year, beginning around the middle of April, the affiliate marketing depart-ments begin the preparation of the marketing plan[2] for the ensuing year.[3] The assistant vice-presidents of marketing for the various areas visit the affiliates and assess the progress being made in preparing the plan. In addition, they transmit information which may affect the projections which are under way.

Regarding the transmission of marketing information which has been compiled through market research studies of operations in foreign and domestic organiza-tions, IFI holds an annual marketing seminar before the yearly preparation of the marketing plans, which is attended by marketing management from the

2. A detailed description of this plan appears in the second part of this case, International Foods, Inc., U. S. A. (B).
3. A summary statement of the marketing plan is presented to the IFI management in the format entitled "Total Marketing Investment" (Figure 4).

headquarters and affiliate operations. In addition, the assistant vice-presidents are responsible for relaying the results of market research studies which may be relevant to the affiliate operations.

Once the marketing plan has been compiled by the affiliate marketing department and approved by the managing director, it is sent to the IFI president. He routes it via the executive vice-president to the vice-president of marketing, who, with the appropriate assistant, then examines the plan rigorously. Any questions are resolved between the marketing departments of the headquarters and affiliates before the plan goes to the board of directors for final approval.

The headquarters marketing staff monitors the operations of affiliate marketing departments. The affiliate facilitates this function by filing a Monthly Moving Marketing Summary (summarizing actual marketing operations for the fiscal year to date and a monthly projection for the ensuing twelve months) and a Quarterly Report of Marketing Expenditures (summarizing on a quarterly basis the marketing operations to date). The expenses incurred for the various elements of the marketing mix—lines three through sixteen in Figure 4—on an absolute and percentage of total marketing budget basis are compared with the projections made in the marketing plan.

The headquarters marketing department has no formally established method for variance analysis. Analysis of results vis-à-vis projections is carried out within the framework of the department's general goals. These include a 4 percent return on sales, maintenance, or expansion of market share, growth in case sales and dollar sales, maximum distribution for the company's products, and maximum channeling of marketing dollars toward the consumer-end of the marketing spectrum. The vice-president of marketing explained, "In terms of the flow of goods from the factory to the consumer, the larger the percentage of expenses that you can throw toward the consumer-end of that spectrum and the less you can spend back toward the factory, the more successful you can expect your product to be."

SPECIAL HEADQUARTERS FUNCTIONS

Overall Long-Term Planning

There is no plan in writing for the long-term growth of either the parent company or IFI. ". . . even within the countries in which we are now doing business, there is no plan in writing for five-year objectives. There are some elements within the marketing plan, including sales projections, product-line extensions, and product programs, but nothing as a whole that relates to capital spending, financial planning, profit projecting and so on." In some cases, the financial department will prepare a five-year profit and loss projection, but only when the company is considering a new product introduction or is evaluating an investment proposal.

FIGURE 4

Quarterly Report of Marketing Expenditures

	1st Quarter Amt. Percent	2nd Quarter Amt. Percent	3rd Quarter Amt. Percent	4th Quarter Amt. Percent	
Unit Sales					1
Gross Sales					2
Consumer Advertising (line 25)					3
Promotional Advertising (line 33)					4
Medical (line 41)					5
Other (line 46)					6
Market Research					7
Commissions					8
Salaries					9
Traveling Expenses					10
Sales Office Expenses					11
					12
					13
Selling Expenses					14
Distribution Expenses					15
Trade Payments (line 53)					16
Total Marketing Investment					17

Consumer Advertising

	1st Quarter Amt. Percent	2nd Quarter Amt. Percent	3rd Quarter Amt. Percent	4th Quarter Amt. Percent	
Cinema					18
Newspaper					19
Periodicals					20
Radio					21
Television					22
Production					23
					24
Subtotal (line 3 above)					25

	1st Quarter Amt. Percent		2nd Quarter Amt. Percent		3rd Quarter Amt. Percent		4th Quarter Amt. Percent		
Promotional Advertising									
Dealer Materials									26
Demonstrations									27
Literature									28
Samples									29
									30
									31
									32
Subtotal (line 4 above)									33
Medical									
Literature									34
Publications									35
Salaries and Expenses									36
Samples									37
									38
									39
									40
Subtotal (line 5 above)									41
Other									
									42
									43
									44
									45
Subtotal (line 6 above)									46

FIGURE 4–*continued*

| | | 1st Quarter | | 2nd Quarter | | 3rd Quarter | | 4th Quarter | |
		Amt.	Percent	Amt.	Percent	Amt.	Percent	Amt.	Percent
	Trade Payments								
47	Discounts (cash)								
48	Discounts (volume)								
49									
50									
51									
52									
53	Subtotal (line 16 above)								

Company _____   Country _____

Currency and Rate _____   Month _____, 19___

Evaluating New Investment Proposals

IFI does not consider a capital spending program in any market where it has not had previous experience on at least an imported basis.[4] Factors the company uses in assessing a new investment proposal are not explicitly stated—"there is no formal procedure." However, at least four variables are known to be important: The country's GNP and its projected growth rate, payback period, size of investment, and rate of return. Although there is no explicitly stated required rate of return for new investments, 15 percent after-tax return to the affiliate on assets managed is an informal rule of thumb. Of course, in high-risk markets this figure would be higher, but by how much and how it would be determined is not clear.

After identifying a market as a potential investment area, the company generally has "someone visit the country, become familiar with it, try and determine what assets the company has that could make for a profitable enterprise in the particular country, and out of this will come a report with some recommendations as to how to attack a particular market, which will then be expanded upon, modified and projected." Generally speaking, there are no minimum investment criteria. "The only time that we would limit the size of the investment and have as a criterion the amount we are prepared to spend is in the acquisition area. Generally speaking, we feel that if we are considering a company that is worth much less than one-half to three-quarters of a million dollars, it probably isn't worth the time and effort involved." For a new product introduction, the company is prepared to lose upwards of a half a million dollars before breaking even if the potential longer term looks satisfactory.

Final approval for such projects rests with the board of directors.

Manpower Planning and Training

Manpower planning in all the functional areas of the business is not formally provided for at present, but attempts are being made to remedy this. In 1969, for the first time, a manpower plan for marketing in Europe was developed for approval by the IFI board of directors.

Management training and development programs within the company are in their infancy but show the company's awareness of their importance. Current efforts to upgrade the managerial expertise of the firm include (1) "recruiting capable individuals"—capable meaning well-educated people who have the characteristics of motivation and intelligence—and placing them in responsible positions as quickly as possible; (2) a year-old, cross-country training program, whereby individuals who have been identified as present or future managers receive periodic training in the home office and other affiliate organizations; and (3) use of executive development programs being offered at major U. S. and European educational institutions.

---

4. This section deals only with capital spending in markets where the company does not now produce. Capital expansion in existing markets is covered in the section on Departmental Planning, Budgeting, and Review under Production.

All hiring for affiliate personnel is handled at the affiliate level by the managing director, according to guidelines he has established in consultation with the headquarters staff. Should the headquarters staff be dissatisfied with the managing director's recruiting and hiring practices, they will themselves become directly involved. IFI makes a concerted effort to see that its affiliate operations are staffed by nationals of the country in which it is operating.

Salary Administration

The HKF board chairman and the IFI president determine which persons constitute "key" executives and set their salaries. Currently, this classification includes all staff positions in the IFI headquarters, the affiliate managing directors and all those individuals who report *directly* to him at the affiliate level.

The affiliate managing director, responsible for recommending salary adjustments at the affiliate level, makes his annual recommendations directly to the HKF board chairman and the IFI president. The heads of the various functional groups at headquarters do some monitoring of salary recommendations, but the amount of review is at best minimal. If the head of one of the headquarters functional groups senses an oversight, he or a representative may suggest that the affiliate managing director review the individual in question.

The basis on which salary levels for headquarters and affiliate personnel are determined is unclear. There are no set criteria. An affiliate managing director's salary is, generally speaking, not related to the profitability of the subsidiary for which he is responsible. There is no bonus or merit pay system except where by law or long-standing custom key employees are entitled to it.

Affiliate Autonomy

It must be kept in mind that "headquarters control" refers to the control exercised by the IFI board of directors, specifically by the board chairman and the HKF president. Apparently the degree of control is a function of the extent to which headquarters can control the affiliate's various operations.

Officially, all company affiliate operations are viewed as "autonomous business entities responsible for profits." This suggests that the company's foreign operations have a relatively free hand, but the IFI concept of autonomy is somewhat different. In actuality, subsidiary operations are rather closely controlled, excepting local purchases of raw materials such as raw milk, labor, fuels, cans, labels, and cartons over which headquarters exercises very little control beyond the board of directors' final authority to approve budgets. This conclusion is based on an expanded definition of the company's concept of autonomy as expressed in interviews between the author and company officials.

Foreign operations are autonomous to the extent that they are profit centers. They are not autonomous to the extent that they raise their own money—the money comes from the headquarters.[5] They [affiliates] have to have their budgets approved by the company's board of directors so that if they are a profitable organization and they don't need a new plant they should be able to get along without any money, and to that degree they are autonomous. For supplemental funds or for changes in approved budgets they must have headquarters' approval. For instance, if in a conference with the chairman of the board and president of IFI's parent company, Herbert Kingsbury Foods (HKF), and officers of IFI, a capital spending program is not acceptable, then ultimately it is the chairman of the board and the president of HKF that make the decision whether or not to accept the proposed plan. This may be a plan that IFI headquarters management has agreed on with the managing director, but if the president and the chairman decide they don't like it, they have the authority and responsibility to change it as they see fit. This is the ultimate authority in the company.

We turn now to the affiliate managing directors' use of autonomy. These men are responsible for the day-to-day operation of the company's foreign businesses. At this point we run into some difficulty since it appears from interviews that the headquarters' concept of autonomy is not equally applied to or accepted by foreign operations. Apparently the system of relationships between headquarters and affiliates retains a great deal of flexibility. The extent to which autonomy is granted and used was summarized:

As a generalization I think you could say that as long as things are going well, management [affiliate] asks for as little help as possible, but when things get bad they want all the help they can get. In addition, utilization of autonomy by affiliate managers is a function of, among other things, differing personalities of the various affiliate managers, ethnic background, culture, and the acceptability of the home-office people who travel to the foreign operations. Also, utilization of autonomy is a function of how good the Profit and Loss Statement looks. If it's good, then headquarters will allow more independence.

Affiliate Organizations

To illustrate the broad socio-cultural-economic-geographic spectrum in which IFI operates, four countries exemplifying some of the different types of organizational structures existing in IFI were selected for concentrated study: West Germany and the United Kingdom in Europe, Peru in South America, and the Philippines in Asia. Among them they represent two advanced and two developing countries. Between them the European countries represent both the European Economic Community (EEC) and the European Free Trade Association (EFTA).

By way of introduction it should be noted that the organization we see in a particular market is not the result of chance events, nor should it be static. To ensure the long-term success of the firm, a company must very carefully determine from an analysis of all factors the kind of operation it wishes to employ in a

---

5. Affiliate operations are financed locally through the use of retained earnings and local borrowings, however the use of affiliate retained earnings or borrowings must be approved by the IFI Board of Directors. Any expense of funds amounting to $2,500 or greater must receive headquarter authorization.

particular market. Furthermore, it should be obvious that these factors are not static. In consequence, the firm must continually assess the effectiveness of a particular organizational structure in meeting the needs of the market, the company, and the personnel who manage it. Of utmost importance, then, is the company's need to employ an organizational structure which allows for the continual growth of operations.

In all cases the managing director of the affiliate organizations is the formal, direct link with headquarters through the office of the IFI president. The managing director is ultimately responsible for the performance of the affiliate operation. It should be made clear that although the formal channel of communication between headquarters and the affiliates exists only between the president of IFI and the affiliate managing director, informal channels are recognized and used routinely. In other words, the managers and staffs of the various headquarters and affiliate functional departments—marketing, production, finance, law—do communicate directly with each other. The formal channel must be used when a change in or deviation from approved budgets or plans is being contemplated or discussed. In this way, the participation of top management at the headquarters and affiliate level is assured.

Affiliate Organizational Structures

Figures 5 through 10 are the organization charts for IFI operations in the four countries chosen for study: West Germany, the United Kingdom, Peru, and the Philippines. The figures show that company operations in these four countries are, like the headquarters operation, organized in departments along functional lines. The charts also reveal marked differences between countries in the functional departments which exist and differences in responsibilities within departments.

FIGURE 5

International Foods, Inc. West Germany[a]

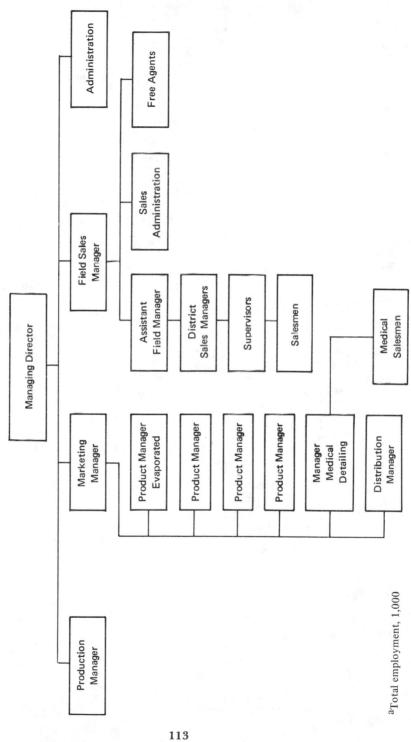

[a]Total employment, 1,000

113

FIGURE 6

International Foods, Inc.—United Kingdom[a]

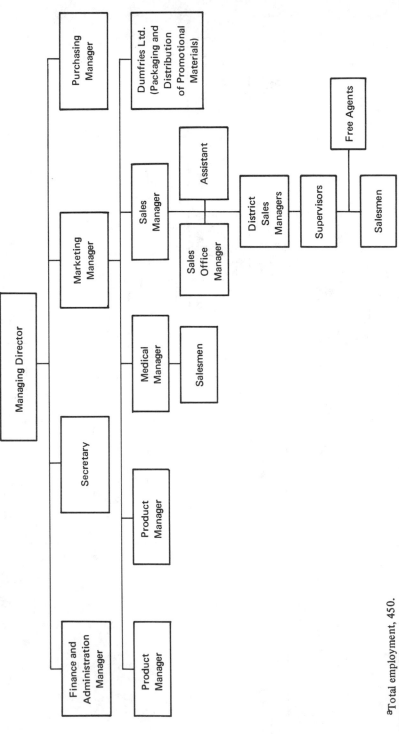

[a]Total employment, 450.

114

FIGURE 7

International Foods, Inc.—Peru[a]

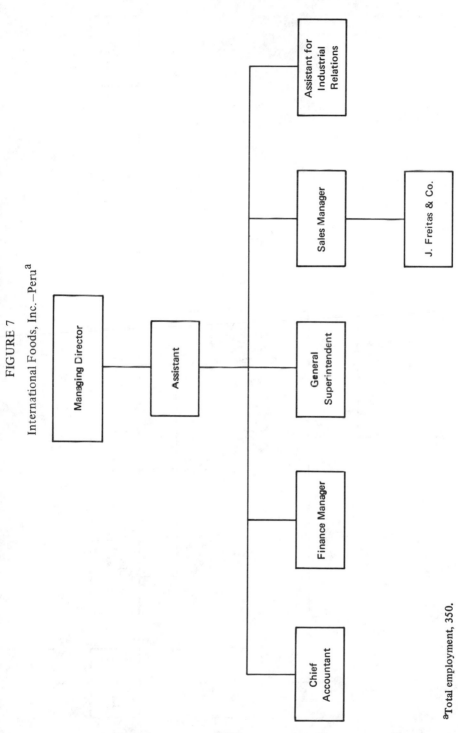

[a]Total employment, 350.

115

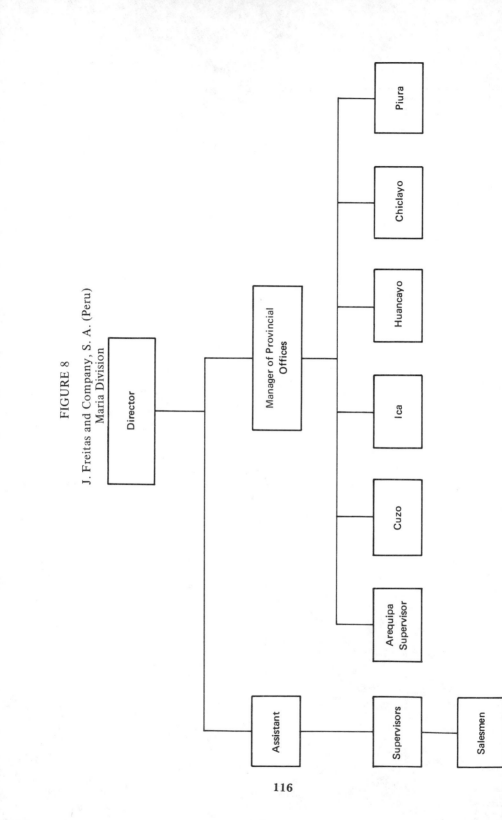

FIGURE 8

J. Freitas and Company, S. A. (Peru)
Maria Division

FIGURE 9

International Foods, Inc.—Philippines

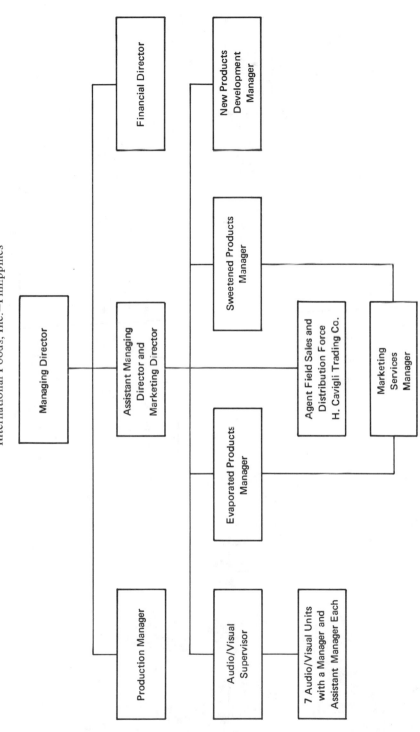

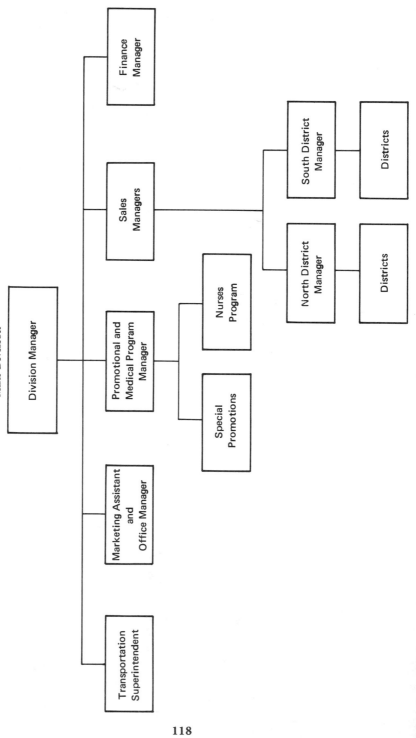

FIGURE 10

H. Cavigli Trading Company—Philippines
Milk Division

CELANESE FIBERS INTERNATIONAL COMPANY, U. S. A.

Development and Training of Foreign Top Management Personnel-Career Path Planning

New York-based Celanese Fibers International Company (CFIC), a division of Celanese Corporation, U. S. A., is responsible for the international fibers interests of Celanese Corporation. An extract of CFIC's organization chart is shown in Figure 1.

The phenomenal overseas growth in the past twenty years has brought CFIC some problems, notably in hiring, training, and developing local people for top overseas managerial positions. This critically important factor, according to a CFIC official, may eventually influence the rate of growth and expansion abroad because of four policy considerations:

1. CFIC's emphasis on joint ventures abroad wherever possible.
2. An absolute minimum of centralized decision-making at New York headquarters, and the fostering of local operational decisions abroad.
3. Staffing of top-level overseas management positions with local personnel to the maximum extent feasible.
4. Movement of top management people between various overseas companies to afford better opportunities for advancement of non-U. S. personnel commensurate with their ability and experience.

To assure success in overseas operations, CFIC headquarters assumes responsibility for the planning and conduct of training and development of non-U. S. personnel slated for top-level management positions. The CFIC personnel department in New York, in conjunction with both New York and overseas home office management, carefully plans and follows the development of every potential manager.

CFIC has had success in retaining and promoting personnel for the overseas companies. Its policies and procedures, evolved over the years, have been tempered by Celanese management philosophy, by problems encountered in a variety of sociopolitical environments, and by motives and rewards sought by people brought up in different cultural frameworks.

The purpose of this case is to study CFIC's policies and procedures in guiding overseas personnel development, and, more important, how they were evolved. To do this effectively the case study follows the career path of one employee, Dr. Jaime Lizarralde, president and chief operating officer of the Colombian company, Celanese Colombiana, S. A. To provide the reader with a clear picture of

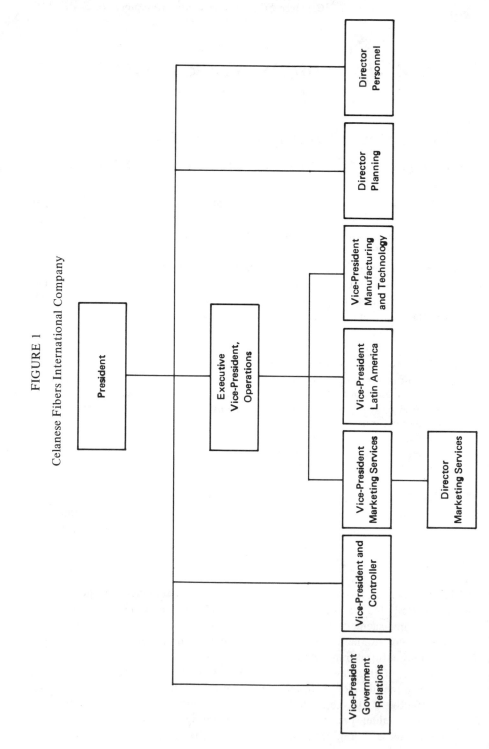

FIGURE 1
Celanese Fibers International Company

President

Executive Vice-President, Operations

Vice-President Government Relations

Vice-President and Controller

Vice-President Marketing Services

Vice-President Latin America

Vice-President Manufacturing and Technology

Director Planning

Director Personnel

Director Marketing Services

the course of events, a question-answer format is used. In the first part of the case, the case writer interviews officials at CFIC's headquarters in New York. A discussion of CFIC's general personnel policies also follows. In the next section, Dr. Lizarralde is interviewed and his observations concerning his career development are recorded.

I. CELANESE FIBERS INTERNATIONAL CO., NEW YORK

Q. When and how did the operations of the Colombian company begin?

A. In 1949 a group of Colombian investors, who owned one of the largest textile mills in Bogota, invited Celanese Corporation to join with them in the manufacture of synthetic fibers. In 1950 this venture was established to manufacture acetate filament. The joint venture was named Celanese Colombiana, S. A.

Q. What were CFIC's responsibilities in the area of executive recruitment, training, and development?

A. Pursuant to agreement, CFIC was to take full responsibility in staffing the plant and administration with supervisory personnel. Local investors were to assist in locating and selecting local applicants. We selected a total of eleven candidates (seven Colombians and four foreigners) for training in the U. S., all with college degrees in textile, chemistry, mechanical, or chemical engineering. Four of the Colombians were educated in the United States.

Q. Where and how were these candidates trained?

A. The candidates brought to the States were trained for six to eight months in all the operational aspects of fibers manufacturing at Celanese Corporation's Narrows, Virginia plant, in the Charlotte, North Carolina Technical Development Laboratories, and in the Cumberland, Maryland; Rome, Georgia; and Rock Hill, South Carolina plants.

Q. What did these people do on their return to Colombia?

A. Immediately on their return, they were put in charge of various departments. They really had a formidable job to do. Not only were they going to set up machinery and equipment but, more important, they had to train unskilled workers and semiskilled shop foremen in the operation and maintenance of equipment.

Q. How did these people move upward in their training?

A. All of these people were expected to train their immediate subordinates in the jobs they were doing. Once a replacement was suitably trained, his instructor would move up to a higher job within the same or another functional area.

Q. What positions do these people hold now?

A. Except for Dr. Jaime Lizarralde, who is now the president of Celanese Colombiana, all others have since left the company.

Q. It seems that Dr. Lizarralde knew from the start that he was slated for bigger and better things—like being pre-ordained. How do you account for this? Does it mean that the other ten persons left the company because even at the early stages of their career they realized that only Lizarralde was going to make it? Or was it that because of slower promotional opportunities, the more ambitious of the trainees left the company?

A. We hired eleven people whom we felt could, with training, effect a smooth plant start-up. They succeeded in this effort. I do not think that those who left were either more or less ambitious. It just happened that way.

Q. I think a survival ratio of one to eleven needs some thinking and explanation. This may mean that the initial screening and selection were poor, or that this is normal for these kinds of jobs in a developing nation, or that the company is not competitive in providing benefits and working environment.

A. You must remember that these eleven men were our first employees. The individuals were selected because they had the talents to learn our technology and to supervise the manufacturing processes of the plant. At that time our first goals were production and sales, not necessarily individual promotability. Today we would stress individual growth more in the selection procedure. I should add, however, that I believe our salaries and fringe benefits have consistently been quite competitive.

Q. What stages of progression did Lizarralde go through before arriving at his present position?

A. After his U.S. training, Lizarralde started almost on the floor, as a section supervisor. Specifically, his moves were as follows:

1. August to October 1951, Celanese Columbiana, Yumbo plant, helped in the installation of equipment, trained personnel, and started production of acetate yarn.
2. November 1951 to April 1953, Production Departments as Head, Extrusion Section; Superintendent Preparation, Extrusion, and Recovery.
3. May 1953 to July 1955, reported to the Plant Manager as Head of Special Projects Department.
4. August 1955 to July 1957, transferred from Yumbo Plant to Celanese Colombiana main offices, then located in Cali. Under the Company General Manager, worked in market research and new product development covering textile yarn, chemicals, and plastics in Colombia. Also acted as yarn salesman for Celanese Colombiana, in which capacity he visited Ecuador and Peru several times.
5. August 1957 to March 1959, Product Manager, Chemicals and Plastics. Duties covered sales, technical services, and product development for Celanese Colombiana and Celanese Corporation of America products. Also helped the Textile Product Manager in yarn sales.
6. April 1959 to October 1959, Assistant to General Manager.
7. November 1959 to May 1960, Manager, Company Production Planning Department.
8. June 1960 to December 1964, Plant Manager, Yumbo (Cali), Celanese Colombiana, S. A.
9. January 1965 to February 1966, General Manager, Rayon and Celanese Peruana, S. A., Lima, Peru.
10. March 1966 to October 1969, Executive Vice-President and General Manager, Celanese Colombiana, S. A.
11. October 1969, President, Celanese Colombiana, S. A.

Q. At what point was the question of fate discarded and actual planning for Lizarralde's individual development decided upon? How was the decision arrived at?

A. I would say that actual planning for Lizarralde started with the management's recognition of his potential for top managerial positions. By the time he became Head of the Special Projects Department, his potential was visible both in Colombia and New York. The process of determination always takes place through a partnership between the local and U.S. management. This was an individual who appeared to have potential for greater responsibility. By whatever means opinion is derived of what is required to rise up and take on higher levels of responsibility, management felt that he had it. It is usually a partnership decision—no one individual ordinarily makes such a decision.

Q. I should like to discuss Lizarralde's assignment in Lima.

A. In January 1965, he was transferred to Peru as the General Manager of the Celanese affiliate there. He stayed for fourteen months before his return to Colombia.

Q. This raises some interesting questions. As I understand, your policy is to encourage promotion of local people for managerial positions in their respective countries, yet in this case a Colombian went to Peru. What other alternatives were considered in filling this position before the selection of Lizarralde?

A. Celanese entered Peru by acquiring equity participation in a company owned by Peruvians and established more than fifteen years ago. An expansion into polyester fibers similar to the one just finished in Cali was immediately started. Our prime concern at that time was to provide the Peruvian affiliate with (a) the technical expertise they needed in manufacturing, (b) Celanese philosophy re new product development and marketing, and (c) a communication bridge between the Peruvian operation and CFIC.

Briefly then:

1. In Peru, it was essential that whoever was to go there had to be totally fluent in Spanish. Jaime filled that bill.
2. It was very important also that Jaime was familiar with Celanese procedure.
3. A substantial amount of the problems there had to do with imparting our manufacturing technology to this younger affiliate, and Jaime was well qualified to do this.
4. It was not our desire to send in a U.S. expatriate who would have had the skills of manufacturing, marketing, or language, but who probably would not have the same element of acceptability to the Peruvian environment.

Q. Since you mentioned that one of the needed qualifications was fluency in Spanish, does it mean that in terms of moving personnel, language would determine the regions within which people move from one place to another?

A. No, not always, but Peru was a special case because the president and main minority stockholder did not speak any English at all.

Q. Did Dr. Lizarralde have any reservations about going to Peru from a family or career viewpoint?

A. No. He looked upon it as personally inconvenient but as a very important and interesting career challenge and step. I think he probably suffered in some respects both financially or in some other ways, but it was a career step, and he recognized it as such. He hoped to some degree it would ultimately pay off, as it did.

Q. Under what circumstances did Dr. Lizarralde return to Colombia?

A. In May 1966, he returned to Bogota as executive vice-president and general manager of Celanese Colombiana, the number two spot in the organization. The president of the company at that time was also a Colombian citizen.

Q. How about other vice-presidents in Celanese Colombiana? Were they also considered for the job?

A. There were three vice-presidents, including Lizarralde, who reported to the president. However, it was felt that Dr. Lizarralde was the best candidate at that time.

Q. Is this a post facto rationalization or can you offer us some explanation?

A. Age was a consideration. One of the three was nearing retirement. The other had been promoted to vice-president only recently and was not yet ready for further promotion locally. Further, he was under consideration for a position in the U.S.A.

Q. These considerations raise some questions regarding CFIC's views concerning top management. Some companies fill top jobs from within. Some companies prefer a man from outside who has had different kinds of top-level management experience. You know, for the top job I'd rather not take a man from the automobile industry; I'd take somebody from electronics, or just machinery development because the nature of the competition is changing, or the industry structure is changing, or we just don't want that much inbreeding in the top echelons of the organization. That sort of reasoning does go into one's calculations, and this is what I was trying to get into in addition to Celanese Colombiana's Lizarralde being in the organization. You could say—with good justification—that Lizarralde doesn't have that much breadth of experience. Would that be a relevant consideration?

A. We are not a strictly promote-from-within organization and never have been. As long as we keep expanding, I hope we never will be. Nor do we prefer to go outside unless we feel honestly we haven't got the skills within. It should be stressed, however, that ours is a very specialized business requiring a depth of knowledge in our processes and technology. Jaime had this plus a lot of other advantages, including significant multifunctional exposure coupled with international experience. And you add it all up and you say O.K. we'll nominate him. You make an educated impartial type of judgment.

Q. How does Lizarralde's compensation—both direct and indirect—compare with similarly placed Colombians in other companies?

A. It's neither higher nor lower. It's in the upper end of the range.

Q. Let's shift the questioning a little bit now. Could we go into the overall personnel policies of CFIC in regard to executive development?

A. Development of employees is an assigned responsibility of management of any affiliate. However, we—Celanese, U.S.—come into the act when they have identified certain outstanding individuals with potential. When the affiliate identifies these people, we, together with top levels of affiliate management, begin to monitor and influence their progress. It's our aim to maximize their development and, not unimportantly, to help staff all affiliates by making individuals of high potential who have an interest in cross-national moves available either for U.S. jobs or other affiliate jobs as part of their own career paths.

Q. What are the criteria you use for identifying people with potential?

A. We do not rely on quantitative measures. I wouldn't know whether it is even possible for us at this juncture or in the near future to define "outstanding" or "above average" in absolute terms. The definitions are used and understood within a common frame of reference which has been developed over a number of years through written communications and face-to-face conversations between various affiliates and the home office staff. Within this frame of reference, an outstanding person, regardless of where he is now, must have the potential to rise to at least a second level of a major affiliate operation. This is the level reporting to the top man. He must have the facility to become the director or vice-president of marketing, manufacturing, finance, or other major function.

Q. Are you using any qualitative scales for measuring various personnel attributes which may give an indication of an employee's potential?

A. I suppose one can come up with a lot of factors, e.g., leadership, good; judgment, good; initiative, excellent; and so on. The point is that the appraisal forms through the years have been full of these trait-oriented buzz words. And the appraisal forms down through the years just as often have been useless.

We have given psychological tests. It is not inevitably a step that somebody must hurdle. We have utilized them; we still utilize them sometimes with some individuals. Some we do not. But again, it's a global view of a man. We try to use all the useful tools available to look at the entire individual. There are no factors that we single out in this.

What I'm trying to get at is this, and it seems to be working now. Two groups must intimately know the person, and the need. The president of CFIC and his senior staff know the needs of the overall organization and the manpower in different areas. Senior management in each country knows the individual intimately. They communicate and come to terms with a common, agreed-upon measure for evaluation. From there on, monitoring begins at the two levels.

Q. But, as you said, the judgment is there, and if that is purely judgmental without any underlying criteria that means that if one of these two groups is significantly changed, the probability that the judgment would change also remains very high. How do you provide for consistency?

A. We've got a couple of things here. First of all, let's separate performance from potential when you look at a man. We evaluate performance as performance against mutually agreed-upon objectives. O.K. There is nothing very new about this. Performance is the easiest of the two to measure, I think.

Potential is tough, and we don't intend to pretend it isn't. We would utilize and have, I think, utilized almost every mechanism for helping us evaluate potential, including psychological examinations and interview, the combination of which is even better from a knowledgeable, hopefully third-party consultant who is well-skilled and well-versed in all of the techniques of the field. We utilize this information and it adds a little bit of a third-party aspect—the objectivity aspect. But we have never been able to separate an organizational format—a structure of an organization—from the style, the skills, the personality of the individuals in it. I don't think we will ever be able to fully separate a high-potential man from some of the subjective interpersonal evaluations made by the company's senior managers. That's why they are senior managers, to make those judgments. All these run the peril and the pitfall; the guy who is the "crowned" hero now might conceivably be the "clown" hero tomorrow. But we attempt to separate it scientifically. We recognize that somewhere in the process somebody makes a subjective judgment. That is, with all the facts in maybe he's filled 60 percent of the pie with good solid information, and there's 40 percent more that says well, "I'll pick Charlie." Let's use him.

Q. All right, one more question. What do you do to protect both the company and the individual involved from the possibility that there might be an actual bias in this system against him from the senior management because he's just too ambitious, too smart, and the senior management—assuming the senior management is one person—is afraid that he might lose his own job, or position, or prestige because this guy would show him up?

A. This question might apply anywhere—in any company. It is rare, however, that the situation would long be tolerated. Our approach is as follows. At no time is an evaluation of an individual merely one judgment. A proposal to put anyone into a senior management position in an overseas company—that would be two levels below a general manager—is reviewed by the CFIC Management Committee. This means that the man (the boss) who has perhaps individually selected this guy has to check against his either selecting in his image or selecting someone who isn't a threat. High-level selections are reviewed with the appropriate U.S. officer on a functional basis. Thus, when a selection is made locally in second and third levels, it is checked with CFIC for the opinion that the New York staff might have regarding the man. All CFIC staff travel very frequently and one of their aims is close contact with those men in second and third levels. Anytime we consider the position of general manager of an overseas company, this proposal is reviewed with the top management committee of Celanese Corporation. So in all cases you have at least two and usually three layers of review to go through. This procedure minimizes the effect of individual selection. It does not specifically state that all three of these levels couldn't be wrong. We could still select an individual who turns out to be a no go, perhaps.

Q. Do they use any independent information or are their reviews based solely on the information furnished by the local companies?

A. The information is gathered through visits by the CFIC people to the field. Should there not be sufficient first-hand knowledge, it is very usual for the man to come to New York for talks. This happens quite frequently. The way we operate is such that by the time someone is being considered for this level, normally he would already be pretty well-known. Communications are this good because of continuing visitations.

Q. How does the number relate to the actual cross-national transfers?

A. In 1969 we had only two such transfers. In 1970 the number is expected to double and is likely to increase even more rapidly in the coming years.

Q. In view of this increasing emphasis, is there additional structuring in your system?

A. Yes. Early in 1970 the procedures for international career path planning were finalized and initiated for use by the overseas companies (Exhibit 1 and Figures 2-6).

EXHIBIT 1

Inter-office Memo of the
Celanese Fibers International Company

To: All International Subsidiaries   July 7, 1970

From:

*Status and Follow-up of
Stewardship Program
Career Pathing*

All of our international subsidiaries and participating affiliates have now completed their 1969 Stewardship Report and have provided us copies. While the principal value of the Stewardship procedure is to provide a basis for your developmental and personnel planning programs, I thought you would be interested in knowing how these reports are utilized here.

Prior to being finally approved, each Stewardship Report is reviewed in its entirety by the president of CFIC. This review normally takes place in the presence of your general manager. The sections of each report dealing with specific functions are also reviewed by the appropriate CFIC functional executive. If there is a disagreement on evaluations, the functional executive here will communicate with his counterpart in your company. Finally, a consolidated Stewardship Report is prepared by our department which the president of CFIC utilizes in making a summary presentation to the Celanese Corporation Management Committee. Consolidated functional summaries are part of this report and I have attached a portion of them, in the form of curves, for your inspection. These curves show total reported performance and potential data for each of the functions, and I think you will be able to make some interesting comparisons and draw some initial conclusions from them.

EXHIBIT 1—*continued*

Stewardship does not stop at the time the report is made. Staff meetings are held in CFIC on a periodic basis, and the status of all the outstanding potential people worldwide and significant personnel problem areas are discussed. These meetings consider whether the career path of a high potential individual may be accelerated by cross-national or cross-functional assignment. The appropriate CFIC functional executive will then review proposed assignments with his counterpart in your organization prior to the final career pathing decision on an individual. I will keep you fully advised of any conversations of this nature. Our *objective* is to make sure maximum development opportunity is given to employees, regardless of location, should their capabilities and interest warrant it.

With this objective in mind, would you please furnish us with copies of your career path plans for high potential persons (those with ratings of 1 or 2). Enclosed are Individual Career Path forms and an example for your use. If you already have a career path format let us know.

As you begin to plan career paths for high potential persons, keep the following points in mind:

1. Does this person need to accelerate development by temporary assignment outside your company?
2. Does he need exposure to another function, either within or outside your company?
3. What types of assignment seem appropriate?
4. How long should these assignments last?
5. What is the final goal of the assignments?

In identifying the career path for an individual, be sure to indicate, at the bottom of the form, the development steps necessary to enable the individual to reach his goal. The reverse side of his Potentiality Forecast Sheet and comments made during performance appraisals should provide the basis for determining these development steps.

If you have any questions, please contact me. Meanwhile, I will keep you informed of any discussions that are held with your management.

II. DR. JAIME LIZARRALDE, BOGOTA, COLOMBIA

Q. Why don't you start by giving me some of your own background: Where you were born, what you did, where you went to school, how did you happen to join Colombiana, and so on. A brief biographical sketch; then I will ask you questions in three or four areas later on.

A. I was born in Cali, Colombia in May of 1927. All my primary and secondary schooling was in Cali with the Jesuit Fathers, who were not only good references, but I was given the benefit of a good school. I went to the U.S. in the summer of 1946 to attend the University of Florida, in Gainesville. I received my degree in Chemical Engineering in June 1950 and in August of the same year returned to Colombia. For four months, I worked as a junior research engineer with Laboratorio Quimco Nacional, Bogota (a government-owned organization) engaged in the survey, research, and study of Colombian mineral ores. I learned about Celanese manufacturing investment in Colombia and the

FIGURE 2

Celanese Colombiana Individual Career Path

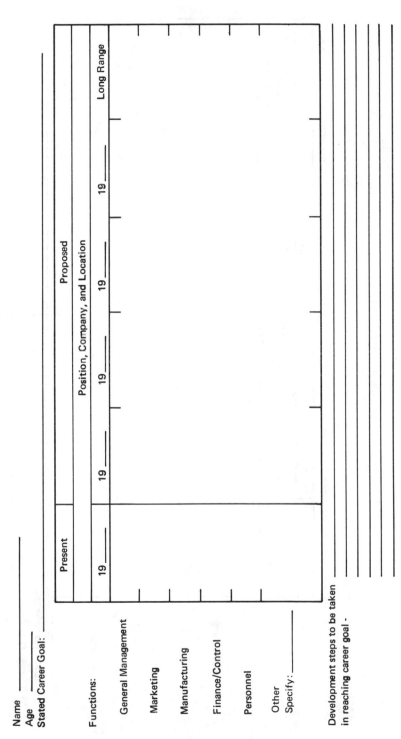

FIGURE 3

Individual Career Path

Name _____

Age _____

Stated Career Goal: _____

Function: Marketing

Direct Sales

End Use Marketing

Customer Service

Product Planning

Marketing Technical

Market Research

Other
Specify: _____

Present	Proposed				
	Position, Company, and Location				
19 ___	19 ___	19 ___	19 ___	19 ___	Long Range

Development steps to be taken
in reaching career goal -

_____
_____
_____
_____
_____

FIGURE 4

Individual Career Path

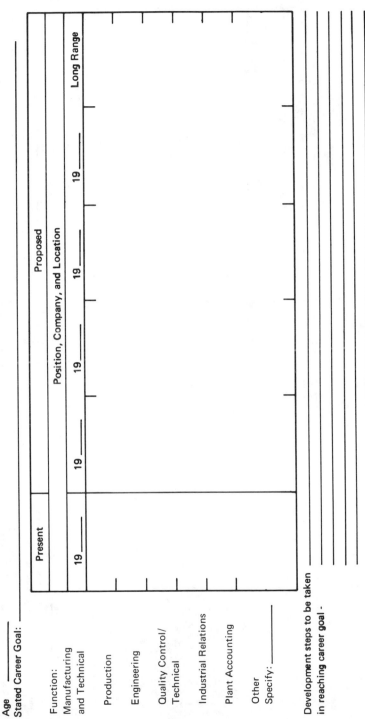

FIGURE 5

Individual Career Path

Name _____

Age _____

Stated Career Goal: _____

Present	Proposed				
	Position, Company, and Location				
19___	19___	19___	19___	19___	Long Range

Function: Financial Accounting, Planning, and Controls

Accounting and Consolidations

Financial Analysis

Controls, Systems, and Audits

Credit

Planning

Administration

Other Specify: _____

Development steps to be taken in reaching career goal - _____

132

FIGURE 6

Individual Career Path

Name _____

Age _____

Stated Career Goal: _____

	Present	Proposed			
Function: Personnel and Industrial Relations	19___	19___	19___	19___	Long Range
Position, Company, and Location					
Organization and Manager Development					
Recruitment					
Personnel Administration					
Labor Relations					
Compensation					
Other Specify: ___					

Development steps to be taken in reaching career goal -

_____
_____
_____
_____
_____

133

desire of their subsidiary to hire people in a very well-known Colombian newspaper. So I answered the ad, and was called for an interview in Cali. I was interviewed and offered a job with Celanese Colombiana to return to the U.S. for training and then to go back to Colombiana and start working for them.

Q. How many people did they interview?

A. I don't know, but I assume many people; they picked out eleven, including myself, to be trained and come back to work for them in Colombia.

Q. Why do you think they selected you?

A. I don't know why, but let me tell you what I could believe are two reasons why they selected me. The first was, I was the only one in that group that had just finished college; I was the youngest one in the whole group. All the others had had some years of experience. And I was from Cali, where they were planning to set up a plant. Maybe the management thought my being from Cali would make me more stable. So actually, I assume that they thought "Well, this young fellow is from Cali, he lives in Cali, is single; so he's a more stable person." And second, there was a little remark that I made to the manager that he liked. He told me, "Mr. Lizarralde, I'm taking a chance with you. You're the last one that I'm offering a job to; you are the eleventh one and you are the youngest, you have had no experience. So I'm taking a chance with you." So I said: "You're taking a chance with me? I'm taking a chance with Celanese too because I don't know your company. So we're even in this game." He laughed at me and said "O.K. you little rascal, you have a job." I told him frankly, straightforward: "It's fifty-fifty."

Q. What kind of background did the other ten people have?

A. Technical, including textile, mechanical, and chemical engineering.

Q. All had U.S. degrees or Colombian degrees?

A. They were looking mostly to people with U.S. degrees, because they wanted to have U.S. training plus the language. I think they were looking for those two things. I remember, as a matter of fact, I still have at home a copy of the ad; I kept it as a souvenir. And they said that they preferred people with a knowledge of English.

Q. When you joined them, did you have an idea that you would be with them all these years?

A. No, I didn't, not by any means. I was looking for a company that would give me a chance to go ahead, to progress, and to move up. I liked the people interviewing, and when I was in college in the U.S., I had learned about Celanese Corporation being a very great company in the textile field, synthetic fibers.

Q. Did they send you back directly for training?

A. Yes, the other ten people and I were sent to the U.S. for training from January through August of 1950—eight months. The training was very interesting because it was both theoretical and practical. Theoretical in the sense that we had lectures by the people of Celanese and people from the outside, on safety, quality control, human relations, industrial relations, and all the other things in the industry. Plus a practical training on the specific things that we were supposed to do after coming back to Colombia. And we did receive a rather practical training in the sense that we did all the work with our hands. We were trained as regular workers. Because we were using processes which had never been known to Colombia, we had to be workers ourselves in order to teach the workers. So for me, the exposure to a theoretical and practical training was excellent. I would say it was like taking a master's degree.

Q. After you all came back, what happened to the rest?

A. Through the years they all left the company for many reasons.

Q. All of them?

A. Yes, all of them. I'm the only one left from that group.

Q. Can you give me some idea of the reasons for which they left the company?

A. I don't exactly recall, but one textile engineer went into his own business in Bogota. Another, a Swiss chemical engineer, left Celanese Colombiana and was hired by Nestlé. Maybe he wanted to leave Colombia. And another Colombian didn't like Celanese Colombiana; he was disappointed and looked for another job. This is what I can remember right now.

Q. Doesn't it seem strange to you, that out of the eleven people they hired, you are the only one that stayed with the company?

A. You're right about that. Sometimes I wonder why they didn't stay with the company, because they went through very good training, had very good treatment, and they didn't last too many years with the company. I think it is significant, however, that the others were all senior to me in age.

Q. Was there something wrong with the selection process? You figure that with eleven people, the normal turnover rate is three or four people, no matter how good a selection process. When you have over 90 percent of the people you hire at the executive level leaving you, you wonder whether it was the selection process which was wrong or was it training. Maybe they didn't get the kind of future they wanted. There must be some rationalization.

A. I agree with you, but remember, we were not hired at executive levels. We were hired to start a plant. I was so involved with my job trying to do well and to do it for myself that the reasons for their departure were actually not my business. I believe the selection process put a premium on technical ability before promotability.

Q. Maybe they were ambitious people, and that's why they left. By the same token, does it imply that the people who remain are not ambitious?

A. I doubt it. Some of them had personal reasons; one man going back to his country and another going into his own business. That's understandable. Remember, these were professional engineers who were given training that made them very desirable to other companies.

Q. You mean they selected more ambitious people than they should have?

A. No, I don't think ambition was the key factor.

Q. Let me rephrase the same question. You stayed with Celanese Colombiana for eight months in the States and all of you must have been quite close to each other. How would you describe the difference between them and you in temperament or attitudes? I know it's twenty years ago.

A. I'm trying to remember. Some of them were men with five, six years of experience—it's hard, because a lot of the time I was working, training, so, frankly, I stopped thinking about their personalities too much. And I was a fairly independent fellow. As a matter of fact, I didn't live in the same house the whole group lived in. I went to another place nearby. I was not close enough to them. We were very friendly, and all that, but after that, I was on my own. I knew English, I could get around here pretty well, I was dedicated to my own life and the company.

Q. What is the executive turnover you have now?

A. It's very little. I wish I could help you more with the group. I think it was a heterogeneous group, because there were all ages there, I think from twenty-three to forty.

Q. Let's get back to your own experience. What did you do after you returned to Colombia?

A. We were assigned to different sections of the plant. I was head of the spinning department. There were about sixty workers and ten supervisors. The first work was to train the people to do the operations we had learned. It was the first worker group that I had in my life. It was rough. I was twenty-three. I remember losing six kilos of weight. It was the first job I had, but I think I did well. I was given another department called "Preparation." Later on I had three departments. They gave me more responsibility. After that I was made Plant Night Chief Superintendent. The time span was two years. Later, the plant manager brought me out from production and set up a new department for the whole plant called Industrial Engineering. But it was more than industrial engineering, it was one of those jobs for which you have special assignments for the plant manager. It was a great experience. Then I started to get assignments not only in production, but also in administration and accounting. So that gave me about four-and-a-half years in the plant. One day they asked me to move to the Cali office in marketing. So I started my marketing career. It was called the Sales Department then, because the total marketing concept didn't come in until the sixties. I started off in Market Research. I didn't know anything about this, so I bought books. I did a lot of self-learning because I was a production-minded man. I also received training in the U.S. and Columbia from the experienced Celanese Corporation marketing staff. I stayed there from 1955 to the end of 1959. One day I was asked to move from there to be an Assistant to the General Manager in Bogota. They say I had production and marketing training and gave me an opportunity to make use of them.

Q. Did you know it was coming?

A. No, they asked me to do it. On December 11, 1958, they had bought another fiber producer in the country. By 1959 it was decided to consolidate this operation with Celanese Colombiana. Indurayon was twice as big as Celanese Colombiana and many of its managers took high positions in the combined company. Both companies were merged in July 1959. In May of 1960, they told me I was going to become the Cali plant manager because the American there was going to be moved to a plant in the U.S. I was the first Colombian to have that job. I was plant manager from 1960 to 1964. To me it was the formative time of my career. First, the plant was away from the main office. Decisions had to be taken in the field. It was a plant of about 500 people, and we had all sorts of problems with labor and production. I was very happy back in my home town, my wife too. It was the best time of my life. It was hard work being plant manager for a plant that works twenty-four hours. One day they asked me if I would work in Peru. I said if my future is there, I can think about it. So a few months later I went to Lima as the General Manager of Celanese Corporation's Peruvian affiliate.

Q. Was it financially more rewarding?

A. It wasn't too much. The salary was good but after I arrived in Lima, it wasn't as good as I had believed, because the cost of living in Lima was very high. I had enough to live very well, but the working conditions and people were so different that it was quite an experience. It opened a completely new life for me.

Q. Why don't you tell me more about the differences between working in Colombia and Peru.

A. I found Peruvians to have a somewhat different business style. Mostly the top people were aggressive. However, the workers' concept of efficiency was very different. All together, it made me realize how different seemingly similar countries can be. My wife and I were lucky; we made good, new friends. The differences were in my work because Celanese technology in the sense of machinery, systems, quality, manufacturing procedures, and the systems of marketing was different. It was a challenge for me because the field was wide open for me to do things.

Q. American companies have tried to transfer personnel among Latin American countries rather than to send someone from the U.S. Do you think a management pool is advantageous so transfers can be made within only certain language areas, or doesn't it matter?

A. Having the language of a country is very good because you understand and communicate more rapidly. There is a lot of difference in translating, so the language plus your background will help solve a situation faster and easier.

Q. How long did you stay in Peru?

A. Thirteen months. After the polyester yarn plant was installed, CFIC, after consulting the Peruvian management, told me there was an opening in Colombia. I almost dropped to the floor. When I went to Peru I thought I'd be there at least a few years.

Q. Did you like returning to Colombia?

A. Yes, to me it was a step forward in my career in a company I had been in for many years. Second, it was my country. Third, it was a distinguished position in that company. So in two weeks I was moved back to Bogota as executive vice-president and general manager of Celanese Colombiana.

Q. How is your company organized?

A. We have a president, a general manager, and then six managers responsible for various functional areas (Figure 7).

FIGURE 7

Celanese Colombiana, S. A. Organization General

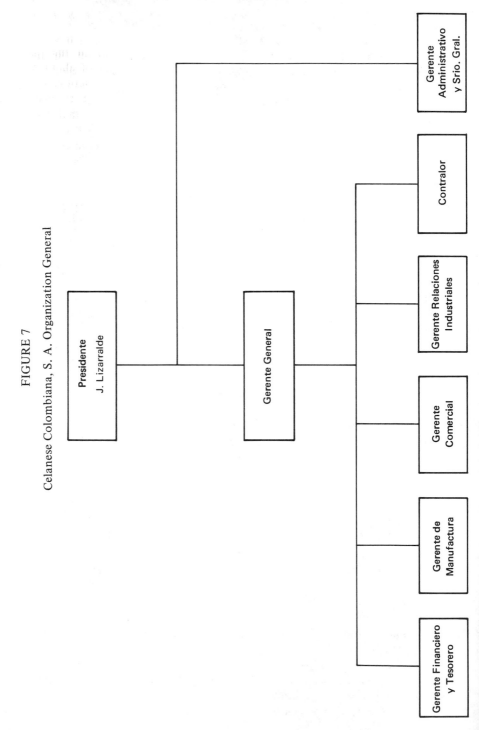

Q. So you were placed over all of these people when you returned to Colombia from Peru as the general manager?

A. Yes. The Board of Celanese Colombiana appointed the CFIC vice-president for Latin America, who was also vice-chairman of the Colombiana Board, as the president of Celanese Colombiana. He served as president till October 1969 when the board elected me the president of the company.

Q. Did you know the presidency would follow in a few months or a year or two after they made you general manager?

A. I'm an ambitious type of fellow; I was going to work to get to the top, but I didn't know when I would get there. I never worried about time. When you try to press time, it fails.

Q. Would you have been disappointed if they had appointed somebody outside, a Colombian, but a non-Celanese Colombiana man as the president?

A. In a sense, yes, but I would have accepted the decision.

Q. You were one of a group of extremely qualified and well-experienced Colombians in Colombia. Did you get offers from any other companies?

A. I had some offers earlier in my career with Colombiana.

Q. What was the nature of the staff reporting to you?

A. When I arrived in Colombia to be the general manager in 1966, the composition of the staff was changed for reasons which could not be anticipated. The manager of operations was moved to the U.S. as assistant director of Latin America and has since returned to become the general manager. There were vacancies in finance and control so I had a number of positions to fill.

Q. What kind of people were hired? What kind of background did they have? What procedure was used?

A. They were hired with the active concurrence of CFIC, a man for industrial relations, another for administration and secretary general, and we moved two men from the lower ranks to be the marketing and manufacturing managers.

Q. Did you have to get CFIC approval for hiring these people or did you do it on your own?

A. I have them help me in interviewing these people. I get a concurrence from them. In some cases, I have them talk with the prospective candidates and give me an opinion, because we believe it is prudent to have more than one interviewer.

Q. Would you send them to New York to be interviewed?

A. A couple of times I did that. When you hire top people, you cannot play with them. It's a very important decision. . . . You have to have the maximum assurance that you have the right man. The higher you go the more careful you have to be in the selection of people.

Q. What are your own future plans? If this company is truly international, it should not discriminate among people regardless of citizenship. Would you consider going to New York and becoming one of the U.S. company's vice-presidents, or would you rather stay in Colombia?

A. I sincerely hope to continue working for Celanese Colombiana many more years, to take an actual part in its challenging growth and development. To be a vice president in New York is quite a nice suggestion.

Q. Do you know any other American companies in Colombia where you think cross-movement between Americans and foreigners is greater than in Celanese?

A. As far as other U.S.-owned companies are concerned, and there are quite a few—for example, Coca-Cola, Goodyear, B. F. Goodrich, Chrysler, etc.—the only other company aside from Celanese Colombiana that has a Colombian president is Chrysler.

Q. What kind of budgetary authority do you have? What is the maximum amount of money you can spend on capital expenditures without further approvals?

A. I report to the Board of Directors and thus exercise the authority granted to me as president in the Celanese Colombiana by laws.

Q. What is the growth rate of Celanese Colombiana? In terms of annual sales?

A. Sales in 1970 will reach 440 MM Colombian pesos compared to 1960 when they were 78.

THE NATIONAL CASH REGISTER CO. (JAPAN),LTD.

Successful Adaptation to Local Conditions— Recruitment and Retention of Skilled Manpower and Managerial Talent

Comments like the following two abound in the offices of personnel directors of American and other foreign corporations trying to do business in the booming Japanese market:

> If he works for an American company, nine chances out of ten he isn't any good." This is the lament of a U.S. businessman in Japan who is trying to recruit employees for his plants there. His problem is that the best Japanese workers shun American owned companies, indeed many Japanese regard all foreign companies with suspicion.[1]
>
> Foreign enterprises planning to do business in Japan will find it most advantageous and profitable to tie up closely with Japanese partners. . . . Ever present is the difficulty of obtaining necessary personnel in a country where labor liquidity is poor.[2]

One company that has proved to be an exception is National Cash Register Co. (Japan), Ltd. (NCR), a 70 percent owned subsidiary of National Cash Register Company of Dayton, Ohio with the remaining 30 percent owned by Japanese stockholders. The company is listed on the Tokyo stock exchange. Through a judicious blend of American personnel policies which emphasize monetary

---

1. "NCR Makes Going Native Pay Off," *Business Week,* 14 December 1968, p. 114.
2. *See* case concerning Caterpillar Mitsubishi Limited, Japan.

incentives and promotion based on merit and Japanese personnel policies which cater to job security and loyalty to the company NCR Japan has been successful in hiring Japanese personnel from the top of the management pool and keeping them with the company in the face of competition from other American and Japanese companies.

NCR cash registers were first introduced to Japan in 1897 by Ushijima & Co., of Yokohama which was taken over by the American Trading Company in 1906. In 1933 the Nippon National Cash Register Co., Ltd. was established, following termination of the agency contract with the American Trading Company. In 1935 the Nippon National Cash Register Co., Ltd. amalgamated with the Nippon Cash Register Company under the name of the former. In 1942 the interests of the Nippon National Cash Register Co., Ltd. were bought by the Fujiyama Holding Company as a result of World War II. At the end of the war in 1945 the Nippon National Cash Register Co., Ltd. was reestablished. In 1957 a manufacturing plant was completed at Oiso, Kanagawa Prefecture. In 1962 the new head office building was completed at Tameike, Tokyo. In 1966 the NCR Institute of Technology was opened at Sagamihara, Kanagawa Prefecture. In 1970 an emulsion plant was completed at Oise, Kanagawa Prefecture.

As of January 1970, NCR Japan is capitalized at ¥ 6,000 million, has 5,554 employees and operates 5 data processing centers, 72 branches and 2 factories throughout the country. Its broad range of products includes cash registers, adding machines, electronic data processing equipment, microform systems and data time sales, and various supply items such as paper rolls and business forms.

NCR's *PHILOSOPHY OF INTERNATIONAL OPERATIONS*

Behind NCR's recruitment policies in Japan and other countries lie the basic principles of the parent company in regard to its overseas operations. These are:

1. A conviction that the citizens of those nations in which NCR operates can best manage the company's affairs in their respective countries.
2. A policy of entering a country only on a permanent basis. Despite wars, revolutions, and severe economic crises, NCR has never voluntarily withdrawn from any country.
3. A belief that a company which operates abroad has an obligation to consistently reinvest part of its profit in the countries where those profits are earned.
4. A recognition that success in overseas markets depends on giving those markets the kind of products they need and want; products which are not necessarily those designed for U.S. markets.
5. A respect for the dignity of all peoples and a recognition that different countries cherish different customs and different religions, with NCR operations conducted accordingly.
6. A procedure under which no product is ever marketed in any country until the necessary steps have been taken to ensure that the user of that product can depend on complete service and maintenance at all times.

RECRUITMENT IN JAPAN

NCR Japan is one of the biggest American employers in Japan and because of its continuing growth maintains a year-round recruiting effort. To assure itself of competent personnel NCR Japan departed from the Japanese practice of hiring from a limited number of elite schools and widened its search process to include a large number of other schools. As Mr. C. McDonald, Director of Personnel, NCR Japan explains:

> . . . To recruit competent employees, we give all qualified applicants an equal opportunity to sit for our employment examinations. Some Japanese firms give such opportunity to only students of those schools designated by them when recruiting employees upon graduation from schools. But there must be competent students in every school. We provide students from every section of Japan who are desirous of joining us with an equal opportunity to take our employment examination, and hire ambitious men and women willing to display their abilities and develop their careers. Our basic recruiting policy is to employ truly competent people without being swayed by their school education, lineage, and family.

Annually the company personnel visit 230 technical high schools, 98 colleges, and universities all over the country in order to acquaint their placement directors, professors, and office managers with NCR's employment plans and to hold employment briefing sessions for students.

This policy is combined by some other practices which are uniquely Japanese. For example, once a candidate is selected, a company representative visits the family of the applicant for a reference check. Personal friendships also play an important role in recruiting qualified applicants. It is not unlikely for the Assistant Personnel Manager, who is a Japanese, to request his Japanese friends on the faculties of various schools to make some time available to him in their seminar to explain the company and its policies. Such favors are usually reciprocated with small gifts or entertainment—which is acceptable in Japan.

The recruiting process is quite formalized and is separate for new employees from graduating classes of schools and for applicants with previous work experience. In the case of graduating classes, selection and hiring goes through the following stages:

> Placing want ads in campus papers and sending representatives to campuses
> Sending job offers to schools
> Receipt of application papers from applicants
> Notice of written examination
> WRITTEN EXAMINATION
> Notice of examination results to schools and applicants and notice of interview to successful applicants
> INTERVIEW
> Notice of interview results to schools and applicants and notice of medical examination to successful interviewees

MEDICAL EXAMINATION
Reference checks
Requesting applicants passing medical examination to submit NCR's pre-scribed papers and sending them notice of employment decision
Second medical examination in February
Notice of employment
Starting with the Company on April 1.

This process is usually completed for all applicants by July of the previous year.

The company does not use any psychological tests to evaluate job applicants. However, aptitude tests are given to applicants for certain job classifications. These are:

1. Aptitude test
   (a) technicians
   (b) system engineers
   (c) EDPS sales specialists
   (d) business machine operators
   (e) instructresses
2. Brain-wave (electroencephalographic) test
   (a) drivers

The result of this process is evidenced in the high ratio of new employees to applicants during the last few years (Table 1).

TABLE 1

Number of Job Applicants and New Hirings
(Skilled Employees Only)

Year	Number of Applicants (A)	Number of New Employees (B)	Ratio (B)/(A)	Ratio (A)/(B)
1967	5,034	635	12.6%	7.9 times
1968	5,297	748	14.1%	7.1 times
1969	5,264	837	15.9%	6.3 times
1970 (first 6 months)	2,990	616	20.6%	4.9 times

COMPENSATION AND PROMOTION

Another departure from the Japanese tradition has been in the areas of compensation and promotion. Unlike most Japanese firms where employees are promoted on the basis of seniority or education, NCR recognizes merit as one of the important elements for promotion. To avoid conflict with the senior people, the company promotes promising young men by transferring people across departmental lines. The company emphasizes not only careful recruitment but also on-going employee training. For example, NCR has established its Institute of Technology at Sagamihara for both new and senior employees who are trained continually to meet the needs of the times generated by new product development and management techniques. Management development seminars are also regular Institute features. From this emphasis on continuing education evolved the NCR motto: "There is no graduation in NCR."

The company has also resorted to the very un-Japanese practice of paying its salesmen commissions instead of straight salaries. The salesmen, whose incomes as a result are considerably higher than comparable jobs in other companies, have responded very well to the policy.

In Japan, NCR has departed from standard U.S. fringe-benefits packages and has adapted to Japanese practices. In addition to a comprehensive employee insurance program, the company gives, for example, bonuses to all its employees (except salesmen) twice a year. In recent years the annual bonus has averaged six months' salary.

NCR maintains five dormitories for bachelor employees who are fresh out of school and live out of commuting distance or who are transferred far from their homes. The dormitories can accommodate from ten to one-hundred and ten persons. At the same time, the company encourages its employees to buy their own homes by providing them with low interest loans.

In the area of recreational activities, NCR maintains more than fifty sports and social clubs, makes large contributions to these activities, providing sports facilities such as swimming pools, baseball and soccer grounds and tennis courts, and giving monetary assistance in the purchase of goods or in the payment of fees to instructors, and has four health resort houses around Tokyo which are open to employees through the year. In addition, summer houses are made available in summer and ski lodges in winter.

MEETING CULTURAL ENVIRONMENT

NCR Japan has always maintained close contacts with the community at large, including scholarships for study in the United States and sister-city ties between Oiso and Dayton. By enhancing the NCR Japan reputation, these activities also help solve labor-shortage problems. Significantly, about 60 percent of the employees at the Oiso factory were recruited locally.

Another case of adaptation to unique Japanese moves was described in *Business Week* on NCR Japan:

> Several years ago, a small branch office asked permission to hire an additional girl to run errands and serve the customary cup of tea to visitors.
>
> "We thought this was an absurd extravagance for a three-man office," Wilson says. "It was only gradually that we learned that serving tea meant a loss of face for the young male clerk in the office and this was hurting our reputation as an employer. Now, we hire young girls to pour tea at all branches as a matter of course."[3]

3. *Business Week*, 14 December 1968, p. 116.

RETRENCHMENT AND RETIREMENT

It is very difficult or almost impossible to discharge employees for reasons of economy during recession periods. According to a company spokesman:

> In NCR Japan, employees are never taken on except when there are definite manpower requirements. No NCR Japan employees have so far been discharged on grounds of a business recession. In our company, which is ever-growing and expanding, there can be no discharge for reasons of economy.

Though most Japanese enterprises fix their retirement age for male employees at fifty-five, NCR Japan employees retire at sixty; females at fifty-five. The company also tries to stabilize the postretirement livelihood of its employees by paying a retirement allowance either in the form of a pension or in a lump sum. Those who leave the company for personal reasons before the age limit receive a lump sum retirement allowance.

ROBERTS-ARUNDEL LTD., ENGLAND

Industrial Relations

The Roberts Company of Sanford, North Carolina, is a successful manufacturer of spinning machines for the textile industry. Recently, it has been pursuing a vigorous program of expansion in overseas markets which has resulted in plants in Belgium and Italy, and one in the works for Spain.

In early 1965 Ellis Bor, a major shareholder of a British manufacturing concern, Arundel Coulthard proposed to the management of Roberts Company that they buy Arundel. At that time Arundel was suffering from heavy losses, was facing liquidation and had not made any profit since 1961. In fact, Arundel's shares were selling for between 17 and 21 shillings per share, considerably below their book value of 39. Sensing a bargain, and recognizing a chance for profitable expansion in Great Britain, Roberts Company president Robert E. Pomeranz and his staff decided to accept Mr. Bor's proposition. Roberts Company's tender offer of 27/6 d per share resulted in their obtaining over 98 percent of the shares in Arundel.

ARUNDEL COULTHARD
BEFORE TAKEOVER

Arundel Coulthard, in operation since 1812, was characterized by obsolete plant facilities, antiquated practices, an outdated line of merchandise, and low worker morale. As of 1965, the company had five plants, two in Stockport and one each in Sanford, Preston, and Ashton-under-Lyne. Commenting on the plant conditions, Mr. Pomeranz was quoted as saying:

> The buildings were very old, mostly without heat, without decent light, and with accumulations of many years of junk and rubbish. Wages were very low, average 14 pounds weekly, and productivity also low. The 620 employees had produced an average turnover of much less than one million pounds for the past three years whereas the figure should have been at least three to four times as great in a modern growing enterprise.[1]

As a manufacturer of textile machinery, Arundel was rapidly losing ground at the time of Roberts Company takeover. After visiting the plants, a young foundry engineer employed by Roberts Company declared:

> I saw something in the Stockport foundry I had read about in foundry history from fifty years before, men taking off their shoes and stockings and stamping the sand in the moulds with their bare feet. We sent a man out into Manchester and bought two air hammers for about 50£ and showed the men that it would do better quality with much less time and less work. But they did not take to it and I doubt they will.[2]

Never a large firm, and described by some as "musty," Arundel used, principally, outmoded factory machinery for which parts were no longer available. More than sixty shop workers were engaged in fashioning spare parts to be used as replacements.

Frank Ridgway, Arundel's chief engineer and managing director at the time of takeover, had been with the company for over forty years. Roberts people described him as "a genius of conceptual and practical engineering designs." Mr. Ridgway, who retired when Roberts Company took over, left behind a wealth of valuable machine blueprints and records of his ideas and experience.

ACQUISITION AND AFTER

In keeping with Roberts Company's international policy, British national John E. Cox, an engineer and former officer of the British Navy, was appointed to the post of Managing Director. Ellis Bor, previously Arundel's major shareholder, was named Director and Company Secretary. As Arundel was unionized and Roberts Company was not, it was decided to leave the responsibility of labor relations with the local staff. Pomeranz and other executives of the Roberts Company, seeking not to appear paternalistic to labor, attempted to make important decisions from a distance.

Roberts Company, upon acquisition in July 1965, launched a vigorous program of plant modernization. The three smaller of the five plants were closed and the

1. *Financial Times* (London), 13 December 1967.
2. Ibid.

remaining two, at Preston and Stockport, were extensively modernized. All outmoded machines were scrapped. The managers were charged to modernize the work place so that every opportunity would be provided to encourage productive work in the future rather than the almost-wasted work efforts in the environment of the past.

Modernization was not confined to plant and equipment alone. Extensive efforts were made to improve the working conditions of the employees. A new heating system was installed; dirt and cobblestone floors were concreted; the plant was cleaned by removing years of rubble and junk; and toilets and washrooms were reequipped and painted. More important, wages were raised to levels commensurate with those in other plants in the area.

All this, however, did not improve the productivity or profitability of the operations of Roberts-Arundel. During 1965 and 1966 the United States textile industry was experiencing a boom and the U. S. plant of Roberts Company was operating at capacity. Consequently, it was decided to manufacture spinning frame components in Stockport, England, for shipment to Sanford, North Carolina. The production was scheduled at the rate of 12 in April 1966, 20 in May, and 32 sets monthly thereafter. However, the Stockport plant fell behind schedule and the first shipment arrived in the U. S. in November, which was too late to be helpful. Among the reasons for late delivery were inadequate planning, undependable suppliers, and low productivity. To gauge some measure of low worker productivity: in 1965, 62 men produced about 12 tons of castings a week, while in Sanford, U.S.A., in 1960 with a nonmechanized foundry, 65 men produced 60 tons a week.

The directors of the company made constant efforts to improve operations and rationalize production through consultations with staff and unions. However, the presence of five unions caused considerable delay in programming operations as each step was taken only after extensive efforts were made to seek cooperation from all concerned.

By January 1966, it was decided that the Stockport foundry should be closed as being inefficient. It was not until June 1966, and after due notice, that the Stockport jobs were declared redundant although some men were transferred to other positions.

Recognizing that it was economically inefficient to operate both the Preston and Stockport plants, as they were only fifty miles apart, Roberts Company shut down the Preston plant. Although the work force in Preston was more productive and would have learned quicker, the company decided to retain the Stockport plant[3] because the company had applied for an Industrial Development Certificate and land adjoining the Stockport plant was available.

The profit picture was equally discouraging. From July through November 1965, losses amounted to £68,000. In fiscal 1966, Stockport lost £208,000. Although losses in fiscal 1967 were somewhat lower than in 1966, they were still quite sizable. In the same period, the consolidated group profits, after accounting for Stockport losses, were £500,000 and £715,000 respectively.

3. Stockport plant and Stockport foundry are two separate entities.

INDUSTRIAL RELATIONS

Worker dissatisfaction proved to be the biggest problem of Roberts-Arundel. Mr. Pomeranz had been careful to select a British subject, Mr. John Cox, as plant manager to insure cooperation of the workers. Cox's training with the British navy did not seem to help him in either improving productivity or workers' morale. A typical example of how the company's labor policies backfired is the controversy over tea breaks. The men had been accustomed to lengthy afternoon tea breaks, a time-honored custom. When Mr. Cox replaced teakettles and mugs with a hot-drink machine, the workers became irate. Searching for a compromise, Mr. Cox returned the teakettles, but stipulated a ten-minute break limit. The workers continued taking their time in tea-brewing, at which point Mr. Cox demanded the cessation of the excess break time and had the teakettles and mugs smashed. The workers also took exception to the new soap dispensers installed in the renovated washrooms—they preferred the original plain cakes of soap.

Workers were also not taking kindly to the new machines or production methods introduced by Roberts-Arundel. As one example, the workers refused to use the two new air hammers, referred to earlier, and insisted on continuing to stamp the sand with their bare feet.

The brewing discontent came to a head when the company announced its intention to close the Preston plant which would render 158 men and women redundant. Some of the machines and operations from Preston were to be transferred to Stockport and the company was willing to transfer thirty men and ten to twenty women to Stockport, with women assigned to jobs previously done by women at Preston. Stockport already had women machine operators, hired for the first time since December 1965 after the takeover of Arundel Coulthard by the Roberts Company. These women received £28 per week, approximately one-half the pay that a man would receive for the same work.

The workers and their union were very angry at the company's actions which resulted in the laying off of men from Stockport on the one hand and employment of additional women at Preston on the other hand. Consequently, they began a series of work stoppages which amounted to an unofficial strike. Faced with this situation, the directors at Stockport recommended to the parent company in Sanford, U.S.A., that all strikers be discharged. The recommendation was approved by several senior directors including Mr. Pomeranz, the president of the parent company.

Back in England, the labor situation in the Roberts Company caught the fancy of Mr. Hugh Scanlon, a regional chief of Britain's largest union, the Amalgamated Engineers. Mr. Scanlon, seeking the highest office in the union, added fuel to the fire by incorporating the Arundel labor disputes in his platform. He was successful in his bid for office.[4]

---

4. The prestigious *Economist,* 16 December 1967, referred to this union as backward, communist, and antifeminist, among other adjectives. Robert Pomeranz stated that if he had known of the communist overtones of the area's trade unionism, he doubted he would have bought the plant.

Mr. Pomeranz was, during this period, closely associated with the proceedings, though he tried to maintain the position of the outsider:

Though I visited Stockport at least every three months and received weekly reports on operations I was not personally involved in the "unofficial strikes" which seemed to occur with regularity. I was quite aware of the inability of Stockport to meet its shipment promises and of our monthly losses. I felt that patience was needed. I had confidence in the Directors to bring it around and implicitly accepted and approved their actions.[5]

But Mr. Pomeranz's record with unions was one neither of experience nor empathy. The Roberts Company plants in the United States were nonunionized, and according to *Newsweek*, Mr. Pomeranz was proud of this fact. In such a position, it is highly possible that his relationship with the workers left something to be desired.

The Amalgamated Engineers Union was the first to go out on strike, and four other unions quickly followed suit. Even at its peak, the strike was never completely successful. The Roberts Company's immediate response to the strike was to fire the strikers and hire strike breakers on the basis that the unions had violated their contracts. Mr. Pomeranz claimed that the unions had not filed their grievances. A wave of violence erupted at the Stockport plant resulting in window breaking, injury to policemen hired to guard the factory, arrests, and other forms of physical violence. In spite of these conditions, many of the workers walked through the picket lines; but work stoppage was almost complete.

Mr. Pomeranz started attempting to negotiate a settlement with the union. Although a tentative compromise agreement was made between the Amalgamated Engineers Union and management in September 1967 in New York, it soon collapsed. In December, Mr. Pomeranz met with Mr. Ray Gunther, the national Minister of Labor, Mr. Scanlon, by then president of the Amalgamated Engineers Union, and Mr. Martin Jakes, Director General of the Engineering Employees Federation. Mr. Pomeranz states that he was looking for a possible compromise agreement. However, Mr. Scanlon was prepared only to offer an ultimatum, which demanded the reinstatement of the fired men, and a guarantee of one year's employment.

Mr. Pomeranz was not prepared to accept Scanlon's offer and consequently issued an order to close down the Stockport plant in mid-January 1968.

APPENDIX I

British Trade Union Conditions—1965

Conditions relative to the status of British trade unionism under which the Roberts Company made its unsuccessful bid for new operations were extreme. The union situation had been under constant attack by leaders in Britain, both Labor and Conservative. Complaints covered claims that the current form of

---

5. "Mr. Pomeranz States His Case," *Financial Times* (London), 13 December 1967.

union organization hampered economic growth and that the set-up was inefficient in its service to union membership. George Woodcock, Trades Union Congress General Secretary, was one of the structure's bitterest critics.

British labor unions originated during the 18th century in response to brutal conditions under the Industrial Revolution. Even as late as the close of the 19th century, labor unions were an underground movement, forming in small groups for a specific purpose and area of concern. Members exercised no voting rights. The "Factory Acts" of 1847 and 1874 were the products of reform groups and not unionism.[1] By 1913, when Labor Party followers found asylum under the crown, unionism had taken the form of a "crazy quilt," with independent groups having popped up around the countryside.[2]

The result of this type of formative period was to maximize local loyalties and minimize national communication. Consequently, the governing body of the unions, the TUC (Trades Union Congress), lacked the necessary power to effect widespread policy changes. Further, only eighty-odd affiliated TUC members were members of the Labor Party itself. Woodcock wanted three changes made in the structure of the labor movement, including (1) fewer unions, organized along industrial lines, (2) more authority at the plant level (where wages were decided in reality), and (3) more authority for the TUC.[3]

A major factor in the unrest existing in the labor movement had been the increasing power of communist-led workers. Roberts Company was under fire from this segment, as were many other companies across the country at that time. The *Economist* writes of one "Jack Dash," but ever cautiously:

> Mr. Dash's reputed eminence in London Docks is not a cause, but a symptom, of the union's inadequacies. Because he is a Communist, it may be a dangerously misleading symptom. The leader of the Barbican Strike Committee is a Communist too. The Communist or near-Communist rump of the Electrical Trades Union had been blamed for last week's roughing-up of the union's general secretary: other Communists and their friends have been involved in the rough stuff at Stockport and Luton.[4]

Whether cause or symptom, the presence of Communist influence of this degree was definitely a new encounter for Roberts Company and Mr. Pomeranz.

Some other figures show the labor situation as below par in 1965. Only one-half of the workers got any form of sick pay. Generally, fringe benefits ran 14 percent of wages in Great Britain, compared to 75 percent in Italy, 50 percent in France, and 30 percent in Belgium. The average worker received $45 for a 47-hour week. A tradition existed for overtime, averaging three hours a week. Critics felt that elimination of overtime and increase in regular wages would both increase productivity and give more free time to the worker. The British reply? Radical, by golly.

> "It's not the way we do things here," said an official of an employees federation. "And anyhow, what would the workers do with their evenings if they didn't work overtime?"[5]

1. Henry Pelling, *A History of British Trade Unionism* (New York: St. Martin's Press, 1963). pp. 71-74.
2. *Business Week,* 13 July 1963.
3. *Business Week,* op. cit., p. 130.
4. "Strikebound," *Economist,* 21 October 1967, p. 254.
5. *Business Week,* op. cit.

3

Long-Range Planning

HEWLETT-PACKARD COMPANY, U. S. A. (B)
Planning for Growth

The continued growth of H-P both domestically and overseas can be attributed substantially to the initial careful planning that precedes expansion and to the subsequent control measures. Both planning and control procedures are designed to insure that growth is in accord with the company's overall objectives and is well ordered and executed.

GROWTH OBJECTIVE

H-P considers a 20 percent annual increase on net sales and an after-tax profit of 8 to 10 percent on each sales dollar as satisfactory goals. The minimum profit goals are strongly stressed, and company profit margins for 1966 and 1967 were 8.3 percent and 8.7 percent respectively.

In addition to the overall growth objective, the company has certain other objectives to which it adheres in its overall operations. These are:

1. The growth should be accomplished through retained earnings. H-P's president states, "H-P's sales growth in any one year is limited to the amount of after-tax profit multiplied by the annual turnover of the funds employed in the business." To this extent long-term financing has been purposely avoided with a total long-term debt of only $2 million at the end of 1967.
2. Acquisitions are invariably 100 percent owned by H-P both in the U. S. and abroad. The only exception has been the operations in Japan where, due to Japanese government restrictions. H-P operates through a joint venture with a Japanese company.
3. Achievement of highest possible rate of return on investment and lowest cost per sales dollar.

The long-term debt policy has been modified in the company's overseas expansion program. Although initial investments have been financed largely by internal funds, international growth has been financed through a higher level of long-term debt. Reasons for this shift in emphasis have been (1) the great need for cash to finance receivables in a rapidly growing business and to provide working capital for the factories and (2) U. S. government regulation policies such as foreign direct investment limitations and the interest equalization tax, which limit the amount of funds which can be invested abroad from the United States.

One company official explains H–P's overseas finance policy as follows:

In Europe we're dealing with extremely mature, mobilized money situations with the highest element of risk at this particular moment due to possible devaluation or revaluation. In Latin America we have money risks of a completely different nature on a daily basis. Involving ourselves in protection of our liquid assets is the fundamental activity. But how you do this differs with each area. In Europe where we are hedging on an active basis, we move money at a tremendous rate among our sales groups and the factories we have there. It's quite a different kind of a daily job dealing in Brazil, with the financial problems as they exist there, or in dealing with Japan.

Calculation of liquidity, leverage activity, and profitability ratios for Hewlett–Packard's consolidated statement reveals an outstanding financial position (Table 1). H–P's wariness of long-term debt is illustrated by its high liquidity position and its phenomenal leverage position. Because of this financial position there have been some efforts to acquire Hewlett–Packard. However, with Messrs. Hewlett and Packard holding 70 percent of H–P stock, acquisition appears highly unlikely.

IMPLEMENTATION STRATEGY— BUDGETING AND PLANNING

H–P has planned carefully to achieve its growth objectives. The general planning policy is built around a semi-annual budget and a five-year plan. All reporting is divided functionally into manufacturing and marketing segments.

Semi-Annual Targets and Budgets

Every manufacturing and marketing entity submits semi-annually its target expectations of performance during the next twelve-month period.

The first form (Figure 1), entitled "Target Statistical Data," indicates allocations for personnel, inventory, collection period on receivables, sales promotion, and capital assets.

The second form (Figure 2), entitled "Orders Quotas and Income/Expense Targets," includes the order quota, forecasted shipments, cost of sales, other expenses, and operating and net profit. Note that item 31 is "Cost Per Order Dollar" which is considered a major evaluation figure by H–P management.

The third form (Figure 3), entitled "Capital Assets Budget Request," is used to budget land and plant improvements. Although the international sales organizations

TABLE 1

Financial Position Ratios for Hewlett-Packard

Ratio	1967	Reference[a]
Liquidity		
Current Ratio (CA/CL)	2.4	3.42
Quick Ratio (CA-Inv/CL)	1.75	2.75
Inv/Working Capital Ratio	61%	81%
Leverage		
Total debt/Total assets	27.75%	100.2%
Fixed assets/Net worth	37%	39.0%
Activity		
Cash velocity	74 times	—
Inventory turnover	6.7 times	5.3 times
Sales/Fixed assets	4.0	3.0
Average collection per	64 days	51 days
Sales/Total assets	1.5	2
Profitability		
Gross operating margin	52%	—
Net operating margin	15%	4.23%
Sales margin (after tax)	8.3%	3.27%
Return on net worth	12%	14.83

[a]Reference figures are from "Electronics, Components and Accessories Industry," *Key Business Ratios* (New York: Dunn & Bradstreet, 1967).

collect the money for products which they sell and the international factories receive payment, if either wants to improve plant facilities, it must go out for funding. Usually the funding for overseas projects is done abroad and not directly from the United States.

The international budgets must be approved by international operations and by corporate headquarters. Once approved, during the course of the time period involved, the manager has the flexibility to deviate from the budget almost at will. The only requirement is that he notify the main office of his intended action. However, the one-year target format is continually measured against the monthly statement,[1] and all deviations from the target must be explained.

Budgets are closely administered by finance officers at international head-quarters. Annually, business managers from the overseas areas gather for a week-long review of uniform financial practices, order processing activities, and communications systems problems and development. These seminars are used to coordinate budgeting and reporting efforts between the overseas operating divisions and the home office.

1. A detailed description of various monthly statements and their uses is given in Part C of this case study.

FIGURE 1

IMC: _____

Target Statistical Data
Fiscal Year Ended 31/10/____

Line No.	Item		Targeted Amounts	
			At 30/4/	At 31/10
1.	Employee Count	Field Engineers		
2.		Service Technicians		
3.		Other		
4.		Total		
5.	Inventory Data			
6.	Instrument Inventory, at cost (1372–75)		$	$
7.	Parts Inventory, at cost (1371)			
8.	Subtotal: Landed Inventory		$	$
9.	Add: Transit Inventory (1361–64)			
10.	Total Inventory		$	$
11.	Demo inventory, *at cost* as a % of *year's* quota		%	%
12.	Instrument inventory supply		mos.	mos.
13.	Parts inventory supply		mos.	mos.
14.	Days Receivables		days	days
15.	Sales Promotion Target Detail			F/Y Ended 31/10/____
16.	Acct. No.	Description		
17.		Media Advertising		$
18.		Application Notes		
19.		Direct Mail		
20.		Data Sheets		
21.		Catalogs		
22.		Addressograph		
23.		HPSA, HPIA, or Export Mktg. Adv. Charge		
24.		Trade Shows		
25.		Demo Bus		
26.		Product Training Seminars		
27.		Promotional Parts		
28.		Other Misc. Matls. and Supplies		
29.		Total		$
30.	Capital Assets Data			
31.	Estimated depreciation/amortization for year			$
32.	Estimated asset purchases for year			$
33.	Intra-Corporate Shipments			$
34.	Intra-Corporate Orders[a]			$

[a]To be shown only by Int'l. Distribution Centers.

154

FIGURE 2

IMC: _____

Orders Quotas and Income/Expense Targets, F/Y Ended 31/10

Fiscal Year-to-Date Targets, as of the end of:

Line No.	Item	Nov. 19	Dec. 19	Jan. 19	Feb. 19	Mar. 19	Apr. 19	May 19	June 19	July 19	Aug. 19	Sept. 19	Oct. 19
1.	Orders Quota—Cumulative —Monthly												
	Shipments:												
2.	Instruments												
3.	Parts												
4.	Repair Parts												
5.	Repair Labor/Ovhd.												
6.													
7.	Total Shipments												
	Cost of Sales												
8.	Instruments												
9.	Parts												
10.	Repair Parts												
11.	Repair Expense												
12.													
13.	Total Cost of Sales												
	Sales Margin												
14.	Net Commission Income												
15.	Gross Income												
16.	Expenses:												
17.	Comm. Exp., O/S Reps.												
18.	Comm. Exp., IC												
19.	FE & SS												
20.	Order Processing												
21.	General												
22.													
23.	Total Expenses												
24.	Operating Profit												
25.	Net Trading Income												
26.	Other Income (Exp.)												
27.	Profit Before Tax												
28.	Less: Income Tax												
29.	Retirement & P/S												
30.	Net Profit—Discount Charge												
31.	Effect on Profit $ Memo: Cost/Order $												

155

FIGURE 3

IMC: _____
Capital Assets Budget Request, 6 Months Ended

Summary	Acct. No.	Budget Requests[a]	6 Mos. Ended[b]	Rental Budget[c]	6 Mos. Ended[d]	Life of Rental Contract[e]	Monthly Rental Cost[e]	Includes Service Contract (Yes/No)[e]
Land and Improvements								
Leasehold and Improvements								
Bldgs. and Improvements								
Machinery and Equipment								
Elec. Test Equipt.								
HP								
Other								
Office Equipt.								
Automotive Equipt.								
Autos								
Other (Large Vans, etc.)								
Other								
Total								

[a]This column summarized requests for Executive Council approval of the next 6 months' budget. The items included are further detailed on the attached continuation sheet(s).

[b]This column summarizes estimated budget requests which will be submitted later for the second half of the fiscal year. Because Executive Council approval will not be sought until later, no detailed continuation sheet listings are necessary.

The remarks listed under Note a, regarding nature of amounts to be shown for individual property accounts, apply to this column also.

[c]Insert purchase price of capital assets to be rented or leased under period in which rental or lease will be started. Classify according to summary accounts at left. This column is used for definite requests for the next six months.

[d]This column is the same as column (3) except that it is used for projecting the requests for the subsequent six months.

[e]In case of multiple lease terms on one class of assets, use continuation sheets as necessary.

156

Five-Year Plans

The five-year plans are prepared annually for the ensuing five years, submitted to Palo Alto for review, and are approved after consultation between the home office and divisional offices (Figures 4 and 5). A *five-year plan* is not a series of financial statements, but rather a statistical and verbalized projection, including the expected operating profit and net profit after tax performance for the five-year period. The manufacturing plan (Figure 4) is filled out by a manufacturing organization's management. Part I calls for a brief description of the organization's objectives and a description of present and future product lines and fields of activity. For example, the German plant might forecast the economic outlook for Germany for the next five years and predict the development of a certain type of computer during that time period. Part II requires notes to be made of anticipated shifts in product and market environment during the next five years.

Dollar goals are listed year by year by major product lines in Part III. Figures from the previous year's five-year plan (target figures) are also included, and major deviations must be explained. The return on assets, operating profit, plant space, personnel, product and market development, inventory, and other dollar figures are also projected. This is supported by a five-year cash forecast.

Part IV lists any significant changes from the previous year's long-range plan, with the emphasis here on changes in future plans, not on unreached targets. Part V includes critical items which must be planned in advance.

The five-year plan for a marketing organization (Figure 5), is drawn on similar lines. As a general practice, Hewlett–Packard does not disclose divisional or regional information for several sensitive reasons, and the five-year plan and the yearly targets as well are considered classified documents.

The unique and most striking feature of H–P's five-year plans is the emphasis on close coordination between manufacturing and sales growth and the need for forecasting and procuring trained personnel in numbers adequate for the expanded needs of the company. A company official explains this approach in the following terms:

We pay utmost attention in our plans for the provision of manpower requirements. Our company specializes in complex products so our growth is dependent on the availability of technically trained people at the right time, in right places, and in right numbers. Managers are closely questioned if their manpower plans seem inadequate for their anticipated growth. Their promotion and the success of the company as a whole are dependent on how well they train and maintain adequate staff to sustain growth on a continuous basis.

FIGURE 4

Long-Range Manufacturing Plan

Prepared _____ , 1967   _____ Division

I. A. Division Objectives, Assumptions:

   B. Markets/Products Field of Activity:
      1. Present:

      2. 1972:

II. Strategic Plans. Anticipated Major Shifts in Market/Product Environment in Next 5 Years and Alternatives of Planned Action:

	Actual	*Target*	*Plans*			
III. Goals—Fiscal Year	*1967*	*1968*	*1969*	*1970*	*1971*	*1972*

Shipments—$K (by Major Product Line and Diversification):

        Total Shipments   _____

Operating Profit—% (by Major Product Line and Diversification)

        Combined Op. Profit   _____

Return on Assets—%

Long-Range Manufacturing Plan   _____ Division

Total Sq. Ft. Avail.—10/31 (K)

158

FIGURE 4—*continued*

IV. Goals—Fiscal Year

	1967	1968	1969	1970	1971	1972
People—10/31						

Graduate Engineers:
Test Technicians:
Total People:

Product Development—$K

New Market Development—$K

Inventory (Mos.)—10/31

Cash Excess (Short.)/Ships.

V. Significant Changes from Last Year's Long-Range Plan:

VI. Outline of Critical Items which must be Planned in Advance to Achieve Goals

FIGURE 5

Long-Range Sales Plan

Prepared _____ , 1967   _____ Region

I. Region Objectives, Assumptions:

II. Strategic Plans. Anticipated Major Shifts in Market/Product Environment in Next 5 Years and Organizational or Other Alternatives or Planned Action.

FIGURE 5–*continued*

III. Goals–Fiscal Year	*Actual* 1967	*Target* 1968	1969	*Plans* 1970	1971	1972
Orders–$K						
Electronic Discipline:						
Medical Discipline:						
Chemical Discipline:						
Other Discipline(s):						
Repair Labor, etc.:	_____					
Total Orders						
Cost/Order Dollar–¢						
Electronic Inst. and Parts						
Medical Inst. and Parts						
Chemical Inst. and Parts	_____					
Combined Cost/Order $						
International						
Net Trading Income (±)						
Regional Cost						
Prov. for Rep. Discount	_____					
Intl. Cost/Order $						

Long-Range Sales Plan   Region

	Actual 1967	*Target* 1968	1969	*Plans* 1970	1971	1972
Repair Billing/Cost–%						
Receivables (Days)–10/31						
Total Sq. Ft. Avail.–10/31						

IV. Goals–Fiscal Year	1967	1968	1969	1970	1971	1972
People–10/31						
Staff and Field Engineers:						
Electronic Discipline:						
Medical Discipline:						
Chemical Discipline:						
Other Discip. and Specs.:	_____					
Subtotal						

Service Technicians:
Admin. and Support: _____

  Total People

<u>Inventory—10/31</u>

  Instr. (% Annual Quota)
  Parts (Months)

V. Significant Changes from Last Year's Long-Range Plan

VI. Outline of Critical Items which must be Planned in Advance to Achieve Goals

KAREY INTERNATIONAL, INC., U. S. A.

Planning for Overseas Expansion and Market Entry

Karey International, Inc.[1] (KII) was established in 1969 as a wholly owned subsidiary of Karey Apparel Company of U. S. A. Karey Apparel, a medium-sized sportswear manufacturer, holds patents on a well-known and internationally accepted permanent press process. In 1969 reported worldwide sales were $81.0 million with after-tax profits of $3.4 million.

1. The name of the company and all other figures used in the case are disguised to protect the company's competitive position.

KII was organized to consolidate the company's overseas operations under one management and to provide for a concerted effort to expand abroad. Mr. Blumenthal, KII vice president of marketing, recognized that to grow successfully it was vital that their expansion moves abroad should be planned for deliberate and steady progress and avoid the risks of overexpanding, missed opportunities, or unforeseen and unplanned implementation. As a first step, he and his staff developed a market plan for the five-year period 1970 to 1974 to assess the growth potential for KII in certain selected countries. Next, Mr. Blumenthal devised a criterion to evaluate individual projects in terms of their profitability and feasibility within the framework of the company's resources and their most efficient use. A copy of these plans is reproduced below:

KII FIVE-YEAR MARKET PLAN: 1970 TO 1974

This plan projects market conditions during the 1970 to 1974 period in the areas designated as primary interest (PI) countries by KII management—Australia, Belgium, Canada, Japan, United Kingdom, and West Germany—and outlines the extent to which KII should expect to grow in these markets. Data for certain other selected (OS) countries are also presented for illustration and comparison purposes.

The development of these plans is based on the following considerations:

1. We have discarded the "accounting" concept of planning which simply projects a certain growth rate based on past sales, growth in GNP, personal income, expenditure, or similar criteria. Those criteria may develop relatively "safe" plans, but they do not perform the planning function which should be action oriented in terms of what we can do and how far we can go rather than passive response to a given set of conditions. Specifically:

(a) Plans based on past performance assume that the future will be similar to the past, assist status quo by not flushing out the strengths and weaknesses of our operations, are likely to overlook emerging areas of growth and exploitation since they did not fit into the earlier pattern of our activities.

(b) Plans based solely on such macro-indicators as GNP, personal income, and so on are also faulty because they assume our progress will be similar to that of the general economic activity. There will be no structural changes in a country's economic activities, and competitive activities will be unchanged in future.

2. These plans are based on analyzing each territory at four levels:

(a) Forecast of general economic conditions
(b) Forecast of those micro-indicators which are more closely related to the sale of our products
(c) Changes in the nature and structure of competition in various countries.
(d) Strengths and weaknesses of KII at the home office and field level which can be utilized to make use of the marketing opportunities offered in these countries.

3. Sales forecasts are based not on what will happen but on what can be accomplished if KII mobilizes its resources to the maximum extent. It must be noted here that these plans have a greater element of uncertainty and risk of unfulfillment than forecasts based on general economic growth or similar indicators because to a large extent they depend on what we do in achieving them. Therefore, it is very important that we incorporate 'he following points in our plans:

(a) Develop criteria for ranking countries and projects in order of their attractiveness as investment prospects for KII.
(b) Establish minimum and maximum investment limits for individual projects on a global basis as well as in individual countries. This is necessary to spread investment risks and avoid undertaking projects which either overextend the company's resources or lock us in projects with heavy start-up costs but low profit potential.
(c) Develop organization structure at the home office level for continuous study, evaluation, and coordination of plans and their execution.
(d) Develop procedures to control and evaluate programs at various stages of execution to avoid mistakes before they become extensive, evaluate performance of local management, and spot future areas of expansion.

Points (c) and (d) will be the subject of a second report.

General Economic Conditions and Factors Affecting Demand for Clothing in Selected Countries

The demand for clothing in a given country depends on two sets of criteria:

1. Growth rates and structural changes in population, changes in growth and distribution of personal income, changes in ratio of savings to consumption, and changes in relative prices of clothing.
2. Differences in life styles of various groups of consumers as reflected in their expenditures for various kinds of clothing as a percentage of their income and consumption.

Tables 1 and 2 present data on these variables for primary interest (PI) and other selected (OS) countries which have a bearing on our projection of demand for clothing on KII's market share in those countries. Some caution is desirable in interpreting these data because of various problems associated with collecting and comparing cross-cultural data. For example, in some countries health and insurance expenses are covered under governmental expenditure thereby depressing the figures for per capita private expenditure. Similarly, in some countries cleaning expenses are included in clothing expenditure. However, as general indicators of overall demand trends these data can supply a useful guide. (*See* Table 3.)

Although a large part of the variation in individual clothing expenditures may reflect different life styles, variation may also result from statistical factors such as the use of conversion and exchange rates which may not be appropriate for comparing the prices of clothing. Age, sex, and distribution of population differences are also important factors. (*See* Table 4.)

TABLE 1

Population Growth and Distribution in Selected Countries

	Population 1968 (Millions)	Population Growth 1962–1967 (Percent/ Year)	Age Distribution of Population 1965–1966		
			10–19	20–29	Columns 3 + 4
			(Percentage of Population)		
	1	2	3	4	5
PI Countries					
Australia	12.0	1.9	18.4	13.6	32.0
Belgium	9.6	0.8	15.0	12.3	27.3
Canada	20.7	1.9	16.2	11.8	28.0
Japan	100.7	1.0	20.3	17.7	38.0
United Kingdom	55.5	0.6	14.5	13.1	27.6
West Germany	59.9	1.0	13.0	15.5	28.5
OS Countries					
Austria	7.3	0.5	13.7	17.8	31.5
Denmark	4.9	0.8	15.4	16.7	32.1
Finland	4.7	0.7	20.2	13.7	33.9
France	50.1	1.0	17.2	12.5	29.7
Italy	52.5	0.8	15.7	14.8	30.6
Netherlands	12.7	1.3	18.4	14.3	32.7
Norway	3.9	0.8	16.4	15.0	31.4
Portugal	9.5	1.1	17.1	13.6	30.7
Sweden	7.9	0.9	15.0	14.2	29.2
Switzerland	6.0	1.2	15.2	16.6	31.8

Source: United Nations Statistical Year Books

Aggregate Expenditures

Aggregate expenditure is a function of the national income. Assuming that differences in national income tend to equalize in the long run, the national income is likely to grow at the same rate as the gross national product (GNP).

The normal GNP growth for Western Europe during 1960 and 1967 was slightly above 4 percent, with EEC and Scandinavian countries reaching 5 percent and the rest of the EFTA countries ranging between 3.2 and 4.0 percent. Australia and Japan have had a growth rate of 5.1 and 9.6 percent, respectively. For the growth rates between 1968 and 1975, Kahn and Wiener[1] predict EEC and Australia keeping their present growth rate, Scandinavia slowing down, U. K. at 4.0 percent, and Japan between 7.0 and 10.0 percent.

Since national income consists mainly of private expenditure, savings, and governmental expenditure, and since savings are influenced by income level, we have used governmental expenditure as the determining variable for the ratio

1. Herman Kahn and Anthony Wiener, *The Year 2000* (New York: Macmillan & Co., 1968).

TABLE 2

Private Spending and Expenditures on Clothing in
Selected Countries, 1968

(Current Prices in U. S. Dollar Equivalents)

	Total Consumers' Expenditure per Head 1	*Consumer Expenditure on Clothing per Head* 2	*As a Percentage of Columns 1 + 2* 3	*Total Consumer Expenditure in Clothing (In Billions)* 4
PI Countries				
Australia	1,410	138	9.8	1.63
Belgium	1,400	130	9.3	1.25
Canada	1,840	143	7.8	3.00
Japan	740	86	11.7	9.70
United Kingdom	1,160	97	8.4	7.20
West Germany	1,280	150	11.7	9.00
OS Countries				
Austria	920	123	13.4	0.91
Denmark	1,600	107	6.7	0.52
Finland	950	88	9.3	0.41
France	1,530	156	10.2	7.80
Italy	840	84	10.0	4.45
Netherlands	1,150	160	13.9	1.65
Norway	1,260	160	12.7	0.63
Portugal	347	30	8.7	0.29
Sweden	1.790	175	9.8	1.39
Switzerland	1,650	130	7.9	0.78

SOURCES: United Nations Yearbook of National Account Statistics 1968; European Free Trade Association (EFTA) Trade 1959-1967, Geneva, March 1969; and European Economic Community's (EEC) Basic Statistics, 1968.

between private expenditure and national income. The cultural climate during the last part of the sixties indicates a greater future role for the government which is likely to cause a decline in the ratio of private expenditure to national income. It also seems probable that the countries with a currently high ratio will lose more in terms of private expenditures than those with the currently lower ratios.

Summary

Our study of economic indicators shows that although no country included in our study has overall superiority, Japan and Australia hold the edge. Otherwise, the range of differences between countries is not large. Nevertheless, some countries may be more suitable than others in some categories due to the presence of other factors such as supply conditions or ease of entry. When all the variables have been considered and equally weighted, the following

TABLE 3

Ratio of Private Expenditure to National Income in
Current Prices (1960 = 100)

	National Income			Private Expenditure			Private Expenditure as a Percentage of National Income	
	1960	*1967*	*1968*	*1960*	*1967*	*1968*	*1960*	*1967*
PI Countries								
Australia	100	164	165	100	158	158	82	78
Belgium	100	167	180	100	159	172	86	82
Canada	100	143	150	100	165	170	86	84
Japan	100	266	322	100	256	320	68	66
United Kingdom	100	150	158	100	150	160	81	81
West Germany	100	158	172	100	165	176	74	78
OS Countries								
Austria	100	167	176	100	171	181	77	79
Denmark	100	198	216	100	198	216	82	81
Finland	100	190	188	100	186	204	74	72
France	100	190	210	100	183	200	84	81
Italy	100	200	226	100	198	222	80	80
Netherlands	100	190	211	100	195	212	69	70
Norway	100	183	187	100	172	184	77	72
Portugal	NA	NA	NA	NA	NA	NA	NA	NA
Sweden	100	190	200	100	180	194	65	62
Switzerland	100	184	NA	100	179	NA	73	70

SOURCE: United Nations Yearbook of National Account Statistics 1968.

general ranking patterns emerge in order of their attractiveness under four
different categories, i.e., economic climate, demand aspect, supply aspect, and
ease of entry:

Economic Climate	*Demand Aspect*	*Supply Aspect*	*Ease of Entry*
1. W. Germany	1. Japan	1. Belgium	1. Canada
2. Japan	2. Australia	2. Netherlands	2. Belgium
3. Belgium	3. Netherlands	3. Sweden	3. Italy
4. Sweden	4. W. Germany	4. Japan	4. Netherlands

2. The above ranking is a subjective conclusion based on both the material in this report and
background material used for this report. Both PI and OS countries were considered with only
the top four in each category being listed.

TABLE 4

Private Expenditure on Clothing
in Current Prices (1960 = 100)

	1960	*1963*	*1965*	*1966*	*1967*
PI Countries					
Australia	100	113	125	130	139
Belgium	100	123	144	152	151
Canada	100	112	125	132	141
Japan	100	132	148	200	225
United Kingdom	100	111	125	129	131
West Germany	100	123	149	155	153
OS Countries					
Austria	100	129	149	157	164
Denmark	100	128	153	170	177
Finland	100	116	133	143	149
France	100	NA	NA	NA	NA
Italy	100	146	162	178	195
Netherlands	100	127	156	164	170
Norway	100	120	134	139	151
Portugal	NA	NA	NA	NA	NA
Sweden	100	123	140	146	150
Switzerland	100	127	141	148	152

SOURCE: United Nations Yearbook of National Account Statistics 1968.

PI *Countries: Sales and Market Penetration Projection 1970 to 1974*

Highlights.

1. Consumer spending on clothing is expected to increase by 55.5 percent between 1969 and 1974.

2. KII's efforts during the 1970 and 1971 period will be confined to exploring opportunities for market entry in selective clothing lines in these countries. The nature of line and method of entry will depend upon the demand, general economic, and competitive conditions, prevailing in those countries. As far as possible, the market entry will be secured through acquisition of existing facilities rather than setting up new plants.

3. Between 1972 and 1974 we will consolidate our position in these markets and establish a strong base from which to launch a vigorous campaign for expansion and diversification.

4. The year-to-year growth in KII's sales during 1970 to 1974 is projected as follows:

Year	Sales Forecast (Million U.S. Dollars)	Percent Increase
1970	5.81	–
1971	16.27	202.00
1972	18.44	13.20
1973	21.08	14.30
1974	24.33	15.40

SPORTSWEAR FIELD

Based on several marketing studies of various international markets, interviews with reliable sources, and considering the Karey family's experience in and knowledge of the sportswear industry, Karey International has decided to concentrate its apparel acquisition program in the sportswear field which apparently offers the greatest growth and profit potential.

Calculations for Canada, Belgium, the United Kingdom, Japan, Australia, and West Germany are based on acquiring total equity in one or partial equity in a few manufacturers of men's or women's sportswear. In Japan 100 percent acquisition is prohibited by law, thus forcing reliance on licensing and joint ventures.

Competition in the sportswear field emanates largely from many small and medium-sized apparel manufacturers in Australia, Belgium, and West Germany, and from large, well-established manufacturers in Canada, Japan, and the United Kingdom.

Growth Rate

In Australia the growth rate within the individual lines of women's sportswear will be substantially higher than the overall growth rate for clothing expenditure. After the first and second years, sales are expected to double because of increased market coverage and production facilities in 1971. The absolute increase is only $300,000 and $600,000 respectively, which will give Karey of Australia only a very small share of the market. The growth will then level off to a slightly more moderate although still very aggressive rate. This will be accomplished by increasing coverage of the market. At the relatively small volume that Karey is initially estimated to do, the projected growth rate requires gaining only a small amount of the total market.

The rate of growth within the individual lines of Australian men's sportswear will increase slowly to 7 percent by 1974. Although this is slightly above the estimated clothing expenditure, it is still realistic considering KII's aggressive marketing policy and substantial penetration.

The clothing expenditure as a percent of private consumption expenditure in Canada has been averaging a modest 8 percent. However, sportswear is projected to increase progressively, therefore making KII's percent growth rate appear very reasonable.

Due to England's austerity program, real GNP was relatively low during the 1967 to 1970 period; however, England's anticipated entry into EEC within the next few years should bring about a definite although small increase in growth rates.

The stiff competition in Germany precludes large growth-rate expectations; therefore they have been estimated at only slightly above the average growth rate.

Growth in Belgium, however, will not be as significant as in Germany due to a less rapidly expanding economy and governmental attempts to curtail inflation. Real GNP is estimated to increase by 4.5 percent in 1970, thus with a price rise of about 4 percent, GNP should increase by 8.5 percent. However, the greatest portion of this increase will be channeled into education, entertainment, and recreation. Belgium has attained a fairly high standard of living for the basic essentials, thus the future should produce more spending on luxury goods.

Japan is realistically forecasting the highest growth rate of any developed country in the world. Therefore, the very aggressive growth rates of 15 and 20 percent we estimate are certainly not overly optimistic especially since price increases account for approximately 4 percent.

Market Target

The Australian market target will be reached in women's sportswear by expanding the capabilities of our existing manufacturer in Australia, and in men's sportswear by acquiring an interest in two Australian manufacturers. Reaching the target in Canada, the U. K., West Germany, and Belgium requires acquisitions or joint ventures. In Japan, with no possibility of a 100 percent acquisition, our market target will be attained via licensing and joint ventures. We will most likely weigh our activities more heavily toward licensing in Japan than in other countries. Joint ventures with Japanese apparel manufacturers have the decisive disadvantage that most of the manufacturers show extremely low after-tax return on investments (2 to 5 percent) and equally low after-tax profits on sales (1 to 2 percent). For this reason licensing will play a major role in reaching our projected Japanese market (*See* Tables 5-10 and Figures 1-6.)

THE SELECTION OF
INVESTMENT ALTERNATIVES

Countries offering opportunities for KII expansion have been analyzed and the growth rates that can be reasonably expected during the next five years projected. Now we focus on developing criteria which should guide KII's selection of projects for execution if it is to realize its goals.

A problem more fundamental than selecting one alternative from many is the process of selecting the alternatives themselves. From all possible investments available, to which ones should resources be allocated for serious consideration?

Ignoring financial capacity for the moment, let us assume that unlimited cash is available and there are no restrictions on amount to be invested. Even under these utopian assumptions not all possible investments should be considered.

It must be recognized at this point that not all alternatives investigated will be selected for investment: a rough rule of thumb is that one of three alternatives is

TABLE 5

Australia: Sales and Market Penetration Projection 1970 to 1974
(in Millions of U.S. Dollars)[a]

Year	Private Consumption Expenditure	Growth Rate (Percent)	Total Expenditure on Clothing	Growth Rate (Percent)	Consumer Expenditure on Specific Clothing (CESC)	Consumer Expenditure on Specific Clothing (CESC) Men	Consumer Expenditure on Specific Clothing (CESC) Women	CESC as Percentage of Total Expenditure on Clothing	CESC as Percentage of Total Expenditure on Clothing Men
1958	9,139	–	1,041	–	–	–	–	–	–
1960	10,640	8.25	1,189	7.0	–	–	–	–	–
1965	14,481	7.10	1,467	6.4	–	–	–	–	–
1966	15,546	7.40	1,545	5.4	–	–	–	–	–
1967	16,800	8.00	1,646	6.1	–	–	–	–	–
1968	18,230	8.50	1,753	6.5	–	–	–	–	–
1969	19,780	8.50	1,867	6.5	643	335	308	34.5	18.0
1970	20,970	6.00	1,960	5.0	675	352	323	34.5	18.0
1971	21,807	4.00	2,019	3.0	698	364	334	34.5	18.0
1972	22,681	4.00	2,079	3.0	708	374	334	34.5	18.0
1973	23,701	4.50	2,152	3.5	740	386	354	34.5	18.0
1974	24,891	5.00	2,238	4.0	772	402	370	34.5	18.0

[a]As KII already owns a women's sportswear manufacturer, and has plans to acquire an interest in a men's sportswear manufacturer, Table 5 has been broken down to show men's and women's sportswear.

Exchange rate: U.S. $1.12 = A $1.

Year	CESC as Percentage of Total Expenditure on Clothing Women	KII's Share of CESC Dollars	KII's Share of CESC Dollars Men	KII's Share of CESC Dollars Women	KII's Share of CESC Percent	KII's Share of CESC Percent Men	KII's Share of CESC (Percent) Women	Growth of Rate (Percent)	Growth of Rate (Percent) Men	Growth of Rate (Percent) Women
1958	—	—	—	—	—	—	—	—	—	—
1960	—	—	—	—	—	—	—	—	—	—
1965	—	—	—	—	—	—	—	—	—	—
1966	—	—	—	—	—	—	—	—	—	—
1967	—	—	—	—	—	—	—	—	—	—
1968	—	—	—	—	—	—	—	—	—	—
1969	16.5	0	0	—	0	0	nil	—	—	—
1970	16.5	1.81	1.51	.30	0.268	0.428	0.093	—	—	100.00
1971	16.5	2.19	1.59	.60	0.314	0.437	0.180	21.0	5.00	100.00
1972	16.5	2.89	1.69	1.20	0.408	0.452	0.350	32.0	6.00	100.00
1973	16.5	3.84	1.80	2.04	0.518	0.467	0.576	33.0	6.50	70.00
1974	16.5	4.79	1.93	2.86	0.620	0.480	0.773	24.8	7.00	40.00

SOURCE: United Nations National Accounts Statistics (actual figures for 1958 to 1967). Business International Investing, Licensing and Trading Editions Abroad Estimates used as basis (estimated figures for 1968 to 1974).

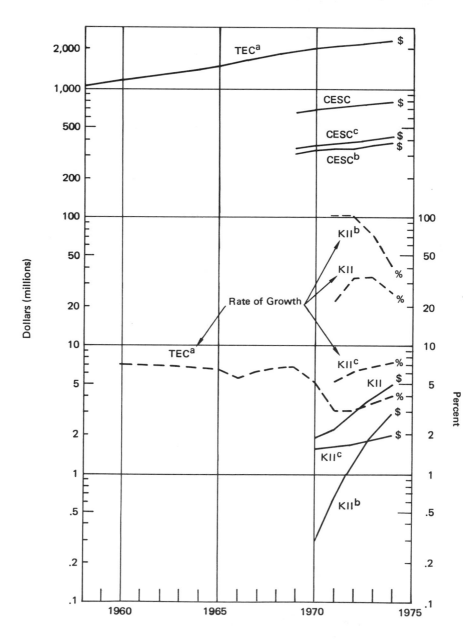

FIGURE 1

Australia

aTEC = Total Expenditure on Clothing
bWomen's Sportswear
cMen's Sportswear

172

TABLE 6

Belgium: Sales and Market Penetration Projection 1970 to 1974
(in Millions of U.S. Dollars)a

Year	Private Consumption Expenditure	Growth Rate (Percent)	Total Expenditure on Clothing	Growth Rate (Percent)	Consumer Expenditure on Specific Clothing (CESC)	CESC as Percentage of Total Expenditure on Clothing	KII's Share of CESC Dollars	KII's Share of CESC Percent	Growth Rate (Percent)
1958	7,140	–	684	–	–	–	–	–	–
1960	7,870	5.00	767	6.50	–	–	–	–	–
1965	11,100	8.00	1,100	7.40	–	–	–	–	–
1966	11,900	7.20	1,175	6.80	–	–	–	–	–
1967	12,500	5.05	1,160	<1.28>	–	–	–	–	–
1968	13,437	7.50	1,207	4.00	–	–	–	–	–
1969	14,507	8.00	1,261	4.50	410	34.0	0	–	–
1970	15,737	8.50	1,324	5.00	428	34.0	0	–	–
1971	17,077	8.50	1,397	5.50	448	34.0	2.50	0.56	–
1972	18,567	9.75	1,481	6.00	476	34.0	2.68	0.57	7.00
1973	20,217	8.90	1,577	6.50	504	34.0	2.90	0.58	7.75
1974	22,057	9.10	1,688	7.10	536	34.0	3.15	0.59	8.75

aExchange rate: U.S. $1 = 50 Bfr.

SOURCE: United Nations National Accounts Statistics (actual figures for 1958 to 1967). Business International Investing, Licensing and Trading Editions Abroad Estimates used as basis (estimated figures for 1968 to 1974).

FIGURE 2

Belgium

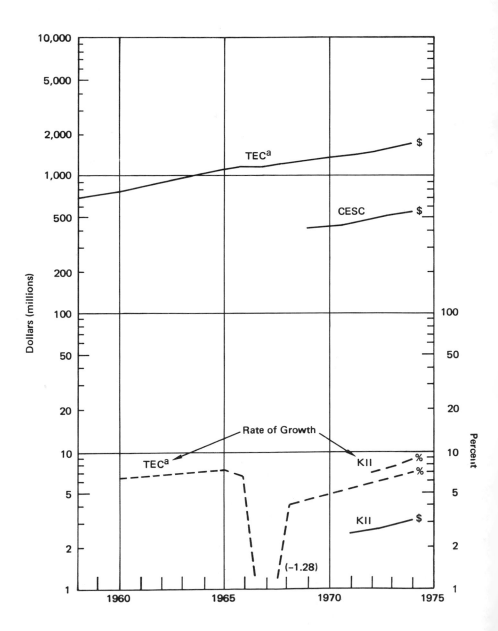

TABLE 7

Canada: Sales and Market Penetration Projection 1970 to 1974
(in Millions of U.S. Dollars)[a]

Year	Private Consumption Expenditure	Growth Rate Percent	Total Expenditure on Clothing	Growth Rate Percent	Consumer Expenditure on Specific Clothing (CESC)	CESC as Percentage of Total Expenditure on Clothing	KII's Share of CESC Dollars	KII's Share of CESC Percent	Growth Rate Percent
1958	19,648	–	1,823	–	–	–	–	–	–
1960	21,774	5.40	1,964	3.85	–	–	–	–	–
1965	29,699	5.10	2,455	5.00	–	–	–	–	–
1966	32,277	8.70	2,593	5.60	–	–	–	–	–
1967	34,909	8.20	2,784	7.35	–	–	–	–	–
1968	37,799	8.00	2,992	7.50	–	–	–	–	–
1969	40,809	8.00	3,224	7.75	1,090	34.0	0	–	–
1970	44,169	8.25	3,476	7.80	1,200	34.5	4.00	0.333	–
1971	47,909	8.50	3,754	8.00	1,310	35.0	4.58	0.350	11.4
1972	52,109	8.75	4,062	8.20	1,440	35.5	5.10	0.355	11.4
1973	56,669	8.75	4,402	8.40	1,590	36.0	5.70	0.358	11.8
1974	61,749	9.00	4,782	8.60	1,740	36.5	6.35	0.365	11.4

[a]Exchange rate: U.S. $1 = C$1.08.

SOURCE: United Nations National Accounts Statistics (actual figures for 1958 to 1967). Business International Investing, Licensing and Trading Editions Abroad Estimates used as basis (estimated figures for 1968 to 1974).

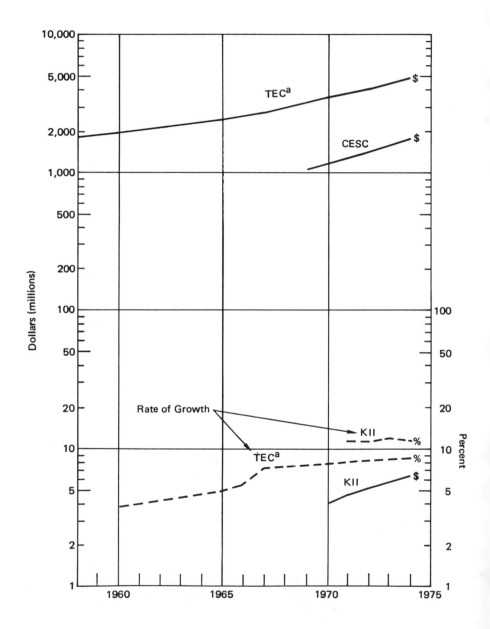

FIGURE 3

Canada

^aTEC = Total Expenditure on Clothing

TABLE 8

Japan: Sales and Market Penetration Projection 1970 to 1974
(in Millions of U.S. Dollars)[a]

Year	Private Consumption Expenditure	Growth Rate (Percent)	Total Expenditure on Clothing	Growth Rate (Percent)	Consumer Expenditure on Specific Clothing (CESC)	CESC as Percentage of Total Expenditure on Clothing	KII's Share of CESC Dollars	KII's Share of CESC Percent	Growth Rate (Percent)
1958	19,100	—	2,560	—	—	—	—	—	—
1960	23,600	11.8	3,120	11.0	—	—	—	—	—
1965	48,000	20.0	5,800	17.0	—	—	—	—	—
1966	54,000	12.6	6,340	9.4	—	—	—	—	—
1967	62,000	14.8	7,100	12.0	—	—	—	—	—
1968	73,800	19.0	8,300	17.0	—	—	—	—	—
1969	85,600	16.0	9,460	14.0	3,220	35.0	0	—	—
1970	98,900	15.5	10,760	13.5	3,680	35.0	0	—	—
1971	114,200	15.5	12,190	13.3	4,120	35.0	2.00	0.048	—
1972	132,000	15.5	13,780	13.1	4,660	35.0	2.30	0.049	15.0
1973	152,400	15.5	15,560	12.9	5,280	35.0	2.76	0.053	20.0
1974	176,000	15.5	17,550	12.8	5,960	35.0	3.31	0.056	20.0

[a]Exchange rate: U.S. $1 = 360 ¥.

SOURCE: United Nations National Accounts Statistics (actual figures for 1958 to 1967). Business International Investing, Licensing and Trading Editions Abroad Estimates used as basis (estimated figures for 1968 to 1974).

FIGURE 4

Japan

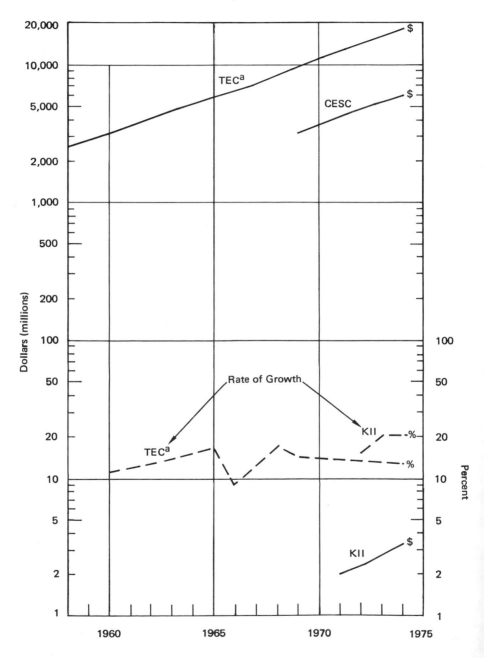

aTEC = Total Expenditure on Clothing

178

TABLE 9

United Kingdom: Sales and Market Penetration Projection 1970 to 1974
(in Millions of U.S. Dollars)[a]

Year	Private Consumption Expenditure	Growth Rate (Percent)	Total Expenditure on Clothing	Growth Rate (Percent)	Consumer Expenditure on Specific Clothing (CESC)	CESC as Percentage of Total Expenditure on Clothing	KII's Share of CESC Dollars	KII's Share of CESC Percent	Growth Rate (Percent)
1958	42,800	–	4,690	–	–	–	–	–	–
1960	47,300	5.75	5,300	6.5	–	–	–	–	–
1965	64,000	7.00	6,660	5.0	–	–	–	–	–
1966	68,000	6.25	6,820	2.4	–	–	–	–	–
1967	70,700	4.00	7,000	2.6	–	–	–	–	–
1968	74,280	5.00	7,210	3.0	–	–	–	–	–
1969	78,740	6.00	7,462	3.5	2,540	34.0	–	–	–
1970	84,240	7.00	7,760	4.0	2,640	34.0	–	–	–
1971	90,340	7.25	8,110	4.5	2,760	34.0	2.50	0.090	–
1972	97,100	7.50	8,515	5.0	2,900	34.0	2.65	0.091	6.0
1973	104,860	8.00	8,983	5.5	3,060	34.0	2.82	0.092	6.5
1974	113,230	8.00	9,517	6.0	3,220	34.0	3.00	0.094	7.0

[a]Change rate: U.S. $2.80 = 1£

SOURCE: United Nations National Accounts Statistics (actual figures for 1958 to 1967). Business International Investing, Licensing and Trading Editions Abroad Estimates used as basis (estimated figures for 1968 to 1974).

FIGURE 5

United Kingdom

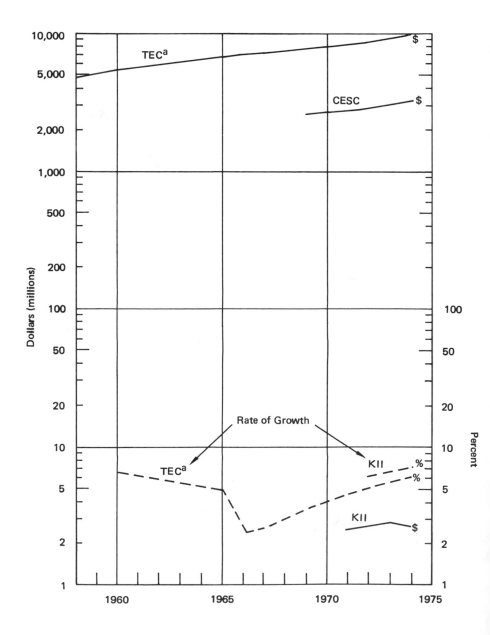

^aTEC = Total Expenditure on Clothing

180

TABLE 10

West Germany: Sales and Market Penetration Projection 1970 to 1974
(in Millions of U. S. Dollars)[a]

Year	Private Consumption Expenditure	Growth Rate (Percent)	Total Expenditure on Clothing	Growth Rate (Percent)	Consumer Expenditure on Specific Clothing (CESC)	CESC as Percentage of Total Expenditure on Clothing	KII's Share of CESC Dollars	KII's Share of CESC Percent	Growth Rate (Percent)
1958	34,200	–	4,330	–	–	–	–	–	–
1960	41,000	10.0	5,150	9.5	–	–	–	–	–
1965	63,500	11.0	7,750	10.0	–	–	–	–	–
1966	68,400	7.7	8,130	4.9	–	–	–	–	–
1967	70,000	2.3	8,040	< 1.1 >	–	–	–	–	–
1968	77,000	10.0	8,762	9.0	–	–	–	–	–
1969	85,000	11.0	9,638	10.0	3,180	33.0	0	–	–
1970	93,930	10.5	10,544	9.5	3,480	33.0	0	–	–
1971	102,430	9.0	11,598	10.0	3,820	33.0	2.50	0.065	–
1972	110,630	8.0	12,758	10.0	4,200	33.0	2.76	0.066	10.5
1973	118,900	7.5	14,034	10.0	4,640	33.0	3.06	0.066	11.0
1974	127,750	7.5	15,437	10.0	5,080	33.0	3.43	0.068	12.0

[a]Exchange rate: U. S. $1 = 3.68 DM

SOURCE: United Nations National Accounts Statistics (actual figures for 1958 to 1967). Business International Investing, Licensing and Trading Editions Abroad Estimates used as basis (estimated figures for 1968 to 1974).

FIGURE 6

West Germany

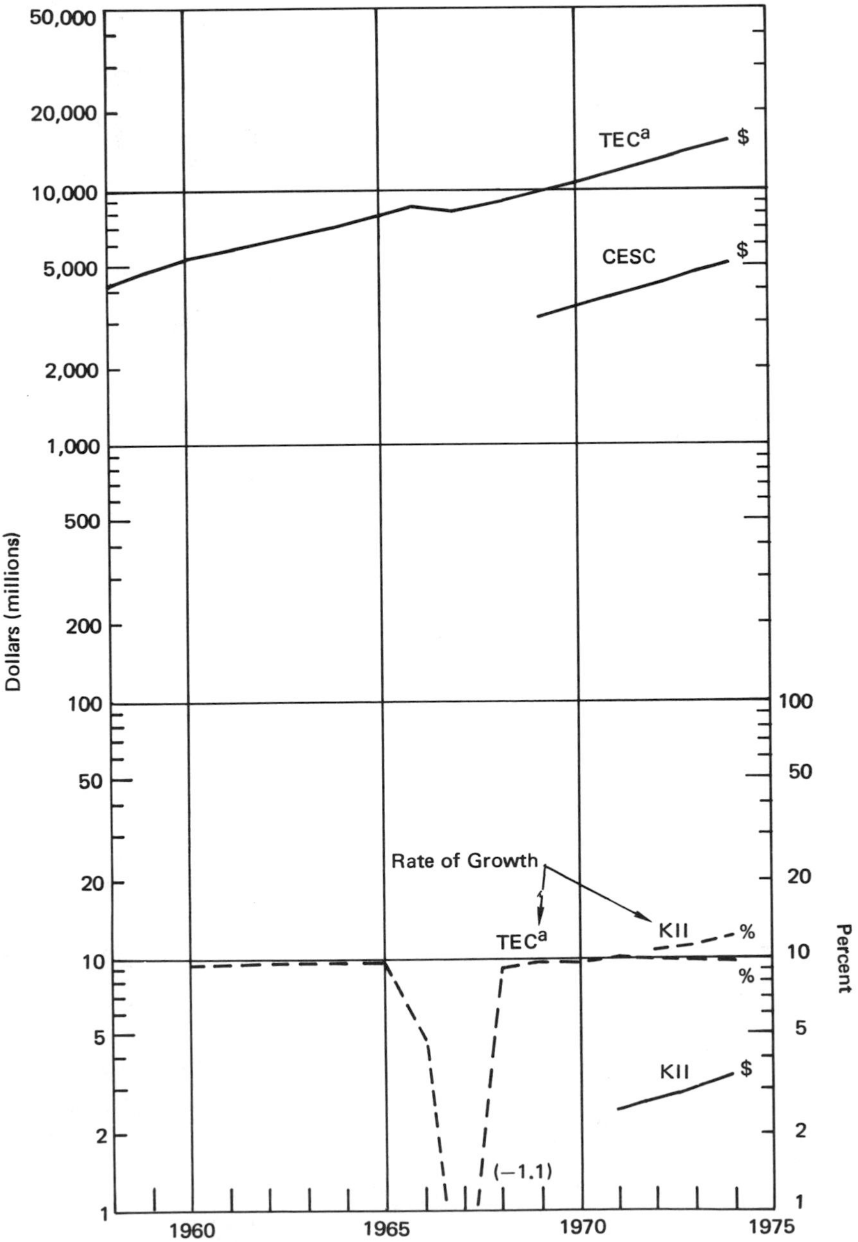

[a]TEC = Total Expenditure on Clothing

deemed worthy. Under such circumstances, the fixed cost of investigation associated with every single *accepted* project is effectively three times the cost of investigating a single *alternative* project.

A further consideration involves the time horizon over which the fixed initial costs should be recaptured. This is a decision based primarily on subjective factors and traditional policies of the firm. It is here suggested that all fixed initial costs should have a planned recovery period of one year from the commencement of operations based on the new investment. As with all rules of thumb, however, this must remain flexible and subject to revisions which experience indicates as necessary changes.

The following criterion has now been established: three times the fixed costs associated with investigative efforts on a single project must be at least covered by the projected first-year profits of any project accepted for consideration.

The question of fixed costs is one to which no specific answer based on experience is available at the moment. Instead, a priori estimates must be employed. Again, this is an area subject to future revision.

The question of potential profits can be answered simply by observing the present profits and sales of the firm being considered. Assume that the firm can maintain its sales level in the coming year and, despite its past profit margin on sales, with the injection of KII's new capital and management skills it will be able to equal the KII domestic profit margin on sales. If this assumption is accepted, estimating first-year profits does not involve arduous investigative efforts (and costs) but merely a cursory examination of the firm's most recent sales figure.

Unfortunately, the analysis to determine a "target" sales figure which can be used as a guide in selecting projects to be investigated depends heavily upon a reasonably accurate dollar figure for fixed costs. As previously mentioned, this figure is not available, and only an educated estimate can be made. The major components of this fixed cost are: accounting fees, traveling and lodging expenses, salaries and wages. A hesitantly offered estimate of this figure is $10,000.

If three times the fixed-cost figure is to be recovered within the first year, net profit must be at least $30,000. An implicit assumption here is that the impact of taxes will be approximately the same as that presently felt by KII. It is impossible to formulate a general rule and still consider the multitude of tax differences among the various countries involved in this study. A satisfactory justification for the use of this "after U. S. tax" figure is that any income repatriated to the United States must pay at least as much as the corporate income tax rate. Whether the income earned is repatriated or not, its treatment is a matter of policy. (The rule stating that fixed costs should be covered is an operating, not a literal, rule of thumb, which does not imply that earnings should literally be earmarked to pay for investigation costs and should therefore be returned to the United States upon realization.)

A matrix of net profits corresponding to various sales and margin levels can be constructed, with a 4 percent return being the historical figure for the company and, therefore, the one upon which we should focus. (*See* Table 11.)

TABLE 11

Net Profit on Sales Which Would be Generated
with Various Profit Margins

Sales (Thousands of Dollars)	*Profit Margin on Sales (Percent)*				
	2.0	3.0	4.0	5.0	6.0
	Total Profit (Thousands of Dollars)				
250	5.0	7.5	10.0	12.5	15.0
500	10.0	15.0	20.0	25.0	30.0
750	15.0	22.5	30.0	37.5	45.0
1,000	20.0	30.0	40.0	50.0	60.0
1,250	25.0	37.5	50.0	62.5	75.0
1,500	30.0	45.0	60.0	75.0	90.0
1,750	35.0	52.5	70.0	87.5	105.0
2,000	40.0	60.0	80.0	100.0	120.0
2,500	50.0	75.0	100.0	125.0	150.0
3,000	60.0	90.0	120.0	150.0	180.0

A more analytical study would involve the assignment of probabilities of achieving each of the profit margins—2 percent may have a probability of 0.9, 4 percent 0.75, 5 percent 0.4, and so on—and computing the *expected* net profits based on outcomes weighted by these probabilities (Table 12). Assigning such probabilities requires an intimate knowledge of the industry and a "feel" for the firm and is primarily subjective in nature. Therefore, since the analysis can continue without these estimates (which would necessarily be based on insufficient background), this probabilistic approach will receive no more than this passing mention. The use of probabilities will be the very elementary one of saying that, based on past experience, we believe that 4 percent will be the most likely profit margin to occur, with 3 percent and 5 percent being possible, and 2 percent and 6 percent being improbable.

A corresponding matrix may be constructed to indicate the percentage claim on profits needed to yield at least $30,000.

Assuming, for the moment, that any percentage of ownership is equally desirable, the following observations can be made:

1. Based on the most likely profit margin (4 percent) we would *never* consider a potential investment with less than $750,000 in total sales.
2. If we wish to be conservative and focus attention on the lower end of the "probable margin" range (3 percent), we would never consider an investment with less than $1,000,000 in sales.
3. The smaller the sales volume, the larger the desired percentage of interest.

If KII had definite leanings toward minority share or otherwise limited holdings, the minimum acceptable sales volume would be increased proportionally. For example, if minority holdings are preferred, the "normal" lower limit will be $1,500,000 in sales, and a "conservative" lower limit will be $2,000,000 in

TABLE 12

Probability of Achieving a Given Profit Margin
with a Specified Sales Volume

Sales (*Thousands of Dollars*)	*Profit Margin on Sales (Percent)*				
	2.00	*3.00*	*4.00*	*5.00*	*6.00*
250	a	a	a	a	a
500	a	a	a	a	1.00
750	a	a	1.00	.80	.67
1,000	a	1.00	.75	.60	.50
1,250	a	.80	.60	.48	.40
1,500	1.00	.67	.50	.40	.33
1,750	.86	.57	.43	.34	.29
2,000	.75	.50	.38	.30	.25
2,500	.60	.40	.30	.24	.20
3,000	.50	.33	.25	.20	.17

[a]Profits do not cover $30,000

sales. The table can be extended as far as necessary so that the appropriate figures may be obtained directly from it.

It is difficult to determine a priori a fixed lower sales limit based on an assumed desired percentage equity because, in most cases, KII will not be able to obtain its equity preference; offers will come on a take-it-or-leave-it basis. Because of this, no fixed limit should be set, but a schedule of limits based on various percentage-of-equity levels should be constructed. This report therefore does not offer any dollar limits on the size of potential investments, but it offers a method by which such limits may be determined. In light of the many assumptions caused by incomplete knowledge and data incorporated here, it is suggested that a restatement of this proposed method be formulated to create a more reliable tool for evaluating alternative projects.

Determining an upper sales limit similarly depends on the percentage of equity interest desired or offered. Also important here, however, is the constraint imposed by limited resources. Attention must be focused on "bottleneck" resources, or those in the most limited supply and without which operations cannot continue. In investment decisions such as those KII faces, cash or financial capital is often believed to be the scarce resource. Here, however, managerial skills appear to be at least as important as capital requirements, if not more so.

If anything more than 15 to 20 percent of a firm is acquired, KII will have a definite interest in sharing the managerial tasks. Indeed, it is exactly in this line that it presumably has some advantage over the local manager, for this must be the primary motivation for entry into such a competitive foreign market. The larger the percentage interest and the larger the firm, the more does KII have at stake, and therefore the more of its scarce management resources it must devote to the success of the project.

It is assumed that KII desires a rather substantial percentage ownership, since it does not want to be a mere shareholder waiting for dividends, and that management participation is expected. Thus, for every project selected, some piece of the "managerial pool" must be assigned to it.

If the popular theory is believed that the complexities of a firm's internal operations are related to the size of the firm as the volume of an object is related to its surface area, then it is apparent that three $X million firms do not require as many managerial resources as one $3X million firm. So, given the apparent lack of abundant, available management personnel at KII, it is desirable to limit the size of investments, preferring several smaller acquisitions to one giant one, *even if financial resources are available*.

This limitation on size is also desirable in light of risk factors. With its limited experience in foreign markets and complete lack of experience in European and Asian markets, KII would do well not to sink all its resources into a single project. This obvious fact requires no further discussion.

Unfortunately, no straightforward method to determine this upper size limit can be devised since the measure of management is elusive and must therefore be determined by someone thoroughly familiar with KII's capacities. The best that can be offered is the suggestion that it is this management factor, the bottleneck resource, which affects the desired upper limit of a single investment project, not necessarily the supply of capital available.

APPENDIX

A Comparative Analysis of Financial and Nonfinancial
Aspects of Entering and Operating Conditions in
Primary Interest Countries

TAX AND FINANCIAL CONSIDERATIONS

I. Comparative Taxes

A. Basic Corporate Tax Rate

1. Australia:	Net profits from all sources—public company to $10,000 40 percent over $10,000 45 percent	
2. Belgium:	On net income from all sources: 30 percent	
3. Canada:	On net profit from all sources: on the first $35,000 21 percent over $35,000 50 percent	
4. Japan:	On net profits: (a) Corporations capitalized at ¥100m. or less, 28 percent on first ¥3m. of profits, 35 percent on profits over ¥3m. (b) Corporations capitalized at over ¥100m., 35 percent of total profits.	

5. United Kingdom: On net profits from all sources: 42.5 percent

6. West Germany: See special corporate taxes.

B. Special Corporate Tax Rates

1. Australia:

Private Company
30 percent on first $10,000
40 percent on remainder
50 percent on undistributed profits
Land Tax
Varies from nil to 3.75 percent
Real Property Taxes
Varies from 3 percent to 27.9 percent

2. Belgium:

Retained income plus nondeductible expenses (in local currency)

to $1,000,000	25 percent
next $250,000	50 percent
over $5,000,000	35 percent

3. Canada:

The following types of income paid to nonresident corporations are subject to a 15 percent withholding tax:

(a) All dividends except those of certain foreign business corporation public utilities and nonresident-owned investment corporations.

(b) All interest except (1) on obligations entered into before December 20, 1960, payable in a foreign currency or issued or guaranteed by the Government of Canada, (2) on foreign currency deposits with certain banks, payable in a foreign currency, and (3) on amounts payable by nonresident-owned investment corporations.

(c) Rents, royalties, or similar payments except in respect to a copyright.

4. Japan:

On income distributed as dividends

(a) Corporations capitalized at ¥100m. or less, 22 percent on first ¥3m. of income, 26 percent of income over ¥3m.

(b) Corporations capitalized at over ¥100m. 26 percent on all income.

5. United Kingdom: None

6. West Germany:

Retained net income: 32.53 percent
Distributed net income: 15.45 percent

For small companies (at least 76 percent held by natural persons and less than 5,000,000 DM capitalization), tax on net retained income (in local currency)

to $10,000	39 percent
$10,000–$20,000	44 percent
$20,000–$30,000	49 percent
$30,000–$40,000	54 percent

$40,000–$50,000   59 percent
over $50,000 $49,000

For small companies on distributed net income: 26.5 percent
For foreign companies on total net income: 49 percent

C. Capital Gains Rate

1. Australia: No special rate

2. Belgium: On gains from property held five years or more: 0.15 percent.

3. Canada: Before 1970 there was no tax on capital gains, however, the new tax reform will probably include a capital gains tax on the U. S. model.

4. Japan: No special rate

5. United Kingdom: No special rate

6. West Germany: No special rate

D. Major Surcharges or Other Taxes

1. Australia: None

2. Belgium: Surcharges on corporate tax: 15 percent
Can be reduced to 0 percent; 3.75 percent, 7.5 percent on advance payment (reduction limited to 3.75 percent or 7.5 percent for foreign corporations)

3. Canada: Dividends received from other corporations will be exempt from Canadian tax if the paying corporation was:
(a) A resident Canadian taxable corporation
(b) A corporation that would have been a Canadian taxable corporation if it were not for special provisions allowing a three-year exemption from tax on income derived from the operation of certain mines.
(c) A nonresident corporation of which more than 25 percent of the voting stock is owned by the recipient.
(d) A "foreign business corporation" of which more than 25 percent of the voting stock is owned by the recipient.

4. Japan: None

5. United Kingdom: None

6. West Germany: None

E. Major Local Taxes

1. Australia: Land tax on unimproved capital value of land: 3.75 percent maximum.

	Other municipal property taxes: about 1 percent on value of property
2. Belgium:	Communal tax on corporation tax: 6 percent
3. Canada:	There is also a provincial corporate tax of 12 percent in Quebec and Ontario, 11 percent in Manitoba, Saskatchewan, and Newfoundland, and 10 percent in other provinces, but it is creditable up to 10 percent against federal taxes. Thus the total effective rate, including the surtax, is 53.5 percent in Quebec and Ontario, and 1 percent or 2 percent less in other provinces. All provinces except Quebec and Ontario have agreements for the collection of their corporate taxes by the federal government.

Each province taxes operations carried on within its boundaries. A corporation that operates in several provinces must allocate its taxable income among them, usually on the basis of sales and wages in each province.

4. Japan: Prefectural enterprise tax on net income (in local currency)

to ¥1.5m.	6 percent
¥1.5-¥3m.	9 percent
over ¥3m.	12 percent

Municipal and prefectural inhabitants tax on corporate income tax payable
(a) Corporations capitalized at over ¥10m. ¥5,000 plus 14.7 percent
(b) Other corporations ¥3,000 plus 14.7 percent

5. United Kingdom: None

6. West Germany: Municipal trade tax on profit: 5 percent (subject to local multiplying factors making effective rate about 13.5 percent)

Municipal trade tax on capital 0.2 percent (subject to local multiplying factors making effective rate about 0.5 percent)

F. Tax Carry-Forwards From Operating Losses

1. Australia:	Seven years
2. Belgium:	Five years
3. Canada:	Five years
4. Japan:	Five years
5. United Kingdom:	Indefinite
6. West Germany:	Five years

G. Tax Carrybacks From Operating Losses

1. Australia:	None

2. Belgium: None

3. Canada: None

4. Japan: One year

5. United Kingdom: One year

6. West Germany: None

II. Selected Financial Factors Affecting Operations

A. Interest Rates

1. Australia:	April 1970	
	(a) Central Bank Discount Rates	not available
	(b) Commercial Bank Prime Rate	7.75 percent
2. Belgium:	April 1970	
	(a) Central Bank Discount Rate	7.50 percent
	(b) Commercial Bank Prime Rate	9.75 percent
3. Canada:	April 1970	
	(a) Central Bank Discount Rate	8.0 percent
	(b) Commercial Bank Prime Rate	8.5 percent
4. Japan:	April 1970	
	(a) Central Bank Discount Rate	6.25 percent
	(b) Commercial Bank Prime Rate	6.50 percent
5. United Kingdom:	April 1970	
	(a) Central Bank Discount Rate	7.5 percent
	(b) Commercial Bank Prime Rate	8.5 percent
	(c) Commercial Bank Average Rate	9.0 percent
6. West Germany:	April 1970	
	(a) Central Bank Discount Rate	7.5 percent
	(b) Commercial Bank Prime Rate	10.5 to 11 percent
	(c) Commercial Bank Average Rate	12.0 percent

B. Inventory Evaluation

1. Australia: Goods may be valued at cost price, market selling value, or replacement price. FIFO or average cost methods may be used; LIFO is not permitted.

2. Belgium: The system must be in accordance with sound accounting practices. Goods must be valued at the lower of cost or market value, and the LIFO method is not recognized.

3. Canada: Businesses are permitted to value inventory for income tax purposes (a) at cost, (b) at the fair market value, or (c) at the lower of cost or market. The method of pricing the opening inventory of one year must be the same as that used for pricing the closing inventory of the preceding year.

4. Japan:
Goods may be valued at replacement cost, adjusted retail price, or the lower of cost or market. Methods of depreciation approved by statute include FIFO, LIFO, weighted average, and moving average. Other methods may be used upon approval of the tax authorities.

5. United Kingdom:
Goods must be valued at the lower of cost or market. The FIFO method of valuation must be used.

6. West Germany:
Goods must be valued at the lower of cost or market. Both LIFO and FIFO methods are permitted, and other methods may be used if justified.

C. Depreciation

1. Australia:
Either straight-line or diminishing-balance methods may be used to calculate depreciable allowances. Rates for the declining-balance method are 1-1/2 times those applied to the straight-line method. Typical rates are: accounting machines straight-line 10 percent, declining-balance 15 percent, motor cars straight-line 20 percent, declining-balance 30 percent.

2. Belgium:
Buildings must be depreciated using the straight-line method. Either straight-line or declining-balance methods may be used on other assets. Typical rates are: 3 percent for industrial buildings and 5 percent for offices. The declining-balance method may employ a maximum rate of double the straight-line rate or 20 percent, whichever is lower.

3. Canada:
Depreciation. Capital cost allowances are ordinarily calculated on a declining-balance basis. The rate for most machinery is 20 percent, for cars, trucks, and mining equipment 30 percent, heavy contractors' equipment 50 percent, wooden buildings 10 percent, and other buildings 5 percent. Dies, jigs, patterns, and tools worth less than $100 can be written off in one year. Investments in depressed areas qualify for accelerated depreciation on the more generous straight-line basis. The rate is 50 percent a year on machinery and equipment, and 20 percent on buildings.

4. Japan:
Either straight-line or declining-balance methods may be used. Different depreciation methods for each classification of assets is permitted, and different methods for assets of the same classification at different business locations may be adopted with the approval of the tax authorities.

5. United Kingdom:
Straight-line method only may be used for industrial buildings and structures. Either straight-line or declining-balance methods may be used on other assets. There is an initial capital allowance in addition to the first year's depreciation of 15 percent for

industrial buildings and structures and 30 percent for machinery, furniture, fixtures, vehicles, etc.

6. West Germany: Straight-line method must be used for immovable fixed assets (buildings, etc.). Other assets may be depreciated on either the straight-line or declining-balance method. The maximum allowable rate under declining-balance is twice the straight-line rate or an overriding maximum of 20 percent.

D. Government Regulations, Attitudes, and Investment Incentives

1. Australia: Australia welcomes foreign investment but prefers that local capital be given an opportunity to participate in new ventures.

Under certain conditions companies may deduct interest paid on convertible securities from taxable income.

If a business controlled from abroad produces either no taxable income or a taxable income less than that which might reasonably be expected to arise, it is liable to pay tax on a taxable income of such amount of the total business receipts as determined by the commissioner.

2. Belgium: Interest rate rebates on loans are granted by banks and semi-public institutions for the financing of new investments. Rates of rebate vary but are generally about 2 percent and extend over a three year period.

Special assistance programs are available for the social and economic development of certain geographic regions. The services include: interest rate rebates, government guarantees for loans, tax exemptions on real estate, and certain capital subsidies. The specific rates and conditions vary widely and are applied on a case-by-case basis.

A National Investment Company assists new enterprises which have difficulty raising funds within the country. It is authorized to subscribe to equity interests in the new company (capital or convertible bonds).

Land in industrial areas is available at low purchase or rental cost.

There are government subsidies to fund the training of Belgian nationals for adaptation to new methods of production.

3. Canada: Foreign investments are generally welcome and are facilitated by the absence of exchange or other controls. They are even more welcome—and often qualify for government assistance—if they broaden the base of foreign ownership (i.e., come from Western Europe or Japan), allow for a degree of Canadian ownership, are designed to export as well as sell in the Canadian

market, locate in surplus labor areas, and generally behave in line with Canadian tastes and customs. None of these conditions are compulsory.

There is no discrimination against foreign firms or local subsidiaries of foreign firms in borrowing funds in Canada. Indeed, foreign-owned subsidiaries have often secured credits at lower rates than local companies by providing parent guarantees.

Canada is not regulated by the Office of Foreign Direct Investment (OFDI), therefore, any investment there is not included in KII's $1 million per year maximum allowable.

4. Japan: Although there is no statutory regulation to its effect, majority interest by foreigners in a Japanese company is rarely allowed.

A general rule is that even minority interests are not allowed unless the foreign investor possesses important technology which would be licensed to the Japanese company.

If less than a 15 percent acquisition via a stock exchange transaction is proposed, there are certain conditions under which it would be automatically approved by the authorities: (a) the share of a single foreign investor does not exceed 7 percent, (b) the share of all foreign investors does not exceed 20 percent (or 15 percent for restricted businesses), and (c) no influence by a foreign investor over the management of the corporation is exercised.

If a direct foreign investment is validated and made with foreign money, investments and resulting profits may be remitted abroad.

If a direct foreign investment is made via the acquisition of shares with yen, no privilege of remittance of investment or resulting profits is extended.

5. United Kingdom: Government holds liberal attitudes toward foreign investment. Companies are allowed to repatriate proceeds from the sale of investments including capital gains. Earnings and dividends are freely transferred.

Incentives are in the form of cash "investment grants" rather than preferential tax treatment. These grants are available for capital expenditures on new plants or machinery in manufacturing at the normal rate of 20 percent.

Development area incentives are available for geographical areas characterized by high and persistent unemployment. Investment grants for these areas may rise to 40 percent, and other incentives include: leases of buildings at favorable rents, building grants of 25 percent to 35 percent toward costs, and loans from the Board of Trade. The Department of

Employment and Productivity will also extend financial aid toward the training and relocation of labor.

6. West Germany: The Federal Bank can restrict foreign investment in German companies. Conditions at present are favorable, however, and include: almost automatic permission for the acquisition of interest in a company, transfer of profits abroad, and the repayment of capital to nonresidents.

German banks are a significant source of borrowed funds and have been a major source of capital to international industry.

In 1969 the banking system was under pressure from the domestic private sector for long-term credit. Consequently a 100 percent reserve requirement was placed on the excess of short-term loans forcing deposits over April 1969 levels.

III. Selected Nonfinancial Factors Affecting Operations

A. Economic Climate

1. Australia: All sectors in the economy show continuing strong growth. Although Japanese competition with Australia is becoming keener, industrial output is at a high level and continues to grow. Consumer demand in Australia is also increasing.

2. Belgium: The economy of Belgium is in an ascendant stage and seems fundamentally healthy. Solid growth is taking place in all sectors. Exports have increased quite a bit, an important factor, since 40 percent of Belgium's GNP is due to foreign trade. Some restrictions have been imposed to prevent overheating.

3. Canada: Canada has weathered the slow-down that followed the 1964 to 1966 boom and is entering a new period of sustained growth. Real GNP growth is expected to be about 4.5 percent in both 1968 and 1969, with a modest easing in price rises to about 3 percent this year. GNP grew by over 6.5 percent in real terms in 1965 and 1966, but eased to a 2.8 percent increase in 1967, while price pressures mounted. Canada's readjustment to the boom came more quickly than it did in the U. S., because the pressure of Vietnam spending was not so intense, and the government moved more rapidly to fight inflation.

4. Japan: The momentum generated by Japan's booming exports, buoyant private investment, and heavy consumer spending in 1968 has carried over into 1969. As a result, continuing expansion is expected. Japan will achieve an overall balance of payments surplus

in 1969, and its international reserves will continue to rise.

5. United Kingdom: The squeeze on the domestic economy in Great Britain has resulted in a lower level of personal consumption and output during the first months of 1969 than in the final growth period of 1968. Trade performance has been erratic, but there is hope that the trade balance will improve. Austerity will be necessary to strengthen the export sector and reduce imports.

6. West Germany: The economic boom in Germany continues. Income and demands are increasing, order backings are growing, and delivery times are lengthening. Consumer prices, however, have been relatively quiescent. Both fiscal and monetary policy have turned restrictive, although the effectiveness of such policies remains circumscribed by balance of payments conditions.

B. Availability of Labor

1. Australia: The employment situation tightened noticeably in Australia during the past year. The number of registered unemployed dropped to a low of 0.96 percent last July (50,000 persons), while the number of vacancies rose to 38,000. Nevertheless, employment increased by 3 percent during February 1969, supplied by a large number of immigrants. Married women are relatively the fastest growing segment of the work force. Wages continue to rise.

2. Belgium: The Belgian government is trying to keep the economy from overheating. Wage and price increases have therefore been slowed down. Excessive increase in labor costs or problems with unions are not expected.

3. Canada: In general, Canada has the youngest and probably the fastest-growing labor force of any industrial country. In the five years to 1968, the number of employed workers grew by 1.2 million, nearly 20 percent.

Unemployment ran at around 5 percent during most of 1968 (but was 8 percent in the Maritime provinces) and is expected to stay near this level in 1969. This will mean a greater supply of unskilled and semiskilled manpower. Canada has always had to import some of its skilled workers and professionals, however, and they remain in short supply.

One of the consequences of the 1965 to 1966 boom was the number of highly inflationary wage settlements. The wage spiral has not yet disappeared, though the pressure is expected to ease in 1969.

4. Japan: The growing scarcity of labor in Japan has had its effect on wages. Along with the rapid growth of the economy, wages have increased by 14 percent in 1968. As in Germany, workers are hard to come by.

5. United Kingdom: The squeeze on the British domestic economy and the reduction of consumption has raised unemployment to 2.3 percent. Lack of productivity increases and the difficulties in negotiating with the many unions (especially with respect to innovations and modernization) make the recovery sluggish.

6. West Germany: The labor market in Germany remains extremely tight with job vacancies far outnumbering the unemployed. The recruiting of 1.4 million foreign workers has not been sufficient to satisfy the demand.

4

Finance, Investment, and Operative Controls

ZIGZAG CORPORATION, U. S. A.

Investment Feasibility Study for Establishing a Sewing Machine Operation in the United Kingdom and the Republic of Ireland

Zigzag is a large U. S. firm whose primary product is consumer and industrial sewing machines.[1] Zigzag supplies close to half of the U. S. sewing machine market and a definitive share of the world market from its plants, both domestic and foreign. Exports to the Latin American countries are supplied from the U. S., and those to the rest of the world come in the main from a West German plant. Marketing operations in overseas territories are handled through wholly owned subsidiaries in various countries.

Since 1960 Zigzag's domestic sales of consumer sewing machines have been steadily declining because American housewives are losing interest in home sewing. To overcome the decline in sales and revenues, the company has taken three steps:

1. Expansion into office equipment field through the purchase of two companies manufacturing desk calculators, typewriters, and other office equipment.
2. Addition to their product mix of new consumer items—vacuum cleaners, phonographs, AM-FM radios, and other low-price domestic appliances.
3. Overseas expansion of their manufacturing and sales activities in sewing machines.

Of these actions, the progress on the first two has been somewhat slow because of stiff competition from established domestic producers. However, the company's efforts in expanding abroad have been remarkably successful.

---

1. All the names and figures used in the case study are fictitious to disguise the identity of the company and protect its competitive position.

In September 1968, Mr. John Hartly, Vice President for the International Division, decided that the current sales of sewing machines in the United Kingdom merited a closer look in terms of establishing manufacturing facilities there. Consequently, he asked Abbott Falsey & Sons, a well-known consulting firm based in London, to do a feasibility study.

The consulting firm's report submitted in March 1969 was highly favorable. However, before submitting it for the approval of Zigzag's board of directors, Mr. Hartly decided to give it a careful study. He asked his administrative assistant, John Hogle, a recent MBA from the University of California, Berkeley, to analyze this study and make recommendations for management's consideration.

A copy of the project report submitted by Abbott Falsey & Sons appears below:

ABBOTT FALSEY & SONS, LONDON
PROJECT REPORT ON THE ESTABLISHMENT
OF A SEWING MACHINE
PLANT IN THE UNITED KINGDOM

Introduction

The Economy of the United Kingdom. The United Kingdom comprises the four geographic entities of England, Scotland, Wales, and Northern Ireland, totaling 94,000 square miles, of which England totals 51,000. The population estimates, in millions, are shown in Table 1.

TABLE 1

Population Estimates

Year	United Kingdom	England
1967	55	49
1977	58	51
1980	60	53
1990	64	57
2000	70	62

Of the present population some 80 percent live in urban areas; about 13 million are under fifteen years of age; another 12 million are between the ages of fifteen and twenty-nine; approximately 21 million are between thirty and sixty; and some 9 million are more than sixty years of age.

The U. K.'s gross national product (GNP) was $86 billion in 1965 compared with $64 billion in 1960: much of this increase was due to rising prices, as economic growth in real terms amounted to only 17 percent. The estimates for 1966 and 1967 for GNP are $91 and $95 billion and for national income (NI) are $84 and $87 billion. Manufacturing accounts for about 35 percent of GNP, and distributive trades and services account for some 27 percent.

Labor. The total working population has hovered around the 25 million mark over the last four years. Of this, 35 percent are in the manufacturing industries and less than 2 percent in agriculture. There is normally a substantial surplus of experienced workers in Northern Ireland, Northern England, Scotland, Wales, Merseyside (the Liverpool area), and South-West England. In the early and middle sixties unemployment was around 1.5 percent; it has since risen to around 2.2 percent.

The average weekly earnings for men over twenty-one in the Engineering and Electrical Goods industries in 1967 was $50; average weekly hours were forty-five, and the average per hour was $1.10.

Fringe Costs. All employers pay a Selective Employment Tax for all employees; for full-time men workers the rate is $3.00. However, this tax is refunded to employers in the manufacturing industries. Furthermore, manufacturers in the Development Areas receive a Selective Employment Tax premium and a Regional Employment Premium together amounting to $4.50 for men workers. These premiums are equal to about 8.5 percent of current wage rates.

About 80 percent of British manual workers have their basic minimum wage rates and other conditions of employment fixed on a nationwide basis by collective agreements or by statutory wage regulation orders.

Nearly everyone who works in Britain, citizen or not, is compulsorily insured under the National Insurance and Industrial Injuries Schemes, to which both employer and employee are required to contribute. In addition, employers are required to pay a pension contribution, graduated according to the employee's earnings, unless an acceptable private pension scheme grants them dispensation.

There are also several optional expenses, such as private pension schemes, medical services, meals, and so on which may be undertaken to attract employees. The statutory payments and optional expenses referred to above, expressed as a percentage of the weekly wage, are shown in Table 2.

Labor productivity is generally lower in the U. K.; for example, from 1960 to 1966 U. S. wage costs per units of output held steady while those in the U. K. rose between 2 and 6 percent. In 1968 and 1969, despite the British Government's efforts to control wage inflation and to dampen price increases, wages rose by 2 to 3 percent more than prices thus increasing by an annual average of 8 percent.

Employment of Aliens. Directors of branches or subsidiaries of American firms encounter little difficulty in obtaining permission to enter and remain in the U. K. Work permits must be obtained for employees of managerial status and key technical personnel required to set up and operate the plant or business. These persons must pay U. K. income taxes on their earnings subject to the provisions of the U. K.-U. S. tax treaty. U. K. exchange control regulations permit American personnel working temporarily (up to four years) in the U. K. to open nonresident sterling bank accounts and to credit their net earnings to these accounts. American personnel may automatically remit the funds to the U. S. A.

TABLE 2

Total Fringe Costs

Payments	Percent
National Insurance Contribution (including S.E.T.)	9 – 12
Paid vacations, sick leave	7
Optional expenditure	2.5 – 5
	18.5 – 24

Refund and Premium	Percent
Refund of S.E.T.	6
Development Areas Refund and Premium	8.5
Total refunds and premiums	14.5
Net fringe costs in Development Areas	4 – 9.5

Investing in the United Kingdom

The Investment Climate. The U.K. generally welcomes foreign investment. Despite occasional cries over "the American take-over of Britain," considerations of the balance of payments and industrial efficiency take precedence. There are a few simple formalities associated with establishing a business in Britain. There is no discrimination between nationals and foreigners in the laws applying to the formation of British companies or in any of the other regulations affecting the establishment or operation of a business. Domestic as well as foreign firms are subject to the same controls over the location of their plant when a new building or a sizable extension to an existing one is contemplated. The present government policy is to channel new industrial development away from the congested areas to localities where industrial sites are available and surplus manpower is found.

Long-term investments by foreign sources have increased rapidly since 1945. It is estimated that in 1962 foreign holdings of common stock in British firms totaled about $2 billion, with close to $100 million in other types of securities. More American private capital is invested in the U. K. than in any other country except Canada. Unofficial estimates have placed U. S. investment at about 7 percent of total investment but accounting for over 10 percent of total domestic production. Official U. S. data show that U. S. direct investment in the U. K. totaled $5.1 billion in 1965. The value of U. S. investment has more than doubled since World War II. It is estimated that there are more than 900 U. S. subsidiaries in the U. K. It is interesting to note that in 1964 some 150 U. S. manufacturing companies accounted for over 12 percent of U. S. exports; and, currently, U. S. firms (controlling more than 10 percent of Britain's modern technology oriented industry) account for about 20 percent of all exports.

Over the last few years the U. K. has been actively encouraging new foreign investment. The government introduced new incentives in 1966, whereby previous tax allowances were replaced by cash investment grants, in the hope that this might even prompt British industry to increase its lamentably low rate of new investment. This system applies only to Great Britain: Northern Ireland has a separate incentive scheme.

Legislation Governing Investment. A U. S. firm wishing to establish an enterprise in Britain need not prove its value to the British balance of payments position. To qualify for later repatriation, however, all investment must receive prior approval from the exchange control authorities. Take-over bids and other proposals not involving direct investment are considered on their individual merits. With respect to new investment, the Bank of England must be satisfied that any proposed investment by nonresidents provides that a reasonable proportion of the capital subscription be made by foreign participation. Earned profits and dividends can be transferred irrespective of the amount. If any capital directly invested in an approved project is withdrawn, the proceeds may be repatriated at any time, together with any net capital gains.

Company Formation. For approval to establish a company in the U. K. it is usually necessary to tell the Treasury, through the Bank of England, the purpose of the company and to describe its capital structure. One may choose between two basic types of limited liability companies:

> *A Private Company*, which may not offer its shares to the public and must restrict the transfer of its shares: it must have not less than two and not more than fifty shareholders.
>
> *A Public Company*, which is not restricted in the ownership of its shares or in the number of its shareholders, provided that they total at least fifty; the public may be invited to subscribe to its shares and debentures.

The majority of incorporated business is formed as private companies, a form that is generally considered the most convenient, unless substantial additional capital is required. The costs of forming a company are small and are directly related to the size of the authorized capital. Total registration fees would come to $120; and to this is added the stamp duty of one-half percent of the nominal capital.

It is recommended that Zigzag establish a wholly owned subsidiary as a *private company* for doing business in the United Kingdom. A subsidiary is a separate legal entity, and the parent company's assets are thus isolated from any possible liabilities of its British business. The minimum capital requirement for a subsidiary is $240,000.

The U.K. has legislation for the protection of patents, trademarks, and industrial designs. The latter are protectable for five years from the date of application and are renewable for two terms of five years.

The U.K.'s Market Potential. The U. K. is, as a highly industrialized economy, a very sophisticated and intensely competitive market. As a consequence of a common language, ancestral ties, and the influence of massive local U. S. investment, it is the market that probably most closely resembles that of the U. S. A. But it nevertheless retains substantial national, and especially regional, dissimilarities to the U. S. market. The outstanding example is the difference of consumer durable goods ownership, particularly of luxury goods.

Between 1956 and 1966 the U. K. National Income per head grew at an annual average of 2.6 percent to $1,550. This contrasts with the U. S. figures of 2.3 percent and $3,500 and with West Germany's 3.9 percent and $1,700. The growth rate was expected to diminish from 1966 to the early seventies.

In 1967 there were 18 million households in the U. K., with an average size of 3.1 persons. Forty-six percent own their house or apartment. The average annual household income is $4,416; of this, taxes and other deductions take 18 percent, leaving an average disposable income of $3,621. The average Briton spends 3.2 percent of this on household durables. The average hire purchase debt (time payment on installment buying) outstanding per household is $183. The increase in the standard of living is shown in Table 3.

TABLE 3

Increase in Standard of Living

Percentage of Households Having	*1956*	*1967*
Car	25	46
Telephone	16	25
TV set	40	88
Refrigerator	7	51
Washing machine	19	61
Vacuum cleaner	51	81

No official figures are available as to percentage ownership of sewing machines; but to judge from trade estimates obtained by the British Consumers' Association, the proportion of households owning an electric sewing machine must be approaching 20 percent.

The Distribution of Personal Income. Official estimates of the overall distribution of personal income in the U. K., both before and after tax, are shown in Table 4.

TABLE 4

Distribution of Personal Income

Range of total income	*Number of families (in Thousands)*			
	1955 to 1956		*1965 to 1966*	
	Before Tax	*After Tax*	*Before Tax*	*After Tax*
Under $ 2,400	19,000	20,000	13,000	15,000
$ 2,400 – $ 4,800	1,500	1,000	8,000	7,000
$ 4,800 – $12,000	250	150	1,000	700
$12,000 – $24,000	47	12	145	90
Over $24,000	14	1	40	25

Clearly there has been a very significant increase in personal incomes. Especially notable is the considerably greater increase in disposable incomes over the last decade. It is evident therefore that with the great rise of disposable incomes and the low percentage of consumer durables ownership, the U. K. market provides excellent sales prospects for a sophisticated range of modern labor-saving machinery. Zigzag should design and price a sewing machine line aimed at the appropriate income sector. The two sectors where disposable incomes have grown the most are the "middle class" levels earning between $2,400 and $4,800. An ideal marketing strategy would be to provide three basic models: (1) a basic electric machine, priced at $35, (2) a simple automatic machine, priced at $50, and (3) a "zig-zag" machine priced at $100. These will be the company's prices to its retailers who will set the final prices to the consumer.

The middle-priced machine would be chiefly aimed at the rapidly expanding group of middle class households; the luxury model would be aimed at the select million or so households of high incomes, prepared to pay higher prices for quality and advanced features. The low-priced model would be aimed at the potential 15 million or so lower income earners, looking for low cost in a reliable machine. This machine, which must generate its profits by mass turnover, would also appeal to the middle class as a combination labor-saving and a quality money-saving device.

Location of Plant in the U. K. With reference to industrial development, the government channels new industry into the labor-surplus regions. As these are by definition removed from the prosperous expanding markets, various forms of assistance are offered to firms establishing there. The rich areas of the Midlands and the southeast are densely populated and highly industrialized with concomitant high land and labor costs. New industries are therefore directed to the Development Areas (north, northeast, and southwest England, Scotland, Wales, and Northern Ireland). The government is able to channel new investment there by requiring the approval of any new industrial building in excess of 5,000 square feet; the Board of Trade generally issues the requisite certificates only to firms locating in the Development Areas.

As a financial incentive, cash grants of 40 percent are made on the cost of new equipment provided for manufacturing in these special areas. In addition, a firm can obtain the refunds and premiums indicated earlier. Governmental assistance is also provided for training costs, normally at the rate of $24 a week for men workers. In areas of exceptionally high unemployment, a five year rent-free period is allowed on factory rents.

Northern Ireland has the most favorable assistance terms in the U. K., as it has generally the highest unemployment rates. It provides the same 40 percent cash grant but also applies it to new buildings as well as to new equipment (to which it adds a further 10 percent in cash). It also provides custom-built factories at 24¢ to 36¢ a square foot, with much lower rents in the first ten years. Considerable help is given toward training the new workers. Despite all these attractive incentives, the recent political and social upheavals would be a serious disadvantage to locating there, in addition to placing Zigzag's plant away from the main U. K. markets.

In all of these areas, of course, all U. K. taxes are payable (which are described later). And there are no special depreciation provisions pertaining to Development Area production.

Choice of Location. In spite of all the financial incentives to locating in a U. K. Development Area or in Northern Ireland, we should select a site which aims at maximizing our profits by minimizing our costs of production and our taxation liabilities. The following procedure for launching our products in the U. K. market is indicated: The plant should be located in a region with the highest unemployment in the whole of the British Isles. Although this situation may be the farthest from the lucrative markets of the U. K., the financial advantages are irresistible. Namely, the proposed location is the Shannon Free Trade Zone in the west of the Republic of Ireland.

Whereas factory costs in the U. K. Development Areas range from 40¢ to 75¢ per square foot, in Eire they are lower even than the 24¢ in Northern Ireland. Property tax rates in the U. K. are about 20¢ a square foot, falling to 10¢ in Northern Ireland. Cost of land in the U. K. is as low as $800 an acre; it is considerably lower in Eire, especially in the West. (Power costs are similar, being about 1-1/2¢ per kilowatt hour.) In the Shannon Industrial Estate (Shannon Free Trade Zone is a part of this estate) the Irish Government provides "nonrepayable loans" covering up to two-thirds of the costs of fixed assets; pays all labor training costs; provides very low cost housing; exempts a firm from property taxes and from import duty on raw materials and partly or wholly manufactured products, in any quantity. But the two greatest advantages are: first, all profits derived from exports are totally tax-free until 1983; second, all imports of Irish manufacture are exempted from U. K. import duty. All these factors are more than sufficient to make up for the extra costs of transportation to the U. K. market. There is the port of Limerick nearby for the normal shipment of our goods.

To sell the products on the U. K. market a sales subsidiary will be established in London to cover the immediate prime area and the rest of the "rich swath" referred to above. To take advantage of the exemption from U. K. import duty, as we would import semi- or wholly manufactured parts (for finishing or assembly) from the U. S. parent, we will establish our plant in the Shannon Industrial Estate. All the profits from the sales in the U. K. market will be taxed at the normal rates. The company will make considerable initial savings in the very low labor costs of manufacturing in Ireland, in the minimal rents, in the freedom from the property tax, and in the freedom from income taxation on the value added by the manufacturing process. To come under the heading of Irish manufacture it is necessary to assemble the parts imported from the U. S. A. with some element of Irish manufacturing. This will qualify the product for exemption from the 26 percent import duty on its sale value within the U. K. We have, by saving the greater cost of manufacturing or assembling in the U. K., lowered our actual overall costs. Furthermore, the fact of import duty exemption on the imported parts means that the high U.K. purchase tax will fall on a much lower end price: this will aid us in setting our prices at a low and competitive level, thus possibly securing an initial marketing advantage.

We now turn to the financial administration of our proposed operations.

Financing the Operation. The most important initial consideration, from the point of view of risk analysis, is that we can rely completely on the unconditional guarantee of the remittance of profits and dividends and the repatriation of capital, in both the U. K. and Ireland. (Ireland even guarantees the repatriation of capital and earnings in the investor's own currency.) Thus the only currency worries are the risk of devaluation of the pound and internal inflation in the U. K. Although the latter is a nuisance, it is not a serious problem from the company's point of view: inflation has been running at the rate of 3 to 4 percent in the U. K. over the last decade, on an annual basis, which compares not unfavorably with the rest of Western Europe. In the last two years prices have risen sharply, but it is hardly likely that this rate would be permitted to continue much longer. The former problem is causing continuing anxiety to all U. S. corporate treasurers, as it requires careful phasing of a firm's forward sales of the sterling receipts destined to be repatriated. At the moment, spot sterling is selling at \$2.3913, with a three-month forward discount of 1.625 cents; three months' forward cover is at an annual interest cost of 2.75 percent, and three months' covered arbitrage margin stands at 2.2 percent in favor of New York (on Treasury bills).

For the operation in Ireland we have available the facilities of the government-sponsored Industrial Credit Corporation, which is generous in its allocations of aid. In the U. K., foreign-owned corporations are required to secure Treasury permission before raising capital there. U. K. resident subsidiaries of U. S. firms must obtain consent from the Treasury before borrowing money there or before issuing shares or other securities. For normal expansion, such consent is freely given. Nonresident controlled companies are normally allowed to borrow in the U. K. to finance short-term assets, provided that their fixed assets are adequately financed by the parent company. Such finance is normally expected to be provided by the parent company from non-U. K. sources. In the U. K. incorporating a sales office as a separate company to handle the entire U. K. marketing operation neatly sidesteps the restrictions on long-term borrowing there (not to mention the cost, since the "prime rate" alone is usually 2 percentage points above bank rate, which now stands at 8 percent. The problem in the U. K. is to sell against the intense and established competition of British firms and Japanese, Italian, and German imports. In each price grouping we have priced our machines at about 10 percent below the modal price in those market sectors, the aim being to sell on a heavily advertised "best value for money" concept—one that is of ever increasing importance in the U. K. The only financing that the sales operation will need will be pure current asset finance. The machine inventories will be acquired on extended trade credit from our Irish plant. The vast majority of sales to end consumers will be on time payment; these will be financed by one of the large British hire purchase finance houses.

Sales to retailers will have to be financed by trade credit. This will be extended to them by the sales subsidiary, usually on 30/60 days net terms. This will also be financed by the subsidiary's parent company in Ireland.

The only immediate and constant cash expenses will be the rent of the office space, salaries and wages, advertising and distribution costs, and costs of warehousing the inventories. The initial insertion of cash into our London sales headquarters operations will be obtained from the Irish plant. Initially funds might not be forthcoming from banks. At a later stage we may take advantage of the British banks' preference for self-liquidating short-term loans—given an adequately low interest rate. The Irish operation will be able to obtain most of its finance from the Irish Government's Industrial Credit Corporation, with a strong argument based on the purely export nature of our operations to the United Kingdom. It is impossible to say whether the entire financial needs could be thus covered, for it would depend on the success of the individual negotiations. If the lesser proportion of the current financial requirements has to be raised elsewhere, the Irish banks and U. S. banks in Ireland are possible sources. Their rates are similar to those of the British banks, as the Irish bank rate moves in accordance with Britain's. As the Eurodollar three-months' deposit rate now stands at 7.75 percent, such loans would be little cheaper; and, frankly, they would be harder to obtain at the initial stage of operations as novel as ours. Novel, that is, in terms of normal British practices. And this may well be the criterion on which Zurich-type gnomes judge our application. All this, of course, is supplementary to the initial injection of equity capital from the U. S. parent, which we shall keep to the minimum for U. S. balance of payments considerations.

The fulcrum of our operations will be the Irish plant. This will be organized as a subsidiary company incorporated under Irish laws. The London sales office will be set up as a subsidiary company, with the express purpose of creating it as a separate legal entity. The special reason for this necessity is that it will be run at no profit. It will introduce the duty-free merchandise into the U. K. market and sell it to the retailer at the price paid to the Irish company. As stated above, the trade credit extended to retailers will be financed by the Irish parent, and the heavy expenses for promotion will also be borne by the Irish company. The crucial point here is that we shall be eliminating the need to pay British Corporation Tax, which stands at a *flat* rate of 42.5 percent, a high rate well worth avoiding. Until a law is passed insisting that firms make large taxable profits, we shall be making them without any tax liability: and if that time comes, all our legal costs for running battles against the Internal Revenue will have been adequately provided for. By then, anyway, our market penetration will be sufficiently great for us to weather any storm. In summary, we shall have neatly maximized our profits by minimizing our taxes. This is the situation in a nutshell: no corporation tax liability in the U. K., no income taxes on export-earned profits in Shannon till 1983, no property taxes, and no import duties to be paid anywhere. In 1984 we will have to reconsider these arrangements. But, by then, rich rewards will have been reaped from this venture. Of course, the experienced salesmen hired in London and the administrators and staff will be subject to personal income taxes averaging 32.1 percent—which is the effective standard rate. But the firm's only tax liabilities will be the purchase tax of about 33.3 percent, imposed on the c.i.f. value, and the S.E.T. and National Insurances taxes (which, as outlined above, will take up 9 to 12 percent of the weekly wage).

Therefore, it is in Ireland that all our costs will ultimately be met—given that all the U. K. costs will be financed from Shannon. Initially, we shall have to provide for only a third of total fixed assets costs, by equity capital. As the firm expands, debt will be acquired locally—or with a Eurodollar loan—given an improvement in borrowing rates. It is assumed that the Irish company will be set up as a private company; therefore, it will not be permitted to issue shares to the public. In the long term it may well be useful to go public and finance further expansion by share issues on the Dublin or London stock exchange, given Treasury permission. By then our size may well warrant such a conversion. At present, our working capital needs will be obtained by local borrowing.

To minimize our tax liabilities on remittances to the U. S. parent, we should reinvest one-half of our earnings, which will be tax free at origin. Fortunately no one yet considers Ireland a tax haven, and our activities are regarded as normal manufacturing and exporting operations. But apart from this neat side-stepping of the U. S. Revenue Act of 1962, there is a much more important reason for retention of half of our net income. This is to finance expansion, particularly to meet Japanese and Italian counter-measures in price-cutting and for increasingly heavy promotional outlays. This has not been specifically accounted for in the sales and expenses figures in the appendix: but after our initial market penetration, damaging competitors, we must make ample provision for countering stiff retaliation. Hence the overriding need to reinvest one-half of our earnings for the strengthening of the company's basic competitive capacity.

Against this, of course, in addition to all other costs of goods sold, will be charged depreciation on generous terms. The Irish Government allows for depreciation at 25 percent initially, and at 20 percent of the declining balance thereafter. These are special rates applicable to export operations such as ours. A further deduction for contingency reserves, for legal fees, etc., will be made where possible. Rapidly expanding retained earnings will be used to finance operations, hence, debt-servicing at high local loan rates will be unnecessary. As expropriation and devaluation considerations are negligible at the present, our initial operations will not be plagued with such concerns. Nevertheless, precaution is a financial virtue; we shall therefore lease our factory from the Irish Government. Ireland will provide us with a custom-built plant of 500,000 square feet, at around 20¢ per square foot. Our annual lease will amount to $100,000 per year. Our tooling costs will be $3 million, the government will furnish a grant of $2 million, and the U. S. parent will inject equity capital of $1 million.

Sales will be limited to England during the first seven years of operations and later expanded to the Sterling Area bloc, the European continent, and EFTA. If the U. K. is admitted into the E.E.C., trade with Europe could be undertaken earlier.

TABLE 5

Proforma Statement of Cost of Goods
Manufactured (Ireland–U. K.) in Thousands of Dollars

	1970	1971	1972	1973	1974
Work in Process	0	0	0	0	0
Raw Materials:					
Inventory	0	22	34	64	29
Purchases	242	265	330	313	390
Available	242	287	364	377	419
Less: Inventory	(22)	(34)	(64)	(29)	(29)
Material Total Cost	220	253	300	348	390
Direct Labor	310	351	410	481	530
Direct Factory	170	203	225	263	290
Indirect Labor	800	905	1050	1240	1350
Indirect Factory	260	291	335	396	430
Total	1540	1750	2020	2380	2600
Less: Work in Process	(0)	(0)	(0)	(0)	(0)
Cost of Goods Manufactured	1760	2003	2320	2728	2990

TABLE 6

Proforma Income Statement
(Ireland–U.K.) in Thousands of Dollars

	1970	1971	1972	1973	1974
Gross Sales	4250	5050	5950	6750	7650
Less: Discounts	(250)	(550)	(850)	(884)	(1000)
Net Sales	4000	4500	5100	5866	6650
Cost of Goods Sold					
Finished Goods	0	40	52	36	68
Cost of Goods Manufactured	1760	2003	2320	2728	2990
Goods Available for Sale	1760	2043	2372	2764	3058
Less: Finished Goods	(40)	(52)	(36)	(68)	(48)
Cost of Goods Sold	1720	1991	2336	2696	3010
Gross Profit on Sales	2280	2509	2764	3170	3640
Operating Expenses					
Advertising	1250	1250	1000	1000	1000
Dealer Administration	1100	1150	1200	1250	1300
Rent	100	100	100	100	100
Total Operating	2450	2500	2300	2350	2400
Net Income Before Tax	(170)	(09)	464	820	1240
Less: Estimated Tax	0	0	0	0	0
Net Income After Tax	(170)	(09)	464	820	1240

TABLE 7

Proforma Balance Sheet
(Ireland–U.K.) in Thousands of Dollars

	1970	1971	1972	1973	1974
Current Assets:					
Cash	300	300	508	1318	1728
Securities	0	225	1000	1000	1000
Accounts Receivable	354	420	495	562	800
Inventory: LCM					
Finished	110	143	88	176	176
Work in Progress	0	0	0	0	0
Raw Material	22	34	64	29	29
Total Current Assets	786	1122	2155	3085	3733
Land (leased)	0	0	0	0	0
Plant and Equipment	3000	3000	3000	3500	4500
Less: Accrued Depreciation	(600)	(1200)	(1800)	(2400)	(3100)
Total Assets	3186	2922	3355	4185	5133
Current Liabilities:					
Accounts Payable, Notes Payable:					
Local Accounts Payable	44	51	60	70	78
Notes Payable	250	0	0	0	0
Income Tax Payable	0	0	0	0	0
Interest Payable	62	50	10	10	10
Total Current Liabilities	356	101	70	80	88
Long-Term Liabilities Debt	0	0	0	0	0
Total Long-Term Liabilities	0	0	0	0	0
Stockholders Equity ($10 par):					
Local	2000	2000	2000	2000	2000
Foreign	1000	1000	1000	1000	1000
Retained Earnings	(170)	(179)	(285)	(1105)	(2045)
Total Liabilities and Capital	3186	2922	3355	4185	5133

TABLE 8

Proforma Retained Earnings Statement
(Ireland–U.K.) in Thousands of Dollars

	1970	1971	1972	1973	1974
Balance	0	(170)	(179)	285	1105
Net Income for Year After Tax	(170)	(09)	464	820	1240
Less: Dividends	0	0	0	0	300
Change in Retained Earnings	(170)	(09)	464	820	940
Balance	(170)	(179)	285	1105	2045

TABLE 9

Proforma Flow of Funds Statement
(Ireland–U.K.) in Thousands of Dollars

	1970	1971	1972	1973	1974
Source of Funds:					
Internal:					
Retained Earnings	(170)	(09)	464	820	1240
Depreciation	600	600	600	600	700
Total	430	591	1064	1420	1940
External:					
Short-Term Liabilities:					
Local	250	0	9	10	8
Foreign	0	0	0	0	0
Long-Term Liabilities:					
Local	0	0	0	0	0
Foreign	0	0	0	0	0
Equity:					
Local	2000	0	0	0	0
Foreign	1000	0	0	0	0
Total Funds Produced	3680	591	1073	1430	1948
Uses of Funds:					
Increase in Assets:					
Cash and Securities	300	225	983	810	410
Accounts Receivable	354	66	75	67	238
Inventory	132	45	41	216	0
Plant and Equipment	3000	0	0	500	1000
Land (leased)	100	100	100	100	100
Total	3886	436	1199	1693	1748
Decrease in Liabilities:					
Short-Term	0	250	0	0	0
Long-Term	0	0	0	0	0
Income Tax	0	0	0	0	0
Dividends	0	0	0	0	300
Interest	62	149	125	75	75
Total Funds Applied	3948	835	1324	1768	2123
Increase (Decrease) in Net Working Capital	(268)	(244)	(251)	(338)	(175)

TABLE 10

Sales (Units)

Machine	1970	1971	1972	1973	1974
A ($ 35)	50,000	60,000	70,000	80,000	90,000
B[a] ($ 50)	30,000	35,000	40,000	45,000	50,000
C[a] ($100)	10,000	12,000	15,000	17,000	20,000
Total	90,000	107,000	125,000	142,000	160,000

[a]Produced only on direct order

TABLE 11

Revenues (Ireland–U.K.)
in Millions of Dollars

Machine	1970	1971	1972	1973	1974
A ($ 35)	1.75	2.10	2.45	2.80	3.15
B ($ 50)	1.50	1.75	2.00	2.25	2.50
C ($100)	1.00	1.20	1.50	1.70	2.00
Total	4.25	5.05	5.95	6.75	7.65

TABLE 12

Production (Units) Totals of all Types (Ireland)

	1970	1971	1972	1973	1974
Planned Production	100,000	110,000	120,000	150,000	160,000
Beginning Inventory	0	10,000	13,000	8,000	16,000
Units Available for Sale	100,000	120,000	133,000	158,000	176,000
Established Sales	90,000	107,000	125,000	142,000	160,000
Ending Inventory	10,000	13,000	8,000	16,000	16,000

TABLE 13

Costs

Variable Dollar Costs	Machine A	Machine B[a]	Machine C[a]
Per unit of production:			
Materials	1.00	2.00	10.00
Direct Labor	2.00	3.00	10.00
Direct Factory Cost	1.00	2.00	5.00
Subtotal	4.00	7.00	25.00
Indirect Labor	5.00	10.00	20.00
Indirect Supplies	2.00	3.00	5.00
Subtotal	7.00	13.00	25.00
Total Variable Costs	11.00	20.00	50.00
Selling Price	35.00	50.00	100.00
Profit Margin	24.00	30.00	50.00

[a]Produced only on direct order

TABLE 14

Direct Materials Costs
Accounts Payable–Accounts Receivable (in Thousands of Dollars)

Machine	1970	1971	1972	1973	1974
A	60	63	70	88	90
B	60	70	80	90	100
C	100	120	150	170	200
Total	220	253	300	348	390
Accounts Payable[a]	44	51	60	70	78
Order Factor–Raw Materials[b]	1.1	1.05	1.1	0.9	1.0
Order (Thousands of Dollars)	242	265	330	313	390
Use	220	253	310	313	390
Carry Forward	22	12	20	0	0
Accounts Receivable 1/12 × Sales	354	420	495	562	800

[a]1/5 × Cost of Materials = Accounts Payable
[b]Factor used to order supplies

TABLE 15

Direct Labor and Material Costs[a] (in Thousands of Dollars)

Machine	Costs	1970	1971	1972	1973	1974
A	Material	60	63	70	88	90
	Labor	120	126	140	176	180
	Factory	60	63	70	88	90
	Total	240	252	280	352	360
B	Material	60	70	80	90	100
	Labor	90	105	120	135	150
	Factory	60	70	80	90	100
	Total	210	245	280	315	350
C	Material	100	120	150	170	200
	Labor	100	120	150	170	200
	Factory	50	60	75	85	100
	Total	250	300	375	425	500

Indirect Operating Costs

Machine	Costs	1970	1971	1972	1973	1974
A	Labor	300	315	350	440	450
	Supplies	120	126	140	176	180
	Total	420	441	490	616	630

TABLE 15—*continued*

Indirect Operating Costs

Machine	Costs	1970	1971	1972	1973	1974
B	Labor	300	350	400	450	500
	Supplies	90	105	120	135	150
	Total	390	455	520	585	650
C	Labor	200	240	300	340	400
	Supplies	50	60	75	85	100
	Total	250	300	375	425	500

[a]For production units see Tables 10 and 12.

TABLE 16

Financial Ratios

Financial Ratios	Formula Used	1970	1971	1972	1973	1974
Liquidity						
1. Current Ratio	$\dfrac{\text{Current Assets}}{\text{Current Liabilities}}$	2.1	11.1	30.7	38.0	42.0
2. Acid Test	$\dfrac{\text{Current Assets} - \text{Inventory}}{\text{Current Liabilities}}$	1.8	9.4	28.6	36.0	40.0
Leverage						
1. Debt to Total Assets	$\dfrac{\text{Total Debts}}{\text{Total Assets}}$	0	0	0	0	0
Activity						
1. Inventory Turnover	$\dfrac{\text{Net Sales}}{\text{Inventory}}$	36.5	31.5	57.5	33.0	38.0
2. Fixed Assets Turnover	$\dfrac{\text{Sales}}{\text{Fixed Assets}}$	1.7	2.5	4.2	5.3	4.7
3. Total Assets Turnover	$\dfrac{\text{Sales}}{\text{Total Assets}}$	1.25	1.5	1.5	1.4	1.3
Profitability						
1. Profit Margin on Sales	$\dfrac{\text{Net Profit After Taxes}}{\text{Sales}}$	–	–	.09	.14	.19
2. Return on Total Assets	$\dfrac{\text{N.P.A.T.}}{\text{Total Assets}}$	–	–	.14	.20	.24
3. Return on Net Worth	$\dfrac{\text{N.P.A.T.}}{\text{Net Worth}}$	–	–	.14	.20	.245

Notes to Financial Statements

1. Depreciation is on a straight line basis—five-year life.
2. Accounts Payable—1/5 x cost of materials necessary for year. *See* Table 14.
3. Accounts Receivable—1/12 x sales per year. Last year Accounts Receivable expanded to $800,000.
4. Work in Progress—Time each machine on assembly line short

Machine	Time on Line
A	0.66 hours
B	1.0
C	3.3

At Labor (with all benefits) $3.00/hour
5. Plant capacity initially 175,000 units.
6. Machine A Production:

Year	Units
1970	60,000
1971	63,000
1972	70,000
1973	88,000
1974	90,000

Machines B and C produced only on direct order.

TANILA MANUFACTURING CO., CHILE

Financial Planning: Decision-Making under Risk

Tanila Manufacturing Company,[1] a wholly owned subsidiary of Golcorp, a U. S.-based conglomerate, was established in Chile in 1963 to participate in the growing Chilean economy. In 1969 Tanila's annual sales were Es. 50 million. Annual growth of sales is 15 percent. Average net operating income since 1967 has been 10 percent of the yearly sales figures.

Golcorp management granted substantial autonomy to its overseas managers whose performance is measured by the profitability of the subsidiaries under their control.

1. All the names and figures used in the case study are fictitious to disguise the identity of the company and protect its competitive position.

THE PROBLEM

In 1969, John Earle, the financial manager of Tanila, has on hand Es. 20 million from the sale of some excess company land. He wants to employ these funds in the best way for the next year and a half, at which time Tanila will need the funds for a planned expansion. There exist two possible ways to invest the funds:

1. A term bank deposit with no possible withdrawal privileges until the end of the eighteen-month period. The interest rate guaranteed for the first twelve months was 36 percent (compounded semi-annually) and the following six months, 26 percent.
2. Government six-month bills paying 5 percent per annum plus the official rate of inflation. Assume no transaction costs.

Because of the planned expansion, Mr. Earle decides to use an eighteen-month planning horizon.

Since the bank rate is assured over the planning horizon, Mr. Earle is interested in seeing if he can, by buying six-month bills, make a better profit on the slight interest rate differential which might occur from the government being better able to evaluate the rate of inflation on the shorter term basis than the bank's two-year projection.

STRATEGIES

Mr. Earle is interested in the strategy which will yield greater expected return when all the risks and uncertainties have been considered and properly discounted (*see* Figure 1). The return on bank deposits is a straightforward compound interest rate calculation. The calculations of the return on the government bills require an expected value payoff matrix with the assignment of subjective probabilities.

To assist him in evaluating the situation and aid him in his judgment of the subjective probabilities of inflation, Mr. Earle has a report from a bank which provides him with economic information on Chile. Reports from this bank have been reliable in the past, and Mr. Earle has confidence in them.

The bank report is reproduced below:

BANK REPORT

Facts about Chile

Government: Democratic; bicameral legislature; Eduardo Frei, President since 1964 (Christian Democrat).

Finance: Consistent budget deficit; high rate of inflation; rising cost of living.

Background of Chile: Chile's experience with currency devaluation and the associated inflation of the domestic economy extends back some forty years in varying degrees of severity. The underlying problems have been many and changing, but perhaps such a long history has produced a certain amount of "inflation psychology" with the governments and the consumers.

FIGURE 1

Possible Decision Strategies

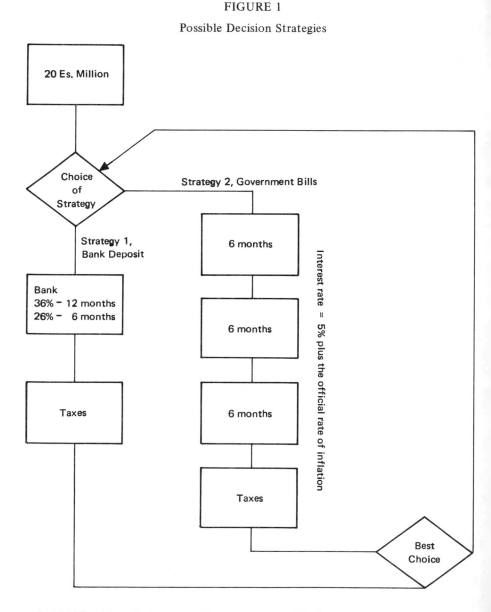

In 1964 President Frei and his Christian Democratic Party were elected to power largely on their promises to overhaul the domestic economy and to maintain the purchasing power of the consumers. The government started ambitious programs of agrarian reform, of revitalizing the social security system, of expanding the educational system, all of which entailed large government expenditures.

The government also protected the consumer by passing a bill authorizing automatic wage increases to match inflation. This bill was strongly opposed in many quarters, particularly by Congress, before its eventual adoption. The result of this additional purchasing power has been the development of a classic wage/price spiral with too much money chasing too few goods. This demand/pull inflation has been further compounded by a growing, cultured middle class who are demanding products before the prices rise even higher.

Some small consolation could be obtained if domestic productivity were increasing at a rapid rate, but the reverse is true. In 1968 the GNP rose 2.1 percent in real quantity, and the forecast for 1969 was for a rise of less than 2.5 percent. Such slow growth in productivity accentuates the inflationary gap produced by the large government expenditures and public consumption.

General Analysis: Chile has a highly inflationary yet recessed economy. There are several reasons for recession. Government investment has failed to expand as rapidly as real wages. Income redistribution has been unsatisfactory. A severe drought, which ended in May 1969, decreased agricultural output and resulted in rationing of electrical power. As a consequence, the production of copper—the country's main export commodity—declined by 6 percent in 1968. Prices rose 14 percent during the first quarter of 1969 (versus a 10 percent rise in the same quarter of 1968). A further price increase of at least 30 percent was expected for 1969, accompanied by a foreign trade deficit (imports of Es. 1.16 billion versus exports of Es. 960 million expected).

Outlook: We believe that 1970 will be a politically significant year for Chile since President Frei and the Christian Democratic Party are required by law to retire from office. The problem of inflation will become a major campaign issue with the candidates again offering new solutions. As past history has shown, however, the problems facing the economy cannot be solved overnight, and it is therefore considered that the short-term policy will necessarily accord with that of the present government.

A study of representative indices showed that the inflationary trend of the first seven months of 1969 was remarkably consistent, and this conclusion was also indicated by the consistent rate of devaluation (*see* Table 1).

The effect of the drought will be felt until the end of 1969. Since the government is making efforts to decrease the rate of inflation (at least to stabilize it at around 25 percent), we feel that by the middle of 1970 production rates and the inflation rate will have returned to approximately mid-1968 levels.

ASSESSMENT OF FUTURE INFLATIONARY CONDITIONS

From the bank report, Mr. Earle derives the graph of inflation as it has occurred in the past (Figure 2). From this he attempts to project what the rate of inflation is likely to be in the next eighteen months.

On the basis of the bank report, Mr. Earle judged that more favorable conditions can be expected in the future. Assuming the inflation rate of 30 percent for the first six months as a certainty, he feels that inflation will ease somewhat and decrease to around the 25 percent rate in about one year.

Mr. Earle derives the following subjective probabilities for the probable rates of inflation for the eighteen months (*see* Table 2). In deriving the probabilities and making the calculations, Mr. Earle assumes that the assessment of the rates of inflation are independent events.

TABLE 1

Representative Indices (Percent)

	1962	1963	1964	1965	1966	1967	1968	1969
Consumer Price Index	69	100	146	188	231	273	346	480
Prices (Home Goods)	68	100	152	202	256	306	391	561
Discount Rate	14.62	14.21	14.63	15.30	15.84	15.84	16.61	19.59

TABLE 2

Projected Inflation

Rate of Inflation / Six-Month Periods	Probability of Occurrence			
	35	30	25	20
1	1.0			
2		.60	.60	.10
3		.10	.70	.20

TAXATION: CHILE

To keep the model simple, Mr. Earle assumes that taxes are paid at the time of the interest realization, i.e., at the end of the eighteen months.

Explanation of Taxes

1. Base Tax: This 30 percent is the basic tax applied to the operating income of Chilean incorporated companies.
2. Cost of Living Surtax: The rationale for this tax is that the government has officially recognized the country's high rate of inflation and, in doing so, has assumed a policy of allowing firms to revalue their entire asset structure by the officially declared rate of inflation. At the same time, it is clear that a portion of the net earnings is due to this inflationary increase; therefore, the government imposes a cost of living surtax to counteract the dilution of tax revenue by inflation. The tax law states that if taxes are paid at the time returns are due, then only 50 percent of this cost of living surtax need be applied, i.e., 15 percent of the net operating income.
3. Housing Tax: The other tax requirement is that of a compulsory housing investment. All business enterprises are required to invest 5 percent of

FIGURE 2
Inflation Projection

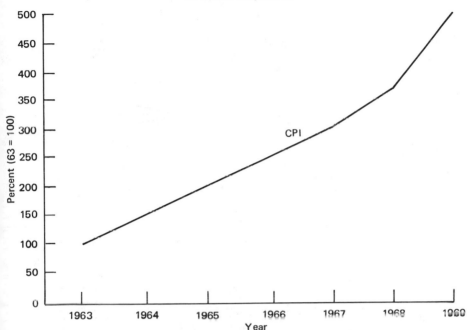

SOURCE: Table 1.

their net taxable income in housing programs, and if such investment is not made within specific periods the amount not invested must be paid as part of the income tax. There is obviously an opportunity for interim investment of these cash flows; to keep the model simple, however, assume that the tax is paid at the end of the eighteen months.

PAYOFF MATRIX

Based on the bank report, and after taking into consideration the impact of Chilean taxes, Mr. Earle then calculated the expected payoffs for the two alternative investment strategies (Tables 3 to 5).

APPENDIX I

Supplemental Information

DECISION-MAKING UNDER CERTAINTY, RISK, AND UNCERTAINTY

Certainty: Decision-making under certainty occurs when we have a decision problem in which we know with certainty which state of nature will occur.

TABLE 3

Expected Value Payoff Matrix
Government Bills

Six-Month Periods[a]

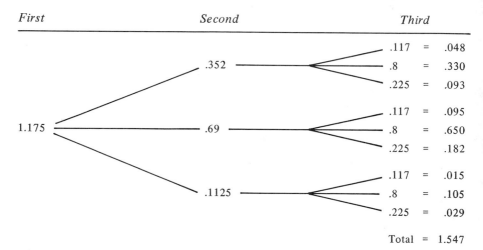

First	Second	Third

1.175

.352
- .117 = .048
- .8 = .330
- .225 = .093

.69
- .117 = .095
- .8 = .650
- .225 = .182

.1125
- .117 = .015
- .8 = .105
- .225 = .029

Total = 1.547

[a]Figures calculated by multiplying probability of rate of inflation (Table 2) by the interest rate per period. .30 probability of rate of 30 percent inflation X 1.175 = .352. For the next period it would be 1.175 X .10 = .117, 1.150 X .70 = .8, 112.5 X .20 = .225, and so on.

TABLE 4

Calculations

Rate of Return – Bank Deposit

	6 months		6 months		6 months		
	36% p.a.		36% p.a.		26% p.a.		
Factor	1.18	X	1.18	X	1.13	=	1.58

Rate of Return – Government Bills

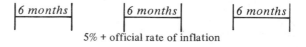

|6 months| |6 months| |6 months|

5% + official rate of inflation

factor (Table 3) – 1.547

Risk: This decision problem occurs where there are a number of states of nature but where the decision-maker knows the probability of occurrence of each of the states of nature. The probability of the various states is determined by how frequently the event has occurred in the past.

TABLE 5

Comparative Returns and Risks

Millions Es.

Return	Bank	Government Bills
Gross Taxable Return		
Es. 20 Million X factor	11.6	10.94
Less Tax 50 percent	(5.8)	(5.47)
Net Gain After Tax		
(Expected Payoff)	5.8	5.47
Risk	None	Some

Conclusion: On the basis of his analysis, Mr. Earle decides to invest his funds in the bank.

Uncertainty: This problem exists where the probability of occurrence of the various states of nature is not known—where there is no basis for estimating probabilities from past experience.

COMPOUND PROBABILITY AND INDEPENDENT EVENTS

Two or more events are said to be joint or compound if they occur in unison or in sequence. Joint events are said to be independent if the outcome of one does not affect, and is not affected by, the other. That is, if events are independent, the occurrence or nonoccurrence of any event in one trial will not in any way affect the probability of any other event in any other trial.

$$P(A \cap B) = P(AB) = P(A)P(B)$$

EXPECTATION

Expectation is called by many other names, such as the mathematical expectation, the expected value, or simply the mean of a random variable. The mathematical expectation of a random variable is the sum of the products that are obtained by multiplying all possible values of the random variables by their corresponding probabilities.

$$E(X) = x_1 f(x_1) + x_2 f(x_2), + \ldots x_n f(x_n)$$

where $f(x)$ = probability of event.

SUBJECTIVE PROBABILITIES

The subjective theorist regards probability as a measure of personal confidence in a particular proposition. A subjectivist would assign a weight between zero and one to an event, according to his degree of belief in its possible occurrence. In general, the probabilities he assigns to various events for a given proposition are weighted averages, adding up to unity.

COMPOUND INTEREST

Formula:

$$s = (1.0 + i)^n$$

where: i = amount of interest per period
n = number of periods paying interest

Example:

36 percent interest per year compounded semi-annually ($n = 2$)

$$s = (1.0 + .18)^2$$

COMMERCIAL NAVIGATION CO., U. S. A.

Hedging Strategy to Protect Against Foreign Exchange Losses in Long-Term Overseas Contracts: Deutschemark Revaluation and Aftermath

Commercial Navigation,[1] a major nonsubsidized shipping company in the domestic and foreign trades, is a leader in both the development of mechanized ship loading and unloading through the use of containerized freight and in the development of specialized vessels for transporting bulk raw sugar, molasses, and automobiles. Their engineering research and development for the design of containers, vessels, and related port facilities, begun early in the 1960s, has brought faster, lower-cost freight service. In the course of developing this innovative freight

---

1. All the names and figures used in the case study are fictitious to disguise the identity of the company and protect its competitive position.

handling service, Commercial Navigation has converted existing freighters to container-type vessels.

There are various reasons for this recent activity. Although the existing operations are primarily between domestic ports, the company anticipates expanding its foreign-trade market share with the transition to containerized vessels. This objective not only stems from the existing potential but from the anticipated increasingly competitive atmosphere in foreign trade. Commercial Navigation is one of the few domestic companies operating completely containerized ships in foreign trade. However, Japanese shipping firms recently have begun operations with such ships, and at least one American carrier has also announced similar plans. It was believed further that many more carriers would begin containerized operations in the near future.

As a result of this increased competitive atmosphere, Commercial Navigation, in addition to conversion activities, decided to purchase two new container ships. This expansion was believed desirable, considering the greater capacity and speed of the newer vessels. For example, in December 1968 the *Economist* wrote:

> A transport revolution is spreading rapidly throughout the industrialized world. The spearhead of that revolution is the cargo container, a simple aluminum or steel box with doors at one end.
>
> The big container operators are now seeking to integrate road, rail, and sea transport by moving containers rapidly and mechanically between each form of transport. The key to this through-transport system lies in the standardization of the containers, and more important, the standardization of the fixtures and fittings needed to carry and fasten the containers on each form of transport.
>
> The result is a radical reduction in transport costs and a big improvement in transit times. But the impact of the cargo container is out of all proportion to the relative simplicity of the idea.

Upon close consideration of the major shipbuilders' bids, it was concluded that a German shipbuilder could provide the best contract. (No construction subsidies were available to Commercial at the time.) Although the Japanese have been the leaders in total ship production, although mostly tankers, and the Swedes have substantially increased their production in the recent past (Figure 1), the German shipyards hold a leading position in the building of special freighter ships. So it was not surprising that the most suitable contract in terms of specifications was presented by a German shipbuilder.

MARITIME SUBSIDIES

A major consideration of any shipping firm is the Maritime Laws and their implications for transporting merchandise between various geographic locations. Commercial Navigation consulted their attorneys on the relevant statutes. Because they intended to use the vessels in foreign trade, there was no apparent violation of the law.

FIGURE 1

Shipbuilding in Selected Countries 1960 to 1967

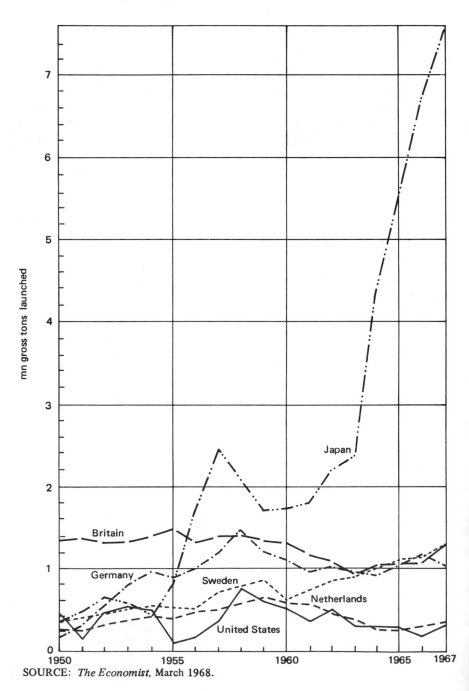

SOURCE: *The Economist,* March 1968.

Specifically:

> No merchandise shall be transported by water, or by land and water, on penalty
> of forfeiture thereof, between points in the United States, including Districts,
> Territories, and possessions thereof embraced within the coastwise laws, either
> directly or via a foreign port, or for any part of the transportation in any other
> vessel than a vessel built in and documented under the laws of the United States
> and owned by persons who are citizens of the United States, or vessels to which
> the privilege of engaging in the coastwise trade is extended by section 13 or 808
> of this title.[1]

Although no incipient violation was evident, certain potential ship-construction
benefits were sacrificed as a result of importing the vessel: the federal government
guarantee on bonds if used to finance domestic construction, and the loss of
potential direct grants of up to 60 percent of construction costs (Table 1).

After taking into consideration the domestic construction differential subsidy,
the German ship was still more desirable in terms of both price and contract
specifications.

The choice of a German builder and the terms and specifications of the contract
placed Commercial Navigation, as the buyer, in a position of having to choose
between major financing alternatives. The contract called for a 5 percent down
payment, then further payments from approximately fifteen months until the end
of the thirty-month contract. The total price for the two vessels was nearly
DM 80 million (U.S. $10 million per vessel).

Since the 1961 revaluation, the Deutschemark, reflecting the state of affairs in
the German economy, had been increasing in strength as an international currency.
Although the trend was evident, it was accompanied by minor fluctuations which
will become more important as this paper progresses.

The German government is pledged under International Monetary Fund rules to
"support" the price of the Deutschemark (DM) by preventing it from fluctuating
more than 1 percent of the originally agreed upon par value in the "spot" market—
the price paid for prompt delivery. Variations in the "future" market; i.e., promise
to sell/buy at some decided future date and price, are of no immediate concern to
the German government and thus fluctuate according to the market's anticipation
of the future value of the mark ("spot" price) plus some small transaction cost.
Consequently major disparities in the "spot" and "future" prices reflect particular
anticipation about the value of the currency in the future. This in fact was the
situation with the Deutschemark at the time of the contract negotiations with the
builder in the spring of 1968. There had been considerable fluctuation of the spot
and future markets during this period (Figure 2).

This situation triggered the buyer's detailed analysis of the financial ramifications
of the contract specifications with the builder. In the initial stages much of the
financial analysis was devoted to alternative methods of contract payment including
provision for prepayment. At the time economists and various government officials

1. Title 46. Merchant Marine Act. Chapter 24.

TABLE 1

Who Gives Subsidies, and How

Country	Direct Grants		Indirect Assistance					Tariff Protection		
	Shipbuilders	Ship-owners	Credits/ Loans	Export Credits	Export Credit Insurance	Tax Relief	Special Depreciation Allowances	Duty Waived on Imported Components	Other	Research Grants
Britain	£37½ million for rationalization	Investment grants for U.K. shipowners	Up to £200 million credit at 5½%	Yes	Yes	Export rebates, investment rebates	Yes	Yes	–	Yes
Japan	–	Subsidies for scrapping	Japan Dev Bank: 5-6 yr loans for up to 60% of price at 8.7%	Two kinds: Ex-IM bank gives 8 yrs covering 56% of price. Government gives 10 yr credits for 70–100%.	Yes	Partial exemption on exports	Yes	For exports ships only	Tariff on imported ships	Yes
France	11% of contract price	Compensation for high operating costs	20 yr modernization loans at 5%	Yes	Yes	Investment rebates	–	Certain goods only	Import licenses	–

Country	Direct Grants		Credits/ Loans	Indirect Assistance				Tariff Protection		
	Shipbuilders	Ship-owners		Export Credit	Export Credit Insurance	Tax Relief	Special Depreciation Allowances	Duty Waived on Imported Components	Other	Research Grants
Italy	12/15% of price	Subsidies for scrapping	15 yr loans for up to 60% of price. Government paying first 3½% of interest	Yes	Yes	Turnover tax exemption	Yes	Partial	Import licenses	Yes
Germany	—	Investment grants	12 yr modernization loans at 5-6%. Shorter term at 5½%	Yes Up to 80% of price	Yes	Investment rebates	—	Yes	—	Yes
Netherlands	—	—	Subsidized credit	—	Yes	Turnover tax exemption, relief on replacement and scrapping	Yes	Yes	—	—
Sweden	Special subsidy to 1 yard	—	Credit guarantees	Yes	Yes	Turnover tax exemption. Investment rebates	Yes	Yes	—	—

TABLE 1 –continued

Country	Direct Grants		Indirect Assistance					Tariff Protection		
	Shipbuilders	Ship-owners	Credits/Loans	Export Credits	Export Credit Insurance	Tax Relief	Special Depreciation Allowances	Duty Waived on Imported Components	Other	Research Grants
Norway	–	Investment grant, subsidies for scrappint	Credit guarantees. Loans for 50–60% of price at 5½–6%.	–	Yes	–	Yes	Duty reimbursed	–	–
Denmark	–	–	Credit guarantees 15 yr loans for up to 80% of price	Yes	Yes	Turnover tax exemption	Yes	Duty reimbursed	–	–
U. S. A.	–	Up to 60% of construction costs. Operating subsidy	Credit guarantees. 25 yr loans for up to 25% of price at 3½%. Ships trading abroad only.	–	Yes	Tax concessions for rebuilding and conversion	Yes	–	Ban on importing ships for domestic trades	Yes

SOURCE: The *Economist*, March 1968.

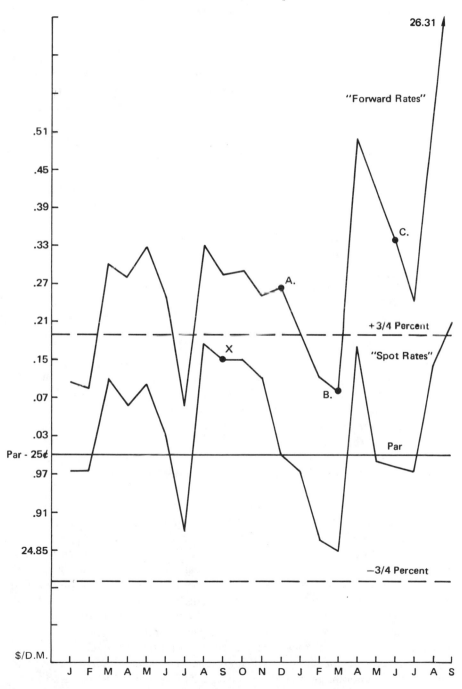

FIGURE 2

Movement of Forward and Spot Rates

229

predicted that should revaluation take place (although German officials denied any possibility of devaluation), the increase in the relationship of the Deutschemark to the U.S. dollar would be approximately 7 percent. With the contract price of DM 80 million and 95 percent exposure (5 percent down payment) the potential dollar loss (based on an assumption, for the moment, that both before and after revaluation the "spot" prices paid would be the old and new par values) would be approximately $1,333,000. This potential loss was sufficient motivation to develop a strategic hedging alternative. An extra impetus was added when during the summer of 1968 there were wide movements in the spot and future rates for the Deutschemark.

In developing a hedging strategy the management insisted that three fundamental objectives must be met.

1. The contract "atmosphere" in no way should be jeopardized.
2. The gain from hedging must be greater than the cost.
3. No violation of U.S. foreign exchange laws would be incurred.

After looking into various options, the management reduced its choices to three basic alternatives for detailed analysis and consideration.

CHOICE OF ALTERNATIVES

The first alternative was prepayment of a large percentage of the contract price. This would be accomplished by September purchase of Deutschemarks in the "spot" foreign exchange market for immediate payment to the builder. The buyer, who had established a line of credit for a revolving term loan with a domestic bank consortium in order to finance the ship purchase, could draw on the term loan for prepayment funds. In addition, the builder had agreed to rebate a percentage of any prepaid amount. The rebate would be based upon the amount over and above the required contract payment schedule. Coincidentally this rebate percentage was exactly equal to the interest rate charged by the domestic bank consortium. Thus the U.S. dollars could be borrowed, exchanged for Deutschemarks, and prepaid to the builder who in turn would rebate the cost of borrowing. It appeared that this form of hedging would result in no cost to the buyer.

There was, however, one major qualitative sacrifice with this alternative. The buyer would lose a certain amount of leverage—negotiating ability—over possible unforeseen detailed contract specifications. Jeopardizing the buyer's future bargaining position by prepaying the contract price was naturally highly undesirable, considering the size and complexity of the project. Somewhat less important, but still a consideration, was the builder's possible default after prepayment. However, after examining the builder's financial position, history, and size, Commercial was satisfied with the builder's ability to honor the contract.

The second alternative action considered was entering the "future" market—rather than the "spot" market as above—so that the forward purchase agreement dates coincided with the payment schedule. The first major payment was approximately eighteen months away; thus the buyer would "promise" to buy, vis-à-vis the forward market, the necessary amount of Deutschemarks to match the payment requirements. There were, however, two major drawbacks associated with this alternative. First, the payment schedule, again reflecting the complexity of the project, could not be accurately predicted.

Second, assuming the prediction could be made, purchasing 60 million DM more than one year in advance would be difficult. The forward market simply did not have the "depth." That is, there was insufficient supply in September at prices that would make the transaction a hedge. Exchange traders were unwilling to risk the exposure without a sizable price concession. This could have been circumvented by purchasing smaller amounts at different intervals or by purchasing the full amount on a three-month future (this market appears to possess the depth to handle a large transaction) and renewing the transaction each time it came due—thus remaining hedged in a price which "traveled" close to the spot price. The cost and confusion of such an alternative certainly left much to be desired. Multiple transactions with their costs calculated on the spread between the spot and future prices could result in the buyer becoming a victim of de facto revaluation. (*See* points A, B, C in Figure 2.) This alternative appeared to be self-defeating.

The third alternative considered was similar to the first in that it entailed borrowing domestically and exchanging for Deutschemarks. The similarity ended there, however. Rather than prepay the builder it was thought wiser to lend the marks at a rate equal to or greater than the domestic borrowing rate—that is, equal to the builder's promised rebate percentage. This appeared to embrace the best of both worlds; i.e., a hedge against revaluation with the loan contracted in marks and no sacrifice of leverage. The builder would continue to finance himself thus assuring the buyer that the builder would remain more willing to satisfy any future reasonable specification demands. In addition, potential default on the part of the builder, although not a major consideration, would not be applicable.

This alternative was not without its problems. Finding a borrower of Deutschemarks who would agree to a fifteen-day call notice—the period of time that the builder agreed to notify the buyer of a payment due—would be extremely difficult. For a loan of marks to a foreigner, the implications of the interest equalization tax or the foreign direct investment restrictions added further discouragement to this alternative.

SELECTION OF A STRATEGY

After close evaluation of all the relevant factors, the second and third alternatives were rejected. Consequently prepaying the builder was believed to be the best hedge against revaluation while at the same time preserving the essence of the original contract. The two most influential factors in the prepayment decision were:

1. A borrower of Deutschemarks who was willing to return them under a proposed schedule and on a fifteen-day call basis proved to be impossible

to locate under reasonable terms and within the time-frame allotted. This simply was a reflection of the low interest rates (in Germany) resulting from an influx of supply of short-term capital hoping to gain from both interest and currency appreciation.

2. The mechanics of matching the payments of the construction schedule with forward purchases of marks proved too costly to undertake. The cost of purchasing forward marks in the volume needed, represented, in fact, a revaluation of nearly 6 percent in September.

The New York Foreign Exchange Market had insufficient marks on the September purchase day, so the buyer went to the German Central Bank. This situation was viewed by the management as an indication that their decision was prudent. The "dried up" market exemplified the desirability of being "long" on Deutschemarks and thus reinforced the buyer's anticipation of a currency revaluation.

One of the major problems with the prepayment alternatives, as was stated above, was the loss of leverage in negotiating any unforeseen specification problems. To circumvent this the buyer prepaid 80 percent of the contract price (including the initial 5 percent down payment). This was estimated to approximate the builder's profit margin. It was calculated that the 20 percent exposure to revaluation was worth the gain in leverage obtained.

Some minor improvements in the basic alternative selected were also considered and discarded. For example:

With a hedging cost of nearly zero, the only other possible motivations for choosing a different alternative would be either a 100 percent reduction of exposure (as opposed to 80 percent), or better yet, no exposure and a net gain from the actions taken. For example, purchase of short-term government obligations could have resulted in a 100 percent reduction in exposure. However, this action was costly due to the interest equalization tax and the difference between the bank term loan rate and the return from the German government obligations.

Although the management was quite satisfied on the soundness of this decision, the financial vice-president had some reservations on the wisdom of the *timing* of their purchase of DM's and wondered if it would have been more prudent for the company to postpone the purchases for another three to five months to prepay the price of the ships.

AFTERMATH OF THE REVALUATION

Shortly after the Deutschemark revaluation, the company found itself deeply rooted in an entirely new, although related, problem: As a consequence of the revaluation, the prepaid DM's resulted in a potential realized gain of nearly $1,200,000. This raised, among others, the following questions:

1. Does Commercial Navigation in fact have a recognizable gain for income tax purposes on the revaluation of the mark?
2. Assuming a gain, what action should the company take to make this gain official and is the gain capital or ordinary?

3. What is the purchase price of the vessels expressed in U.S. dollars for tax purposes (depreciation)?

The vice-president for finance asked his financial analyst to make a study of all aspects of the situation and to outline a course of action for the company to follow.

CATERPILLAR MITSUBISHI LIMITED, JAPAN

Organization and Management of U. S. - Japan Joint Venture Operation

In the fall of 1963 Caterpillar Tractor Co., U.S.A., the world's largest manufacturer of earth-moving equipment, and Mitsubishi Heavy Industries, Ltd., a large Japanese conglomerate entered into a joint venture (Caterpillar Mitsubishi Limited) to manufacture tractors and other earthmoving equipment in Japan. The project was the culmination of more than four years of intensive study of the Japanese market by Caterpillar and included all facets of operating in the Japanese economy by a foreign company. The resulting plant, located in Sagamihara, thirty-five miles southeast of Tokyo, covers an area of 2.3 million square feet, and is one of the largest specialized tractor manufacturing plants in the Far East. It is also the largest subsidiary in Caterpillar's network of overseas operations.

Caterpillar Tractor Company, U. S. A., headquartered in Peoria, Illinois, ranked forty-second in Fortune's list of 500 U.S. manufacturing corporations in 1969. It manufactures more than 150 items of heavy earthmoving equipment. Its advancement from a major domestic manufacturing company into a multinational corporation is typical of a large exporter expanding its manufacturing facilities into the major markets of the world. Chairman of the Board, W. Blackie, and President, W. H. Franklin, are very much aware of the company's growing dependence on foreign subsidiaries and affiliated companies for sales and revenues. A great proportion of the potential for Caterpillar growth lies outside the U.S. where its machines and equipment are needed for the economic development of nations. Caterpillar sales outside the U.S. generally exceed 40 percent of its total annual volume and the company is understood to be one of the nation's largest exporters.[1] In 1969 Caterpillar's total sales amounted to $2,001.6 million, of which $951.7 million, or 47 percent, were foreign sales.

Caterpillar employment increased to a record of 65,862 people at 1969 year end, of whom 13,161 worked abroad. This multinational organization has twenty-nine

1. Caterpillar Tractor Company, U.S.A., Annual Report, 1969.

plants and parts warehouses in the U.S. with nineteen similar units located throughout the world. The operations are grouped into four regional divisions: U.S. Commercial Division, Canada-Latin America, Europe-Africa-Middle East, and Australia-New Zealand-Asia.

Caterpillar's product policy is, "When it bears the brand name Caterpillar, it is Caterpillar, and the source of manufacture is of no consequence. Design and quality are the same everywhere as is parts' interchangeability."[2]

CATERPILLAR'S ENTRY
INTO JAPAN

Caterpillar became aware of Japan's market when various Japanese firms showed interest in establishing a relationship with them. According to a company spokesman, "Initial surveys began in 1959 and 1960, and it might be well to say that as a result of these early surveys and the potential that was available there, the conditions under which a company would have to be organized were not felt to be satisfactory and our company turned down the proposition."[3]

Continued requests from Japanese firms prompted Caterpillar to make additional surveys in 1961 and 1962. The results were more favorable as the Japanese market for tractors had grown tremendously since the last survey (Table 1). The comparable figures for tractor and bulldozer production in the United States and Japan are presented in Table 2. From these facts, it was evident that there was a lucrative and expanding market potential for someone who might want to get in there and work with the Japanese and establish a market for a good product. It was also learned that imports into Japan were negligible due to tariff protection and import quotas. The survey team described the machines then being manufactured in Japan as "copies of American built machines." The company decided that with the growth potential and the state of technology which existed in Japan, there was room for one more competitor and Caterpillar could probably fill that role.

TABLE 1

Production of Tractors in Japan

Year	Number of Units
1955	500
1960	4,800
1961	7,500
1962	11,000

The market alone was not the overriding factor that nudged Caterpillar into the manufacturing business in the Far East. Other considerations were pertinent to this decision. After World War II most of the countries of the world, both developed and underdeveloped, encouraged industrialization within their borders, often

2. Ibid.
3. Interview with the author.

TABLE 2

Tractor and Bulldozer Production Comparisons: United States and Japan
(in Thousands of Units and Millions of U.S. Dollars)

Item and Country	1963 Units	1963 Dollars	1964 Units	1964 Dollars	1965 Units	1965 Dollars	1966 Units	1966 Dollars	1967 Units	1967 Dollars	1968 Units	1968 Dollars
Crawler Tractors												
U.S.	34.1	$454	39.3	$548	39.7	$594	40.0	$623	29.3	$504	32.0	$600
Japan	12.9	176	13.4	179	11.2	154	15.7	203	20.3	257	26.9	349
Bulldozers												
U.S.	22.6	314	26.9	393	27.2	428	28.6	476	20.9	378	22.5	453
Japan	—	—	—	—	6.3	90	7.7	101	9.6	125	13.3	180
Tractor Shovels												
U.S.	11.5	140	12.4	154	12.5	166	11.4	147	3.4	126	9.5	146
Japan	—	—	—	—	4.9	64	8.0	102	10.7	133	13.9	169
Crawler Tractors												
Under 100 hp												
U.S.	—	—	—	—	18.3	—	19.0		12.3		13.9	
Japan	—	—	—	—	3.1	—	5.7		7.5		11.5	
Over 100 hp												
U.S.	—	—	—	—	21.4	—	21.0		16.9		18.0	
Japan	—	—	—	—	8.1	—	10.0		12.7		15.4	
Bulldozers												
Under 100 hp												
U.S.	—	—	—	—	11.6	—	12.0		7.8		8.6	
Japan	—	—	—	—	1.8	—	3.3		4.0		6.0	
Over 100 hp												
U.S.	—	—	—	—	15.6	—	16.6		13.1		13.9	
Japan	—	—	—	—	4.6	—	4.4		5.5		7.5	
Tractor Shovels												
U.S.	—	—	—	—	6.7	—	7.0		4.5		5.3	
Japan	—	—	—	—	1.3	—	2.4		3.5		6.0	

behind high tariff walls to dissuade imports of all kinds including those of tractors. A dollar shortage prevailed over much of the world and many countries found it difficult to purchase American tractors because of their foreign exchange situation. Under such adverse conditions for American exports, Caterpillar sought to protect its foreign markets and overseas sales by establishing its own subsidiaries abroad. By producing tractors locally in foreign countries, the tariff barriers could be circumvented. Much of the freight costs could be eliminated. Most important, these subsidiaries would become an important part of the local economies by contributing to wages, taxes, and overall growth. Thus, the expansion into Japan was the result of a policy that even today plays a dominant role in Caterpillar's worldwide sales effort.

One of the main reasons not yet mentioned for the entrance into Japan was to establish a foothold in the Far East, which at that time had no foreign-owned manufacturing plants.

MINISTRY OF TRADE AND INDUSTRY (MITI), JAPAN

Establishing a foothold in Japan is difficult. No other country in the world presents such impregnable barriers and constraints. The rules and regulations for entry into Japan are established and enforced by the Ministry of Trade and Industry (MITI).

In the early 1960s the rules for a foreign-owned company to enter into Japan were quite restrictive and often not clear-cut. Since then MITI has gradually relaxed the entry conditions and has allowed foreign capital to establish facilities or buy into Japanese-owned companies. The ambiguity of the entry requirements notwithstanding, the major aim of the Japanese government has been to protect domestic industries and firms from foreign competition and dominance. MITI and Japan have been hesitant about allowing American giants to gain a foothold in the Japanese market for fear that some day they might emerge as dominant economic forces outside government control.

In 1963 it was a considerable accomplishment for Caterpillar to gain entry into such a market, where the Japanese were so ill-prepared to compete with an American firm. A company spokesman stated:

> In practice, MITI was very reluctant to approve joint venture companies where the foreign investors had more than 15 to 20 percent equity. In our particular case, they were anxious to have our company in Japan because they felt we did have considerable technical knowledge to contribute to the general art and industrial development.

Knowing how unyielding MITI had been in previous situations, Caterpillar, which had hitherto adhered to a policy of 100 percent ownership of its overseas subsidiaries, accepted that such a move would never be allowed by MITI. Caterpillar, therefore, started looking for a Japanese partner in order to establish operations in Japan.

THE BUSINESS ENVIRONMENT

A corporation desiring to enter a foreign market must proceed cautiously. Regardless of the extent of its experience, each venture is unique and must be handled separately from any other. However, some general guidelines can be established to develop a basis for conducting an overseas business venture.

In many ways MITI's hard-nosed attitude toward joint ventures can be considered a blessing in disguise. For any company establishing an enterprise in the unfamiliar business environment of Japan, the initial phases can be disastrous without some knowledge of Japanese business ethics and procedures. As any company who has had the experience could testify, an understanding of the customs and practices of Japanese firms and industries is mandatory before undertaking a business venture.

Kogoro Uemura, President of Keidanaren, the Japan Federation of Economic Organizations, advocates the use of joint ventures:

> Foreign enterprises planning to do business in Japan will find it most advantageous and profitable to tie up closely with Japanese partners. Ever present is the difficulty of obtaining necessary personnel in a country where labor liquidity is poor. It is deemed advisable for foreign enterprises cooperating with their Japanese counterparts for doing business in this country to make good use of their Japanese partner's experiences and personnel for better management results.
>
> Numerous foreign enterprises have advanced into Japan in the past. In many cases, they have failed as they unilaterally adopted their own methods of management without understanding precisely the specific and unique conditions inherent in this country. On the other hand, some foreign enterprises starting business in Japan on a fifty-fifty basis with Japanese partners have achieved more favorable results.[4]

SELECTION OF A JAPANESE PARTNER

When it was considered more advantageous to enter Japan through a joint venture, the next decision was to select a partner. But how was this to be done? A Caterpillar executive explains:

> The survey team had various thoughts—about the kinds of things that should be desirable in a potential Japanese partner, notably the management structure. As far as the survey team was concerned, some of the potential associates were ruled out because of their philosophies of doing business and (Caterpillar's) rigid desire to exercise and maintain strict quality control.

The Japanese market for crawler-type tractors was dominated by two manufacturers with 90 percent of the market. The remaining 10 percent of the market was shared by three other companies. The distribution was as follows:

4. Kogoro Uemura, "Keidanaren's Attitude Toward Capital Liberation," *Keidanaren's Review* (Spring 1969).

	Percentage of Market Share
Komatsu Seisakusho	53
Mitsubishi Nihon Juko	35
Nittoku Kinzoku	7
Hitachi	4
Sumitomo Kikai	1

A prospective candidate for partnership, Mitsubishi Heavy Industries Reorganized (MHIR), became interested in the bulldozer market, although it was not making a crawler tractor at that time. Mitsubishi had previously manufactured bicycles, scooters, and tricycles and then added paper, petroleum, and textile machines. Finally, it was decided that the manufacture of automobiles would be its principal purpose. Efforts to find and develop additional products in new fields prompted Mitsubishi (MHIR) to seek a means of entering into the manufacture of crawler-type tractors.

Other companies desired some sort of affiliation with Caterpillar. Some only wanted to advance their technical knowledge through licensing agreements; others wanted a controlling interest in a joint venture. However, after taking all the relevant factors into consideration, Caterpillar decided to go ahead with Mitsubishi in a fifty-fifty joint venture.

There were many reasons for the partnership between these two companies. The many similar views they shared would enhance the close coordination necessary for a joint venture. For instance, they both believed in a progressive management and shared a willingness to contribute to national wealth through corporate activities. From a structural point of view, the two companies were similar in size, number of employees, and sales. Other similar traits included rational and conservative corporate financing, market policy, and employee relations.

A major goal of Caterpillar was to maintain quality control. As one company spokesman explained, "The survey team also believed that the management of Mitsubishi had the ability and desire to maintain its standards of quality control." Mitsubishi had excellent management personnel and proven ability as an integrated machine-maker. A very interesting factor that had a great deal to do with the formation of the partnership was the personality of Mr. Makita. He was Mitsubishi's managing director at that time and maintained the initiative throughout the negotiations. Both Caterpillar and Mitsubishi feel strongly that the basis for their association was due largely to Makita's personality and the trust he engendered. Another reason why Caterpillar found Mitsubishi especially attractive as a potential partner was that Mitsubishi was the only suitor company with the capability to manufacture crawler-type tractors which was not yet manufacturing them. All other potentially interested partners were those companies which were already in the field, and there was serious question in the mind of Caterpillar's management about protecting its technical secrets from potential competitors, even during the period of mutual investigations and preliminary discussions.

FINANCING THE JOINT VENTURE

The capital needs of the new company were estimated at ¥ 44 billion with ¥ 20 billion to come from equity financing and another ¥ 24 billion to be borrowed funds. Caterpillar and Mitsubishi Heavy Industries Reorganized would be equal partners. In the event of any increases in the capital, the two partners were to subscribe to the newly issued shares on an equal basis.

There is one area where the two companies do not share equal responsibility. All debentures to be issued by the new company were subscribed by Mitsubishi Heavy Industries Reorganized. Any future borrowings by the new company were to be guaranteed 50 percent by Mitsubishi Heavy Industries Reorganized and Caterpillar Mitsubishi, and 50 percent by Caterpillar. Actually, Caterpillar Overseas Corporation of Geneva, a wholly owned subsidiary of Caterpillar Tractor Company, is the parent company of Caterpillar Mitsubishi and is in control of the joint venture.

Licensing and Royalty Arrangements

Caterpillar granted an exclusive license to the new company to manufacture in Japan, for a period of ten years, Caterpillar products utilizing patents and know-how belonging to Caterpillar. These licensed products are limited to those deemed suitable by Caterpillar for marketing in Japan and the Far East. In consideration of the granting of this license, the new company will pay Caterpillar a license fee with no initiation or minimum fee.

Product Line

Since the first D4D tractor was completed in 1965, Caterpillar Mitsubishi has expanded its product line to include eleven models: six track-type tractors, three track-type loaders, two wheel loaders. In addition two new diesel engines were also developed for use in the tractors. As to future product policy, the joint venture will specialize in the production of small and medium-size tractors whereas the U.S. Caterpillar Company will concentrate on larger-sized tractors such as the twenty-five and thirty-five–ton models. In this way, the partners will achieve the economy of mass production and promote the scheme of international division of labor. Costs can be reduced and a further expansion of sales in the worldwide market will be achieved.

Marketing Arrangements

Caterpillar Mitsubishi could not duplicate the marketing arrangements and practices followed in the U.S. because there were few individuals with large enough financial resources to establish and maintain suitable dealerships. It was, therefore, decided that Caterpillar Mitsubishi would market throughout Japan, thereby serving as a direct sales agency to the customer. This was also a first for Caterpillar, U.S.A.

Management Structure

The management of Caterpillar Mitsubishi is carried out by nine Americans from the U.S. and nine Japanese from Mitsubishi or Caterpillar Mitsubishi. Some

American directors live in Japan and in addition to serving as directors, act as advisors in their particular specialties. The management structure is such that the chairman of the board is always an American and the president is always a Japanese. There are two managing directors from Caterpillar and three from Mitsubishi. An auditor from each company is also represented. The official language used in the board meetings is Japanese.

From the president on down, the company is operated by the Japanese, with American personnel acting as advisors to the various department levels. This advice is at management level and is not given to the line personnel. All matters of significance are considered by the board of directors after which the operating personnel put them into action. If the "advice" is accepted by board action, then it must be followed.

The Problems of a Joint Venture

The major problems that Caterpillar encountered were communication, cooperation, and coordination of business methods, the company reported.

Communication. This was, by far, the major problem. You never really know whether the idea is being communicated or properly understood until action is taken, but without communication, you couldn't even reach the point of knowing whether you had any of the other problems. Interpreters were used but this was very time consuming and had poor results. However, it was the only way that we could reach even the beginning of understanding. As we became better acquainted with our counterparts, whom we were advising, we discovered that even though most of them professed not to know English or speak English, they could read and understand written English to a degree. We then began a series of chalk talks for training purposes which permitted everyone to participate in the translation of the thoughts. While most of them can read English, they had no experience in speaking or listening to it. This new idea proved to be more effective but it was still extremely slow.

Cooperation. This was another large area that required a major effort to overcome. Cooperation requires at least a fifty-fifty burden on the part of both parties in any partnership, and unilateral action only creates additional problems. We all learned that ideas must be sold on their merits and acceptance of them not forced. Consequently, much patience and considerable explanation were required. In a situation such as ours, the old adage was never truer, "A person convinced against his will is of the same opinion still."

Coordination of Business Methods and Procedures. It is obvious that two different societies and cultures view problems in a different light and the proposed solutions will also vary. Time and again our methods and our procedures were so different from what they were used to that it was extremely difficult for them to accept the fact that our system was workable. This required considerable explanation and selling.

A company spokesman noted: In Japan, perhaps far more than in any other place that I have visited in the world, the use of school chums, favors, and honoring recommendations is used many, many times over.

In regard to sales representatives: They are inclined to respect other manufacturer's territories and will not even call on prospective customers. In fact, it is the general custom and practice to wait for an invitation to call on prospective customers. It took us two years to learn that.

On obtaining bids: By custom, they do not like to give quotations; they will only give estimates. According to their thinking, after the estimates are reviewed, it is always possible to go back and make further negotiations. It is not considered disgraceful if their estimates are not accepted, but to lose a bid after a quotation is made is a serious loss of face. "Losing face" is very important to the Japanese. Also very prominent in Japanese business is the desire to make last-minute revisions in their estimates. We are quite sure that this is the cause of information leaks and the rapid information flow that occurs in Japan. In fact, it could almost be said that there are no real secrets in business.

HEWLETT-PACKARD COMPANY, U. S. A. (C)

Operative Controls

H-P International continually evaluates the performance of its various overseas organizations to make sure that they will achieve their semi-annual targets and will be well within the projected performance range for their five-year plans.

Each international organization submits a set of monthly reports covering all aspects of its operations. The content and format of these reports for an international marketing organization are reproduced in Tables 1-10. Similar reports are required from the manufacturing divisions as well.

The data furnished in these reports are used to compare actual conditions against the semi-annual budget and the five-year plan. The monthly statements are also of great value in preparing future semi-annual budgets and five-year plans. A close accounting and coordination between the corporate headquarters and the international manufacturing and marketing organizations are necessary to keep up in a fast-moving field with an entirely technological emphasis. The company must plan for product obsolescence since five years of product life is considered maximum. The overriding factor here is the problem of capitalization (sunk costs) since once the company is committed to a product, it must be sold.[1]

---

1. *See* Hewlett–Packard Company, U.S.A. (D).

TABLE 1

International Marketing Company: Schedule 1
Statement of Condition as of _____

Assets

Current Assets:

Cash		$
Accounts Receivable		
Trade	$	
Intra-Corporate	$ _____	$
Inventories		$
Other		$
Total		$

Property, Plant, Equipment:

Land, Leasehold, and Leasehold Improvements	$	
Buildings and Building Improvements	$	
Equipment	$	
Construction Work in Progress	$	
Total	$	
Less: Accumulated Depreciation	$ _____	$

Intangible and Other Assets $ _____

    Total Assets $ _____

Liabilities and Net Worth

Current Liabilities:

Bank Overdraft		$ Credit Balances
Accounts Payable		
Trade	$	
Intra-Corporate	$ _____	$
Accrued Expenses		$
Retirement Provision		$
Estimated Income Tax		$
Other (Specify)		$
Total		$

Long-Term Liabilities and Reserves $_____

    Total Liabilities $

Net Worth

Capital		$
Retained Earnings, Nov. 1,	$	
Earnings Year-to-Date from Schedule 2	$ _____	$ _____

    Total Net Worth $ _____

    Total $ _____

TABLE 2—*continued*

International Marketing Company: Schedule 2

Statement of Earnings
_____ Months Ended _____

____Months Ended_____ Target	Month of _____ Actual		Percentage of Shipments		
			_____Months Ended_____ Actual	Target	12 Months Target
(From Target WS)		1. Shipments Target			
(Line 1 minus Line 8)		2. Deviation			
		3. Shipments			
		4. Instruments			
		5. Parts			
		6. Repair Parts			
_____	_____ _____	7. Repair Labor/ Overhead _____	_____	_____	_____
		8. Total Shipments			
		9. Cost of Sales[a]			
		10. Instruments			
		11. Parts			
		12. Repair Parts			
(From Line 20 Sch. 7)		13. Repair Expense _____	_____	_____	_____
		14. Total Cost of Sales			
(Line 8 minus Line 14)		15. Sales Margin			
		16. Rental Income			
_____	_____ _____	17. Net Commission Income _____	_____	_____	_____
(Sum of Lines 15 + 16 + 17)		18. Gross Income			
(From Line 27, Sch. 4)		19. Expenses			
(From Line 12, Sch. 5)		20. F/E and S/S			
(From Line 15, Sch. 6)		21. Order Proc.			
_____	_____ _____	22. General _____	_____	_____	_____
(Sum of Lines 20 + 21 + 22)		23. Total Expenses			
(Line 18 minus Line 23)		24. Operating Profit			
(From Line 19, Sch. 8)		25. Net Trading Inc.			
_____	_____ _____	26. Other Inc. (Exp.) _____	_____	_____	_____
(Sum of Lines 24 + 25 + 26)		27. Profit Before Tax			
_____	_____ _____	28. Less: Income Tax _____	_____	_____	_____
(Line 27 minus Line 28)		29. Net Profit			

[a]Individual COS actual and targeted percentages are expressed as percentages of corresponding types of shipments. Total COS percentages are expressed as percentages of total shipments.

TABLE 3

International Marketing Company: Schedule 2A
Schedule of Cost per Order Dollar by Discipline
_____ Months Ended _____

Actual Dollars, Fiscal Year-to-Date

		Elect.	Med.	Anal.	Data Pr.	Calc.	Total
Orders Received							
1.	Instruments	(Direct)					(Sch. 3, Line 2)
2.	Parts, etc.	(On Basis of Instrument Orders)					(Sch. 3, Line 3)
3.	Total Orders Received						(Sch. 3, Line 4)
Expenses Incurred							
Field Engineers and Sales Support:							
5.	Salaries: Field Engineers	(Alloc. per FE Effort [$Dist., Part 2, p. 10B])					(Sch. 4, Line 2)
6.	Sales Support	(Alloc. per FE Effort [Time Dist., Part 1, p. 10B])					(Sch. 4, Line 3)
7.	Total Salaries						(Sch. 4, Line 4)
8.	Payroll Taxes and Benefits	(Allocate per Above "Total Salaries")					(Sch. 4, Line 5)
9.	Travel	(Allocate per FE Effort [Time					(Sch. 4, Line 9)
10.	Promotion	Distribution] Except for Distribution					(Sch. 4, Line 17)
11.	Other (all Other Including Distribution to S.S.)	to Sales Support which Is Direct.)					(Sch. 4, Lines 18–26
12.	Total Field Eng. and Sls. Supt.						(Sch. 4, Line 27)
13.	Order Processing Expense	(Allocate per Number of Line Items in Instrument Order [or Number of Orders if Line Item Totals Not Available].)					(Sch. 5, Line 12)
14.	General Expense	(Allocate per Above [Line 12].)					(Sch. 6, Line 15)
15.	Total Expenses Incurred						(Sch. 2, Line 23)
16.	Cost per Order Dollar	(Line 15 ÷ Line 3 [Should be in ¢])					
17.	Number of FEs per Discipline						
18.	Target C.P.O.D.						

TABLE 4

International Marketing Company: Schedule 3
Statistical Data

		Month of	___ Mos. Ended	___ Mos. Ended	12 Months Target
1.	Orders Received				
2.	Total Orders Received	$ (V-3, 5.1)	$	(Same as Corporate Statistics amt.)	
3.	Percent of Quota	%		%	
4.	Expenses Incurred				
5.	Fld. Eng. and Sls. Supt.	$ (Sch. 2, Line 20)	$	¢	¢
6.	Order Processing	(Sch. 2, Lire 21)		¢	¢
7.	General	(Sch. 2, Line 22)	$	¢	¢
8.	Subtotal	$ (Lines 5 + 6 + 7)	$	¢	¢
9.	Net Repair Expense	(Sch. 7, line 18)			
10.	Total Exp. Incurred	$(Lines 8 + 9)	$		
11.	Total Exp. Targeted	$ (From Target WS)	$		
12.	Intra-Corp. Orders Received		$		
13.	Intra-Corp. Shipments		$		
14.	Cap. Asset Commitments				

		Actual, 6 Mos. to Date	6 Mos. Budget
15.	Land and Bldgs. (Commitments=Cash Expenditures)	$	$
16.	Equipment (Commitments=P.O.'s Issued)		
17.	Total	$	$
18.	Employee Count		
19.	Field Engineers		
20.	Service Technicians		
21.	Other		
22.	Days' Receivables (No. of Days)		
23.	Inv. Supply (Mos.) - Instruments		
24.	- Parts		

TABLE 5

International Marketing Company: Schedule 3A
Inventory Analysis

25.	Transit Instrument Inventory		
26.	Total Transit Instruments	Total of $ _____	$ _____ (Line 9) [b]
27.	Landed Instrument Inventory		
28.	Stock	$ _____	
29.	Demo	$ _____	
30.	Committed	$ _____	
31.	Total Landed Instruments	(Total of $ Lines 28, 29, 30)	
32.	Total Instruments	(Total of $ Lines 26 and 31)	$ _____ (Line 6) [b]
33.	Freight and Duty on Instruments	$ _____	
34.	Total Instrument Inventory		$ _____ (Total of Lines 32 and 33)
35.	Parts Inventory		
36.	Parts, HP	$ _____	
37.	Parts, Outside	$ _____	
38.	Total Parts	$ _____	$ _____ (Line 7) [b]
39.	Freight and Duty on Parts	$ _____	
40.	Total Parts Inventory		$ _____ (Total of Lines 38 and 39)
41.	Total Inventory	(Total of Lines 34 and 40) [a]	

[a] Must equal the amount of Inventory shown on Balance Sheet.
[b] Use appropriate "6 Month" or "12 Month" figure from Target Form 1M-3.

TABLE 6

International Marketing Company: Schedule 4
Field Engineering and Sales Support Expense
_____ Months Ended _____

				Percent of Shipments _____ Mos. Ended _____ 12 Months		
_____ Months Ended						
Target	Actual			Actual	Target	Target
		1.	Wages and Salaries			
		2.	Field Engineers			
		3.	Sales Support			
(Sum of Lines 2 + 3.)		4.	Total Wages and Salaries			
		5.	Payroll Taxes and Benefits			
		6.	FE/SS Travel			
		7.	Automobile			
		8.	Other			
(Sum of Lines 7 + 8.)		9.	Total FE/SS Travel			
		10.	Promotion			
		11.	Media Advertising			
		12.	Direct Mail			
		13.	Shows			
		14.	Demo Vehicles			
		15.	Prod. Training			
		16.	Other			
(Sum of Lines 11 thru 16.)		17.	Total Promotion			
		18.	Other Operating Expense			
		19.	Operating Materials and Supplies			
		20.	Warranty Expense			
(Sum of Lines 4 + 5 + 9 + 17–20.)		21.	Total Direct Expense			
		22.	Allocated Expense			
		23.	Tel. and Tel.			
		24.	Equipment Costs			
		25.	Occupancy Costs			
		26.	Dist. from Repair Exp.			
		27.	Total Expense			

TABLE 7

International Marketing Company: Schedule 5
Order Processing Expense
_____Months Ended __________

_____ *Months Ended*				*Percent of Shipments* _____ *Mos. Ended*	__________ *12 Months*	
Target	*Actual*			*Actual*	*Target*	*Target*
		1.	Wages and Salaries			
		2.	Payroll Taxes and Benefits			
		3.	Operating Materials and Supplies			
		4.	Operating Expense			
		5.	Travel			
		6.	Other			
(Sum of Lines 1 thru 5.)		7.	Total Direct Expense			
		8.	Allocated Expense			
		9.	Tel. and Tel.			
		10.	Equipment Costs			
		11.	Occupancy Costs			
(Sum of Lines 7 thru 11.)		12.	Total Expense			

TABLE 8

International Marketing Company: Schedule 6
General Expense
_____Months Ended __________

_____ *Months Ended*				*Percent of Shipments* _____ *Mos. Ended*	__________ *12 Months*	
Target	*Actual*			*Actual*	*Target*	*Target*
		1.	Wages and Salaries			
		2.	Payroll Taxes and Benefits			
		3.	Operating Materials and Supplies			
		4.	Automobile Expense			
		5.	Operating Expense			
		6.	Postage			
		7.	Bad Debts			
		8.	Travel			
		9.	Other			
(Sum of Lines 1 thru 9.)		10.	Total Direct Expense			
		11.	Allocated Expense			
		12.	Tel. and Tel.			
		13.	Equipment Costs			
		14.	Occupancy Costs			
(Sum of Lines 10 thru 14.)		15.	Total Expense			

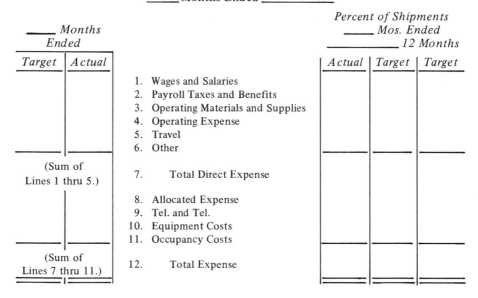

TABLE 9

International Marketing Company: Schedule 7
Repair Expense
_____ Months Ended_____

| _____Months Ended | | | | _____ Mos. Ended _____ 12 Months | | |
Target	Actual			Actual	Target	Target
		1.	Wages and Salaries			
		2.	Payroll Taxes and Benefits			
		3.	Service Department Travel			
		4.	Automobile			
		5.	Other			
(Sum of Lines 4 & 5.)		6.	Total S/D Travel			
		7.	Operating Materials and Supplies			
		8.	Operating Expense			
(Sum of Lines 1 + 2 + 6 + 7 + 8.)		9.	Total Direct Expense			
		10.	Allocated Expense			
		11.	Tel. and Tel.			
		12.	Equipment Costs			
		13.	Occupancy Costs			
(Sum of Lines 9 thru 13.)		14.	Total Expense Incurred			
		15.	Less: Dist. to:			
		16.	Sales Support			
		17.	Trading Expense			
(Line 14 minus Lines 16 & 17.)		18.	Net Repair Expense	100.0	100.0	100.0
		19.	Add: Service Center Charges			
		20.	Cos, Repair Expense[a]			
		21.	Sales, In-House Repairs	$		
		22.	Sales, Service Center Charges			
		23.	Total Repair L/OH Sales per Sch. 2, Line. 7	$		

[a]The Line 20 dollar figures must equal those shown on Schedule 2, Line 13.

TABLE 10

International Marketing Company: Schedule 8
Statement of Trading Income
_____ Months Ended _____

Percent of Shipments

	Months Ended ___		Month of ___		Months Ended ___		Month of ___ 12 Months	
	Target	Actual	Target	Actual	Actual	Target	Target	Target
1. Trading Income								
2. Less: Trading Expense								
3. Interest								
4. Surcharge								
5. Freight								
6. Warehousing								
7. Frt. For'der.								
8. Duty								
9. Turn-over Tax								
10. Misc. Tax								
11. Delivery Exp.								
12. Common Carrier								
13. Van								
14. Driver								
15. Total Del. Expense (Sum of Lines 12 thru 14.)								
16. Subtotal (Sum of Lines 3-10 + Line 15.)								
17. Dist. from Repair Expense								
18. Total Trading Expense (Sum of Lines 16 + 17.)								
19. Net Trading Inc. (Line 1 minus Line 18.)								

GENERATION BANK OF SAN FRANCISCO

Development of Joint Banking Operations in Latin America, Sensitivity to Local Operating Conditions

Generation Bank of San Francisco, California,[1] made its first joint-venture overseas direct investment in a commercial bank in 1966 with its purchase of 19.2 percent of the outstanding stock of the Banco de Nicaragua. The $1.9 million investment, made in two installments—50,000 shares in July and 1,000 shares in September—was made through Generation Bank International Corporation, a subsidiary organized under the Edge Act to make investments in Latin America. For a large U.S. commercial bank this external investment was slow in coming. Although Generation Bank had previously participated in investment companies and financieras overseas, this Nicaraguan venture was unique because it was equity participation in a commercial bank.

Generation Bank (hereafter abbreviated as GB), in 1968 was among the top twenty U.S. banks in terms of capital funds, loans outstanding, and net revenues. Even in Europe, where it has substantial clientele and banking operations, it serves both U.S. and overseas clients through a large network of local correspondent banks. GB and the correspondent banks in various countries serve each other's customers by reciprocal agreement, a policy in sharp contrast to that of the "big three"[2] which maintain their own overseas branches. In explaining the differences between GB's approach to overseas expansion and those of the three other U.S. banks, one bank official stated:

I would think that our ends are not too different from the First National City Bank, the Chase Manhattan Bank, and the Bank of America. It is only that our method is different for various reasons.

All these banks have been operating in Europe and other foreign countries since before World War II and consequently have established an extensive network of branches which are well versed in local customs and business practices. If we were to compete with them with any degree of effectiveness in overseas markets we would have to establish an equally large number of branches in five years that took these banks over twenty years to accomplish. Given our resources and

1. Pseudonym.
2. The "big three" of U.S. banks are First National City and Chase Manhattan Banks of New York and Bank of America in San Francisco.

the competitive conditions such an action would have been impossible for us to pursue. Nonetheless, we had to expand overseas for two major considerations which are common with other international banks: (1) to better serve our U.S. business clients who were rapidly expanding overseas and expected their domestic bank to provide them with banking services overseas, and (2) to secure a source of earnings off shore.

We feel that to establish branches around the globe has certain disadvantages—first of all, the cost involved is prohibitive, and second, the personnel requirements are practically impossible. Third, we feel that nationalism in various countries will have a detrimental influence on the branches abroad.

Our policy has been to look at investment opportunities for participation by Generation Bank on a minority basis with good commercial banks in the various countries which will enable us to give perhaps even better service to our domestic customers which are active overseas.

If a bank sets up a branch banking system, taking a substantial amount of its own capital, then it probably will not be seeing a return on its investment for three to five years. This is a very costly operation. We, therefore, have chosen good working relationships with only a minority interest in each case.

For similar reasons we also decided that we will not go into overseas markets in collaboration with another U.S. bank. We may, however, consider going in with another European or other foreign banks.[3]

ENTRY INTO NICARAGUA

Before the direct investment, GB had developed strong personal business ties with Banco de Nicaragua over a number of years. These strong ties were held through a San Francisco coffee and sugar importer whose top executive was related to the influential Nicaraguan family which helped to establish Banco de Nicaragua.

Nicaragua has a long history of constitutional government and revolution. New governments have been established either by election or *coup d'état*, both being commonplace. The first national constitution was adopted by a constituent assembly in 1825. At that time, the conservatives, centered in the city of Granada on Lake Nicaragua, and the liberals, centering around León near the Pacific coast, warred for control of the government. Since then, the Liberal Party has dominated Nicaraguan politics much of the time and, headed by the Somoza family since 1937, has ruled the country continuously. The geographical headquarters for the two parties remain the same after 140 years of conflict.

Banco de Nicaragua was established in 1952 by members of the country's opposition party (Conservative Party). Prior to that Nicaragua had only one government owned and operated commercial bank and a branch of the Bank of London and Montreal. Therefore, Banco de Nicaragua was Nicaragua's first private commercial bank. The officials of Banco de Nicaragua claim that although the principal shareholders are members of the Conservative Party, they still maintain a good relationship with the government. The Liberals have given the country political stability,

3. Unless otherwise specified, all references to comments or statements by the various officials of Generation Bank pertain to either written or oral communications with the author.

and the economy has grown over the years. Banco has, in fact, financed a number of government projects.

GB officials state that person-to-person relationships weigh heavily in doing business in Nicaragua:

> In a small community like the Nicaraguan one, you obviously have this kind of thing. They, the guys, grew up together, they know each other; society is small so they've known each other ever since they were kids. They know whether they can trust a guy or not.

Nicaragua is one of the five nations making up the Central American Common Market (CACM).[4] One of the foremost objectives of this market is to get all countries to agree on a common external tariff and to abolish all internal tariffs. The direct investment in Banco de Nicaragua was one way to establish services within the boundaries of CACM. Bank officials claim that Nicaragua was not necessarily preferred to any other Central American country.

The reasons for GB's selection of Nicaragua as the first Latin American country for its direct investment were manifold. First, as mentioned earlier, Banco de Nicaragua was chosen on the basis of an old personal relationship.

Generation Bank had in fact helped establish Banco de Nicaragua in 1952. At that time a high-ranking GB official took a leave of absence to coordinate the Banco's establishment and became its first manager.

Nicaragua is one of the most progressive Central American countries as far as trying to attract foreign capital is concerned. The country's development program, under the direction of the president, is on a selective basis. There is no problem of repatriating profits in Nicaragua since there is no foreign exchange control. But recently the country suffered losses in its foreign exchange reserves, causing a balance of payments problem. The net loss on Nicaragua's current account was somewhere around $60 million which resulted in a net drain on foreign exchange of some $14 million. But the program to attract foreign capital is presently helping to wipe out that large deficit.

Nicaragua affords a great market for agricultural loans. In Central America, a very large portion of a country's GNP is directly related to agriculture. Private capital inflow is believed to be one way to offset this imbalance. In Nicaragua, diversification of agricultural crop assortment is the approach now taken as one step toward true industrialization. The country is trying to get away from cotton, its main crop, and put more money into rice and cattle development. The government feels that this cushion is necessary as a growth base to provide for contingencies. As the agricultural base grows, GB will find growing opportunities for industrial and commercial loans. GB, like other California banks, is interested in agribusiness and because of its experiences in the U.S., is uniquely equipped to assist in similar ventures overseas. At present, however,

---

4. The other nations in the CACM are: Honduras, El Salvador, Guatemala, and Costa Rica.

Nicaragua's export-based growth is being reinforced by government emphasis on primary products and deemphasis on import substitution investments.

In describing the bank's outlook on Latin American investment an official stated:

> We believe that Central America, even though it is a small area, can be quite important from the viewpoint of our business interests. We believe that an increasingly large number of our U.S. customers are likely to become interested in business opportunities in this area. We followed this investment by having a representative in this area to look into, analyze, and evaluate the activities of various U.S. corporations in CACM. As a result, we are now actually exploring other investment possibilities in the area.

TERMS OF PARTICIPATION

Banco de Nicaragua encouraged the GB investment. Banco wanted increased capital and the benefits of the technical know-how of American institutions. Other American banks were showing an interest in Banco de Nicaragua at the time of the GB investment. This prompted GB to take action. The other principal bidder wanted 50 percent of Banco de Nicaragua, but Banco, wanting to remain under local control, took the San Francisco offer.

Banco de Nicaragua gained certain commitments from Generation Bank as a result of the purchase. It gained a sizable commitment for continuous capital outlays with regard to credit. GB extended substantial loans to the Nicaraguan bankers enabling them to capture a large share of the market. It also committed a continuous supply of technical and managerial assistance, agreeing to send people to Nicaragua to inspect the bank's position and loan policy, accounting procedures, and other technical activities.

In explaining GB's reasons for accepting a minority share in Banco de Nicaragua, an official stated:

> The figure of 19.2 percent is not a magic figure. It was considered by us as being substantial for an institution of this size without impairing their local bank image. Immediately after we made the investment, the competing bank started saying that *it* was the *only* Nicaraguan bank. While one could successfully counteract this argument when only 20 percent of one's stock is foreign owned, it might have been a little inconvenient for the Banco de Nicaragua to claim Nicaraguan nationality in the eyes of the public if we owned, say, 49 percent of that stock. Moreover, our influence in terms of giving advice and its acceptance by the Banco people was far greater than our 19.2 percent equity reflected. In fact I don't believe we would have been any more effective even if we had owned 49 percent of their stock.

There were no written agreements between the participants concerning expansion of the capital base of Banco or taking in new American or local partners except for an implicit understanding that Banco would not do so without GB's consent.[5] However, a GB official conceded that if they were to do it all over again they would prefer to have this and similar other conditions in writing.

Generation Bank was also not obliged to confine its operations in Nicaragua to Banco de Nicaragua alone. In fact, it has maintained a business relationship and equity participation with a local financiera (translated as development bank), where GB had invested $200,000 by the end of 1968.

GENERATION BANK'S ORGANIZATION DEVELOPMENT AND OVERSEAS EXPANSION POLICIES: EXPERIENCE OF BANCO DE NICARAGUA

As GB's first commercial bank investment participation, officials viewed Banco de Nicaragua as a "pilot project." From this experience GB has formulated its overseas expansion policy, which is to take up a minority interest in local commercial banks. Referring to Central America in general, and CACM in particular, bank officials outline their long-range goals as follows:

There are five countries in that common market. Our thinking here, when looking at the situation in long-range terms, is to put a banking group together on a regional basis, starting with Nicaragua where we have the present investment, and then moving into other countries. We are in El Salvador, not in a bank, but in the financing area—a medium-term/long-term lending institution—and we have contracts already in the other countries and some ideas as to how to enter the financial fields there, banking or otherwise.

Once we have these investments, we will pull them all together. We would probably put a company over all of them—a holding company. In other words, try to get a regional Generation Bank with local partnership networks in the financial field. With very many American companies becoming interested in Central America, they could establish a plant in one of the countries, knowing that there would be financing of sufficient size to enable large plant and marketing activities in the five countries involved in the common market.

The relationship between GB's International Division and the subsidiary GB International Corporation can be studied in Figure 1.

The organization chart reveals that the International Corporation works with the International Division through its investment officer. This investment officer maintains close communications with the Central American representative in Managua, Nicaragua, and GB's Central American investments.

Generation Bank International Division divides its responsibility into four geographic areas among Europe (including the Middle East and Africa), U.S.A. (exports), the Far East (including Asia and Australia), and Latin America. The Division's line of communication to Banco de Nicaragua is through the Central American representative who is directly responsible to the Latin American

5. Banco de Nicaragua has so far not violated this understanding.

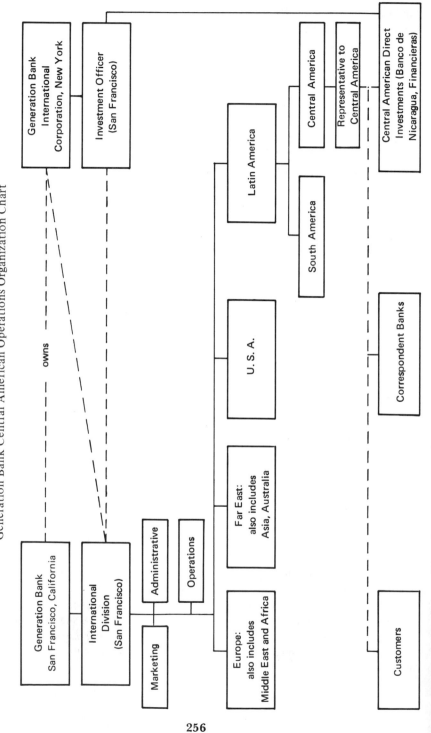

FIGURE 1

Generation Bank Central American Operations Organization Chart

supervisor in San Francisco, but he directs most of his communications through the Central American desk which also works directly under the Latin American supervisor in San Francisco.

The Central American representative maintains a "dotted line" relationship with Banco de Nicaragua and the other GB interests in Central America, including bank customers and correspondent banks. A GB official explains the correspondent relationship as follows:

> We look pretty heavily to our correspondents overseas. We rely on them a great deal. In turn, they rely on us to an extent. If we had a branch, then we would be in direct competition with the correspondents. This way we can associate very strongly with the bank in the country without alienating or being offensive to the other banks. In Managua, for instance, we have correspondent relations with several banks in addition to the Banco de Nicaragua. They in turn have very extensive correspondent relationships with other U.S. banks.

PROBLEMS OF OPERATING AS A MINORITY PARTNER

Since GB's minority ownership in Banco de Nicaragua was not accompanied by any legal agreement, its only protection was through the rights of a normal shareholder. Therefore, to gain power it had to rely on its image as an advanced and powerful western banking institution.

Despite the recognized advantages of being a minority owner, there were also certain risks for GB which were inherent in such an arrangement. First, there was the higher-than-normal risk of making a loan. The second risk was political, with remote possibilities of revolution and nationalization of banks. The third risk was the possibility of a falling out with the majority partners.

In meeting the higher-than-normal risk of loan making, the bank could attach higher interest rates, stiffer terms, and greater selectivity in accepting customers. (In meeting the above-normal loan risk, Banco de Nicaragua earns approximately 10 to 12 percent on its net worth, and retains a good share of its capital.) Since the country was ruled by the strong Somoza family, providing Nicaragua with a stable government and economy, political risks for equity investment were not considered as high as in other underdeveloped countries.

Banco de Nicaragua may at any time change the capital ownership structure of the bank, and possibly can invite another major foreign investor. GB is, of course, opposed to any such action since its influence would be significantly reduced. In the words of a GB official:

> You lose a lot of leverage if you go in with another guy. In the case of a commercial bank, we will not go in with another U.S. bank. We may consider going in with another European bank, however.
> . . . There has been no actual fist shaking or anything like that. The Banco de Nicaragua executives are very interested in taking on another American corporation for the sake of prestige. This would be a New York bank. This, of course, would diminish our influence, and we don't like that one bit. We won't go along with it. Banco de Nicaragua is over-capitalized now.

The only thing which we have not done specifically with Banco de Nicaragua which we might do in the future is to make a definite agreement that they would not take on any other foreign investors without our approval.

GENERATION BANK

In 1966 GB decided to experiment by sending a personal representative into the country. This representative did not become an employee of Banco de Nicaragua, but after the direct investment he was assigned to attend all director's meetings. His function has become advising and liaison. The first representative to Central America describes the early period of his orientation as follows:

When I was appointed to this job, Managua was chosen as my headquarters only by coincidence. The office could have been anywhere else—El Salvador, or anyplace in the Central American Market. However, I was more acquainted with the people there, and I knew the people at Banco de Nicaragua.

I went to Managua on October 23,1966. The first few months were actually spent in Managua, with no travel to other countries. I was simply getting my bearings and learning more of the language. I had an office in Banco de Nicaragua because we didn't want to open an office. We weren't at all sure that we were going to stay in Central America. It was an experiment.

It is quite an undertaking to open a formal office in any country because when you establish such an office, then you are committed more or less to maintaining it. It could really injure your reputation if you went in and decided for some reason that you couldn't stay. If you pulled out then, you would do more harm than good.

Before the Generation Bank purchase of stock, Banco de Nicaragua had shown a rapid rate of growth and was therefore an attractive investment. Since 1966, however, Banco de Nicaragua's progress had slowed down and GB officials felt that there was room for improvement. In an effort to improve their return on investment, GB assumed the role of advisor by sending a management team to Managua in June of 1968.

Banco de Nicaragua's board of directors looks to GB for advice and appears to weight its advisory contributions by a ratio greater than the 19.2 percent investment. GB has attempted not to exhibit a strictly U.S. point of view since its senior vice-president has seventeen years of experience in Latin America and its representative has ten years experience in that area.

In giving advice GB has made sure that Banco de Nicaragua does not rely too heavily upon its help and has been careful to retain the image of minority partner. Only recently has GB toyed with the idea of sending an official to Banco de Nicaragua for the purpose of assuming a role in direct management. The reasoning behind the consideration of this lies more in the traditional banking structure of the CACM area. With loanable funds considered scarce, banks do not tend to build an active marketing program for the purpose of finding new business. GB feels that a U.S. manager would be more forward in his approach to marketing.

At the present time, GB is content to make its major advisory contribution to Banco de Nicaragua in the form of technical knowledge. In a growing country such as Nicaragua certain systems and procedures soon become inadequate for a growing bank. For this purpose, as well as the one cited above, GB provided the June 1968 management research team.

MANAGEMENT RESEARCH TEAM

The June 1968 research team sent to Banco de Nicaragua consisted of three members—one loan expert and two vice-presidents—whose purpose was to investigate present methods of operation.[6] The team's findings brought improvements to many areas among which were included:

1. The creation of a loan review and examination department to examine and report on the bank's loan portfolio;
2. The instigation of an officer development and management training program; and
3. Revision of branch supervision and operating procedures including written operating manuals and employee information booklets.

An investigation of the loan portfolio of Banco de Nicaragua revealed a very good credit analysis system and an excellent system of credit reports and statements. However, the team noted that the responsibility for a loan was not placed on the lending officer but was passed on to a committee. GB felt that the committee was just a legal entity and that the responsibility for the loan should be placed with the officer recommending it. Even if the amount was beyond his limit, thus requiring approval by a higher officer, he still should recommend the loan and be responsible for it from the time it was granted until the time it was collected.

Even more important was the discovery by the research team that the responsibility for making and reviewing loans was vested in the same unit reporting to the local management. Generation Bank felt that loan review should be the responsibility of someone who is not subject to direct authority of bank administration, someone who could review each loan after it had been on the books and who had not been charged with the responsibility actually to make the loan. Therefore, a separate loan review and examination board was created whose job it was to review all separate branch office loan recommendations. This body was separate from the loan division and could therefore give a freer opinion on the justification for the loan.

An analysis of the credit department included a survey of statements, existence of cost programs, system for checking overdrafts, system for reviewing loans, proper follow-up methods, and collection procedure for past-due loans. The team noted that Banco de Nicaragua had in the past concerned itself more with past-due than

6. In 1967, GB also sent a personnel expert to assist Banco's management with their personnel policies.

with current loans. GB felt that all loans should come under the scrutiny of the review board.

The research team found that of the sixteen branches, only a few had lending authority and only small loans could be made. Most large loans had to go through the main office and involved heavy paper work and loss of time with inconvenience to the customer. The team suggested that loan limits be increased so that most loans could be processed immediately.

Training programs were recommended by the management team to replace the very loose programs then in use. The team found that a newly appointed branch manager visited the head office and spent a few weeks familiarizing himself with the different departments. Some of them had not been bankers before and had come from insurance companies and other fields of work. Therefore, a new training program was suggested for branch officers to improve their knowledge of loan analysis. In special cases, candidates for bank positions were sent to Mexico where a training program is offered in Spanish at Banco de Nationale. Those who spoke English were sometimes brought to the United States for a period of training.

The research team took the initiative to provide a certain amount of on-the-job training in accounting techniques, credit analysis, and other business aspects. One member of the team spoke fluent Spanish and was able to supply the needed training in the employees' native tongue.

As part of its expansion of services, Banco de Nicaragua is organizing a trust department. But Nicaragua has no trust law. To meet the need, one of the bank officers—a graduate attorney from the University of Madrid—has written the entire trust law now suggested for adoption by the Nicaraguan government. The Association of Bankers, an organization of all foreign and domestic banks in the country, is presenting the proposed law to the congress.

GB officials state, concerning the suggestions made:

If the local bank doesn't accept a suggestion, perhaps they will give us a reason, a valid reason, why our recommendation is not applicable in certain areas. In this case we would have to reevaluate.

We are not trying to tell them how they have to run their business, but merely trying to help at their request. We are not trying to impose our systems or impose our ideas. We have no problem in this respect.

APPENDIX I

Banco de Nicaragua, Nicaragua—Comparative Balance Sheet
(in Millions of C$)

Assets	*1965*	*1966*	*1967*	*1968*
Cash and Bank Notes	41.230	55.621	39.901	39.868
Loans	105.815	135.486	132.546	126.003
Fixed Assets	7.695[a]	8.486[a]	9.236[a]	7.370
Central Bank Bonds	–	19.350	25.160	25.160
Other Investments	1.674	1.669	3.792	8.928
Agencies and Branches	3.882	5.161	–	–
Interest Receivables	2.015[a]	3.414[a]	3.658	3.945
Other Assets	5.307	2.693	9.222	8.364
Total	167.618	231.880	223.516	219.638

Capital and Shareholders' Equity	1965	1966	1967	1968
Shareholders' Equity	20.000	26.500	26.500	26.500
Capital Reserve	8.907	20.231	21.136	21.894
Reserve for Dividend Stabilization	.102	.833	1.161	1.161
Retained Earnings	3.257	4.892	4.673	5.338
Reserve for Portfolio	1.386	1.912	2.176	2.388
Reserve for Taxes	1.586	2.145	1.791	1.750
Deposits	113.543	135.919	129.770	128.260
Credit Obligations	1.515	3.913	1.545	3.653
Foreign Loans	14.000	33.600	32.900	27.300
Other Liabilities	3.322	1.934	1.865	1.393
Total	167.618	231.880	223.516	219.638

[a](minus reserve)

APPENDIX II

The Central American Common Market

Latin America's most successful regional economic bloc passed through a stormy period last year. The Central American Common Market (CACM), beset by balance-of-payments difficulties and intra-regional imbalances, appeared to be on the brink of disintegration in mid-1968, until a meeting of the Presidents of the five member countries bridged conflicting national viewpoints. But although measures taken at that time eased immediate difficulties, they did not resolve CACM's basic problems, which may affect further integration.

Since its founding in 1960, CACM has expanded domestic markets through gradual elimination of regional trade barriers. This has helped attract foreign investment and speed the industrial development of the member countries—Costa Rica, El Salvador, Guatemala, Honduras and Nicaragua. Indicators of the progress during the 1960 to 1968 period include:

1. An increase in intra-regional trade from $33 million to about $260 million, thus raising the share of such imports in the regional total from 6 percent to over 20 percent.
2. A thirteen-fold growth of trade in manufactured goods, to an estimated $140 million.
3. A 5.2 percent annual rate of economic growth for the region, which has pushed up per capita incomes from $257 to over $300.

Together with these benefits, regionalism has also brought a paradoxical heightening of nationalistic feelings among the CACM countries—a strong desire to prevent other members from taking undue advantage of the regional arrangements. These disagreements have been especially aggravated over the past two years by the region's balance-of-payments difficulties, which in turn have brought slower and uneven economic growth. Earnings from coffee, cotton, bananas, and cocoa—the principal exports—have been curbed by either weak world prices or droughts, insects, and other natural disasters. At the same time, newly established industries are generating an increased demand for imports of capital goods and raw materials, while rising incomes are stimulating purchases of more durables and luxury goods from abroad. Expanding imports have combined with sluggish exports to escalate CACM's external trade deficit to $176 million in 1967, more than double that of 1960.

The trade picture within CACM has also tended to worsen differences among members. El Salvador and Guatemala, the relatively more developed countries, have been enjoying trade surpluses in intra-CACM exchanges, primarily due to their export of manufactured goods. Honduras and Nicaragua, on the other hand, have recorded sizable deficits due to slow gains in their predominantly agricultural exports. Further problems arise from national rivalries with regard to locating new, regionally oriented industries within their own borders.

Easing Payments Strains

In an effort to ease balance-of-payments strains, the CACM Finance Ministers drew up in June 1968 the Protocol of San José, an amendment to the Integration Treaty. The Protocol imposes a general 30 percent tariff surcharge on all imports from outside CACM, except for a number of essential items. It also permits a regional sales tax of 10 to 20 percent on luxury goods, regardless of origin; implementation and the level of taxation were to be decided individually by members.

Business opposition to the Protocol in most of the countries delayed ratification and brought last year's crisis to a head. President Johnson's trip to Central America in July and his "summit" meeting with the five Central American Presidents provided a needed conciliatory environment. The outcome of this meeting was threefold: (1) The Presidents agreed to work towards ending the balance-of-payments conflicts in the area and to ratify the Protocol of San José; (2) Future goals of the Common Market were discussed; and (3) New U.S. financial assistance amounting to $65 million was pledged. Of this, $35 million will go to the Central American Integration Fund for a regional telecommunications network and joint electricity supply. The remainder is to be split among the members and will be utilized for expanding agriculture, education and electrification.

In spite of the eagerness of CACM Presidents to alleviate their balance-of-payments problems, the Protocol is still not completely operative. Honduras has delayed formal notification of its ratification to the Organization of Central American States (ODECA). Also, the Costa Rican legislature has still to vote for ratification, although executive approval has been obtained.

Expanding Regional Ties

At the Presidents' summit meeting and subsequent conferences, the CACM countries have reached agreement in many areas vital to the effective functioning of a true common market, including:

1. Completion of trade integration by extending the common external tariff to products now exempt and by removing remaining restrictions on intra-CACM trade.
2. Coordination of national monetary policies and creation of a Central American Stabilization Fund.
3. Harmonization of customs duty and tax incentives offered to investors.
4. Allowing labor to move freely within the region.
5. Coordinating activities of national planning agencies to permit planning on a regional scale.

In addition to consolidating their own integration plans, CACM members are working towards closer economic ties with other Latin American states. Most likely, CACM will expand trading relationships with neighboring countries and

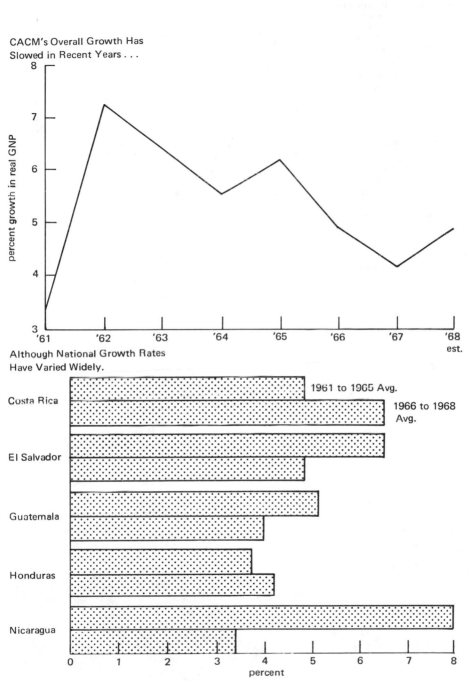

CACM's Overall Growth Has
Slowed in Recent Years . . .

percent growth in real GNP

'61 '62 '63 '64 '65 '66 '67 '68
                                      est.

Although National Growth Rates
Have Varied Widely.

1961 to 1965 Avg.

1966 to 1968
Avg.

Costa Rica

El Salvador

Guatemala

Honduras

Nicaragua

0   1   2   3   4   5   6   7   8
                  percent

SOURCE: Agency for International Development, CMB estimates.

other economic blocs rather than enlarge its own membership. However, Panama appears to be a possible exception and may join at some future date. Although the question of Panamanian membership has been explored for many years, progress towards closer ties is apparently being hindered by a number of difficulties. These include Panama's relatively more developed economy, its higher labor costs vis-a-vis the CACM countries, and the already high concentration of foreign investment there.

A joint commission is currently studying ways of expanding CACM exports to Mexico, while closer trade links with Colombia may also be in the offing. With regard to the other regional economic groupings, CACM hopes to arrange special relationships with both the Andean Common Market and the Latin American Free Trade Association (LAFTA). A joint LAFTA-CACM commission has already met to discuss possibilities for cooperation.

Financing Economic Integration

The prime source of much-needed financial assistance for CACM regional projects has been the Central American Bank for Economic Integration (CABEI), founded in 1960. To promote economic integration and balanced development, the Bank has focused its lending activities towards: (1) major infrastructure projects; (2) investments in industries large enough to supply the region; and (3) agricultural projects aimed at greater regional self-sufficiency.

Since CABEI's founding, loans made for these purposes have totaled about $125 million. To permit expanding lending activity, the Bank's original

MANUFACTURES HAVE INCREASED THEIR SHARE IN INTRA-CACM IMPORTS

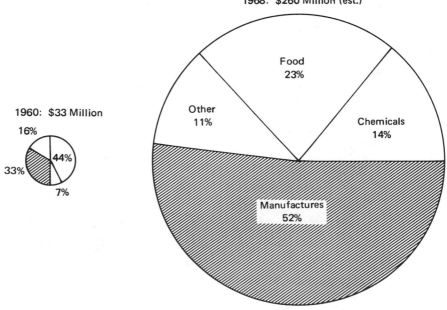

SOURCE: SIECA, CMB estimates.

authorized capital has been tripled, to $60 million. These resources have been supplemented by various foreign loans, so that CABEI's disposable funds are now estimated at close to $200 million. Industrial financing approached a $50 million total in 1968, or about 40 percent of CABEI's loan portfolio. An additional $70 million of industrial lending is scheduled for the next five years. Emphasis is now being given to intermediate industry, such as chemicals and basic metals, as contrasted with earlier priorities for consumer industries. Special attention will be given to projects involving natural resources, tourism, and transport.

The private sector appears likely to increase its role in financing regional development. Major private *financieras* in each of the CACM countries have recently combined to form a new investment bank, Banco de Inversiones Centroamericano (BICA). BICA will direct its financing activities towards projects of benefit to more than one CACM member, in part by encouraging mergers among small national firms. It will also try to develop an effective regional market for CACM securities, underwrite new corporate issues, and create an acceptance market for commercial paper.

CHASE MANHATTAN BANK, N. A., PANAMA

Innovative Use of a Bank's Resources to Contribute to the Economic Development of Panama

In 1950, the David Branch of the Chase Manhattan Bank, Republic of Panama, issued the first loan under a program designed to aid the then-troubled Panamanian cattle industry. To meet its needs at that time, Panama imported 20,000 head of cattle annually. As the industry grew in the ensuing seventeen years, it met the country's demand for beef, then, exceeding demand, became an exporter of 10,000 head per year. The value of the country's cattle and improved pasture land is now estimated at more than $200 million, spread among 31,000 ranchers. A major influence in this growth has been the 17,000 Chase Manhattan loans totaling about $50 million which have been issued since 1950.

Immediately following World War II, Panama's banks had a surplus of funds, a result of wartime productivity and the country's unique geographical position. But by the end of the war there was a considerable decline in the general activity of the Panama Canal, causing an overall business slump and fear of a recession. This started a flight of capital from the country and a diminution of bank deposits as business looked elsewhere for higher-return investment opportunities.

The American manager of the Chase Manhattan in Panama, Mr. J. Edward Healy, Jr., saw an opportunity for using his bank's funds in a manner which would not only be profitable for the bank but also would contribute to the economic development of Panama. In a sense, the attitude of this official was typical of the outlook of the top management of Chase Manhattan which had been very actively involved in the economic development of many underdeveloped countries in Latin America, Africa, and Asia. This philosophy was best summarized in a recent statement by the bank's president, David Rockefeller: ". . . business is not an end in itself but only a means to an end. That end is the happiness and fulfillment of the people . . . (I)n any business we must look beyond the strictly financial figures to the broader moral balance sheet."

Mr. Healy suggested a loan program for building the cattle industry in Panama whereby native Panamanians educated in modern techniques would be hired to aid the local ranchers in making necessary technological improvements. This program also included different criteria for the granting of loans. Instead of loans based on existing wealth, they would be based on potential and desire to improve. After some deliberation in the New York office, the program was given a go ahead with full authority for implementation to Mr. Healy.

INITIAL STAGE

The government of Panama allowed a maximum interest charge of 7 percent annually. Under this requirement, Chase set up a schedule of cattle credit "service charges" in addition to the 7 percent annual interest rate. These charges were based on the size of loans and their servicing requirements. Initially, the services were not out of the ordinary, but as the program progressed, more services were added which became an integral part of the program. (*See* "Maturing Stage" below).

The schedule of service charges was as follows:

Up to $20,000	1%	Minimum $25.00
$20,001 to $40,000	1/2%	
$40,001 to $70,000	1/4%	
$70,001 and over	1/8%	Maximum $500.00

Thus, an application of these rates on a $100,000 loan would be as follows:

$ 20,000	1%	$200.00
20,000	1/2%	100.00
30,000	1/4%	75.00
30,000	1/8%	37.50
$100,000		$412.50

Under local management, the bank hired Panamanian graduates of various agricultural colleges in the United States to instruct the local ranchers. Mr. Enrique Real was the first of Chase's "Bankers on Horseback," being the first agronomist hired by the bank to investigate credit applications. The local manager hired only those people who were trained agronomists and were willing to learn banking in order to go into the field and assist cattle ranchers not only in their financing, but in their ranching problems as well.

The key to "supervised credit" has been the "agricultural technician," the bank's title for the combination credit investigator/agronomist who travels the countryside on horseback, such as the above-mentioned Mr. Real. The ideal technician is a native who has exhibited self-motivated interests in agriculture and can pick up banking fundamentals with ease. He knows the idiosyncrasies of the rural people and can get their confidence. Often the relationship between client and technician becomes personal.

There were other problems of a procedural nature which had to be solved if the program was to be mutually successful for the bank and the rancher. The prime concern was to evolve a working pattern which would affect the desired social change. First the ranchers' needs for advice on ranch improvement had to be balanced against their distrust of city experts with their new ideas. The second balance then was between the bank's security requirements and the potential of the ranchers for improvement.

Some of the problems were procedural. Things that might seem innocuous and natural to a person used to the methods of modern financing might easily frighten a would-be rural borrower. From the very start, the bank was confronted with the problem of the ranchers' point of contact with the bank. Should the rancher be required to come to the bank? After a few cases, the bank decided although large cattle ranchers found it convenient to come, the small ranchers—those with most potential and greatest need—found the city environment overpowering and were reluctant to come to the bank's offices to seek financial help from strangers. Consequently, they preferred to stay with the local money lenders. To overcome this problem, the bank decided to go out and meet the ranchers on their home ground, thus creating "bankers on horseback."

These field agents encouraged ranchers to seek bank assistance to improve their stock. Once an application was made, a thorough credit investigation was undertaken. Following this, an agent visited the applicant's ranch to make a detailed investigation. A complete inventory was taken of the herd, with special attention paid to preventive sanitary practices. Also included was an inspection of the land topography, type and condition of the soil, pastures and fences, and approximate area. From this information came a projected budget, compiled by the technician and the rancher, based on the amount of money applied for and agreed uses to which it would be put.

Steers used as collateral for loans were branded with the bank's "CMB" marking in addition to the recorded brand of the customer. "The Chase brand has become a source of pride to the ranchers," says Mr. Real. "It identifies them as progressive cattlemen who are following the latest and most efficient methods of cattle raising."

The main concern of the bank was that the debtor would stay in the business indefinitely. Luis H. Moreno, Jr., Assistant Treasurer of Chase Manhattan, explained it this way:

> If you give a rancher credit purely on collateral, you don't care what he does. Whatever he does with the money is his business and if he fails you always have recourse to the land that has been mortgaged.

But we are concerned with productivity. Every once in a while, a case is picked and supervised, either by visits to the ranch or by having the rancher come to the bank and inform us of the progress—how his sales are doing, how much profit he is getting out of his sales, following to see if he gets behind, and why he gets behind. This is what is called "supervised credit." Lines of credit are reviewed yearly, which usually includes a survey or visit of the ranch. Once the ranchers understand that the real motive behind these visits is to assess their land, they often request these visits.

INNOVATION DIFFUSION
AND ADOPTION

The bank officials were conscious of the vital role of the "change agent" in the diffusion of new ideas. This concern was reflected in their insistence on hiring Panamanian agronomists and not bankers as "bankers on horseback." However, the process of change involved much more than acceptance of advanced technology and business methods. It meant changing life-long habits and modes of behavior, and developing trust in people apart from their traditional social group. One bank officer related how the young agronomists were accepted by the local people:

. . . Many of them would say, "I don't know fellows: you are very young to tell me what to do and you think that whatever has been done in other countries is good here. I think you are wrong." And sometimes they would just flatly tell you, "Listen: I have been working my ranch for forty years and I have done my best without the need of any advice or any opposition from anybody, so this is the way I am going to do it."

. . . The man who is going to handle this program has to know the idiosyncrasies of the rural people so that they can have the right approach to them and get their confidence as soon as possible. Talk in their language. Know how to sit down at the river side and have lunch right there on the ground. They see you as a human being and they understand that you are not infallible, and, if you make a mistake, they will understand it as a mistake made in good faith.

. . . One of the things that happened to me . . . (was that) I was working in one of these corrals and, of course, I was riding a horse and there were about six or seven of the neighbors that wanted to come to meet the banker. Perhaps not only with maliciousness but with the idea that they may get to know him and then later on they may come to the bank and be financed. This is a very human way to operate. So one of them called to me and asked: "How much do you think is the worth of these animals?" Now this is a very interesting question. You value cattle according to different concepts and if I am the owner, I would say $500 mainly because there were a lot of people around, and I want to hear that I value my animals very high. But if I were not the owner I would value the animals at an average price or if I were interested in buying the animals I would value them as low as I can. You see the different concepts. So what happened was this. I had to think twice what I was going to say, but honesty always leads you to the best way out. I mean when you are honest and you can explain why. So, I said $200. The man said: "I don't think so, I think you are wrong. This animal is worth much more." I said, "Yes, you could have paid much more but what I am saying is that what you paid for this animal is too much for the purpose for which you purchased it because you don't need this kind of an animal. It doesn't have the quality for the purpose you intended."

They really put you on the spot, but you must answer in as frank and casual a way as possible. By answering in a very honest way you can gain their confidence.

Therefore, in confronting the problem of implementing change, the agronomists approached each problem from the native angle, operating on the premise that "many of them may feel that floor without concrete is better because it gives them fresher air." Necessary changes were encouraged through subtle demands.

The cattle fattening program was encouraged through the following means. A farmer was given money to fatten his cattle, and as soon as the cattle were marketed, the loan was paid back. However, some animals were low quality and would take three or four years to fatten. Rather than refuse all of them as collateral, the banker would refuse a few at a time, perhaps twenty to twenty-five out of a hundred. In this way the rancher soon got the point and started improving.

Vaccination was encouraged by similar means. Farmers were told that if they did not vaccinate, they would not get the loan. All that was required was proof that the rancher was trying. Resistance to adoption of accounting methods was a major obstacle. The ranchers were shown the importance of simple accounting by practical questioning on a person-to-person basis. Small steps were encouraged such as being able to answer "How many calves did you lose this summer or dry season?" From there, simple accounting books were introduced.

PROGRAM'S PROGRESS

Chase Manhattan started in 1950 with one trained agronomist and only four bank branches in Panama: in late 1968, there were sixteen technicians and seven bank branches.

The median size of loan has increased from the initial $500 to the current $3,000. The smallest loan so far has been $100 and the largest, $250,000. A new program has just been started encouraging the youngsters to get involved by offering $50 to $100 loans to members of a club who range from ten to eighteen years of age. This is not only a potential market for the future, but also a great public relations idea.

There has been a steady increase in the absolute volume of outstanding loans to the agricultural sector by the banks in Panama. The figures are presented in Table 1.

In eighteen years of its operation, Chase Manhattan has yet to suffer a loss on a cattle financing loan in Panama. The bank has learned a great deal from this program and is now applying the techniques tried in Panama in developing similar programs in other Latin American countries, namely, Dominican Republic, Trinidad, Venezuela, Honduras, Colombia, and Brazil.

In Panama, the program has sparked activity by other commercial banks most of which have launched or are in the process of developing similar programs.

Other encouraging results from the cattle program have been:

1. Creation of job opportunities in rural sectors;
2. Increased interest by businessmen in the rural sector;
3. Four fold cattle inventory increases for 95 percent of long-term clients;

TABLE 1

Loans Outstanding by Commercial Banks in the Republic of Panama
(in Thousands of Balboas)[a]

	1963		1964		1965		1966		1967	
	Amount	%	Amount	%	Amount	%	Amount	%	Amount	%
Total Bank Loans	122,720		144,553		198,216		287,750		329,132	
Total for Agri-cultural Sector	9,541	7.8	13,005	9.0	12,211	6.2	12,287	4.3	20,930	6.4
Chase Manhattan's Share of Agri-cultural Sector Loans	5,761	60.4	8,912	68.5	6,428	52.6	4,496	36.6[b]	11,001	52.6

[a]Exchange rate: 1 Balboa = 1 U.S. $1.00
[b]This drop is due to an erroneous interpretation and misclassification of some loans guaranteed by land, which were classified by the Panamanian banking authorities according to the security and not its purpose.

SOURCE: Chase Manhattan Bank, New York.

4. Rising land values;
5. Improved quality of cattle.

By 1968, the cattle industry in Panama was firmly established, and although many problems remained to be solved, the industry showed every sign of continued growth. A conservative estimate of the industry's worth in 1966 was put at $180 million—cattle worth $65 million, land worth $100 million, and installations valued at $15 million. Ranches account for six million man-days of employment each year, making cattle ranching Panama's largest private employer with an annual payroll of over $10 million. The industry accounts for about 7 percent of the gross national product.[1]

A further view of the progress of the Panama cattle industry can be seen in Table 2.

TABLE 2

Population, Slaughter, and Export of Cattle
from the Republic of Panama

Year	Population	Slaughtered	Exports	Sale to Canal Zone
1950	570,000	73,359	NA	3,407
1951	NA	73,713	NA	2,677
1952	NA	68,373	NA	4,817
1953	NA	73,906	NA	5,618
1954	NA	73,841	2,726	4,981
1955	NA	77,743	3,030	4,655
1956	NA	79,588	400	5,199
1957	NA	87,475	1,597	3,422
1958	NA	91,949	1,522	2,709
1959	NA	94,411	2,899	2,230
1960	665,600	93,083	900	2,084
1961	760,935	106,115	385	2,494
1962	835,400	117,601	7,337	Insignificant
1963	842,400	122,126	4,418	Insignificant
1964	896,000	124,370	7,361	Insignificant
1965	968,600	134,029	5,214	Insignificant
1966	1,010,700	144,189	4,958	Insignificant
1967	1,036,600 (est.)	NA	NA	Insignificant

SOURCES: Moreno, Luis H., Jr., *La Ganderia de Ceba en Panama* (New York: The Chase Manhattan Bank, 1963), p. 110.
Chase Manhattan Bank, New York.

1. "Panama's Cattle Industry," *The Panama Canal Review*, May 1966, p. 3.

5

Marketing Management

AMIT OIL COMPANY LTD.

Market Research in Western Europe

INTRODUCTION

The Initial Problem

In 1963 the Amit Oil Company Limited (AOC)[1] was a multibillion dollar holding company with subsidiaries engaged in all aspects of petroleum production, refining, transportation, and distribution. Its 1962 sales of £718.0 million resulted in net profits of £70.5 million.

Early in 1963, AOC's marketing executives undertook a careful review of the company's European retail outlets. They had grown increasingly concerned over the brand's performance on the continent, for sales had not kept pace with potential in several of the rapidly growing European markets.

The Dynamar Study

As a result of their concern over these market trends, AOC's marketing executives asked Dynamar—the company's market research facility—to perform brand image studies in six European countries: Switzerland, Belgium, France, Denmark, Sweden, and the Netherlands. Dynamar's research group designed and administered a survey to carefully chosen samples ranging from 595 respondents in Belgium to 875 in Denmark.

---

1. All the names and figures used in the case are disguised to protect the company's identity and competitive position.

Professor Claude Faucheux, who played a central role in planning and interpreting the study, expressed its purpose as follows:

> To provide a framework for the selection of advertising themes and strategies.
> To delineate the market profiles and the actions required to communicate the desired image of the firm.
> To establish the characteristics of an optimum clientele.
> To propose a theory of purchasing behavior with respect to the products and their essential characteristics.
> To indicate the nature of contemporary psychological needs relating to the use of the automobile.

The Focus on Switzerland and Sweden

The initial analysis of the data led Professor Faucheux to conclude that Switzerland and Sweden should be selected for further analysis. Several factors encouraged the selection of these two countries:

> Switzerland and Sweden occupy polar positions along a multi-dimensional continuum with garage-orientation at one end and service station-orientation at the other;
> The data are most complete and comparable for these two countries;
> AOC enjoys differing images and degrees of market penetration in each.

Professor Faucheux noticed that the six countries fall into place along a hierarchy according to the prevailing degree of service station usage in each. As extremes in this hierarchy, Switzerland and Sweden particularly illustrate the differences associated with the degree of service station-orientation.

AOC's positions in the Swiss and Swedish markets differed considerably. In Switzerland, AOC led all brands in number of outlets, but trailed Shell in market share. Meanwhile, in Sweden, AOC fell behind Esso, Shell, Gulf, and IC/OK in number of outlets or in reported market share. (*See* Table 1.)

The Main Issue

The main issue of this case hinges on the differences that Dynamar found between the Swiss and Swedish gasoline markets and between AOC's position therein. Upon completion of the study, AOC executives faced the problem of how to approach these two markets in the formulation of different marketing strategies appropriate to each.

In the following sections data are presented relevant to the problem of which strategies to adopt in the two markets. Tables containing information on all the six countries are presented first. These are followed by tables with joint data on Sweden and Switzerland and then by tables with separate data on each country. Within each group, data pertaining to gasoline buying are presented first, followed by data pertaining to oil buying and gas station/garage patronage. We begin with a discussion of the general theory which guided Dynamar's research program. The

TABLE 1

Size of Network, 1963

	Switzerland			Sweden		
	Service Stations	Others	Market Share (Percent)	Service Stations	Others	Market Share (Percent)
Shell	88	763	27.8	812	854	19.8
Esso	79	910	20.8	759	867	20.4
IC/OK	—	—	—	303	577	16.5
Gulf	23	301	2.9	722	705	14.0
Caltex	31	138	2.9	612	626	10.6
AOC	50	989	21.3	586	318	11.4

Central Issue section discusses the implications for action and some of the general results of the study as revealed by the data. This is followed by the presentation of the market research data. Tables 2 and 3 provide market information for the six European nations. The aggregate data on the Swiss and Swedish markets are presented in Tables 4 through 8. Tables 9 through 13 present the data for the individual Swiss market, while Tables 14 through 16 provide similar information for Sweden.

BACKGROUND: MARKET DEVELOPMENT AND THE MOTORIST'S NEEDS

The Pattern of National Development in Automotive Services (an Historical View)

In undertaking its research assignment, the Dynamar staff worked with an implicit theory of the development pattern in a national market for automotive services. According to their view, a market evolves naturally, as automobile ownership increases and car usage becomes more complex, from an early predominant reliance on the garage toward an increasing use of service stations.

In the early stages of motorization, the garage is the only place serving the motorist. Later, with more automobiles, better communications, and specialization, the garage continues to provide technical service, but the service station increasingly handles everything else.

The Two Universes

In Dynamar's view, this garage/service station bifurcation brought about the motorist's participation in two universes: the garage universe and the service station universe.

The garage universe involves those aspects of service pertaining to the engine, and therefore, assumes slightly unpleasant connotations for the motorist. He perceives the engine as a constraint; as something dirty and greasy; and something strange uncontrolled, and full of uncertainty.

The service station universe, on the other hand, relates to the external and easily accessible aspects of the car. It therefore takes on pleasantly familiar and comfortable connotations. The motorist perceives the service station as a familiar agent of freedom; as a clean place to relax and refresh; as part of a controlled and predictable environment.

The motorist associates motor oil with the garage universe. In general, he views this product as one for which great differences exist between brands. Conversely, he associates gasoline with the service station universe. For the most part he judges all gasoline brands to be alike.

Finally, the motorist attaches different significance to the garage mechanic and the service station dealer. As custodian of the mysteries under the hood, the garageman assumes the role of expert and adviser; the motorist must frequently ask for his advice and follow it. But, with the service station dealer the motorist enters into a personal relationship; he expects friendly interaction. But he solicits and follows the dealer's technical advice far less frequently.

The Motorist's Needs

Dynamar's concept of the two universes aligns quite consistently with conclusions about the motivations of the motorist in an advanced economy drawn from a 1956 study performed by National Analysts, Inc. for Du Pont de Nemours & Co. In this study the Philadelphia research firm attempted to isolate "the reasons behind the motorist's actions." It began by conducting a series of in-depth interviews aimed at developing a method which would show.

> What motivations, impulses, habit patterns, or other facets of human behavior produce consumer action in the buying of petroleum products;
> The origin of this behavior, how ingrained the patterns are, and the degree to which these patterns may be manipulated.

Information gleaned from these open-ended questioning sessions enabled National Analysts to design a motivational questionnaire which it administered to an area sample of 2,036 motorists drawn from a universe of all U.S. motorists who had made purchases in service stations during the previous month.

The Du Pont study singled out *four key motives* which operate in automobile-related buyer behavior:

> *The play need* (the need to relax and amuse oneself; to seek diversion and entertainment). In satisfying this need the car is used for recreational purposes—for pleasure and amusement.
> *The aggression need* (the need to get ahead—to belittle another or to prove one's superiority over someone). . . . It's been seen, perhaps, in those drivers who must be first off at a traffic light and who must pass the other drivers on the road. . . .
> *The conservance need* (to collect, repair, clean, and preserve things). This is perhaps expressed in the need to take care of the car, to keep it in good running order. . . .
> *The infavoidance need* (to avoid failure, shame, humiliation, ridicule). It is the need to *avoid* appearing . . . inferior . . . a person of inferior position, qualities, or tastes.

THE CENTRAL ISSUE:
IMPLICATIONS FOR ACTION

The task before the AOC executives, therefore, was to analyze the Dynamar data in a manner that would provide guidelines for marketing and advertising strategies. Specifically, they wanted to know:

1. How should the gas users be classified on physical and sociological dimensions so that significant consumer classification can be developed for cultivation by AOC?
2. What kind of brand/product image would be most favorable for AOC?
3. What kind of product and service policies would yield maximum customer satisfaction, high brand loyalty, and brand differentiation for the target customers selected by AOC?

In their development of significant customer classifications, AOC marketing executives wanted to do further study of the four key motives of automobile-related buyer behavior in the light of their data. However, they did not want to confine their search to these four categories alone, but were willing to look for other sociopsychological consumer categories if they offered a better explanation of buyer behavior and were more available to development through operational strategies.

AOC executives were also faced with the issue of what marketing strategies to adopt toward Switzerland and Sweden—most especially how these strategies should resemble one another and how they should differ. In approaching this decision, AOC marketing executives recognized numerous variables which affect the brand's image in the marketplace. They viewed some of these as "direct" in that the company could directly control them at the consumer or retailer level while they considered some of them "indirect" in that the company had less control over them (though some argued that AOC could effectively manipulate these "indirect" variables through retailer training programs, information campaigns, and so on).

The following list suggests some of the variables which AOC executives included in their emerging model of the petroleum market as relevant dimensions for company action in appealing to the motorist:

Direct Variables:

Advertising	Outlet location
Network of service stations	Outlet design
Price and margin	Sign and color
Sales force	Technical equipment
Financial aid to dealer	

Indirect Variables:

Behavior of personnel in their personal relations with consumer
Status: Technical abilities with respect to care of car vs. mere sales
Personal services provided—e.g., cleaning windows, checking water, checking oil, and so on

These variables serve to identify and differentiate those factors which are critical in appealing to the motorists in various markets in general, and in Switzerland and Sweden in particular.

TABLE 2

1. Where do you usually buy your petrol?

	Denmark		France		Belgium		Holland		Sweden		Switzerland	
	No.	%	No.	%	No.	%	No.	%	No.	%	No.	%
	875 = 100		600 = 100		595 = 100		695 = 100		639 = 100		600 = 100	
(a) At a large service station	430	49.0	240	40	216	36.4	151	21	439	68	73	12.2
(b) At a garage	90	10.3	81	14	175	29.4	310	45	17	3	257	42.7
(c) At a small service station	160	18.3	113	19	86	14.4	47	7	126	20	70	11.7
(d) At a large garage	48	5.6	38	6	24	4.0	64	9	14	2	28	4.7
(e) Anywhere	147	16.8	128	21	94	15.8	123	18	43	7	150	25.0
(f) Working place/Owner of tank	–	–	–	–	–	–	–	–	–	–	22	3.7

2. If you don't change oil yourself, who does it?

	Denmark		France		Belgium		Holland		Sweden		Switzerland	
	726 = 100		81 = 100		505 = 100		616 = 100		471 = 100		458 = 100	
(a) Garage	267	36.5	62	76	426	84.4	524	85	80	17	412	90.0
(b) Big service station	422	58.4	14	18	70	14.0	52	8	293	63	18	3.9
(c) Filling station	3	0.5	–	–	3	0.6	24	4	96	20	20	4.4
(d) Don't know	34	4.6	5	6	6	1.0	16	3	2	–	8	1.7

277

TABLE 3

Six-country Average (Percent)

1. *In your opinion, have the oil and petrol brands very distinct qualities?*

	Petrol Brands	Oil Brands
(a) Yes	29	47
(b) No	48	29
(c) Don't know/no answer	23	24
	100	100

2. *Regular and super brand of petrol can be mixed.*

(a) Agree	51
(b) Disagree	30
(c) No opinion	19
	100

3. *Mixing brands of oil is dangerous.*

(a) Agree	72
(b) Disagree	13
(c) No opinion	15
	100

TABLE 4

	Sweden		Switzerland	
	No.	%	No.	%
1. *Why did you buy a car?*	698 = 100		600 = 100	
(a) For use while working	285	40.8	354	59.0
(b) For weekends	–	–	–	–
(c) For holiday trips	287	41.1	145	24.2
(d) For going to and from your place of work	109	15.6	79	13.2
(e) For other reasons	17	2.4	22	3.6
2. *How many kilometers a year do you do on an average?*	639 = 100		600 = 100	
(a) 0 to 5,000 km	24	3.8	22	3.6
(b) 5,001 to 10,000 km	268	41.9	123	20.5
(c) 10,001 to 15,000 km	153	23.9	169	28.2
(d) 15,001 to 20,000 km	98	15.3	119	19.8
(e) 20,001 to 30,000 km	66	10.3	102	17.0
(f) 30,001 to 50,000 km	21	3.3	59	9.8
(g) 50,001 to 80,000 km	1	0.2	6	1.0
(h) 80,001 to 100,000 km	2	0.3	–	–
(i) More than 100,000 km	6	0.9	–	–

TABLE 5

	Sweden		Switzerland	
	No.	%	No.	%
A. We are giving some opinions. Could you say whether you agree with them or not, or whether you have no opinion.	639 = 100		600 = 100	
1. Service stations are more pleasant than garages				
(a) Agree	490	76.7	241	40.2
(b) Disagree	78	12.2	259	43.2
(c) No opinion	71	11.1	100	16.6
2. One likes chatting with the dealer				
(a) Agree	524	82.0	195	32.5
(b) Disagree	64	10.0	329	54.8
(c) No opinion	51	8.0	76	12.7
3. The welcome at a filling station is most important				
(a) Agree	543	85.0	406	67.7
(b) Disagree	83	13.0	116	19.3
(c) No opinion	13	2.0	78	13.0
4. It is pleasant to relax while having the car refueled				
(a) Agree	447	70.0	177	29.5
(b) Disagree	147	23.0	363	60.5
(c) No opinion	45	7.0	60	10.0
5. The reception of dealers is different according to brands				
(a) Agree	256	40.1	90	15.0
(b) Disagree	268	41.9	377	62.8
(c) No opinion	115	18.0	133	22.2
B. Do you think a motorist has extra advantages when using the same service station?	639 = 100		600 = 100	
(a) Yes	567	88.7	361	60.2
(b) No	72	11.3	239	39.2
C. To what do you attach most importance when you stop at a service station?	639 = 100		600 = 100	
(a) To the brand	314	49.1	346	57.7
(b) To the appearance	27	4.2	51	8.5
(c) To the man who serves you	210	32.9	17	2.8
(d) To the technical equipment	62	9.7	26	4.3
(e) Others	26	4.1	115	19.2
(f) Don't know/no answer	–	–	45	7.5

TABLE 5—*continued*

	Sweden		Switzerland	
	No.	%	No.	%
D. *From the following reasons, which one in your opinion, makes you choose a service station other than the usual one?*	639 = 100		288 = 100	
(a) They sell the same brand that I am used to	431	67.5	128	44.5
(b) They are situated on my side of the road	67	10.5	57	19.8
(c) They are not too busy	43	6.7	13	4.5
(d) They look modern	13	2.0	3	1.0
(e) No particular reason, I like to change sometimes	11	1.7	13	4.5
(f) My friends have recommended it	5	0.8	2	0.7
(g) Other reasons	30	4.7	64	22.2
(h) Don't know/no answer	39	6.1	8	2.8
E. *What would you appreciate in a service station?*	639 = 100		600 = 100	
(a) Pleasant situation	25	3.8	44	7.3
(b) Quick service	77	12.1	389	64.8
(c) Repair facilities	96	15.0	53	8.8
(d) Facilities to relax	108	16.9	4	0.7
(e) A bar	96	15.0	9	1.5
(f) Pleasant service	77	12.1	67	11.2
(g) Eating facilities	32	5.0	1	0.2
(h) Others	77	12.1	24	4.0
(i) Don't know/no answer	51	8.0	9	1.5
F. *Do you appreciate extra services after the filling up of your tank?*	639 = 100		600 = 100	
(a) Yes	620	97.0	517	86.2
(b) No	19	3.0	83	13.8
G. *If yes to question F, which ones?*	620 = 100		517 = 100	
1. Checking the oil				
(a) Yes	552	89.0	269	52.0
(b) No	68	11.0	248	48.0
2. Checking the water				
(a) Yes	515	83.1	244	47.2
(b) No	105	16.9	273	52.8
3. Checking the tire pressure				
(a) Yes	570	91.9	306	59.2
(b) No	50	8.1	211	40.8
4. Cleaning the windshield				
(a) Yes	608	98.1	506	97.9
(b) No	12	1.9	11	2.1

TABLE 5—*continued*

	Sweden		Switzerland	
	No.	%	No.	%
H. What do you appreciate most in the dealer?	639 = 100		600 = 100	
(a) His technical agility	320	50.1	141	23.5
(b) His welcome	102	16.0	84	14.0
(c) His goodwill	194	30.3	339	56.5
(d) His discretion	21	3.3	24	4.0
(e) Don't know/no answer	2	0.3	12	2.0
I. Do you ever ask for advice?	639 = 100		600 = 100	
1. From the dealer?				
(a) Very often	25	3.9	4	0.7
(b) Often	149	23.2	43	7.2
(c) Seldom	301	47.1	180	30.0
(d) Never	164	25.7	373	62.1
2. From the mechanic?				
(a) Very often	28	4.4	29	4.8
(b) Often	191	29.9	155	25.8
(c) Seldom	283	44.3	244	40.7
(d) Never	137	21.4	172	28.7
J. Do you follow their advice?				
1. The dealer's	475 = 100		227 = 100	
(a) Always	235	49.5	102	44.9
(b) Often	235	49.5	115	50.7
(c) Never	5	1.0	7	3.1
(d) Don't know/no answer	—	—	3	1.3
2. The mechanic's	502 = 100		428 = 100	
(a) Always	311	61.9	240	56.1
(b) Often	188	37.5	181	42.3
(c) Never	3	0.6	4	0.9
(d) Don't know/no answer	—	—	3	0.7

TABLE 6

	Sweden		Switzerland	
	No.	%	No.	%
A. Do you usually get your gasoline from the same place?	639 = 100		600 = 100	
(a) Yes	592	92.6	402	67.0
(b) No	47	7.4	198	33.0
B. How many times a week do you get your gasoline from a service station other than your usual one? (apart from during holidays)	639 = 100		600 = 100	
(a) Never	361	56.5	163	27.2
(b) Once a month	250	39.1	155	25.8
(c) Once a week	21	3.3	18	3.0
(d) Not faithful to a service station	5	0.8	176	29.3

TABLE 6—*continued*

		Sweden		Switzerland	
		No.	%	No.	%
(e)	Less often	–	–	7	1.2
(f)	Don't know/no answer	2	0.3	81	13.5

C. *Do you normally buy the same brand of gasoline?*

		639 = 100		600 = 100	
(a)	Yes	605	94.7	408	68.0
(b)	No	34	5.3	192	32.0

D. *If yes to question C, what is the name of the brand?*

		605 = 100		408 = 100	
(a)	Shell	119	19.8	113	27.8
(b)	Esso	123	20.4	85	20.8
(c)	AOC	69	11.4	87	21.3
(d)	Gulf	84	14.0	12	2.9
(e)	Caltex	64	10.6	12	2.9
(f)	Castrol	–	–	2	0.5
(g)	Migrol	–	–	32	7.8
(h)	Agip	–	–	–	–
(i)	Fina	–	–	–	–
(j)	Azur	–	–	–	–
(k)	Total	–	–	–	–
(l)	Mobil	–	–	–	–
(m)	Nynas	12	2.0	–	–
(n)	IC/OK	99	16.5	–	–
(o)	Unc-X	–	–	–	–
(p)	Outsiders	–	–	–	–
(q)	Others	32	5.3	48	11.8
(r)	Don't know/no answer	–	–	17	4.2

E. *At the moment are you using the gasoline of the brand you mentioned?*

		605 = 100		408 = 100	
(a)	Yes	574	94.9	371	90.9
(b)	No	31	5.1	37	9.1

F. *If yes to Question C, do you always ask for the brand when you drive on the road?*

		605 = 100		408 = 100	
(a)	Always	509	84.1	231	56.6
(b)	Sometimes	72	11.9	105	25.7
(c)	Never	24	4.0	66	16.2
(d)	Don't know/no answer	–	–	6	1.5

G. *What do you think is most appealing in a brand?*

		639 = 100		600 = 100	
(a)	The quality of its products	210	32.9	362	60.4
(b)	Its service stations	33	5.2	39	6.5
(c)	Its dealers	134	21.0	17	2.8
(d)	Its advertising	7	1.1	24	4.0
(e)	That it can be found everywhere	199	31.1	59	9.8
(f)	Other answers	52	8.1	63	10.5
(g)	Don't know/no answer	4	0.6	36	6.0

TABLE 6—*continued*

	Sweden		Switzerland	
	No.	*%*	*No.*	*%*
H. *Why, in your opinion, do people keep to one brand?*	*639*	*= 100*	*600*	*= 100*
(a) It is always the same presentation	28	4.4	40	6.7
(b) One can be sure of the quality of the products	172	26.9	391	65.2
(c) One can be sure of the dealer's welcome	49	7.7	21	3.5
(d) One can be sure of the quality of the services	99	15.5	30	5.0
(e) By habit	—	—	—	—
(f) One can get bonus	283	44.2	—	—
(g) Others	3	0.5	71	11.8
(h) Don't know/no answer	5	0.8	47	7.8
I. *Would you think a motorist has extra advantages when using the same brand of gasoline?*	*639*	*= 100*	*600*	*= 100*
(a) Yes	522	81.7	358	59.7
(b) No	117	18.3	242	40.3
J. *Do you think loyalty to one brand should be rewarded?*	*639*	*= 100*	*600*	*= 100*
(a) Yes	552	86.4	356	59.3
(b) No	86	13.5	243	40.5
(c) Don't know	1	0.1	1	0.2
K. *Do all companies sell gasoline at the same price?*	*639*	*= 100*	*600*	*= 100*
(a) Yes	245	38.3	112	18.7
(b) No	381	59.6	472	78.7
(c) Don't know/no answer	13	2.1	16	2.6
L. *If no to Question K, is there a noticeable difference between prices of gasoline?*	*381*	*= 100*	*472*	*= 100*
(a) Yes	113	29.7	224	47.5
(b) No	264	69.3	224	47.5
(c) Don't know/no answer	4	1.0	24	5.0
M. *Besides gasoline, do you buy anything else in a service station?*	*639*	*= 100*	*600*	*= 100*
(a) Yes	471	73.7	121	20.2
(b) No	168	26.3	479	79.8
(c) Don't know/no answer	—	—	—	—

TABLE 7

	Sweden		Switzerland	
	No.	%	No.	%
A. Do you usually change the oil yourself?	575 = 100		600 = 100	
(a) Yes	104	18.1	142	23.7
(b) No	471	81.9	458	76.3
B. Do you usually get your oil change done at the same place?	471 = 100		458 = 100	
(a) Yes	438	93.0	411	89.8
(b) No	31	6.6	46	10.0
(c) Don't know	2	0.4	1	0.2
C. Do you usually keep a can of oil in your car?	564 = 100		598 = 100	
(a) Yes	60	10.6	115	19.2
(b) No	504	89.4	483	80.8
D. What brand of oil have you in the engine of your car now?	181 = 100		600 = 100	
(a) Shell	23	12.7	133	22.2
(b) Esso	33	18.2	90	15.0
(c) AOC	27	14.9	85	14.2
(d) Gulf	17	9.4	19	3.2
(e) Caltex	21	11.6	18	3.0
(f) Castrol	–	–	9	1.5
(g) Migrol	–	–	19	3.1
(h) IC/OK	33	18.2	–	–
(i) Nynas	4	2.3	–	–
(j) Fina	–	–	–	–
(k) Antar	–	–	–	–
(l) Mobil	–	–	–	–
(m) Labo	–	–	–	–
(n) Other brands	18	9.9	159	26.5
(o) Don't know/no answer	5	2.8	68	11.3
E. After how many km do you usually have chassis lubrication carried out?	623 = 100		547 = 100	
(a) Less than 2,000 km	355	57.0	193	35.3
(b) 2,000 km	120	19.3	163	29.8
(c) From 2,000 to 3,000 km	108	17.3	155	28.3
(d) More than 3,000 km	40	6.4	36	6.6
F. Do you change your oil and have your car greased at the same time?	495 = 100		494 = 100	
(a) Yes	200	40.4	314	63.6
(b) No	295	59.6	167	33.8
(c) It does not need to be greased	–	–	13	2.6

TABLE 8

	Sweden		Switzerland	
	No.	%	No.	%
A. In your opinion, have the gasoline and oil brands very distinct qualities?	639 =	100	600 =	100
1. Gasoline brands				
(a) Yes	208	32.6	165	27.5
(b) No	390	61.0	305	50.8
(c) Don't know/no answer	41	6.4	130	21.7
2. Oil brands				
(a) Yes	343	53.7	253	42.2
(b) No	250	39.1	201	33.5
(c) Don't know/no answer	46	7.2	146	24.3
B. Do you think it necessary always to use the same brand of gasoline or the same brand of oil?	639 =	100	600 =	100
1. Gasoline				
(a) Yes	434	67.9	245	40.8
(b) No	198	31.0	315	52.5
(c) Don't know/no answer	7	1.1	40	6.7
2. Oil				
(a) Yes	550	86.1	449	74.8
(b) No	77	12.1	116	19.3
(c) Don't know/no answer	12	1.8	35	5.9
C. Different brands of gasoline or oil can be mixed provided they are of the same quality.	639 =	100	600 =	100
(a) Agree	320	50.1	244	40.7
(b) Disagree	249	39.0	182	30.3
(c) No opinion	70	10.9	174	29.0
D. Regular and super grades of gasoline can be mixed.	639 =	100	600 =	100
(a) Agree	275	43.0	353	58.8
(b) Disagree	235	36.8	119	19.8
(c) No opinion	129	21.2	128	21.4
E. If you changed your brand of gasoline, would you do it:	639 =	100	600 =	100
(a) On your own initiative?	357	55.9	314	52.3
(b) Following a friend's advice?	6	0.9	13	2.2
(c) Following a mechanic's advice?	52	8.1	180	30.0
(d) Following a dealer's advice?	24	3.8	13	2.2
(e) Following the car maker's advice?	196	30.7	45	7.5
(f) Don't know/no answer	4	0.6	35	5.8

285

TABLE 8—*continued*

	Sweden		Switzerland	
	No.	*%*	*No.*	*%*
F. *If you changed your brand of oil, would you do it:*	*639* = *100*		*600* = *100*	
(a) On your own initiative?	295	46.2	280	46.7
(b) Following a friend's advice?	6	0.8	13	2.2
(c) Following a mechanic's advice?	74	11.6	206	34.3
(d) Following a dealer's advice?	33	5.2	10	1.6
(e) Following the car maker's advice?	226	35.4	55	9.2
(f) Don't know/no answer	5	0.8	36	6.0
G. *We are giving some opinions about gasolines and oils. Could you say whether you agree with them or not, or whether you have no opinion.*	*639* = *100*		*600* = *100*	
1. Service stations sell a better quality of gasoline and oils than garages				
(a) Agree	83	13.0	20	3.3
(b) Disagree	435	68.1	473	78.9
(c) No opinion	121	18.9	107	17.8
2. Garages are not suited to the sale of gasoline				
(a) Agree	250	39.1	81	13.5
(b) Disagree	306	47.9	468	78.0
(c) No opinion	83	13.0	51	8.5

TABLE 9
Switzerland

A. *How would you like loyalty to one brand to be rewarded?*	*Advertising Gift*		*Special Service*		*More Zeal From the Dealer*		*Quicker Service*	
	No.	*%*	*No.*	*%*	*No.*	*%*	*No.*	*%*
1. Why did you buy your car?	*96* = *100*		*59* = *100*		*55* = *100*		*67* = *100*	
(a) For my work	51	53.1	34	57.6	36	65.5	41	71.9
(b) For holidays and to go to work	45	46.9	25	42.4	19	34.5	16	28.1
2. Do you follow the dealer's advice?	*46* = *100*		*20* = *100*		*23* = *100*		*24* = *100*	
(a) Always	25	54.3	6	30.0	11	47.8	11	45.8
(b) Sometimes and never	21	45.7	14	70.0	12	52.2	13	54.2
3. Do you follow the garage mechanic's advice?	*78* = *100*		*44* = *100*		*42* = *100*		*42* = *100*	
(a) Always	49	62.8	20	45.5	23	54.8	24	57.1
(b) Sometimes and never	29	37.2	24	54.5	19	45.2	18	42.9

TABLE 9—*continued*

	Agree		Disagree	
B. *Service stations are more pleasant than garages*	No.	%	No.	%
1. Where do you buy your gasoline?	164 =	100	195 =	100
(a) Large service station	41	25.0	23	11.8
(b) Small service station	29	17.7	26	13.3
(c) Garage (large and small)	94	57.3	146	74.9
2. What do you like most of all about the dealer?	228 =	100	244 =	100
(a) His technical ability	50	21.9	58	23.8
(b) His welcome	40	17.6	29	11.9
(c) His goodwill	138	60.5	157	64.3
3. Do you buy the same brand of gasoline?	194 =	100	328 =	100
(a) Yes	141	72.7	214	65.2
(b) No	53	27.3	114	34.8
C. *One likes chatting with the dealer*				
1. Do you follow the dealer's advice?	75 =	100	124 =	100
(a) Always	32	42.7	61	49.2
(b) Sometimes and never	43	57.3	63	50.8
2. What do you appreciate most in the dealer?	183 =	100	310 =	100
(a) His technical ability	38	20.8	87	28.1
(b) His welcome	36	19.7	34	11.0
(c) His goodwill	109	59.5	189	60.9

TABLE 10
Switzerland

A. As you know, there are quite a lot of brands of petrol. What is your opinion about the following brands?

	Shell		Migrol		AOC		Esso		Gulf	
	No.	%	No.	%	No.	%	No.	%	No.	%
	No. = 600						% = 100			
(a) Large brand	581	96.8	199	33.2	548	91.3	553	92.2	227	37.8
(b) Small brand	3	0.5	275	45.8	20	3.3	14	2.3	250	41.7
(c) Don't know	16	2.7	126	21.0	32	5.4	33	5.5	123	20.5
(a) Well known	580	96.7	330	55.0	555	92.5	569	94.8	223	37.2
(b) Not well known	6	1.0	196	32.7	22	3.7	13	2.2	295	49.2
(c) Don't know	14	2.3	74	12.3	23	3.8	18	3.0	82	13.6
(a) It is everywhere	567	94.5	174	29.0	543	90.5	550	91.7	171	28.5
(b) It is not everywhere	15	2.5	357	59.5	30	5.0	27	4.5	322	53.7
(c) Don't know	18	3.0	69	11.5	27	4.5	23	3.8	107	17.8
(a) Service stations are attractive	487	81.2	200	33.3	475	79.2	478	79.7	267	44.5
(b) Service stations are ordinary	12	2.0	168	28.0	19	3.1	17	2.8	101	16.8
(c) Don't know	101	16.8	232	38.7	106	17.7	105	17.5	232	38.7
(a) A brand which endeavors to modernize and keep up to date	414	69.0	276	46.0	411	68.5	409	68.2	202	33.7
(b) A brand which does not try to modernize	45	7.5	104	17.3	34	5.7	39	6.5	108	18.0
(c) Don't know	141	23.5	220	36.7	155	25.8	152	25.3	290	48.3
(a) Its advertising is interesting	334	55.7	134	22.3	291	48.5	306	51.0	86	14.3
(b) Its advertising is ordinary	46	7.6	168	28.0	68	11.3	59	9.8	145	24.2
(c) Don't know	220	36.7	298	49.7	241	40.2	235	39.2	369	61.5
(a) Has a good prestige	533	88.8	156	26.0	496	82.7	514	85.7	193	32.2
(b) Has no prestige	13	2.2	270	45.0	21	3.5	24	4.0	178	29.7
(c) Don't know	54	9.0	174	29.0	83	13.8	62	10.3	229	38.1

	Shell		Migrol		AOC		Esso		Gulf	
	No.	%	No.	%	No.	%	No.	%	No.	%
			No. = 600				% = 100			
(a) People talk a lot about it	455	75.8	328	54.7	420	70.0	435	72.5	108	18.0
(b) People do not talk about it	53	8.8	142	23.7	77	12.8	70	11.7	304	50.7
(c) Don't know	92	15.4	130	21.6	103	17.2	95	15.8	188	31.3
(a) It is a popular brand	530	88.3	289	48.2	493	82.1	506	84.3	163	27.3
(b) It is not a very popular brand	8	1.4	169	28.2	28	4.7	24	4.0	241	40.3
(c) Don't know	62	10.3	142	23.6	79	13.2	70	11.7	194	32.4

B. *Do you think it necessary always to use the same brand of gasoline?*

	Yes		No	
	No.	%	No.	%
1. Where do you usually buy gasoline?	193	= 100	252	= 100
(a) Large service station	39	20.2	32	12.7
(b) Garage	114	59.1	122	48.4
(c) Anywhere	40	20.7	98	38.9
2. Do you ask the garage mechanic for advice?	244	= 100	314	= 100
(a) Very often and often	62	25.4	108	34.4
(b) Seldom and never	182	74.6	206	65.6
3. Do you ask the dealers for advice?	240	= 100	309	100
(a) Very often, often, and seldom	98	40.8	110	35.6
(b) Never	142	59.2	199	64.4

TABLE 10—continued

C. Gasoline brands are similar

	Agree		Disagree	
	No.	%	No.	%
1. Do you usually buy the same brand of gasoline?	267 =	100	243 =	100
(a) Yes	151	56.6	193	79.4
(b) No	116	43.4	50	20.6
2. What do you like most of all about the dealer?	256 =	100	225 =	100
(a) His technical ability	55	21.5	67	29.7
(b) His welcome	46	18.0	26	11.6
(c) His goodwill	155	60.5	132	58.7
3. Do you follow the dealer's advice?	89 =	100	98 =	100
(a) Always	37	41.6	49	50.0
(b) Sometimes and never	52	58.4	49	50.0

D. Where do you usually buy your gasoline?

	Large Service Station		Small Service Station		Garage		Anywhere	
	No.	%	No.	%	No.	%	No.	%
1. Do you normally buy gasoline of the same brand?	73 =	100	69 =	100	285 =	100	149 =	100
(a) Yes	61	83.6	57	82.6	217	76.1	52	34.9
(b) No	12	16.4	12	17.4	68	23.9	97	65.1

E. Which brand of gasoline do you normally buy?

	Shell		Essc		AOC	
	No.	%	No.	%	No.	%
1. After how many km do you have your oil changed?	103	100	73	100	78	100
(a) Less than 2,000 km	19	18.4	11	15.1	7	9.0
(b) Every 2,000 km or more	84	81.6	62	84.9	71	91.0
2. After how many km do you have a chassis lubrication?	97	100	72	100	80	100
(a) Less than 2,000 km	38	39.2	23	31.9	23	28.8
(b) Every 2,000 km	29	29.9	23	31.9	24	30.0
(c) More than 2,000 km	30	30.9	26	36.2	33	41.2

F. Apart from holiday periods, how many times a week/month do you buy your gasoline from a service station other than your usual one?

	Never		Once a Month		Once a Week and Do Not Keep to the Same Service Station	
	No.	%	No.	%	No.	%
1. How many kilometers do you drive annually?	156	100	150	100	189	100
(a) Under 10,000 km	46	29.5	30	20.0	46	24.3
(b) 10,000 to 20,000 km	75	48.1	83	55.3	79	41.8
(c) Over 20,000 km	35	22.4	37	24.7	64	33.9
2. Do you buy the same brand of gasoline?	163	100	153	100	176	100
(a) Yes	149	91.4	109	71.2	69	39.2
(b) No	14	8.6	44	28.8	107	60.8

291

TABLE 10–*continued*

G. *Do you look for this brand when traveling?*

1. Where do you usually buy your gasoline?

	Always		Sometimes and Never	
	No.	%	No.	%
	217 =	100	147 =	100
(a) Large service station	41	18.9	16	10.9
(b) Large garage	17	7.9	7	4.8
(c) Small service station	30	13.8	22	15.0
(d) Small garage	99	45.6	80	54.3
(e) Anywhere	30	13.8	22	15.0

TABLE 11

Switzerland

			Under 2,000 km or Every 2,000 km			Over 2,000 km		
			No.		%	No.		%
A.	*After how many kilometers do you change oil?*							
	1. How many kilometers do you drive annually?		308	=	100	246	=	100
		(a) Under 15,000 km	176		57.1	114		46.0
		(b) Over 15,000 km	132		42.9	132		54.0
	2. Where do you usually buy gasoline?		297	=	100	219	=	100
		(a) Garages	143		48.2	93		42.5
		(b) Large service stations	47		15.8	24		11.0
		(c) Small service stations	31		10.4	34		15.5
		(d) Anywhere	76		25.6	68		31.0
	3. Do you follow the advice of the garage mechanic?		230	=	100	172	=	100
		(a) Always	135		58.7	88		51.2
		(b) Sometimes and never	95		41.3	84		48.8
B.	*After how many kilometers do you have chassis lubrication?*							
	1. How long have you had your car?		190	=	100	190	=	100
		(a) Less than one year	43		22.7	79		41.6
		(b) One to two years	47		24.7	58		30.5
		(c) More than two years	100		52.6	53		27.9

TABLE 11—continued

C. Do you perform chassis lubrication and change oil yourself?

	Yes No.	Yes %	No No.	No %
	115 =	100	381 =	100
(a) Executives (senior and lower)	24	20.9	137	36.0
(b) Independent professions	5	4.3	51	13.4
(c) Employees	29	25.3	118	31.0
(d) Farmers	12	10.4	16	4.1
(e) Workers	45	39.1	59	15.5

D. In your opinion, do the different oil brands have distinct qualities?

	Yes No.	Yes %	No No.	No %	No Opinion No.	No Opinion %
1. Do you have a regular gasoline brand?	252 =	100	200 =	100	146 =	100
(a) Yes	179	71.0	111	55.5	97	66.4
(b) No	73	29.0	89	44.5	49	33.6
2. Do you ask the dealer for advice?	199 =	100	196 =	100	142 =	100
(a) Very often, often, and seldom	38	19.1	72	36.7	62	43.7
(b) Never	161	80.9	124	63.3	80	56.3
3. Do you ask the garage mechanic for advice?	252 =	100	199 =	100	146 =	100
(a) Very often, often, and seldom	174	69.0	140	70.4	111	76.0
(b) Never	78	31.0	59	29.6	35	24.0
4. Do you follow the dealer's advice?	87 =	100	71 =	100	61 =	100
(a) Always	42	48.3	24	33.8	34	55.7
(b) Sometimes and never	45	51.7	47	66.2	27	44.3
5. Do you follow the garage mechanics's advice?	173 =	100	139 =	100	110 =	100
(a) Always	99	57.2	73	52.5	67	60.9
(b) Sometimes and never	74	42.8	66	47.5	43	39.1

E. *Do you think it necessary always to use the same oil brand?*

1. Do you normally buy gasoline of the same brand?

	Yes No.	Yes %	No No.	No %
	448 =	100	116 =	100
(a) Yes	313	69.9	51	44.0
(b) No	135	30.1	65	56.0

2. On whose advice would you change oil brand?

	Yes No.	Yes %	No No.	No %
	400 =	100	107 =	100
(a) Own initiative	199	49.8	65	60.7
(b) Garage mechanic's	159	39.7	30	28.0
(c) Car manufacturer's	42	10.5	12	11.3

3. Do you follow the dealer's advice?

	Yes No.	Yes %	No No.	No %
	163 =	100	42 =	100
(a) Always	75	46.0	17	40.5
(b) Sometimes and never	88	54.0	25	59.5

4. Do you follow the garage mechanic's advice?

	Yes No.	Yes %	No No.	No %
	311 =	100	86 =	100
(a) Always	179	57.6	45	52.3
(b) Sometimes and never	132	42.4	41	47.7

F. *Oil brands can be mixed if they are of the same quality*

1. On whose advice would you change oil brand?

	Agree No.	Agree %	Disagree No.	Disagree %	No Opinion No.	No Opinion %
	223 =	100	168 =	100	148 =	100
(a) Own initiative	124	55.6	95	56.5	60	40.5
(b) Garage mechanic's	78	35.0	48	28.6	79	53.4
(c) Car manufacturer's	21	9.4	25	14.9	9	6.1

2. Do you ask the garage mechanic for advice?

	Agree No.	Agree %	Disagree No.	Disagree %	No Opinion No.	No Opinion %
	243 =	100	181 =	100	172 =	100
(a) Very often, often, and seldom	167	68.7	124	68.5	134	77.9
(b) Never	76	31.3	57	31.5	38	22.1

3. Do you follow the garage mechanic's advice?

	Agree No.	Agree %	Disagree No.	Disagree %	No Opinion No.	No Opinion %
	167 =	100	123 =	100	132 =	100
(a) Always	89	53.3	66	53.7	84	63.6
(b) Sometimes and never	78	46.7	57	46.3	48	36.4

TABLE 11 – continued

	Shell		Esso		AOC	
	No.	%	No.	%	No.	%
G. Which oil brand do you have in your engine?						
1. Where do you usually buy your gasoline?	130 =	100	87 =	100	81 =	100
(a) Garage (large and small)	58	44.6	42	48.3	49	60.5
(b) Service stations	32	24.6	21	24.1	20	24.7
(c) Anywhere	40	30.8	24	27.6	12	14.8
2. After how many km do you change oil?	126 =	100	80 =	100	81 =	100
(a) Less than 2,000 km	21	16.7	6	7.5	8	9.9
(b) Every 2,000 km	49	38.9	39	48.8	33	40.7
(c) More than 2,000 km	56	44.4	35	43.7	40	49.4
H. Which oil brand is sold at the place where you have your oil changed?						
1. After how many km do you change oil?	100 =	100	68 =	100	68 =	100
(a) Less than 2,000 km	18	18.0	4	5.9	8	11.8
(b) Every 2,000 km	38	38.0	40	58.8	26	38.2
(c) More than 2,000 km	44	44.0	24	35.3	34	50.0
2. After how many km do you have a chassis lubrication?	93 =	100	67 =	100	68 =	100
(a) Less than 2,000 km	36	38.7	19	28.4	23	33.8
(b) Every 2,000 km	23	24.7	26	38.8	19	27.9
(c) More than 2,000 km	34	36.6	22	32.8	26	39.3

TABLE 12

Switzerland

A. On whose advice would you change gasoline or oil brands?	Own Initiative		Garage Mechanic's		Car Manu-facturer's	
	No.	%	No.	%	No.	%
1. Do you ask the dealer for advice?						
(a) Gasoline:	310 = 100		174 = 100		44 = 100	
very often, often, and seldom	101	32.6	77	44.3	18	40.9
never	209	67.4	97	55.7	26	59.1
(b) Oil:	277 = 100		199 = 100		54 = 100	
very often, often, and seldom	90	32.5	83	41.7	22	40.7
never	187	67.5	116	58.3	32	59.3
2. Do you follow the dealer's advice?						
(a) Gasoline:	99 = 100		77 = 100		78 = 100	
always	40	40.4	39	50.6	67	85.9
sometimes and never	59	59.6	38	49.4	11	14.1
(b) Oil:	89 = 100		83 = 100		21 = 100	
always	36	40.4	43	51.8	7	33.3
sometimes and never	53	59.6	40	48.2	14	66.7
3. Do you ask the garage mechanic for advice?						
(a) Gasoline:	312 = 100		179 = 100		45 = 100	
very often and often	78	25.0	76	42.5	14	31.1
seldom	113	36.2	79	44.1	·21	46.7
never	121	38.8	24	13.4	10	22.2
(b) Oil:	278 = 100		205 = 100		55 = 100	
very often, often, and seldom	163	58.6	174	84.9	43	78.2
never	115	41.4	31	15.1	12	21.8
4. Do you follow the garage mechanic's advice?						
(a) Gasoline:	189 = 100		155 = 100		34 = 100	
always	106	56.1	96	61.9	17	50.0
sometimes and never	83	43.9	59	38.1	17	50.0
(b) Oil:	162 = 100		174 = 100		42 = 100	
always	89	54.9	108	62.1	19	45.2
sometimes and never	73	45.1	66	37.9	23	54.8

TABLE 13

Switzerland

	French Switzerland		German Switzerland	
	No.	%	No.	%
1. Gasoline brands are similar	163 =	100	347 =	100
(a) Yes	113	69.3	154	44.4
(b) No	50	30.7	193	55.6

TABLE 13—*continued*

	French Switzerland		German Switzerland	
	No.	*%*	*No.*	*%*
2. Do you usually buy the same brand of gasoline?	*174* =	*100*	*418* =	*100*
(a) Yes	99	56.9	282	67.5
(b) No	75	43.1	136	32.5
3. Do you look for this brand when traveling?	*78* =	*100*	*205* =	*100*
(a) Always	56	71.8	164	80.0
(b) Sometimes/never	22	28.2	41	20.0
4. Do you think there are extra advantages in using the same brand?	*174* =	*100*	*412* =	*100*
(a) Yes	88	50.6	263	63.8
(b) No	86	49.4	149	36.2
5. One likes chatting with the dealer	*145* =	*100*	*377* =	*100*
(a) Agree	70	48.3	124	32.9
(b) Don't agree	75	51.7	253	67.1
6. What is the most important thing to make a service station attractive?	*98* =	*100*	*259* =	*100*
(a) General appearance	47	48.0	156	60.2
(b) Clearly indicated/well-lit	51	52.0	103	39.8
7. How would you like brand loyalty to be rewarded?	*62* =	*100*	*214* =	*100*
(a) Advertising gift	27	43.5	72	33.6
(b) Special service	18	29.0	43	20.1
(c) More zeal from the dealer	6	9.7	52	24.3
(d) Quicker service	11	17.8	47	22.0
8. Service stations are more pleasant than garages	*144* =	*100*	*354* =	*100*
(a) Agree	87	60.4	153	43.2
(b) Disagree	57	39.6	201	56.8
9. Where do you usually buy your gasoline?	*173* =	*100*	*398* =	*100*
(a) Large service station	26	15.0	47	11.8
(b) Small service station	18	10.4	51	12.8
(c) Garage	79	45.7	201	50.5
(d) Anywhere	50	28.9	99	24.9
10. On whose advice would you change gasoline brands?	*152* =	*100*	*385* =	*100*
(a) Own initiative	71	46.7	242	62.9
(b) Garage mechanic's	61	40.1	118	30.6
(c) Car manufacturer's	20	13.2	25	6.5
11. On whose advice would you change oil brands?	*157* =	*100*	*382* =	*100*
(a) Own initiative	52	33.1	227	59.4
(b) Garage mechanic's	80	51.0	125	32.7
(c) Car manufacturer's	25	15.9	30	7.9

TABLE 14

Sweden

A. To what do you attach most importance when you stop at a service station?

	Appearance of the Service Station		Dealer		Brand		Technical Equipment	
	No.	%	No.	%	No.	%	No.	%
1. Do you ask the dealer for advice?	26 =	100	194 =	100	303 =	100	60 =	100
(a) Often	10	38.5	55	28.3	68	22.4	9	15.0
(b) Seldom	7	26.9	89	45.9	159	52.5	31	51.7
(c) Never	9	34.6	50	25.8	76	25.1	20	33.3
2. Do you ask the garage mechanic for advice?	25 =	100	195 =	100	300 =	100	60 =	100
(a) Often	11	44.0	68	34.9	88	29.3	16	26.7
(b) Seldom	7	28.0	79	40.5	154	51.4	29	48.3
(c) Never	7	28.0	48	24.6	58	19.3	15	25.0

B. Does it ever happen that you ask advice of the dealer?

	Always		Often		Seldom		Never	
	No.	%	No.	%	No.	%	No.	%
1. Frequency of oil changing	22 =	100	130 =	100	260 =	100	140 =	100
(a) Less than 2,000 km	9	40.9	43	33.1	50	19.2	27	19.3
(b) 2,000 km	4	18.2	30	23.1	68	26.2	37	26.4
(c) 2,000–3,000 km	8	36.4	39	30.0	95	36.5	49	35.0
(d) More than 3,000 km	1	4.5	18	13.8	47	18.1	27	19.3
2. Frequency of chassis lubrication	24 =	100	144 =	100	292 =	100	157 =	100
(a) Less than 2,000 km	16	66.7	85	59.0	163	55.8	88	56.1
(b) 2,000 km	5	20.8	33	22.9	57	19.5	22	14.0
(c) 2,000–3,000 km	2	8.3	19	13.2	53	18.2	34	21.7
(d) More than 3,000 km	1	4.2	7	4.9	19	6.5	13	8.2

TABLE 14—continued

	Always		Often		Seldom		Never	
	No.	%	No.	%	No.	%	No.	%
3. The place where the oil change is made	19 =	100	122 =	100	224 =	100	100 =	100
(a) Car workshop	1	5.3	10	8.2	45	20.1	23	23.0
(b) Large service station	10	52.6	86	70.5	140	62.5	55	55.0
(c) Small service station	8	42.1	26	21.3	39	17.4	22	22.0
4. Do you follow the garage mechanic's advice?	23 =	100	137 =	100	266 =	100	67 =	100
(a) Always	13	56.5	97	70.8	163	61.3	36	53.7
(b) Sometimes	10	43.5	40	29.2	103	38.7	31	46.3
5. Do you follow the dealer's advice?	24 =	100	147 =	100	293 =	100	NA	NA
(a) Always	13	54.2	87	59.2	132	45.1	NA	
(b) Sometimes	11	45.8	60	40.8	161	54.9	NA	

	Always		Often		Sometimes		Seldom		Never	
	No.	%	No.	%	No.	%	No.	%	No.	%
C. Do you follow the advice of the dealer?										
1. Frequency of chassis lubrication	228 =	100	173 =	100	229 =	100	238 =	100	118 =	100
(a) Less than 2,000 km	142	62.3	52	30.1	122	53.3	47	19.7	19	16.1
(b) 2,000 km	44	19.3	44	25.4	49	21.4	61	25.6	31	26.3
(c) 2,000–3,000 km	28	12.3			46	20.1				
(d) More than 3,000 km	14	6.1			12	5.2				
D. Does it ever happen that you ask advice of the garage mechanic?										
1. Frequency of oil changes	24 =	100								
(a) Less than 2,000 km	12	50.0								
(b) 2,000 km	4	16.3								

	Always		Often		Seldom		Never	
	No.	%	No.	%	No.	%	No.	%
(c) 2,000–3,000 km	6	25.0	51	29.5	88	37.0	45	38.1
(d) More than 3,000 km	2	8.7	26	15.0	42	17.7	23	19.5
2. Frequency of chassis lubrication	28 =	100	181 =	100	275 =	100	134 =	100
(a) Less than 2,000 km	19	67.9	108	59.7	148	53.8	77	57.5
(b) 2,000 km	4	14.3	40	22.1	55	20.0	19	14.2
(c) 2,000–3,000 km	3	10.7	27	14.9	50	18.2	28	20.9
(d) More than 3,000 km	2	7.1	6	3.3	22	8.0	10	7.4
3. Place where the oil change is made	19 =	100	160 =	100	200 =	100	88 =	100
(a) Car workshop	3	15.8	19	11.9	37	18.5	20	22.7
(b) Large service station	11	57.9	104	65.0	125	62.5	52	59.1
(c) Small service station	5	26.3	37	23.1	38	19.0	16	18.2
4. Do you follow the garage mechanic's advice?	28 =	100	188 =	100	278 =	100	NA	NA
(a) Always	16	57.1	130	69.1	162	58.3		
(b) Sometimes	12	42.9	58	30.9	116	41.7		
5. Do you follow the dealer's advice?	28 =	100	166 =	100	233 =	100	41 =	100
(a) Always	11	42.3	79	47.6	119	51.1	24	58.5
(b) Sometimes	15	57.7	87	52.4	114	48.9	17	41.5
6. Do you keep to the same fueling point?	28 =	100	188 =	100	279 =	100	137 =	100
(a) Very much	19	67.9	98	52.1	160	57.3	81	59.1
(b) Little or not at all	9	32.1	90	47.9	119	42.7	56	40.9

TABLE 14—continued

		Always			Sometimes	
E. Do you follow the advice of the garage mechanic?	No.	=	%	No.	=	%
1. Frequency of chassis lubrication	301		100	181		100
(a) Less than 2,000 km and 2,000 km	245		81.4	129		71.3
(b) 2,000–3,000 km and more than 3,000 km	56		18.6	52		28.7

302

TABLE 15

Sweden

A. What attracts one most to a brand of gasoline?	Quality of Products		Personnel		Brand can be Found Anywhere	
	No.	%	No.	%	No.	%
1. Do you ask the dealer for advice?	197	100	126	100	189	100
(a) Often	40	20.3	39	31.0	48	25.4
(b) Sometimes	92	46.7	59	46.8	97	51.3
(c) Never	65	33.0	28	22.2	44	23.3
2. Do you follow the dealer's advice?	141	100	105	100	152	100
(a) Always	77	54.6	49	46.7	74	48.7
(b) Sometimes	64	45.4	56	53.3	78	51.3
3. Do you ask the garage mechanic for advice?	198	100	129	160	188	100
(a) Often	54	27.3	47	36.4	62	33.0
(b) Sometimes	94	47.5	62	48.1	87	46.3
(c) Never	50	25.2	20	15.5	39	20.7
4. Do you follow the garage mechanic's advice?	156	100	113	100	159	100
(a) Always	99	63.5	71	62.8	97	61.0
(b) Sometimes	57	36.5	42	37.2	62	39.0
5. Do you look for brand when driving far from home?	204	100	123	100	187	100
(a) Always	180	88.2	97	78.9	163	87.2
(b) Sometimes and never	24	11.8	26	21.1	24	12.8

TABLE 15—continued

	Quality of Products		Personnel		Brand can be Found Anywhere	
	No.	%	No.	%	No.	%
6. Do you keep to the same fueling point?	207 =	100	132 =	100	198 =	100
(a) Very much	118	57.0	80	60.6	109	55.1
(b) Little and not at all	89	43.0	52	39.4	89	44.9

	Yes				No	
	No.	%			No.	%
B. *Do the various gasoline brands have distinct qualities?*						
1. Do you ask the dealer for advice?	206 =	100			387 =	100
(a) Very often and often	62	30.1			93	24.0
(b) Seldom and never	144	69.9			294	76.0
2. Do you follow the dealer's advice?	149 =	100			285 =	100
(a) Always	82	55.0			129	45.3
(b) Sometimes	67	45.0			156	54.7
3. Do you ask the garage mechanic for advice?	205 =	100			397 =	100
(a) Very often and often	82	40.0			122	30.7
(b) Seldom and never	123	60.0			275	69.3
4. Do you follow the mechanic's advice?	168 =	100			297 =	100
(a) Always	116	69.0			171	57.6
(b) Sometimes	52	31.0			126	42.4
C. *Do you think it is necessary to keep to the same brand of gasoline?*						
1. Do you ask the dealer for advice?	429 =	100			197 =	100
(a) Very often and often	129	30.1			39	19.8
(b) Seldom and never	300	69.9			158	80.2

	Yes		No	
	No.	%	No.	%
2. Do you follow the dealer's advice?	319 =	100	142 =	100
(a) Always	165	51.7	65	45.8
(b) Sometimes	154	48.3	77	54.2
3. Do you ask the garage mechanic's advice?	414 =	100	185 =	100
(a) Often	135	32.6	52	28.1
(b) Seldom	198	47.8	81	43.8
(c) Never	81	19.6	52	28.1
4. Do you follow the mechanic's advice?	346 =	100	146 =	100
(a) Always	219	63.3	88	60.3
(b) Sometimes	127	36.7	58	39.7
5. Do you keep to the same fueling point?	428 =	100	198 =	100
(a) Very much	258	60.3	98	49.5
(b) Little or not at all	170	39.7	100	50.5

D. If you keep to the same brand of gasoline, which one is it?

	Shell		Esso		AOC		Gulf		Caltex		IC/OK	
	No.	%	No.	%	No.	%	No.	%	No.	%	No.	%
1. Do you ask the dealer's advice?	114 =	100	117 =	100	65 =	100	79 =	100	61 =	100	95 =	100
(a) Often	42	36.8	25	21.4	14	21.5	18	22.8	13	21.3	21	22.1
(b) Seldom	47	41.2	57	48.7	36	55.4	33	41.8	28	45.9	55	57.9
(c) Never	25	22.0	35	29.9	15	23.1	28	35.4	20	32.8	19	20.0
2. Do you follow the dealer's advice?	94 =	100	88 =	100	53 =	100	54 =	100	42 =	100	80 =	100
(a) Always	53	56.4	46	52.3	25	47.2	30	55.6	20	47.6	34	42.5
(b) Sometimes	41	43.6	42	47.7	28	52.8	24	44.4	22	52.4	46	57.5

TABLE 15—continued

3. Do you ask the garage mechanic's advice?

	Shell No.	Shell %	Esso No.	Esso %	AOC No.	AOC %	Gulf No.	Gulf %	Caltex No.	Caltex %	IC/OK No.	IC/OK %
	116 =	100	120 =	100	61 =	100	78 =	100	61 =	100	92 =	100
(a) Often	45	38.8	34	28.3	16	26.2	25	32.0	23	37.7	27	29.3
(b) Seldom	47	40.5	58	48.3	32	52.5	30	38.5	25	41.0	48	52.2
(c) Never	24	20.7	28	23.4	13	21.3	23	29.5	13	21.3	17	18.5

4. Do you follow the mechanic's advice?

	Shell No.	Shell %	Esso No.	Esso %	AOC No.	AOC %	Gulf No.	Gulf %	Caltex No.	Caltex %	IC/OK No.	IC/OK %
	94 =	100	94 =	100	56 =	100	60 =	100	49 =	100	82 =	100
(a) Always	65	69.1	54	57.4	35	62.5	38	63.3	33	67.3	50	61.0
(b) Sometimes	29	30.9	40	42.6	21	37.5	22	36.7	16	32.7	32	39.0

E. As you know, there are quite a lot of brands of petrol. What is your opinion about the following brands?

	Shell No.	Shell %	IC/OK No.	IC/OK %	Gulf No.	Gulf %	AOC %	AOC %	Esso No.	Esso %	Nynns No.	Nynns %
					No. = 639		% = 100					
(a) Large brand	575	90.0	364	57.0	364	57.0	390	61.0	569	89.1	115	18.0
(b) Small brand	32	5.0	198	31.0	198	31.0	192	30.0	38	5.9	435	68.0
(c) Don't know	32	5.0	77	12.0	77	12.0	57	9.0	32	5.0	89	14.0
(a) Well known	588	92.0	396	62.0	422	66.0	454	71.1	581	90.9	173	27.0
(b) Not well known	32	5.0	204	32.0	166	26.0	153	23.9	32	5.0	415	65.0
(c) Don't know	19	3.0	39	6.0	51	8.0	32	5.0	26	4.1	51	8.0
(a) It is everywhere	556	87.0	262	41.0	377	59.0	403	63.1	581	90.9	96	15.0
(b) It is not everywhere	64	10.0	332	52.0	211	33.0	198	31.0	32	5.0	492	77.0
(c) Don't know	19	3.0	45	7.0	51	8.0	38	5.9	26	4.1	51	8.0

		Shell		IC/OK		Gulf		AOC		Esso		Nynns	
		No.	%	No.	%	No.	%	No.	%	No.	%	No.	%
				No. = 639				% = 160					
(a)	Service stations are attractive	498	77.9	383	60.0	428	67.0	447	70.0	511	80.0	294	46.0
(b)	Service stations look ordinary	32	5.0	83	13.0	51	8.0	51	8.0	25	3.9	115	18.0
(c)	Don't know	109	17.1	173	27.0	160	25.0	141	22.0	103	16.1	230	36.0
(a)	A brand which endeavors to modernize and keep up to date	294	46.0	288	45.0	230	36.0	256	40.1	364	57.0	121	19.0
(b)	A brand which does not try to modernize	160	25.0	115	18.0	192	30.0	173	27.1	103	16.1	268	42.0
(c)	Don't know	185	29.0	236	37.0	217	34.0	210	32.8	172	26.9	250	39.0
(a)	Its advertising is interesting	224	35.1	185	29.0	166	26.0	173	27.1	268	41.9	64	10.0
(b)	Its advertising is ordinary	127	19.9	147	23.0	160	25.0	160	25.0	103	16.1	230	36.0
(c)	Don't know	288	45.0	307	48.0	313	49.0	306	47.9	268	42.0	345	54.0
(a)	Has a good prestige	294	46.0	224	35.0	243	38.0	236	36.9	313	49.0	128	20.0
(b)	Has no prestige	45	7.0	77	12.0	58	9.0	58	9.1	32	5.0	141	22.0
(c)	Don't know	300	47.0	338	53.0	338	53.0	345	54.0	294	46.0	370	58.0
(a)	People talk a lot about it	505	79.0	383	60.0	345	54.0	371	58.1	518	81.1	128	20.0
(b)	People talk little about it	83	13.0	192	30.0	211	33.0	198	31.0	64	10.0	422	66.0
(c)	Don't know	51	8.0	64	10.0	83	13.0	70	10.9	57	8.9	89	14.0
(a)	It is a popular brand	447	70.0	326	51.0	307	48.0	326	51.0	498	77.9	96	15.0
(b)	It is not a very popular brand	71	11.1	166	26.0	166	26.0	173	27.1	39	6.1	345	54.0
(c)	Don't know	121	18.9	147	23.0	166	26.0	140	21.9	102	16.0	198	31.0

TABLE 16
Sweden

A. Chassis and oil maintenance	Do You Usually Do Your Own Chassis Lubrication?				Do You Usually Change the Oil Yourself?			
	Yes		No		Yes		No	
	No. =	% =	No. =	% =	No. =	% =	No. =	% =
1. Frequency of chassis lubrication	108	100	511	100	101	100	456	100
(a) Less than 2,000 km	66	61.1	287	56.2	60	59.4	255	55.9
(b) 2,000 km	22	20.4	96	18.8	22	21.8	84	18.4
(c) 2,000–3,000 km	15	13.9	93	18.2	10	9.9	90	19.7
(d) More than 3,000 km	5	4.6	35	6.8	9	9.9	27	6.0
2. Frequency of oil change	85	100	463	100	99	100	455	100
(a) Less than 2,000 km	14	16.5	111	24.0	20	20.2	110	24.2
(b) 2,000 km	33	38.8	107	23.1	33	33.3	107	23.5
(c) 2,000–3,000 km	22	25.9	169	36.5	30	30.3	161	35.4
(d) More than 3,000 km	16	18.8	76	16.4	16	16.2	77	16.9
3. Do you ask the dealer's advice?	107	100	500	100	100	100	448	100
(a) Often	12	11.2	135	27.0	14	14.0	122	27.2
(b) Seldom	52	48.6	245	49.0	43	43.0	226	50.4
(c) Never	43	40.2	120	24.0	43	43.0	100	22.4
4. Do you follow the dealer's advice?	65	100	401	100	NA		NA	
(a) Always	25	38.5	208	51.9	NA		NA	
(b) Sometimes	40	61.5	193	48.1	NA		NA	

Questions 5–7

	Do You Usually Do Your Own Chassis Lubrication?				Do You Usually Change the Oil Yourself?			
	Yes		No		Yes		No	
	No.	%	No.	%	No.	%	No.	%
5. Do you ask the garage mechanic for advice?	106 = 100		499 = 100		97 = 100		450 = 100	
(a) Often	18	17.0	171	34.3	21	21.6	160	35.6
(b) Seldom	52	49.1	227	45.5	44	45.4	202	44.9
(c) Never	36	33.9	101	20.2	32	33.0	88	19.5
6. Do you follow the garage mechanic's advice?	73 = 100		421 = 100		NA		NA	
(a) Always	37	50.7	271	64.4	NA		NA	
(b) Sometimes	36	49.3	150	35.6				
7. Do you change oil on:	99 = 100		420 = 100		86 = 100		381 = 100	
(a) Your own initiative	60	60.6	234	55.7	53	61.6	213	55.9
(b) Car manufacturer's advice	39	39.4	186	44.3	33	38.4	168	44.1

B. After how many kilometers do you normally have a chassis lubrication?

	Less Than 2,000 km		2,000 km		2,000–3,000 km		More Than 3,000 km	
	No.	%	No.	%	No.	%	No.	%
	296 = 100		102 = 100		93 = 100		38 = 100	
(a) Engineers	29	9.8	11	10.7	22	23.6	6	15.8
(b) Independent professionals	27	9.1	15	14.7	11	11.8	5	13.2
(c) Managers	40	13.5	17	16.7	18	19.4	12	31.6
(d) Employees	86	29.1	22	21.6	21	22.6	7	18.4
(e) Workers	114	38.5	37	36.3	21	22.6	8	21.0

TABLE 16—continued

		2,000 Kilometers or Less		More Than 2,000 Kilometers	
		No.	%	No.	%
C.	**Frequency of oil changes**				
1.	How much do you drive annually?	243	100	261	100
	(a) 5,000 to 10,000 km	129	53.1	100	38.3
	(b) 10,000 to 15,000 km	54	22.2	79	30.3
	(c) 15,000 to 20,000 km	36	14.8	50	19.1
	(d) 20,000 to 30,000 km	24	9.9	32	12.3
2.	Do you ask the dealer for advice?	255	100	275	100
	(a) Often	73	28.6	57	20.7
	(b) Seldom	118	46.3	142	51.6
	(c) Never	64	25.1	76	27.7
3.	Do you ask the garage mechanic for advice?	255	100	275	100
	(a) Often	96	37.6	77	28.0
	(b) Seldom	109	42.8	130	47.3
	(c) Never	50	19.6	68	24.7
D.	**Frequency of chassis lubrication**				
1.	Do you ask the dealer for advice?	448	100	140	100
	(a) Often	118	26.3	21	15.0
	(b) Seldom	220	49.1	72	51.4
	(c) Never	110	24.6	47	33.6
2.	Do you ask the garage mechanic for advice?	448	100	143	100
	(a) Often	148	33.1	33	23.1
	(b) Seldom	204	45.5	72	50.3
	(c) Never	96	21.4	38	26.6

E. *Do you think that the different oil brands have distinct qualities?*

	Yes		No	
	No.	%	No.	%
1. Professions	325 =	100	241 =	100
(a) Engineers	32	9.8	37	15.4
(b) Independent professionals	27	8.3	27	11.2
(c) Managers	39	12.0	41	17.0
(d) Employees	76	23.3	49	20.3
(e) Farmers	45	13.8	18	7.5
(f) Workers	107	32.8	69	28.6
2. Do you ask the dealer for advice?	328 =	100	236 =	100
(a) Often	89	27.1	40	16.9
(b) Seldom	143	43.6	135	57.2
(c) Never	96	29.3	61	25.9
3. Do you ask the garage mechanic for advice?	323 =	100	239 =	100
(a) Often	117	36.2	59	24.7
(b) Seldom	138	42.7	122	51.0
(c) Never	68	21.1	58	24.3
4. Do you follow the garage mechanic's advice?	271 =	100	191 =	100
(a) Always	179	66.1	106	55.5
(b) Sometimes	92	33.9	85	44.5
5. Do you change oil on:	190 =	100	152 =	100
(a) Own initiative	146	76.8	128	84.2
(b) Car manufacturer's advice	44	23.2	24	15.8

F. *One can mix oils of different brands as long as they belong to the same quality*

	Yes		No	
1. Brand of place of oil changing	245 =	100	193 =	100
(a) Shell	54	22.1	45	23.3
(b) Esso	55	22.4	50	25.9

311

TABLE 16—continued

	Yes		No	
	No.	%	No.	%
(c) AOC	39	15.9	21	11.0
(d) Gulf	28	11.4	23	11.9
(e) Caltex	27	11.1	20	10.4
(f) IC/OK	42	17.1	24	12.5

G. *If you were to change oil brands would it be:*

	On Your Own Initiative		On Advice of Garage Mechanic		On Advice of Dealer		On Advice of Car Manufacturer	
	No.	%	No.	%	No.	%	No.	%
1. Do you ask the advice of the garage mechanic?	280 =	100	72 =	100	30 =	100	213 =	100
(a) Often	85	30.3	23	31.9	13	43.3	66	31.0
(b) Seldom	127	45.4	38	52.8	12	40.0	97	45.5
(c) Never	68	24.3	11	15.3	5	16.7	50	23.5
2. Do you follow the dealer's advice?	213 =	100	61 =	100	25 =	100	162 =	100
(a) Always	102	47.9	31	50.8	16	64.0	82	50.6
(b) Sometimes	111	52.1	30	49.2	9	36.0	80	49.4

SHARPES, INC. U. S. A.

A Feasibility Study to Estimate Market Potential for a Consumer Product

Sharpes, Inc.[1] is a large, diversified multinational company whose production of razor blades accounts for about half of its total sales. During the past ten years, Sharpes has been expanding its overseas manufacturing facilities significantly (Table 1). During Sharpes' 1969 fiscal year (September 1968 to August 1969) approximately 55 percent of its earnings were generated through its overseas subsidiaries.

Sharpes' international operations are largely autonomous with respect to its domestic operations. The international subsidiaries are overseen by the International Group Vice-President who reports directly to the Chairman of the Board. Under him are four geographical group general managers, who coordinate the subsidiary companies, and an export market manager. Capital expansion is generally left up to these men for anything short of setting up operations in a new country. Since all such expansion is made solely from funds generated by Sharpes' overseas operations and from local investment, the International Group Vice-President has only to approve the venture for it to begin (Figure 1).

The Group Vice-President for International Operations, Jack Anthony, was most anxious to expand Sharpes' manufacturing operations abroad, not only to continue the rapid increase in overseas profits, but also to absorb the steady decline in its market share in West Europe where it was experiencing stiff competition from local manufacturers. Moreover, import restrictions in an increasingly large number of underdeveloped countries were also beginning to hurt sales and stunt growth.

The Group General Manager for Australasia, Robert Klammer, had been thinking for some time about extending Sharpes' operations in India. Klammer's territory, which included India and Pakistan, was one of the largest in terms of sales potential and future growth, though it was the smallest in terms of its contribution to Sharpes' current international sales and profits. Before approaching International Division for investment authority, Mr. Klammer decided to explore the possibility of investment opportunities in India. Consequently, Klammer hired Emrich Research Associates, Inc. of New York to do a study about the sales and

---

1. All figures and names used in this case are disguised to protect the company's competitive position.

TABLE 1

Sharpes' Total Sales and Profits from Razor Blades 1959 to 1968
(in Thousands of Dollars)

Fiscal Year	Net Sales	Net Income Before Taxes	Net Income
1959	73,347	22,627	10,901
1960	78,426	26,562	13,008
1961	88,502	30,212	14,926
1962	96,514	32,406	15,806
1963	103,112	29,812	14,518
1964	104,021	25,608	13,372
1965	117,064	25,714	14,823
1966	138,590	32,067	17,421
1967	149,998	36,104	19,623
1968	194,214	43,501	21,795

FIGURE 1

Sharpes' International Organization Chart

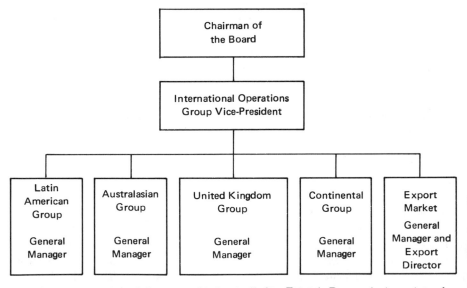

manufacturing potential for razor blades in India. Emrich Research Associates has had extensive experience in conducting area market studies in foreign countries. In addition, through their branch office in India, they were uniquely equipped to carry out this assignment. The terms of reference given to Emrich Associates by Mr. Klammer were as follows:

1. Assess the political, social, and economic climate for private foreign investment in India.

2. Estimate the demand for razor blades in India during the next five years.
3. Study the nature and structure of both current and anticipated competition in the manufacture and marketing of razor blades in India.
4. Ascertain the source and availability of raw materials.
5. Assess the marketing and distribution costs.

In March 1969 Emrich Associates submitted their findings to Mr. Klammer which confirmed his expectations of a good potential market for razor blades in India (Appendix I). Mr. Klammer sent the report to Mr. Anthony in New York, recommending that approval be given for:

1. Equity capital investment (dollar outlay) of $2.7 million ± 5 percent starting in 1969 and spread over three years. Actual outlays to be determined later in accordance with the payment schedule for plant and equipment to be purchased outside India.
2. Entering the Indian market on a minority basis (49 percent) in collaboration with Messrs. Dahmi & Sons, New Delhi, India.
3. Aiming at market penetration of 40 percent within four years from the start of full-scale operations.
4. Authorization of an outlay of $40,000 to start engineering studies, site selection, and further marketing studies.

Mr. Anthony and his staff were quite impressed with the study. However, they had some reservations about entering the market in a joint venture as a minority partner.

Questions

1. Analyze the findings of Emrich Research Associates' Report.
   (a) How far do you agree with their projection of consumer demand?
   (b) Are there any other factors which should be included in the report to enable Sharpes' executives to make a better decision?
2. Evaluate the recommendations as to size of investment, degree of market penetration, and manner of market entry recommended by Klammer to Anthony.
   (a) What is the reasoning behind the recommendations made by Klammer?
   (b) Do you agree with these recommendations? If not, what other alternative course of action would you suggest and why?
3. What techniques or arguments would you use to get the Indian Government to allow you rather than a competitor (or both of you) to set up operations in India?
4. Based on studies 1, 2, and 3 above:
   (a) Recommend whether Sharpes should enter the Indian market, and if so how and to what extent.
   (b) Estimate the amount of investment which will be required to make a successful entry.
   (c) Project future sales, growth, market penetration and profitability.
   (d) Identify important razor blade market segments. Characterize the attitudes and buying habits of each segment so that the best appeals can be utilized to persuade Indians to buy Sharpes' razor blades.

APPENDIX I

A Feasibility Study for the Manufacture and Marketing of
Razor Blades in India

CONDUCTED FOR SHARPES' INTERNATIONAL, SIDNEY, AUSTRALIA BY EMRICH RESEARCH ASSOCIATES, NEW YORK, U. S. A.

Submitted December 1968

INTRODUCTION—GENERAL OBSERVATIONS

As the largest noncommunist country in the world, with a population of over 500 million, India has unlimited potential as a razor blade market. However, India offers an environment which has many problems characteristic both of underdeveloped and highly advanced countries. If any one word were used to describe India, it would have to be "paradoxical," not only in geography, but also in her people. Urban India has a large and growing middle class, many of whom are college educated. Those who have assimilated Western ideas and habits with their own rich Indian heritage present a very sophisticated and knowledgeable market. On the other hand, the rural majority is relatively uneducated and strongly tradition oriented. The use of the safety-razor is virtually nonexistent among members of this segment of the population.

India offers virtually unlimited potential as a razor blade market, but also offers a stiff challenge that only innovative and adaptive management can meet. We believe that Sharpes can provide the management and technical skill to meet this challenge. In addition, we were contacted by representatives of the Dahmi family who are interested in going into partnership with Sharpes. In return for supplying the machinery and approximately twenty marketing, technical, and managerial experts for the first year, we believe the Dahmi family will pay all other expenses and set-up costs for the year. The Dahmi family has an extremely large amount of capital at its disposal and will not need to borrow. Moreover, the Dahmi's political influence should encourage the government licensing committee to act quickly in approving our partnership.

We estimate a total cost of $3 million ($2.7 million for equipment and $.3 million for salaries). It is also necessary to act quickly since we believe that the razor blade market will be open to foreign investment for two months at the most.

The Sharpes name will, in our opinion, attract 20 percent of the market initially (at present approximately half of the illegally imported blades are Sharpes). We expect that our sales will grow at the rate of 20 percent annually during 1970 to 1975 compared with an increase in the total consumption of blades at the rate of 10 percent per annum. This will have the effect of gradually increasing our market penetration as well which we hope will stabilize around 35 percent at the end of the fifth year. For this reason we feel that the most modern stainless steel production equipment is the best choice. Once distribution and manufacturing operations have reached 35 percent, we see no reason why return on equity before taxes cannot surpass the present 22 percent average on domestic capital. We also expect a small profit in the first year of operation.

MARKET SIZE AND POTENTIAL GROWTH IN THE DEMAND FOR RAZOR BLADES

The total market for razor blades is subject to several constraints:

1. Males over fifteen years of age constitute the basic market for blades.
2. Some religious sects do not shave (particularly the Sikhs) and others shave only weekly before religious services.
3. The sale of blades is predominantly limited to urban areas which constitute only 20 percent of the total population. Urban areas are those cities and towns with over 20,000 people (there are 634 towns with over 20,000 people and 107 cities over 100,000). Rural inhabitants do buy razor blades, but they purchase them in periodic trips to urban centers.
4. Per capita income is very low in India. This income is unevenly distributed, with most of the higher income people living in the cities. Rural areas are pretty much out of the money economy.

Given below is a brief summary of the step-by-step process used for determining the size of the razor blade market:

General Population Statistics[1]

Total population (U. N. est. 1969): 526,500,000

1. Annual rate of increase—2.5 percent
2. 987 females per 1,000 males
3. 82.2 percent rural, 17.8 percent urban (1961)

Age Structure, 1961

Age Group	Percentage of Total Population
0 to 4	15.0
5 to 14	26.0
15 to 24	16.7
25 to 34	15.4
35 to 44	11.0
45 to 54	8.0
55 to 64	4.8
65 to 74	2.1
75 and over	1.0

[a]Fifteen and over = 59 percent of total population.

Number of individuals in four major religious groups (1961)

1.	Hindu	366.2 million
2.	Moslem	46.9 million
3.	Christian	10.5 million
4.	Sikhs	7.8 million

1. Sources: U. N. Statistical Publications and Government of India Reference Manuals.

Population Projections

Total Population (in Millions)

1970	539.7
1971	553.2
1972	567.0
1973	581.2
1974	595.7
1975	610.6

To allow for an increasing migration of people from rural to urban areas since the 1961 census, we have adjusted the rural/urban percentage breakdown from 82.2/17.8 to 80.0/20.0.

Year	Rural (in Millions)	Urban (in Millions)
1970	431.7	107.9
1971	442.5	110.6
1972	453.6	113.4
1973	464.9	116.2
1974	476.5	119.1
1975	488.5	122.1

Potential Shaving Market—
Males Fifteen and Over

Assume that 987 females for every 1,000 males or 50.3 percent of the total population is male. Further, assuming the percentage of the total population which is fifteen or over constitutes 59 percent of the total population, then 59 percent of approximately 50.3 percent of the total population represents a potential market.

Year	Total Population	Male: 15 and Over	Urban	Rural
		(in Millions)		
1970	539.7	159.2	31.8	127.4
1971	553.1	163.2	32.6	130.5
1972	567.0	167.3	33.5	133.8
1973	581.2	171.4	34.3	137.2
1974	595.7	175.7	35.1	140.6
1975	610.6	180.1	36.0	144.1

Urban Males, Fifteen and Over, Using Shavers. The computations here necessitated that we first determine, by projection, the number of urban males, fifteen and over, using shavers. To do this we first had to determine the number of urban males, fifteen and over, who were shaving in 1961, and increase this figure at a rate of 10 percent per year.

Total Population 1961	439.1 (in Millions)
17.8% total population (urban):	78.2
59% total population—15 and over:	46.0
50% total population—male 15 and over:	23.0
30% males 15 and over shaving:	6.9

Year	Males Shaving	*Not Shaving (in Millions)*	*Total Urban Males 15 and Over*
1970	16.5	15.4	31.8
1971	18.1	14.5	32.6
1972	19.9	13.5	33.5
1973	21.9	12.4	34.3
1974	24.1	11.0	35.1
1975	26.5	9.5	36.0

Rural Shaving Market. This market represents, by far, the greatest potential for future razor blade sales. Assuming that at time zero (1970), a negligible projection of the rural population is shaving, we have projected the increase in razor usage assuming a modest growth of 1.0 percent per year.

Year	*Total Rural-Male Pop. over 15 (in Millions)*	*Number Using Razor Blades at 1% per Year (in Millions)*
1970	127.4	0.100
1971	130.5	0.101
1972	133.8	0.102
1973	137.2	0.103
1974	140.6	0.104
1975	144.1	0.106

Market Summary

Based on the above data, we project the demand for razor blades to grow as follows:

The Male User 15 Years and Older

No. of Persons (in Millions)	*Blade Shaving Habits*	*1970 No. Blade Shaving (in Millions)*	*Estimated Growth Rate*	*1975 No. Blade Shaving (in Millions)*
Rural				
1970 – 127.4	Daily	.020	1%	.021
1975 – 144.1	Biweekly	.040	1%	.042
	Weekly	.040	1%	.042
Urban				
1970 – 31.8	Daily	3.3	10%	5.3
1975 – 36.0	Biweekly	6.6	10%	10.6
	Weekly	6.6	10%	10.6
		16.5		26.5

Total Demand for Blades

1970	*1975*
3.3 × 360/year 1.188 × 10^9	5.5 × 360/year 1.980 × 10^9
6.6 × 100/year .660 × 10^9	10.6 × 100/year 1.060 × 10^9
6.6 × 50/year .330 × 10^9	10.6 × 50/year .530 × 10^9
2.178 × 10^9	3.570 × 10^9

Income Projections

India has a per capita income of slightly less than $80 per year. This is largely because 72 percent of the work force is engaged in agriculture on a subsistence level and is not in the money economy, rather living largely on what it can grow and barter.

Year	Average Factory Worker Wages in Rupees	Working Class Consumer Index with 1951 as Base
1960	1,375	143
1961	1,417	148
1962	1,465	150
1963	1,479	151
1964	1,522	169
1965	NA	190
1966	NA	203
1967	NA	215

Source: *Statistical Abstract of the Indian Union 1967.*

Year	Factory Workers in all Factories (including Government) in Thousands
1960	3,764
1961	3,918
1962	4,111
1963	4,374
1964	4,616
1965	4,682

Source: *Statistical Abstract of the Indian Union 1967.*

Year	Estimated Per Capita Income
1958	$64
1963	$80
1965	$91
1966	$77

Source: *Yearbook of National Accounts, 1967*, p. 825.

Projecting a 3 percent increase in average factory wages, a 5 percent increase in the price index, and a 5 percent increase in the number of factory workers, we have:

Year	No. of Workers (in Thousands)	Average Wages in Rupees	Consumer Index 1951 Base
1965	4,682	1,570	190
1966	4,940	1,620	203

Year	No. of Workers (in Thousands)	Average Wages in Rupees	Consumer Index 1951 Base
1967	5,200	1,680	215
1968	5,460	1,730	228
1969	5,850	1,780	239
1970	6,150	1,835	251
1971	6,460	1,890	263
1972	6,800	1,950	274
1973	7,150	2,010	288
1974	7,520	2,080	302
1975	7,910	2,140	316
1976	8,420	2,200	332
1977	8,850	2,270	348
1978	9,310	2,340	357
1979	9,800	2,410	385
1980	10,290	2,490	404

LOCAL OPERATING CONDITIONS

Government Attitude
Toward Foreign Investment

The government's role in industry is to insure that the nation's scarce resources are utilized as efficiently as possible as to minimize balance of payments deficits, avoid economic chaos, and provide maximum economic growth. For this reason the overall attitude of the Indian Government toward foreign participation in its economy is favorable; still, such investment can only be made under conditions that the government feels will minimize the cost in foreign exchange and capital repatriation. Presently all foreign investment in India must be a joint venture with majority Indian equity participation. All such investment arrangements must have governmental approval. At present the government has established three lists of industries in order to provide guidelines for acceptance of foreign investment. The first list is composed of key industries, in which foreign participation is strongly encouraged and automatically approved. The second list contains industries in which participation is ordinarily spared reference to the licensing committee. The third list is composed of industries in which foreign participation must be approved and negotiated with the licensing committee. New lists are published monthly as new licenses are granted and economic conditions change. The trend has been for more and more industries to be added to the second list. At present, razor blades are on list three, but because domestic razor blade production improved tremendously in the past year, it is highly probable that razor blades will move to list two very soon. For this reason a quick decision is important.

Although there are no antitrust or competition statutes, the government is showing concern over the increasing amount of economic concentration in a few hands and may intervene in the activities of a firm should its conduct be deemed harmful to the public good.

Pricing

The government encourages independent pricing, subject to two restrictions:

Under the Essential Commodities Act any item declared "essential" may be subjected to price control. Such control seems to be loosening at this time.

The state encourages arms-length pricing of capital goods and components.

The freedom to sell at any price implies that no minimum resale pricing law is in effect and that discounts to sales agents and distributors are permissible.

Repatriation of Capital and Profits

Because of a chronic shortage of foreign exchange the Reserve Bank of India applies strict controls to the movement of foreign currencies. The transfer of profits in the investors' currency is permissible without limitation, provided, of course, that all tax obligations have been fulfilled. There are no restrictions on the repatriation of capital in government approved projects. However, in cases where investment has been made in areas which the Indian Government has accorded on priority, the Government reserves the right to put limitations on repatriation at times of foreign exchange shortage. USAID guarantees, however, are available against inconvertibility.

Taxation

India is characterized by very high taxation schedules and low tax morality. The large tax burden is exemplified by a basic corporate income tax rate of 50 percent, plus a 40 percent surtax. This is applicable only to federal taxation, in addition to which there are numerous state and local taxes, as well as nuisance taxes, such as the "Octroi" tax on trucking between cities.

The principle of arms-length pricing is important to avoid taxation of extra-Indian earnings derived from "business connections in India."

Losses may be carried forward for eight years for tax purposes. The threat of double taxation by India and the U. S. is avoided because of a taxation treaty.

Depreciation schedules are set by the government. Although they are not particularly liberal in themselves (buildings—5 percent; capital equipment—7 to 15 percent, usually the former), if a firm operates multiple shifts the depreciation schedule is increased 50 percent. Depreciation expenses may be carried forward without limitation.

Sources of Funds

The prime concern of any foreign firm investing in India is the federal limitation to a minority interest of 49 percent. The present trend of financing is broken down into three sources: (1) cash 35 to 45 percent; (2) local firm 25 percent, and (3) public equity issue 30 to 40 percent. Although new investment equity capital is scarce, there does exist in India a financial infrastructure (principally eight equity exchanges) which can float the necessary funds. The cost of equity financing on the local market is approximately 5 percent.

The principal sources of debt financing are twofold: (1) For medium- and long-term funds the Cooley Funds are available at 8 percent. These funds are the repayment of American foreign aid, which by contractual agreement cannot be remitted to the U. S. (2) For short-term funds the local development banks are available, with the Industrial Credit and Investment Corporation of India (ICICI) receiving very strong world bank backing.

Labor

Although nationally India is extremely labor-intensive, skilled workers are scarce and managers even scarcer. Yet, foreign firms are expected by the state to "Indianize" their local operations. Thus, foreign firms must engage in long talent hunts and extensive training programs.

Union organization, although supported by the government, is small yet its proponents are very vocal. Unions are essentially organized on a plant basis, but there are four major national organizations which are affiliated with the major political parties of India (Congress, Socialist, and Communist).

Federal intervention in labor relations is common in the guise of compulsory conciliation under the "Code of Discipline in Industry." The government also controls wage administration, which is based on a crawling peg to keep pace with the consumer price index increases.

There are three main features to labor compensation standards other than the tie-in of the consumer price index to basic wages and they are: (1) compulsory profit sharing of 60 percent of "available surplus" (gross profits minus direct taxes plus preferred dividends plus 8.5 percent return on investment and depreciation) (2) social security tax of 6.25 percent on the basic wage for up to a total of forty-five days.

The basic work week is forty-eight hours, with overtime being double-time.

MARKETING IN INDIA

Competition

In 1957, the last year importation of foreign razor blades was permitted, the razor blade consumption was as follows (uncoated carbon blades were generally the only blades available throughout the world at that time):

Brand	Quantity (Millions)	Retail Price Per Hundred Blades[1]
Imported		
Sharpes	100	Rs. 10.00
Diamond	50	7.50
Other imported	50	7.50
Domestic	150	3.50

Domestic production rose rapidly as follows:

1957	150 million
1960	500 million
1965	1,000 million
1966	1,100 million
1967	1,200 million

1. $1.00 = Rs. 7.50

Domestic blade production in 1968 was estimated at nearly 1,400 million. During the period 1957 to 1968, domestic production changed from a homogeneous group selling at a cheap price to a broader range with several premium blades selling at higher prices in 1967.

Brand	Price Per Hundred Blades	Volume (in Millions)
Panama (German partner)	Rs. 9.00	42
Swish Stainless	7.50	84
Ahok Stainless	6.75	84
Bengal	6.75	63
Sharpedge Erasmic	6.00	205
Maharaja	6.00	84
Viceroy	6.00	42
Prince	5.25	415
Six others	5.25	221
Total		1,240

There is a great deal of dissatisfaction with domestic blades and poor brand loyalty, with frequent trial of new brands. The sources of dissatisfaction were as follows:

There were few shaves per blade.
The shaving action was generally unsatisfactory with much pull and many nicks.
Many blades per pack had to be discarded because they were dull or rusty.
Many consumers pointed out that there was no uniformity of quality; two blades from the same pack were often very different in quality.

The most surprising finding was that 40 percent of shavers were still using imported blades (smuggled) purchased at Rs. 35.00 per 100. These consumers explained that

Imported blades gave at least five close shaves per carbon steel blade and at least fifteen shaves per stainless blade.
They gave greater shaving satisfaction.

These consumers also stated that they had tried all the domestic brands, including the premium brands, and all the new introductions as they appeared in the market. However, they invariably reverted to imported brands because of dissatisfaction.

Distribution Channels

Only a small segment of the total population is part of India's market economy. The actual market for consumer goods other than food and locally made necessities is less than 10 percent of the population. This segment is growing rapidly and totals nearly 40 million.

Much consumer selling is done by door-to-door peddlers, called *wallahs*, or through government emporia. The vast majority of consumer marketing is in produce grown and sold locally through barter.

India is naturally divided into four main distribution regions with one of the four major cities—Delhi, Calcutta, Madras, or Bombay—at the center. Most wholesalers are confined to one of these regions. A few wholesalers, however, are nationwide with branches in all four regions. In all regions, sales marketing channels are varied and flexible, with retailers and wholesalers either separate or combined. Sometimes large families organize an integrated distribution system. Open-air bazaars and a few modern metropolitan variety stores and cooperatives are the main retail outlets.

In India the marketing system tends to work in reverse of the marketing in the United States. That is, pressure comes from below rather than from above. Very few manufacturers have sales representatives who try to encourage wholesalers and retailers to buy more of their product. The same applies to wholesalers trying to sell more to retailers. Usually, in India, the retailers go to the wholesalers who go to the manufacturers to get orders.

Typical Marketing Channels

1. Consumer Purchase Level
   (a) *Wallahs* (door-to-door)
   (b) Government Emporia (retail)
   (c) Bazaars
   (d) Metropolitan Variety Stores
   (e) Cooperatives
2. Natural Distributions Centers
   (a) Delhi (North)
   (b) Calcutta (East)
   (c) Madras (South)
   (d) Bombay (West)
3. Channels and Estimated Sales
   (a) Nationwide Wholesalers   20%
   (b) Local Wholesalers (including cooperatives)   50%
   (c) Family Integrated System   30%
4. Freight Handling

Type	Amount of Freight Moved
Railroad (35,000 miles)	80%
Highways (440,000 miles)	3%
Airlines (35,000 miles)	7%
Shipping	10%

Promotion: Media

1. Newspapers—(1966) 49 daily newspapers with circulation of 6,253,000.

Name	Language	City	Type
Indian Express	English	Madras	Evening Daily
Navbharat Times	Hindi	Bombay	Morning Daily
Hindustan Times	English	New Delhi	Morning Daily
Anada Bazar Patrika	Bengali	Calcutta	Morning Daily
Sunday Standard	English	Bombay	Sunday
Anada Vikatan	Tamil	Madras	Sunday

2. Magazines—predominantly Life-International (biweekly)

3. Radio—Radio Ceylon (India-Pakistan-Ceylon-Burma coverage) (1964) number of receivers 6,485,000. New regulations permit advertising now on state-controlled radio and TV stations.
4. Television—(1966) 4,000 receivers
5. Billboards
6. Movie Shorts—(1964) Number of theaters 3,843, number of seats 3,200,000.

Trademark

It is possible that the trademark or colors presently used to package Sharpes' blades may have to be changed. Certain colors, symbols, and even names have special religious significance to either the Hindus or Moslems. The use of such a color, symbol, or name in promotion or packaging could alienate members of the offended sect. Further research in the area is vitally important.

The "Sharpes" name should probably be retained, since most Indians associate quality with foreign brands, especially British, Swedish, U. S., German, and Dutch.

A marketing strategy that could appeal to some religious ethics might be extremely successful. Many Hindus believe that personal cleanliness is extremely important and an association of Sharpes' blades with, say, soap might have a dramatic appeal.

Consumer Profile of Razor Blade
Users: Habits, Attitudes, and
Social Connotations

The majority of Indian men who shave do so with razor blades. However, the electric razor and the straight edge or "barber's" razor do constitute a small segment of the market.

Used razor blades are not thrown away but are either used by women (new blades are too sharp) or are kept for use as a cutting tool. Shaving is done with shaving cream or with regular soap.

Most Indian shavers are dissatisfied with present domestic blades. The poor attributes of domestic blades stated in the case are valid and force many men to use "smuggled" blades, although 40 percent was felt to be a high figure. There is no brand loyalty with respect to blades, but price and quality are significant in motivating brand selection. Indians feel that a foreign blade is superior to a domestic blade.

Shaving, and blades in particular, does not carry any social stigma, although one caste does not shave (the Sikhs). This is too small a segment for us to worry about. Therefore, with a carefully chosen brand and brand name, we will be able to appeal to the Hindu and the Moslem religious sectors.

MANUFACTURING

The carbon steel blade is made of steel containing 1.2 percent carbon. Such steel is abundant and relatively cheap but corrodes easily. The stainless steel blade is composed of 11.5 percent chromium. Stainless steel resists corrosion exceptionally well and retains its edge much longer. However, stainless steel is relatively scarce, about twice as expensive, and is much more difficult to grind and temper. To insure an adequate supply at a stated price, Sharpes has negotiated a long-term contract with Sandvik, Ltd. to be their exclusive supplier.

An uncoated razor blade edge under a microscope looks as "ragged as a saw." The uncoated stainless steel edge looks even more ragged than the uncoated carbon steel edge. A special plastic coating fills in the jagged edges so that blades not only appear smooth but also last somewhat longer.

In the U. S. men average about two shaves with the uncoated carbon steel blade, about four shaves with the coated carbon steel blade, and about eight shaves with the coated stainless steel blade. In the U. S. the number of shavers using the stainless blade increased steadily after its introduction and has stabilized at about 70 percent. The coated carbon steel blade takes a finer edge. For this reason the first and second shaves on this blade are somewhat closer and smoother than those using the coated stainless steel blade. All subsequent shaves are much better with the stainless blade.

Packaging costs represent about 50 percent of the factory costs for the coated carbon steel blades. Stainless blades are marketed in the same size container. The potential exists for cutting packaging costs in half since fewer blades represent a supply for an equal time.

Although stainless cost more than carbon blades, they yield so many more good shaves that the consumer will spend less per shave. Such has been Sharpes' experience in the U. S. and other markets, and profit margins have fallen. For this reason, unless competition has forced it to introduce a stainless blade, it has generally refrained from doing so. A major exception has been South America, which greatly surprised Sharpes. Its introduction in South America of a stainless blade virtually wiped out all competition there and the decreased profit margins were more than offset by an increased market share.

To assure a uniform product quality, Sharpes' engineers design all production equipment which is then manufactured in Sharpes' own machine shops.

Uncoated carbon blades/hundred:

1. Steel
   Carbon   Rs. 1.52
   Carbon w/coating   1.61
   Chromium (stainless) including coating   3.36
2. Labor   .32
3. Packaging
   (a) Inner wrapper
       Outer wrapper
       Tuck, cellophane
       Outer wrapper
       Outer box   1.32
   (b) Crates   .34

Factory Costs	*Cost (Millions)*	*Personnel*
Uncoated Carbon Blade		
Automated computerized factory	Rs. 0.144	500
Automated factory	0.093	1,000
Semi-automated factory	0.056	1,500

Factory Costs	Cost (Millions)	Personnel
Plastic Coated Carbon Blade		
Automated computerized factory	Rs. 0.160	550
Automated factory	0.104	1,100
Semi-automated factory	0.056	1,650
Stainless Steel Plastic Coated Blade		
Automated computerized factory	0.192	605
Automated factory	0.125	1,210
Semi-automated factory	0.069	1,810

All four kinds of blades can be produced in one factory—coated and uncoated carbon steel and stainless steel.

HEWLETT-PACKARD COMPANY U. S. A. (D)

Market Planning and Strategy of Implementation

The overseas marketing policies of H-P reflect, with some variation, the marketing policies pursued domestically. The company is primarily product oriented, and marketing is used mainly as an ancillary arm of the organization. Therefore, the success of marketing effort depends largely on the nature of products developed and manufactured by the company.

PRODUCT DEVELOPMENT

The prime emphasis in Hewlett-Packard is on product development with about 11 percent of the sales dollar spent on R & D. The company markets some 2,500 diverse items. The sales of each individual item are, however, relatively small. Each manufacturing division R & D manager and every R & D employee has a responsibility for the continued development of new products. Periodic product development reports are prepared and circulated among design personnel in the various divisions to preclude duplication of effort, to ensure that products of the various divisions will work together, and to provide for the early establishment of promotional plans.

Hewlett-Packard's product planning program is internally oriented and the company relies heavily on executive judgment for choice of product ideas. H-P managers do not consider consumer surveys to be an effective method of analyzing the product needs of the market. Since the company hierarchy is made up of electronic engineers, and its employment practices provide mainly for engineers, the bulk of product ideas represents electronic instruments for electronic engineers.

The company's feeling toward new product development is illustrated by a quote from one company official:

> For many of our products, which are electronic in nature and designed to help electronic engineers, we are our own best source of marketing information because the people in our laboratories are doing exactly what our customers are doing. If our people find a quicker way of doing things you can bet that our customers will want to know that method. Therefore, we are our own guinea pig for much of this process. However, in the medical and chemical areas, this is not true, and we must go outside for product ideas. The source of an idea can be a new technique developed by somebody else and reported in the literature. It can be a processing breakthrough in making certain kinds of crystals or a manufacturing breakthrough. It can be the development of a key element in, say, a signal generator. A signal generator is made up of a source, a monitoring section, and various subelements. It could be a breakthrough in attenuation that makes it possible to redesign a whole series of generators. Also, a product idea can be suggested to us by our customers, or it may come from some alert sales engineer.

Another company official remarked about the change in product development as follows:

> We are faced with the rising importance of computer related activity. Traditionally, our instruments have measured something and displayed it on a meter or with a series of lights or numbers which a person reads or interprets. Now with the computer most of these activities can be analyzed inside the instrument package. The responding action is determined by the machine. This places a strain on the organization to direct its development activities so that hardware which fits these needs will be developed. Miniaturization is another step which must be considered in each instance.

Still another company official characterized his company's R & D efforts and its heavy sunk cost in product development:

> Ours is basically a development oriented company dealing with electronic products of a specialized nature. Even in the case of bread-and-butter items, we are talking in terms of only a few hundred units per month which would not be considered particularly large in many other industries.
>
> The basic ideas for products are created in our labs. Our manufacturing people decide which of the ideas have practical possibilities in terms of improved performance over existing products and uses. This process of in-company winnowing out is possible because to a large extent our customers put our products to the same uses as we put them in our labs, our machine shops, and in our plants. Moreover, it's a question of demonstrating to the customer what a new product can do and, in fact, creating a demand for it because many a time a customer has no idea that existing performance standards can be improved.

The big expense is in design and development and not manufacturing.
Once we go through the steps of designing an instrument, putting the
prototypes through environmental tests, etc., we have pretty well accomplished the bulk of the work. It is a fixed cost and like an iceberg the
manufacturing costs are only the tip. Once development has been accomplished we go into production, even though somebody might, at that
point, take a few units out and make a very intensive survey and find
out there's not a very big market for the new product. We would still
go into production because for the most part the production processes
are relatively simple. Sometimes it's merely a question of bending some
sheet metal in different directions and cutting some holes. So even
though our market may be somewhat less than expected when we went
into development, we would still go into it.[1]

Recently, the company developed a computer which can be used for
engineering tasks. Further developments have brought to the forefront a desk
calculator for engineers. It sells for $5,000 and could be altered with little
difficulty to handle business problems. Company officials are well aware of
this possibility but have not concluded that Hewlett-Packard should branch
out into commercial product development. They emphasize that to this time,
Hewlett-Packard has considered itself as being in the industrial products
industry and manufactures what could be classified as "machine tools." One
manager gives the following rebuttal to the idea of developing and marketing
commercial products:

> This is a debatable question: Should Hewlett-Packard enter the consumer
> market in depth? We are selling engineering talent. We charge for it and
> expect to get good returns from it. The calculator is the first step in a
> series of engineering related tools that are not strictly measuring devices.
> I expect we will have a lot of fun with it, but whether we should get
> into other fields is a good question. I think marketing a business
> product would be getting into a field with an entirely different orienta-
> tion. Whether we would be successful in it is really problematical. For
> example, many people ask: "Why don't you get involved in designing
> and manufacturing machine tool control equipment?" We already have
> considerable know-how in this field, but we are physically removed from
> where the machine tool people are—Milwaukee, Pittsburgh, and Chicago—
> and might face a considerable overall disadvantage.

Hewlett-Packard's international factories were initially established to produce
products designed in the United States but which faced high duty rates and/or
strong local competition. Later emphasis, especially as a consequence of the duty
reductions resulting from the Kennedy Round, has been placed on the hiring of
qualified engineers and the development of proprietary products. H-P currently
tends to encourage each factory in developing its own new product ideas and to
discourage sole reliance on transferred products. However, each marketing
organization is expected to market products from all the factories.

1. Unless otherwise stated, all references to statements by company officials pertain to oral
or written communications with the author.

MARKET PLANNING AND CONTROL

Customer Targets

Science, medicine, industry, government, and education are considered to be the broad market categories for Hewlett-Packard products. In the United States the company maintains some 10,000 active consumer accounts while competing with approximately 200 similar firms. Hewlett-Packard customers can be divided into three basic groups: research and development laboratories, product manufacturers, and service and maintenance people.

The company feels that it maintains a more integrated marketing program than does its competitors. One manager states:

> I think that Hewlett-Packard maintains a really customer-oriented approach and tries to approach marketing from a problem solving point of view. We say to the customer: "You have a measurement problem, and we feel that we have the best solution. We are not going to just give you a box with the hardware in it, but we are going to help you make the best of it."
>
> For example, there is no catalog that approaches the quality of the Hewlett-Packard catalog. Also, the written supporting material we have available for any instrument is far superior to any of those published by the competition—the documentation, the descriptive material, the ease with which repairs and maintenance can be handled because they are well described, the speed with which replacement parts can be identified and secured.

H-P's international marketing strategy is primarily subjective. Company managers know the current level of sales and the types of instruments that are being sold in each area. One marketing manager explains:

> We do quite a lot of traveling; through visits we have an impression of how well things are going in certain areas. So we have some idea of which markets we feel are being handled well and which are not. And, of course, we have some idea of what the potential is. So it's a question of lining up your bets and looking for what changes must be made. Perhaps the marketing effort is being handled indifferently; the manager has too much to do. Perhaps an insufficient number of sales engineers are being employed, or perhaps the area is not following our pricing policies. All these and many other factors have to be weighed and decisions made.

Company officials do not place much emphasis on in-depth market analysis. They feel that since the quantities sold of each product are small and because the industry is tightly knit, executive judgment of market potential is sufficient. Results have been impressive. For example the projected sales level in one region in 1968 was accurate to within one percent. Company officials were also able to predict Australia's sales within five percent and Japan's within three percent. Overall international forecast accuracy was within ten percent in 1968.

Marketing Costs

H-P roughly allocates 10c of every sales dollar to the "sales activity." The sales activity is defined to include part of the directly related support functions (discussed earlier), such as order processing and shipment. The approximate breakdown of marketing costs per sales dollar is:

Support function (related to sales)	3¢
Advertising	1¢
Direct selling—including personal contact and follow-up service related to sales	6¢
Total costs per sales dollar	10¢

Advertising and Promotion

The main thrust of H-P sales promotion is through personal contact as is indicated by the 60 percent allocation of total marketing costs to this item. H-P considers this heavy emphasis on personal contact quite appropriate in view of the technical nature of the product, the small volume of unit sales with high unit prices, the custom usage of the product by a large number of customers, and the need for after-sales service.

Next in order of importance perhaps is the Hewlett-Packard *Journal*, a monthly publication describing new measurement techniques and products. The H-P *Journal* is directed personally to scientists and engineers and has a circulation of over 200,000. It has grown as a result of the close-knit nature of the worldwide electronics community. Most important men in electronics are on the mailing list.

The international advertising dollar is under the control of regional marketing groups. The Latin American area requests money from Hewlett-Packard Inter-Americas in Palo Alto, while the Western European advertising program is coordinated by Hewlett-Packard, S. A. in Geneva. The funds expended on local levels within the various countries are minimal and usually come in the form of grants.

H-P international markets also get the benefit of spill-over of advertising placed by domestic divisions in engineering and electronics journals. The overseas offices are not charged with any portion of the costs of placing these ads. This is a greater advantage than may appear on the surface, since most foreign engineers rely heavily on American publications for information about activities in their professional fields (Tables 1 and 2).

In 1968, H-P tried another somewhat novel method of reaching its customers and demonstrating its products. H-P acquired a DC-6 airplane and filled it with company products. This plane was flown over a large portion of the world to bring the latest H-P equipment to customers. Each trip was carefully planned with advance arrangements made at every stop to bring together the most prominent and strategically placed decision makers in government and the private sector who were potential buyers for H-P products. The plane also carried experts from Palo Alto to give technical demonstrations and handle

TABLE 1

Foreign Circulation in Reader/Pages for Top Fifteen Most Advertised-in Publications

Magazine	Pages of Ads	Foreign Circulation	Reader/Pages
Electronics	170	11,949	2,031,330
Electronic Design	96	4,179[a]	401,184
Spectrum	81	6,513	527,553
Science Split-run?	79	10,243	745,918
Microwave Journal	66	9,163	604,758
Electro-Technology	56	461	25,816
Instruments and Control Systems	51	2,595	132,345
Analytical Chemistry	46	8,499	390,954
Microwaves	44	4,727	207,988
Aviation Week	40	5,391	215,640
Physics Today	38	4,253	161,614
EEE	37	334	12,358
Chemical and Engineering News	35	8,768	302,995
Scientific Research	34	5,449	185,266
Circulation	21	000	000
Total	894	81,612	5,945,719

American Scientist	Split-run?	Yes	2,728
Medical World News	Split-run?	Yes ($300 min.)	1,187
Science and Technology	Split-run?	Yes	11,456
Scientific American	Split-run?	Yes	69,149

[a]Includes Canadian circulation

TABLE 2

Foreign Circulation of Publications Carrying the Bulk of H-P Advertising

Publication	No. of Ad Pages	Insertions	U.K.	Ireland	Austria	Belgium	Eastern Bloc[a]	Scandinavia[b]	France	Germany	Greece	Netherlands	Italy	Portugal and Spain	Switzerland	U.S.S.R.	Total European Circulation	Total Potential Advertisement Exposure[d]
Electronics	159	143	1773	11	50	321	319	1156	1275	929	24	387	1059	164	402	60	7930	1,133,990
Electronic Design	96	88	1646	10	11	–	–	55	906	555	13	–	789	66	136	–	4187	368,456
Spectrum	75	56	944	53	12	101	56	425	310	242	44	5	333	67	259	20	2871	160,776
Science	69	60	995	50	91	216	279	800	738	689	58	4	715	169	304	25	5133	307,980
Microwave Journal	66	62	2987	35	45	170	238	792	818	817	16	322	835	78	200	–	7353	455,886
Electro-Technology	48	47	–	–	–	–	–	–	–	–	–	–	–	–	–	–	461[c]	21,667
Instrument and Control Systems	51	49	305	4	3	47	173	239	211	146	3	128	144	34	27	20	1484	72,716
Analytical Chemistry	46	44	1200	32	50	181	452	587	716	583	41	292	567	190	168	–	5059	222,596
Microwaves	44	40	1019	9	16	131	86	380	517	479	30	–	607	33	116	–	3423	136,920
Aviation Week	30	29	1147	12	11	97	39	406	793	448	14	129	320	76	140	66	3698	107,242
Physics Today	30	27	583	29	18	79	93	310	435	346	26	–	178	40	217	67	2421	65,367
EEE	37	37	21	–	1	–	–	–	28	19	–	–	21	5	2	–	97	3,589
Chemical and Engineering News	27	20	944	19	53	206	227	485	616	562	52	315	564	183	378	17	4621	92,420
Scientific Research	34	32	3501	81	95	249	1	509	826	818	40	270	621	188	342	–	7541	241,312
Circulation	21	13	–	–	–	–	–	–	–	–	–	–	–	–	–	–	3661[c]	47,593
Science and Technology	18	12	872	41	44	83	28	430	296	194	9	152	121	51	127	7	2455	29,460
Scientific American	12	6	20173	686	259	1423	376	5571	3352	3214	214	4134	2331	687	2175	151	44746	268,476
Medical World News	18	9	–	–	–	–	–	–	–	–	–	–	–	–	–	–	1187[c]	10,683
Totals:	881	774	38110	1072	759	3304	2367	12145	11837	10041	584	6138	9205	2031	4993	433	103,019 / 108,328	3,747,129

a Includes: Bulgaria, Czechoslovakia, Hungary, Poland, and Yugoslavia
b Includes: Denmark, Finland, Sweden, and Norway
c Total Foreign excluding Canada—per SRDS 4/24/68
d Number of insertions times total European circulation
Source: *Foreign Circulation of Selected Technical and Scientific Publications for Hewlett-Packard Corporation*, Lennen & Newell, Incorporated, March 1968.

inquiries from these visitors. There was also an effective follow-up program to convert inquiries into orders.

Pricing Policy

H-P follows a policy of uniform pricing on a world-wide basis. Although some rare exceptions are made to accommodate local competitive conditions, the company generally maintains a rigid, constant pricing policy and requires all foreign marketing organizations to sell at the same price level (Exhibit 1). Volume discounts are allowed on large purchases, but discounts are not allowed on any other basis: if the quantities are similar, the customer on the street may purchase at the same price as the large industrial buyer.

H-P's overseas marketing organizations work from the same basic price list but are allowed to charge for import duties, local taxes, and other incidentals. Tables 3 and 4 give examples of the calculative procedure for overseas sales and the nature of charges that can be included in the prices.

Processing and Handling of Orders

Another important feature of H-P marketing policy is that *all* H-P owned or controlled international sales organizations funnel their orders to the appropriate manufacturing factory. Orders from independent sales organizations and direct customer orders are handled by H-P's regional sales organizations.

Exhibits 2 and 3, entitled "Corporate Marketing Policy: International Orders," and "International Marketing Policy: Procedures for the Handling of Non-Routine Inquiries and Orders," describe the process of handling international inquiries and orders in the U. S. and outside the U. S. respectively. Both policy statements are accompanied by flow charts to show points of action for various organizational units.

EXHIBIT 1

International Policy

1 December 1968

SALES COMPANY PRICING PROCEDURES

It is H-P policy to sell its products throughout the world at the lowest possible price consistent with corporate objectives and local pricing and competitive situations. Prices in local currency should not exceed the total cost incurred if purchase had been made in the country of manufacture and importation made directly by the customer.

Local currency f.o.b. duty-paid prices shall be established for the complete corporate product line by each International Sales Company Manager in such a manner as to ensure complete recovery of:

EXHIBIT 1—*continued*

1. Full f.o.b. factory catalog price.
2. Transportation, handling, insurance and warehousing costs from factory to f.o.b. destination.
3. Local duty, import, turnover, added value and sales taxes.
4. Interest charges in those countries where normal payment terms exceed 45 days.
5. Provisions for currency devaluation exposure when recommended by International Corporate Finance.

Each International Sales Company is expected to produce a profit in its trading income account. This account is defined in the H-P International Accounting Manual, which fully describes appropriate debit and credit charges. Profit in this account shall reflect H-P ability to realize savings in transportation, insurance and handling costs because of its large shipping volume compared to the customer's ability to import in his own account.

In some countries it is desirable to provide multiple pricing schedules for identical products to cover special prepaid warranty periods in excess of H-P standard policy, special customer training and unusual length of payment terms. Such pricing variations are acceptable; however, they must have advance approval from the Vice President, International Operations.

International Sales Company Managers shall submit pricing formulas for each category of duty rate to their International Sales Region Managers for approval or revision. A recommended format is attached. Upon approval by the International Sales Region Manager, one copy of each pricing schedule shall be forwarded to the International Operations Administrative Manager.

The setting of U. S. dollar prices of products from International manufacturing plants for sale in the United States, shall be the responsibility of the International Operations Import Products Manager. The Import Products Manager shall submit pricing formulas, using the same procedure described above, to the International Operations Administrative Manager for approval or revision.

TABLE 3

Local Selling Price Formula
(Quotes in Local Currency)

Duty-Paid Sales

1. List Price (Local Currency)	100.00
2. CIF Port of Entry Costs	
3. Duty	10.90
4. Forwarder Fees (Local)	0.40
5. Local Transportation	
6. Local Handling	1.00
7. Other: (Describe)	
8. Taxes: (Describe)	

TABLE 3–*continued*

Duty-Paid Sales

	(a)	____
	(b)	____
	(c)	
9.	Insurance	0.10
10.	Interest on deposits (if any)	
11.	Interest on financing terms at 6% per year	0.30
12.	Contingency Interest: (Devaluation exposure etc.)	
13.	Trading Income	4.80
14.	Other (Describe)	
	Total: Invoice amount customer pays for goods[a]	117.50

[a]Amount customer pays for goods will be calculated as follows:

List Price (local currency)
+ Surcharge (if any)

Subtotal × 1.175   =   Local Sales Price
                                  + 10% Value Add Tax

                                  Total = amount customer pays for goods

TABLE 4

Local Selling Price Formula
(Quotes in Local Currency)

Duty-Free Sales

1.	List Price (Local Currency)	100.00
2.	CIF Port of Entry Cost	
3.	Duty	
4.	Forwarder Fees (Local)	0.40
5.	Local Transportation	
6.	Local Handling	1.00
7.	Other: (Describe)	
8.	Taxes: (Describe)	
	(a)	
	(b)	
	(c)	
9.	Insurance	0.10
10.	Interest on deposits (if any)	
11.	Interest on financing terms at 6% per year	0.30
12.	Contingency Interest: (Devaluation exposure etc.)	
13.	Trading Income	3.20
14.	Other: (Describe)	
	Total: Invoice amount customer pays for goods[a]	105.00

[a]Amount customer pays for goods will be calculated as follows:

List Price (local currency)
+ Surcharge (if any)

Subtotal × 1.05   =   Local Sales Price
                                  + 10% Value Add Tax

                                  Total = amount customer pays for goods

EXHIBIT 2

Corporate Marketing Policy

June 1, 1967

INTERNATIONAL ORDERS

Definition. International orders are generally defined as orders for material for use outside the fifty United States. International orders cannot be exclusively identified by where they are written or the type of characteristics of the items requested. However, orders indicating exportation or that have one or more of the following characteristics are usually classified as international orders:

1. 230 volt or 50 Hz power line operation.
2. Export packing and/or marking.
3. Export documentation, such as:
   (a) cubic volumes and/or metric weights;
   (b) U. S. Government Schedule B and/or export licensing information;
   (c) AID etc. documentation;
   (d) special international banking requirements.
4. Delivery to an intermediate consignee known to be an overseas shipper or freight forwarder.

Policy. It is the policy of the Hewlett-Packard Company to have the maximum number of international orders placed with the local H-P sales offices outside the United States for three major reasons:

1. The H-P sales offices outside the United States contact and render service to the end users of our instruments.
2. Customers in Europe and Japan receive faster delivery from H-P international factories and warehousing facilities. Local delivery outside the United States strengthens the international manufacturing program and broadens the base of the entire company.
3. All H-P international activities must operate in conformance with the Export Control Regulations of the U. S. Government. The intent of these regulations is to prevent H-P instruments classified as "strategic" from leaving the free world. Violations carry penalties, including prohibition from sending material out of the United States and even fines and imprisonment. International orders must be processed in accordance with these regulations.

Domestic Sales Offices. The primary nature of the customer's business activity and whether or not H-P is required to provide exportation assistance determines the extent of the participation by the domestic sales offices. To implement this policy and to define the businesses to be handled by the U. S. sales offices, customers desiring equipment for use outside the United States have been divided into the various categories shown.

Quota Credit and Commissions. Sales quota credit and commission compensation on orders involving split situations between Domestic and International Sales Regions shall adhere to the Corporate Marketing Policy on Commissions. The definitions of Specifier, Purchaser and User determines the mathematical split to be used for both quota credit and commission.

EXHIBIT 2—*continued*

Requests from Export-Import Houses. H-P Sales Offices located in or near U. S. Centers of International Commerce are frequently called upon by Export-Import Houses who buy from U. S. sources for distribution or resale outside the United States. Requests of this type should be sent to H-P International, Palo Alto, for further handling. It is H-P's belief that there are relatively few occasions where export-import houses are able to provide a useful function in supplying H-P products. Instead, they isolate their customers from the technical assistance available from the local International H-P Sales Offices and raise the cost of H-P instruments by including substantial profit margins and charging their customers for exportation services which H-P provides either free or at cost.

For these reasons, orders are rarely accepted from export-import houses. Instead, International Operations supplies the names and addresses of the International H-P Sales Offices and requests the export-import house to ask the prospective purchaser (whose identity is usually carefully concealed) to contact his local office or, if he prefers, the appropriate H-P International Regional Marketing Organization (HPSA, HPIA, Export Marketing).

Export-import houses occasionally perform useful functions for the purchasers of H-P equipment. For example, they may provide unusual credit terms, combine a number of small shipments to reduce handling, shipping and export-import charges, or secure all of their customer's requirements—the troublesome, small items as well as the big profitable ones. Under these circumstances and on receipt of a written request from the foreign customer, International Operations will accept export-import house orders. Export-import house orders supported by customer letters are handled promptly at full catalog prices. In addition, complete information is sent to the H-P sales office in the foreign area so the customer may receive the proper technical assistance.

Summary. International orders are those for material destined for shipment outside of the United States. Customers should be encouraged to place these orders with the local H-P International Sales Offices for ease in order handling, better local (outside the United States) follow-up and speedier delivery. Local U. S. assistance should be given to help maximize our overall sales.

EXHIBIT 3

International Marketing Policy

March 25, 1966

PROCEDURES FOR THE HANDLING OF NON-ROUTINE INQUIRIES AND ORDERS

The majority of H-P's international customers receive assistance and place their orders through the local H-P sales offices in their countries. This is proper and in line with H-P's policy of providing its customers with the most direct service, adapted, as far as possible, to meet local conditions.

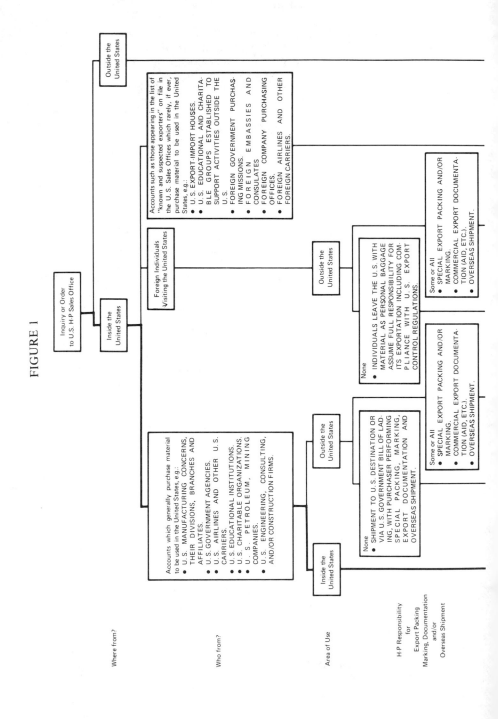

FIGURE 1

Action

Quote and Accept Orders

- IN ACCORD WITH U.S. MARKETING POLICY.

Quote and Accept Orders

- MAKE SURE THE MATERIAL WILL OPERATE ON THE POWER LINE VOLTAGE AND FREQUENCY AVAILABLE IN THE FOREIGN AREA.
- TREAT U.S. GOVERNMENT ORDERS FOR U.S. GOVERNMENT USE AND ORDERS WHERE THE FOREIGN DESTINATION IS UNKNOWN AS U.S. ORDERS WITH FULL SALES QUOTA CREDIT AND COMPENSATION RETAINED BY THE U.S. SALES OFFICE INVOLVED.
- SPLIT SALES QUOTA CREDIT AND COMPENSATION ON OTHER ORDERS WHERE THE FOREIGN DESTINATION IS KNOWN IN ACCORDANCE WITH U.S. MARKETING POLICY. SEND COPY OF INVOICE, NAME AND ADDRESS OF THE END-USER, IF KNOWN, AND CHECK FOR APPROPRIATE AMOUNT OF COMPENSATION TO H-P INTERNATIONAL OPERATIONS, PALO ALTO FOR DISTRIBUTION TO H-P INTERNATIONAL SALES OFFICE IN THE AREA OF THE END USER.

Do Not Quote or Accept Orders

- SEND ALL INQUIRIES AND ORDERS TO H-P INTERNATIONAL OPERATIONS, PALO ALTO, FOR QUOTATION AND/OR ACCEPTANCE.
- H-P INTERNATIONAL OPERATIONS WILL SEE THAT (1) THE U.S. SALES OFFICE INVOLVED RECEIVES APPROPRIATE SPLIT SALES QUOTA CREDIT AND COMPENSATION ACCORDING TO U.S. MARKETING POLICY AND (2) SIMILAR TREATMENT ACCORDING TO INTERNATIONAL MARKETING POLICY IS RECEIVED BY THE INTERNATIONAL SALES OFFICE IN THE AREA OF THE END-USER.

Quote and Accept Orders

- DETERMINE INDIVIDUAL IS ACTING FOR HIMSELF AND NOT FOR EXPORT-IMPORT HOUSE OR FOREIGN EMBASSY, CONSULATE, PURCHASING MISSION, ETC.
- MAKE SURE THE MATERIAL WILL OPERATE ON THE POWER LINE VOLTAGE AND FREQUENCY AVAILABLE IN THE FOREIGN AREA.
- ARRANGE SUITABLE PURCHASE TERMS (I.E., CASH).
- SECURE NAME AND COMPLETE ADDRESS OF END-USER IN FOREIGN AREA
- SPLIT SALES QUOTA CREDIT AND COMPENSATION ACCORDING TO U.S. MARKETING POLICY SENDING CHECK FOR APPROPRIATE AMOUNT AND END-USER INFORMATION TO H-P INTERNATIONAL OPERATIONS, PALO ALTO FOR DISTRIBUTION TO H-P INTERNATIONAL SALES OFFICE IN AREA OF END-USER.

Do Not Quote or Accept Orders

- SEND ALL INQUIRIES AND ORDERS TO HP INTERNATIONAL OPERATIONS, PALO ALTO, FOR QUOTATION AND/OR ACCEPTANCE.
- HP INTERNATIONAL OPERATIONS WILL SEE THAT (1) THE U.S. SALES OFFICE INVOLVED RECEIVES APPROPRIATE SPLIT SALES QUOTA CREDIT AND COMPENSATION ACCORDING TO U.S. MARKETING POLICY AND (2) SIMILAR TREATMENT ACCORDING TO INTERNATIONAL MARKETING POLICY IS RECEIVED BY THE INTERNATIONAL SALES OFFICE IN THE AREA OF THE END-USER.

Do Not Quote or Accept Orders

- SEND TO H-P INTERNATIONAL OPERATIONS, PALO ALTO FOR FURTHER HANDLING.

341

EXHIBIT 3—*continued*

From time to time, however, the local H-P sales offices receive inquiries and orders for equipment which is to be used outside their territories. These non-routine requests should be handled in as simple and direct a manner as possible to avoid unnecessary delays which lead to customer dissatisfaction. At the same time, care must be taken to protect the interests of H-P sales offices in the receiving area and to observe the export control regulations of the United States and other countries which may be concerned.[1] Particular attention must be given to this last point. H-P holds the local sales offices responsible for seeing that H-P products are resold to legitimate customers and that all reasonable care is taken against subsequent diversion to unauthorized destinations. Carelessness on the part of a local sales office could result in loss of U. S. import privileges by the sales office and even, perhaps, loss of U. S. export privileges by the Hewlett-Packard Company.

The general procedures to be followed in handling these non-routine requests are summarized in the flow-chart attached to this memorandum. Although the flow-chart and its associated notes are largely self-explanatory, special attention must be given to five general questions.

1. Who is making the inquiry?

Find out about the prospective purchaser and the nature of his business. The goals here are: (1) to provide the best possible service to all legitimate customers, (2) to ensure that export control regulations are not violated, and (3) to provide protection to the H-P sales offices in other territories.

A special problem exists with firms and individuals who are engaged in export-import activities and who are not original equipment manufacturers. Inquiries and orders from these firms and individuals must be approached carefully, for supplying products through these people effectively undercuts the activities of the local H-P sales offices who supply services directly to the end-users. On the other hand, in cases where these intermediaries serve useful purposes a flexible attitude is required so the customers are helped rather than hindered in their purchases of H-P products.

2. What is the destination of the equipment?

Even though it is known that the material will be used outside the sales territory, it must be determined if it will be used elsewhere in the freeworld or is intended for use in an area subject to more severe export controls. The objective is to know as much as possible about the ultimate and any intermediate destination of the material to protect the purchaser, the local H-P sales office, and the H-P Company. Also, it should be understood that accurate information of this type is essential to determine appropriate compensation

---

1. Electronic instrumentation, considered to be of high strategic value, is subject to special U. S. controls. H-P field sales people thus have the dual responsibility of conforming to the export control policies of their own governments while at the same time, understanding and working within the frequently more restrictive U. S. controls. For a basic survey of the development of export controls from the viewpoint of the United States see the notes attached to this memorandum.

EXHIBIT 3—*continued*

splits and to notify the H-P sales offices in the receiving areas of their post delivery responsibilities.

3. What is the end-use of the equipment?

The use of the item, by whom and for what purpose, is important. For example; approval to use U. S. material in a free world country to manufacture products for use in that country or elsewhere in the free world is not difficult to obtain. Yet, approval would be difficult to secure if the same products were to be exported to the Soviet bloc and virtually impossible if their destination was to be Communist China, North Korea, North Viet Nam or Cuba. As another example; approval to export or re-export an oscilloscope to a Soviet hospital for, say, cancer research, would be much easier to obtain than to send the same scope to a Polish Center which might be working on some aspect of nuclear weaponry.

4. Where should the order be placed?

It is important to accurately determine this point to minimize duplication of effort, speed the flow of internal paperwork and, of course, provide the customer with the fastest delivery.

5. What documentation is required?

Many of these non-routine requests are likely to require special export/import documentation for each country involved. Since a large variety of documentation requests is possible, only a few general guide lines have been included in the flow-chart. It is the responsibility of the local H-P sales offices to make the appropriate inquiries as soon as possible. Do not assume that someone else is looking after the documentation requirements. It costs very little to ask questions but mistakes and delays can be very costly.

We believe a thoughtful use of the attached flow-chart, within the framework of these questions, will assist the local H-P sales offices in the proper handling of their non-routine inquiries in a manner which is both convenient and practical. Obviously, no flow-chart can cover all the situations which may be encountered. Where exceptions occur and the flow-chart does not seem to fit, be sure to contact the H-P regional organization covering the sales territory (HPSA, HPIA, or H-P Export Marketing) for advice *before proceeding* with the request.

FIGURE 2

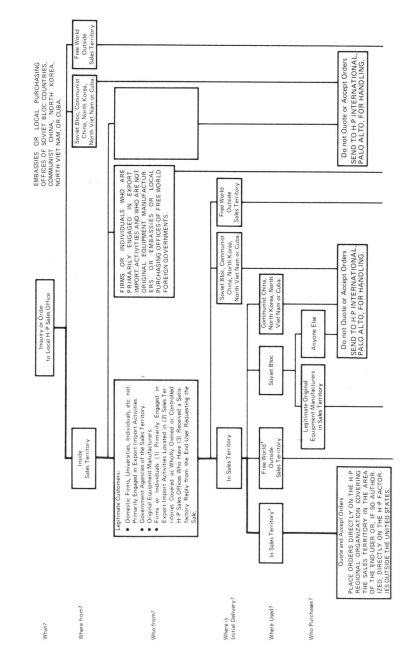

344

Action

Channels and Procedures for Handling International Inquiries and Orders

Quote and Accept Orders

PLACE ORDERS DIRECTLY ON H-P REGIONAL ORGANIZATION COVERING THE SALES TERRITORY (HPSA, HPIA, OR H-P EXPORT MARKETING) OR, IF SO AUTHORIZED, DIRECTLY ON THE H-P FACTORIES OUTSIDE THE UNITED STATES.

IDENTIFY DESTINATION WHEN ORDERING SO APPROPRIATE COMPENSATION SPLITS CAN BE MADE AND THE LOCAL H-P SALES OFFICES IN THE AREA OF THE END-USER NOTIFIED OF THEIR POST DELIVERY RESPONSIBILITIES.

Quote and Accept Orders

PLACE ORDERS DIRECTLY ON H-P REGIONAL ORGANIZATION COVERING THE SALES TERRITORY (HPSA, HPIA, OR H-P EXPORT MARKETING) OR, IF SO AUTHORIZED, DIRECTLY ON THE H-P FACTORIES OUTSIDE THE UNITED STATES.

Subject to the Following Limitations:

ALL INSTRUMENTS AND PARTS OF U.S. MANUFACTURE REQUIRE SPECIFIC AUTHORIZATION FROM THE U.S. GOVERNMENT. TO OBTAIN AUTHORIZATION SUBMIT, WITH THE ORDER, AN APPROPRIATE FOREIGN GOVERNMENT IMPORT CERTIFICATE OR, IF THIS IS NOT AVAILABLE OR CANNOT BE OBTAINED, A PROPERLY COMPLETED END-USE STATEMENT (U.S. FORM FC 842 OR 843, SAMPLE COPIES ATTACHED. ADDITIONAL FORMS CAN BE OBTAINED FROM LOCAL U.S. EMBASSIES OR CONSULATES.)

INSTRUMENTS AND PARTS MANUFACTURED OUTSIDE THE UNITED STATES REQUIRE AUTHORIZATION OF THE GOVERNMENT OF THE MANUFACTURING COUNTRY. INFORMATION AS TO THESE REQUIREMENTS CAN BE OBTAINED FROM THE RESPECTIVE FACTORIES WHOSE RESPONSIBILITY IT IS TO SEE THESE REGULATIONS ARE MET. IN ADDITION, ITEMS SUBJECTED TO INTERNATIONAL (COCOM) CONTROLS—MAINLY THOSE MARKED VL ON THE H-P PRICE LISTS—REQUIRE PERMISSION OF THE U.S. TREASURY DEPARTMENT SINCE THE H-P FACTORIES OUTSIDE THE UNITED STATES ARE WHOLLY OWNED OR UNDER SUBSTANTIAL CONTROL OF H-P, A U.S. FIRM. TO OBTAIN AUTHORIZATION SUBMIT WITH THE ORDER AS MUCH INFORMATION AS POSSIBLE REGARDING THE PROPOSED DESTINATION OF THE MATERIAL, THE H-P ITEMS AND THEIR END-USE, AND THE SYSTEM IN WHICH THEY ARE TO BE USED AND ITS VALUE.

Quote and Accept Orders

WHOLLY OWNED OR CONTROLLED H-P SALES OFFICES IN HPSA AREA ORDER FROM HPSA, AND/OR THE EUROPEAN H-P FACTORIES IF THE MATERIAL WILL BE SHIPPED TO DESTINATIONS WITHIN HPSA'S AREA. IF DESTINATION IS OUTSIDE HPSA'S AREA, ORDER FROM H-P REGIONAL ORGANIZATION (HPIA OR H-P EXPORT MARKETING) COVERING THE AREA INTO WHICH THE MATERIAL WILL BE SHIPPED.

INDEPENDENT H-P SALES OFFICES AND WHOLLY OWNED OR CONTROLLED H-P SALES OFFICES OUTSIDE HPSA'S AREA ORDER FROM H-P REGIONAL ORGANIZATION COVERING THEIR OWN SALES TERRITORIES.

PAY SPECIAL ATTENTION TO DOCUMENTATION REQUIREMENTS OF EXPORTING AND IMPORTING COUNTRIES.

SUPPLY COMPLETE SHIPPING INSTRUCTIONS AND IDENTIFY DESTINATION WHEN ORDERING SO APPROPRIATE COMPENSATION SPLITS CAN BE MADE AND THE LOCAL H-P SALES OFFICES IN THE AREA OF THE END-USER NOTIFIED OF THEIR POST DELIVERY RESPONSIBILITIES.

Do Not Quote or Accept Orders

WHOLLY OWNED OR CONTROLLED H-P SALES OFFICES INFORM PROSPECTIVE PURCHASER, EITHER BY LETTER OR VERBALLY, OF H-P POLICY—SEE SUGGESTED FORM LETTER ATTACHED.

INDEPENDENT H-P SALES OFFICES ASK PROSPECTIVE PURCHASER TO REFER CUSTOMER TO THE H-P SALES OFFICE IN HIS LOCAL AREA. IF NO H-P SALES OFFICE HAS YET BEEN ESTABLISHED, ASK PROSPECTIVE PURCHASER TO REFER CUSTOMER TO H-P REGIONAL ORGANIZATION COVERING HIS LOCAL AREA (HPSA, HPIA OR H-P EXPORT MARKETING.)

Do Not Quote or Accept Orders

UNLESS INSTRUCTED OTHERWISE, SEND TO H-P REGIONAL ORGANIZATION COVERING SALES TERRITORY (HPSA, HPIA OR H-P EXPORT MARKETING) FOR HANDLING—USUALLY TRANSMITTAL TO APPROPRIATE LOCAL H-P SALES OFFICE EITHER DIRECTLY OR THROUGH ANOTHER H-P REGIONAL ORGANIZATION.

---

*If, After delivery it is learned that U.S. manufactured material is intended to be re-exported to the Soviet Bloc, Communist China, North Korea, North Viet Nam or Cuba, inform Purchaser of U.S. Control Regulations and request Authorization by providing the H-P Regional Organization covering the sales territory with as much information as possible regarding the proposed destination of the material, The H-P items and their end-use and the system in which they are to be used and its value.

If, after delivery, it is learned that H-P Products manufactured outside the United States subject to International (COCOM) Controls—mainly those marked VL on the H-P Price Lists are intended to be re-exported to the Soviet Bloc, Communist China, North Korea, North Viet Nam or Cuba, request authorization by supplying as much information as possible (described above) to the H-P Regional Organization or H-P factory outside the Unites States originally shipping the material into the sales territory.

NOTE: Under some circumstances approval may be granted if the Soviet Bloc is involved; however the chance of obtaining approval for the other destinations is very remote.

INTERNATIONAL FOODS INC., U.S.A. (B)

Development of Marketing Mix for Operating in Foreign Countries at Different Levels of Economic Growth

THE MARKET STRUCTURE

Four large companies dominate the international canned milk industry. Although they accounted for more than 70 percent of 1969 worldwide condensed and evaporated milk sales, none dominates in all markets, none is known worldwide as a premium brand, and in some areas local brands preempt a significant market share. As one IFI official puts it: "Not even on a regional basis such as the European Economic Community can we say that a particular brand is number one in terms of acceptance."[1]

OBJECTIVES OF THE MARKET MIX— CORPORATE PHILOSOPHY

The parent company has established fairly explicit marketing mix goals for the affiliates. In view of the oligopolistic structure of the evaporated milk market, IFI needs to maximize its market share or at least maintain its historical share. To this end, one objective is to increase case-sales volume. Price margins are very narrow because the pricing structure is essentially set by the competition or by the local governments. In consequence, case sales are emphasized rather than dollar sales. To maximize case sales, IFI aims for maximum possible distribution in a given market in retail outlets and in institutions such as hospitals and schools. Given the inherent differences between markets with respect to distribution channels, type of retail market structure, and extent of the spatial dispersion of retail outlets (primarily a function of the geography of population centers), maximizing product distribution provides the basis for the fundamental marketing objective of IFI—to maximize the dollar expenditure toward the consumer end of the marketing spectrum. That is, marketing expenditures should be concentrated in directly sales-related areas such as discounts to retailers, media and promotional advertising, and the like.

---

1. All the names and figures in this study are fictitious to disguise the identity of the company and protect its competitive position.

In the following sections the IFI markets are analyzed in four countries—United Kingdom, West Germany, Philippines, Peru—and their marketing objectives and strategies for 1970 are described. These descriptions include discussions of all elements of the marketing mix except advertising and promotion which is dealt with in Part C of this case. The 1970 data used are based on annual marketing budgets submitted by the overseas affiliates and approved, after revisions, by the New York home office of IFI.

Tables 1 through 4 present a comparative picture of the evaporated milk industry in the four countries under study, extent of market penetration by IFI in various countries during 1956 to 1969, and IFI market forecasts for the next five years. Tables 5 through 9 present comparative data for various marketing expenditures by IFI in the four markets.

UNITED KINGDOM

Objectives of the Marketing Mix

In January 1968 the company instituted a "New Marketing Strategy" with the following elements:

1. To increase total volume sales of the brand,
2. To protect the brand nationally from private-label encroachment,
3. To protect the brand nationally from major price cutting by competitors,
4. To exploit opportunities to increase sales volume in those areas of high evaporated milk consumption where product brand loyalty is historically weak, and
5. To launch a brand image revitalization program.

A 1969 study showed that the objectives of the new marketing strategy were being broadly achieved.

The U.K. affiliate recommended that the objectives of the new marketing strategy should be continued without any general revisions. The minor changes are to be in those areas in which weaknesses are apparent in the performance of the firm in achieving those objectives.

To ensure the successful attainment of the general goals, the following objectives have been recommended as the central focus of the marketing mix for the current year:

1. To maintain the volume sales growth of the IFI brands at a rate at least equal to that of the total market growth, thereby minimally maintaining brand market share, and
2. To implement the first objective, the firm will strengthen and consolidate the new brand image as a multi-use, naturally nutritious, and modern product.

TABLE 1

Summary of Industry Sales and Growth Rates

	1965		1966		1967		1968		1969	
	Case Sales (Thousands)	Change %	Case Sales (Thousands)	Change %	Case Sales (Thousands)	Change %	Case Sales (Thousands)	Change %	Case Sales (Thousands)	Change %
United Kingdom										
Lancer (IFI)[a]	2,305		2,342	1.6	2,216	(5.4)	2,461	11.1	2,510	2.0
Perfect[a]	1,220		1,329	8.9	1,129	(15.0)	1,161	2.8	NA	—
Crown[b]	NA		NA	—	NA	—	NA	—	NA	—
Turm[a]	NA		NA	—	NA	—	NA	—	NA	—
Private labels and co-op[b]	957		1,041	8.8	1,285	23.4	1,494	16.3	NA	—
Total industry	5,147		5,423	5.4	5,180	(4.5)	5,777	11.5	5,893	2.0
West Germany										
S&A 1&2 (IFI)[a]	4,741		4,749	0.2	4,441	(6.5)	4,044	(8.9)	3,789	(6.3)
Yukon[b]	NA		6,300	—	6,200	(1.6)	6,100	(1.6)	6,000	(1.6)
Blanc[a]	NA		3,401	—	5,759	69.3	5,756	(0.1)	4,011	(30.3)
Turm[a]	3,200		3,250	1.6	3,100	(4.6)	2,900	(6.5)	2,700	(6.9)
All other	10,000		10,000	0	9,500	(5.0)	9,200	(3.2)	10,500	14.1
Total industry	28,200		27,700	(1.8)	29,000	4.7	28,000	(3.4)	27,000	(3.6)
Philippines										
Maria (IFI)[a]	800	(10.6)	853	6.7	750	(12.1)	777	3.5	780	0.4
Neema[b]	1,719	(5.2)	1,781	3.6	1,693	(5.0)	1,761	4.0	1,650	(6.3)
Tulip[a]	327	(27.3)	495	51.4	480	(3.0)	500	4.1	485	3.0
Total industry	2,846	(9.8)	3,129	10.0	2,923	(6.6)	3,038	3.9	2,915	(4.0)

Peru

	1965		1966		1967		1968		1969	
	Case Sales (Thousands)	Change %	Case Sales (Thousands)	Change %	Case Sales (Thousands)	Change %	Case Sales (Thousands)	Change %	Case Sales (Thousands)	Change %
Maria 1&2 (IFI)[a]	1,963		2,094	6.7	2,367	13.0	2,394	1.1	2,535	5.9
Perfect[a]	268		287	7.1	338	17.8	359	6.2	NA	–
Imports	452		485	7.3	671	38.4	836	24.6	NA	–
Total industry	2,683		2,866	6.8	3,376	17.8	3,589	6.3	3,652	1.8

[a]Foreign owned brands.
[b]Locally owned brands.

349

TABLE 2

Market Penetration by Brand/Company Share 1965 to 1969

Market Area	Brand	1965 Market Share Percent	1966 Market Share Percent	1967 Market Share Percent	1968 Market Share Percent	1969 Market Share Percent
United Kingdom	Lancer (IFI)	44	43	43	43	42
	Private label brands	19	19	25	26	–
	Perfect	24	26	21	20	–
	Crown and others (major local brands)	13	13	11	11	–
	Total market share	100	100	100	100	100
	Total industry sales volume (thousands of cases)	5,147	5,423	5,180	5,777	5,893
West Germany	All S&A brands (IFI)	17	17	15	14	14
	Turm	11	12	11	10	10
	Yukon	24	23	21	22	22
	Blanc	12	12	20	21	15
	All others	36	36	33	33	39
	Total market share	100	100	100	100	100
	Total industry sales volume (thousands of cases)	28,200	27,700	29,000	28,000	27,000
Philippine Islands	Maria (IFI)	28	27	26	26	27
	Neema	60	57	58	58	57
	Tulip	12	16	16	16	16
	Total market share	100	100	100	100	100
	Total industry sales volume (thousands of cases)	2,846	3,129	2,923	3,038	2,915

Market Area	Brand	1965 Market Share Percent	1966 Market Share Percent	1967 Market Share Percent	1968 Market Share Percent	1969 Market Share Percent
Peru	All Maria brands (IFI)	73	73	70	67	70
	Perfect	10	10	10	10	NA
	Imports	17	17	20	23	NA
	Total market share	100	100	100	100	100
	Total industry sales volume (thousands of cases)	2,683	2,866	3,376	3,589	3,652

TABLE 3

Sales Summary (IFI Brands) 1965 to 1969

	1965		1966		1967		1968		1969	
	Case Sales (Thousands)	Change (%)	Case Sales (Thousands)	Change (%)	Case Sales (Thousands)	Change (%)	Case Sales (Thousands)	Change (%)	Case Sales (Thousands)	Change (%)
United Kingdom—Lancer										
Tall	1,079		1,133	5.0	1,075	(5.1)	1,248	16.1	1,280	2.6
Baby	1,226		1,209	(1.4)	1,141	(5.6)	1,213	6.3	1,230	1.4
Total	2,305		2,342	1.6	2,216	(5.4)	2,461	11.1	2,510	2.0
West Germany—S&A										
S&A 1:										
Tall	NA		2,431	–	2,260	(7.0)	2,092	(7.4)	1,996	(4.6)
Baby	NA		2,203	–	2,097	(4.8)	1,765	(15.8)	1,636	(7.3)
Total	4,307		4,634	7.6	4,357	(6.0)	3,909[a]	(10.3)	3,679[b]	(5.9)
S&A 2:										
Tall	–		–	–	–	–	57	–	48	(16.7)
Baby	–		–	–	–	–	78	–	62	(19.9)
Total	–		–	–	–	–	135	–	110	(18.5)
Total S&A 1&2	4,741		4,749	0.2	4,441	(6.5)	4,044	(8.9)	3,789	(6.3)
Philippines—Maria										
Tall	NA		NA	–	NA	–	551	–	585	6.3
Baby	NA		NA	–	NA	–	226	–	195	(13.8)
Total	800		853	6.7	750	(12.1)	777	3.5	780	0.4
Peru—Maria 1&2										
Total Maria 1&2	1,963		2,094	6.7	2,367	13.0	2,394	1.1	2,535	5.9

[a]Includes tube sales of 52,000.
[b]Includes tube sales of 47,000.

TABLE 4

Sales Forecast (IFI Brands) 1970 to 1974

	1970		1971		1972		1973		1974	
	Case Sales (Thousands)	Change (%)	Case Sales (Thousands)	Change (%)	Case Sales (Thousands)	Change (%)	Case Sales (Thousands)	Change (%)	Case Sales (Thousands)	Change (%)
United Kingdom—Lancer										
Tall	1,339	4.6	1,381	3.1	1,425	3.2	1,471	3.2	1,518	3.2
Baby	1,236	0.5	1,249	1.1	1,264	1.2	1,278	1.1	1,293	1.2
Total	2,575	2.6	2,630	2.1	2,689	2.2	2,749	2.2	2,811	2.3
West Germany—S&A										
S&A 1:										
Tall	2,037	2.06	2,127	4.42	2,177	2.4	2,205	1.3	2,227	1.0
Baby	1,773	8.38	1,873	5.65	1,923	2.7	1,948	1.3	1,973	1.3
Total[a]	3,860	4.9	4,050	4.9	4,150	2.5	4,203	1.3	4,250	1.1
S&A 2:										
Tall	50	4.2	50	1.01	50	0	50	0	50	0
Baby	62	0	65	4.0	65	0	65	0	65	0
Total	112	1.8	115	2.68	115	0	115	0	115	0
Total S&A 1&2	3,972	4.83	4,165	4.86	4,265	2.4	4,318	1.2	4,365	1.1
Philippines—Maria										
Tall	590	0.9	600	1.7	620	3.3	650	4.8	680	4.6
Baby	190	(2.6)	180	(5.3)	190	5.6	200	5.3	220	10.0
Total	780	0	780	0	810	3.8	850	4.9	900	5.9
Peru—Maria										
Maria 1	2,708	14.0	2,849	5.2	2,968	4.2	3,059	3.1	3,151	3.0
Maria 2	192	20.0	196	2.1	199	1.5	203	2.0	209	3.0
Total Maria 1&2	2,900	14.4	3,045	5.0	3,167	4.0	3,262	3.0	3,360	3.0

[a]Includes tube sales of 50,000.

TABLE 5

Marketing Expenditures as a Percentage of 1970 Sales
(Budget Estimates)

	United Kingdom	West Germany	Philippines	Peru
Sales (cases)	2,575,000	3,972,000	780,000	2,900,000
Gross sales (U.S. dollars)[a]	16,505,000	30,073,000	4,516,410[b]	17,062,988
Total marketing expense (U.S. dollars)	3,119,000	5,151,000	677,000	1,200,678
Marketing expense (dollars) per case	1.20	1.30	0.87	0.41
Marketing expense (dollars) per gross sales	0.19	0.17	0.15	0.07

[a]Exchange rates: United Kingdom $2.40/£1
  West Germany   DM 3.7/$1
  Philippines   ₱3.90/$1
  Peru   S 52/$1

[b]Filled evaporated milk only.

The marketing strategy IFI chose to implement the general objectives includes: the aggressive protection of the brand from increased private-label penetration, and the increased exploitation of areas of high evaporated milk consumption, especially in those sales regions in which brand loyalty is low, and the aggressive pursuit of IFI's Lancer label in its few remaining areas of weakness.

The Market

Four producers, all domiciled within the country, dominate the United Kingdom evaporated milk industry (Tables 1 and 2). Their labels are Lancer (IFI), Perfect, Crown, and Turm. The balance of the market is supplied by private labels and co-ops.

In terms of case sales, the U.K. market for evaporated milk is only 18 to 20 percent as large as the West German market. Total industry case sales in the U.K. grew approximately 14.5 percent between 1965 and 1969 (Table 1). In that same period, case sales of IFI's Lancer label increased about 8.8 percent, but private labels increased approximately 56.1 percent. The private label increase is further demonstrated in Table 2 which shows that their market share increased from 18.6 percent in 1965 to 25.9 percent in 1968. Between 1965 and 1969, although its market share dropped from 44.8 to 42.5 percent, IFI remained a dominant factor in the market. From 1965 to 1968 the competition's Perfect label sales dropped approximately 4.8 percent, a market-share loss of roughly 3.6 percent.

IFI projected a 1970 to 1974 sales increase of approximately 9.2 percent. Table 4 gives a year-by-year projection for sales of IFI's Lancer label. Data on projected industry and competitive growth for this period are not available.

TABLE 6
Budgeted Marketing Expenses, 1970

Expense Category	United Kingdom			West Germany			Philippines			Peru		
	£	Total Marketing Expense (%)	Unit[a] Cost ($)	DM	Total Marketing Expense (%)	Unit Cost ($)	Pesos	Total Marketing Expense (%)	Unit Cost ($)	Sols	Total Marketing Expense (%)	Unit Cost ($)
Consumer advertising	412,379	31.7	.38	3,600,000	18.9	.25	906,400	34.3	.2980	2,957,000	4.7	.0196
Promotional advertising[b]	61,365	4.7	.06	941,000	4.9	.06	203,500	7.7	.0669	488,000	0.8	.0032
Medical[c]	58,314	4.5	.05	366,500	1.9	.03	54,100	2.0	.0179	1,214,000	1.9	.0080
Market research	7,000	0.5	.01	82,000	0.4	.01	14,300	0.5	.0047	220,400	0.4	.0014
Salaries	175,800	13.5	.16	4,700,000	24.7	.32	26,200	1.0	.0086	733,000	1.2	.0048
Traveling expenses	69,000	5.3	.06	2,420,000	12.7	.17	39,200	1.5	.0129	200,000	0.3	.0013
Sales office expenses	none	—	—	140,000	0.7	.01	6,900	0.3	.0023	42,000	0.1	.0002
Commissions	850	0.1	nil	275,000	1.4	.02	315,000	11.9	.1036	16,474,500	26.4	.11
Distribution expenses	489,250	37.6	.46	3,903,200	20.5	.27	209,000	7.9	.0687	40,076,340	64.2	.2657
Discounts	22,600	1.7	.02	2,566,600	13.5	.18	172,000	6.5	.0565	none	—	—
Salesmen contests	none	—	—	65,000	0.3	nil	23,600	0.9	.0078	30,000	—	.0001
Insurance	25	nil	nil	none	—	—	none	—	—	none	—	—
School campaign	3,000	0.4	nil	none	—	—	56,200	2.1	.0185	none	—	—
Seminars	none	—	—	none	—	—	8,400	0.3	.0028	none	—	—
Redistribution	none	—	—	none	—	—	37,500	1.4	.0123	none	—	—
Space rental/display allow.	none	—	—	none	—	—	22,000	0.8	.0072	none	—	—
Promotional trucks	none	—	—	none	—	—	431,000	16.3	.1417	none	—	—
Relabeling	none	—	—	none	—	—	115,000	4.4	.0378	none	—	—
Total	1,299,583	100.0	1.20	19,059,300	100.0	1.30	2,640,300	100.0	.87	62,435,240	100.0	.4140

[a] $ unit cost calculated by converting expense in local currency to U.S. dollar equivalent. Based on projected case sales for fiscal year 1969–1970. Unit = case.

Exchange rates:			Projected Case Sales
	United Kingdom	$2.40/£1	2,575,000
	West Germany	DM 3.7/$1	3,972,000
	Philippines	P 3.90/$1	780,000
	Peru	S 52/$1	2,900,000

[b] Point of purchase promotion.

[c] Advertising and promotion to medical profession (includes salaries and expenses of sales personnel).

TABLE 7

Budgeted Direct Selling Expenses, 1970[a]

Expense Category	United Kingdom		West Germany		Philippines		Peru	
	£	U.S. $[b]	DM	U.S. $	Pesos	U.S. $	Sols	U.S. $
Audio-visual	None	—	None	—	79,700	20,436	None	—
Discounts	22,600	54,240	2,566,600	693,676	172,000	44,102	None	—
Seminars	None	—	None	—	8,400	2,154	None	—
Salesmen contests	None	—	65,000	17,568	23,600	6,051	30,000	579
Redistribution	None	—	None	—	37,500	9,615	None	—
Medical salaries	28,050	67,320	157,500	42,568	16,100	4,128	435,413	8,373
Medical expenses	12,587	30,209	55,000	14,865	22,500	5,769	194,587	3,742
Distribution	489,250	1,174,200	3,903,200	1,054,919	209,000	53,590	40,076,340	770,699
Promotional trucks	None	—	None	—	431,000	110,513	None	—
Relabeling	None	—	None	—	115,000	29,487	None	—
Travel	69,000	165,600	2,420,000	654,054	39,200	10,051	200,000	3,846
Sales office	None	—	140,000	37,838	6,900	1,769	42,000	808
Salaries	175,800	421,920	4,700,000	1,270,270	26,200	6,718	733,000	14,096
Commissions	850	2,040	275,000	74,324	315,000	80,769	16,474,500	316,817
Special promotions	None	—	200,000	54,054	None	—	None	—
Total	798,137	1,915,529	14,582,300	3,914,054	1,502,100	385,153	58,185,840	1,118,958

[a]All item expense categories shown here are also included in Table 6.

[b]Conversion rates:

United Kingdom	$2.40/£1
West Germany	DM 3.7/$1
Philippines	P3.90/$1
Peru	S 52/$1

356

TABLE 8

Sales Personnel—1966 to 1970

	United Kingdom					West Germany				
	1966	1967	1968	1969	1970	1966	1967	1968	1969	1970
District sales managers	8	8	8	8	8	7	7	7	7	7
Supervisors	8	8	9	10	10	18	18	19	24	24
Salesmen										
Wholesale	–	–	–	–	–	84	85	87	89	92
Retail	72	72	72	72	72	122	129	130	173	171
Medical sales representatives	15	15	14	13	13	7	7	7	7	7
Trainees	–	–	–	–	–	–	–	–	1	1
Free agents	2	2	2	2	2	6	6	6	6	5
Others	1	1	1	1	1	–	–	–	–	–
Total sales force[c]	106	106	106	106	106	244	252	256	307	307
Total retail outlets covered regularly (thousands)	10.05	10.23	12.00	14.57	10.57	NA	NA	NA	42.00	40.00
These do percentage of total food business	30	31	40	55	57	NA	NA	NA	55	52

[a] Only the Lima-Callao region has a sales manager.
[b] The top line is for the Lima-Callao area and the lower line is for the provinces.
[c] Includes administrative and supervisorial personnel.

TABLE 8–*continued*

	Philippine Islands					Peru				
	1966	*1967*	*1968*	*1969*	*1970*	*1966*	*1967*	*1968*	*1969*	*1970*
District sales managers	1	1	2	2	2	1[a]	1	1	1	1
Supervisors	10	10	11	13	13	2	2	2	3	3
Salesmen										
Wholesale	–	–	–	–	–	16[b]	16	16	16	16
Retail	124	124	124	140	140	15	15	15	15	15
Medical sales representatives	14	17	15	12	15	2	2	2	2	2
Trainees	–	–	2	2	–	–	–	–	–	–
Free agents	–	–	–	–	–	–	–	–	–	–
Others	8	8	10	10	8	–	–	–	–	–
Total sales force[c]	156	160	164	179	178	36	36	36	37	37
Total retail outlets covered regularly (thousands)	NA	NA	48.98	53.80	59.12	17.00	17.27	17.57	17.87	18.00
These do percentage of total food business	NA	NA	NA	NA	NA	90	90	90	90	90

[a]Only the Lima-Callao region has a sales manager.

[b]The top line is for the Lima-Callao area and the lower line is for the provinces.

[c]Includes administrative and supervisorial personnel.

TABLE 9

Sales Personnel Performance, 1966 to 1970

	United Kingdom					Germany				
	1966	1967	1968	1969	1970	1966	1967	1968	1969	1970
Sales: Thousands of Cases	2,342	2,216	2,461	2,510	2,575	4,749	4,441	4,044	3,789	3,972
Sales: $U.S.[a]	—	—	15,781,090	16,089,600	16,504,800	—	—	30,324,000	27,894,432	30,072,919
Total salesmen[b]	90	90	89	88	88	219	227	230	276	276
Average case sales per salesman	26,022	24,622	27,651	28,522	29,261	21,685	19,564	17,583	13,728	14,391
Average $U.S. sales per salesman	—	—	177,315	182,836	187,554	—	—	131,843	101,067	108,960

[a] In converting local currencies into $U.S. the following exchange rates were used:

United Kingdom	$2.40/£1
Germany	DM3.7/$U.S.
Philippine Islands	₱3.9/$U.S.
Peru	S52/$U.S.

[b] The number of salesmen excludes administrative and supervisorial personnel.

TABLE 9—*continued*

	Philippine Islands					Peru				
	1966	1967	1968	1969	1970	1966	1967	1968	1969	1970
Sales: Thousands of Cases	853.2	750.3	776.7	780.0	780.0	2,094	2,367	2,394	2,535	2,900
Sales: $U.S.[a]	—	—	—	4,491,795	4,516,410	—	—	12,572,079	14,629,291	17,062,988
Total salesmen[b]	146	149	151	164	163	33	33	33	33	33
Average case sales per salesman	5,844	5,036	5,144	4,756	4,785	63,455	71,727	72,545	76,818	87,879
Average $U.S. sales per salesman	—	—	—	27,389	27,708	—	—	380,972	443,312	517,060

[a] In converting local currencies into $U.S. the following exchange rates were used:

United Kingdom	$2.40/£1
Germany	DM3.7/$U.S.
Philippine Islands	₱3.9/$U.S.
Peru	S52/$U.S.

[b] The number of salesmen excludes administrative and supervisorial personnel.

Milk consumption in the United Kingdom has changed during the past few years. Table 10 shows that canned and dehydrated milks have shown the most consistent and by far the largest rate of growth. Between 1964 and 1968 this category exhibited a dramatic 47 percent growth in pound sterling sales. Primary uses of evaporated milk include dessert creamer, cooking, coffee creamer, and baby feeding.

Pricing

In the U.K. market IFI appears to base its pricing policy upon two factors: its strong competitive position in the market and the cost of producing and marketing the product. As the brand leader, despite pressure from the private labels, IFI attempts to price Lancer at the highest level consistent with maintaining current sales volume (Table 11). The Perfect label, under the constant pressure of declining sales and market share, has resorted to using pricing as a competitive tool in the large chain outlets. The Perfect brand has not followed this policy throughout all store types—in the cooperatives the price has been significantly higher than Lancer, while in the independents the price has been quite volatile from year to year. The private labels have been priced significantly lower than Lancer—the maximum spread was 24.3 percent in 1965 and the minimum difference was 14.2 percent in 1968. This large price differential no doubt is the primary factor behind the growth of the private labels' market penetration, and the price differential is possible largely because private labels use price as the only competitive device, thus eliminating the use of other marketing tools such as advertising, store promotion, and so on.

For the second element which appears to determine the brand's pricing policy—cost of producing and marketing the product—the only data we have pertain to the marketing cost per case. Table 11 demonstrates that there has been a 21.6 percent increase in marketing costs per case between 1965 and 1968 which is surely

TABLE 10

Related Grocery Business Trends in the United Kingdom
1964 to 1968

	1964	1965	1966	1967	1968
	Sales £ Millions	Sales £ Millions	Sales £ Millions	Sales £ Millions	Sales £ Millions
All commodities	2,607	2,755	2,873	2,988	3,198
Evaporated milk	12.745	12.529	12.475	12.787	13.692
Canned and packaged cream	8.404	9.500	10.343	11.354	12.312
Powdered[a]	0.297	NA	1.836	1.902	2.051
Custard powders	3.491	5.500	3.304	3.286	3.198
Yogurt	NA	NA	NA	4.482	5.916

[a]Company estimates place the value of the total powdered milk market at £2,954,000 in 1968 with one competitive brand holding about 70 percent of the market.

TABLE 11

Historical Retail Price Schedule – United Kingdom

	Store Type[a]	1965	1966	1967	1968	1969	1970
Retail price (per can) for IFI brand–local currency (pence)	M	14.8	14.7	15.5	15.5	15.5	15.5
	C	15.2	15.2	15.8	15.9	15.9	15.9
	IND	15.8	15.8	16.1	16.4	16.4	16.4
Retail price (per can) for Perfect label	M	14.6	14.6	15.5	15.1	15.1	15.1
	C	15.6	15.7	16.2	16.2	16.2	16.2
	IND	15.8	15.6	16.4	15.8	15.8	15.8
Retail price (per can) for private labels (average)		11.2	12.4	12.7	13.3	13.5	13.5
IFI market share in percentages		44.8	43.2	42.8	42.6	42.5	42.8
IFI marketing cost per case (shillings)		5.1	6.0	5.6	6.2	6.0	6.2

[a]Store type abbreviations: M = Multiples, C = Cooperatives, IND = Independents.

362

reflected in the 4.7 percent increase in consumer price over the same years. Thus, it appears that IFI utilizes some method of cost-plus pricing. IFI's volume discount schedule is reflected in the gradation of retail prices which mirror purchase volume and the narrow profit margin characteristic of the retail grocery business.

Sales Organization

IFI's own sales organization markets throughout the United Kingdom, excepting Northern Ireland and the Channel Islands which are handled through independent distributors. Table 8 shows that direct-sales personnel and total number of sales personnel have remained constant during the past five years; supervisory personnel have increased, and medical sales representatives have declined. The productivity of the sales personnel engaged in direct field sales—salesmen, medical sales representatives, and free agents—has increased slowly in a slow-growing market. While total case sales increased 2 percent from 1968 to 1969, the average case sales per salesman increased 3.2 percent, and the average dollar sales climbed 3.1 percent. The estimated figures for the current year show a forecasted total case sales increase of 2.6 percent with corresponding increases in average case sales and dollar sales (Table 9).

Distribution Network and Distribution Costs

The structure of trade in the United Kingdom is dominated by three types of outlets multiples (or chains), co-ops, and independents (of which Symbols is the largest). *See* Table 12.

The budgeted distribution costs for 1970 stand at £489,000, an increase of 6.4 percent over 1969. To promote increased volume business, IFI offers the trade a direct factory discount of six pence (six cents U.S.) per case.

Market Research

In January 1968 IFI instituted its "New Marketing Strategy" which stressed the "multiple use" of the product in its promotional campaigns. This strategy has been maintained essentially through 1969 and will be followed in 1970. In 1969 a national accountability study was conducted which showed generally favorable results of the implementation of the "New Marketing Strategy." The basic findings of the study of relevance to the 1970 plans are as follows:

Product penetration has increased significantly since 1965. It was also found that Lancer maintained its share of the increase, whereas Perfect suffered a loss; improved considerably in the AB[2] socioeconomic groups, whereas Perfect lost heavily; improved in the important London and Southeastern Region, and also considerably in Wales and the West. Consumers record a higher number of uses for Lancer than for competitive brands; think it more "natural" than the competitive brands, more "modern" than Perfect, but less modern than the private labels.

---

2. A = high income, B = middle income, C = low income, and D = poor income.

TABLE 12

Product/Volume Distribution by Store Type in the United Kingdom, 1969

Store Type	Total Retail Outlets %	Total Food Business Handled (%)	Evaporated Milk Industry Sales Handled (%)	Evaporated Milk Products Handled %	IFI Evaporated Milk Products Handled (%)	Total IFI Sales Originating from Store %
Multiple	12.1	39.1	53.1	100	98	48
Co-ops	8.6	16.0	14.0	100	75	15
Independents	79.3	45.0	33.0	100	87	37
Symbol	31.7	20.0	18.0	100	86	15
Other	47.6	25.0	15.0	100	89	22

Housewives tend to believe that it has more vitamins than the competition. The study also found that television is communicating the advertising theme very satisfactorily to the mass market; the press campaign has contributed significantly in redressing the imbalance of television impact in favor of the ABCone socio-economic classifications; Lancer is equally acceptable in all socioeconomic groups; the main copy themes are being well communicated, especially the slogan, "has many uses," the testimonial by famous gourmets; and the central theme, "Has Many Uses" appears to be more effective in the print media than on television.

Additionally, in 1969 IFI commissioned the Bureau of Commercial Research to study the effectiveness of the advertising campaign, product usage, and the trends in can size. The survey was taken in four regions, each with a field interview sample size of 450. The results of this study were not completed when the Marketing Plan was drawn up for 1970.

The 1970 allocation for market research was £7,000 for a monthly Nielsen Food Index survey which provides a regional breakdown of such factors as brand share, consumer sales trends, retail outlet penetration, consumption per capita, seasonality of sales, promotional expenditures by brand, and other related elements.

Aside from the main market research efforts, the firm also planned to allocate a small sum for a postal survey in conjunction with a school campaign. This study was designed to assist the firm in evaluating the acceptance and usefulness of the recipe box as a teaching aid in the domestic science classes and to obtain teachers' opinions on the program's future development.

WEST GERMANY

Objectives of the Marketing Mix

The West German affiliate, in its analysis of its brands' competitive environment during 1970, developed a five-point program of objectives of the marketing mix to maintain and improve its competitive position. In general terms, the objectives are:

1. A 3.5 percent increase over 1969 (to 3,922,000 cases) in volume sales.
2. The plan is to reach a midyear national numerical distribution level of 68 percent of the total retail outlets by sales region (the level for mid-1969 was 61.8 percent) and a weighted—on the basis of volume—level of 75 percent (last year's level was 65.1 percent), and to emphasize those sales regions in which brand performance is weak. Additionally, the company desires to increase its numerical distribution in the large consumer markets and discount houses from 27 to 40 percent and thereby increase the weighted distribution of the product in that particular store type from 35 to 50 percent.
3. To increase the brand market share from 14 percent in 1969 to 16.8 percent by the end of 1970.
4. To change the present brand profile to result in an increased brand loyalty and the development of heavier usage patterns among the twenty- to twenty-four-year-old segment of the target market. A general view of the target audience is all housewives twenty to thirty-four years of age

who live in cities of more than 20,000 inhabitants. More specifically, the target customers should be young, up-to-date pacesetters, who are nonetheless experienced housewives who appreciate a good quality product.

5. To introduce new terms and conditions to the trade in order to increase volume sales with the larger clients through inventory pressure so that more direct influence can be exerted upon those customers who are currently purchasing the product cooperatively.

In its formulation of the marketing mix objectives, the company recognized that its successful performance during 1970 depended upon the resolution of four major problem areas:

1. The need to increase sales in both can sizes. To achieve this end the firm proposed new advertising and promotional campaigns, new terms and conditions for the trade and, most important in the company's view, cancellation of the price maintenance system. Under the price maintenance system the company must, by law, sell at the same price throughout all regions of West Germany and in all types of retail outlets. This prevents the company and the retail trade from periodic promotions through special campaigns. This places the company at a small disadvantage where its prices are consistently higher than the private brands. In a mature market, such as that of evaporated milk, where significant product differences are nonexistent, IFI believes that periodic price promotions in combination with conventional advertising and other promotional techniques are necessary to hold and improve its market share.

2. The need to improve the company's profit margin. The proposed solution was to increase the ex-factory price per case by DM 1.00. However, such an increase depended upon resolving the agricultural question within the European Economic Community (EEC) and its adoption of a Common Agricultural Policy (CAP).

3. The improvement of brand market share in the consumer markets and discount houses. IFI anticipated that cancelling the price maintenance agreements and introducing the new terms of trade would increase the brand's market penetration considerably. Additionally, the frequency of sales calls was shortened from eight weeks to six weeks.

4. The need to improve the distribution of the product in three specific sales regions where the numerical percentage level of distribution was less than 50 percent in 1969. The affiliate proposed, after receiving the cancellation of the price maintenance agreements and introducing the new terms of trade, to secure the active cooperation of the wholesalers in these areas by offering special sales programs and promotions.

The Market

In the evaporated milk industry in West Germany, four major brands dominate— S & A (IFI), Yukon, Blanc, and Turm. Except for Blanc, which is a low-priced import, all three major brands are produced locally. In addition, there are a host of other locally produced and imported labels (category All Others) which are available in the lower price range.

Except for 1967, the West German evaporated milk market has diminished every year since 1965. During that time per capita consumption of fresh milk dropped 4.1 percent (from 85.9 kgm to 82.3 kgm). Fresh milk represents approximately 90 percent of the total milk consumption in West Germany. Primary uses for evaporated milk in this market are coffee creaming and baby feeding. As shown in Table 1, 1965 industry case sales stood at 28.2 million but by 1969 had dropped 4.2 percent to 27 million. On a label by label basis, sales of IFI's S & A labels dropped approximately 20 percent; Yukon sales (1966 to 1969) were down by about 4.7 percent, Blanc sales (1966 to 1969) increased by 17.9 percent, Turm (1965 to 1969) dropped 15.6 percent, and All Others rose approximately 5 percent during the period 1965 to 1969.

According to data contained in the IFI Marketing Plan for 1970, the company projected that its case sales would increase by 687,130 (17.4 percent) over the next five years (Table 4). Projected industry growth during this period is not available.

Pricing

The German affiliate finds the product in the midst of very aggressive competitive marketing campaigns: "It's a struggle to keep it [their present market share] because we're being bombarded on all sides. You have high-priced and low-priced locally produced, and you have low-priced products coming in from France and Holland and you're caught in the middle."[3] This situation is unique among IFI's European operations, for in most markets the brand is quite strong if not the brand leader. Thus, the pricing policy that IFI follows reflects the battle to remain competitive. The basic principle in such a situation is to estimate how much lower than the brand leader the product must be priced to achieve the forecasted volume sales objectives.

Table 13 gives the impression that the S & A brand is the price leader in the market. However, it does not demonstrate a true perspective of the total market. The Turm label, which is losing its 10 percent market share, is the weakest major brand in the market. The brand leader, Yukon, a premium priced local label with a market share of 22.2 percent in 1969, is not mentioned in the historical price schedule. The Blanc brand has penetrated the market with approximately the same success as S & A. A large number of low-priced imported and locally produced brands have an aggregate share of 38.9 percent.

Thus, it is apparent that the analysis of the brand's position in the market, as formulated by IFI's New York marketing staff, is based on a solid foundation. The brand has shown a declining market share while maintaining middle ground in regard to the pricing differential in the market. The company's competitive dilemma is reflected in the fact that on May 1, 1968, the product's retail price was decreased 2.6 percent (this reflects a decrease of 3 percent in the per case wholesale price) while the other brands mentioned in Table 13 either maintained their existing prices or increased them in response to rising costs—

Interview with IFI vice-president of marketing.

TABLE 13

Historical Retail Price Schedule—West Germany

	Size	1965	1966	1967	1968	1969
Consumer price for IFI product–local currency (DM)	Tall	0.72	0.74	0.78	0.78[a]	0.76
					0.76	
Consumer price for Turm label	Tall	0.72	0.66[b]	0.69	0.69	0.69
Consumer price for private label	Tall	0.60	0.62	0.64	0.66	0.66
Consumer price for Blanc	Tall	0.60	0.58	0.59	0.60	0.62
IFI market share in percentages	–	16.8	17.1	15.3	14.4	14.0
IFI marketing cost per case (DM)	–	NA	NA	NA	4.57	4.76

[a]Price change during 1968 from 0.78 to 0.76.
[b]In 1966 the can size was reduced from 410 grams (the size of the other brands' cans), to 340 grams.

the increase in the IFI West German affiliate's marketing costs between 1968 and 1969 was 4.1 percent.

Sales Organization

To provide adequate coverage for new products, such as baby foods, the sales force was increased to more than 300 within the past five years (a 25.8 percent gain). Although retail salesmen account for a major portion of that increase, total case sales have declined 20.2 percent. Estimates for 1970 are for a 4.8 percent increase both in total case sales and average case sales per salesman and an average dollar sales increase of 7.8 percent (*see* Tables 8 and 9).

Distribution Network and Distribution Costs

IFI's evaporated milk bearing the S & A label is available in nearly all of West Germany's 187,000 food and 14,200 drug stores. Table 14 gives pertinent information on the structure of West German retail outlets.

The firm budgeted DM 3,918,000 to cover the 1970 costs of distribution throughout the market, a 7.1 percent decrease from 1969, and estimated that case sales would increase by 205,600 cases.

One of IFI's basic marketing objectives for 1970 was to introduce new trade terms and conditions designed to increase sales to its large customers through inventory pressure and to exert a more direct influence on customers who were pooling their purchases. The new terms were to be introduced in conjunction with two other objectives of the marketing mix: canceling the price-binding agreements to stimulate sales volume, and increasing the price per case ex-factory. Table 15 shows the current and proposed wholesale price schedule designed to accomplish these ends.

The three high-volume categories, in addition to the discount structure, entail free delivery from the factory to the outlet, while the lower four classifications carry a DM 0.20 per case delivery charge. IFI allocated DM 2,556,000 for the costs of the discount structure during 1970.

Market Research

The firm allocated DM 82,000 for a study of the evaporated milk market to be conducted by Nielsen Research. Proposals for a consumer panel study and a major market study were also made for 1970, although no funds were then allocated for these studies.

On the basis of market and consumer survey data conducted in 1969, the firm recognized its weak position in the market and its poor brand image. It therefore changed advertising agencies and created a new copy strategy.

TABLE 14

Product/Volume Distribution by Store Type in West Germany, 1969

Store Type	Total Retail Outlets %	Total Food Business Handled (%)	Evaporated Milk Industry Sales Handled (%)	Evaporated Milk Products Handled %	IFI Evaporated Milk Products Handled (%)	Total IFI Sales Originating from Store (%)
Consumer markets and discounters	1	10	16	100	27	2
Self-service—super	3	21	18	100	83	17
Self-service—large	6	16	15	100	78	17
Self-service—medium	10	14	13	100	74	15
Self-service—small	28	16	16	100	65	21
Clerk service—large	13	11	10	99	78	15
Clerk service—small	39	12	12	99	47	13

TABLE 15

IFI Brands' Wholesale Price Schedule—West Germany

No. of Cases	Price Per Case 14 Oz. (Tall) Can		No. of Cases	Price Per Case 6 Oz. (Baby) Can	
	Now	*Proposed*		*Now*	*Proposed*
From 1,000	DM 27.75	DM 27.55	From 1,035	DM 26.55	DM 26.35
720	27.75	27.65	720	26.55	26.45
480	28.15	27.75	495	26.95	26.55
240	28.50	27.75	240	27.30	26.55
120	28.75	28.00	120	27.55	26.80
40	29.00	28.25	40	27.80	27.05
10	29.25	28.50	10	28.05	27.30

PHILIPPINES

Objectives of the Marketing Mix

IFI anticipated that the market-depressing conditions of the past five years would continue during 1969 and estimated a market decrease of approximately 2,815,000 cases (3.5 percent) of which IFI's share would be 780,000 cases. The forecast represented an increase in the purchase of the tall can size (14 oz.) of .85 percent or 5,000 cases, and a decrease in the consumption of the small can (6 oz.) of 7.7 percent or 5,000 cases, which corresponded to the historical sales trend for the previous three years. The firm stated that the decrease in the sales of the "baby" can was primarily due to the increased competition of lower priced imported brands.

Thus, IFI formulated a set of marketing objectives which it felt would maintain its sales volume at 780,000 cases in the declining market. To achieve this basic goal the affiliate proposed the following activities: (1) improve the distribution of the product, (2) enlarge the brand's consumer base, (3) maintain the firm's services, and, most important, (4) launch a new advertising campaign, which IFI considered to be absolutely vital to the successful achievement of its marketing objectives.

The Market

Milk production in the Philippines consists primarily of evaporated milk and sweetened milk products which accounted for an average of 96 percent, by volume, of all milk products produced in the country between 1965 and 1969. Total milk production (all categories) increased by 46.2 percent. Per capita consumption of evaporated and sweetened milk increased from 3.33 kgm in 1965 to 4.34 kgm in 1968. That of whole and skimmed powdered milk remained constant at 0.13 kgm during the same period (Table 16).

The evaporated milk market in the Philippines consists of three types of products: condensed, made from cow's milk with water removed; filled, made from milk solids but with vegetable fat replacing butter fat; and recombined,

TABLE 16

Milk Production and Brand Shares in Philippines

A. Type of Milk Produced 1965 to 1969

Year	Evaporated	Sweetened	Fresh
		(percentage of total)	
1965	70.4	25.8	3.8
1966	72.6	24.6	2.8
1967	65.8	30.3	3.9
1968	66.9	30.2	2.9
1969	64.0	32.0	4.0

B. Projected Filled Evaporated Milk Sales as a Percentage of All Evaporated Milk Sales 1970 to 1974

	Sales (Thousands of Cases)		
Year	All Evaporated	Filled (Sweetened) Evaporated	Filled Sales as a Percentage of All Evaporated Sales
1970	5,620.0	2,815.0	50.0
1971	5,745.0	2,815.0	48.9
1972	6,030.3	2,955.8	49.0
1973	6,328.2	3,103.0	49.4
1974	6,597.4	3,258.8	49.3

C. Projected Brand Shares of Filled Evaporated Milk Sales 1970 to 1974

		Projected Market Share (%)		
Year	Case Sales	Maria	Neema	Tulip
1970	2,815,000	27.7	55.0	17.3
1971	2,815,000	27.7	55.2	17.1
1972	2,955,800	27.4	56.4	16.2
1973	3,103,000	27.4	57.1	15.5
1974	3,258,800	27.6	57.7	14.7

made from imported milk powder and butter oil. In the filled evaporated milk product market, the major competition to IFI's Maria label is the locally produced Neema and Tulip labels (Table 16).

The increase in per capita consumption of evaporated and sweetened milk during 1965 to 1969 primarily reflects the increased consumer change from evaporated to sweetened milk products. Also notable is the complete lack of fresh milk consumption, a response to its zero production between 1965 and 1969, as reported in the IFI Marketing Plan for 1970. IFI's experience in the Philippines has shown that more than 90 percent of its volume is used for coffee creaming, dessert and fruit creaming, and for drinking and cooking. Note that the Maria label product is not used for baby feeding. The Philippine health authorities will not allow IFI to advertise it as an infant feeder because it contains vegetable fats which they believe to be harmful to an infant's health. Company research findings disagree with this conclusion, but the agreement not to encourage the use of the product for infant feeding is honored.

Total industry sales of filled evaporated milk grew by a meager 2.4 percent between 1965 and 1969 (Table 1), but Maria sales dropped 2.4 percent and Neema sales 4 percent, while Tulip sales increased by a dramatic 48.3 percent. The large increase in Tulip's sales is primarily a function of its price. Tulip's pricing, according to company information, posed a threat to Maria and Neema sales in institutional-consumer markets where price is a very important factor. Further, Tulip's pricing resulted in a decline of Maria's sales of the baby-size can (Table 3). The IFI marketing plan noted a discernible market shift from filled to sweetened milk. Market share statistics for the three brands between 1965 and 1969 are given in Table 2. A Maria label sales forecast for 1970 to 1974 (Table 4) projected a sales increase of approximately 15.3 percent. During that same period the company anticipated that Neema sales would grow by about 21.2 percent and Tulip sales decrease by 1 percent. Table 15 gives relevant data concerning production of various milk types during 1965 to 1969, and projected future consumption and market shares by brand types from 1970 to 1974.

Pricing

IFI prices filled evaporated milk lower than that containing butter fat on the premise that only the price differential permits general milk market penetration. The historical retail price schedule appears in Table 17. Although the local management recommends an appropriate price, the staff of the parent organization actually sets the final price. IFI's pricing policy in this market is based upon two elements, each of which exerts its influence at successive stages of the product's life cycle. The initial recommended price is based essentially on the changes in the cost of raw materials and labor plus a "reasonable" profit. Once approved, this is the wholesale list price.

It is at this point that the second element enters into the price strategy. The wholesale list price is set not only to reflect production cost plus profit margin but also to allow the retailer to set a shelf price determined by the competitive environment. Although currently there are no institutionalized product price controls,

TABLE 17

Historical Retail Price Schedule—Philippine Islands

	Size	1965	1966	1967	1968	1969
Consumer price for Maria (IFI) label—local currency (P)	Tall	.45	.45	.50	.50	.50
Consumer price for Neema label	Tall	.45	.45	.50	.50	.50
Consumer price for Tulip label	Tall	NA	NA	NA	NA	NA
IFI market share in percentages	—	28.1	27.3	25.7	25.6	26.8
IFI marketing cost per case (P)	—	NA	2.68	3.12	2.53	2.84

Table 16 shows that the two major competitive brands uniformly follow the product's retail price level. This uniformity indicates that there is no price leader in the locally produced filled milk market in that the major brands all sell for identical shelf prices. IFI has indicated that using price as a competitive marketing tool in this particular market is futile, because a price increase shifts customers to lower priced brands. Similarly, no major competitor would lower the price because he knows that the competition would meet this strategic move. A company spokesman said, "By lowering your price you would not sell more milk, you would only reduce your profit margins."

Sales Organization

As its sales organization in the Philippines market, IFI uses the H. Cavigli Trading Company (HCTC), a wholly owned subsidiary of New York-based H. Cavigli Corporation. This use of HCTC is based on both economic and legal grounds. To avoid the potentially costly introductory stages when it began local production in 1957, especially with respect to the handling of local credit sales, IFI contracted with HCTC to manage the sales and distribution functions. HCTC is compensated solely on an annual per case commission basis. Figure 1 presents the organizational chart of the Milk Division of HCTC. It can be seen that the Milk Division is organized along functional lines which stress the sales and distribution aspects of the overall marketing function.

An additional consideration was the Retail Trade Act involving aliens. This legislation grants preferential status and exemption from the Act's statutes to American firms involved in retail operations if those firms can prove and substantiate that the ownership is wholly American. Because IFI could not verify that all outstanding stock in the parent organization was American owned, and because it was impossible to discriminate in the stock's sale on the open exchange, the firm chose to align itself with HCTC, which could prove to the satisfaction of the national government that it was a totally American-owned organization. Using an independent, outside agency in a function which forms such an important and integral part of the firm's successful performance necessitates some means to coordinate activities and policy between the two organizations. This is done through the IFI-HCTC Marketing Committee, a joint policy committee comprised of three members of the IFI marketing staff (with the noticeable absence of HCTC's sales manager). The committee performs two vital functions: it formulates general sales policy, and it provides the final local approval of forecasts submitted by the sales force in the field.

International Foods generally regards the sales manager of Cavigli's Milk Division as their own general sales manager: "That's the way we treat him, and that's the way we work with him." However, his decision-making authority is limited to implementing policy changes in the daily field operations of the sales force. Major marketing mix decision-making authority, such as instituting changes in the pricing policy or granting special incentives to the trade, are outside his functional jurisdiction, as they are for IFI's own sales managers. Such authority is

FIGURE 1

H. Cavigli Trading Company—Milk Division, Philippines

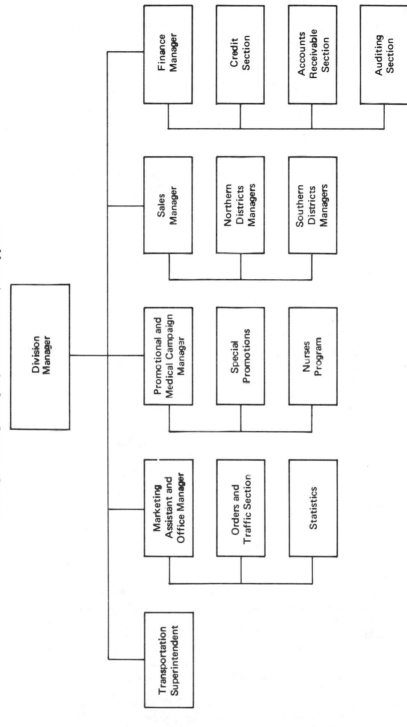

retained by the top local management and ultimately by the staff in the parent office in New York.

The sales manager does play an important role in formulating the sales forecasts initially submitted by the sales force in the field. Each of the thirteen sales regions is headed by a sales supervisor whose function is to forecast sales for the coming year. The company states that these estimates are overly optimistic, in that they often are founded on the assumption that special allowances, incentives, or promotions will be used within a particular sales region. The forecasts are submitted to the sales manager for approval. He considers the estimates, and if he finds that they generally conform to the growth rate of product sales over the previous three to five years within each district, he passes the forecasts along to the marketing staff of the affiliate. Should he consider the estimate to be unrealistic, he returns it to the regional supervisor for reconsideration.

When HCTC submits its best estimates to the marketing staff of IFI an additional round of review is begun. The IFI personnel review the estimates, not solely in light of historical growth patterns, but also in light of their more general knowledge of the Filipino economy and, especially, governmental intervention or restrictions within the evaporated milk market. If IFI and HCTC projections differ, which is usual, then the joint IFI-HCTC Marketing Committee meets and develops a final estimate which is submitted to the New York headquarters for ultimate approval.

That approval depends upon how well the sales force met the objectives set by the joint policy committee. These objectives are essentially oriented toward increasing sales force efficiency. Table 9 shows that the company anticipates a minimal improvement in sales force efficiency: 0.6 percent in case sales and 1.1 percent in average dollar sales. Contributing to the low expected improvement is the turnover ratio of the sales force which in 1968 was 25.3 percent and for the first seven months of 1969 was 12.3 percent, or eighteen salesmen either terminated or resigned. Table 8 provides the breakdown of the sales organization.

To improve the performance of the HCTC organization, five objectives and specific plans for achieving those objectives were proposed by the joint policy committee:

1. To ensure closer supervision over the approximately 30 percent of the field sales force who are presently assigned to five sales regions the firm proposed to realign the districts to take advantage of the new surface transportation networks completed by the government.
2. To upgrade the quality of the sales personnel and reduce the turnover ratio, it was recommended that the sales training program be continued by means of quarterly workshops. In addition, the company proposed to align its compensation schedule with that of the general industry and to provide increased motivation through salesmen incentive programs.
3. To minimize credit risks and to improve the level of product distribution, the dealership base in the key cities and in the secondary sales areas was to be expanded.
4. To improve the implementation and control of the quarterly sales promotion activities, the company proposed to develop an annual

program of quarterly sales promotions and to institute a method of reporting and evaluating the success of these programs.

5. A final proposal was to complete the census of retail outlets and develop a cycle of coverage frequency for each of the promotional vans.

In implementing changes in sales force performance IFI found that, because HCTC is an independent, outside agency, IFI management had to follow constantly the efforts of the sales organization. This was not because the two groups operated under different policies, but rather because they did not view those policies in the same perspective. Thus, IFI's management generally instituted changes and reform.

Sales Training

One of the objectives is to upgrade the quality of the sales personnel. To accomplish this aim partially, the company proposed to conduct a national convention in Manila for all supervisors, salesmen, and merchandisers, during which the marketing objectives and strategies would be presented. The company also proposed to hold quarterly seminars in each of the ten supervisorial districts outside of Manila, essentially a program of continuing sales education during which sales methods are improved and an assessment and evaluation of quarterly objectives of performance are discussed in relation to the overall marketing objective of the subsidiary. To fulfill these proposals, IFI allocated ₱ 8,400 to cover the expenses incurred for transportation, board, and lodging for all participants.

Distribution Network and Costs

Details on the structure of the Philippine trade are not available except that there are approximately 59,213 food stores and 4,257 drug stores in the Philippines. A detailed survey of the store types was slated for 1970.

The stated objective of the company is to achieve its sales forecast under the identical policies on credit, discounts, and delivery as were employed during 1969. In 1969 IFI met the Tulip brand underpricing of from ₱ 0.50 to ₱ 1.50 per case to the institutional buyers. IFI's average cost during 1969 was ₱ 0.81 per case on approximately 97,000 cases, which represents 24 percent of the total institutional volume. The objective of the firm for 1970 was to increase its share of the institutional market to 33 percent (or about 130,000 cases) while maintaining the same average cost of underpricing.

The company employs a program of discounts designed to induce prompt payment of its accounts receivable. An allocation of ₱ 172,000 has been made to cover the costs of a trade discount of ₱ 0.25 per case on invoices paid within fifteen days. The costs are computed on sales to dealers and do not apply to sales made to the HCTC. Table 18 gives IFI's trade discount structure.

Theoretically, credit is available to anyone purchasing the product, even a single case. However, credit sales generally are based on carloads. To encourage volume purchasing by the trade, the company has established a volume price schedule in which one to one hundred cases are priced at the maximum, 101 to 249 cases at the

TABLE 18

Discount Structure—Philippines

Can Size	Highest List Price	Highest Cash Discount	Highest Volume Discount	Direct Factory Discount	Highest Promotional Allowance	Other	Best Net Price
Tall	₱22.45	₱0.25	None	₱0.10	None	None	₱21.80
Baby	24.50	0.25	None	0.10	None	None	23.85

median, and 250 or more at the best price available. But the wholesaler's profit margin is practically eliminated if he does not purchase in 250 case lots. Thus, the company creates additional pressure for volume purchasing.

Credit sales, which account for nearly all of total sales, are carried for an average of forty-five to sixty days. Credit sales dominate because cash sales are almost impossible to obtain except in off-truck sales to very small retail outlets. The basis for this situation is the adverse performance of the economy and the shortage of the money supply. The regional assistant vice-president of marketing in New York stated, in response to a question about the efficacy of granting credit to retailers with marginal incomes, that "you could eliminate your credit, but you also would have no sales in six months. Your trade continues to buy only as long as you keep supplying them so they can keep the money flowing—cash flow is very important." He further stated that the competition is subject to similar pressures. Historically, the company did generate large cash sales and thus could offer a discount of ₱ 0.25, or 2/10 net 30, but as economic conditions worsened the policy was discontinued.

In 1970 ₱ 97,000 was allocated to cover the costs of an allowance of ₱ 0.10 per case to customers who took delivery of the merchandise at the plant and for the cost of delivery, F.O.B. Manila, through contract truckers. The company estimated that the combined cost would average ₱ 0.14 per case.

Special Programs

The 1970 budget for marketing operations included several items peculiar to IFI's Philippines operations: expenses peculiar to the particular year and those responding to distinctive characteristics of the competitive environment which are carried as continuing programs.

The audio-visual program is designed to promote consumption in those rural areas where standard promotional campaigns and activities have little effect. The program operates seven mobile audio-visual units which show two movies a night, six days a week, with an average of 600 movies per truck per year, to a conservatively estimated audience per showing of 1,500 persons. The movies are accompanied by short commercials which stress the nutritional value of the product in infant feeding and every day use. These are supplemented by lectures given by the two-man operating crews. These teams also conduct the school campaign in their respective areas during the academic year (see Part C for a discussion of this campaign) and during the summer months engage in off-truck sales to small retail outlets and to ultimate consumers. The budgetary allocation of ₱ 79,700 covers the cost of operating the trucks and the salaries and expenses of the fourteen operating personnel. The cost allocation of the total expenditure is broken down between advertising costs (80 percent, or ₱ 63,760) and the marketing function (20 percent, or ₱ 15,940). The allocation for 1970 represented an increase of 3.5 percent over 1969 in this continuing program.

IFI's promotional trucks are another marketing expense classification unique to the Philippines. These vans and their operators are somewhat comparable to the retail salesmen in the firm's domestic operations in the United States. The operators are considered to be promotional salesmen and merchandisers whose function is to promote the use of the product in their respective sales areas. In addition to their function of actively promoting the brand, the vans distribute the product for the wholesaler, a function traditionally allocated to the manufacturer or importer of a product in the general Southeastern Asia area. Continuance of this type of distribution service is based also on an additional factor: by using the wholesaler the problem of retail trade credit is shifted from the company to the wholesaler. The firm views the problems associated with the wholesale trade and their associated expenses as minor when compared with the problems inherent in the retail trade.

In 1970 this program, jointly conducted and financed by IFI and HCTC, was allocated ₱ 431,000 (an increase of 4.9 percent over 1969) to cover the operational costs of the seventy promotional vans and the salaries and expenses of all the promotional salesmen and merchandisers, as well as the workers hired to assist the operators of the larger trucks. The increased allocation included a provision for upgrading the salary scales of the operating personnel so that the firm's salary administration would be competitive with prevailing industry rates.

The budgetary classification is somewhat a misnomer in that the vans' only daily promotional activity is putting up posters or signs. Because this is considered an essential element of the vans' activities, its cost has not been isolated. Thus, while the expense classification implies a promotional cost, there is no allocable advertising cost on the vans. The basis for this costing decision is that, while promotional postering is an integral part of the vans' operations, their principal function is the redistribution of the product. The redistribution function entails shifting the old product on retail shelves—the shelf-life of the brand is considered to be three months—to outlets where inventory turnover is faster. The budgetary allocation to cover the expenses of this program during 1969 was computed on the basis of 8 percent of the total share of the product in promotional van expense. For 1970 this was computed to be ₱ 37,500, an increase of 4.2 percent.

The final special budgetary category of the proposed total marketing investment was relabeling. This allocation represents the difference in cost (loss) between the manufacturing cost of over-age milk plus the cost of freight and handling for its return to the production facility minus the resale value at a reduced price. The allocation of ₱ 115,000 was based on average returns of 1.52 percent from the market. It covered the firm's estimate of the cost of labor and materials used to relabel the product for the trade. The allocation represented an increase over 1969 of 35.3 percent which is accounted for by the inclusion of a provision for the relabeling of trade inventories in connection with implementing the new advertising campaign.

Market Research

In 1969 IFI commissioned MARFAC Research Associates to conduct "Project Maria," a consumer survey designed to measure consumer attitudes about the brand. It appears that the brand's sales had been decreasing and that the firm had been unable to reverse the trend. The field sales force indicated that the brand's label, which featured a historic monument, did not appeal to the consumer. IFI had the label tested by a market research group which found that the label as such tested well. The firm then commissioned MARFAC to test the product with three primary objectives in mind:

1. To determine the housewives' opinions about milk additives and the functions they should perform,
2. To determine if some vitamin-like additives actually improved the brand to such an extent that an advertising campaign would stand the test of credibility, and
3. To evaluate the acceptability of the brand among the consumers in direct comparison with its primary competitors.

The direct results of the study indicated that, for reasons of economy, the housewives would prefer an additive that would "improve the overall quality of milk." In the blind home-placement study, to test the third objective, the survey revealed that the Maria brand performed better and was better appreciated by the sample than were its main competitors, Neema and Tulip. However, the study also revealed that the consumer, when testing identical evaporated milk in brand labeled cans, invariably preferred the Neema brand. Thus, MARFAC concluded that Maria's label had some inherent brand-linked prejudices, and therefore, recommended that the firm undertake the large commitment of relabeling the brand in an attempt to change its image.

Continued market research in this area was scheduled for 1970. Also the firm was to continue its participation in Excelsior Research Company's Pantry and Distribution checks so that it could continually assess the product's brand share in the consumers' homes as well as the penetration of retail outlets in the key sales regions of the country. IFI planned to commission two consumer attitude studies— one on coffee creaming and one on infant feeding. The infant feeding survey was based upon a suggestion by the vice-president of marketing in IFI's New York headquarters that would determine the infant feeding habits and trends within Filipino society. The total amount allocated for market research on the product during 1970 was ₱ 14,300.

The firm also attempted to conduct a census survey of the nation's retail outlets for the product through the HCTC field sales force. This census had been in progress for several years and the firm hoped to complete it in 1970. An IFI spokesman in New York gave his opinion that "If the sales people were in our own control we would have accomplished the census in a matter of months, but it has taken these people a long time."

PERU

Objectives of the Marketing Mix

The immediate and long-term goal of the IFI Peruvian affiliate is to increase its sales volume. The Maria label market share was 69.4 percent, with imports providing 23.3 percent and the remaining 7.3 percent coming from small local producers. In 1970 the company planned to increase its market share to 76.4 percent of the total consumption.

The marketing objectives of the firm are summarized as:

1. To strengthen the brand's image as a natural milk, which is delicious, fresh, 100 percent pure cow's milk.
2. To persuade mothers that the brand is better than any other milk, fresh or canned, for nourishing their children from infancy onwards.
3. To attempt to reach those socioeconomic groups which represent 90 percent of the households in the Lima-Callao region and 81.1 percent of the provincial households.
4. To intensify the brand's usage for infant feeding by increasing the budgetary allocation for the infant-oriented medical promotions campaign.
5. To strive for 100 percent distribution coverage of the retail grocery outlets and the *bodegas* (small neighborhood stores).
6. The Peruvian national government has banned the import of evaporated milk. Therefore, the affiliate recommends that the firm introduce a new locally produced brand in 1970 aimed at the infant market. The firm further recommends that an independent advertising campaign be established. Immediate action would take up the gap in the market created by the ban on imports.

The Market

Until mid-1969 there were three major segments in the Peruvian evaporated milk industry: IFI with its locally produced, medium-priced Maria 1 and 2 labels; the locally produced, medium-priced Perfect label; and imported, premium-priced evaporated milk originating primarily from a single European producer (see section on pricing). However, the Peruvian government banned imports of evaporated milk for 1970, thus eliminating a major source of competition for the two locally produced labels.

In recent years the evaporated milk market in Peru has increased dramatically. As shown in Table 1, industry sales increased by approximately 36.1 percent between 1965 and 1969. During that same period, while Maria's sales increased by 29.1 percent, the imports increased a startling 84.9 percent. Data showing market share for each segment appear in Table 2.

IFI projections for sales from 1970 to 1974 are given in Table 4. During this period the company expects case sales to increase by approximately 15.8 percent which reflects company feelings that the industry's dramatic growth of the past five years will not continue indefinitely. The most important factor in sales estimating for 1970, according to company spokesmen, was the ban on imports. It was estimated that the Maria 1 and 2 labels would take approximately 55 to 60 percent of the normal import volume, an approximate increase of 14 to 15 percent in company sales volume over the 1969 level. The ban on imports also spurred the company to study the possibility of the European producers establishing a manufacturing operation in Peru. The IFI management felt that a manufacturing operation would not be established because import volume before the ban would not justify such a move, and a locally produced product would probably not enjoy the same brand image as the imported product.

According to company market research conducted in the Lima-Callao area—which accounts for approximately 66 percent of total Maria sales—98.8 percent of the homes use milk, of which 39 percent by volume is fresh and at least 59 percent evaporated. The three main uses of evaporated milk in the Peruvian market are coffee creaming and drinking (67 percent), infant feeding (29 percent), and cooking additive (4 percent). Table 19 summarizes relevant information on milk consumption by socioeconomic groups.

Pricing

IFI's pricing strategy, or that of any milk firm in Peru, is predetermined by the national government. Because milk is considered a staple commodity in the Peruvian economy, and because of severe inflationary pressures, the government has assumed total control in the milk market both of wholesale and retail prices.

Table 20 shows that the two major brands, both produced locally, have experienced a five-year retail price increase of 59.5 percent which conforms generally with the increased cost-of-living index (caused by devaluation of sols and inflation). The table also shows that the imported brands, now denied entry into the market, were generally premium-priced because the import tariff was added to the basic cost of the product. However, it seems that future price increases may be hard to come by in view of the "revolutionary" military government stabilizing prices, thereby exerting heavy pressure on the company's profit margins.

TABLE 19

Milk Consumption by Socioeconomic Groups—Peru
Lima-Callao Area

Socioeconomic Group	Percentage of Population	*Milk Consumption*			
		Evaporated	Fresh	Powdered	Total[a]
High income	5	31	69	0	100
Medium	30	54	45	1	100
Low	40	66	31	3	100
Poor	25	NA	NA	NA	—

[a]In the Lima–Callao area, 98.8 percent of all homes consume milk. Of the total milk consumed, 59 percent is evaporated, 39 percent is fresh, and 2 percent is powdered.

TABLE 20

Historical Retail Price Schedule—Peru

	Size	1965	1966	1967	1968	1969
Consumer price for IFI products—local currency (s/)	Tall	4.20	4.20	4.90	6.70	6.70
Consumer price for Perfect label	Tall	4.20	4.20	4.90	6.70	6.70
Consumer price for Dutch imports	Tall	5.20	5.20	5.90	7.70	8.00
Consumer price for French and German imports	Tall	NA	NA	NA	NA	6.50[a] 7.20
IFI market share in percentages	–	73.2	73.1	70.1	66.7	69.4
IFI marketing cost per case in U.S. dollars[b]	–	0.24	0.23	0.25	0.18	0.41

[a]S/6.50 for French brand and s/7.20 for German brand.

[b]Figures for 1965 to 1968 do not include distribution expenses which are included in 1969 data.

Sales Organization

Since their entry into the Peruvian milk market some thirty years ago, IFI has used J. Freitas & Co. (JFC) as its sales and distribution organization. This is a family-owned Peruvian firm. Economically, IFI feels that its market share is sufficiently strong that its sales operations can be handled through an independent distributorship far more cheaply than through its own sales organization. International Foods has contracted for JFC's services on an annual per case commission basis. The budgetary allocation for commissions during the current fiscal year is s/16,474,500 or 73.7 percent of direct selling expenses. JFC also supplies the distribution network through branch offices and warehouses. The warehouse facilities in the seven major cities have a storage capacity of 219,000 cases, with the Lima warehouse accounting for 68.5 percent of the total capacity. The distribution expenses, warehousing, freight, and insurance, incurred by JFC, are assumed by IFI and were budgeted at s/40,076,340 for 1970.

JFC never purchases the product, but it has total responsibility for the invoicing, done in the name of IFI, in addition to functional responsibility for storage, transportation, and both retail and wholesale sales coverage.

The medium of coordination between the two organizations is the marketing manager, or sales manager as he is designated in IFI (see Part A). The sales manager has direct responsibility for the development of the annual Marketing Plan. Physically located in the Lima offices of JFC, he theoretically provides only the liaison between the two firms and the source of the marketing mix guidelines. However, in actuality, he effectively manages the Maria Division of JFC in that his function as liaison officer means that the policies formulated by the top local management in New York are transmitted to JFC through him, without discussion.

The decision making authority of the sales manager is quite limited within the narrow confines of the authority granted to any manager in any of the affiliates. He is allowed to implement general policy changes only in those areas that affect daily field operations, such as the extension of credit in most cases. However, he has no authority to institute changes in the major parameters of the marketing mix without prior approval of the headquarters' staff. Thus, the essential function of the sales manager is to distill the sales reports and forecasts into a reasonable estimate of actions for the coming fiscal year. During the fiscal year he also has the initial responsibility of budget review.

Of course, final approval of the Marketing Plan and its operational budget rests in the New York offices of IFI. Their approval is based upon the successful achievement of the objectives of the sales force. The goal of the JFC organization during the current fiscal year is to reach 100 percent distribution of the product in the bodegas and wholesale outlets with a large enough inventory to cover these outlets within the fifteen-day frequency of salesman calls. The specific recommendations for action to accomplish this objective are as follows:

1. The salesmen's area of coverage is to be reorganized so that the customers are classified by a logical order of visits. This is being implemented to ensure that the salesmen do not alter the order of sales calls without specific authorization.
2. To implement a new daily sales report which enumerates the salesman's daily visits by numerical order, the number of cases sold in each visit, the size of the customer's inventory of the brand, and the size of the competitive brand's inventory.
3. To implement two new reports designed to provide both direct and indirect supervision and control by the appropriate supervisor over his group of salesmen.
4. To institute periodic sales contests in order to motivate the salesmen to increase sales and distribution.

All the proposed actions are aimed primarily at increasing the productivity of the salesmen in their respective regions. Tables 8 and 9 show that, while the size of the sales force has remained constant over the past five years, its performance has shown considerable improvement. In 1969 the sales force showed an average case increase over the previous year of 4,273 per salesman, or 5.9 percent. The comparable estimate figures for the current fiscal year are 11,061 cases, or 14.4 percent. The ban on imports accounts for the large estimated increase in salesman productivity.

Distribution Network and Marketing Costs

Unfortunately, data on retail outlets in Peru are not as complete as for West Germany and the United Kingdom. The available information is summarized in Tables 21 and 22.

As stated in the Marketing Plan, IFI did not contemplate any changes during 1970 in the policies regarding the company's terms of trade. IFI-Peru does not have

TABLE 21

Number of Retail Outlets by Type and Location—Peru

Store Type	Lima-Callao	Numbers/Location Provinces	Total Peru
Grocery Stores	8,500[a]	16,000[b]	24,500
Drug Stores	630	770	1,400

[a]Does not include Municipal Open Market shops (40,000) or peddlers (13,500).
[b]Does not include Municipal Open Market shops (31,800) or peddlers (11,900).

TABLE 22

Source of IFI Sales by Region—Peru

Zone	Percentage of Total Population	Percentage of Total IFI Sales
Lima-Callao	25.2	66.4
Central	24.4	12.6
South	19.6	6.3
North	27.1	13.6
Interior	3.7	1.1
Total	100.0	100.0

a discount structure available to the wholesale or retail trade. The extension of credit to customers is divided into three primary categories. For the large customers, credit is extended up to sixty days. For smaller customers, it is fifteen to thirty days. Very small accounts have to pay cash.

The local marketing manager generally determines if credit terms are to be extended to a specific customer. However, should a customer's outstanding account become too large, or a controversy develop, then the ultimate responsibility rests with the subsidiary's managing director.

Thus, the only motivation the trade has to purchase the brand, especially in light of its price structure, is to help sell other items and to gain access to the credit facilities that the firm extends to buy other IFI products.

Competitive firms use terms of trade extensively as a marketing tool. The primary competitor, the Perfect label, uses a 2 percent discount on all invoices paid within thirty days regardless of the order size. They also conduct special discount campaigns throughout the country, in which a discount of 2 to 10 percent is given to the trade, plus additional free cases for displays and special promotions. The free cases are given on the following basis: with the purchase of fifteen cases the customer receives one-half case gratis, with fifty-five cases he receives two cases free, and for every 105 cases he receives four free cases.

Market Research

IFI allocated s/220,400 for 1970 market research. This budget allocation was to cover two independent studies. The first, a "Brand Barometer," conducted by

Indices "U," was to indicate quarterly the position and share of the market held by each evaporated milk brand. The second study, conducted by Instituto Verificador de Medios Publicitarios, was to give the firm the annual market share of each brand, not only in the Lima-Callao area, but also in the eight principal provincial cities. Both surveys were to use a personal interview technique among all socioeconomic groups.

MOHAN ICE CREAM COMPANY, PHILIPPINES

Pricing Strategy, Anticipating Competition's Responses, Home Office-Subsidiary Relationship

In January 1969, the International Division of Mohan Ice Cream Company, U.S.A.[1] was faced with a set of major problems in its Philippines operation. Although the company's sales and revenues were growing every year, it was rapidly losing its lead in market share to its major competitor, Yanqui Ice Cream Company. In terms of sales revenue, the Philippines was Mohan's second largest overseas market (largest in the Far East), and was the only market in the world, including the United States, where its market share was larger than Yanqui's. Therefore, the International Division decided to reevaluate completely its marketing policies in the Philippines with a view to developing new strategies to enable its Philippines subsidiary to recapture its earlier market dominance and continue to grow.

Mohan Ice Cream Company was established in the United States in 1905 to sell a special flavor of vanilla ice cream. However, at this time its subsequent arch rival, Yanqui Ice Cream, was twenty years old, well-established domestically, and already started on its overseas expansion program.

From the outset Mohan was beset with "image" problems. To the competition's label of "imitator," Mohan was unable to retort effectively. Consequently, it remained essentially a small regional company, was unable to achieve national distribution, and constantly lost money. In 1930, when the company was almost bankrupt, Mr. D. C. Emrich acquired it and expanded company operations by building new plants in various parts of the country. During the depression, Mr. Emrich expanded Mohan's sales by offering greater quantities of ice cream than the competition, capitalizing on appeals such as "Super-Pack at Regular Price."

Table 1 compares net sales and net income for the two companies during the period 1930 to 1950.

---

1. All the names used in the case study are fictitious to disguise the identities of the company and its offices.

TABLE 1

Net Sales and Net Income: 1930 to 1950
(in Millions of Dollars)

| Year | Mohan Ice Cream Company | | Yanqui Ice Cream Company | |
	Net Sales	*Net Income*	*Net Sales*	*Net Income*
1930	5.7	no profits	40.3	13.4
—	—	—	—	—
1935	10.8	1.9	41.8	16.2
—	—	—	—	
1940	24.4	4.3	100.2	30.2
1941	38.2	6.1	136.6	25.3
1942	41.4	8.7	135.0	25.1
1943	48.2	6.2	136.5	25.4
1944	45.3	5.8	142.0	27.2
1945	43.4	5.1	139.5	25.6
1946	46.6	5.9	129.3	25.3
1947	50.3	7.2	151.5	28.3
1948	49.2	8.9	180.4	32.4
1949	47.4	2.3	230.3	35.3
1950	39.2	1.6	210.9	28.2

However, what was good during the depression and the war period was not necessarily good after the war. Beginning in 1948, postwar inflation plunged Mohan into trouble. The larger sizes at lower prices cut deeply into Mohan's profits and the company was again on the brink of bankruptcy. Mr. Emrich virtually conceded to Yanqui. In a last-ditch effort, and realizing that the company's real troubles lay in its marketing, Mr. Emrich hired Mr. Harold Klein, a former Yanqui executive, as executive vice-president.

The battle royal between the two companies began after March 1950 when Klein took over as the president and chief executive officer of Mohan Ice Cream. By means of aggressive marketing and promotion, Mohan's sales rose from $39 million in 1950 to $158 million in 1960 and $848 million in 1968. The net profits for the same period rose from $1.6 million in 1950 to $14.0 million in 1960 and $45.45 million in 1968, a sharp increase of about eight times. Mohan also consistently narrowed the gap between its market share and that of Yanqui. Figures in Table 2 tell this story.

PHILIPPINE MARKET

Mohan entered the Philippine market in 1945. By this time Yanqui was well-established there and in other Far Eastern markets. Yanqui operated in the Philippines through an exclusive franchise arrangement with Soriano Inc., one of the most powerful companies in the islands and producer of the only indigenous beer, San Miguel. Soriano has many financial and real estate interests spread throughout the Philippines. It was and still is the only producer of glass, glass

TABLE 2

Shares of Domestic (U.S.) Market

Yanqui vs. Mohan, 1940 to 1968 (Percent)

Year	Yanqui	Mohan	All Other
1940	53	11	36
–	–	–	–
1950	48.4	11.8	39.8
1951	47.0	13.6	39.4
1952	46.9	13.9	39.2
1953	45.4	16.2	38.4
1954	44.1	18.3	37.6
1955	43.8	20.3	35.9
1956	40.2	22.0	37.8
1957	39.8	25.2	35.0
1958	36.0	26.0	34.0
1959	35.1	25.3	39.6
1960	37.2	20.7	42.1
1961	35.8	19.8	44.4
1962	33.1	17.2	49.7
1963	32.0	17.2	50.8
1964	32.4	16.3	51.3
1965	31.8	15.8	52.4
1966	30.7	14.2	55.1
1967	31.3	14.3	54.4
1968	31.1	13.8	55.1

bottles, and glass containers in the archipelago. Not only does Soriano manufacture the containers for its beer (and for soft drinks), it also owns paper mills and a plastics plant in which cardboard and plastic containers are manufactured. Until the advent of plastics, Soriano's cardboard cartons were the best solution for ice cream packaging in the Philippines, given their competitive advantage and the prevailing conditions in the area.

MOHAN'S ENTRY INTO THE PHILIPPINE MARKET

Mohan entered the market in 1945 through a franchise manufacturer in which it had a minority equity interest. Initially, Mohan offered one basic flavor, pineapple, which is the largest selling and the most popular flavor in that country. Yanqui Ice Cream was available in the market *only* in pineapple flavor, and came in a 15 centiliter size which was sold to consumers for a retail price of 15 centavos. The situation persisted for about five years and Mohan found that it was getting nowhere in terms of market penetration. The company's local management was not overanxious to expand its facilities and invest capital in developing a strong distribution network.

In 1950, with the change in Mohan's U.S. management, the Philippines management changed its development and marketing strategies.

1. To achieve more flexibility in its expansion program and greater control in its distribution, the company switched from its policy of franchised operations to company-owned plants. Most of the existing franchises were bought out and new plants set up with the result that by 1960, in terms of market penetration, Mohan achieved parity with Yanqui, and by 1961, Mohan's products were available nationally.
2. At the same time (1950), Mohan decided to introduce the 20 centiliter size at 15 centavos, thus offering consumers a greater volume of ice cream for their money than Yanqui.
3. The introduction of plastic containers for ice cream proved particularly successful. The inadequacy of transportation and storage facilities, both at the point of purchase and at the consumers' homes, made cardboard packaging more vulnerable to damage and deterioration. A further advantage of plastic was that the empty containers had a variety of uses, especially for storing foodstuffs.
4. This price-package strategy, backed by heavy promotion to make the consumer aware of the larger size at the same price, appealed especially to the large segment of the Philippine population with very low per capita income.

The result of these strategies was that Mohan's sales starting in 1950 really skyrocketed. Despite extensive expansion, Mohan's plants have been working at full capacity ever since. (*See* Appendix I, Tables 1 through 9.) The gap between the market shares of Mohan and Yanqui kept narrowing, and in 1963 Mohan's sales for the first time exceeded Yanqui's. The changes in the market shares of the two competitors between 1950 and 1968 are shown in Table 3.

Yanqui Ice Cream stayed with the 15 centiliter size and did not reduce its price. Consequently, it lost the initiative and its market share kept declining. In retrospect, the following explanations can be offered for Yanqui's action:

1. Yanqui's U.S. management had pursued similar policies in the U.S. during the depression and the years immediately following World War II, thereby losing their formerly dominant position in the U.S. markets. The Philippines company followed the parent company's philosophy.
2. Soriano Inc., Yanqui's Philippine partner, was involved in a variety of businesses of which ice cream was but a small part of the total. Second, Soriano did not believe in low profit margins and high volume to the extent that food and beverage companies do in the United States. Third, a change-over to a larger size would have involved writing off existing stocks of cardboard containers, which Soriano was unwilling to assume.
3. While Mohan absorbed the cost of changeover and assisted its local subsidiary with additional funds, Yanqui offered only long-term loans which local franchisers were reluctant to accept because of high carrying costs.

Soriano made two kinds of efforts to stem the downturn in its market share. One, the advertising strategy was changed at least twice during the period 1950 to 1963. The appeals were (a) Yanqui's Ice Cream is Fresh and Tasty, and (b) Yanqui's Ice Cream Gives Energy. Second, Soriano threatened to cut off retailers' supplies of San

TABLE 3

Shares of Philippines Market[a]

Yanqui vs. Mohan 1945 to 1965 (Percent)

	Yanqui		Mohan			
Year	Pineapple Flavor	All Other Flavors	Pineapple Flavor	All Other Flavors	Other Companies	Total Ice Cream Market
1945	68	–	5	–	27	100
–	–	–	–	–	–	–
1950	65	–	6	–	29	100
1952	59	–	10	–	31	100
1954	57	–	14	–	29	100
1956	54	–	16	–	30	100
1958	49	–	19	–	32	100
1960	42	–	25	–	33	100
1961	37	–	28	–	35	100
1962	32	–	32	–	36	100
1963	30	–	31	–	39	100
1964	32	–	36	3[b]	29	100
1965	30	–	39	5	26	100
1966	28	3[b]	42	8	19	100
1967	32	4	35[c]	9	19	100
1968	33	5	33	9	20	100

[a]Market share figures are estimates based in part on government data and in part on Mohan's market intelligence.

[b]Introduced for the first time.

[c]Price increase affected.

Miguel beer if they carried Mohan's Ice Cream. However, none of these strategies was successful because of the tremendous consumer demand which compelled retailers to stock Mohan's. Mohan, in the meantime, stayed with its basic advertising appeal of "More for Your Money."

COMPETITIVE CONDITIONS IN THE PHILIPPINES DURING 1963 TO 1968 AND MOHAN'S MARKETING STRATEGY

To appreciate Mohan's problems during this period it is necessary to understand the organizational relationship between Mohan's subsidiaries and those of the head office.

1. Mohan is a highly decentralized company (Figures 1 and 2). Each subsidiary is responsible for showing profits in its territory. The compensation of local management is composed of salaries and of

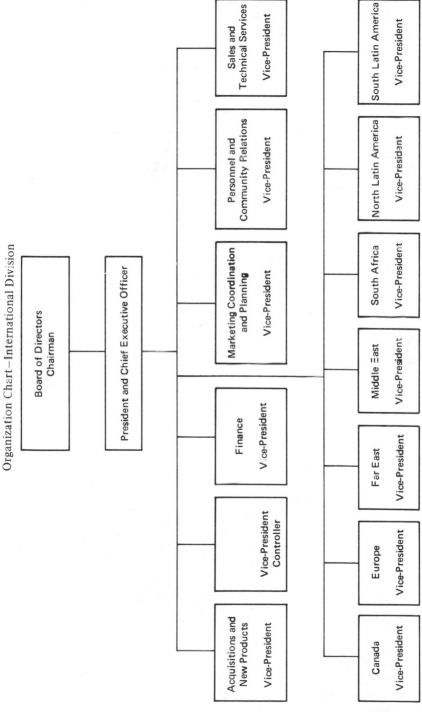

FIGURE 1

Organization Chart—International Division

FIGURE 2

Area Organization—Far Eastern Region

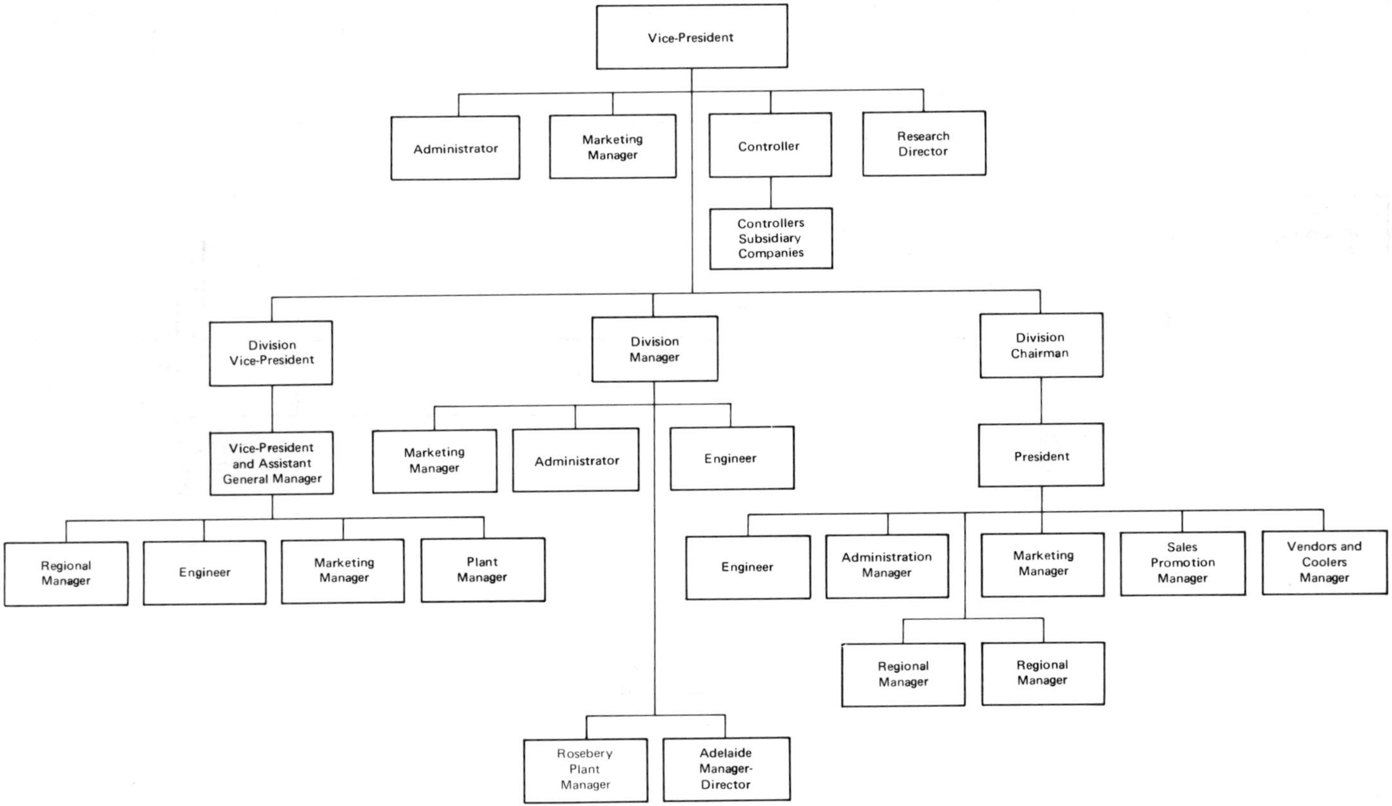

FIGURE 3

Philippine Sales History

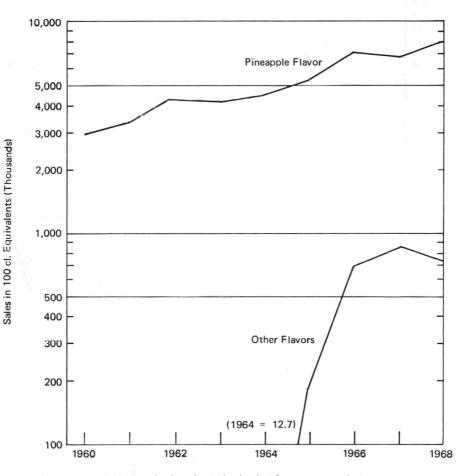

bonuses which are calculated on the basis of current year's income. Thus, local management is very reluctant to make any changes such as introducing a new type of package which would reduce their subsidiaries' current income and therefore their own compensation.

2. Capital requirements, on the other hand, are met by the head office and do not affect local subsidiaries' earnings. The local management, therefore, is anxious to support such projects which require head office capital so long as their earning potential is greater than their carrying costs.

3. Although field offices are responsible to area management in the home office for all major policy decisions, the home office is reluctant to impose any decision contrary to the wishes of local management, except under extreme circumstances, because of the responsibility of local management for showing profits.

FIGURE 4

Philippine Sales—Two-Year Monthly Breakdown

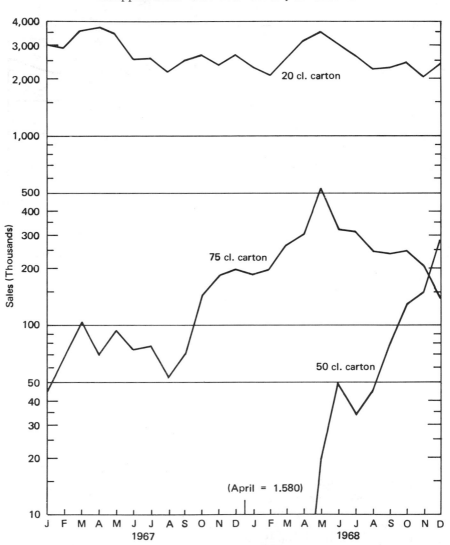

4. Although Mohan's U.S.-Philippine management relations could be improved and coordinated by periodically interchanging management personnel between the field and home office, the field managers were reluctant to leave the islands. First, a manager would have substantially less power and status in New York, where instead of ranking high in position he would deal with many managers of equal or superior rank. Second, Mohan's compensation plan extended a bonus for quota-plus profits in the islands which would be lost to a manager who left.

5. Very little market research is done by the local subsidiaries—the first consumer survey in the Philippines was conducted in 1967. The local arrangements are generally satisfied if they achieve increases in sales. No effort is made to relate growth in sales to market potential.

The Philippine's situation remained favorable for Mohan between 1963 and 1966 and its market share kept increasing. During this period, the home office market research staff assigned to the Far East region constantly recommended to the Philippine office to bring out larger size containers, e.g., 25 cl. and 50 cl. and even 75 cl. However, the field office resisted these recommendations and offered the following arguments against adopting them.

1. Larger sizes are not suitable for the Philippine market because retailers have limited freezer capacity.
2. Consumers by and large do not have refrigerators and therefore cannot store ice cream. They prefer to buy in sizes which can be consumed individually shortly after purchase.
3. The potential market for larger sizes, up to 50 cl., was not more than 5 percent of the total market. They rejected 75 cl. size as out of hand and being unsuitable for the Philippine market. The estimates of the head office research staff made on the basis of two market surveys in 1964 and 1965 yielded a potential market share for larger sizes in the order of 15 to 20 percent. However, the general philosophy regarding this question was "while we have the upper hand we can afford to let our competitor make the first move."

In January 1967, Soriano brought out a 50 cl. plastic package which was an immediate success. The introduction was accompanied by a two-pronged attack in terms of give-aways and advertising campaign.

1. A two-for-one sale—one free 50 cl. container of ice cream with one purchase of the same size.
2. Following the introduction of the larger package the words "big, big" were injected into all the advertising appeals for Yanqui Ice Cream, thus largely nullifying the effect of Mohan's advertising.
3. Mohan's head office was caught completely off-balance. The local management claimed it was unaware of Soriano's plans to bring out a larger size. The head office tried to import larger sizes from the U.S. to meet the competition. However, in the first three months of 1967, it could bring in only 300 cases compared to thousands of cases of Yanqui's Ice Cream in larger sizes which were flooding the market by then.
4. Mohan brought out a 50 cl. size in January 1968 and by the end of the year their sales were back to their April 1967 level. During 1968, the sales growth was maintained, but they could not recover their market share position. Moreover, the recovery in sales volume was achieved with the help of a large increase in promotion effort and expenses. The comparative figures are given in Table 4.

TABLE 4

Media and Promotion Expenses for the
Period 1960 to 1968

		Percentage Increase	
Year	Amount Spent	From Previous Year	From 1960
1960	444,000	–	–
1961	392,000	−11.72	−11.72
1962	417,000	6.37	−6.09
1963	506,000	21.34	13.96
1964	779,000	53.95	75.45
1965	868,000	11.42	95.49
1966	1,201,000	38.36	170.49
1967	1,781,000	48.29	301.12
1968	1,669,000	−6.29	275.90

5. Sales of the 50 cl. size by the end of 1968 had stabilized at 15 percent of the total sales and were still growing, albeit slowly. However, this percentage share was three times larger than estimated by the local management of Mohan (Figures 3 and 4).

PRICING POLICIES

During 1964 to 1965 Mohan's local management initiated talks with Soriano to see if the two could agree on a price increase for their ice creams.[2] There had been no price increase since 1960, and inflation was squeezing the profit margins. At first, Soriano was not interested. However, shortly before they were to introduce the larger package, Soriano approached Mohan's local management with the suggestion that the price of the 20 cl. package be increased from 15 to 20 centavos. This hefty increase was strongly opposed by Mohan's head office market research staff on the following grounds:

1. Yanqui has a prestige image in the Philippine markets; it appeals to upper income groups and therefore has less price elasticity.
2. Mohan's Ice Cream is considered average man's ice cream and has a large following among the middle and lower income groups, and its demand is therefore very sensitive to changes in prices.

It therefore recommended a maximum price increase of two centavos. Soriano, however, would not consider anything less than five centavos. Mohan's local management, although concurring with the head office arguments, recommended that Mohan go along with Soriano on the premise that a large increase was better than none at all. Moreover, they argued that price parity between local independent manufacturers and Mohan and Yanqui would be maintained as the seriously

2. Such discussions are not illegal in the Philippines.

undercapitalized local producers would be tempted to raise their prices as well in order to generate additional capital.

However, events proved these predictions wrong. Kalano, the major local producer, did not increase his prices. Mohan lost some market share to Yanqui's introduction of the larger package. The price increase further compounded the company's problem. Mohan was caught in the middle with catastrophic results on sales and profits. The reverberations reached New York. Many staff changes were made in the Philippine subsidiary's management. Although the general manager of the subsidiary was not fired, his powers were removed by the appointment of a deputy general manager in charge of day-to-day operations. The general manager was reduced to a figurehead but he could not be removed as he was a personal friend of President Marcos of the Philippines. His stay in the islands may not have been a positive factor, but it was considered that his removal against his wishes would definitely be a negative factor and might have political repercussions.

In July 1968 the company contracted with the Manila office of Mitchell Associates, Inc. a reputable U.S. market research firm, to conduct a study in the Philippines of consumer attitudes, consumption patterns, and strengths and weaknesses in Mohan's promotion and distribution strategies. A copy of the summary of findings of the survey by the market research firm appears in Appendix II.

Mohan Ice Cream Co., Inc., Philippines
Sales History

TABLE 1

Sales of Mohan Pineapple Flavor Ice Cream—Greater Manila

Year[a]	Qty. per box 20 cl. No. of Cases[b]	Qty. per box 75 cl. No. of Cases[b]	Total Qty. per box 100 cl. equiv. No. of Cases[b]
1960	7,405,521		1,481,104
1961	7,760,595		1,552,119
1962	10,146,033		2,029,206
1963	7,535,909		1,507,182
1964	8,280,889		1,656,178
1965	9,114,443		1,822,889
1966	10,273,916	13,481	2,064,895
1967			
January	672,910	42,112	
February	669,587	62,457	
March	829,321	84,756	
April	801,596	58,691	
May	820,347	68,519	
June	534,444	52,627	
July	608,602	56,529	
August	448,248	36,217	
September	545,751	46,344	
October	600,012	59,161	
November	458,491	58,874	
December	518,252	78,284	
Total	7,507,561	704,571	2,029,941
1968			
January	477,569	70,922	
February	440,060	62,489	
March	578,219	90,497	
April	677,103	115,891	
May	853,876	160,081	
June	776,192	149,484	
July	678,810	133,292	
August	524,418	101,876	
September	541,300	95,899	
October	582,733	103,071	
November	464,683	85,285	
December	559,615	114,694	
Total	7,154,578	1,283,481	2,392,535

[a]There were no sales of 50 cl. size during this period.
[b]Each case contains 24 boxes

TABLE 2

Sales of Mohan Pineapple Flavor Ice Cream—Bacolod Area

Year	Qty. per box 20 cl. No. of Cases[a]	Qty. per box 50 cl. No. of Cases[a]	Qty. per box 75 cl. No. of Cases[a]	Total Qty. per box 100 cl. equiv. No. of Cases[a]
1960	653,966			130,792
1961	792,384			158,477
1962	1,109,854			221,971
1963	1,147,821			229,566
1964	1,834,587			366,913
1965	1,723,302			344,660
1966	2,120,116			424,023
1967				
January	169,250			
February	150,858			
March	213,313			
April	241,617			
May	186,114			
June	156,647			
July	127,323			
August	119,891			
September	133,971			
October	129,739		2,812	
November	133,613		1,498	
December	150,751		4,105	
Total	1,913,087		8,425	388,926
1968				
January	136,495		5,497	
February	127,654		12,320	
March	154,189		14,255	
April	184,073		9,103	
May	183,153		16,126	
June	169,691		4,207	
July	162,141		2,458	
August	128,034	5,597	4,727	
September	122,262	13,740		
October	133,037	16,158		
November	117,430	15,794		
December	149,124	21,518		
Total	1,767,283	72,807	68,693	397,779

[a]Each case contains 24 boxes.

TABLE 3

Sales of Mohan Pineapple Flavor Ice Cream—Rest of Philippines

Year	Qty. per box 20 cl. No. of Cases[a]	Qty. per box 50 cl. No. of Cases[a]	Qty. per box 75 cl. No. of Cases[a]	Total Qty. per box 100 cl. equiv. No. of Cases[a]
1960	6,623,597			1,324,719
1961	8,116,092			1,623,218
1962	10,139,727			2,027,945
1963	12,045,666			2,409,133
1964	15,689,401			3,137,990
1965	19,159,401			4,583,392
1966	22,916,960			
1967				
January	1,893,008		1,924	
February	1,732,825		5,159	
March	2,064,189		19,799	
April	2,270,737		10,387	
May	1,996,606		25,629	
June	1,574,683		21,587	
July	1,453,598		21,908	
August	1,422,497		16,245	
September	1,465,858		23,850	
October[b]	1,586,476		79,706	
November	1,453,850		120,613	
December	1,616,748		116,756	
Total	20,531,075		346,807	4,366,320
1968				
January	1,367,238		108,120	
February	1,226,550		120,440	
March	1,469,742		160,399	
April	1,913,054	1,580	178,451	
May	2,097,901	19,949	212,406	
June	1,746,447	48,738	168,949	
July	1,527,077	34,045	180,826	
August	1,341,561	40,343	141,679	
September	1,357,661	64,120	143,406	
October	1,444,297	99,983	145,457	
November	1,259,580	110,247	124,627	
December	1,433,132	113,497	138,550	
Total	18,184,240	532,502	1,725,310	5,197,080

[a]Each case contains 24 boxes.
[b]The seasonal variation has been offset in some instances due to the introduction of Pineapple in a new market area.

TABLE 4

Sales of Mohan Orange Flavor Ice Cream—Greater Manila

Year[a]	Qty. per box 20 cl. No. of Cases[b]	Qty. per box 50 cl. No. of Cases[b]	Total Qty. per box 100 cl. equiv. No. of Cases[b]
1960			
1961			
1962			
1963			
1964			
1965			
1966	1,574,222		314,844
1967			
January	98,123		
February	84,535		
March	118,303		
April	83,461		
May	125,937		
June	76,556		
July	80,245		
August	61,948		
September	81,740		
October	92,996		
November	59,008		
December	65,010		
Total	1,027,862		205,572
1968			
January	64,532		
February	59,474		
March	79,234		
April	78,523		
May	93,606		
June	90,689		
July	81,490		
August	63,475		
September	65,197		
October	66,717		
November	50,594	4,054	
December	55,711	4,372	
Total	849,242	8,426	174,061

[a]There were no sales of 75 cl. size during this period.
[b]Each case contains 24 boxes.

TABLE 5

Sales of Mohan Orange Flavor Ice Cream – Bacolod Area

Year	Qty. per box 20 cl. No. of Cases[b]	Qty. per box 50 cl. No. of Cases[b]	Total Qty. per box 100 cl. equiv. No. of Cases[b]
1960			
1961			
1962			
1963			
1964			
1965	287,175		57,435
1966	204,664		40,933
1967			
January	14,755		
February	13,586		
March	19,970		
April	20,471		
May	17,660		
June	13,253		
July	9,719		
August	9,472		
September	9,613		
October	3,688		
November	10,235		
December	10,892		
Total	153,314		30,663
1968			
January	10,292		
February	9,492		
March	11,414		
April	11,563		
May	11,369		
June	11,187		
July	9,328		
August	7,540		
September	7,835		
October	8,778		
November	6,451	1,980	
December	7,142	1,149	
Total	112,391	3,129	24,042

[a]There were no sales of 75 cl. size during this period.
[b]Each case contains 24 boxes.

TABLE 6

Sales of Mohan Chocolate Flavor Ice Cream— Rest of Philippines

Year[a]	Qty. per box 20 cl. No. of Cases[b]	Qty. per box 50 cl. No. of Cases[b]	Total Qty. per box 100 cl. equiv. No. of Cases[b]
1960			
1961			
1962			
1963			
1964	63,502		12,700
1965	655,937		131,187
1966	1,702,240		340,448
1967			
January	199,472		
February	225,867		
March	287,510		
April	295,413		
May	285,542		
June	216,188		
July	249,547		
August	215,793		
September	226,048		
October	233,075		
November	197,205		
December	243,617		575,055
Total	2,875,277		
1968			
January	211,503		
February	192,907		
March	202,077		
April	245,907		
May	232,238		
June	217,731		
July	185,155		
August	161,703		
September	166,134		
October	163,861	9,636	
November	132,064	15,952	
December	130,918	20,172	
Total	2,242,198	45,760	471,319

[a]There were no sales of 75 cl. size during this period.
[b]Each case contains 24 boxes.

TABLE 7

Sales of Mohan Chocolate Flavor Ice Cream—Greater Manila

Year[a]	Qty. per box 20 cl No. of Cases[b]	Total Qty. per box 100 cl. equiv. No. of Cases[b]
1960		
1961		
1962		
1963		
1964		
1965		
1966		
1967		
January		
February		
March		
April		
May		
June		
July		
August		
September		
October		
November	11,556	
December	33,051	
Total	44,607	8,921
1968		
January	13,667	
February	9,808	
March	10,751	
April	7,347	
May	7,689	
June	7,329	
July	187	
August	6,126	
September	5,861	
October	6,106	
November	4,113	
December	3,865	
Total	82,849	16,569

[a]There were no sales of the 50 or 75 cl. size during this period.
[b]Each case contains 24 boxes.

404

TABLE 8

Sales of Mohan Chocolate Flavor Ice Cream—Bacolod Area

Year[a]	Qty. per box 20 cl. No. of Cases[b]	Total Qty. per box 100 cl. equiv. No. of Cases[b]
1960		
1961		
1962		
1963		
1964		
1965		
1966		
1967		
January		
February		
March		
April		
May		
June		
July		
August		
September	3,070	
October	7,120	
November	3,505	
December	2,479	
Total	16,174	3,235
1968		
January	1,749	
February	1,633	
March	1,707	
April	1,540	
May	1,126	
June	1,309	
July	1,493	
August	1,005	
September	862	
October	800	
November	693	
December	530	
Total	14,447	2,889

[a]There were no sales of the 50 or 75 cl. size during this period.
[b]Each case contains 24 boxes.

TABLE 9

Sales of Mohan Chocolate Flavor Ice Cream—Rest of Philippines

Year[a]	Qty. per box 20 cl. No. of Cases[b]	Total Qty. per box 100 cl. equiv. No. of Cases[b]
1960		
1961		
1962		
1963		
1964		
1965		
1966		
1967		
January		
February		
March		
April		
May		
June		
July		
August		
September	29,109	
October	23,693	
November	42,759	
December	51,215	
Total	146,776	29,355
1968		
January	32,706	
February	27,835	
March	27,961	
April	24,746	
May	20,850	
June	17,649	
July	16,813	
August	14,062	
September	13,934	
October	17,119	
November	12,735	
December	10,914	
Total	237,324	47,465

[a]There were no sales of the 50 or 75 cl. size during this period.
[b]Each case contains 24 boxes.

APPENDIX II

Mitchell Associates, Inc., Manila, Philippines
July 1968

A Study of Consumer Brand Preferences, Advertising Recall, Consumption Habits, and Competitive Structure of Ice Cream Market in Philippines

FOR GREATER MANILA, BACOLOD, CEBU, AND TANUAN

Part I — Consumer Research

TABLE 1

Unaided Recall of Brand Advertising
(in Percent)

Brands	*Gr. Manila*		*Bacolod*	*Cebu*	*Tanuan*
Base: Total Interviews	*1967*	*1968*	*1968*	*1968*	*1968*
Recalled	90	85	84	62	69
Mohan's Pineapple	83	79	80	57	61
Yanqui's Pineapple	79	77	78	56	61
Kalano's Pinvan					
(Pineapple and Vanilla)	50	54	1	1	1
Eric's Vanilla	38	54	24	33	13
Mohan's Orange	55	46	52	33	36
Yanqui's Orange	43	39	46	24	24
Vanita Orange	11	31	a	a	1
Yanqui's Lem-O-Lime	14	18	20	13	7
Mohan's Chocolate	–	15	23	18	11
Yanqui's Lemon	13	14	1	9	6

aLess than 1%.

407

TABLE 2

Brands of Ice Cream Ever Consumed (in Percent)

| Brands | Gr. Manila | | Bacolod | Cebu | Tanuan |
Base: Total Interviews	1967	1968	1968	1968	1968
Mohan's Pineapple (U.S.)	94	96	90	78	78
Yanqui's Pineapple (U.S.)	94	95	85	77	78
Kalano's Pinvan (Pineapple) and Vanilla) (Local)	90	91	5	–	26
Eric's Vanilla (Danish)	89	90	50	73	61
Yanqui's Orange (U.S.)	88	89	71	71	74
Kalano's Vanita Orange (Local)	85	68	2	1	7
Mohan's Orange (U.S.)	84	85	66	69	40
Yanqui's Lem-O-Lime (U.S.)	73	69	37	47	51
Yanqui's Lemon (U.S.)	66	58	34	37	41
Vignette (British)	61	49	2	2	9
Paradise (Local)	49	45	25	49	19
Mohan's Chocolate (U.S.)	–	39	32	36	33
Banto (Local)	2	36	1	1	5
Filipino Coffee (U.S.)	–	13	–	–	2
Zandy (Local	–	–	–	32	2
Others	15	1	a	14	a

[a]Less than 1%

TABLE 3

Profile of Ice Cream Consumers (in Percent)

| Population Groups | Gr. Manila | | Bacolod | Cebu | Tanuan |
Base: Total Interviews	1967	1968	1968	1968	1968
Total Population:	73	75	68	46	42
Age Groups					
14–18	67	80	79	42	40
19–25	78	76	73	51	37
26–35	78	76	62	51	45
36–50	68	65	64	39	45
Sex					
Male	75	75	68	46	43
Female	72	74	67	45	41
Economic Class					
AB	79	83	88	79	88
C	77	79	84	62	63
D	66	63	65	35	37
Area					
Urban	–	–	84	65	60
Rural	–	–	51	26	24

TABLE 4

Total Market
Brand Shares—By Major Markets (in Percent)

Brands	Gr. Manila		Bacolod	Cebu	Tanuan
Base: Total Occasions	1967	1968	1968	1968	1968
Mohan's Pineapple	43	38	74	49	58
Regular	37	29	65	36	34
Half-Liter		—	—	—	21
Family	6	9	9	13	3
Yanqui's Pineapple	21	26	18	30	32
Regular	17	17	16	16	24
Family	4	9	2	14	8
Yanqui's Orange	8	6	6	7	7
Regular	7	4	6	6	7
Family	—	1	—	1	—
Lem-O-Lime	1	1	a	—	—
Kalano's Flavors	20	18		—	—
Mohan's Orange	3	2	2	3	2
Mohan's Chocolate	—	1	a	—	—
Mohan Unspecified	—	a	—	—	—
Eric's Vanilla	4	6	—	—	—
All Others	1	3	—	4	—

aLess than 1%.

TABLE 5

Preference for Ice Cream Brands (in Percent)

Brands	Gr. Manila		Bacolod	Cebu	Tanuan
Base: Total Interviews	1967	1968	1968	1968	1968
Mohan's Pineapple	53	46	72	46	46
Yanqui's Pineapple	20	22	13	17	19
Kalano's Pinvan (Pineapple and Vanilla)	8	10	—	a	—
Yanqui's Orange	8	7	6	4	9
Eric's Vanilla	—	5	—	3	—
Vanita Orange	2	2	—	—	—
Mohan's Orange	3	2	1	3	4
Paradise	—	1	a	1	a

aLess than 1%.

TABLE 6

Selected Brand Image Factors (in Percent)

Brands	Gr. Manila		Bacolod	Cebu	Tanuan
Base: Total Interviews	1967	1968	1968	1968	1968
"Best Value for Money"					
Mohan's Pineapple	40	35	70	46	42
Yanqui's Pineapple	18	16	14	16	20
Kalano's Pinvan (Pineapple and Vanilla)	21	26	–	1	1
"Preferred by Those Under 25"					
Mohan's Pineapple	43	32	66	35	25
Yanqui's Pineapple	20	16	12	15	19
Kalano's Pinvan (Pineapple and Vanilla	16	20	–	1	1
"Becoming More Popular"					
Mohan's Pineapple	50	38	74	49	42
Yanqui's Pineapple	23	18	10	17	19
Kalano's Pinvan (Pineapple and Vanilla)	11	16	–	a	a

aLess than 1%.

Part II—Outlet Research

TABLE 7

Distribution of Major Brands and Packages (in Percent)

Brands	Gr. Manila	Bacolod	Cebu	Tanuan
Base: Total Outlets				
Mohan's Pineapple	88	87	89	92
Regular	88	87	89	92
Half-Liter	–	–	–	84
Family	42	32	36	2
Yanqui's Pineapple	66	83	78	84
Regular	66	83	78	84
Family	44	30	59	70
Mohan	60	56	67	71
Orange	60	56	67	71
Chocolate	15	19	29	28
Eric's Vanilla	58	5	66	11
Yanqui's Orange	54	74	71	73
Regular	54	74	71	73
Family	36	a	40	32
Lem-O-Lime	10	16	3	5
Lemon	4	6	3	2
Kalano's Pinvan (Pineapple and Vanilla)	29	–	–	–
Kalano's Vanita Orange	19	–	–	–

aLess than 1%.

TABLE 8

Major Brands and Packages, Out of Stock (in Percent)

Brands Base: Total Outlets	Gr. Manila	Bacolod	Cebu	Tanuan
Mohan's Pineapple	10	9	8	8
Regular	10	9	8	8
Half-Liter	–	–	–	9
Family	26	42	37	a
Yanqui's Pineapple	20	10	15	15
Regular	20	10	15	15
Family	19	44	22	14
Mohan	18	20	14	22
Orange	18	20	14	22
Chocolate	7	6	3	7
Eric's Vanilla	24	4	16	4
Yanqui's Orange	21	16	17	21
Regular	21	16	17	21
Family	13	a	20	17
Lem-O-Lime	5	3	1	–
Lemon	3	2	1	1
Kalano's Pinvan (Pine- apple and Vanilla)	18	a	–	–
Kalano's Vanita Orange	24	–	–	–

aLess than 1%.

TABLE 9

Brand Shares of Total Ice Cream Sales (in Percent)

Brands Base: Total Containers	Gr. Manila		Bacolod	Cebu	Tanuan
	1967	1968			
Mohan's Pineapple	31	35	45	35	42
Regular	29	31	40	30	32
Half-Liter	–	–	–	–	10
Family	2	4	5	5	a
Yanqui's Pineapple	17	28	30	26	33
Regular	15	24	26	21	25
Family	2	4	4	5	8
Yanqui's Orange		6	11	12	13
Regular		5	11	10	11
Family		1	a	2	2
Mohan's Orange		4	8	6	9
Kalano's Pinvan (Pine- apple and Vanilla)		15			
Kalano's Vanita Orange		10			
All Others	52	2	6	21	3

aContainer sales during week prior to interview.

TABLE 10

Share of Total Ice Cream Stock in the Stores
Major Brands and Packages (in Percent)

Brands

Base: Total Full Stock (Containers)	Gr. Manila	Bacolod	Cebu	Tanuan
Mohan's Pineapple	*30*	*40*	*33*	*43*
Regular	27	38	29	38
Half-Liter	—	—	—	5
Family	3	2	3	a
Yanqui's Pineapple	*18*	*30*	*25*	*29*
Regular	15	27	20	22
Family	3	3	5	7
Yanqui's Orange	*10*	*13*	*10*	*12*
Regular	8	13	8	10
Family	2	a	2	2
Mohan	*9*	*12*	*10*	*14*
Orange	8	9	8	11
Chocolate	1	3	2	3
Eric's Vanilla	10	1	11	2
Kalano's Pinvan (Pineapple and Vanilla)	13	—	—	—
Kalano's Vanita Orange	5	—	—	—
Others	5	4	11	—

aLess than 1%.

TABLE 11

Participation in Special Promotions (in Percent)

Brands

Base: Total Outlets	Gr. Manila	Bacolod	Cebu	Tanuan
Participated	*73*	*40*	*62*	*56*
Mohan's Pineapple	70	36	58	47
Yanqui's Pineapple	62	37	58	54
Mohan's Orange	a	—	a	a
Yanqui's Orange	a	a	—	—
Eric's Vanilla	a	—	a	—
Did Not Participate	*27*	*60*	*38*	*44*

aLess than 1%.

TABLE 12

Trade's General Opinions on Family Size Container
Mohan's Pineapple and Yanqui's Pineapple
(in Percent)

	Gr. Manila		Bacolod		Cebu		Tanuan	
Base: Total Outlets	MP	YP	MP	YP	MP	YP	MP	YP
Positive Opinions	*102*	*93*	*124*	*100*	*155*	*142*	*114*	*118*
Economical/Cheap	39	39	39	40	60	64	47	56
Agreeable Taste/ Good/Delicious/ Sweet/Savory	25	19	36	19	15	8	4	1
More Salable/ Profitable	21	19	24	15	35	31	46	42
More Contents/ Equivalent to Three Regular Containers/ Big Size	13	12	13	14	30	30	46	8
Other	4	4	12	12	15	9	7	11
Negative Opinions	*11*	*17*	*14*	*33*	*4*	*5*	*19*	*18*
Unsalability (Not Popular, etc.) Not in Demand	5	6	3	9	2	3	17	16
Disagreeable Smell/ Taste (Tart/Very Sweet)	4	6	3	10	[a]	1	1	1
Other	2	5	8	14	2	1	1	1
Same Taste as Regular	*4*	*5*	*5*	*4*	*a*	*a*	*—*	*a*
No Comment	*12*	*14*	*10*	*13*	*3*	*3*	*5*	*12*
Grand Total[b]	129	129	153	150	162	150	138	148

[a]Less than 1%.
[b]Columns do not add to 100 due to multiple responses.

TABLE 13

Trade's Likes/Dislikes About Selling Family Size Container (in Percent)

Base: Outlets Selling Family Size	Gr. Manila	Bacolod	Cebu	Tanuan
Likes				
Salability	59	78	76	62
Big/Most Profit	34	20	27	40
Economical/Cheap	18	28	25	28
Has More Content	3	12	7	5
Attractive/Cute Container	2	11	1	3
Other	5	18	4	9
No Comment	6	3	3	7
Total	127	170	143	154
Dislikes				
Unsalability/Regular Size More Salability	5	4	6	9
Inconvenience in Handling/Heavy Containers/Occupies Much Space	4	1	4	4
High Price/Small Profit/ Bigger Deposit for Containers/Big Capital Required	3	4	5	2
Other	5	8	4	3
No Comment	84	85	81	82
Total	101	102	100	100

aColumns do not total 100 due to multiple responses.

TABLE 14

Frequency of Service Calls
Mohan's Pineapple and Yanqui's Pineapple (in Percent)

	Gr. Manila	Bacolod	Cebu	Tanuan
Mohan's Pineapple	100	100	100	100
Two or More Times a Week	53	74	62	66
Once a Week	36	19	30	29
Less than Once a Week	6	2	3	5
Visits Outlets not Carrying Mohan's Pineapple	5	5	5	a
Yanqui's Pineapple	100	100	100	100
Two or More Times a Week	34	63	50	55
Once a Week	42	31	40	35
Less than Once a Week	10	1	5	9
Visits Outlets not Carrying Yanqui's Pineapple	14	5	5	1

aLess than 1%.

414

TABLE 15

Brand and Size Switching Resulting from Family Size Container

Base: Outlets Selling Family Size	Gr. Manila	Bacolod	Cebu	Tunuan
Has There Been *Brand* Switching		(Between Mohan's and Yanqui's)		
Yes	*47*	*85*	*54*	*49*
Yanqui's Pineapple to Mohan's Pineapple	12	11	17	7
Mohan's Pineapple to Yanqui's Pineapple	1	1	9	1
Both	34	73	28	10[a]
Mohan's Pineapple Family to MP 1/2 Liter	–	–	–	31
No	*53*	*15*	*46*	*51*
Has There Been *Size* Switching				
Yes	*72*	*94*	*80*	*90*
Regular to 1/1 Liter	–	–	–	5
Regular to Family	31	6	40	6
Family to Regular	2	1	7	6
Both	39	87	33	73[a]
No	*28*	*6*	*20*	*10*

[a]Includes Mohan's Pineapple 1/2 liter container.

COROMANDEL FERTILIZERS LIMITED, INDIA

Marketing of Fertilizers in an Underdeveloped Country

On December 10, 1967, the Deputy Prime Minister of India, Mr. Morarji Desai, dedicated the Coromandel fertilizer plant in the port city of Visakhapatnam in the State of Andhra Pradesh. This was the official opening of not only the largest but the first U. S.-backed private fertilizer plant in India.

Built at a cost of approximately $70 million, the plant took four years to complete and was designed for an annual production capacity of 365,000 tons of ammonium phosphate fertilizer and 15,000 tons of prilled urea. Production at full capacity requires annual imports of 73,000 tons of sulfur and 235,000 tons of phosphate rock. The remaining primary raw material is naphtha which is supplied by the Caltex refinery, also at Visakhapatnam.[1] The 10 million jute bags required annually provide Rs. 2 crore[2] in sales to the Indian jute industry.

Coromandel is the first joint venture fertilizer project in the private sector, with equity participation by two U. S. companies, the government of India, Indian private companies, and the Indian public. The composition of the equity ownership is shown in Tables 1 and 2.

TABLE 1

Equity Ownership of Coromandel

Name of Company	*Percent of Equity Ownership*
Chevron Chemical (subsidiary of Standard Oil of California)	25
International Minerals and Chemical Corporation, U. S. A. (IMC)	24
EID-Parry, Ltd., India	7
Industrial Development Bank of India and other government of India-controlled or backed underwriters and the Indian general public[a]	44
	100

[a]Due to poor public response at the time of the stock offering, the underwriters had to buy most of the stock designated for the public-at-large. However, it is expected that the underwriters will gradually be able to liquidate their holdings by selling to the general public as the sales and profitability of Coromandel improve.

TABLE 2

Initial Investment in Coromandel

	Amount Invested	
Name of Investor	*Indian Currency (in crores of Rs.)*	*U. S. Dollars (Millions)*
Chevron		5.5
IMC		5.5
Indian Investors	4.57	
U. S. government through Export/Import Bank	20.25	
U. S. AID (under P. L. 480)	8.38	
Industrial Bank of India	7.0	

1. Naphtha is a product of crude petroleum refining.
2. $1.00 = Rs. 7.50; Rs. 1 Crore = 10 million rupees.

ENVIRONMENTAL FACTORS
FOR COROMANDEL PLANT:
AGRICULTURE IN INDIA
AND ANDHRA PRADESH

Approximately 80 percent of all Indians live in rural areas. There are basically two types of farmers. By far the largest group is the small, subsistence-level farmer who typically grows rice or another food crop. If he is successful, he grows enough to feed his family and to have a small residual with which to barter for local products in his village market. Frequently he is not this successful.

According to the *United Nations Monthly Bulletin of Statistics* for October 1967, the Indian per capita income in 1965 was $86, down from $88 in 1964; 1965 per capita income was $2,893 for the U. S., and $130 for Ceylon. Indian farmers are generally found in the lower end of the income scale and a large number of them are at or below subsistence levels. The typical small farmer uses primitive means to grow his crops. Families are traditionally large, and no practice comparable to primogeniture is followed. As a result, the acreage farmed by each generation of farmers is progressively smaller. This fragmentation of the family lands is often carried to extremes. If a father has two sons and two fields of equal size, he will most often give half of each field to each son. The few young men who find jobs in the city typically live very austerely so that they can send much of their income back to their families on the farm in order to perpetuate their life style.

Another problem frustrating the farmer is the extremely inadequate distribution system for getting rice and other food crops to areas which need them most. Much of the fertile land lies along large rivers, such as the Godavari. Mr. Thomas G. Hughes, Chairman of Chevron and a director of Coromandel, points out:

> One of the things we are most actively trying to get corrected is the distribution system so that there is a mechanism for pulling this excess of rice out of the local areas [where it was grown]. You've got the Godavari River—like our Mississippi. You've got fertile land on both sides of it, and that's about it. The local Godavari River area gets a glut of rice and sugar cane very quickly unless there's a mechanism for getting it out into Kerala and the other states that need it. You go into the nearby villages and you see in the little shops bag after bag after bag of rice.

DEMAND FOR FERTILIZERS

In terms of need for fertilizers to improve production in a country where agricultural productivity is among the lowest in the world, where the domestic supply of food is insufficient to feed the growing population even at the current low-calorie intake, and where every increase in real income for a long time is going to be spent on food products, one could imagine an almost unlimited and insatiable continuing demand for fertilizers. However, this huge potential demand cannot be effectively converted to real demand of any significant proportion for a variety of reasons, notably the farmer's conservatism, the element of luck (nature) in his financial success or failure, and his low staying power in the face of abundant crops. As Mr. Hughes points out:

> How do you persuade a farmer who knows that there is local excess of rice, who most typically does not read or write and only knows what he can see in his local area? Now you come to him and you say, "Mr. Farmer, if you would only use our fertilizer, you would grow a lot more." He would say, "I have to put out some rupees for fertilizer and already I am having trouble disposing of the rice I've got. Now, if I grow more, then I'm going to have more trouble disposing of it and instead of getting my money back that I've spent for fertilizer, I'm going to drive the price down. So why buy fertilizer?"
>
> If the farmers in Andhra Pradesh would use half the amount of fertilizer that theoretically should be used, we would be expanding that plant *just* to supply Andhra Pradesh! When I raise that question, however, I must point out that even in the most sophisticated market in the United States, which is Iowa, and where many of our customers have gone to M.I.T., the theoretically optimal quantities are not used either. And there are a lot of reasons behind this. You have to be a farmer to understand all of them. In the first place putting fertilizer on crops is very much like putting food in people. When I eat, I get fat; yet some of my colleagues eat more than I do and are skinny as rails. Now you also try to outguess the "business" part of this. What's the price for my crop going to be? How much can I afford to put on in terms of fertilizer and how much do I get back for having done it? . . . It might not rain or it might rain at the wrong time. Disease, fungus, bugs, or what-have-you might show up. . . . The farmer has all that on his mind. . . . The theoretical optimum is arrived at by calculation of first how big an area is going to be planted. Secondly, what the plant population is going to be and how much, if known, to get its maximum growth it will take out of the ground in terms of plant nutrients. So you multiply this out and you get some real nice big numbers which make any fertilizer man happy.

The small Indian farmers most often do not use fertilizers at all, and those few who do use some, use very little. The small farmer is typically outside the monetized sector of the economy. The purchase of fertilizer requires rupees which he typically does not have. Credit is generally unavailable since the small farmers do not grow a crop they can sell for money. (To virtually all Indians, family land has such high intrinsic value that it is unthinkable to risk borrowing on it.) Even if the small farmer has rupees, he may have no understanding of the use of fertilizers. Having both the rupees and knowledge of fertilizers, the small farmer may still be reluctant to buy. It is virtually impossible to explain in the small farmer's frame of reference that optimal quantities of fertilizers, pesticides, and high-quality seed will produce quantum increases in productivity. Commenting on the Indian farmer's reluctance to buy fertilizer, Mr. Hughes states:

> A farmer who is about to spend some cash money for something like fertilizers often because of his past experience, says to himself, "I'm not going to get too heavily in debt to the bank. . . . I'm going to hedge my bet; I'm going to use half as much." A very great number do this. . . . Different farmers have had different experiences. One farmer may have two or three years ago piled on the

fertilizer just like the university recommended and didn't get any improvement in his crop at all. This can happen. He's pretty hard to sell, particularly if the following year or the year before he put half that much on and got the same crop. Again, he may someday try it and the next time get the full benefit of his piling on the fertilizer. But since he didn't once, he's pretty cagey about it. The other thing is that all farmers are alert to hazards of weather. You can't control the weather, so the farmer takes as much of the risk out by not having any more cash input if something goes wrong with the weather.

There is also the problem of timing. Fertilizer is an extremely seasonal product. When the farmer has made up his mind he needs the fertilizer, he needs it now and cannot wait for it. This is characteristic of not only Indian farmers, but also farmers in Iowa. As was pointed out by Mr. Hughes, "In Iowa, at planting time, trucks will be lined up for several miles outside the manufacturing site waiting to pick up fertilizer. Yet several days later, there will be absolutely no trucks."

SUPPLY OF FERTILIZER

Before December 1965, the Central Fertilizer Pool (CFP), organized and controlled by the Government of India, received the entire Indian fertilizer output plus all imports of nitrogenous fertilizers. At that date the Government of India instituted a new policy whereby all fertilizer plants were free to sell their products in the open market with the proviso that the CFP had the option to buy and distribute up to 30 percent of a plant's annual production. This provision was to insure the supply of fertilizer to state-sponsored village cooperatives in times of scarcity. This policy was extended to all new plants licensed before December 1967 and was to remain in force for seven years from the date they went into commercial production.

India has been engaged for several years in an aggressive program to achieve self-sufficiency in fertilizer production. Efforts to encourage investment include permitting the free marketability of the output and specifying fertilizer production as among those industries eligible for a rebate of corporation income taxes equivalent to 10 percent of their normal income tax and super tax and 20 percent of the surtax. Although production never met the ambitious goals set by the government, it did increase substantially. As shown in Tables 3 and 4, production failed to meet government expectations but consumption missed even more. This fact, plus increased imports, led to a surplus in fertilizer which is expected to continue.

COROMANDEL'S PROBLEMS

Construction and Start-Up Costs

Coromandel's operations, beset by a series of construction delays, operational difficulties, and marketing problems, incurred a loss of Rs. 38,737,450 for the fiscal year October 1, 1967 to September 30, 1968, and a total accumulated loss carried forward of Rs. 39,610,246. Some of these problems were not entirely unexpected, considering the size of the project; the difficulties of building and operating in a

TABLE 3

Nitrogen Fertilizers
Production, Imports, and Consumption
(Millions of Tons)

Year	1. Target	2. Consumption	3. Production	4. Imports	5. Total of Cols. 3 and 4
1961–62	0.400	0.307	0.154	0.138	0.292
1962–63	0.525	0.328	0.194	0.285	0.479
1963–64	0.650	0.426	0.219	0.223	0.442
1964–65	0.800	0.492	0.243	0.235	0.478
1965–66	0.800[a]	0.582	0.238	0.376	0.614
1966–67	1.000	0.830	0.309	0.575	0.884

[a]Revised target following mid-term appraisal. Production figures relate to agricultural year July 1 to June 30.

SOURCE: *Report of the Fertilizer Credit Committee of the Fertilizer Association of India* (1968), p. 29.

TABLE 4

Index Numbers of Fertilizer Production
(Base: 1956 = 100)[a]

Year			
1951	21.7	December 1966	484.1
1955	98.4	October 1967	541.7
1960	152.7	November 1967	553.9
1965	382.4	December 1967	637.1
1966	410.2		
1967	504.7		

[a]Production figures relate to industrial year July 1 to June 30.

SOURCE: *Records and Statistics*, Quarterly Bulletin of the Eastern Economist, New Delhi (May 1968), p. 143.

developing economy; a complex plant requiring continuous high volume operations; lack of skilled labor both in the construction and operational phases; and government procedures. However, much of this loss can be attributed to the difficulty in making forecasts both by Coromandel executives and government officials due to lack of statistical data. Looking back at Coromandel's operations during the past four years, Mr. Hughes commented:

The Indian farmer does not adapt to the use of optimum quantities of fertilizer as fast as his government or most of the various technical groups, foundations, and so forth hoped and predicted. As a consequence of this, we have built up some tremendous inventories of fertilizer. . . . The traditional Indian marketing problem has been one of scarcity, and never one of abundance, which is what our problem is.

Constraint in Plant Operations

Coromandel's manufacturing facility was designed to produce large amounts of fertilizer efficiently. However, such a facility requires a heavy initial investment, raising the breakeven point to 80 percent of capacity. As one company official commented:

> Fixed costs represent a much larger component of total costs than similar manufacturing operations in other parts of the world. Electric power, normally a variable cost in other countries, is provided at a flat monthly rate regardless of the quantity actually consumed. While at first glance this might appear favorable for the company, this is not the case. The flat rate is based on the unrealistic assumption of peak power consumption a hundred percent of the time. Furthermore, power failures occur frequently and no credit is given for periods without power. Power failures—regardless of their length—create serious problems in the manufacture of fertilizer. Safety requires that elaborate shutdown procedures must be followed when any power failure occurs because of the explosive nature of the indredients at stages prior to completion. This makes the breakeven point, in fact, higher than 80 percent under optimal conditions and more difficult to attain. Fertilizer plants in the private sector are not permitted to have their own electrical generating stations. The electrical company's service has shown significant improvement; few power failures are now anticipated, and at this time manufacturing is proceeding rather smoothly.

Structure of Industry
and Nature of Competition

In Andhra Pradesh, Coromandel's main competition is from the government-operated plants at Trombay in the State of Maharashtra, and Sindri in the State of Bihar. These plants face fewer uncertainties than does Coromandel; government cooperatives and agricultural programs supply a captive market, and they have their own private sources of electrical power.

The government-operated factories manufacture a product which is less uniform in quality and consistency than Coromandel's, whose products are as fine as any manufactured in the world. The Trombay plant produces a cheaper fertilizer with the same analysis as Coromandel's GROMOR 20-20-0 but lacks its water solubility. The Sindri plant's product is identical to GROMOR 20-20-0 both in analysis and water solubility. Many Indians, however, have grown to place less reliance on the quality of government made products.

Imports from the United States financed by U. S. AID are also a formidable source of competition. These imports cost less than domestically produced fertilizers to the Government. The farmer, nevertheless, pays the same price for both the imported and domestically produced fertilizers.

Figure 1 shows the large number of fertilizer plants that were in production or planned at the time Coromandel's plant began operations.

FIGURE 1

Location of Fertilizer Factories (as on September 30, 1967)

State		Name of the Factory
		In Production
Andhra Pradesh	1	Andhra Fertilisers, Tadepalle
	2	Andhra Sugars, Tanuku
	3	Hyderabad Chemicals & Fertilisers, Maula Ali
	4	Krishna Industrial Corporation, Nadadavole
Assam	5	Associated Industries (Assam), Chandrapur
Bihar	6	Bararee Coke Co., Loyabad
	7	Burrakur Coal Co., Bansjora
	8	Bihar State Superphosphate Factory, Sindri
	9	Fertilizer Corporation of India Ltd., Sindri
	10	Tata Iron & Steel Co., Jamshedpur
Delhi	11	D.C.M. Chemical Works, Delhi
Gujarat	12	Adarsh Chemicals & Fertilisers, Navsari
	13	Alembic Chemical Works, Baroda
	14	Anil Starch Products, Bhavnagar
	15	Atul Products, Bulsar
	16	Gujarat State Fertilizers Co. Ltd., Baroda
Kerala	17	Fertilisers & Chemicals, Travancore, Alwaye
Madhya Pradesh	18	Dharamsi Morarji Chemical Co., Kumhari
	19	Hindustan Steel Ltd., Bhilai
Madras	20	Blue Mountain Estates & Industries, Ennore
	21	Coimbatore Pioneer Fertilisers, Coimbatore
	22	E.I.D.-Parry Ltd., Ennore
	23	E.I.D.-Parry Ltd., Ranipet
	24	Neyveli Lignite Corporation, Neyveli
	25	Premier Fertilisers, Cuddalore
	26	Shaw Wallace & Co. Ltd., Avadi
Maharashtra	27	Dharamsi Morarji Chemical Co. Ltd., Ambernath
	28	Eastern Chemical Co., Bombay
	29	Fertilizer Corporation of India Ltd., Trombay
	30	Western Chemical Industries, Bombay
	31	West India Chemicals, Kharadi, Poona
	32	West India Chemicals, Loni-Kalbhore, Poona
Mysore	33	Chamundi Chemicals & Fertilisers, Munirabad
	34	Mysore Chemicals & Fertilisers, Belagula
Orissa	35	Hindustan Steel Ltd., Rourkela
Punjab	36	Fertilizer Corporation of India Ltd., Nangal
Uttar Pradesh	37	New Central Jute Mills Co., Ltd., Varanasi
	38	Ralli Chemicals Ltd., Magarwara
West Bengal	39	Hindustan Steel Ltd., Durgapur
	40	Indian Iron & Steel Co., Burnpur-Kulti
	41	Jay Shree Chemicals & Fertilisers Ltd., Khardah
	42	Phosphate Co. Ltd., Rishra
		Under Implementation
Andhra Pradesh	43	Coromandel Fertilisers, Visakhapatnam
Assam	44	Fertilizer Corporation of India Ltd., Namrup
Bihar	45	Fertilizer Corporation of India Ltd., Barauni
Kerala	46	Cochin Fertiliser Project, Cochin
Madras	47	Madras Fertiliser Project, Madras
Maharashtra	48	Bharat Fertiliser Industries, Bombay
Rajasthan	49	Hindustan Zinc Ltd., Udaipur
	50	Sriram Fertilisers & Chemicals Ltd., Kotah
Uttar Pradesh	51	Fertilizer Corporation of India Ltd., Gorakhpur
	52	Indian Explosives Ltd., Kanpur
	53	J.K. Cotton Spg. Wvg. Mills, Kanpur
West Bengal	54	Fertilizer Corporation of India Ltd., Durgapur
		Approved in Principle
Maharashtra	55	Maharashtra Agr.-Industries Corporation, Bombay
	56	Thana Distt. Coop. Industrial Association, Thana
Mysore	57	Mangalore Project, Mangalore
Rajasthan	58	Khetri Project, Jhunjhunu
Goa	59	Birla Gwalior. Goa
		Proposed for Implementation
Uttar Pradesh	60	Modipon, Ghaziabad
West Bengal	61	Haldia Fertiliser Project, Haldia.

SOURCE: *Records and Statistics,* Quarterly Bulletin Of Eastern Economist, New Delhi, August 1968, pages 222 and 223.

FIGURE 1—*continued*

	IN PRODUCTION	UNDER IMPLEMENTATION	APPROVED IN PRINCIPLE	PROPOSED FOR IMPLEMENTATION
AMMONIUM SULPHATE	⬡	⬡		
AMMONIUM SULPHATE NITRATE	◇			
CALCIUM AMMONIUM NITRATE	□	□	□	
UREA	⬡	⬡	⬡	⬡
AMMONIUM CHLORIDE	○	○	○	
AMMONIUM PHOSPHATE SULPHATE	△	△	△	△
NITROPHOSPHATE	○			
SUPERPHOSPHATE	◇	◇	◇	
DIAMMONIUM PHOSPHATE		○	○	
DICALCIUM PHOSPHATE	▽			
TRIPLE SUPERPHOSPHATE		◇	◇	

423

Government and Agriculture

The Indian Constitution gives the central government very little jurisdiction in agricultural matters, and the state governments vigorously resist any attempts by the central government to move into this area. Although a farm price support program does exist, support prices are less than growing costs.

Coromandel agronomists tried to get permission for a few thousand dollars worth of foreign exchange in order to import IRA Philippine hybrid rice for seed development. This rice is now grown throughout most of Asia because of its extremely high yield per acre. Its major disadvantage, a layer of starch on the outside of the grains which makes it somewhat sticky, caused many Indians to reject it. This was the initial reaction of Asians in other countries, but shortly the rice gained wide acceptance. Coromandel's reasoning was that the IRA Philippine rice would cause a dramatic increase in rice production to the point that India would become self-sufficient or even an exporter of rice. The foreign exchange request was denied largely because the government felt that within a few years agronomists would develop a high-yield rice without the sticky layer. There is no sense of urgency displayed by many government officials, and the immediate problem of rice shortages in those few years was obviously not considered.

Several government actions have frustrated efforts to increase agricultural productivity in the State of Andhra Pradesh. In 1967 the state government imposed a 3.3 percent state sales tax on fertilizer (despite the recent severe food shortages there), and April 1, 1969, the central government added a 10.0 percent excise tax

Between these tax dates came Andhra Pradesh's bumper 1968 rice crop. For an Indian incumbent seeking reelection, a rice surplus is as desirable as lowering taxes. Therefore, the state government insured its surplus by permitting only 20 percent of the excess to be shipped outside the state. Such action can be defended on the grounds that supplies on hand are highly desirable and a surplus might lower prices within the state, but parts of Andhra Pradesh were glutted while people in the State of Kerala were actually starving to death.

COROMANDEL'S MARKETING PROGRAM AND STRATEGIES

At the end of 1968, Coromandel's large inventories and financial losses resulting from poor sales had reached the critical state. Company officials attributed their woes partly to the effect of external marketing factors on their operation and partly to difficulties attributed to the introduction of a sophisticated product in an underdeveloped market.

Choice of Product

The development and packaging of the product is an important ingredient for any successful marketing strategy. In addition to being made available at the right time, place, and price, a product should be offered in the most convenient form for handling and use by the ultimate consumers, as well as the intermediaries, the wholesale and the retail distributors.

Initially Coromandel's primary product was a 28 percent ammonium and a 28 percent phosphate fertilizer called **GROMOR** 28-28-0 (0 percent potash). This product represents a significant engineering achievement and has the highest nutrient concentration of any ammonium phosphate fertilizer in the world. Because of its higher concentration, 28-28-0 fertilizer provides more nutrient per unit cost than lower concentration fertilizers. Savings are realized on packaging, transportation, and handling costs. In spite of its many advantages, GROMOR 28-28-0 encountered serious competition from the less costly 20-20-0. Commenting on its lack of success, a company spokesman said:

> We were trying to market the most sophisticated fertilizer in the world in the least sophisticated agricultural market. . . . The small Indian farmer has no idea what those numbers on the fertilizer bag mean. He only knows that one bag costs 64 rupees and another bag costs 47. . . . Even in the United States, our largest selling complex fertilizer is a 16-16-0 product. . . .

In June 1969 Coromandel began marketing GROMOR 20-20-0 (20 percent ammonium and 20 percent phosphate). The 28-28-0 fertilizer has 40 percent more nutrient but a bag of 20-20-0 costs less.

A risk that the Indian farmer faces when he buys fertilizer is that the bag may have been opened and much of the fertilizer replaced by inert material such as sand, and then the bag sewn back together. To ensure that its product is not adulterated, Coromandel bags are constructed in such a manner that once the bag has been opened it cannot be sewn together without it being very evident to the purchaser.

In Andhra Pradesh fertilizer is sold in greatest quantity for the rice crop; thus, storage life is a most important consideration. In addition, climatic conditions, pestilence, and the market price for agricultural commodities may also affect fertilizer demand. Generally a bag produced for one growing season may be sold at the beginning of the following season. As the fertilizer approaches two years of age, lumps may begin to form and the bag to rot.

Pricing

In Andhra Pradesh the consumer pays Rs. 64 for a 50 kilogram bag of 28-28-0 fertilizer and Rs. 47 for a bag of 20-20-0.

While there is no government price control, Coromandel must keep prices very close to those of competitors. A higher price, it is felt, would result in even lower sales revenue through loss of volume. A lower price is not desirable: the break-even point would be higher than the present 80 percent and retaliating competitors could start a price war.

Prices to the consumer in other states are somewhat lower than in Andhra Pradesh even though additional freight must be charged. This is because the cost of rail transportation is very low and there is no sales tax on fertilizer sold outside Andhra Pradesh. The "net back" in sales in other states is modestly less because the difference between Andhra Pradesh's taxes and transportation charges for out of state customers is partially absorbed by Coromandel.

Costs per Ton of Fertilizer in Andhra Pradesh

28-28-0

Cost to customer		Rs.	1,270
Less:			
Discounts	143		
Taxes	127		
Transportation from:			
Factory to warehouse	8		

28-28-0

Warehouse to customer (average)	30		
Warehousing (average)	15		323
Net realization at Plant		Rs.	947

20-20-0

Cost to customer		Rs.	921
Less:			
Discounts	89		
Taxes	92		
Transportation from:			
Factory to warehouse	8		
Warehouse to customer (average)	30		
Warehousing (average)	15		234
Net Realization at Plant:		Rs.	687

Promotion

Coromandel's initial step in marketing was a "seeding program" which started with smaller amounts of fertilizer imports in 1963 and grew to an annual import of 92,000 tons of 20-20-0 into Andhra Pradesh in 1965 and sold under the Coromandel trademark. The purpose of this seeding program was to ascertain and establish a market for complex—containing more than one nutrient—fertilizer. Although the Central Fertilizer Pool exercised its right to purchase part of these imports directly, the seeding program was largely successful in establishing a market for 20-20-0 fertilizer. Neither the 10.0 percent excise tax nor the 3.3 sales tax were in effect at the time of the seeding program, and the cost to the consumer was Rs. 820 per ton. Since Coromandel initially marketed only the 28-28-0 fertilizer which had an after-tax cost of Rs. 1,270, their competition was able to move in and exploit the market Coromandel had created.

In an effort to get farmers to use more fertilizer, two vans travel the countryside and show movies on using Coromandel fertilizer. Even though these movies are shown in several languages, they are also visually presented in such a manner that even if one does not understand the language, he can understand the message. The fact that most of Andhra Pradesh is very flat and that the vans can be seen from a great distance enables them to attract very large crowds.

Demonstration tracts have also been used successfully to show the effects of fertilizer. These demonstration plots, of which there are about 300, include some of sugar cane because it provides highly dramatic results. Normally, Indian sugar cane is grown without fertilizer and is a small, bush-like, yellow-green plant. In the demonstration tracts, the fertilizer is poured on without regard to economy. The resulting cane is a bright green color and grows so tall and thick that it is necessary to make a bamboo-lattice-work to keep the cane standing upright. Other promotion includes stalls in the regional agricultural fairs and brochures demonstrating the advantages of fertilizer. Seasonal and quantity discounts are given to the distributors, but the extent to which they are passed on to the customer is unknown. Contests both at the customer and the dealer level are also used to promote sales. Prizes are not large because of the small margin on the fertilizer. By far the most popular prize has been a tiffin-carrier, a type of lunch box. To attract dealers, some newspaper advertising is utilized but this has not been successful and has been largely discontinued.

Marketing research has not been very successful because few basic statistics are available and very few products are marketed competitively. Further, it was believed that fertilizer would be a scarce commodity and there would be no problem selling it.

It is difficult to determine the effectiveness of the marketing effort until the end of the growing season. In Andhra Pradesh, the predominant crop is rice; thus sales are largely tied to this one growing season. In an effort to determine sales progress prior to the end of the season, requests were sent to all distributors to find out their inventories. Less than 40 percent of the distributors responded to these requests because sales could easily be determined from inventory figures. Distributors receive their inventory on credit; thus when sales are made the distributor is supposed to pay for that part of the inventory he sells. As a result the only distributors who responded were those who made few or no sales at all.

Distribution

EID-Parry, Ltd. markets a complementary line of pesticides, seed, and other fertilizer through its 1,500 dealers. For its efforts, Parry receives a commission on the net F.O.B. plant realization of the fertilizer. Parry also will guarantee a minimum sales beginning in 1970 based on a percentage of the two-year period, 1968 to 1969. Parry's contract is for five years with an option for an additional five-year period. Because of the low sales rate and high promotion, Coromandel sales have been a losing proposition for Parry. These sales, however, have probably been beneficial to Parry's complementary product lines such as seeds and pesticides. Parry initially paid for everything received from the factory and financed dealer inventories. Because of high interest rates and in an effort to push sales, many exceptions exist to this policy and Coromandel pays some interest costs and accepts some credit risks. Coromandel sets all prices at the consumer level and maintains a marketing force of about fourteen men.

Most of Parry's salesmen are young graduates of agricultural colleges and are provided with motorcycles so that they can reach all distributors. These young men have a good background in theory but little practical growing experience. Both Parry and Coromandel also employ graduate agronomists. Parry's agronomists are largely employed as "missionary salesmen" who instruct the farmers directly, while Coromandel's agronomists instruct Parry's salesmen and manage demonstration plots.

Although Coromandel's principal distribution agent, EID-Parry, Ltd., is one of the most efficient in India and has extensive experience in marketing to the agricultural community, it has had virtually no experience in highly competitive marketing. Traditionally, shortages have characterized the supply of nearly everything in India. Parry's great ability lies in the establishment of a distribution system and its efficient functioning once established.

Coromandel is unable to take over the marketing effort itself because:

1. The cost of such an effort will exceed Parry's commission.
2. Coromandel does not have nor could it readily acquire Parry's experience or knowledge in determining distributors' credit-worthiness. India has nothing comparable to the Dun and Bradstreet credit rating system.
3. The existence of several languages in the State of Andhra Pradesh alone makes marketing much more difficult.

Initially Coromandel was licensed to sell only in Andhra Pradesh, but now sales are made in Maharashtra, Gujarat, Orissa, Kerala, Madhya Pradesh, Madras, Mysore, and the Punjab. The extremely low rail freight rates makes this possible. These sales are made largely through government cooperatives. Additional quantities are also marketed through Parry's fifty outlets for pesticides in Orissa. Coromandel is also sold in the government cooperatives in Andhra Pradesh. Commenting on the variety of distribution, Mr. Hughes states: "We have reached the stage of concern where everybody is a salesman, even me. We've just got to move this product."

The cost of railroad transportation is indeed very low, but the service is equally slow. Many sales were lost because distributors did not have inventories on hand. Coromandel has literally loaded down the local distributors with all the fertilizer they can possibly sell in the current growing season.

COROMANDEL'S FUTURE

Mr. Hughes summarizes the future of Coromandel and what he believes is necessary for this joint venture to succeed.

I think that a great deal needs to be done in providing for the farmer, for the time that he is growing his crops, so that he may purchase the necessary seed, fertilizer, and pesticides. We must also assume that there will be a continuation of the educational process we have started in educating our salesmen, distributors, and the farmers. Those people with the necessary skills must impart to others their skills. . . . When the farmer did not start using fertilizer as rapidly as we had hoped, it was really not that surprising. The real glaring lack here is a distribution system. Again this should not come as a surprise because this was evident with the wheat shipments the U. S. made to India. Anything that comes in abundance causes the whole system to break down. Much of this wheat never reached those for whom it was intended. When a couple of ships come into Visakhapatnam with cargoes of wheat, we have to stop shipments of fertilizer because the railroads can't handle it. The appreciation of all the problems India has is acquired with difficulty. It seems that almost everyway you turn you are faced with some shortage or lack of something.

JOHNS-MANVILLE INC., U. S. A.

Development of Sales Territories and Determination of Direct Selling Expenses for Industrial Products in Overseas Markets

The Johns-Manville Corporation (J-M Corp.),[1] one of the world's largest vertically integrated producer and distributor of industrial and commercial construction materials,[2] is in the process of evaluating its financial reporting system. Specific attention is being paid to the effect of expense allocation on a standard cost basis on company export sales development and sales maintenance.

Organizationally, the company presents a mixture of product[3] and functional diversification. Specifically, company operations may be placed into three functional categories: raw material products, industrial products, and construction materials. The markets for J-M raw material products include J-M operating divisions and outside customers. "Seventy-three percent of J-M mineral output in 1967 went to outside customers, representing 13 percent of J-M total sales volume.[4] J-M products[5] containing company produced raw materials accounted for 44 percent of total sales."[6]

J-M industrial products accounted for 20 percent of total company sales in 1967.[7] Demand for J-M industrial products reflects the level, nationally and internationally, of construction activity and spending on production equipment

1. All figures used in the case are disguised to protect the competitive position of the company.

2. A list of the company's principal products includes roofing and building materials, insulation products, friction materials including brake linings, acoustical materials, packings, asbestos cement pipe, asbestos fiber, fiberglass, electrical tape, and specialties.

3. *See* Appendix 1.

4. *See* Appendix 2.

5. "Characteristically most J-M products are developed from the raw materials of its own mines," 1967 Annual Report, Johns-Manville Corporation, p. 1.

6. 1967 Annual Report, p. 2.

7. Ibid., p. 4.

which utilizes J-M industrial products. Sales of J-M construction materials make the greatest contribution to total company sales, in 1966 accounting for 67 percent of total J-M business. These sales were divided approximately as in Table 1. Alike its industrial products, the demand for J-M construction materials will reflect the level of construction activity.

TABLE 1

J-M's Share of Major Categories of Construction Markets

Category	Percent
Institutional and commercial construction	13
Industrial building	9
Maintenance, remodeling, and repair (all types of existing structures)	16
New residential construction	14
Water and sewer systems	15

SOURCE: J-M Corporation.

INTERNATIONAL DIVISION– EXPORT SALES

The operations of the International Division may be divided into two categories: the manufacturing and sale of goods in U. S. and Canadian markets; the export of goods produced by the eleven U. S.-Canadian divisions. In 1967 export sales amounted to approximately $129.5 million (Table 2). In addition to selling J-M products, the company sells a limited line of products from outside companies. These products complement the existing J-M product line. In 1967 these sales amounted to approximately $6.1 million.

Export sales are handled by the sales force of the International Division. Salesmen's territories are presently determined on a geographical basis. On the average, territorial coverage per salesman per year amounts to $300 to 350 thousand. Salesmen in the U. S., by comparison, generally run about $400 to 500 thousand per year in volume. Currently, salesmen are paid solely on commission. The commission is calculated on the basis of a product's contribution to net earnings.

EXPENSE ALLOCATION–EXPORTS

There are essentially two kinds of expenses involved in export sales: those incurred by the divisions which produce and transfer the goods to the International Division; those incurred by the International Division in the sale of these goods. Because each of the twelve operating divisions is managed as a profit center, the International Division has had to devise a method for determining the cost of export sales. Currently, the company uses a standard cost formula for allocating such expenses. The standard cost formula is determined by the corporate finance department and is expressed as a percent of gross sales dollars and net sales dollars. Table 3 presents the standard costs utilized in the calculation of net earnings accruing from export sales in 1967.

TABLE 2

1967 Total Export

Sales to customers		$129,482,745
Products of outside vendors		6,146,252
Less:		
Transportation	$13,143,088	
Returns	72,079	
Cash discounts	72,834	
Allowances	1,184,771	
Net sales		121,156,225
Cost of shipments to customers	74,151,784	
Products of outside vendors	4,400,158	
Total standard cost shipped products	78,551,942	
Earnings after standard cost shipped products		42,604,283
Transferred plant costs - net[a]	5,919,746	
Gross earnings		36,684,537
Division expense:[b]		
Salesmen	4,842,390	
Sales office	10,168,214	
Warehouses		
Inbound freight	724,584	
Warehouse expense	670,859	
Total division expense	16,406,047	
Earnings after division expense		20,278,490
General and administrative:		
Advertising	1,338,239	
Research	672,070	
Engineering and technical projects	22,897	
Division administrative	490,083	
General company administrative	1,535,100	
Misc. income and deductions	2,618	
Pre-tax earnings		16,217,483
Net earnings		9,150,190

[a]". . . allocations of fixed expense applied on the basis of actual costs incurred to cover portions of division overhead and management utilized by the producing division in the manufacture and transfer of the products to the International Division. It may be considered as an allocation of fixed expenses established by formula within the corporate finance department." Mr. Hartley Sandt, Vice President and General Marketing Manager, J–M Corporation, letter dated November 24, 1969.

[b]All expenses incurred by the International Division in the sale of exports, i.e., includes local management services, salesmen, etc., Ibid.

SOURCE: J-M Corporation.

TABLE 3

Standard Cost Allocation to Various Expense Categories

Expense Category	Percent of Gross Sales Value
Cost of shipments to customers	57.3
Products of outside vendors	71.6

Expense Category	Percent of Net Sales Value
Transferred plant costs: net	4.9
Salesmen	4.0
Sales office	8.4
Warehouses:	
Inbound freight	0.6
Warehouse expense	0.6
Advertising	1.1
Research	0.6
Engineering and technical projects	0.01
Division administrative	0.4
General company administrative	1.3
Miscellaneous income and deductions	0.002

NOTE: On the basis of these standard costs the company has prepared a forecast of net earnings from exports for 1968 (Table 4). With this information the International Division will devise its export sales strategies and allocate funds to implement these strategies.

SOURCE: J-M Corporation.

TABLE 4

Estimated 1968 Export Sales
(Thousands of Dollars)

Product Group[a]	Gross Sales Value[b]	Net Earnings[c]	Percent
A	16,800	602	3.6
B	40,012	5,285	13.2
C	19,152	630	3.3
D	7,770	917	11.8
E	1,820	21	1.1
F	12,957	350	2.7
G	3,437	224	6.6
H	2,975	293	9.8
I	9,527	63	0.7
J	4,200	238	5.7
K	350	7	2.0
Total Export	119,000	8,630	7.2

[a]Product groups may be thought of as consisting of the product package available from each of the eleven operating divisions.
[b]Equivalent to the category "Sales to Customers" shown in Table 2.
[c]After taxes.
SOURCE: J-M Corporation.

APPENDIX I

J-M Corporation—Operating Divisions

Asbestos Fiber. Headquartered in Asbestos, Quebec, this division is responsible for the worldwide exploration, mining, and milling of asbestos fiber.

Building Products. The Building Products Division is a major national producer and supplier of building materials for residential, commercial, and industrial construction. Operations include fifteen manufacturing facilities. Division sales offices service all major markets throughout the United States.

Canadian Products. With headquarters at Toronto, Ontario, this division is responsible for the manufacture and sale of J-M product lines throughout the Canadian market. Production operations are located at Asbestos, Quebec; North Bay and Toronto, Ontario, Canadian-made products are marketed overseas through the company's International Division.

Celite. The Celite Division is a major miner and supplier of diatomite for industrial applications. The division also mines perlite ore and manufactures synthetic silicates.

Dutch Brand. This division produces pressure-sensitive plastic, rubber, cloth, and paper tapes for original equipment manufacturers, heating and air conditioning, electrical, industrial, and government markets.

Fiber Glass. The Fiber Glass Division is a leading national producer of fiber glass. It markets textile fiber glass and reinforcement materials. Insulations produced by the division are marketed by the company's Building Products and Industrial Insulations Division.

Flooring. This division manufactures and markets a broad line of asphalt-asbestos and vinyl-asbestos floor tile for residential, commercial, institutional, and industrial applications. Floor tile products are produced in four locations in the U. S. and are sold by leading dealers throughout the United States.

Industrial Insulations. The Industrial Insulations Division is a prime supplier of industrial and commercial insulating materials. Production is handled by the division's seven plants.

International. The International Division is responsible for production and marketing of J-M product lines outside the United States and Canada. American and Canadian-made products are sold to 103 countries throughout the world. The division operates eight plants overseas and maintains an extensive program of licensing and technical assistance and minority investments involving sixty-one companies, operating eighty-two plants in twenty-nine countries.

Melamite. This division produces a wide variety of high-pressure plastic decorative laminates. The division's products are available to furniture manufacturers and the do-it-yourself market through leading lumber dealers.

Packings and Friction Materials. This division manufactures and markets a broad line of packings, gaskets, asbestos textiles, automotive and industrial brake linings, brake blocks, and clutch facings. The division also produces a composition brake shoe for the railroad industry.

Pipe. J-M pipe products are manufactured by this division in eight plants and are marketed for application in such diverse activities as public works; water and sewer systems; commercial, institutional, and residential construction; farm and turf irrigation; etc.

APPENDIX II

Ten-Year Review of Operations

(All Dollar Figures in Millions except those per Share)

	1967	1966	1965	1964	1963	1962	1961	1960	1959	1958
Sales	$510.4	512.5	480.2	458.9	414.9	392.3	377.8	365.2	377.6	331.7
Earnings Before Income Taxes	$60.4	72.3	63.5	58.3	52.6	43.8	43.0	49.9	55.7	42.2
Income Taxes	$27.8	34.3	29.4	26.2	24.9	19.9	19.1	23.4	24.1	18.8
Net Earnings	$32.6	38.0	34.1	32.1	27.7	23.9	23.9	26.5	31.6	23.4
Earnings per share[a]	$3.91	4.50	4.03	3.77	3.25	2.81	2.81	3.12	3.74	2.83
Percent of Earnings to Sales	6.4	7.4	7.1	7.0	6.7	6.1	6.3	7.3	8.4	7.0
Stockholders' Investment	$351.7	337.0	324.5	307.8	297.3	287.2	283.6	275.7	265.4	245.5
Percent of Earnings to Investment at Start of Year	9.7	11.7	11.1	10.8	9.6	8.4	8.7	10.0	12.4	11.1
Dividends	$18.3	18.6	17.4	17.0	17.0	17.0	17.0	17.0	16.7	14.3
Dividends per Share	$2.20	2.20	2.05	2.00	2.00	2.00	2.00	2.00	2.00	2.00
Cash Flow	$55.4	60.4	54.1	50.8	46.9	43.5	40.8	43.3	48.4	39.2
Cash Flow per Share[a]	$6.64	7.15	6.38	5.97	5.51	5.11	4.80	5.10	5.73	4.74
Capital Expenditures	$34.4	28.3	21.2	20.1	15.8	11.4	20.0	20.0	16.2	12.0
Investments[b]	$1.3	8.1	3.5	6.3	5.8	6.6	1.8	2.9	.9	.9
Depreciation and Depletion	$22.8	22.3	20.0	18.7	19.2	19.6	16.9	16.8	16.8	15.8
Research Development and Engineering Expense	$11.4	11.6	11.4	12.1	9.9	11.5	11.6	10.3	8.6	7.7
Book Value per Share	$42.16	40.44	38.29	36.32	34.89	33.71	33.30	32.47	31.32	29.63
Shares Outstanding at End of Year	8,341,276	8,332,880	8,475,233	8,474,778	8,510,248	8,519,900	8,517,613	8,490,038	8,474,214	8,283,192
Stockholders	26,100	27,600	27,700	30,000	31,000	30,500	29,400	29,600	30,100	23,800
Employees	21,800	21,500	21,200	20,600	19,900	19,700	20,300	20,200	20,000	18,300
Wages, Salaries, and Employee Benefits	$198.1	189.6	174.6	165.5	151.8	147.0	142.1	138.6	131.0	114.3

[a]On average shares outstanding.
[b]Additional investments in unconsolidated foreign subsidiaries and other companies.

SOURCE: Johns-Manville Annual Report 1967, p. 17.

434

APPENDIX III

International Operating Facilities

Plants

Bellegarde, France
Casalpusterlengo, Italy
Ghent, Belgium
Hull, England
Mexico City, Mexico
Mol, Belgium
St. Marcellin, France
Wissembourg, France

Mines

Lake Myvatyn, Iceland
Santa Catarina, Mexico

Sales Offices

Beirut, Lebanon
Buenos Aires, Argentina
Goteborg, Sweden
Hong Kong
Husavik, Iceland
Johannesburg, South Africa
Lagos, Nigeria
Lima, Peru
London, England
Lyon, France
Madrid, Spain
Mexico City, Mexico
Milan, Italy
Mol-Donk, Belgium
Nairobi, Kenya
Paris, France
San Juan, Puerto Rico
Sao Paulo, Brazil
Sydney, Australia
Wiesbaden, Germany
Zurich, Switzerland

SOURCE: Johns-Manville Annual Report 1967, p. 16.

STILLE-WERNER, SWEDEN

Advertising Strategy in the Introduction of New Sanitary Napkins in a Different Culture

Stille-Werner is a Swedish Company primarily engaged in manufacturing and distributing infirmary supplies and paper products in the Swedish market. The company had 750 employees and an annual turnover of 60 million Swiss Croners in 1969.

Stille had manufactured and sold sanitary napkins in Sweden before World War II but had not been in the market since then. However, in 1967, Stille found an opportunity to enter the market in a dramatic manner. The company's New Products Group had developed a new sanitary napkin. Based on an invention by SPA, a paper mill company, this napkin had two important features in convenient usage and disposal which distinguished it from and made it superior to other sanitary napkins available in the market. One, it could be attached to the underwear with a tape and therefore no belt was needed to wear it. Two, it could be flushed in the toilet.

At first Stille's management doubted the marketing possibilities of the product in view of the competitive structure and novel product design. However, before making a decision, they decided to conduct a market survey to make a more realistic assessment of the situation.

GENERAL MARKET CONDITIONS

As a first step, Stille conducted a study to determine the market size of sanitary protection (SP) items and the nature of existing competition. Their findings are briefly summarized here:

The SP market in Sweden amounted to 68 million Sw. Crs. in 1968 (in retail prices), of which Sw. Crs. 42 million were for sanitary napkins and Sw. Cr. 18 million for tampons. The SP market has grown about 10 percent during the sixties. The napkin market has been growing at the rate of 5 to 6 percent, and the tampon market at 15 to 20 percent a year.

The number of consumers has been somewhat constant, there being about 1.8 million females between the ages of thirteen and fifty. However, the market size may increase through more intensive usage. On an average, a consumer changed protection two to three times a day with eighteen to twenty changes per menstruation period. Gynecologists, however, recommended twice this rate. About 95 percent of all consumers used industry produced SP products.

Grocery stores are the principal outlets for SP handling about 65 percent of the total retail sales, with the remaining 35 percent being sold through department stores and cosmetic shops etc. In 1968 SP worth Sw. Crs. 6 million were sold through grocery stores (including supermarkets), Sw. Crs. 15 million through department stores, and Sw. Crs. 9 million through cosmetics and other shops. The independent food stores (non co-op) have 50 percent of the sanitary napkin and 40 percent of the tampon sales.

Mölnlycke is the major brand in the market and accounted for 75 percent of the napkin market and 95 percent of the tampon market in 1968. Co-op brand Lady was number two. Other brands like Silkesept, Formita, and Tampax had smaller shares. In 1965, Mölnlycke had sold 25 million ten-unit packages of SP of which 18 million were napkins and 9 million tampons.

MARKET RESEARCH—
ATTITUDE STUDY

The next step for Stilles was to do a consumer study about product acceptability. This research was conducted in Stockholm and a small religious town. The study found that 54 percent of the consumers interviewed liked the product and 82 percent of the latter group said that they were willing to pay a higher price for this napkin. The research also showed that the SP consumption was proportionally much higher in the small town. The explanation was that the women in Stockholm consumed more birth-control pills which caused lighter menstruations.

Buying Habits. The attitude study showed that women buy SP only when they need it. Women are accordingly not very open for low-price campaigns or other such promotions.

Information Need. The research told that communication between women about SP products hardly existed. It was found that the women preferred real information and not victorian language. This was especially true for women in the age group below twenty-five.

Package. The market research showed that women normally kept the SP package in a concealed place.

The results of this survey were quite encouraging and Stilles decided to test market the product. The choice of location, however, presented some problems. Stilles was afraid that if the product was test marketed anywhere in Sweden, Mölnlycke was likely to interfere with the test by reducing prices of their products in the test market area, thereby distorting the test findings. Consequently, the product was test marketed in 1968 in Tammersfors, Finland. The results of the test market showed a somewhat higher repurchase disposition than the consumer test had indicated.

INTRODUCTION OF STILLES SANISEPT

Stille was now ready to introduce its brand, Stilles Sanisept, in the Swedish market. To market its product, it made the following basic decisions concerning marketing and promotional strategies:

1. Distribution—National: all channels carrying SP products were to be used.
2. Pricing—Price Stilles Sanisept slightly lower than the premium brand of the major competitor. The price of Stilles Sanisept compared with Mölnlycke follows:

Brand	Package	Average Retail Price (including 10% purchase tax) Sw. Crs.
Mimosept Mölnlycke	10 in a plastic bag	2.70
Mimosept Lady (low price)	10 in a plastic bag	1.97
Mimosept Lady (low price)	20 in a plastic bag	3.32
OB tampon	10 in a plastic bag	2.88
Stilles Sanisept	10 in a plastic bag	2.44

There were to be no price promotions or rebates.

3. Package—To give the product a high visibility, a package was designed which could be hung on a bathroom hook. Stilles used a base design and color-combination which was found on the most widely sold brand of bathroom towels, i.e., Cannon (made by a Swedish subsidiary of the U. S. textile company of the same name). *See* Exhibit 1.

4. Advertising—To be the heart of their sales campaign, was primarily concentrated in women's magazines. The basic theme was to emphasize the functional aspect of the product and provide information in a no-nonsense manner.

The advertising campaign hammered at the superiority of Stilles Sanisept over the competitors' products by showing the two products side by side. Although the rules for such advertising had been relaxed during the last few years, the Stille ads were nevertheless extreme examples of comparative advertising. Four examples of ads used in the campaign are reproduced in Exhibits 2 to 5.

Exhibit 2 is an ad from a women's magazine. It describes the qualities of the napkin. Headline: "You can apply the new sanitary napkin Stilles Sanisept in this simple manner and it can be flushed down." The text informs the reader that a belt is unnecessary, a tape attaches it to the underwear, the napkin is only 12 mm thick and not 25 mm as ordinary sanitary napkins, and that it is the only napkin that is permitted by the Stockholm Health Department for flushing in the toilet (ordinary sanitary napkins are prohibited from being flushed down).

Exhibit 3 is an ad from a teenage magazine directed at young women. The text gives in a summarized form the same information as in Exhibit 2.

Exhibit 4 is an ad published in a women's magazine in April 1969. Headline: "No more tangled belt, troublesome ropes, ties and clasps which rub, this is the new sanitary napkin Stilles Sanisept and it can be flushed down." The text gives the same information as in Exhibit 2.

Exhibit 5 is an ad from a women's fashion magazine published in November 1969. It describes the possibilities for combining the layers of wadding.

Stille spent heavily on mass advertising in promoting Stilles Sanisept. The brand was introduced nationally in March 1969. During the period March to December 1969, Stille spent about Sw. Crs. 824,000 which was approximately 46 percent of the total press advertising done by all manufacturers on all SP products during 1969 (Tables 1 and 2).

RESULTS

By January 1970, ten months after the market introduction Stilles Sanisept had gained 22 percent of the *total* SP market. The market shares for various brands of SP in *grocery stores* (which account for 65 percent of the total SP retail sales) during September 1969 to February 1970 were as follows:

Brand	*Market Share*
Mölnlycke	69 percent
Stilles Sanisept	12 percent

Brand	Market Share
KF Sanetta (co-op)	11 percent
Tampax	2 percent
Other	6 percent

The total consumption of SP products in Sweden in 1970 was expected to be worth 70 million Sw. Crs. Another important change in the market was the increased frequency of usage. This was expected to rise to twenty-five changes per menstruation period in 1970 as against eighteen to twenty during 1968.

The Stilles Sanisept ads were adjudged as among the best in Sweden in 1969 by a jury of the Association of Advertising Agencies and were awarded a prize for excellence.

Molnlycke reported the Stilles Sanisept ads to Naringslivets Opinions-namnd, a court of honor with the task of improving Swedish advertising. Molnlycke complained that this kind of comparative advertising insulted Molnlycke and other producers of ordinary sanitary napkins. After an inquiry, Naringslivets Opinionnamnd declared that the ad contained in Exhibit 4 gave a wrong and insulting description of the ordinary sanitary napkins. The data about the thickness of the napkins was wrong. They said that ads did not follow the rules of the International Chamber of Commerce.

Sweden has since passed a new law concerning unfair competition which will come into force in 1971. It is likely that ads like Stilles Sanisept will be prohibited under the new law.

EXHIBIT 1

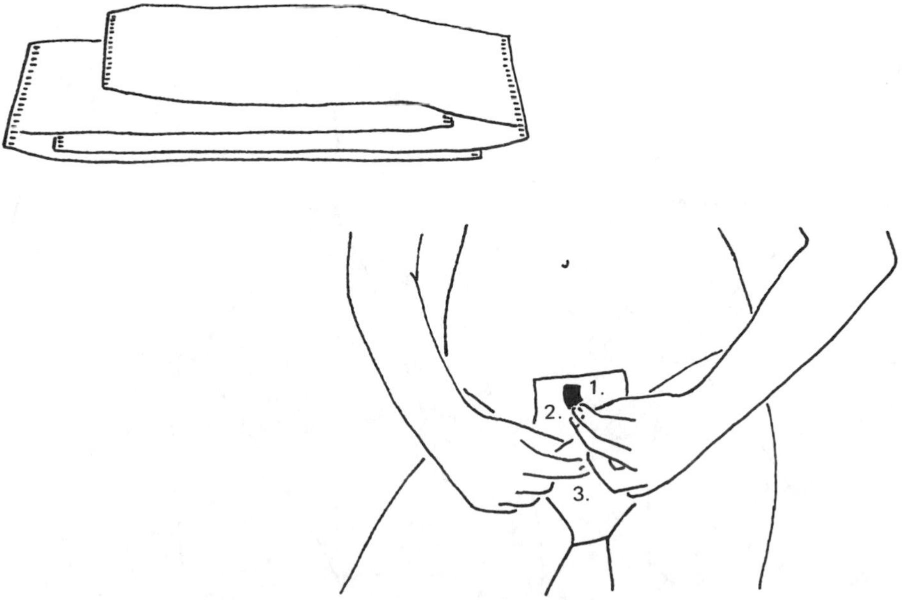

EXHIBIT 2

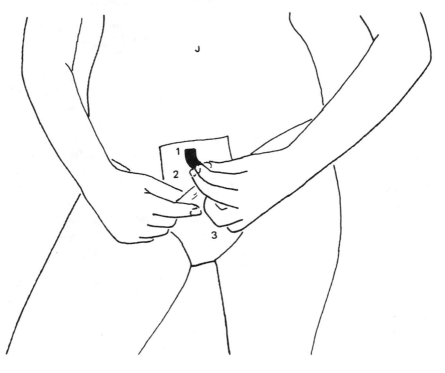

EXHIBIT 3

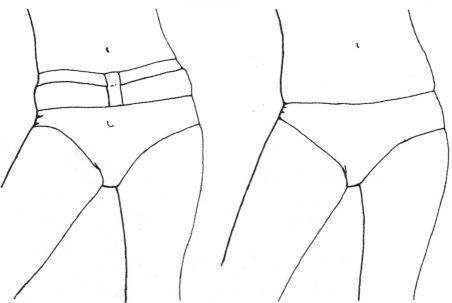

EXHIBIT 4

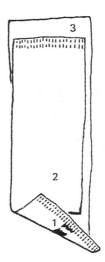

EXHIBIT 5

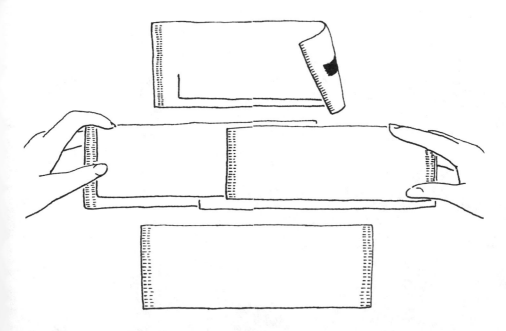

TABLE 1

Sanitary Protection Advertising Expenditures—Sweden

Space Costs in Thousands of Sw. Crs.

Brand	1967	1968	1969
Formita	227	15	31
Kronosept	12	0.4	0.3
Mölnlycke:			
Mimosept	100	140	77
Mimosept Lady	233	103	166
OB	527	542	175
Mölnlycke Others	78	14	104
Sanetta (co-op)	3	–	–
Silkesept	100	63	–
Stilles Sanisept	–	–	824
Tampax	295	374	413
Total:	1,575	1,249	1,794

TABLE 2

Breakdown of Advertising Expenditures for Sanitary Products—Sweden

Brand Name and Nature of Medium	1967			1968			1969		
	No. of Ads	Column Space Centimeters	Total Space Cost Sw. Crs.	No. of Ads	Column Space Centimeters	Total Space Cost Sw. Crs.	No. of Ads	Column Space Centimeters	Total Space Cost Sw. Crs.
Formita									
Daily Press, Stockholm, Gothenberg, Malmö	4	1,260	45,060	–	–	–	8	629	11,781
Daily Press, provincial	–	–	–	–	–	–	24	1,869	18,866
Magazines	31	3,049	155,075	2	159	11,670	–	–	–
Trade Press	7	1,160	26,546	3	212	3,440	–	–	–
Total	42	5,469	226,681	5	371	15,110	32	2,498	30,647
Kronosept									
Daily Press, Stockholm, Gothenberg, Malmö	14	606	11,681	1	27	378	2	146	3,281
Daily Press, provincial	1	77	704	–	–	–	–	–	–
Total	15	683	12,385	1	27	378	2	146	3,281
Mimosept									
Daily Press, Stockholm, Gothenberg, Malmö	66	1,517	35,403	–	–	–	–	–	–
Daily Press, provincial	1	12	60	1	7	35	1	7	35
Magazines	18	968	57,760	14	1,298	128,923	8	971	77,015
Trade Press	2	308	7,223	2	445	11,030	–	–	–
Total	87	2,804	100,446	17	1,750	139,968	9	978	77,050

TABLE 2–continued

Brand Name and Nature of Medium	1967			1968			1969		
	No. of Ads	Column Space Centimeters	Total Space Cost Sw. Crs.	No. of Ads	Column Space Centimeters	Total Space Cost Sw. Crs.	No. of Ads	Column Space Centimeters	Total Space Cost Sw. Crs.
Mimosept Lady									
Daily Press, Stockholm, Gothenberg, Malmö	1	193	3,754	14	2,366	61,638	–	–	–
Daily Press, provincial	–	–	–	1	8	40	–	–	–
Magazines	49	3,246	221,655	2	212	17,990	19	2,254	166,365
Trade Press	2	305	7,168	4	890	22,060	–	–	–
Total	52	3,743	232,577	21	3,476	101,728	19	2,254	166,365
Mölnlycke Others									
Daily Press, provincial	–	–	–	1	8	40	–	–	–
Magazines	13	356	270,095	1	86	13,500	14	1,548	94,920
Trade Press	13	2,530	50,506	–	–	–	2	445	9,068
Total	26	2,886	277,601	2	94	13,540	16	1,993	103,988
Mölnlycke, Ob									
Daily Press, Stockholm, Gothenberg, Malmö	1	28	434	–	–	–	–	–	–
Daily Press, provincial	16	455	3,738	–	–	–	–	–	–
Magazines	69	6,893	464,350	69	8,033	511,043	27	2,873	175,440
Trade Press	23	2,653	58,960	10	1,291	30,510	–	–	–
Total	109	10,029	527,482	79	9,324	541,553	27	2,873	175,440
Sanetta									
Daily Press, provincial	6	363	3,360	–	–	–	–	–	–
Total	6	363	3,360	–	–	–	–	–	–

Brand Name and Nature of Medium	1967			1968			1969		
	No. of Ads	Column Space Centi-meters	Total Space Cost Sw. Crs.	No. of Ads	Column Space Centi-meters	Total Space Cost Sw. Crs.	No. of Ads	Column Space Centi-meters	Total Space Cost Sw. Crs.
Silkesept									
Magazines	19	2,044	99,940	–	–	–	–	–	–
Total	19	2,044	99,940	–	–	–	–	–	–
Tampax									
Magazines	179	5,039	29,765	210	6,940	374,115	198	7,617	409,260
Trade Press	–	–	–	–	–	–	1	220	4,180
Total	179	5,039	29,765	210	6,940	374,115	199	7,837	413,440
Stilles Sanisept									
Daily Press, Stockholm, Gothenberg, Malmö	–	–	–	–	–	–	1	195	13,790
Daily Press, provincial	–	–	–	–	–	–	2	25	232
Magazines	–	–	–	–	–	–	62	14,325	742,380
Trade Press	–	–	–	–	–	–	11	1,964	62,781
Total	–	–	–	–	–	–	76	16,509	823,683
All SP Products									
Daily Press, Stockholm, Gothenberg, Malmö	86	3,604	96,332	15	2,393	62,016	11	969	28,852
Daily Press, provincial	24	907	7,862	3	23	115	27	1,901	19,133
Magazines	378	21,594	1,320,640	311	18,089	1,120,270	328	29,587	1,665,380
Trade Press	47	6,956	150,403	19	2,838	67,040	14	2,629	80,529
Total	535	33,060	1,575,237	343	23,343	1,249,442	380	35,086	1,793,894

INTERNATIONAL FOODS, INC., U. S. A. (C)

Implementing the Advertising and Promotional Strategies

ROLE OF ADVERTISING IN THE MARKETING MIX

The role of advertising within the marketing mix is to implement product flow through the distribution channels, to act as a catalyst in the dynamic process of acquainting the consumer with the available means of satisfying his hierarchy of needs and wants, often to create a channel of release for the consumer's latent needs and drives, and ultimately to induce consumer action which benefits the initiator of the communications process—the firm. However, advertising is only one element in the total marketing mix, which includes all decisions relevant to the nature of the product and packaging, pricing policy, channels of distribution utilized, the compilation and selection of consumer profiles and targets, and promotion. Notwithstanding the internal decision-making processes related to the product, the marketing mix must depend on the nature of the demand for the product and the state of existing competition.

The task of advertising is effectively to communicate information concerning the product and physical and psychic satisfactions to be derived from it to the potential consumers. The fundamental requirements for formulating a strategy and promotional communications, such as media availability, method of placement, agency availability, and quality are fixed and static with respect to time. The individual decision components must be decided upon in a dynamic environment which reflects the economic subsystem within which the firm operates. Thus, the strategic role of advertising within the overall marketing mix varies with time, place, objectives of the firm, and the institution itself. It requires a set of meanings and definitions commonly agreed to by the firm as an institution in order to function in pursuit of its objectives. The role of advertising is not solely related to its detailed message and media goals, nor to the objectives of the marketing mix. It must also reflect the overall corporate objectives.

It is within this framework that we now turn to a description and understanding of IFI's[1] advertising strategies. The emphasis is on a comparative analysis of IFI's advertising and promotional policies as pursued in the four countries under study: the United Kingdom, West Germany, the Phillippines, and Peru. Our primary

---

1. All the names and figures in this study are fictitious to disguise the identity of the company and protect its competitive position.

objectives are to measure the extent to which these various advertising strategies and tactics:

1. Conform with the consumer profiles of the selected target customers in each market;
2. Form an integral part of the total marketing mix.

The secondary objectives of this study are:

1. To understand the conditions under which media and copy themes may be generalized over different markets;
2. To analyze the organizational requirements of decentralized decision-making which must be met if the peculiar needs of different national markets can be harmonized with the overall corporate objectives and marketing goals of a multinational company.

The corporate objectives of IFI are primarily defined on two dimensions. Affiliate performance is measured essentially on basis: (1) 15 percent after-tax return on the assets managed by the affiliate, and (2) 4 percent after-tax return on affiliate sales. (*See* Part A.) These standards are not rigid and may vary with the circumstances of the local profit centers. The goals which can be inferred from the marketing plans focus upon maintaining the corporate image of a firm which produces a high quality product and is genuinely concerned with the quality of life of its consumers.

GENERAL NATURE OF THE ADVERTISING STRATEGY

Corporate Advertising Philosophy

To implement IFI's central objectives, the goals of the marketing mix are much more explicit. As discussed in Part B, the fundamental corporate philosophy is to maximize product distribution, which in turn undergirds IFI's central marketing objective—to maximize the dollar expenditure toward the consumer end of the marketing spectrum. This marketing objective keystone provides the framework for implementing the marketing communications goals (Figure 1).

The principle of minimizing expenditures to the trade and to fixed overhead cost classifications and maximizing expenditures toward elements with direct impact on the consumer depends largely upon the nature of competition and the availability of adequate distribution channels. A member of the IFI marketing staff said that the degree of success the firm has in each market in meeting the dictates of this principle is the basis for the affiliates' profitability: "In terms of the flow of the goods from the factory to the consumer, the larger the percentage of expenses that you can throw toward the consumer end of the spectrum and the less you can spend back toward the factory, the more successful you can expect your product to be." The basis for such a guiding principle is that the firm visualizes the international evaporated milk market as a consumer product-oriented oligopolistic structure in which the product is essentially nondifferentiable.

FIGURE 1

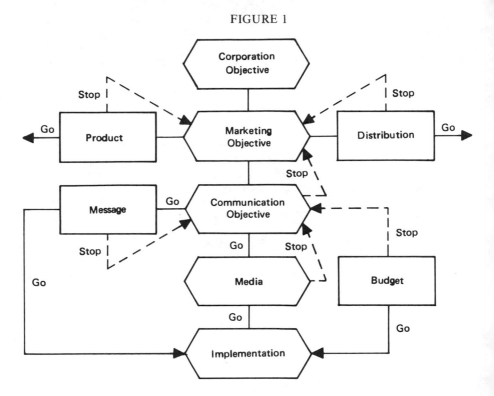

In such an environment it becomes necessary to orient the major portion of the marketing effort toward the consuming public so that they may perceive some differentiation among the products on the market, psychological or otherwise.

Problem Areas in Multinational Advertising Strategies

Any firm marketing a consumer-oriented product necessarily faces consumers with different needs, motivations, and desires, and who, within a culture, generally rely on certain common values for all types of personal decision-making. Cultural differentiation is critical to the successful promotion of a firm's product. If it is neglected, the consumer will conceive it irrelevant to her cultural traits, hence useless in her life-style.

Sommers and Kernan recognized this problem when they investigated the degree of product acceptance in the multinational environment.

The promotional information which supports products in culturally differentiated markets must also be individualized. The product claims made by promotional information can be thought of as including three components—the meaningful, the plausible, and the verifiable. The cultural values of the market will strongly influence the kinds of topics that are meaningful. Similarly they will control the type of product claims people are predisposed to consider plausible. Finally, they will influence the basis upon which claims can be rendered verifiable.[2]

Thus, cultural variables confront market planners in two critically distinct but related ways: they determine the position of culturally sanctioned products in the market; the dominant value orientation of the markets provides invaluable insight for product marketing.

The critical nature of product sanctioning and perceived differentiation heavily burdens the role of advertising in the marketing mix. IFI recognized the importance of this role but had difficulty exploiting it properly. This difficulty can be traced to two critical areas in the firm's marketing activities. advertising must be selected specifically for a given market, and the knowledge of local market conditions must be both broad and intimate.

Selecting advertising to be implemented in a specific market is vital to the consumer's acceptance and perceived differentiation of that product. It is the creativity of the advertising theme, and its accompanying copy and artwork, which creates within the consumer a sense of identification, and therefore her ultimate acceptance. However, because evaporated milk can be viewed as being in the final stage of Raymond Vernon's product cycle (where product differentiability becomes almost impossible and where competitive pressures become increasingly strong) theme creativity becomes difficult to obtain.

IFI recognized the creativity need in its basic decision to use a local advertising agency in each market, rather than to centralize through an internal staff or a domestic agency. By delegating such authority to local agencies, IFI hopes to maximize its effectiveness in several critical areas: (1) effectuate a cost savings by not having a large, specialized, internal staff, (2) avoid having to find, and retain the highly qualified personnel necessary to implement a local in-house campaign, (3) maximize the placement of advertising by using an experienced local agency, and (4) gain as broad and intimate a knowledge of local market conditions as possible.

It has been the general experience of multinational firms, including IFI, that the scope and reliability of promotional research conducted in the local markets does not approach the quality of information available domestically. Such accepted measures as Starch Readership Data, Nielsen Ratings, and advertising media impact studies are generally unavailable in all but the most sophisticated markets. As noted in Part B, research methods are usually restricted to pantry checks, brand awareness studies, and other simple methods. Therefore, IFI has been unable to test the impact of its creative campaigns upon its target consumers, and thus cannot know if the promotional campaigns are effective. Should such impact data be available, their reliability is immediately questioned and their relevance and importance to future creative planning are instantly diminished. Thus, IFI has found that the analytical methods used in its home market are of small value internationally. This problem is especially acute in the area of developing systematic research methods

2. Sommers, Montrose and Jerome Kernan, "Why Products Flourish Here, Fizzle There," *Columbia Journal of World Business* 11, no. 2 (March–April 1967): 93.

applicable in comparative cross-cultural analysis of consumer attitudes and promotional impact. IFI feels that it can partially resolve this problem by conducting analytical methods research in conjunction with the large multinational advertising agencies and various research organizations.

Advertising and Promotion Budgets for the Four IFI Markets

A demonstration of how the principle works of concentrating marketing expenditure toward the consumer end of the marketing spectrum in the four markets, is presented in Table 1. By utilizing the category of "Total Advertising Expenditures" as those costs which are directly oriented toward the consumer, the table presents these costs as a percentage of the other categories. "Total Fixed Marketing Expenditures" includes total advertising costs in addition to such expenditure categories as market research, salaries, administrative, and sales expenses. "Total Marketing Investment" includes the above classifications plus the total proportional costs—commissions, distribution expenses, and trade payments. Tables 2 through 4 show the allocation of the 1970 advertising budget among various broad media categories. Tables 5 through 15 provide detailed data for the disbursement of these funds within each category. All tables include data pertaining to the four countries under study and are referred to in the subsequent sections when individual countries are discussed separately.

The marketing plans for each market should reflect its distinctive characteristics within the general philosophical framework. Similarly, the advertising budgets of the affiliates and their use of the promotional media should be tailored individually to the environment of each specific market. A comparison of the total advertising budgets for 1970 show an unusually close comparability of the percentages of the total budget across each broad media classification. In markets with such different characteristics this seems unusual. Table 2 shows that the primary emphasis of the communications efforts in the four markets is concentrated in mass media advertising, with at least 67.8 percent (in Peru) of the budget allocation in this segment of the promotional strategy. It also demonstrates that point-of-purchase promotional activities assume secondary importance across the markets, obtaining a maximum of 17.9 percent in the Philippines. The category of special promotions essentially features the medical promotional expenditures and the school campaigns.

As a general observation, it can be said that the growth and availability of promotional communications networks usually correspond to the growth of the individual country's economic development. In a growing consumer-oriented economy, increased promotional facilities are a prerequisite to an increased awareness of the product's availability, and thus to its increased distribution within the market. A corollary to this premise is that the type and quantity of the available advertising media typically reflect the development of a country's marketing system. Thus, in considering the four markets it should not be surprising that the types of media and their frequency of availability would be more diverse in such markets as Germany and the United Kingdom, and less so in the markets of the Philippines and Peru.

TABLE 1

The Relationship of Advertising Expenditures to Gross Sales
and Overall Marketing Expenditures—1970

	United Kingdom (£)	Germany (DM)	Philippine Is. (P)	Peru (s/)
Total advertising expenditures	503,245	4,912,500	1,186,200	4,654,500
Gross sales	6,877,000	111,269,800	17,614,000	887,275,400
Total fixed marketing expenditures	787,733	12,314,500	2,201,100	22,358,900
Total marketing investment	1,299,583	19,059,300	2,604,100	62,435,200
Total advertising costs as a percentage of:				
Gross sales	7.3%	4.4%	6.7%	0.5%
Total fixed marketing expenditures	63.9	39.9	53.9	20.8
Total marketing investment	38.7	25.8	45.6	7.5

TABLE 2

Total Advertising Budget by Market Area—1970

Media	United Kingdom (£)			Germany (DM)			Philippine Is. (₱)			Peru (s/)		
	Media Costs	%	Cost per Case[a]	Media Costs	%	Cost per Case[a]	Media Costs	%	Cost per Case[a]	Media Costs	%	Cost per Case[a]
Mass media	383,138	81.6	0.149	3,605,000	79.6	0.913	885,100	72.4	1.135	2,913,500	67.8	1.005
Institutional advertising[b]	4,500	1.0	.002	–	–	–	–	–	–	108,000	2.5	.037
Special promotions[c]	17,855	3.8	.007	307,000	6.8	.078	99,260	8.1	.127	574,000	13.3	.198
Point of purchase advertising	56,865	12.1	.022	536,000	11.8	.136	225,500	18.4	.289	488,000	11.3	.168
Marketing research	7,250	1.5	.003	82,000	1.8	.021	14,300	1.1	.018	220,400	5.1	.076
Total	469,608	100	.183	4,530,000	100	1.148	1,224,160	100	1.569	4,303,900	100	1.484

[a]Based on 1970 forecasted case sales in the local currency.
[b]Includes public relations, institutional advertisements, and courtesy ads.
[c]Includes school campaigns, medical promotional efforts, and special items.

452

These two characteristics of the availability of media manifest the type of elements reflected in the differences inherent in the promotional strategies of the markets. The elements of strategy determination and composition include, as a basis, some of the following, although all elements are not identically important in all markets.

1. In itself, the physical geography of a country not only determines the type of market in which the product must compete, but also the socio-economic breakdown of the population, the population distribution, the channels of distribution, the availability of local production facilities, and a number of additional factors. The influence of such a major determinant of the marketing structure upon the advertising strategies within those countries must necessarily be profound. IFI's operations in Peru provide an excellent study of such a case. Effectively, two-thirds of the area of the country is dismissed as being relatively minor to the success of the firm's marketing operations and profitability.

2. The maturity of the market is another important determinant of the communications objectives. Appeals to young and to mature markets differ significantly. Witness the situation in the United Kingdom where a host of private labels together comprise the competition, not one specific competitor.

3. Governmental restrictions, aside from limiting a firm's degree of freedom in establishing its general marketing objectives, can impose constraints upon the implemented strategies. The prohibition of commercial broadcasting on the BBC and of comparative advertising in Germany can be cited as minimal examples

4. Product usage varies dramatically among the markets. In the United Kingdom evaporated milk is primarily a food creamer; in Germany, its major use is as a coffee creamer; and in Peru and the Philippines both coffee and infant feeding are the major uses. IFI reflects such differences in both strategy and copy.

5. The differences in target market groups are naturally reflected in the strategies. In countries with a high rate of illiteracy, advertising strategies generally must stress symbolic representations, especially with the use of trademarks and point-of-purchase materials. Specific media selection is determined by their socio-politico-economic orientation, thus strategies which attempt to appeal to a distinct segment of the population must use the media with the greatest impact upon that target audience.

6. The distribution of the product throughout the market and whether its usage is concentrated in one specific region (as in Peru and the Philippines) has much the same impact upon promotional strategies as do the limitations imposed upon market penetration by geography and inadequate communications.

Although the varying degrees of importance of these elements are reflected in the individual promotional strategies, it would be easy to assume also that these differences are reflected in the importance attached to specific media usage in the different markets. Yet, when the budget allocations for each medium are compared as percentages of the total advertising mass media budget, the primacy of television and radio is readily apparent. With the exceptions of the German strategy, Table 3

TABLE 3
Advertising Budgets—Mass Media/Market Area 1970

Media	United Kingdom (£) Space Costs	%	Germany (DM) Space Costs	%	Philippine Is. (P) Space Costs	%	Peru (s/) Space Costs	%
Broadcast:								
Television	325,048		1,494,000		193,500		1,925,500	
Radio	–		–		346,300		663,500	
Total space costs	325,048		1,494,000		539,800		2,589,000	
Production costs	13,000		100,000		205,900		167,000	
Total broadcast	338,048	88.2	1,594,000	44.2	745,700	84.3	2,756,000	94.6
Print:								
Newspapers	25,408		–		56,500		38,000	
Consumer magazines	–		1,872,000		69,900		–	
Lay baby magazines	14,610		–		–		–	
Total space costs	40,018		1,872,000		126,400		38,000	
Production costs	2,500		60,000		13,000		20,000	
Total print	42,518	11.1	1,932,000	53.6	139,400	15.7	58,000	2.0
Professional and Trade:								
Medical journals	2,322		39,000[a]		–		10,000[b]	
Trade press	–		30,000		–		35,500[b]	
Total space costs	2,322		69,000		–		45,500	
Production costs	250		10,000		–		–	
Total professional and trade	2,572	0.7	79,000	2.2	–	–	45,500	1.6

[a] The space cost figure includes 3,000 to 4,000 DM of production costs.
[b] No production costs are involved.

454

	United Kingdom (£)		Germany (DM)		Philippine Is. (P)		Peru (s/)	
	Space Costs	%	Space Costs	%	Space Costs	%	Space Costs	%
Outdoor:								
Total space costs	—		—		—		54,000[c]	
Production costs	—		—		—		—	
Total outdoor	—		—		—		54,000	1.8
Grand Total	383,138	100	3,605,000	100	885,100	100	2,913,500	100
Expenditure per case	£0.149		DM 0.913		₱ 1.135		s/ 1.005	

[c]The cost breakdown of the total space costs is as follows: (1) rental for twelve (12) months, s/39,000; and (2) rental of billboard locations, s/15,000. Although no production costs are budgeted, the space costs include maintenance costs for the painted billboards.

shows that allocations for airwave media account for a minimum of 84.3 percent of the total budget. Such large portions of total expenditures can be explained possibly by three factors: (1) In developed countries television provides an effective outlet with potentially 100 percent penetration of the national market; (2) in the less-developed markets, television is available only in the urban centers where the product's sales are concentrated, and (3) also in the less-developed markets radio is used to ensure that the provincial segment of the market is not neglected.

Again excepting Germany, the print media support the emphasis on radio and television. Their purpose appears to be a specialized orientation in each market whose function it is to rectify biases which can be political, linguistic, or social in nature, imposed upon the overall strategies by the primary importance of radio and television or to appeal to specific market segments within the total market on special occasions (e.g., Mother's Day in Peru). Newspapers appear to be used for principal supportive promotions only if a publication exists whose circulation qualifies it as a national influence. General interest consumer magazines, essentially a woman-oriented medium, are used as a primary tool only in Germany, where they have very wide circulation over all socioeconomic classes within the target audience.

The professional and trade media are used primarily to keep the firm's name and product before the trade and the medical profession. The medical journals perform the strategy objective of providing the profession with periodic reinforcement of the brand's advantages as a supplement to mother's milk.

An interesting aside to the importance of the different media is the very close comparability of the mass media production costs as a percentage of the total advertising budget. Table 4 shows that, excepting the Philippine Islands, these costs differ only by 1.2 percent at the maximum. It would appear reasonable to have expected a much wider divergence, given the differences in production facilities and state of the art available locally and the different scales of cost-of-living.

MARKET DESCRIPTIONS OF
PROMOTIONAL COMMUNICATIONS

United Kingdom

Consumer Profile. The present profile of the brand's existing consumers is that of the middle- and lower-income housewives, thirty-five years of age and older, who live in the central and northern regions of the country.

Promotional Strategy. To ensure the successful attainment of the general marketing objectives, the central goal of the firm's promotional activities is to consolidate and strengthen the product's brand image in the consumers' minds. As implemented by the "New Marketing Strategy," the image projected is of a versatile, naturally nutritious, modern product differentiated from competing products by its distinctive advantages. By strengthening the product image, IFI hopes to increase the degree of brand loyalty within the target audience and also to set the foundation for achieving the primary marketing goal—to maintain or increase its present brand market share.

TABLE 4

Total Mass Media Advertising Production Costs by Market Area—1970

Media	United Kingdom (£)	Germany (DM)	Philippine Is. (P)	Peru (s/)
Radio	–	–	169,900	17,000
Television	13,000	100,000	36,000	150,000
Newspapers	2,000	–	3,000	20,000
Trade press	–	10,000	–	a
Consumer magazines	–	60,000	10,000	–
Medical journals	250	– b	–	– a
Lay baby magazines	500	–	–	–
Outdoor	–		–	– c
School campaign	2,750	–	–	–
Public relations	2,000	–	–	30,000
Total	£20,500	170,000 DM	P218,900	s/217,000
Percentage of total advertising budget	4.4	3.8	17.9	5.0

aNo production cost is involved (*see* Tables 9 and 11).

bThe space cost figure (*see* Table 9) of 39,000 DM includes 3,000 to 4,000 DM of production costs.

cNo production costs to be allocated as the firm will use copy that was charged to previous budgets.

IFI's chosen strategy to implement this promotional objective includes the following elements:

1. Continuation of the "many uses" theme;
2. Continuation of the television weighting strategy;
3. Extension of television advertising to cover the entire year in selected areas;
4. Development of a special newspaper campaign to redress the down-scale bias of television;
5. Introduction of new recipes on the can labels to augment the "many uses" theme;
6. Production of a new recipe book;
7. Completion of the school campaign recipe file box promotion;
8. Continuation of the infant feeding campaign, and
9. Continuation of the distribution of free samples and recipe books through the Gas Boards.

The general advertising strategy emphasizes the successful multi-use theme. IFI wants to strengthen and develop that theme to promote increased brand usage for potentially high volume, everyday cooking, such as in egg dishes, custards and puddings, soups, cereals, hot drinks, casseroles and stews, and welsh rabbit.

TABLE 5

Radio Airtime Costs by Market Area—1970

Country	Geographical Region	Radio Homes (Thousands)	Penetration Percent	Number of Channels Used	Total Number of Spots	
					60 sec.	30 sec.
United Kingdom		Not in use at present				
Germany		Not in use at present				
Philippine Is.	Manila	488	88	2	1,248	–
	NW Luzon	196	54	7	4,992	8,736
	NE Luzon	192	46	3	2,496	–
	Central Luzon	131	52	2	–	2,912
	S. Tagalog	191	40	2	2,496	2,912
	Bicol Region	200	48	5	1,248	2,912
	Cent./E. Visayas	292	36	6	6,240	4,368
	W. Visayas	281	36	7	12,480	8,736
	W. Mindanao	201	42	4	3,744	14,560
	E. Mindanao	218	42	5	5,824	5,824
	Total	2,390^b		43	40,768	50,960
Peru	R.P.P.^{d}	774.0^f	–	1	–	1,520
	Total			1		1,520

[a]Rating points are not available for the spot campaign, as all spots are run-of-station. Therefore, the buying of spot space is done on the basis of the dominant radio station per area. However, historical surveys of the sustaining radio programs sponsored by the firm in the key areas have an average rating of 12 percent of the total potential listening audience.

[b]The total number of radio homes in the Philippine Islands is 2,393,000. Thus, the ten main radio areas listed comprise 99.9 percent of the total figure.

[c]A breakdown of costs on a regional basis is not available for the revised campaign.

[d]Radioprogramas del Peru (R.P.P.) is a national network that covers the main urban areas of Lima, Iquitos, Piura, Chiclayo, Trujillo, Chimbote, Huancayo, Ica, Arequipa, Cuzco, Barranca, and Tumbes.

[e]An average figure; thus a discrepancy exists between the total number of spots and its components due to the rounding-off process.

[f]The estimated number of radio homes in Peru is 2,000,000. Thus, the twelve (12) main urban radio areas listed in footnote d comprise 38.7 percent of the total figure.

Country	Geographical Region	Number of Weeks		Spots Per Week		Coverage Rating Points	Cost per Thousand Coverage	Total Cost	Percentage of Total Advertising Budget
		60 sec.	30 sec.	60 sec.	30 sec.				
United Kingdom		Not in use at present							
Germany		Not in use at present							
Philippine Is.	Manila	52	—	24	—	a	N/A		
	NW Luzon	52	52	96	168				
	NE Luzon	52	—	48	—				
	Central Luzon	—	52	—	56				
	S. Tagalog	52	52	48	56				
	Bicol Region	52	52	24	56				
	Cent./E. Visayas	52	52	120	84				
	W. Visayas	52	52	240	168				
	W. Mindanao	52	52	72	280				
	E. Mindanao	52	52	112	112				
	Total			784	980			₱346,300[c]	28.3
Peru	R.P.P.[d]	—	36	—	42[e]	N/A	N/A	663,500	
	Total				42			s/663,500	15.4

[a] Rating points are not available for the spot campaign, as all spots are run-of-station. Therefore, the buying of spot space is done on the basis of the dominant radio station per area. However, historical surveys of the sustaining radio programs sponsored by the firm in the key areas have an average rating of 12 percent of the total potential listening audience.

[b] The total number of radio homes in the Philippine Islands is 2,393,000. Thus, the ten main radio areas listed comprise 99.9 percent of the total figure.

[c] A breakdown of costs on a regional basis is not available for the revised campaign.

[d] Radioprogramas del Peru (R.P.P.) is a national network that covers the main urban areas of Lima, Iquitos, Piura, Chiclayo, Trujillo, Chimbote, Huancayo, Ica, Arequipa, Cuzco, Barranca, and Tumbes.

[e] An average figure; thus a discrepancy exists between the total number of spots and its components due to the rounding-off process.

[f] The estimated number of radio homes in Peru is 2,000,000. Thus, the twelve (12) main urban radio areas listed in footnote d comprise 38.7 percent of the total figure.

TABLE 6
Television Air Time Costs by Market Area—1970

Country	Region	TV Homes (Thousands)	Percentage of Penetration[a]	Number of Weeks	Average Total Spots and Length of Spots (Sec.)	Gross Rating Points[b]	Average Cost per Thousand	Total Cost	Percentage of Total Advertising Budget
United Kingdom (£)	London	4,136	83	36	122x30	2916	19/3		
	Midlands	2,545	83	31	98x30	2275	18/5		
	Lancashire	2,357	86	20	63x30	1680	17/2		
	Yorkshire	1,822	72	18	56x30	1332	18/8		
	C. Scotland	1,146	84	14	42x30	1092	14/9		
	Southern	1,204	72	37	159x30	3498	16/8		
	Harlech	1,206	79	31	98x30	2340	16/2		
	Tyne-Tees	824	89	23	72x30	1968	15/5		
	Anglia	993	70	37	150x30	2900	17/7		
	Westward	436	77	31	101x30	2546	14/6		
	Border	162	85	14	42x30	812	22/8		
	Grampian	311	59	14	44x30	899	22/10		
	Total	17,142	90[c]					£325,048	84.8
Germany (DM)	North	3,130							
	West	4,320							
	Hessia	1,280							
	South/S.W.	2,600							
	Bavaria	2,150							
	Berlin	700			30x30				
	Saar	270			52x15				
	Total	14,450	85.8[d]	N/A		–	5.30/3.40[e]	1,494,000 DM[f]	33.0
Philippine Is. (₱)	Greater Manila	350	7.3	52	554x26[g]	N/A	N/A	193,500	
	Cebu[h]	10	3.0	–	–	–	–	–	
	Bacolod[h]	5	0.9	–	–	–	–	–	
	Davao[h]	3	2.0	–	–	–	–	–	
	Total	368	4.7	52	554x26	–	–	₱193,500	15.8

Country	Region	TV Homes (Thousands)	Percentage of Penetration[a]	Number of Weeks	Average Total Spots and Length of Spots (Sec.)	Gross Rating Points[b]	Average Cost per Thousand	Total Cost	Percentage of Total Advertising Budget
Peru (s/)	Lima-Callao	250.0	44	33	890x10&20	N/A	14.6	1,925,500	44.7
	Arequipa	17.6	40	—	—	—	—	—	
	Chiclayo	18.8	19	—	—	—	—	—	
	Trujillo	8.2	20	—	—	—	—	—	
	Piura	4.5	14	—	—	—	—	—	
	Chimbote	4.5	25	—	—	—	—	—	
	Provincial Spillover[i]	20.7	—	—	—	N/A	—	—	
	Total	324.3	34[j]	33	890x10&20	—	s/14.6	s/1,925,500	44.7

[a]The percentages are based upon the rate of television home penetration within each region by the channels utilized by International Foods.

[b]Gross rating points are established through a national panel which incorporates the use of SET meters, which are attached to the receivers in the home to record on/off and channel changes, and diaries which detail home audience participation. The reports show home and individual ratings in quarter-hour segments as percentages of the maximum potential audience. This information is used to project estimates of future rating expectations. Thus, for example, if 35 percent of the potential audience viewed a particular segment and the advertising campaign showed fifty spots, then the gross rating points for this campaign would be 50 times 35, totaling 1,750.

[c]Only one commercial channel (ITV) is available, as the two BBC channels are noncommercial.

[d]Represents the utilization of two channels—ARD (Channel I) and ZDT (Channel II).

[e]This figure represents an average cost per 1,000 viewers of 5.30 DM for Channel I and 3.40 DM for Channel II.

[f]The total cost figure represents the combined costs of ARD (743,000 DM) and ZDT (751,000 DM).

[g]The average total spots are broken down into average introductory spots per week (21) and average sustaining spots per week (14).

[h]Bonus replays in these three areas by the Manila channels of four programs in which International Foods participates as a sponsor.

[i]Provincial spillover represents fringe penetration of broadcasts from the six urban areas. Channel 5 covers the areas of Piura, Trujillo, Chimbote, Cuzco, Huancayo, and Arequipa, while Channel 4 covers some small towns.

[j]Based on the utilization of two channels and the number of urban homes (954,200) with urban television homes (324,300).

461

TABLE 7

Newspaper Costs by Market Area—1970

Country	Publication	Circulation	Cost per Full Page	Number of Inserts	Percentage Coverage Male	Percentage Coverage Female	Cost per Thousand Circulation		Total Cost	Percentage of Total Advertising Budget
United Kingdom (£)	Sunday Times color supplement	1,461,000	3,176[a]	8	12[b]	10[b]	£1/7/1		25,408	
	Total	1,461,000		8					£25,408	5.4
Germany (DM)	Not used at this time as no newspaper qualifies as a national publication.									
Philippine Is. (₱)	Manila Times	223,800		10[c]	50	50	₱5.39		56,500[d]	
	Total	223,800		10					₱56,500	4.6
Peru (s/)	El Pueblo[e]	14,000	12,000	5	47.9[f]	52.1[f]	Male s/1194	Female s/1096		
	Correo[e]	12,000	6,480	5	40.0	60.0	1350	900		
	Total	26,000		10					s/38,000	0.9

[a] A four-color specially negotiated rate.
[b] Percent of the national population.
[c] The size of the insert is 7 by 20 column inches—approximately 4/5 page.
[d] In addition to the general introductory "Dairy Fresh" campaign this figure also includes the space costs of cooperative ads with the supermarkets during special sales and in-store promotions.
[e] Both newspapers are located in Arequipa—no newspaper campaign is conducted in other Peruvian cities.
[f] Percentage of circulation.

462

TABLE 8

Consumer Magazines Costs by Market Area—1970

Country	Publication	Circulation (Thousands)	Issue Frequency	Number of Inserts	S-E.C. Reached	Page Costs	
						B/W	Color
United Kingdom (£)		Not used at this time					
Germany (DM)	Stern	1,689.0	Weekly	9	All	28,400	51,200
	TV Hören und Sehen	1,525.8	Weekly	9	All	22,000	35,200
	Für Sie	1,110.4	Biweekly	9	All	20,000	36,000
	Brigitte	1,001.1	Biweekly	6	All	19,000	34,000
	Eltern	1,002.8	Monthly	4	All	18,600	32,000
	Ich und Meine Familie	347.0	Monthly	4	All		24,000
	Total	7,176.1	—	41	—		—
Philippine Is. (₱)	Bisaya	80.1	Weekly	24	C,D	459	596
	Weekly Women's	105.6	Weekly	28	B,C	1,062	1,513
	Hiligaynon	52.7	Weekly	24	C,D	459	596
	Total	238.4		76			
Peru (s/)		Not used at this time					

[a] A breakdown of audience coverage rates on a male-female basis is not available. The firm has stated that the magazine covers 2.1 percent of the total population with a circulation of 847,000.

TABLE 8—continued

| Country | Publication | Coverage | | | | Cost per Thousand Circulation | | Total Costs | Percentage of Total Advertising Budget |
		Percentage Male	Total Audience (Thousands)	Percentage Female	Total Audience (Thousands)	Male	Female		
United Kingdom (£)		Not used at this time							
Germany (DM)	Stern	26.9		22.8		9.36	9.93	495,000	
	TV Hören und Sehen	11.0		10.3		15.80	15.21	353,000	
	Für Sie	5.7		15.7		31.57	10.32	385,000	
	Brigitte	5.2		14.9		29.61	9.21	261,000	
	Eltern	10.6		14.5		15.15	9.96	217,000	
	Ich und Meine Familie	a		a		N/A	N/A	132,000	
	Total					–	–	1,872,000	41.3
Philippine Is. (₱)	Bisaya Weekly	48	38.5	52	41.7	1.55	1.43	13,200	
	Women's	36	38.0	64	67.6	4.19	2.36	43,500	
	Hiligaynon	48	25.3	52	27.4	2.36	2.18	13,200	
	Total							69,900	5.7
Peru (s/)		Not used at this time							

[a] A breakdown of audience coverage rates on a male-female basis is not available. The firm has stated that the magazine covers 2.1 percent of the total population with a circulation of 847,000.

464

TABLE 9

Medical Journals Costs by Market Area—1970

Country	Publication	Circulation (Thousands)	Issue Frequency	Number of Inserts	Size of Inserts	Page Cost	Total Cost	Percentage of Total Advertising Budget
United Kingdom (£)	Archives of Disease in Childhood	3.60	Bimonthly	6	Page (all publications)	53	318	
	Medical Officer	1.85	Biweekly	6[a]		35	210	
	Midwives Chronicle and Nursing Notes	17.00	Monthly	6[a]		57	342	
	Health Visitor	5.00	Monthly	6[a]		55	330	
	M.I.M.S.	28.70	Quarterly	4[a]		102	408	
	Paediatric Practitioner	33.69	Monthly	6		119	714	
	Total	89.84		34			£2,322	0.5
Germany (DM)	4 pediatric journals	7.75	Monthly	16	Page or similar size (all publications)	Average price per page is 900 DM		
	Gynaecology Journal	4.00	Monthly	4				
	Medical Nutrition	6.00	Monthly	6				
	2 general medical journals	48.20	Monthly	8				
	2 nursing journals and calendars	}	Monthly	} 17				
	2 midwives journals and calendars	66.90	Monthly					
	Total	132.85		51			39,000 DM[b]	0.9
Philippine Is. (₱)			Not used at this time					
Peru (s/)	Revista Peruana de Pediatría	2.00	Quarterly	4	Page	2,500	10,000	
	Total	2.00		4			s/10,000	0.2

[a]Special Series Rates
[b]Includes Production Costs of 3,000 to 4,000 DM.

TABLE 10

Lay Baby Periodicals Costs by Market Area—1970

Country	Publication	Circulation (Thousands)	Issue Frequency	Number of Inserts	Page Costs	Total Space Costs	Percentage of Total Advertising Budget
United Kingdom (£)	Mother and Baby	16.00	Monthly	6	180	1,080	
	You and Your Baby	300.00	Annually	1	3,852	3,852	
	Mother	115.16	Monthly	6	420	2,520	
	Mother Magazine						
	Book of Baby Care	720.00	Annually	1	3,334[a]	3,334	
	Baby Pictorial	100.00	Quarterly	4	206[b]	824	
	Bounty Baby Book	600.00	Annually	1	3,000	3,000	
	Total	1,851.16		19		£14,610	3.1
Germany (DM)			Not used at this time				
Philippine Is. (₱)			Not used at this time				
Peru (s/)			Not used at this time				

[a]Accounts for a 16-2/3 percent discount in consideration of the twelve-page series.
[b]One-half page B/W—all other inserts are two facing pages B/W.

466

TABLE 11

Trade Magazine Costs by Market Area—1970

Country	Publication	Circulation	Issue Frequency	Number of Inserts	Page Costs	Coverage Percentages	Total Cost	Percentage of Total Advertising Budget
United Kingdom (£)			Not used at this time					
Germany (DM)	Lebensmittelzeitung		Weekly	4	3,750		15,000	
	Ten others		Biweekly and Monthly	10	1,500		15,000	
	Total	167,700		14			30,000	0.7
Philippine Island (₱)			Not used at this time					
Peru (s/)	Man Shing Po	5,000	Daily	7	4,400	40/50[a]	6,000	
	La Voz de la Colonia China	5,000	Daily	8	5,000	40/50	7,000	
	Oriental[b]	10,000	Monthly	2	15,000	70/80	16,000	
	Nikko[b]	8,000	Monthly	1	12,000	70/80	6,500	
	Total	28,000		18			s/35,500	0.8

[a]These readership percentages are for wholesalers and for bodegas.
[b]Oriental is aimed at the Chinese community, while Nikko is devoted to the Japanese community.

TABLE 12

Medical Promotion Costs by Market Area—1970[a]

	United Kingdom (£)	Germany (DM)	Philippine Is. (P)	Peru (s/)
Medical literature	10,630	49,000	–	364,000
Medical samples	850	46,000	15,500	160,000[b]
Medical exhibitions, congresses, and conventions	1,325	16,000	–	50,000
Other medical	2,300	21,000	–	–
Total	£15,105	132,000 DM	₱15,500	s/574,000
Percentage of total advertising budget	3.2	2.9	1.3	13.3

[a]Excludes medical journal advertising and appropriate salaries.
[b]A composite figure of samples distributed to doctors (s/60,000) and a bonus program of one free case per every ten purchased by hospitals (s/100,000).

The broad spectrum of potential uses and the free recipe book appeal to the wide range of tastes within the target market.

The major 1970 TV innovation, aside from new color commercials, was revising the regional marketing weight priority schedule to reflect the latest available data on product consumption, brand consumption, and brand competitiveness. Other media simply support the major role of television, to which 88 percent of the mass media budget is allocated. Newspapers are used to counteract the downward bias of the television audience, thereby assuring increased impact among the upper-class housewives. Baby periodicals for laymen and the medical journals are used to implement the infant feeding campaign.

The media campaigns are augmented by a school program, a public relations campaign, and consumer promotions. Yet, the supplemental nature of these programs is clear when the mass media budget as a percentage of the total advertising budget is calculated—approximately 81 percent.

Development Pattern.

(i) *Radio.* Because the British Broadcasting Company bans commercials, radio promotion is not possible in the United Kingdom. Neither of the two possible alternatives—Radio Luxemburg and Radio Manx—appeals to the target audience, and both have low penetration of the total potential audience. A decisive factor in precluding radio advertising is the need for visual demonstration of the overall creative strategy of the brand—"Open a can of Lancer. It has many uses."

(ii) *Television.* Because the BBC cannot use commercial advertising, IFI has resorted to the Independent Television Authority (ITA) network in its promotional strategy. As Table 6 shows, ITA has a penetration ratio of 90 percent of the 17.1 million households which can receive its programming.

IFI's policy of media strategy is "to concentrate the bulk of our effort into National Television using thirty-second spots on all channels . . . [and] to generate

TABLE 13

Promotional Advertising Costs by Market Area—1970

	United Kingdom (£)	Germany (DM)	Philippine Is. (P)	Peru (s/)
Dealer materials	25,000	200,000[a]	92,000	263,000
Consumer promotions	10,000	190,000[b]	100,000	–
Demonstrations	–	146,000	–	–
Literature	21,865	–	–	–
Samples	–	–	11,500	–
Store promotion	–	–	22,000[c]	225,000[d]
Total	£56,865	536,000 DM	₱225,500	s/488,000
Percentage of total advertising budget	12.1	11.8	18.4	11.3

[a]Includes 54,000 DM for production costs.
[b]This amount is essentially for prizes in consumer contests which are conducted in connection with special print media advertisements and television spots. The media costs for this campaign are included in the appropriate media schedules.
[c]To purchase choice display space positions in the larger retail outlets. (see Table 3).
[d]This represents additional press cost figures to purchase space in the special weekly newspaper advertisements of the supermarket chain stores, plus the value of one free case in every 100 they purchase for this special.

TABLE 14

Special Promotional Expenditures by Market Area—1970

	United Kingdom		Germany		Philippine Is.		Peru	
	£	Percent	DM	Percent	₱	Percent	s/	Percent
Medical promotion	15,105	84.6	132,000	42.9	15,500	15.6	574,000	100
School campaigns	2,750	15.4	–	–	20,000	20.2	–	–
Audio visual	–	–	–	–	63,760	64.2	–	–
Free samples	–	–	175,000	57.1	–	–	–	–
Total special promotions	17,855	100	307,000	100	99,260	100	574,000	100

TABLE 15

Marketing and Advertising Research Costs by Market Area—1970

	United Kingdom (£)	Germany (DM)	Philippine Is. (₱)	Peru (s/)
Market and advertising research	7,000	82,000	14,300	220,400
School campaign research	250	–	–	–
Total	7,250	82,000	14,300	220,400
Percentage of total advertising budget	1.5	1.8	1.2	5.1

increased awareness, a more favorable attitude and higher consumption amongst younger, better-off housewives by making a special effort against this sector of the market." National television is an effective medium to reach the mass housewife market, as 87 percent of all households have TV. It is equally evident, from Table 6, that the promotional strategy is not implemented uniformly across the different Nielsen areas. To meet competitive factors and to strengthen IFI's market share in these areas, the promotional strategy calls for weighting television advertising to meet regional requirements and to increase the rate of media exposure frequency in the areas of maximum need.

To ascertain the marketing priority weights IFI identified three vital and interrelated factors:

1. Total evaporated milk consumption expressed on a cans-per-capita basis;
2. Consumption per capita [of Lancer milk and other IFI brands], and
3. Consumption per capita of private labels which constitute the primary marketing threat to IFI.

Using the data generated by these factors a simple weighting formula is applied: (1) – (2) + (3). The first phase of the formula, (1) – (2), gives priority to areas with a high per capita consumption pattern of evaporated milk, while identifying those areas in which IFI has maximum potential for increasing its market share. By adding (3), per capita consumption of private labels, the priorities are increased in those areas which show the greatest strength of the private labels. Once derived, these marketing weights are used to ascertain the most efficient deployment strategy for budget allocation: they show the areas in which the firm faces the greatest competition and those in which the largest gains can be obtained. From the number of weeks and total number of spots in Table 6, it is clear that the areas to which the weighting system gives priority are Southern, Anglia, and London, followed, as an intermediate cluster, by Westward, Midlands, and Harlech. These areas will receive increased exposure frequency as a result of competitive pressures and because the seasonal consumption pattern in the southern portion of the country appears to be leveling out from the summer sales peak to a relatively uniform annual sales pattern. The strategy for the remaining areas (Lancashire, Yorkshire, Tyne-Tees, Central Scotland, Border, and Grampian) is confined to the seasonally peak sales period between late April and November. The firm also states that the budget allocation for each area should be used to purchase spots in a series of short, relatively concentrated bursts to maximize consumer impact. The length of each burst and the time lag between them varies according to the allocated number of peak viewing audience spots (TG30E's) for each area. This allocation of peak spots is obtained by applying marketing priority weights and a newly introduced system of impact equalization which attempts to relate the dynamic characteristics of the viewing audience to the marketing needs. The general principle is that it is necessary to reach a realistic compromise between the demands of obtaining the maximum possible impact during the burst and reducing the periods of no audience coverage to a minimum.

The creative execution of the strategy for the year is to introduce three new commercials. These new spots will retain and develop the essential qualities of the famous gourmets who are very well remembered and well liked. In addition, the commercials will present a variety of suggestions for everyday usage of Lancer to underscore the product's versatility and value in food preparation.

In November 1969 ITA introduced color television in London and almost simultaneously on the larger regional stations. IFI was ready with three new color commercials made at a budgeted cost of £13,000 (2.8 percent of the total advertising budget). The budgeted space costs were £325,048 (84.8 percent), a 2.2 percent increase over 1969 to reflect increased space costs.

(iii) *Newspapers.* Because television viewing patterns are relatively weaker in the higher socioeconomic classifications, IFI continues to use the *Sunday Times Magazine*[3] color supplement in the belief that it is more effective with this audience than the less expensive women's weekly magazines. To implement this strategy the firm commissioned six new full-page color advertisements which develop the versatility theme and offer a free recipe book.

(iv) *Consumer Magazines.* IFI has stated that the color supplements are believed to be more effective in communicating the brand's message to the younger, AB housewives than the superficially more economical women's weekly magazines. The three magazines which have an AB upward bias (*Radio Times, TV Times,* and the *Reader's Digest*) have a per issue circulation of 8,746,000. These titles provide an average coverage ratio of 26 percent of adult women at a cost per 1,000 women of 15 shillings 3 pence.

(v) *Trade Press.* International Foods engaged in a trade press campaign during the current fiscal year. However, the relevant expenditures are budgeted as public relations costs (*see* Section x).

(vi) *Outdoor.* IFI does not use outdoor advertising in the United Kingdom.

(vii) *Infant Feeding Campaign.* The infant feeding campaign strategy in the United Kingdom differs from that followed in the other markets in that the promotional efforts are oriented both to the medical profession and to the relevant sector of the consumer market.

IFI's medical campaign objective, to remind the medical profession continually of the appropriateness of the brand as a bottle feeder, is implemented by constant support for the medical detailists in their contacts with the profession. This objective is further pursued through two distinct strategies: a medical journal campaign and a medical promotional effort. The campaign's objective in the print media is to remind the target market of the convenience and excellence of the brand which they can recommend with confidence as a substitute for mother's milk. The creative strategy, detailed in Table 9, utilizes one new full-page advertisement in six journals. The use of a single advertisement is designed to present a consistent message to the target audience.

---

3. The *Sunday Times Magazine* is a part of the Thomson Newspaper Ltd. chain which includes sixteen dailies, thirty-three weeklies, and two Sunday editions, in addition to its subsidiary, Scotsman Publications.

The medical promotional strategy is detailed in Table 12. This effort consists of distributing literature, distributing samples to the medical profession, setting up exhibitions at the medical congresses and conventions, and miscellaneous expenses incurred in this effort (excluding salaries and selling expenses). The total allocated budget amounts to £15,105 (3.2 percent of the total advertising budget).

The other portion of the overall infant feeding campaign is advertisements in six publications, generically called lay-baby periodicals (*see* Table 10), whose objective it is to promote the advantages of the brand to expectant and new mothers as an easy, pure, and safe natural milk substitute. This objective requires the use of specially-oriented baby interest magazines and annuals. Because the competition also uses these media heavily, IFI has allocated £14,610 (or 3.1 percent of the total advertising budget) to purchase large, usually double-facing pages, spaced to insure maximum impact upon the audience.

(viii) *School Campaign.* The objective of this campaign is to develop early awareness and brand loyalty among domestic science students; especially to instill, through the formal environment of the school and the teaching personnel, an appreciation of the brand's versatility and ease of usage in elementary cooking.

This program was implemented in 1969 with the distribution of a "teaching aid box file" and four recipe cards in sets of twenty-five to the 3,897 schools which represented a 65 percent response to a direct-mailing campaign. Two additional cards were distributed later. The strategy for 1970 was to complete the basic design of the recipe cards with the distribution of two new cards, to conduct a postal research program to assist in evaluating the program, and to obtain the teachers' estimation of the utility of pursuing the program further.

(ix) *Consumer Promotion.* The consumer promotional activities of the firm are oriented toward achieving two elements of the overall marketing objectives. First, a completely new recipe book highlighting specific uses for the brand in food preparation was to be developed. These recipe books, introduced in October 1970, were to continue the promotional strategy of mailing free cookbooks upon request. The promotional medium has been to offer the consumer the recipe book through the print media advertising and by an offer on the brand's label.

Second, the sampling program for purchasers of new gas stoves was to be continued. IFI, in conjunction with other firms, contracted with Gift Pax Ltd. for the distribution of a free parcel of goods, including a six-ounce can of Lancer and the Lancer recipe book. Consumer surveys found that the program conducted during 1969 was successful, especially in influencing the younger age groups and newlyweds, a particularly difficult segment to influence.

International Foods, Ltd. also allocated expenditures for additional consumer promotional activities: in-store contests and an arrangement with Belfast Distribution Ltd. to promote the brand in the somewhat neglected area of Northern Ireland. IFI's three seasonal promotions—during Christmas, Easter, and the summer—featured special theme units and posters, stack cards, shelf talkers, and recipe folders, at a total budgeted expense of £12,450. The packaging and distribution of the dealer materials was contracted out to Dumfries Ltd. at a cost of £4,550. Thus the total expenditure budgeted for the dealer materials involved in the consumer promotional campaign is £25,000 (*see* Table 14). This allocation does not include the tie-in advertising expenses involved.

(x) *Public Relations*. International Foods Ltd. has contracted with the Bureau of Commercial Information Ltd., at a fee of £2,500 plus expenses, for a public relations campaign to feature three objectives within the total configuration of the firm's general marketing objectives. First, the firm desires to consolidate the Lancer Milk Bureau and the Junior Tasting Panel by the efficient servicing of the printed media's home economist editors. The firm also wishes to develop a Lancer demonstration program with the various Gas Boards and Electricity Councils. Lastly, the firm desires to develop a strong relationship between the company and the grocery trade press. The expenses, at cost, to implement these programs have been allocated at £2,000. These expenditures cover such items as photography, demonstrations, postage, stationery, trade press releases, and entertainment. The detailed proposals for these public relations campaigns are contained in a separate, all-products document entitled *Public Relations Plans for 1970.*

Advertising Copy Themes. Although television plays the dominant advertising role for the product, the copy discussed below pertains to the print media and point of purchase activities. However, this emphasis does not detract from the presentation as a whole in that this material is essentially an inanimate duplication of the visual themes presented in the television advertisements. The central theme dominating all copy, excepting the specially-oriented infant feeding campaign materials, is that of the multiplicity of uses for the product.

Domination of all copy by the brand's name and logotype is achieved by using color solely to represent the can and by placing the can to dominate the entire page. Once the consumer's attention is held, a short verbal text reinforces the central theme by demonstrating some of the product's potential uses and by offering a free recipe book. Figure 2, as an example, graphically shows this entire advertising format by depicting a can of Lancer and saying that the brand can be used in many ways.

Both the mass print media and the consumer promotional activities stress the multiplicity of Lancer's uses. The point-of-purchase campaigns also emphasize Lancer's creaminess and ease of use. During holiday seasons the in-store promotions, as distinct from the mass print media, exude an aura of friendliness and personal rapport with the consumer while maintaining the versatility theme.

The copy used in the infant feeding campaign relates to the brand's use in bottle feeding and does not emphasize the multiple use theme which is stressed in all other target markets. Again, however, the potential consumer's attention is drawn to the brand by means of color and dominant location. The copy emphasis is on the brand's naturalness, the safety of its use, and its ease of preparation. These three central elements of the copy provide the consumer with an overall tone for the brand that stresses the baby's happiness, the complete confidence that a mother can have in the product, and a sense of perceiving the baby and IFI as being inseparable.

FIGURE 2

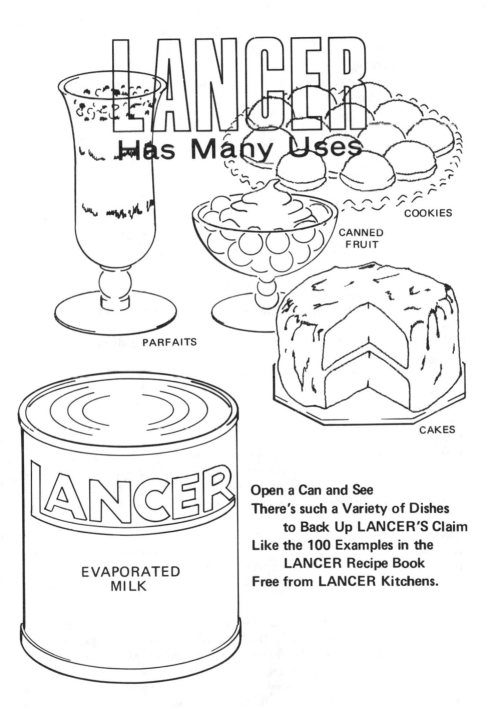

LANCER
Has Many Uses

PARFAITS

COOKIES

CANNED
FRUIT

CAKES

LANCER
EVAPORATED
MILK

Open a Can and See
There's such a Variety of Dishes
    to Back Up LANCER'S Claim
Like the 100 Examples in the
    LANCER Recipe Book
Free from LANCER Kitchens.

Germany

Consumer Profile. IFI's typical S&A brand consumer is an older, conservative housewife who views the product as a typical evaporated milk. But she does not see S & A milk as a typical coffee creamer.

Promotional Strategy. IFI's promotional goal is to create the response that S & A is the best evaporated milk. The communications objectives should specifically accomplish the following:

1. Secure brand leadership of S & A.
2. Attract the indifferent consumers—those who are not quality or price conscious, those who buy by cheapest price, and those new consumers who have not formed attitudes regarding the product.
3. Attract consumers away from the competition.
4. Create brand loyalty among S & A consumers to prevent their defection to the competition.
5. Evoke a strong positive association in the minds of potential consumers.
6. Create a brand image conducive to a strong sympathetic response among the target audience.

The problem in the market is twofold: the brand image is weak and product sales must be motivated through consumer involvement in the product, its advertising, and promotion.

If the creative strategists fulfill their function, the target audience should notice the promotional activities, be activated by them, and find them interesting and original. To counteract previous advertising, which was deemed inconspicuous and boring, IFI changed advertising agencies in 1969.

The creative strategy relies primarily upon two media as the principal vehicles for creating this new brand image: television and consumer magazines. IFI regards television as a suggestive medium which establishes rapid comprehension of the promotional message by combining audio and visual stimuli to create a profound impact upon the consumers' perceptive senses. It also offers comprehensive coverage of the target market. IFI restricts its use of the print media to general-interest, woman-oriented periodicals which cover all socio-economic groupings.

For supportive and specialized coverage, IFI also employs a medical campaign emphasizing S & A's advantages for infant feeding, a limited trade press campaign aimed at the retail outlets, and an active point-of-purchase campaign. These promotional efforts are supported by magazine advertisements. Above all, the primary target is the young, active housewife.

Deployment Pattern.

(i) *Radio.* This medium is not used by IFI in that no national network is available, but rather radio programming is conducted by a myriad of regional stations. Thus, the inherent costs of advertisement development and placement are regarded to be prohibitive in light of the potential impact upon the target audience.

(ii) *Television.* Nine separate and independent but similarly organized broadcasting corporations were set up in West Germany after World War II. Each corporation received a federal tax exemption and was totally financed by advertising and radio-receiver licensing fees. Although all corporations cooperate informally on programming exchanges, technical and legal problems, and long-term planning, the need for a central coordinating agency was recognized.

On June 9, 1950 such an agency was formed, the Arbeitsgemeinschaft der Öffentlich-Rechtlichen Rundfunkanstalten der Bundesrepublik Deutschland (The Consortium of Chartered Broadcasting Corporations of the Federal Republic of Germany), commonly known as ARD. Its stated purposes are "to further the common interests of the broadcasting organizations" and "to deal with common program problems and common questions of a legal, technical, and operational nature."[4] ARD began television programming in 1954, but it was not until November 3, 1956 that commercial advertising was instituted for the first time by the Munich channel.

To offset ARD's monopoly position, the West German states established on April 1, 1963 a second national public network with similar organizational structure, the Zweites Deutsches Fernsehen (ZDF) [second German television]. ZDF, not subject to direct government control, enjoys total autonomy and does not belong to ARD, although the two networks are required by law to cooperate in assuring balanced and contrasting programming. To avoid taxation of licensing fees and total income, both networks established special subsidiaries to manage advertising income.

The use of television as a promotional medium is subject to several general restrictions applicable to both networks equally, in addition to constraints applicable to specific products. The following list represents some of the major limitations:

1. Commercial spot advertisements are permitted only during the six weekday hours of six to eight p.m. during four time blocks—two of seven-minutes and two of six-minutes.
2. The length of the spots is limited to fifteen, twenty, thirty, forty-five, or sixty seconds.
3. Only products may be advertised—promotional spots for individuals, organizations, and services are prohibited.
4. The use of comparatives or superlatives in the copy must be provable.
5. The words "best" or "better" cannot be used except with reference to another product, and then must be provable.
6. Contests promoted via the medium must be open to everyone.
7. The value of gifts or premiums offered in a spot are controlled as a percentage of the value of the product.
8. Samples offered are restricted to one-use units.
9. Medical or dental testimonials are prohibited.
10. The advertisement cannot refer to, or imitate, competitors.
11. Sponsorship of programming is prohibited.

Despite the restrictions, especially those relating to the amount of commercial time available, the medium accounts for approximately 10 percent of the total

---

4. Burton Palu, *Broadcasting on the European Continent* (Minneapolis: University of Minnesota Press, 1967), p. 65.

advertising expenditures of Germany. The demand for advertising spots far exceeds the supply available, leading to allegations of influence peddling. It is common practice among the advertising agencies who purchase commercial time to overbook their clients' needs, knowing that any excess can be easily redistributed. As one ad executive stated, "We must overestimate our clients' time needs. It's only self-defense."[5] As a result, it is common for all the available commercial time to be sold by September 1 of the previous year.

IFI adheres to a single criterion in its use of television: to purchase the maximum available time in order to minimize the restrictions on commercial advertising spots. Of the West German TV audience, estimated at 78 percent of the 21.6 million households, ARD and ZDF claim a coverage ratio of 85.8 percent of those households with television (14.45 million).

The deployment pattern of IFI's campaign emphasized spots of fifteen and thirty seconds duration. ARD will air fifteen thirty-second spots and twenty-six fifteen-second spots at an average cost per 1,000 contacts of DM 5.30. IFI's total space costs for ARD are DM 743,000. Deployment on ZDF features the identical number and type of spots, although the average cost per 1,000 viewers is substantially less, DM 3.40, based on a total space times cost of DM 751,000. Thus, with a total space expenditure of DM 1,494,000 (in addition to DM 100,000 for production costs) which represents 44.6 percent of the total advertising budget, IFI has purchased a total of 82 spots, or an average of 1.6 spots per week (*see* Table 5). This limited number of spots is spread over the entire year, making the frequency of the spots quite marginal. As a consequence of the spot restrictions and the strength of the medium's impact, IFI does not utilize a rating point system in assessing the impact of its specific spots and time allocations.

(iii) *Newspapers.* International Foods follows a policy of utilizing this medium only when a newspaper's circulation figures imply national coverage. Currently the newspapers of West Germany are regionally oriented, and as such, do not satisfy the criterion of being a national publication.

(iv) *Consumer Magazines.* The German print media have changed significantly since World War II. Growth has been very rapid, with more than 5,000 publications of all types having a per-issue circulation of more than 75 million. Pictorial newspapers and magazines have had the greatest growth. Although deplored by "responsible" journalists, the "illustrated" print media is defended as a bona fide addition to a complete and dynamic press industry.[6] The degree cf success of consumer magazines is indicated by the fact that the fourteen major general interest magazines have an audience coverage ratio of 83 percent of the total population. *Stern*, the magazine with the largest circulation, excepting *Hor Zu* (an equivalent of *TV Guide* with a circulation of more than 4.1 million), personifies the nature of the "illustrated" general interest magazines—modified sensationalism which emphasizes the use of gaudy color and photography.

IFI budgeted DM 1,843,000 for consumer magazines (excluding DM 60,000 for production costs), or 53.2 percent of the total advertising budget, predicated upon

5. "German Sponsors Fight for TV Time," *Business Week,* 21 January 1967, p. 94.
6. John C. Merrill, et al., *The Foreign Press* (Baton Rouge: Louisiana State University Press, 1970), p. 137.

a two-point media selection philosophy. The primary emphasis is upon television: ". . . get as much television time as possible, which is limited to twenty minutes per day only." Once the available television time is obtained, the remainder of the advertising media budget oriented toward the general consumer is allocated on the criteria of percentage coverage of the target audience and the cost of reaching 1,000 individuals of that group. The target audience of IFI's promotional campaign is housewives between the ages of twenty and thirty-four in urban areas with more than 20,000 inhabitants.

The deployment pattern of the forty-one inserts (sixteen double pages and twenty-five single pages) is concentrated into five bursts:

1. The beginning of the fiscal year with five single-page inserts.
2. The pre-Christmas season with five double-page advertisements.
3. The first six weeks of 1970 with five double pages and six single pages.
4. April and May with two double pages and six single-page inserts.
5. Mid-summer with six single-page inserts and two double-page advertisements.

These concentrated bursts of print media activity are designed to coincide with the introduction of the various consumer promotional campaigns and contests (*see* Section ix).

(v) *Trade Press.* In an effort to keep the brand before the trade IFI allocated DM 300,000 to purchase space in the trade press (*see* Table 11). Campaign emphasis was on the weekly *Lebensmittelzeitung* (Grocery News) with four full-page black and white inserts. Ten other biweekly and monthly trade publications are also utilized with one full-page insert in each. The deployment pattern called for all the inserts to be concentrated in October 1969. The production of the campaign was budgeted at DM 10,000.

(vi) *Outdoor.* Despite the wide national use of the outdoor medium, especially in the introductory phases of promotional campaigns, the firm did not allocate any funds to this medium for 1970.

(vii) *Infant Feeding Campaign.* The infant feeding campaign focused on the medical profession, concentrating on the five major cities with good distribution in every sales area. In other areas, literature was distributed to doctors, nurses, and midwives.

The literature, including weighing cards, doctor booklets, and medical reprints, was distributed both by the seven medical salesmen (in their approximately 7,000 calls per year) and by mail. Mailing expense covered literature and 960 cases of samples—380 to hospitals, 500 to doctors, and 80 to the parents of triplets, at a total cost of DM 26,000. The total allocation for the cost of the literature was DM 49,000 (*see* Table 12).

An allocation of DM 21,000 was made to cover such promotional items as clinical tests, periodical subscriptions, and medical sales promotion.

The attention of the medical profession is obtained by advertisements in twelve professional monthly periodicals (pediatrics, gynecology, nutrition, general medicine, nursing, and midwifery) with a total circulation per issue of 132,850. Table 9 shows that a total of fifty-one full-page inserts were purchased at a cost (including art and production costs) of DM 39,000. The firm also allocated DM 19,000 for exhibitions at seven medical congresses and five midwives' conventions.

(viii) *School Campaign.* Promotional efforts are not oriented toward the schools, because the primary target audience, twenty to twenty-four years of age, has essentially left the school environment.

(ix) *Consumer Promotion.* The firm's promotional activities during 1969 included a Christmas campaign and a contest for both the consumers and the trade featuring a "Trip to France." The basis for the consumer promotions for 1970 was the brand's trademark and the supporting slogan, "It tastes good." In addition to the in-store promotional efforts, this campaign was supported by short relevant advertisements in consumer magazines.

Four consumer promotions were conducted during the year, in connection with special advertisements and television spots. The first programs, the "Christmas Contest," conducted during November and December 1969, was allotted DM 70,000 to cover the expenditures for fifty winners, who could win whatever they liked within the maximum allowable amount per winner of DM 1,500. To support this contest, DM 5,000 was budgeted for special-theme dealer materials (Christmas posters). Second, a contest featuring verdant fields and dairy cows was conducted during January and February 1970, with ten spring vacations as prizes. The budgeted cost of this contest was DM 50,000 plus DM 40,000 for supportive dealer materials. To stress the slogan, the third promotion—conducted in May and June—used the theme, "S & A tastes good because. . . ." Each of 300 winners was to receive DM 100 in cash. The dealer materials used to call attention to the brand and the contest cost DM 50,000. The final consumer promotion of the year, conducted during July and August, promoted two posters (80,000 in all were available). Budgeted at DM 40,000, the posters were supported by DM 40,000 of dealer materials and were partially self-liquidating.

To supplement these contests, the firm allocated DM 65,000 for additional consumer promotional materials (can openers, plastic bags, and sales programs). Thus, the total budget for dealer materials was DM 200,000 and the final allocated cost of the consumer promotional contest was DM 190,000.

To substantiate the media claims of the brand, and to provide a center of attraction, the firm used eight demonstrators. Each girl presented 220 demonstrations per year in supermarkets, cooperatives, and the larger retail outlets in the district sales region assigned to her. At a cost of DM 83 per demonstration, the total budgeted cost for this supportive campaign was DM 146,000.

Also allocated to demonstration expense was the cost of 800 cases of samples for free distribution. In total, 6,470 cases of free samples were distributed as part of the consumer promotional efforts. These were distributed to salesmen (5,000 cases), production facility visitors (250 cases), exhibitions (70 cases), schools (350 cases), and at demonstrations. The total budgeted costs of this distribution is DM 175,000.

(x) *Public Relations.* The public relations campaign originated by the firm is oriented toward the trade. Thus, the allocated expenditures are described in the section on the trade press (*see* Section v).

Advertising Copy Themes. In the United Kingdom, Peru, and the Philippines, promotional emphasis was upon television, but in Germany, with minimal television space available, the print media and an active in-store promotional campaign were stressed. The campaign stress was perforce verbal rather than visual.

Throughout the year the advertising campaigns carried the central theme of the new campaign—"It tastes good." Point-of-purchase materials reinforced the target consumers' brand awareness. The new theme responded to the existing consumer profile which did not perceive S & A as a typical coffee creamer. Thus, all advertising copy emphasized taste quality as a coffee creamer in an attempt to alter the existing consumers' sense of brand differentiation and to create brand loyalty among the new target market of young urban housewives (Figure 3). As further theme reinforcement, the advertisements emphasized taste enhancement by using rich brown tones as the dominant color. Such tones, conveying warmth, fullness of body, and depth of taste, were augmented in the verbal copy by phrases which emphasized the rich, golden color of coffee creamed with S & A.

In past campaigns both IFI and competitors have emphasized heavily the pastoral origins of milk by depicting verdant fields and herds of dairy cows. This theme was carried into the new S & A campaign by using green extensively as a background color, either for a cup of coffee or the brand's can.

Point-of-purchase advertising, while continuing the campaigns conducted in the print media, also emphasized a distinctive campaign. This was a heavy campaign of consumer contests which, while using the central theme of the brand as a coffee creamer, was singular in its use of artwork in a Peter Max style. The emphasis on vibrant colors and animated representation catches the consumer's eye immediately.

Philippine Islands

Consumer Profile. The profile of the firm's existing consumers of filled evaporated milk is all consumers in the B, C, and D income class homes and the household help in the upper-class (A) homes who purchase the brand for general use.

Promotional Strategy. The basic premise upon which the marketing communications strategy and objectives of IFI-Philippines is formulated is that the filled evaporated milk market is declining. The estimated decrease of approximately 3.5 percent from 1969 to 1970 in industry volume, but with IFI's volume constant at 780,000 cases, produced an increased IFI market share of 278.7 versus 26.8 percent.

IFI's basic objectives are to improve distribution, enlarge the consumer base, and maintain services at an acceptable level. The promotional and advertising campaigns are aimed primarily at efficiently contacting the middle and lower socioeconomic class homes. IFI's market researchers, MARFAC, found that approximately 88 percent of these homes are filled evaporated milk consumers, and that in this

FIGURE 3

It Tastes So Good!

EVAPORATED
MILK

Enjoy the Rich and Creamy Taste of Your Morning Coffee Creamed with S&A

particular market segment the firm's major competitor, Neema, enjoys an approximate three to one advantage over Maria. Population projections for 1969 indicate that approximately 49 percent of the total C and D class homes were on Luzon, 31 percent in the Visayas, and 20 percent on Mindanao. Wherever possible the marketing strategy attempted to align promotional activities with this population distribution.

To achieve the general marketing objectives IFI established five specific campaigns: (1) continued participation in the school promotional program during the first half of the year; (2) continued point-of-purchase promotional efforts, (3) meeting the competition whenever and wherever they resorted to price cutting; (4) continual promotion of Maria for general and kitchen use and for infant feeding (through introduction by the nursery staff at selected large hospitals); and (5) launching a new advertising campaign. IFI felt that attaining these marketing objectives hinged directly on this new campaign. The campaign's introduction was to be delayed until the beginning of 1972 to allow the firm to make the necessary prelaunch preparations; to reduce its inventories, to change the label, and to prepare the advertising campaign. Once launched, the campaign is scheduled to continue for the balance of the year with all programs and promotional activities designed to support it.

In conducting a consumer survey, MARFAC found that in a blind product test, where Maria was measured against the Neema and Tulip brands in home placements, Maria clearly performed better and was better appreciated by consumer housewives than were its primary competitors. With blind test preference high and actual market share low, MARFAC deduced that a brand-linked image prejudice was operating. To counteract this prejudice, IFI completely changed Maria's label.

The advertising strategy emphasized the benefits the consumer housewife would derive from the "new quality product." The historical media mix was used in an attempt to reach every potential consumer housewife:(1) to gain an efficient coverage of the C and D socioeconomic classes in all key areas with maximum frequency and penetration. The emphasis of the effort was in the Greater Manila area, which accounts for the bulk of volume sales, while the balance was divided between Mindanao and the Visayas commensurate to their potential business volume. (2) To employ the media mix which will give the firm the greatest opportunity to accomplish the communications exchange necessary to meet the brand's objectives.

To achieve the objectives of maximum frequency and penetration of C and D socioeconomic households, the firm uses radio nationally as its primary medium to provide maximum impact with television secondary. Print is used extensively to augment the introductory period of the "new" product and to support copy aimed at encouraging the brand's usage in the home. In Manila, however, an entirely different media mix is employed. Television is the primary medium, with radio and print acting as supplements. Both the Manila and the national campaigns are supported by point-of-purchase materials which augment the creative strategy utilized in the other media.

For the first quarter after the introduction of the "new" product the media strategy will employ a heavy frequency of run-of-the-station television spots, radio spots, and print media support to create the maximum impact possible. Subsequently, the product's advertising weights and inserts decreased to a sustaining strategy basis, with the exception of radio.

The creative execution is based on those product claims which received the highest ratings in MARFAC's blind product usage test—as a coffee creamer, a chocolate drink additive, a health drink, and an infant feeder. The firm breaks down the usage on a percentage share of volume sales as follows, although some are not used as a basis for the distribution of expenditures: coffee creamer, 50 percent; drinking food creamer, 25 percent; and fruit creamer, 25 percent.

Promotional Communications Mix.

(i) *Radio.* Philippine radio communications can be divided into four sectors: (1) the central government operating 21 stations, (2) religious organizations with 30 stations, (3) the United States government which controls and operates 47 stations, and (4) private stations, making up the remainder of the 280 station total, are owned by individuals or families with no appearance of a network chain. The stations are well distributed throughout the islands, although 22 percent of the AM stations and all of the FM stations are concentrated in Manila, thus ensuring the total coverage of the estimated 2,393,000 radio homes (or an estimated penetration ratio of 24 percent of the total national population).

The Philippines' population sees radio as its primary communications line for entertainment especially and general news. The medium's importance is further enhanced by the traditional importance placed upon interpersonal communication by the Filipino social structure, for radio is viewed as an interpersonal medium, thus giving it a high degree of credibility. In the provinces radio carried the principal burden of the campaign, and in Manila it played a supportive role to television (*see* Table 5—note the concentration of spots per week, the number of weeks, and the total number of spots). For example, in Manila, with 488,000 radio homes, the radio campaign called for a deployment plan of 1,248 sixty-second spots, while in Western Visayas, with 281,000 radio homes, the deployment plan called for 21,216 spots (12,480 sixty-second spots and 8,736 thirty-second spots), or a total commercial allocation of 280 hours forty-eight minutes of broadcast time.

(ii) *Television.* Television is probably the most popular communications medium in the urban environment, but because of low transmitting power it cannot be received outside the immediate suburbs. Of the 5.5 million national total households, only an estimated 7.3 percent have television sets (401,500 households), of which 42 percent are in the Greater Manila region. Of the thirteen TV stations, six are in Manila and seven are sprinkled throughout the other islands (Cebu, Bacolod, Davao, Minanao, and Luzon).

Television in the Philippines can and should be regarded as two distinct media, depending on the program format and the language spoken. The general style of programming is quite similar to that of the United States, although there are fewer live programs and minimal out-of-studio hook-ups. Yet, within the stylistic format, unlike most other markets, there are definite audience segments in terms of viewing patterns. Programming can be broken into upper class and lower class. It happens that the AB socioeconomic oriented programs are primarily in English, mostly canned American imports—for example, Dean Martin, Tom Jones, Gunsmoke, Walt Disney, and Perry Mason. The programs oriented toward the C and D classes, the firm's target audience, use Tagalog. Like viewers in many parts of the world, Filipinos detest reruns and insist on new programming at all times.

The firm's television strategy, to maximize the brand's impact among the C and D income groups, is implemented by using two methods: (1) Participation in four television programs broadcast in Manila, which have "bonus" replays in Cebu, Bacolod, and Davao. IFI purchases all television properties on the basis of the target audience. Thus, for Maria the firm has bought sponsorship of live, full-length Tagalog programs which feature well-known Filipino personalities in either a comedy or dramatic role. The firm, for another of its products which is oriented toward the AB classifications, also has purchased time on several English-language shows. (2) Purchasing premium, twenty-six second spots over the entire fiscal year. The deployment pattern concentrated heavily on the introduction of the lead-in for the new advertising campaign (twenty-one spots per week) and after the first three months introduced a sustaining program of fourteen advertising spots per week. The total budget allocation was ₱ 193,500 for space costs, plus ₱ 36,000 for commercial production costs. The high percentage of the total advertising budget that production costs assume, as shown in Table 4, is directly related to the firm's participation in live broadcasts.

(iii) *Newspapers.* The extensive Philippines newspaper media are delineated by rural-urban newspaper consumption patterns. In 1968, eighteen of the twenty-two dailies were published in the Greater Manila area, ten in English. Only one newspaper, the *Manila Times*, with a total circulation of 223,800, has enough provincial circulation to warrant attributing to it any national influence. The rural preference for weekly news magazines is reflected in the considerable number of weeklies and biweeklies, most of which are published in Tagalog or are bilingual. The most popular, the *Philippines Free Press*, with a circulation of approximately 100,000 is a grass roots opinion forum.

IFI allocated a total of ₱ 56,000 for space costs, as shown in Table 7, plus ₱ 3,000 for production costs to implement a dually oriented newspaper campaign. The main emphasis of the media efforts was the three-month introductory campaign. To implement this supportive campaign the firm purchased ten 4/5th page inserts (7 by 20 column inches) in the *Manila Times*, to ensure maximum national coverage.

The other portion of the newspaper media activities is a series of cooperative advertisements with retail supermarket outlets during special sales or in-store promotions for the brand. The inserts for these advertisements were fractional pages in black and white. The breakdown between these two distinct campaigns appeared to be as follows: the increased allocation over the 1969 budget of ₱ 30,900 was attributed to the new campaign—i.e., ₱ 25,600.

(iv) *Consumer Magazines.* Both urban and rural residents rely on the general periodical media (with more than 800 titles ranging from weeklies to annuals) for information and reading entertainment. Although 65 percent of the total circulation is within Manila, the rural readership is catered to with the publication of many periodicals either in the local vernacular tongue or in a bilingual format. The most important chain of vernacular publications is the Liwayway group, owned by the Róces family.

These periodicals are auxiliary to radio and television. IFI allocated ₱ 69,900 for space costs and ₱ 10,000 for production costs. The firm bases its media selection upon four criteria: readership profile, circulation, cost, and reproduction (*see* Table 8 for the appropriate figures). IFI uses three periodicals, all owned by the Roces family chain, which represent an example of each type of periodical available in the Philippines:

1. *Weekly Woman's Magazine*, with a circulation of 132,852 is an English language publication with articles of general interest to women. Its penetration of the general marketing target audience (C and D socioeconomic classes) is biased toward the higher income side: C, 55 percent, which ranks the periodical fourth in the ten most popular Filipino publications; and D, 4 percent, which is the lowest rate of penetration.

2. *Hiligaynon* is a weekly bilingual (English and Hiligaynon) publication which stresses entertainment and general news. Its orientation of readership is on the lower part of the target audience: C, 28 percent, or a rank of 9th; and D, 58 percent, which is the second highest penetration ratio.

3. *Bisaya* is a weekly, general interest Cebano language magazine with a circulation of 80,143. Its target penetration rates indicate that its readership is somewhat more uniform among the C and D classifications than the other two periodicals employed: C, 33 percent, which is the eighth ranked rate; and D, 65 percent, which is the highest rate of penetration for the particular socioeconomic class.

(v) *Trade Press.* The firm did not use this medium during 1970.

(vi) *Outdoor.* Although no specific allocations are made for outdoor advertising expenditures, the firm does use small enameled tin signs designed for external advertising. Such signs are especially prevalent in regions such as the Philippines where heat, humidity, and other severe weather conditions make the use of less sturdy signs impractical. The signs feature the brand name and an image of the can. The allocation of P 12,000 for 30,000 signs is contained within the category of dealer materials for consumer promotion in that the primary function of the sign is to call attention to the availability of the brand at a specific retail outlet (*see* Table 14).

(vii) *Infant Feeding Campaign.* The strategy of the infant feeding campaign is to promote the brand's usage in hospital kitchens, as well as for infant feeding in hospitals, health centers, and clinics. To accomplish these efforts the firm employs a field staff of fifteen nurses, whose function it is to contact hospitals, clinics, and doctors, and to demonstrate the advantages of the brand. The nursing staff, made available through the H. Cavigli Trading Company, spends the major portion of its time promoting IFI's other milk products.

The medical representatives pay minimal attention to Maria, a filled milk, because the Philippine health authorities contend that the palm and coconut oil additives, especially the coconut oil, are potentially dangerous to infants. IFI contends that its studies show the filled milk with its oil additives to be every bit as useful to the infant as regular milk.

The inability of IFI and the central government to resolve this difference resulted in a "gentleman's agreement" in which the firm will not publicly advocate the use of filled evaporated milk for infant feeding. Thus, IFI concentrates its infant feeding campaign on its other milk products which have not encountered such difficulties. IFI's basic reason for using the oil additives was its desire to contribute to the development of the Filipino economy. Both parties felt that of the possible indigenous materials available, using the abundant coconut oil would make the best contribution. The government originally fostered the idea, and the Filipino government knew that IFI and its competitors in the domestic American markets had made a similarly constituted product. With this in mind the central government "invited" the industry to consider its usage.

Thus, because of what is essentially a prohibition from any direct consumer-oriented advertising, the firm, through the field nursing staff, promotes the brand indirectly. With the premise that consumers view the medical profession as authoritative opinion leaders, IFI uses the strategy of distributing 650 cases of free samples (at a cost of ₽ 15,500): 450 to hospitals and 100 each to clinics and doctors. Table 12 also shows that the strategy does not utilize any medically oriented literature, periodicals, or exhibitions.

(viii) *School Campaign.* The school campaign can be viewed as two distinct campaigns. In conjunction with the infant feeding campaign, the fifteen-member nursing staff conducts lectures and demonstrations for parent groups in the schools and distributes free samples. The costs of these lectures and of the samples are borne by the infant feeding campaign.

The second program within the total campaign is a label redemption promotion. IFI found that this promotion, conducted during the first half of 1969, contributed to their relatively favorable sales and that the campaign was gaining additional support from the school authorities. The allocation of ₽ 56,200 for 1970, a 30 percent increase over 1969, was intended to expand the program to cover 450 schools all over the country, including the Greater Manila area for the first time. The specific design of the program was to conduct two rounds of promotions, each lasting five months, during the year. Children were to turn in Maria labels, which were assigned points, and accumulated points were exchangeable for school equipment, garden tools, and home economics utensils. The total allocated cost of ₽ 56,200 (*see* Table 13) included the cost for the prizes, the printing of brochures and forms, and the transportation and freight of the materials. The actual handling of this portion of the school campaign was conducted by the audio-visual teams.

(ix) *Consumer Promotions.* IFI's consumer promotional activities are designed to increase brand awareness among the consumers once they are in the retail outlet, to support producer benefits indicated by MARFAC's survey research, and to provide continual reinforcement for the message impact of the advertising media.

The campaign consists of four essential elements: distribution of samples, special in-store promotions, prime space rentals for display, and the distribution of dealer materials (*see* Table 14).

The distribution of free samples is confined to a program of limited consumer sampling and as premiums for the contestants on selected radio and television programs. The use of product prizes is essentially an exchange for brand mention during the show. Of the ₱ 11,500 budgeted for 500 cases, 300 cases go to consumers (including the broadcast giveaways) and 100 cases each go to retailers and wholesalers.

In-store promotion is a continuing program using premiums or special giveaways at supermarkets and large retail outlets. The campaign is designed to increase the consumer's purchasing power by using suitable premiums. The program, instituted on a limited basis and later expanded nationally, used Domino, a cooking oil used almost universally in all household segments of the market. The promotional campaign for 1970 offered a six-pack of tall cans (fourteen ounces) at the regular price plus a free can of Domino worth ₱ 0.45. The cost to IFI for the cooking oil, under a special arrangement with the manufacturer, was ₱ 0.26 per bottle. The special advertising inherent in the campaign consisted of special posters and tie-in advertisements with the supermarkets announcing the offer. The cost per case of this premium offer is broken down as follows:

Cost of premium	8 × ₱ 0.26	₱ 2.08
Packaging		.04
Special posters		.02
Per case		₱ 2.14

IFI considers the feasibility of additional tie-ins to be quite good.

The in-store promotion campaign was also designed to increase Maria's competitiveness in relation to the low price structure of the imported evaporated milks. IFI feels that the campaign was successful in meeting competitive promotional activities. The program was considered an important phase of the total promotional mix for the product in that there is an impressive development of supermarket retailing, both in Manila and the other large population centers of the country. To implement the in-store promotion campaign the firm budgeted ₱ 100,000.

To provide increased competitive leverage in obtaining the prime display positions and shelf space in the supermarkets and large retail outlets IFI allocated ₱ 22,000. This amount permitted rental of choice display space in five supermarkets and included the provision of payment for display space in the smaller retail outlets whenever it was necessary to meet the competition.

An allocation of ₱ 92,000 was made for the cost of producing dealer materials (such as shelf talkers, special price tags, sales banners, streamers, special promotional posters, shopping bags, display units, calendars, and T-shirts). This expenditure also included the costs of developing new materials for the increasing supermarket trade, such as special window posters and in-store streamers. Also included within the total expenditure figure was the cost of materials inherent to introducing the new advertising campaign.

The creative execution for all consumer promotional materials was based on the product claims which derived the highest ratio ratings exhibited in the blind home-usage panel survey conducted by MARFAC.

(x) *Public Relations.* The firm did not make a budgetary allocation for public relations for 1970.

(xi) *Special Promotions.* Table 13 demonstrates a unique feature of IFI's advertising activities in the Philippines—the audio-visual trucks (*see* Part B). The budget allocation covered the cost of operating the trucks and the salaries and expenses of the two-man crews of each unit. The cost allocation of the total appropriation was broken down between advertising costs (80 percent or P 63,760) and the marketing function (20 percent or P 15,940).

Advertising Copy Themes. The advertising copy seeks to emphasize the benefits that the consumer housewife will derive from using the brand. These benefits are based upon those product claims which received the highest ratings in the blind consumer panel conducted by MARFAC. Thus, the primary emphasis of the creative campaign is oriented toward the product's attributes as a coffee creamer (Figure 4). The copy stresses the "rich and creamy" texture of Maria and how its delicious taste improves the coffee. A unique feature of the themes utilized in the mass media campaigns is that much of the copy is aimed, not at the housewife as the purchaser of the product, but at the husband as the major coffee consumer. He is told how fortunate he is to have a good wife who makes him happy by using the brand in his morning coffee. Another campaign, while addressed to the housewife, attempts to relate the firm's infant feeding promotional campaigns to the husband by viewing him as another baby who will squeal with happiness when the housewife creams his coffee with Maria.

The mass media campaigns also employ copy emphasizing Maria's healthful qualities by stressing nutrient value in terms both of original food value and vitamin enrichment. To offset competitive advertising and to augment its own infant feeder promotional activities, IFI stresses that Maria is good for the whole family. This emphasis allows an easy entry into multiple use promotion as a drink for the children, a coffee creamer for the husband, and a cooking ingredient for the housewife. Thus, the rankings of product uses found in the MARFAC research are fully exploited in the advertising themes.

IFI uses two additional themes which are basically unrelated to the brand's product characteristics. The first is a jingle urging the consumers to enjoy the product together. The second calls upon the consumer to share Maria's delicious taste. Both of these themes have implied attributes of the sociability of the consumer and her role in the community as an experienced housewife whose friends regard her opinion highly.

The point-of-purchase campaigns are a direct reflection of the mass media copy, although as is typical in such campaigns, the copy is briefer and more direct in its emphasis. This ensures that the consumer, while recalling the mass media campaigns, is quickly drawn to the product. The in-store materials emphasize the can through graphic representation and the predominant use of the brand's colors—blue and white.

FIGURE 4

Share the Good Taste of

MARIA

MARIA

LECHE EVAPORADA

Rich and Creamy

Nutritious

Good for the Whole Family

Although most of the population speaks Tagalog, and only half speak English, both written and spoken advertising is in English. The audio-visual campaigns of television and radio, which account for 59 percent of the total advertising budget, emphasize English but use Tagalog in jingles. The print media and point-of-purchase campaigns essentially use English, with only the consumer magazines receiving copy in the local dialect.

An interesting aside is that while the mass media production costs are very high, artwork and reproduction quality is quite crude. The major portion of these costs are directly related to the live campaigns on television and the massive campaigns on radio.

Peru

Consumer Profile. The profile of the Maria brand's existing consumer transcends any specific socioeconomic class segmentation in that 72 percent of all Lima/Callao households use evaporated milk. Of the four major uses of milk products infant feeding, cooking, creamers, beverage Maria is especially strong as a creamer, shows relative strength as a mother's milk substitute, but is quite weak in cooking and as a cooking additive.

Promotional Strategy. IFI's marketing communications strategy concentrates upon the A to D socioeconomic classes. The advertisements appeal basically to housewives as the persons who decide upon and direct the family diet. The campaign concentrates primarily in Lima/Callao, where 70 percent of the brand's sales are, using an intensive television campaign, and in the provincial urban centers, using Radioprogramas del Peru as the principal medium. Point-of-purchase consumer promotions and medical promotions are the central supportive strategies.

The basic sales proposition is that both Maria labels will healthfully nourish the entire family because they are 100 percent pure, fresh milk, and that Maria II is enriched with Vitamins A, C, and D and contains less fat.

The objectives of the advertising copy concentrate on three elements: (1) To convince the housewife that Maria is the best milk for every member of the family, regardless of age, (2) to increase housewife awareness of its purity, flavor, freshness, and total nutritional value, and (3) to induce more mothers to use it for infant and child feeding, and in other ways as well.

The creative execution of the promotional efforts emphasizes six elements:

1. To demonstrate specific uses for the product and to illustrate the facility and rapidity of preparation.
2. For the infant feeding market, the copy emphasizes a subtle approach in which the tone and atmosphere is one of human tenderness, while illustrating the health and strength achieved as a result of the brand's use.
3. Adult liquid usage is illustrated by family scenes which exude optimism, health, and joie de vivre.
4. For cooking and baking, the campaign is oriented toward the "taste appeal" of dishes and desserts prepared with Maria.

5. For the enriched label (Maria II), the copy outlines specific advantages of its use in realistic situations.

6. The continued use of the current popular jingle.

Promotional Communications Mix.

(i) *Radio*. Radio is the principal communications medium outside the Greater Lima/Callao area. Because of print media distribution difficulties and extensive rural ownership of transistor radios, radio reaches the largest audience of any medium. It is estimated that there are more than two million radio homes in the country with a national penetration ratio of 76 percent. The popularity of the medium spans all socioeconomic classes throughout Peru, and in many villages and small towns speakers are mounted in the central plaza and played throughout the day.

A profile of the listening audience shows that more than 50 percent of the audience is women plus a very large number of children. On the weekends the differences based on sex are not as marked, but women still dominate. In the urban areas the medium is most widely listened to by the lower socioeconomic groups (50+ percent at peak hours as opposed to 16 percent among the highest classes). Listenership in the rural areas can be presumed to be relatively higher than among the urban lower classifications because of a high rate of illiteracy and the limited available forms of diversion. The peak listening hours, on a national basis, are the late morning to late afternoon (varies between 32 to 42 percent of all radios), while listenership during the evenings approximates 15 to 20 percent. Programming, which tends to be local in scope, relies heavily on music and news. The language of the programming is primarily Spanish, although the two major Indian languages, Aymara and Quechua, are also utilized.

Radio stations must be licensed and conducted in accordance with the General Telecommunications Regulation of 1957. There are 216 legal stations, and many operate illegally. The government-owned station, Radio Nacional, is the largest. Radioprogramas del Peru (RPP), which IFI uses, is the largest private station. Station proliferation doubtless accounts for RPP's small coverage—only 43,500 radio homes per spot in 1969 based on the ratings for 1968. It is estimated that RPP, with its provincial network of stations in the major urban centers (*see* Table 16), covers 60 percent of the total number of urban radio homes (774,000) which have an average number of listeners per set of 4.2 and an average rate of utilization of 57.7 percent at any one time.

In addition to the excellent provincial ranking, several other factors are relevant to IFI's choice of RPP. The station sends and transmits taped programming to all affiliated stations which assures that a standardized high quality programming is transmitted throughout the country. Regional transmission is assured in a medium where contracted regional transmissions are haphazardly followed. There are only thirty four-minute commercial station breaks per day, as opposed to as many as eighty on other regular stations, thereby maximizing impact of each spot.

The firm's use of radio, in conjunction with a massive television campaign in the urban centers, is designed to maximize the marketing objective of maintaining

TABLE 16

Radioprogramas Del Peru

City	Penetration Percentage	Radio Homes	Number of Radio Stations	RPP Ranking
Iquitos	NA	7,600	8	1
Piura	80	23,800	6	1
Chiclayo	91	40,300	8	1
Trujillo	88	36,000	8	1
Chimbote	81	14,700	7	2
Huancayo	78	21,200	12	1
Arequipa	87	38,300	9	2
Cuzco	86	18,900	7	2
Lima/Callao	94	530,800	32	5
Ica	NA	15,100	7	3
Barranca	NA	21,400	2	2
Tumbes	NA	6,900	4	2
Total	—	775,000	111	—

continual advertising pressure on the A to D socioeconomic classifications, which represent 90 percent of the Lima/Callao population and 81.1 percent of the provincial population.

The deployment plan for radio allocates s/663,500 for space costs (plus s/17,000 for production costs) which will provide a frequency pattern of an average of forty-two spots over thirty-six weeks (*see* Table 5).

The creative strategy attempts to strengthen the housewives' brand image of naturalness, purity, flavor, freshness, and total nutritional value. At the same time, the naturalness and healthfulness of the brand is stressed in an attempt to persuade mothers to use Maria for nutritional infant and child feeding. This strategy is promoted by dramatically expounding the advantages of the brand over fresh milk.

(ii) *Television.* Television is probably the most popular communications medium where it is available—the principal urban centers and their periphery. Since commercial television was introduced in 1958, radio listenership and film attendance have declined, but TV continues to grow. There were sixteen TV stations in 1964 (only one more by 1969), but by 1969, of the 954,200 total urban homes, one-third had TV sets. It is estimated that there are 250,000 television sets in the Lima/Callao area with an average of 3.7 viewers per set, or a potential audience of 946,000 persons. The daily average penetration is 45 percent, or 112,500 television receivers in use, with an audience of approximately 416,000 viewers. It has also been estimated that approximately 40 to 50 percent of all sets are in use in the greater Lima area from noon to midnight, with the participation increasing to 67 percent during the peak audience hours of eight to ten p.m. Television set ownership by socioeconomic group is shown in Table 17. The I.V.M.P. survey of June 1968 indicates the following distribution of television ownership in Lima/Callao:

TABLE 17

Distribution of Television Ownership by Socioeconomic Group–Lima/Callao

Socioeconomic Group	Number of Homes (Thousands)	Television Homes (Thousands)	Percentage of Homes with Television
A, B, and C-1	55.0	52.5	95
C-2	165.0	85.2	52
C-3 and D	275.0	105.0	38
E	55.0	7.5	14

There are three essential reasons, both structural and pragmatic, for the emphasis on the Lima/Callao area in the data presented: (1) The medium is concentrated in Lima, with urban provincial coverage effectively distributed by stations in Lima through video tape or retransmission, (2) Data collection outside the capital is haphazard, thus making such data's validity dubious (although the validity of the data collected in Lima/Callao might also be questioned with reason), and (3) 70 percent of IFI's sales are concentrated in the greater Lima area.

The average ratings and share of viewers in Lima from January to April 1969, according to a I.V.M.P. survey, are shown in Table 18.

TABLE 18

Ratings and Viewers

Channel	Average Rating	Average Percentage Share[a]
2	3.9	7.2
4	17.9	43.2
5	19.4	47.0
9	2.2	5.0
11	1.1	2.1

[a]In that these are average figures the total does not equal 100 percent.

In view of the above ratings and percentage share of the audience, the firm decided to use channels 4 and 5 exclusively in Lima, as they cover 90.2 percent of the total potential television audience, thus insuring the maximum consumer impact.

Further grounds for choosing channels 4 and 5 are that they both have regional provincial transmission networks, thus insuring national urban coverage. Channel 4, by using repeating transmission techniques, supplies daily programming directly to the smaller cities of Casma, Huacho, Chancay, Nazca, Ica, Chincha, and Marcona. Using video tape, Channel 5 programming is transmitted, on a one week's delay basis, to the larger cities of Piura, Huancayo, Trujillo, Chimbote, Arequipa, and Cuzco. The provincial retransmission of programming by both stations represents no additional cost to IFI for production or spot coverage.

(iii) *Newspapers.* In 1964 there were 210 newspapers in Peru, 63 of which were highly competitive dailies in the larger urban areas, especially Lima. In the Lima/Callao center there were eleven dailies with a total circulation of 762,000 and an estimated total readership of approximately three times the circulation figure.

In general, Peruvian newspapers used to be strongly political in their editorial tone with the conservative spectrum being the predominant political force. Conservatism was to be expected for the influential dailies were owned and controlled by the wealthy oligarchic elite of Peru. The most influential daily, *El Comercio*, represents the viewpoint of the land-owning elite.[7]

The regional network of newspapers is dominated by three factors: (1) the provincial readership shows a definite preference for newspapers from the capital (*El Pueblo* in Arequipa has the largest circulation of any provincial paper—14,000), (2) the large Lima newspapers provide the national and international news coverage for the local regional papers, and (3) no national media chains exist, excepting the *Correo* which maintains a local staff in those cities where it publishes provincial editions—Arequipa, Piura, Tacna, Huancayo, and Cuzco. The *Correo*, with approximately half of its circulation in Lima, relies on a sensational approach which emphasizes sex and pictures.

IFI's newspaper strategy is to place institutional advertisements in two of the Arequipa dailies, *El Pueblo* and *Correo* (see Table 7). Ten half-page advertisements (five in each newspaper) are run only when the heavy seasonal promotional campaigns overload the effectiveness of the other media: Mother's Day, National Independence Day, the occasion of the Livestock Fair in Arequipa (October), and Christmas. The total space costs for the inserts is s/38,000 and the production costs are s/20,000.

(iv) *Consumer Magazines.* Consumer magazines in Peru are in a constant state of flux, with periodicals appearing and disappearing with regularity. A factor in this problem of turnover is that these general interest magazines are very often strongly political in nature, and thus subject to the shifting winds of public opinion and governmental tolerance.

The most popular Peruvian consumer press, with a combined total circulation per issue of 216,000 (59.8 percent of which are adult women), appeals primarily to the high to medium socioeconomic classes. The most widely read general interest magazines are the Spanish editions of *Reader's Digest* and *Life*, with the leading Peruvian publication (*Caretas*, a biweekly) ranking third with a total circulation of 40,000. These two factors of the distribution of consumer magazine readership confirm a survey conducted in the early 1960s which found that the more

7. Although in March 1970 two of these newspapers were confiscated by the revolutionary military junta, the *Expreso*, begun in October 1961, had adopted a liberal editorial policy on what was called the "liveliest editorial page of any Lima daily," which promoted social and economic reform. The paper was often accused of Communist sympathies. With its confiscation the paper was turned over to the leftist oriented journalists' union. The *Cronica* was more recently confiscated as part of the nationalization (85 percent) of the Banco Popular Del Peru, Peru's largest banking network, of the Prado family. The total holdings of the bank, which included the two television stations in Lima, two textile factories, and the *Cronica*, were part of the nationalization move. (*The Wall Street Journal*, 26 June 1970, p. 8.)

cosmopolitan upper classes were the large majority of magazine readers and that almost all of the upper classes were magazine readers, while only two-thirds of the middle classes and less than one-third of the lower classes were magazine readers.

Because of the socioeconomic orientation, the high page cost (the mean four-color cost being s/23,743 with a range of s/28,350 to s/19,000), and the relatively small audience exposed to the advertisements, IFI decided to refrain from using this medium.

(v) *Trade Press.* The trade press in Peru is not very well developed. It exists because of the proliferation of periodicals in general, 75 percent of which are aimed at special interest groups. IFI used four Oriental periodicals and newspapers for its trade advertising (*see* Table 11). Although not strictly classified as trade press, being essentially general interest publications designed for Peru's sizable Oriental community, these publications, with a total circulation of 28,000, are read by a large percentage of the trade wholesalers and retail bodega owners. Utilizing primarily the two daily publications, *Man Shing Po* and *La Voz de la Colonia China* (fifteen of the eighteen total inserts) the firm has allocated a total of s/35,500.

(vi) *Outdoor.* Outdoor advertising is one of the major promotional media throughout the world. However, the medium is seldom centrally owned, the widely varying rates are often subject to negotiation, and municipal taxes and ordinances range broadly. Such local diversity makes it imperative that placement be handled locally by someone intimately familiar with local conditions.

IFI utilizes outdoor advertising in Arequipa. The s/54,000 allocated for three billboards covers s/39,000 for rental costs for twelve months and s/15,000 for rental of locations. Although no production costs were allocated for the 1970 budget because the copy was charged against previous years' budgets, the space costs included maintenance costs for painted billboards.

(vii) *Infant Feeding Campaign.* To implement the general marketing strategy objective of increasing the brand's usage for infant feeding, the firm employs two medical detailists from the J. Freitas organization. They call on the doctors which administer to the highest socioeconomic classifications (especially the A group) and the maternity hospitals in Lima/Callao and the provinces. To make the medical profession, and thereby indirectly the primary target audience of housewives, aware of the brand's advantages as a substitute for mother's milk, IFI distributes literature, feeding bottles, and identification cards to the doctors and hospitals. It also conducts a doctor and nurse oriented audio-visual campaign in the hospitals.

The budget allocates s/364,000 for the production of the following materials: 75,000 booklets entitled *Baby's Bottle*, 25,000 booklets entitled *Mother and Baby*, 1,000 medical posters, 40,000 identification cards, 2,000 clinical thermometers embossed with the Maria logotype, and 10,000 "Convenient" glass feeding bottles. The 1970 budget represented an increase over 1969 of 218 percent because the firm has increased its coverage of the hospitals, clinics, and pediatricians throughout the country, thereby necessitating an increased distribution of promotional materials. The audio-visual presentations of "How to Bathe the Baby" (primarily for new and expectant mothers) and "H-60," a highly successful Spanish-language film directed to the medical profession, are not included in the budget allocation because their production costs were budgeted in previous years.

The infant feeding campaign also maintains two distribution programs of free samples. To promote the use of Maria for baby feeding the medical detailists receive an allocation of s/60,000 to cover the distribution of samples to doctors (150 cases) and hospitals (50 cases). However, the main impetus of the campaign is the hospital plan, in which the hospital receives one free case for every ten purchased. Budgeted for s/100,000 (or 333 cases), this program is designed to promote the use of Maria in the hospital formula rooms on the maternity wards.

To reinforce the hospital plan, IFI presented an exhibit at the Latin American Nutritional and Dietitian Congress in Lima. The firm's impact was extremely important to the overall success of the marketing objectives because all the hospital dietitians in the formula rooms have complete authority over the composition of ingredients for the babies' bottles. Therefore, it was imperative that the firm represent its brand's advantages in a comprehensive manner. To accomplish this objective, s/50,000 were allocated for the Congress. An additional factor necessitating representation at the Congress was that of competitive pressure—Perfect brand had also budgeted s/50,000 for the meeting.

Space was also bought in the quarterly *Peruvian Review of Pediatrics (Revista Peruana de Pediatria)* at a cost of s/10,000 (*see* Table 9). The four full-page inserts serve as additional mediums of referral to the brand's advantages for the medical profession.

(viii) *School Campaign.* The firm did not allocate funds for a school campaign for 1970.

(ix) *Consumer Promotion.* As supplemental support to the television and radio campaign, IFI continued its program of in-store promotion. An allocation of s/225,000 was budgeted for the 1970 campaign to purchase space in the weekly newspaper advertisements of the different supermarket chain stores in the larger urban centers, especially the Lima/Callao region. In return the product will receive a special weekend price and choice end-base display areas in the retail outlet. This 12.5 percent cost increase over 1969 is accounted for by increased space costs in the newspapers and the increased cost per case of the product during the special sales in which the firm gives one free case for every hundred cases utilized.

The promotional campaign was also supported by the use of point-of-purchase materials. The firm allocated s/100,000 for giveaways (bean bags and pocket protectors for pens) and s/163,000 for promotional dealer materials (can hangers and small banners) to be displayed in the store.

No provision was made for free sample distribution to the consumers, contests, or demonstrations in the overall promotional campaign.

(x) *Public Relations.* The firm views its use of the newspaper media in Arequipa as essentially a public relations campaign in that the inserts in the two newspapers cover only local holidays—Mother's Day, Independence Day, the Livestock Fair, and Christmas.

(xi) *Special Promotions.* IFI allocated s/45,000 to cover the costs involved for courtesy insertions in charity, religious, and governmental publications.

Advertising Copy Themes. The role of advertising in the marketing mix has been minimized by the strength of the brand's market penetration and the concentration of its sales volume in the Lima/Callao region. These two factors, in conjunction with the fact that the target audience encompasses the entire monetized segment of the country's population, have logically forced the promotional copy themes to be very general in nature, without any specific appeal to an individual socioeconomic segment of the target consumers. This generic nature of the copy themes is seen in the creative execution of the brand's promotional activities which emphasize the following general themes (Figure 5):

1. The product's many uses are demonstrated.
2. The facility and rapidity of preparing the brand are illustrated.
3. Adult liquid usage, essentially as a coffee creamer, is illustrated by family scenes exuding optimism, health, and joie de vivre.
4. For the cooking and baking market segment, theme orientation is toward the "taste appeal" and ease of preparation.
5. For the infant feeding market, the copy emphasizes a subtle approach in which the tone and atmosphere are of human tenderness and the health and strength resulting from the brand's use are illustrated.
6. For enriched Maria II, the copy outlines the specific advantages of its use in realistic homelife situations.

This generality of appeal used in the mass media advertising campaigns is carried over to the supportive point-of-purchase campaigns. However, the principal role of these campaigns is as a quick and direct reinforcement in the consumer's mind of the brand's existence. This is accomplished in all in-store promotions by using the product's brand name and color scheme as the dominant elements of the copy. The use of printed text is held to a minimum, and when used, is extremely general in orientation. For example, "Maria, the evaporated milk of Peru for more than two generations." This type of appeal, while not directly related to any specific market segment, instills public confidence in the product.

A unique element of IFI's promotional activities is its use of courtesy advertisements in the print media on national festive occasions. This type of advertisement appeals to the Peruvian public to view IFI as an integral partner in Peru's national development and progress. Thus, essentially these advertisements should be viewed as a vital element of the firm's public image.

Throughout the promotional activities, the firm's name or a graphic representation of the Maria can dominate the advertisement. The advertisements generally use a very subtle color scheme as a background, while the corporate colors are vibrant and direct. Thus, the consumer's awareness is first of the product, and then incidentally of its uses.

FIGURE 5

LECHE
EVAPORADA

The Evaporated Milk Enjoyed by
Peruvians of
All Ages